A New English Music

ALSO BY TIM RAYBORN

*Against the Friars: Antifraternalism in
Medieval France and England* (McFarland, 2014)

*The Violent Pilgrimage: Christians, Muslims
and Holy Conflicts, 850–1150* (McFarland, 2013)

A New English Music

*Composers and Folk Traditions
in England's Musical
Renaissance from the Late 19th
to the Mid–20th Century*

TIM RAYBORN

Foreword by EM MARSHALL-LUCK

McFarland & Company, Inc., Publishers
Jefferson, North Carolina

LIBRARY OF CONGRESS CATALOGUING-IN-PUBLICATION DATA

Names: Rayborn, Tim, 1968– author. | Marshall-Luck, Em, writer of foreword.
Title: A new English music : composers and folk traditions in England's musical renaissance from the late 19th to the mid-20th century / Tim Rayborn ; foreword by Em Marshall-Luck.
Description: Jefferson, North Carolina : McFarland & Company, Inc., Publishers, 2016. | Includes bibliographical references and index.
Identifiers: LCCN 2016010883 | ISBN 9780786496341 (softcover : acid free paper) ∞
Subjects: LCSH: Composers—England—Biography. | Music—England—19th century—History and criticism. | Music—England—20th century—History and criticism. | Folk music—England—History and criticism.
Classification: LCC ML390 .R206 2016 | DDC 780.92/242—dc23
LC record available at http://lccn.loc.gov/2016010883

BRITISH LIBRARY CATALOGUING DATA ARE AVAILABLE

ISBN 978-0-7864-9634-1 (softcover : acid free paper)
ISBN 978-1-4766-2494-5 (ebook)

© 2016 Tim Rayborn. All rights reserved

No part of this book may be reproduced or transmitted in any form or by any means, electronic or mechanical, including photocopying or recording, or by any information storage and retrieval system, without permission in writing from the publisher.

Front cover: sunset in Cornwall photograph by Em Marshall-Luck

Printed in the United States of America

McFarland & Company, Inc., Publishers
 Box 611, Jefferson, North Carolina 28640
 www.mcfarlandpub.com

Table of Contents

Foreword by Em Marshall-Luck   1

Preface   2

Introduction   4

1. English Music from the Later 19th Century: A Renaissance and a Revival   11
2. The Revival of Folk and Early Traditions   39
3. Ralph Vaughan Williams (1872–1958)   60
4. Gustav Holst (1874–1934)   90
5. George Butterworth (1885–1916)   112
6. Ernest J. Moeran (1894–1950)   130
7. Philip Heseltine / Peter Warlock (1894–1930)   149
8. Gerald Finzi (1901–1956)   169
9. Percy Grainger (1882–1961)   190

Conclusion   217

Appendix A: A.E. Housman (1859–1936)   221

Appendix B: Online Resources—Societies and Other Organizations   223

Chapter Notes   227

Bibliography   277

Index   299

Foreword
by Em Marshall-Luck

The late nineteenth and early twentieth centuries witnessed an explosion of talent in English music that is justly described as its "golden renaissance." Myriad composers poured forth music of innovation, power, drama and beauty, inspired by Vaughan Williams, who was arguably the first to venture beyond Elgar's natural "Englishness" of sound to actively create music that was intentionally "English." Many of these composers have since lain in obscurity; overlooked and neglected for far too long, and their music is only now starting to enjoy again its deserved recognition. How welcome this volume is, then, in this time of renewed interest in English music.

Tim Rayborn's writing is accessible and informative; the composers he portrays are brought to life by anecdotes and stories and the text is illuminated by contemporary opinions and references. Numerous footnotes provide valuable information and demonstrate a rigorously scholarly approach, while also facilitating further reading and cross-referencing. Importantly, Rayborn explores the music of each composer as much as their fascinating lives, and he does both of these with an eye to the wider musical and cultural context, and in an engaging manner.

As a guide for musician, student and layman alike, this book will surely act as not just a reference book, giving informative biographical information and supplying context for some of the composers' best-known pieces, but, with its extensive notes and bibliography, will prove the starting point for a voyage of discovery. It is my sincere wish that any reader of this book will be provoked by what they find and do further research into these sometimes extraordinarily eccentric, sometimes more down-to-earth, but always idiosyncratic individuals, who produced such powerful music.

Em Marshall-Luck is the founder and director of the English Music Festival and the director of EM Records & EM Publishing. She is the author of Music in the Landscape: How the British Countryside Inspired Our Greatest Composers *(2011).*

Preface

This book is the product of a love I have had for many years for the remarkable repertoire of English music from the early decades of the 20th century. The years immediately before and after 1900 were times of great changes in Britain, many of them unwelcome. The British Empire saw its influence around the world waning and its traditional social structures challenged. There was a growing weariness of industrialism, and a desire to rediscover traditions and the perceived roots of English heritage. From "back to the land" movements and campaigns for social justice, to a revived interest in history, and medieval and Tudor studies, many different factors played a part in people's reactions to the times. A new interest in English folk songs and dance was to have a significant effect on art music, which many then (and many have since) maintained was undergoing a renaissance after a period of stagnation for much for the later 18th and 19th centuries.

This work is a survey of that time and in particular, the lives of seven composers whose works were deeply influenced by folk songs and early music: Ralph Vaughan Williams, Gustav Holst, George Butterworth, Ernest Moeran, Philip Heseltine (Peter Warlock), Gerald Finzi, and Percy Grainger. All of them to varying degrees drew inspiration from history and tradition when crafting their compositions. This practice did not define them as composers, but it certainly contributed to their individual styles. Many were also active collectors of English folk songs, enthusiastic folk dancers, historical musicologists, and avid lovers of the outdoors. Each chapter tells the fascinating story of a musical life, and also of the many factors that influenced their output. Their lives share some remarkable similarities, but also some pointed differences.

The book is intended as a general introduction; no knowledge of music theory is necessary, as we will not be examining musical scores. It can be enjoyed by newcomers to the subject, as well as those who have previous knowledge, but might wish to study specific topics in greater depth. Detailed notes

Preface

and a lengthy bibliography will help readers delve much further into any individual subjects that they find of interest.

Many thanks are due to those who helped me to create what has become a labor of love. Thanks to Em Marshall-Luck for writing the Foreword, and for her continuing encouragement and support. Special thanks to Lewis Foreman for contributing many fine photographs from his collection for inclusion here. Thanks also to Anthea Ionides for the George Butterworth photographs, Josephine Finzi and the Finzi Trust for images of Gerald Finzi and his family, Sara Salvidge and the Holst Birthplace Museum for the portrait of Gustav Holst, Laura Smyth and the English Folk Dance and Song Society for the picture of Cecil Sharp, and Jennifer Hill and the Grainger Museum for the photograph of Percy and Rose Grainger.

Several subject experts have read these chapters and offered corrections, suggestions, additional information, and help, and I am very grateful to all of them: Brian Allison, Michael Barlow, Simon Brackenborough, Josephine and Clare Finzi, Alison Hall, Katie Heathman, Ian Maxwell, John Mitchell, Graham Muncy, Anthony Murphy, Liz Pooley and the Finzi Trust, and Barry Smith. They have made this a better work, and any remaining errors are my own. Thanks also to Hugh Cobbe (The Vaughan Williams Charitable Trust), Simon Coombs (The Vaughan Williams Society), and Adrian Lucas (The British Music Society).

Once again, thanks to McFarland for their continuing support, and special thanks and love to Abby and our always-entertaining little creatures.

Introduction

England witnessed what many have seen as a remarkable revolution in its art music from the later 19th century onward. Those who were involved with the new movement were eager to announce it as a latter-day renaissance, a time of renewed creativity from native English composers, the likes of which had not been seen since the age of Henry Purcell in the second half of the 17th century. At first based on solid Germanic foundations, this movement was to undergo major transitions shortly after 1900, with many composers abandoning the most obvious of these Germanic musical influences and seeking out new forms of inspiration. Some found this in the innovations of the Russian or the French composers, when the works of Tchaikovsky, Debussy, and Ravel crossed the channel and found their way into concert halls and smaller venues. However, other composers were drawn to more native sources of inspiration, seeking out folk songs in country villages and reviving early music from medieval and Tudor England. They used these motifs as a means to create new works that would give this new English music its own unique identity. These composers are the subject of this study.

Some clarification is needed for the terms "English" and "British." Often used interchangeably, they are, of course, different in meaning, with England being a country, Britain including Wales and Scotland as well, while the United Kingdom encompasses these three plus Northern Ireland. Nevertheless, sometimes one will encounter a reference to the "British Musical Renaissance" as opposed to the English, which can cause some confusion. While this may include contributions from Irish or Scottish composers, it may just as easily refer to the English-centric view of the renaissance with its London base. The term "English Musical Renaissance" is preferred here, while occasionally referring to the nation of Britain as needed.

This book is largely concerned with biographies of composers who were born, lived, and worked in England and the English folk songs that inspired some of their music from the beginning of the 20th century. However, we have a slightly amusing dilemma about what constitutes "English music" when we look at the composers featured herein: Vaughan Williams and Heseltine had Welsh ancestry, Holst had Germanic and Scandinavian blood, Moeran's father was Irish, Finzi came from families of Italian and German Jews, and Grainger was northern European by way of Australia. Only Butterworth might have been able to claim "authentic" English ancestry, and his family name may ultimately derive from Norman or Scandinavian origins in the Middle Ages. How can they therefore claim to be English? For all of them, regardless of their own backgrounds, the folk and early music of England played a significant part in molding their musical identities. Their language was English, not "British," and all recognized the importance of London (in England), from which much of the musical culture of the time emanated, and where the renaissance, if there were such a thing, began. Moeran and Heseltine also drew inspiration from Celtic folk songs and landscapes, but England remained very important to them, though both lived in Ireland for a time. Indeed, all of the composers surveyed here spent significant portions, if not all of, their lives in England. Only Grainger would leave England behind at the advent of World War I to settle in America. Thus we speak of an English music of the time, partially rooted in English folk songs and traditions, and seeking to set aside some of the more heavy-handed Germanic influences that had dominated Victorian music.[1]

The qualities of such English music are often difficult to identify. There was more than one school of composition, and this book will mainly examine those who worked in the "pastoral school" of English music, with its folk song influences, melancholia, and longings for the countryside. This is not a simple categorization, however, and as we will see, composers often blended many different influences and practices into their works, crossing over to create new hybrids. Holst was particularly notable in this regard, and Vaughan Williams certainly owed some of his style to his studies with Ravel. Thus, in trying to define essential qualities in English music of the early 20th century, there are often disagreements. Calum McDonald offered one interesting observation when he noted that there is frequently a wistfulness, an acceptance of change in these compositions: "A sense of evanescence, of mortality, underlies the music of such diverse yet 'quintessentially English' geniuses as Elgar, Delius, Vaughan Williams, Holst [...] it deepens their lyricism, which often operates with music's metaphors for landscape and pastoral, suggesting the loss of the natural harmony of the countryside and so giving rise to a mysterious sense of tragedy [...]."[2] The fear of losing a national identity was a growing concern in the late Victorian era, and certainly the catastrophic effects of World War I after the romanticized "Edwardian Summer" only deepened this sense of loss.

The very word "pastoral" in music is difficult to define,[3] but seems already to have been in use by the beginning of the 20th century, with no real attempts to explain it. As Eric Saylor notes, "English pastoralism is frequently treated as an obvious and clearly defined musical style, even though such quantification is almost entirely absent from the secondary literature."[4] In some circles of musical criticism (then and now) it is a pejorative term, used to describe parochial, insular, idealized, and backward-looking compositions, a criticism frequently leveled at several of the composers examined in this book. Such work, critics asserted, was not the way forward, and would have little appeal beyond the local and the sentimental.[5] Especially after the carnage of World War I, many argued that pastoral yearnings and folk song settings had no place in a harsh new world cruelly stripped of its naïve innocence. Others countered that the pastoral in the arts could be "a brighter, more appealing world that exists parallel to (or interspersed within) the grimmer trappings of modernity,"[6] one of the ways that a nation so torn apart could hold onto its identity. Such a utopian vision was essential to the Arts and Crafts movement of the late 19th century, and the growing popularity of socialism as a means of reform, even among some in the upper classes, as we will see. The pastoral in English music could also be used to illustrate very dark areas, often preoccupied with change and death, as well as agnostic transcendence, especially by 1918.[7] Daniel Grimly has observed that, "[...] the pastoral reemerges, surprisingly (and even shockingly), as a default mode of response to the First World War. The intimation of mortality—*et in arcadia ego*—that has always been a central trope of the pastoral thus takes on an entirely new significance."[8] Sayler concludes that English pastoral music, with all of its diverse components, "has either been overlooked or undervalued by generations of critics and scholars, many of whom have minimized the innovative aspects of the works in that repertory and thus marginalized their socio-cultural significance."[9]

In trying to identify specific English musical and artistic traits, Lewis Foreman has offered a list of characteristics often found in such music from about 1900, including folk song and folk material, early music and dance, use of English literature, use of English legend, forms and moods specifically created for the style, the use of religious and liturgical material, and the evocation of place.[10] The vocal music can frequently be characterized by its attempts to reach "a state of visionary ecstasy,"[11] and one that is not always religious in tone; the main composers surveyed in this work were all either agnostics or atheists.

The sense of place in this music is particularly strong, as Giles Auty notes, speaking of the arts in general: "Most of the more enduring strains in British art are linked indissolubly with our countryside."[12] More recently, Em Marshall-Luck has written *Music in the Landscape*, a fine survey of British composers and their relationship to the land,[13] showing that even those composers more associated with Impressionism and modern developments regarded their native landscape with love, and even awe. Many of the individuals detailed in this book came from rural backgrounds, and never lost that love of the country, and the closeness that they felt for it.[14] Whether they were wandering the land between small villages during the golden age of folk song collecting material (Vaughan Williams, Butterworth, Grainger), or making their homes in quiet, rural environments to better concentrate on their work (Finzi, Holst, Moeran, and occasionally Heseltine), the English (and for a few, Irish) countryside played an important role in shaping their art.

Chapter 1 explores the background of the English Musical Renaissance, from its origins in late Victorian England to the challenges of World War I and beyond. In this age when the Empire was at its height, but also in danger of beginning to crumble, English music underwent a number of important changes. There was a conscious effort to create a new training center with higher standards, which would allow England to take its place among the musical nations of Europe. The idea of a renaissance in musical quality and output was actively encouraged and promoted at the time by everyone from the press to the Royal Family.

Chapter 2 looks at the revival of folk music and folk customs, primarily through the efforts of various composers and other collectors to gather and codify the vast amounts of native folk songs that were still being sung in country villages, but which were in danger of dying out. This enterprise was long seen as noble, and a means not only to preserve an authentic English tradition, but to provide composers of art music with a new source of inspiration from which to craft their compositions (as had been done in various countries such as Hungary and Bohemia), newly liberated from the yolk of Germanic influence. However, there are different ways of viewing this process, not all of them complimentary to those who engaged in the recording and notating of folk song. Their agendas and motives have since been questioned.

From chapter 3 onward, we begin a survey of the fascinating lives of several composers who made use of both folk songs and early music in their works. Regardless of the motivations of the folk song collectors, it is clear that deriving inspiration from such sources gave early 20th-century English music a very different sound from that of the later Victorian age, or indeed, the continent.

Chapter 3 is devoted to Ralph Vaughan Williams, or "Uncle Ralph" as he was affectionately known by many. He was the Grand Man of the pastoral/folk song movement (though not its academic leader), whose work in the field set the standard for those who came after him. His love of both folk and early music would shine through repeatedly in his works throughout his long life, but he was also frequently the subject of criticism, of being backward-looking and possessing limited technique, a "cow pat" composer whose music offered little more than musical impressions of field animals and naïve pastoralism. He was certainly not hide-bound to the folk song ethic, however, as works such as his *Fourth* and *Sixth Symphonies* demonstrably prove.

Chapter 4 looks at the life of Gustav Holst, who was Vaughan Williams' best friend, and like him, devoted to the idea of folk song in his younger days. Throughout their lives, he and Vaughan Williams were always eager to review each other's new compositions and offer comments and criticisms. However, Holst's interests would lead him into different musical directions than that of his friend, and while folk song influence was certainly one element of his output, it was by no means the only one. His most famous work, *The Planets*, is proof enough of this. His interest in Middle Eastern, Indian, and Asian cultures also inspired a number of notable works.

After surveying the lives of these two most famous figures, we look at the story of George Butterworth in chapter 5, whose life was tragically cut short in August 1916 during the Battle of the Somme in World War I. Butterworth was considered one of the most talented of the younger generation of composers, with an enthusiasm for folk song collecting and Morris dancing, at which he excelled. His potential was sadly never realized, and he unfortunately destroyed many of his works before the larger world could hear them.

In chapter 6, we examine the life of Ernest Moeran, a lesser-known figure in the folk song movement. A native of Norfolk, Moeran suffered an injury in World War I, and later lost the battle with alcoholism, but his music was imbued with motifs of folk-like melodies from his native land, even if they were mostly of his own invention. He was a student of the composer John Ireland, and so he also incorporated Impressionistic elements into his works, bringing together the styles of what were at the time two different schools.

Chapter 7 is devoted to the life of the notorious Philip Heseltine, better known to the classical music world by his *nom de plume* Peter Warlock. A rebel against the trends of the establishment, he frequently found himself at odds with its most notable representatives, and was not shy about insulting them in creative and vulgar ways. His interest in folk song came in part from his friendship with Moeran, and the two lived together for some years from 1925, carrying on a life of artistic debauchery. He was interested in the occult (hence his pen name) and probably took his own life at the young age of 36, but his passion for Tudor music led him to rediscover and produce many fine editions of music from the 16th and 17th centuries, doing a great service to the field of historical musicology.

In chapter 8, we examine the life of Gerald Finzi, who, being born in 1901, grew up after the first great wave of folk song collectors. He would follow in the footsteps of Vaughan Williams (who he came to regard as a mentor and true friend), making use of folk motifs, if not actual tunes, in many of his works. He was also devoted to the country life, and spent considerable time rescuing and cultivating a large number of apple varieties in his rural home, before his life was tragically cut short by complications from cancer in 1956.

Finally, chapter 9 surveys the remarkable life of the talented and eccentric Australian composer, Percy Grainger. A brilliant pianist, he was also a dedicated collector of folk songs in both England and later in Denmark. He was determined to capture these pieces accurately by using recording equipment, a practice that was, by and large, dismissed by his contemporaries. He brought a modern ethnomusicologist's sensibilities to such collecting, and his arrangements of these tunes are still popular, as they were in his own time. He was also dominated by his increasingly mentally ill mother, and had a semi-hidden fetish for masochism, as well as many peculiar habits.

Owing to limits of space, we must necessarily pass over some important composers in this story of British music from 1880 onward. One such talent with much potential was Ivor Gurney (1890–1937), a young composer and poet who showed great promise, who was injured by gas in World War I and was afflicted with mental illness, dying in a mental hospital many years after the war.[15] Likewise, there was John Ireland (1879–1962), a contemporary of Vaughan Williams and Holst, and later a teacher of Moeran, whose work, while at times evoking English pastoral themes,[16] was nevertheless more representative of the Impressionist style of such composers as Debussy and Ravel.[17] Another omission is Herbert Howells (1892–1982), considered by some to be a part of the pastoral school, though his harmonies were sometimes more experimental and could recall other influences, such as Ravel.[18] However, some of his earlier works show the influence of Vaughan Williams,[19] with whom he was friends (he was also later friends with Finzi), and he was enamored of early music. He is remembered primarily for his output of Anglican Church pieces.

Women played an important role in the development of music at the time, both as composers and teachers. Space does not permit a detailed investigation of their lives, but music historian Sophie Fuller has given much-needed attention to some prominent women composers from the period.[20] Likewise, Paula Gillett has produced an important study on the experience of women as musicians in later Victorian and Edwardian society.[21] In the field of folk song-collecting, women such as Lucy Broadwood and Maud Karpeles played very important roles, both in the early stages and well into the 20th century, as we will see.[22] Imogen Holst, Gustav's daughter, and a noted composer and music educator in her own right, did much to revive interest in her father's works, with the help of both Vaughan Williams and Benjamin Britten.[23] Ursula Vaughan Williams (a writer and poet, rather than a musician) was crucial in cultivating interest in her husband's works in the immediate decades after his death.[24]

We must also omit a detailed survey of some of the major musical luminaries of the time. One such figure is Frederick Delius (1862–1934), who was a friend of and inspiration to Heseltine, Moeran, and Grainger, but who lived outside of England for much of his life, followed his own compositional path, and cannot be called an "English" composer in the sense of the others in this work. We will examine Delius briefly in chapter 1, as well as in chapter 7 (owing to his close association with and influence on Heseltine) and chapter 9 (Delius promoted Grainger's music). Equally important in any history of the time is Benjamin Britten (1913–76). However, despite making settings of various English folk songs, he did not collect them from original sources, and was opposed to the pastoral school of Vaughan Williams, seeing it as parochial and outdated by the time he was composing in earnest.[25]

This book, then, is an introduction to a selection of remarkable composers who lived at a time of both great artistic and even greater social changes. It does not offer musical analysis of their works (there are many fine studies for that), but rather details their lives and their impact on the musical world of early 20th-century Britain. No previous knowledge of music theory is necessary to read these studies.

While their music could possess a yearning for folk traditions and Renaissance aesthetics, none of them simply naïvely looked backward for inspiration, and in their mature years, most produced works that were shockingly experimental and not "pastoral" in any real way. Each of these individuals deserves, and has, far more detailed biographies than can be presented here, but this book can serve as a useful guide, a summary of their lives and a point of departure for further study. The notes and bibliography will allow interested readers to investigate topics and biographies that they may wish to explore in more depth.

All but Butterworth have societies or trusts devoted to them,[26] and these are listed in Appendix B with their website addresses, along with many related organizations. Discographies tend to date fairly quickly, and so readers are directed to these societies for up-to-date online recommendations of recordings and key works, which they can pursue at their leisure.

1

English Music from the Later 19th Century
A Renaissance and a Revival

The "English Musical Renaissance"[1] is a complex and controversial term, not to be confused with the music and culture of the Tudor period. It describes a perceived rebirth of native musical activity in England (and to some degree, Britain as a whole) from the later Victorian age, often dated to 1880 (see below), and continuing into the mid–20th century. It was viewed as the time when England began to produce its own talent, throwing off the yoke of German artistic influence and finding its own voice by creating a national music rooted in English traditions.[2] The term first came into use in 1882, when music critic Joseph Bennett wrote in a review of Hubert Parry's *Symphony in G* that the work was, "capital proof that English music has arrived at a renaissance period."[3] The idea quickly became popular, and the term continued to be cited with some confidence for many decades. Music critic J.A. Fuller Maitland (1856–1936) was one of the staunchest supporters of the idea. His *English Music in the XIXth Century* from 1902 is divided into two sections: "Book I: Before the Renaissance (1801–1850)," and "Book II: The Renaissance (1851–1900)."[4]

Various studies have detailed the movement, including those of Frank Howes in 1966,[5] Peter J. Pirie in 1979,[6] and Michael Trend.[7] More recently, Meirion Hughes and Robert Stradling wrote a reappraisal of the movement from 1840 to 1940 (1993, updated in 2001) that aroused considerable controversy by questioning many 20th-century assumptions. The authors argue that music is just as subject to external forces and influences as any other topic, and that the "English Musical Renaissance," as it has been understood, was largely a convenient fiction. It was essentially a creation of those in the social and intellectual elite (George Grove, the Board of Education, and even the Royal family), rather than a response to a need based on national pride and a rediscovery of lost heritage, and served only to benefit those few.[8] Reaction from the musical establishment to this thesis was frequently not favorable, but it shows the degree to which ideas can become entrenched and need to be revisited.[9] Many critics had their own valid points of rebuttal.[10] More recently, Siobhan McAndrew and Martin Everett undertook a detailed statistical study of British composers and their networks, encompassing the years 1870 to 1969. Their work, a social network analysis, showed that the theory that a group of self-appointed elites deliberately excluded certain composers and movements from the renaissance is not supported by the evidence.[11]

Returning to what we can call the "renaissance thesis," it proposed that the last great truly "English" composer had been Henry Purcell (1659–96), an undoubted genius whose life was tragically cut short,[12] but whose music was rediscovered and promoted with pride by the turn of the 20th century. Purcell was the final name in a glorious roster of native English composers, stretching back to Tudor and Elizabethan times, including such luminaries as Tallis, Byrd, Dowland, Weelkes, and Wilbye. Indeed, the revival of Tudor music was to play an important role in English musical life from the later Victorian era; in the 20th century,[13] it was enthusiastically embraced by composers such as Vaughan Williams, Gustav Holst, and Philip Heseltine (Peter Warlock).

After Purcell's death, the theory proposes that the identity of English art music was almost entirely dominated by foreign (mainly Germanic) influence, beginning with the works of George Frideric Handel (1685–1759), who was German but naturalized himself in England from 1710. Later writers and the Victorians would extoll Handel's "Englishness,"[14] but he was still a foreigner in the minds of the early exponents of the renaissance idea. Handel, of course, is considered one of the two great late Baroque composers, along with Bach, his exact contemporary. Mozart (1756–91), Haydn (1732–1809), and Beethoven (1770–1827) each exerted their own considerable influences on European musical life, while their English contemporaries such as William Boyce (1711–79) and Thomas Arne (1710–78) lived in relative obscurity.[15]

This continental dominance over English art music continued with the popularity of Felix Mendelssohn (1809–47), who spent some 20 months of his life in Britain, endearing himself to the population and influencing compositional styles. He was also responsible for reviving interest in Bach's music some 80 years after his death. We will discuss Mendelssohn more below.

This Teutonic musical shadow over England continued to be long during the Victorian age, especially as cast by the imposing figures of Richard Wagner (1813–83) and Johannes Brahms (1833–97). Their influence was undoubtedly tremendous on generations of young composers, and yet while

1. English Music from the Later 19th Century 13

many wholeheartedly embraced them, there would be a struggle by certain composers in England to break free from these influences at the turn of the 20th century. Some were more successful in this attempt than others.

By contrast, the 19th century had been a time when it was often said in all seriousness that the English had no need for music, so preoccupied were they with empire-building; it was "a land without music," as the Germans later maintained.[16] The arts were often seen as a luxury for the better-off when a more utilitarian philosophy was in vogue. Music, not being "useful," but rather a pleasant decoration, was therefore not held in high regard.[17] It was a diversion, not a topic of serious study. As a nation and world-spanning empire that so often imported what it needed, some charged that Britain seemed content with importing music and musical styles, as well.[18] Vaughan Williams referred to it as the "cigar theory of music," that is, that quality music, like a quality cigar, had to be imported since its ingredients did not flourish on English soil.[19] Additionally, many with deeply-held religious convictions (which encompassed a new and growing movement) felt that music was simply immoral, or at least presented the danger of being so.

These were not universal attitudes, however. While church music had become fairly banal and art music was eclipsed by the output of composers on the continent (or else merely written in imitation of it), music still flourished in homes, where pianos and songs remained very popular as part of the middle and upper-class Victorian parlor social scene.[20] Likewise, folk songs were sung by those less well-off, as were musical hall tunes and urban songs. However, music was not fashionable or desirable as a career for the upwardly-mobile Victorian gentleman, who tended to aspire to be a successful businessman or a captain of industry. If he had an interest in the arts, it was more often directed toward literature and writing. Further complicating the problem was the lack of any real government support for music, in sharp contrast to the funding given to the British Museum and the National Gallery, for example.[21]

Many were unhappy about this situation. In 1871 the Reverend H.R. Haweis wrote *Music and Morals*, an attempt to refute the negative opinions that many held about music.[22] This was a crucial work in the history of reviving English music, "one of the ur-texts of the English Musical Renaissance, [it] not only passionately advocated music as a force for moral and social good, but also promoted the idea of an English national school of music as an essential aspect of cultural well-being."[23] The book also advocated against Wagner and the "descriptive" school of music-making, arguing that proper music awakens emotions, rather than describing events.[24] Haweis was not convinced that the English were, at the time, especially suited for music, writing: "[...] although we are inclined to admit that the English are on the whole a Religious People, we arrive at the sad conviction that, however improving and improvable, the English are not, as a nation, an artistic people, *and the English are not a Musical People.*"[25] However, he believed that this could change with the introduction of proper education and standards, and a genuine desire to create a native English voice: "We must not be content with foreign models [...] with German music composed in England, or even with little bits of ballad music [...] supposed to be English, but we must aim at forming a real national school, with a tone and temper as expressive of, and as appropriate to England, as French music is to France, Italian to Italy, and German to Germany."[26] This must be done, he continued, by keeping alive a love for music and encouraging native talent to create a true national school that would elevate music to its proper role as "an instrument of civilization."[27]

Haweis' book went through multiple printings over the next few decades, and was a major new perspective on how music might be viewed. Indeed, it stressed that "not only *could* England become a musical nation, but it *should* be so."[28] His thesis is primarily Christian, given his clerical background, and he dismissed forms such as opera for its decadence and music hall for its questionable morality. And yet, with no irony, he held up the German Felix Mendelssohn as the musical model that Britain should follow, as many had before him, stating with confidence: "Like Beethoven [another German!], he had the highest conception of the dignity of art and the moral responsibility of the artist[29].[...] Mendelssohn towers over his contemporaries like a moral lighthouse in the midst of a dark and troubled sea."[30]

Indeed, the German royalty who ruled England had nothing but admiration for Mendelssohn, and this affection spread outward to the people[31]; Haweis was simply restating what was already a popular view. The rise of an evangelical movement that feared England was losing its Christian soul to industrialization further spread the young composer's popularity. Mendelssohn, a Jewish convert to Christianity, won their hearts with his sincere faith. He brought musical Romanticism to England, but not the Romanticism of hedonistic excess that characterized so many of its expressions on the continent.[32] His was a safe, conservative, religious vision of musical progress that accorded with the growing conservatism of the time. His death at the young age of 38 in 1847 caused a profound sense of grief and loss, and many hoped to find a replacement who could continue his work, a hope that was in vain for some decades.[33]

There were, of course, notable composers from the late Victorian age, such as the Irishman Charles Villiers Stanford (1852–1924), Hubert Parry (1848–1918), and even Arthur Sullivan (1842–1900, of "Gilbert and Sullivan" fame), who would play a key role in revitalizing musical life and establishing composition as a serious activity. Parry's choral work *Prometheus Unbound,* which premiered on September 7, 1880, at the Three Choirs Festival,[34] was in later years held to be the starting point of a renaissance in English music. Stanford considered it to be the best serious composition by a native Englishman since the works of Purcell, though at the time reaction was mixed, and some saw it as too avant-garde; most did not see it as the beginning of anything new. Music critic and scholar Fuller Maitland promoted the piece as the first spark of a rekindling[35]; we will discuss his efforts below. Fuller Maitland was crucial in fostering the idea of a rebirth of English music, though his methods and exclusions later on were strongly criticized.

It is curious that Sullivan's "serious" music has largely been ignored, and indeed, many would consider it worthy of such a fate. He initially had begun composing art music, and had garnered considerable praise for his early efforts. However, the lure of financial gain from theater music and operetta was enough to persuade him to turn his creative efforts to that direction, though he continued with serious works, and saw no contradiction in writing both. While Parry and Stanford were very gifted composers, their compositions are little-known in modern times outside of a somewhat small circle of admirers and connoisseurs. By contrast, the light operas of Gilbert and Sullivan are famous worldwide; it seems that hardly a concert season can go by in the Western world without one or more of their works making an appearance. Yet Sullivan is frequently given little credit for helping to reignite the English musical flame during the latter 19th century.[36]

A positive development came after the Great Exhibition of 1851, which had been the brainchild of Albert, the Prince Consort.[37] The Crystal Palace, built for the exhibition, was reconstructed in 1854 in the suburb of Sydenham, and from 1855, an orchestra was connected to it. Thereafter, a regular series of Saturday afternoon Crystal Palace concerts and other

Sir Hubert Parry (courtesy of the Lewis Foreman collection).

events became ever more popular, as the public flocked to hear music.[38] Colin Eatock notes, "By the 1880s, bourgeois audiences were not only attending concerts in droves, but choosing repertoire by popular vote."[39]

It was decided that the South Kensington area of London would thereafter be a location for institutions devoted to the arts and sciences, including a new college for music.[40] Plans were made under the direction of Sir Henry Cole. By the 1860s, a study was conducted on the state of music education in Britain, and how it compared with similar programs in other countries.[41] A Royal Academy of Music already existed, but it had been weak for some time, with financial troubles, poor oversight, and a backwards-looking philosophy. The idea of a new center of learning that could be equal to those on the continent was an exciting proposition. Initially, some hoped that this new undertaking would merge with or replace the Royal Academy, since the latter had already existed since 1822, and had its charters and patronage schemes in place. The Academy pushed back hard, however, refusing to be absorbed into another entity and attacking Cole and his ideas. The Academy was able to save itself, and Cole was forced from 1873 to abandon the idea of a merger, and instead pursue a National Training School of Music,[42] which by 1876 was under the directorship of Arthur Sullivan.[43]

This decade was significant in seeing the passage of a new Education Act in 1870,[44] and for the tight grip of Victorian mores being slightly loosened, despite Haweis' call for Christian English music based on Mendelssohn's model. Two books of the time, Jakob Burckhardt's *The Civilization of the Period of the Renaissance in Italy* (translated into English in 1878)[45] and Walter Pater's *Studies in the History of the Renaissance* (1873) were to have a significant impact on attitudes toward the arts.[46] Pater, a champion of Burckhardt, coined the term "art for art's sake," and called for a new renaissance in art for England. That "call duly received its response: 'renaissances' sprouted and flourished as Pater's work inspired a whole generation."[47] Pater believed in the human spirit flourishing when art was free, intellectualism for its own sake, free imagination, and a liberal way of viewing things. All of these notions were in contrast to the stern Christianity of the Victorians and the beloved musical morality of Mendelssohn, but such rigid ideas began to give way under the infectious idealism of a new artistic rebirth, of which music would be one component.

The successful unifications of political power in Germany and Italy in 1871 may well have given some Englishmen a further impetus to support a new, native music. Given that German and Italian music (the latter with opera) had so dominated the international music scene, now that they were becoming major political powers that could possibly rival that of the British, many later Victorians may well have seen the necessity of improving their own artistic output.⁴⁸ It was important that music not only be revived in England, but that there should be a truly "English music" as an expression of nationalism. By 1900, no fewer than 18 conservatories and colleges of music had been founded.⁴⁹ Music came to be seen as important socially; it could help form a bond between people of different classes and so strengthen the nation, as well as help guard against more unsavory lower-class pursuits, such as heavy drinking; Victorian morality still had a significant influence in the culture.⁵⁰

Despite this sense of urgency, the National Training School was at first a disappointment, failing to secure the government funding that it needed, and only admitting a small number of students. By 1878, the school seemed destined to fail, but Cole pulled the proverbial rabbit out of the hat in securing additional royal patronage for the venture, from the Prince of Wales and the Duke of Albany (who was especially supportive of public funding for music and music education). This led to the institution being renamed as the Royal College of Music, and a new charter being drawn up in 1880.⁵¹ George Grove was brought in to oversee fundraising, and proved to be quite capable in this effort.⁵² An architect and engineer,⁵³ he nevertheless had a passion for music.⁵⁴ He promoted concerts and oversaw the creation of the famed *Dictionary of Music and Musicians* (first produced between 1879 and 1889), later named for him. Having been through several editions, it is still one of the most important research tools available to modern music students.⁵⁵ At the time, it gave important coverage to English music and the nascent attempts to revive musical activity in England. Its 1874 Prospectus, which outlined the multi-volume work, was "nothing less than the first 'manifesto' of the English Musical Renaissance."⁵⁶ Indeed, it featured entries for obscure English composers long forgotten, an extended listing for Henry Purcell, and even entries for contemporary composers such as Parry and Stanford, who were also contributors.⁵⁷ If this seems suspiciously like deliberate self-promotion for a new wave of English music, it also helped to place England on the same map as its continental rivals and soon became an indispensable reference tool.

Indeed, supporters held that English music had every right to be in such lofty company. No less than Leopold, Duke of Albany proclaimed (with Grove's delighted participation as he read the duke's words) that the English were the most musical of nations, dating back to the Middle Ages.⁵⁸ At a major fundraising event in Manchester in December 1881, Albany/Grove continued by stating with confidence that the famous 13th-century English round *Sumer Is Icumen In*, "is the germ of modern music, the direct and absolute progenitor to the oratorios of Handel, the symphonies of Beethoven, the operas of Wagner.[...]"⁵⁹ This pompous and fairly ludicrous statement was clearly an attempt to credit England with kick-starting art music in Europe, an absurd proposition that no serious musicologist would now support. It not only attempted to place England confidently in the musical firmament, it also made the audacious assertion that Germany's music was originally English.[60]

Regardless of that noble ancestry, German and Italian forms had come to dominate England since Handel's time, the speech continued, but the ever-resilient English had carried on with their own musical traditions in the church, the glee clubs, the music halls, the inns, and light operas. Now it was time for art music to reclaim its greatness, as it had been diluted and obscured after Purcell's death.[61] The Royal College would see to that, becoming a shining beacon in the musical world, to rival the best conservatories in Europe, such as the one in Berlin.[62] Edward the Prince of Wales (later King Edward VII) stated that this was essential, because such an institution would improve "colonial co-operation and sympathy," and "by inspiring among our fellow-subjects in every part of the Empire these emotions of patriotism which national music is calculated to evoke [English music would] strengthen a common love of country."[63] A new national music would thus be an essential ingredient in preserving the British Empire. This contrasted with how some other European countries viewed nationalism in music, relating it instead to revolutions and social changes.[64]

This royal support and the urgency of its message proved to be irresistible, as Hughes and Stradling note: "Grove's was a seminal influence in the history of English Music. He launched a revolution from above, with the royal brothers themselves as its willing figureheads. He set a programme and a vision which has dominated his country's musical culture, arguably down to the present day."[65]

Parry and Stanford were the logical choices for the main professorships in the new institution, and they would remain integral to the functions of the College for decades,[66] with Parry teaching composition and music history, and Stanford teaching composition and directing the college orchestra. A third professor, Walter Parratt, taught organ.

Parry is rightly credited with bringing higher standards to compositional instruction, and raising the respectability of the profession considerably. He was an essential part of the new College faculty, though his reputation has waxed and waned over the last century. Often thought to be conservative in outlook and a somewhat facile establishment composer who did not think enough about what he wrote, his daughter Dorothea set the record straight in 1956, when she noted that he was a radical and opposed to conservative politics. He was non-religious, preferred not to associate with the upper class, and despite his hard work, struggled with depression.[67]

Stanford would prove to be an essential figure in this story.[68] A composer schooled in the Germanic tradition (and a great admirer of the "three Bs": Bach, Beethoven, and Brahms), he would teach an impressive number of young men who would be significant composers in the first decades of the 20th century, including Ralph Vaughan Williams, Gustav Holst, Samuel Coleridge-Taylor, John Ireland, E.J. Moeran, and Frank Bridge,[69] several of whom also studied with Parry. Stanford's reputation as a teacher eclipsed that of his standing as a composer, and several of his students (most notably Vaughan Williams, Holst, and Ireland) achieved greater fame than he did, as did his self-taught contemporary Elgar, surely a frustrating development. Nevertheless, "he, more than any other single man, created the modern English school by his work as a teacher [...] in so far as one can speak of a school of English composition he was its maker."[70]

Further, Stanford was an early voice for recognizing the importance of folk songs, though not those gathered from oral traditions, but rather those which had already found their way into print. As a conservative opposed to socialism, he felt such songs could be national and used to teach a patriotic way of thinking that endorsed the established order.[71] In a lecture to the managers of the London Board of Schools in 1889 regarding music education, he observed:

Sir Charles Villiers Stanford (courtesy of the Lewis Foreman collection).

> And what should be the kind of music taught? Without doubt, national music, folk-music—the music which from the earliest times has grown up amongst the people. Without the foundation of such music no healthy taste can be fostered in the population. From all times it has been the germ from which great composers have come. Need I point out to you as a proof, that those countries which have the greatest store of national music have also produced the greatest amount of creative genius as well as of general appreciative power?[72]

He went on to note that teachers were particularly blessed with a rich treasure-trove of folk music:

> But if you will admit my proposition that the healthy musical taste

of a nation depends upon the wealth of its literature of folk-music, I will, as a result of your admission, point out that in the British Isles you have the greatest and most varied storehouse of national music in existence. You have two distinct schools—Saxon and Celtic; and four distinct styles—English, Welsh, Scotch, and Irish.[73]

The best way to introduce these tunes to children, he posited, was to give each their own folk music first; English songs to English children, Welsh songs to Welsh children, etc., and schools would then play an important role in preserving and passing on such music.[74]

Despite this devotion to native musical tradition, Stanford and Parry were both equally committed to the Brahms/Schuman school of composition, and felt that this was the way forward for young English composers. The idea of throwing off such influences would have to wait until the next generation. Indeed, Foreman notes that sometime later, the "criticism of Stanford's approach to folk-song was that he placed the tunes within the straight-jacket of his essentially Germanic musical culture,"[75] making them little more than English "Lieder."

Wagner stirred great controversy, then as now. Parry was enamored of his earlier output, especially the *Ring Cycle*, but rejected some of his later works, as well as his distasteful anti–Semitic philosophies, as did Grove. Parry's earlier pieces, including *Prometheus Unbound*, show Wagnerian influence.[76] Stanford was impressed by Wagner's operatic talents, but equally offended by his personal views. The rivalry between supporters of Brahms and supporters of Wagner was well established in Germany, and neither Parry nor Stanford had a desire to see such opposing camps set up in England; Brahms became their man.[77] They differed in their opinion of opera, however. Despite his earlier enthusiasm, Parry later came to dislike it, describing it as "the shallowest fraud that man ever achieved in the name of art,"[78] while Stanford embraced the genre. However, his own operas, such as *The Veiled Prophet* and *Savonarola*, are largely unknown today. Nevertheless, Wagner's popularity grew in England during the 1890s, and his music found many supporters, among them the composer Granville Bantock[79] and George Bernard Shaw, who saw Wagner's work as heralding the future.[80]

A rivalry closer to home was also averted, that between the Royal Academy and the Royal College. Scottish composer Alexander Mackenzie took over the principal's role at the Academy from 1888, and broke with the stubborn attitudes of his predecessor, embracing the idea of a renaissance, and forging a friendship with Grove and the Royal College. He wisely realized that for music to flourish and to attract patronage, the two institutions had to present as allies rather than competitors. Any rivalry would have to be friendly and artistic; there was both Oxford and Cambridge, for example, so there could also be a Royal Academy and a Royal College.[81]

With the establishment of two institutions, it was inevitable that the press and others would begin to talk about an "English school" of composition. The first members of this school were seen as Parry, Stanford, Mackenzie, and two other lesser-known figures, Frederic Cowen and Arthur Goring Thomas.[82] The latter two are mostly forgotten today, but at the time were seen as important in helping to create the new national style.

Grove was particularly eager that the British press give good coverage of his efforts, and went to great lengths to court sympathetic views and allies within it.[83] The most influential of these was Fuller Maitland, chosen as Grove's successor to edit the *Dictionary*, and who later became chief music critic for the *Times*. For those seeking legitimacy for the movement, Fuller Maitland was the perfect choice. He was, in addition to his *Dictionary* duties, the music editor for the *Encyclopedia Britannica*, and he contributed to the *Oxford History of Music*. He was an ardent advocate of the concept of the English Musical Renaissance, as we have seen, and was devoted to the ideal of a national movement, as well as the study of folk song and the revival of interest in the Tudor composers and Henry Purcell.[84] He was convinced of his own importance, titling his 1929 autobiography *A Door-Keeper of Music*.[85]

Enthusiasm for these earlier composers had been building in the last decades of the 19th century. Mendelssohn had previously brought the music of Bach into newfound popularity, and a society dedicated to Bach had formed in 1849. Purcell also had a society dedicated to his works, founded in 1876. In some ways he was even more important, for his Englishness gave a legitimate claim to English greatness. Here was a Baroque composer on par with Bach and Handel, just what the advocates for the renaissance needed.

The growing interest in earlier music also saw the revival of music from Tudor times. As early as 1840, the Musical Antiquarian Society had been formed to promote music of the 16th and 17th centuries,[86] though its scholarship was hardly acceptable by later standards.[87] More significant was the later work of Arnold Dolmetsch, who we will discuss in more detail below. Interest in madrigals and other vocal pieces began to flourish, as did a desire to improve church music. Fuller Maitland was equally devoted to Elizabethan and Jacobean music, especially instrumental works, and he oversaw the publication of an edition of the *Fitzwilliam Virginal Book* (a large collection of 16th and early 17th-century music for keyboard) in 1899.[88] Later, composers such as Vaughan Williams and Philip Heseltine would be passionately devoted to Tudor music.[89]

This infatuation with the 16th and 17th centuries certainly had been fueled by Bennett's declaration of a new musical renaissance. By utilizing a term tied to the Elizabethan and Jacobean periods, he (whether consciously or not) evoked a nostalgic feeling in the minds of many, linking this new musical movement with the great English Renaissance of the past, the age of Elizabeth I and Shakespeare, of Sir Walter Raleigh and Francis Bacon. The celebration of the third centenary of the defeat of the Spanish Armada 1888 only strengthened this connection, as did the convenient coincidence that England was ruled by a queen who presided over an empire. Indeed, the memorial statue of Prince Albert at the Albert Hall (erected in 1871) depicts him in Elizabethan garb.[90] There was no doubt that this was a conscious attempt at promoting the notion of a new golden age by linking that time with an idealized past some 300 years earlier.[91]

Another important, if colorful, figure in the re-establishment of early music in England was Arnold Dolmetsch (1858–1940).[92] Born in Le Mans, France, and the son of a successful piano maker of Swiss-German ancestry, Dolmetsch learned the instrument-making craft from his father before studying violin at the Brussels Conservatoire and then attending the Royal College in its early days, earning a Bachelor of Music degree in 1889; thereafter he adopted England as his permanent home. He became interested in early instruments by seeing those relics from earlier times on display in the British Museum. Bringing his instrument-making skills into play, he conducted an extensive amount of study, researching how to reconstruct and build his own contemporary copies of lutes, viols, and harpsichords, among others. He was convinced that not only the instruments, but the playing styles, as well as the performance environments, needed to be recreated to do the music justice. As such, he was a pioneer in the period-instrument movement that would gain increasing acceptance from the mid–20th century. He was the first to attempt to reproduce authentic instruments that were of high quality.[93]

It was only through knowledge of ancient music, he asserted, that new music could be made: "No art can develop healthily unless grounded upon a real, direct comprehension of the achievement of past generations. The neglect of this truth is the principal cause of the futile striving after originality and the misguided experiments which have brought music to its present chaos."[94] He held that the early music he was researching and playing deserved the same respect accorded to later music, stating: "This music is of absolute and not antiquarian importance; it must be played as the composer intended and on the instruments for which it was written with their correct technique; and through it personal music-making can be restored to the home, from which two centuries of professionalism have divorced it."[95]

Indeed, he was not interested in professional performance, as could be seen in his own family's concerts, for he enlisted his children in his musical activities, whether they wanted to be involved or not.[96] They were not nearly as polished as was to be expected (he would even stop them mid-piece and start over if the playing was not to his liking), with the result that, "for many in the outside world early music performance was synonymous with well-meaning ineptitude."[97] There were those, however, who were charmed by his quirky performances in costume,[98] particularly those outside of the mainstream in early 20th-century British society. As Campbell notes for a concert he gave in December 1891:

> The best-known progressives in London had turned out for the occasions—artists, poets, writers: they were fascinated by this little Frenchman whose very appearance was more pre-Raphaelite than the pre-Raphaelites themselves with velvet suit, lace ruffles and silver buckles on his shoes. His music recaptured for them the delights of a lost enchantment [...] he was loved on sight and when the concert was over they applauded uproariously. At last Dolmetsch had found his audience.[99]

Dolmetsch did not specifically focus on English music, though he was greatly impressed by the consort music for viols from the age of Elizabeth I, James I, and Charles I. His other great contribution to the early music revival was the popularizing of the recorder, begun in earnest after he lost his favorite historical recorder in 1919. He decided to make modern copies of his Baroque original, and soon the instrument was proving to be hugely popular with amateur musicians and in schools, a position that it has retained to this day.[100] At the end of his life, he was awarded the Croix de la Légion d'Honneur in France, and given an honorary doctorate by the University of Durham in acknowledgement of his efforts to revive old music.[101]

From 1931, he had also developed a friendship with Percy Grainger.[102] Grainger was very interested in his work, and arranged for publication of his editions of viol consort music, for both viols and modern instruments, after his death.[103] Not all composers were enamored of the idea of historical performance practices, however. Vaughan Williams, perhaps surprisingly, given his attachment to the Tudor composers and Bach, had no interest in reviving early instruments. It was enough that the music itself should be saved, he felt, and this should be done with modern instruments that he felt were superior to those that had been made in earlier times.[104]

Returning to the late 19th century, the Royal College was eager to endorse the idea of a renaissance in bloom, and of itself as fostering it. Further, Stanford noted in 1894 that the press had an active role to play:

> In view of the great renaissance of music in England which is becoming every day more marked, it is incumbent upon those responsible for the management of the daily newspapers to place musical criticism in a position worthy of the art with which it deals. To do so will be to ensure greater self-respect both in critics and criticised, and, as a result, better feeling between them.[105]

In other words, the press needed to be careful about how it chose its reviewers, who should be knowledgeable and presumably, supportive of the efforts to revive music. He is more explicit when discussing letting reviewers choose which concerts to review: "There remains, indeed, one danger from such a policy: namely, that editors, who happen themselves to be ignorant of music, should engage the services of writers almost equally ignorant merely because they possess the gift of literary style."[106] It was not fitting, therefore, that those ignorant of music or the importance of this musical rebirth be allowed to comment on those aspects of it of which they may have insufficient knowledge. The renaissance was too important to be damaged by faulty press reports.[107]

For all of these precautions, instruction in style and technique at the College and the Academy still proceeded in the Germanic style, with the three Bs being prominent, as well as Mendelssohn and Schuman. Interestingly, Mozart and Haydn seemed to have been downplayed; this may have been due to their Catholicism.[108] As both London institutions began to prosper in this revitalized environment, a third entity appeared from 1880, the Guildhall School of Music, with the initial mission of offering musical training to non-professionals. Many of the Academy faculty also taught here, and it goals and purpose were clearly in line with those of the other two schools.[109] The College suffered a scandal in the early 1890s over the conduct of one of its teachers, Henry Holmes, who had seduced more than one female student[110]; he was sacked and he eventually relocated to San Francisco; the reputation of the College was saved, but it had been an embarrassing series of incidents. Grove himself retired in 1894, leaving the directorship of the College in the capable hands of Parry.

The 1890s would see a major influx of new students, arguably the most important of which were Vaughan Williams and Holst; we will discuss their time at the College (when the two first met and became the best of friends) in their respective chapters.

By this time, there was a growing sense of Englishness in other creative spheres. This "artistic nationalism" was a complex brew of various factors. Encompassing many aspects, its strands were "responses to socio-economic issues—and indeed to the movements in the other arts associated with them—that stretched back as far as John Ruskin and William Morris, perhaps even back to Wordsworth.[...]"[111] With a focus on a pastoral sentiment and a sense of history and preservation, as well as natural conservation and a rejection of modernist values, "this aesthetic, locatable in some form or another ever since in most of the arts in Britain, gathered strength as a very long-drawn-out reaction against the nation's industrial revolution."[112]

This could be seen clearly in the Arts and Crafts Movement, which

> developed in 19th-century Britain as a rebellion against the fashion for inventive sham and over-elaborate design and as an attempt to reverse the growing dehumanisation of work in society. It was based on simple forms, truth to materials and the use of nature as

the source of pattern. [...] Music and drama played a significant part in the movement. Composers such as Ralph Vaughan Williams and Gustav Holst shared the Arts & Crafts' love of the countryside and folk traditions. As part of the movement, Arnold Dolmetsch pioneered the revival of early English music while Cecil Sharp and others collected traditional folk songs and dances.[113]

The movement was closely associated with William Morris (1834–96), the writer, textile designer, and social reformer. His work "transformed a vision of Old (quasi-medieval) England into a semi-feudal socialism potentially realizable in the modern world."[114] Reformist and socialist views, as we will see, were held in varying degrees by many of the composers discussed in this book. The idea of recovering a "lost England" in its folk traditions must have seemed irresistible to many, disillusioned as they were by the ravages of the Industrial Revolution, and the dehumanizing effects it had brought to so many.[115]

At the same time, academics still worked hard to engender a love of the Teutonic traditions in musical excellence. However, by the turn of the 20th century, there were those who were seeing other ways forward for a national English school of music. Wagner was held in high esteem by many young composers, but his appeal as the new voice made the English school's adherence to older Germanic traditions seem somewhat dated.[116] Soon, however, folk song and Impressionism would find their way into the works of this new generation of British musicians and composers, greatly transforming the sound and character of English music.

There was some degree of arrogance about what had already been accomplished by Parry, Stanford, and Mackenzie. Fuller Maitland proclaimed in his *English Music* from 1902,

> that more genius will be manifested in the future than has been in the recent past is most unlikely; but still more improbable is it that the renaissance of which I have traced the beginnings should cease to exert its influence in the years to come. During the last quarter of the XIXth century England has regained a position she has not held for at least two centuries.[...][117]

He was correct that the movement would continue to exert an influence, partially correct about the status of English music in the world of the turn of the century, and mostly incorrect in his assessment of the talent that would yet reveal itself. It is easy to look at one's own age as an apogee and not realize that it may be eclipsed by later generations. Soon after this pronouncement, a second wave of astonishingly talented English composers would begin to make themselves known in new and unexpected ways.

Fuller Maitland worked for the *Times* until 1911 (employing George Butterworth, among others), in addition to editing *Grove's Dictionary* (the 1904–10 edition). His involvement with folk song was important, however, and predated the efforts of Cecil Sharp and Vaughan Williams by more than a decade. He and Lucy Broadwood published *English County Songs* in 1893.[118]

As we have seen, Stanford was already a strong advocate of using folk song to instruct children in music, and interest in the subject stretched back several decades. Sharp and Broadwood were beginning their important work in uncovering and collecting folk music in the still-untouched rural areas of England. For Vaughan Williams, the watershed moment came in December of 1903, when he had a "conversion experience" to the possibilities that these indigenous works held; Holst soon followed him, and then Butterworth, Grainger, and a host of others. The idea of using folk and popular tunes in art music was not new to England; the Elizabethan and Jacobean composers had previously done so to great effect,[119] as had Purcell and Handel.[120]

While some at the time saw these tunes as a salvation for English music, they could not be the only remedy. C.W. Orr observed in 1931:

> Folk-tunes became all the rage; young composers diligently flattened their sevenths and modalised their tunes; parties of enthusiast went back to the land, where they implored the rustics to warble songs their mothers taught them, which effusions were noted down to be worked up into *English Suites, English Rhapsodies,* and *English dance tunes.* [...] It was, in fact, a healthy reaction against the foreign musician-worship that had gone on too long, but it overlooked the truth that you cannot create a ready-made renaissance by a form of folk-tune serum.[121]

We will discuss the folk revival in detail in chapter 2.

An outlier in this story is Edward Elgar (1857–1934).[122] He was not a part of the academic circle of the Kensington renaissance movement, being instead self-taught and from a village near Worcester; his father was a piano tuner, so he had exposure to music from an early age. He was conscious of his own nature as an outsider, from his humble beginnings to his Roman Catholicism, and he was frequently annoyed at his exclusion from the certain musical circles. He was an anomaly in the music revival of the time. The irony is that with his pieces, the *Enigma Variations* (1898–99) and *The Dream of Gerontius* (1900), recognized ever after as works of monumental genius, he established himself as a major force without having taken part in the training so strongly advocated by Parry and Stanford. Indeed, his schooling had ended when he was 15, and he taught himself composition and music in his father's shop. With the support and encouragement of his wife, Caroline (from 1889), he was able to enter into a life of professional music and make a name for himself with virtually no acknowledgement from the College or the Academy. Anthony Murphy notes that arts patron Frank Schuster had important connections that later helped Elgar immensely, introducing him to high society and royalty. Elgar would dedicate his overture *In the South* (1904) to Schuster.[123]

An important early supporter was one Henry Embleton, a Leeds-based businessman who commissioned Elgar's *Caractacus*, and also Arthur Sullivan, who as chief conductor of the Leeds Festival saw to it that the work was premiered there in 1898. Elgar was grateful for the opportunity, noting that "it contrasts very much with what some people do to a person unconnected with the schools—friendless and alone."[124] This was not the first harsh statement he would make about his treatment, and it reveals the resentment he felt not to be a member of the "club." He noted in correspondence with his friend August Jaeger that Parry, Stanford, and Mackenzie were all very busy performing one another's music, because no one else would. He later added, "the stuff I hate and which I know is ruining any chance for good music in England is stuff like Stanford's which is neither fish, flesh, fowl nor good red herring!"[125] In contrast, he did admire Parry and his work.[126]

Elgar was firmly in the camp of Wagnerian music, which further alienated him from some in the establishment, and he and Caroline made trips to Bayreuth in the 1890s. He likewise admired Richard Strauss and held Berlioz as a great influence, all figures which the guardians of the renaissance mistrusted. Strauss would equally hold Elgar in esteem, proclaiming in 1902, "I raise my glass to the welfare and success of the first English progressivist, Meister Edward Elgar."[127] However, with the advent of his *Enigma Variations*, attitudes toward him changed, perhaps out of necessity. This work proved to be immensely popular, and the establishment finally reached out to Elgar. He was offered honorary degrees, including that of a DMus from Cambridge. Though he was initially reluctant to accept, he was gratified that he was finally being recognized. He received further degrees from Leeds and Oxford Universities.

Unfortunately, with these honors came responsibilities and ties to the establishment that began to make him uncomfortable.[128] He attracted the attention of the new king, Edward, and wrote the *Coronation Ode* for him in 1902. Elgar's fame sored and his music was widely popular. His music was conservative and seemed to extol the great virtues of the British Empire at a time when such reassurance was needed.[129] It must have been galling on some level for Parry and Stanford to see this level of success come to a lower-class outsider, when they had labored for so long in the heart of the establishment. In some ways, that success continues today, for while Elgar's *Enigma Variations* and *Pomp and Circumstance Marches*[130] continue to enjoy world-wide fame, the music of Parry and Stanford is unknown except for a select few. Vaughan Williams, however, later questioned how much of an outsider from the academic establishment Elgar really was, attributing much of this story to exaggerations by Bernard Shaw.[131]

In any case, the academics won out over Elgar in their teaching legacies.

Edward Elgar in 1903 (courtesy of the Lewis Foreman collection).

Elgar produced no students of worth, and he did not inaugurate a school of his own. Parry and Stanford helped to educate Vaughan Williams, Holst, Ireland, and many more. While these men did not emulate their instructors and found their own voices, that influence must be noted.

Relations between Elgar and Stanford were never warm, given their differences of opinion and background, and by 1904–05, that relationship became quite strained, when Elgar withdrew a symphony commissioned by the Leeds Festival, which Stanford had helped him to secure. Further, he rejected the offer of a teaching position at the University of Leeds, which again, Stanford had helped to bring about. Instead, he opted for a position as Chair of Music at the University of Birmingham. Stanford was furious and the two broke off relations.[132] Elgar's decision was understandable in that it offered a generous salary and did not require him to live in the city. Further, he undoubtedly felt a loyalty to the region in which he was born.[133] To be fair to Stanford, however, he had reached out and genuinely tried to promote Elgar once the latter had gained some prominence, so one can see why he would have been so offended in receiving two major rebuffs for his efforts.

Now firmly established with academic credibility and commercial success, Elgar delivered a series of talks known as the Peyton Lectures at Birmingham University. These offered a way of looking at music that was at odds with the renaissance approach. He sought to create a center for musical learning in Birmingham that would rival those on the continent, a direct challenge to the supremacy of the Kensington schools. His lectures, though praising Parry, took direct aim at what he saw as the failures of the music revival, which he believed had become elitist and alienating. Despite its efforts, it had left English music in the state of being hopelessly boring and backward-looking. Indeed, he said, reaching back to revive old music served no purpose, and slavishly imitating continental styles, such as the popular new "rhapsody" form, was "inconceivably inept."[134] Elgar had never shown any interest in folk music as a basis for composition, boldly proclaiming, "I am folk music."[135] He held that it was the role of a composer to create new music, not borrow existing melodies and try to do new things with them.[136] He further dismissed Tudor and 17th-century works as "museum-pieces," relics of a long-gone age that were not worth reviving.[137] Now, with these lectures, he had the bully pulpit at last and was reveling in the chance to use it.

Unfortunately, he overplayed his hand, and his ambition to become the leader of his own renaissance failed miserably. A major reason was simply that these lectures were badly written and rambling. As Moore notes,

> Elgar's lectures are not easy to read, nor were they easy to listen to half a century ago. The form of the individual lectures is loose in the extreme, and sometimes barely discernible. Each lecture bears the signs of laborious composition over a long period of time, followed by a tortuous fitting together of disparate parts. Digressions are very frequent, and are made upon every imaginable aesthetic subject: again and again Elgar's attempt to unify the arts brings his considerations near to chaos. All of this compositional difficulty reveals the unpracticed hand.[138]

In attempting to speak with authority, he showed his own lack of education and eloquence, which damaged his image. The reaction to these lectures was so hostile that they took a toll on his health, and he was obliged to resign from the university, never to return. Elgar would thereafter focus solely on writing music, and stay away from the politics of the renaissance and the minutiae of the academic world. He certainly continued to have his backers and public support, though the academics would never again court him. For Elgar, this withdrawal was the right choice, as the pieces that he produced afterward (including his two symphonies and his *Violin Concerto*) were of very high quality. He had hoped to reform what he saw as the stultifying effects of the Kensington institutions by introducing a progressive, Wagnerian-Straussian aesthetic into English music, but he had overstepped, and perhaps became his own worst enemy.

A few years later, however, he was part of a movement to create a new society, The Musical League, dedicated to holding annual festivals for new works by established composers and equally featuring works by young and undiscovered composers. A letter to the *Times* on March 23, 1908, had made the case for such an enterprise. It was signed by Elgar, Frederick Delius (see below), Mackenzie, and others. The League succeeded in promoting concerts to these ends, and gave some young composers, such as Percy Grainger, a chance for their works to be heard.[139]

Another important composer who can only receive a small amount of attention here is Frederick Delius (1862–1934). He was English by birth (born in Bradford, in Yorkshire), but spent much of his life abroad, in the United States and then in Germany and France, making only occasional return visits to England. Delius was a cosmopolitan figure and as such, was not involved in the South Kensington efforts to establish an English music. His work drew from such influences as African-American spirituals (heard during a brief period when he lived in Florida from 1884–86, managing a family orange plantation) and contemporaries, including Grieg and Richard Wagner. Studying in Leipzig, he then relocated to Paris. He was to reside in France for the rest of his life, except during World War I, when he moved to south England.

He notably contrasted with his contemporaries, as Philip Heseltine (one of his greatest admirers) noted, writing in 1915 that he

> holds no official position in the musical life of the country [i.e., England]; he does not teach in any of the academies, he is not even an honorary professor or doctor of music. He never gives concerts or makes propaganda for his music; he never conducts an orchestra, or plays an instrument in public (even Berlioz played the tambourine!). A composer who cares for none of these things is indeed a strange phenomenon.[140]

Delius was not a part the Parry/Stanford/Grove renaissance, and English folk song held little interest for him; he once wrote of Vaughan Williams: "If he turns out anything interesting *ever*, I shall be a very astonished person."[141] Vaughan Williams would comment in 1941 that Delius' music would "have more backbone" if he had not spent much of his life in the luxurious and cut-off world of his French villa.[142] However, Delius' setting of *Brigg Fair*, a Lincolnshire folk song given to him by Percy Grainger, is one of his better-known and loved pieces, and he once proposed that the two of them go to America for the purpose of collecting folk songs.[143] Grainger was a great admirer of Delius (the feeling was mutual), and when the two met, they discovered that they shared a similar harmonic language, even though they had previously been unaware of each other's works.[144] Delius' complex harmonies and challenging compositions were greeted with mixed reactions; some loved his new ideas, others hated them.

His work had a tremendous influence on the young Philip Heseltine, whose hero-worship of the older man became excessive at times, and pointed to the lack of a true father-figure in Heseltine's life. The two became great friends, however, and we will discuss their relationship in more detail in chapter 7. Moeran was also to draw influence from Delius, though he was more committed to the folk song aesthetic.

By the turn of the 20th century, various new developments were happening in English music, with the rise in the interest of folk song being one of the most important. The "heirs and rebels," as Vaughan Williams and Holst described

1. English Music from the Later 19th Century 31

themselves, were among those emerging from the aftermath of the Kensington/Elgar musical civil war with fresh ideas about how English music could progress; they were not alone. Drawing from French developments, certain young composers were attracted to the idea of Impressionism, famously expounded by Debussy and then Ravel. These two new schools of composition were to develop separately and they were frequently in opposition to one another over the next few decades.[145]

Indeed, composer Edmund Rubbra (1901–86) later noted, regarding two of his teachers, Evlyn Howard-Jones and Holst:

> Howard-Jones [...] was a friend of John Ireland, Bax, Goossens, and that school of music. [...] On the other hand, Holst was a friend of Vaughan Williams, and the two schools of thought were much opposed to each other. Howard-Jones said rather nasty things about Vaughan Williams's school, and the other side said equally nasty things (although not quite so much) about the school that Howard-Jones championed. [...] It was odd that at that time there were these two schools that never came together; they were entirely separate from each other.[146]

More recently, Michael White has suggested additional factions and no clear vision about what new English music was:

> There was not much consensus among English Musical Renaissance figures. Elgar denied that there ever was a renaissance in the sense of a meaningful movement, calling it "an egotism of several." With hindsight, the movement breaks down into barely amicable factions: English pastoralists (Vaughan Williams, Gustav Holst, Herbert Howells, Gerald Finzi, George Butterworth); Celtic mystics (Rutland Boughton, E. J. Moeran, Arnold Bax); modernists (Arthur Bliss, William Walton, [Constant] Lambert); crypto-modernists (Frank Bridge); and new boys waiting in the wings (Michael Tippett and Benjamin Britten).[147]

However, as Stephen Banfield has pointed out, there were certainly cordial relations between some members of the opposing schools (Vaughan Williams with Ireland[148] and Bax, for example), and Holst's *Planets* was by no means limited to English pastoralism, but rather featured many Franco-Russian influences.[149] Ernest Moeran, as we will see, was strongly influenced by his teacher John Ireland, and he blended his traditional Norfolk-sounding melodies into this Impressionistic harmonic vocabulary. For his part, Ireland's *Downland Suite* certainly contains elements of pastoral and folk music.

Such crossovers did not stop Constant Lambert from making his famous sarcastic quip about the limited nature of folk song: "the whole trouble with a folksong is that once you have played it through, there is nothing much you can do except play it again, and play it rather louder."[150] In contrast, Vaughan Williams admitted that such a song might become "wearisome" after twenty verses, but still saw this as a strength, asserting that a folk song might not reveal its true character for several of those verses.¹⁵¹ Bax also was not interested in a folk or pastoral school of music, and though he admired Vaughan Williams and Holst (the feeling was mutual),¹⁵² he had no time for Cecil Sharp and his folk activities.¹⁵³ He further believed that a "national English style" was not feasible in any case, noting, "Now in my view it seems that [...] a national school [...] is quite impossible in the British Isles. The only distinctively English features towards which we the British composer may turn for inspiration are the lovely landscapes and the unequalled light of our showery north."¹⁵⁴ He did, however, have a fondness for Irish melodies, and their shapes influenced his compositions to a certain extent, if not to the point of direct borrowing.¹⁵⁵

Grainger noted that the conductor Sir Thomas Beecham had remarked that "these little tunes [folk songs] have done more to spoil British Music than any other single factor."¹⁵⁶ Many of the Impressionists held that their work was forward-looking, breaking the mold of the Germanic templates, while folk song enthusiasts were by contrast merely wallowing in an imaginary past, writing "cow pat" music (a derogatory term coined by the composer Elisabeth Lutyens)¹⁵⁷ that was neither challenging nor original. The irony, of course, was that composers in other countries (such as Bartók in Hungary and Janáček in Bohemia) were praised for their use of folk songs in crafting a national identity and music. Vaughan Williams noted, "We had our critics, who took the curious line that, though it was perfectly right and proper for a Russian or a Norwegian to build up his style on his own national melodies, if an Englishman tried to do so, he was being what they described by that appalling, invented word 'folky.'"¹⁵⁸ He also noted that "National music is not necessarily folk-song; on the other hand folk-song is, by nature, necessarily national."¹⁵⁹ He always dismissed the charge that using folk songs in composition was a kind of cheat, or evidence of a lack of originality.¹⁶⁰

The new music was not limited to these folk or Impressionist influences. The theater was also an important component in the musical revival of the late 19th and early 20th centuries. Drawing inspiration from the Elizabethan Age, composers of the new English renaissance period often sought to promote England's own artistic theatrical culture, to give it a life separate from the operas of Italy and Germany, as well as from American vaudeville, though there was less success in this area than in others.¹⁶¹ This was in contrast to music hall shows and revue, which were popular with the masses, but did not rate as true art in the minds of the reformers. Indeed, Victorians had frequently seen this form of entertainment, which had its origins in pubs in the early decades of the 19th century, as lowbrow and even scandalous.¹⁶²

The Edwardian years heralded a new era in music and culture, and would perhaps be looked back on as a time of artistic innocence and naivety, given the horrors of war that would soon follow. It was the golden age of folk song collecting, but this yearning for a pastoral, rural salvation from the ravages of the Industrial Revolution would soon face the realities of the most appalling use of new technologies yet, in the mass slaughter that the Great War brought. As the drums of war began to beat in 1914, and all things German came to be vilified, many composers and musicians felt that it was their patriotic duty to join the war effort. Not enlisting or worse, demonstrating a conscientious objector's philosophy, could lead to prosecution and imprisonment. Vaughan Williams served in the Royal Army Medical Corps,[163] while Percy Grainger left for the United States, though he did join the army in a band capacity when America entered the war in 1917.[164] Holst was prevented from enlisting due to various medical conditions,[165] while Heseltine seems to have faked a medical problem to gain an exemption.[166] Several opted for active combat duty, and promising young composers such as George Butterworth and Ernest Farrar were killed, while others such as Ivor Gurney and Ernest Moeran suffered injuries that would remain with them for the rest of their lives.[167]

During and immediately after World War I, there was naturally a rejection of the Germanic influence, and indeed, all things German. Teutonic music was removed from concert programs, and German musicians were fired from orchestras and other groups, replaced with sometimes less qualified English equivalents. This mood was significant enough for the royal family to change its name to "Windsor" from "Saxe-Coburg." On a much smaller level, it may have been one of several factors that led Philip Heseltine to adopt the less German-sounding (though arguably more provocative) *nom de plume* of Peter Warlock for at least some of his compositions and criticism.[168] Holst was obliged to drop the "von" from his name before embarking on YMCA musical work for the British troops stationed in the Eastern Mediterranean in 1918.[169]

During the war, the government did not have an official policy on the use of music for propaganda, though some composers, particularly Elgar, produced works crafted to inspire the English and honor the fallen.[170] Those composers serving in the war most often had little time to create new works, other than jotting down sketches and ideas. Stanford and Parry, perhaps surprisingly, did not produce a significant amount of patriotic music during the period. Both detested the war and perhaps could not bring themselves to write much in its support, especially since both had for so long extolled the German tradition.[171]

Stanford, the conservative Irishman who had adopted all things English, was doubly troubled by the Easter Rising in his native Ireland in 1916, the first major rebellion by Irish republicans determined to secede from the United Kingdom and establish self-rule. It failed, but opened the door to the movement that ultimately succeeded in establishing the Republic of Ireland.[172] Stanford also had been so concerned by German air raids on London that he relocated to Windsor[173]; as the war progressed, he was very troubled to learn of the fates of former Royal College students such as Gurney and Butterworth. He had a falling-out with Parry in late 1916. However, when Parry died in October 1918 from the flu epidemic, Stanford saw to it that he was buried in St. Paul's Cathedral.[174]

Parry, who had long loved Germanic culture, was thrown into despair over the war, which he had always assumed would not happen. As Jeremy Dibble notes, "During the war he watched a life's work of progress and education being wiped away as the male population, particularly the new fertile generation of composing talent—of the Royal College, dwindled."[175] It is sad and ironic that he died only a month before the formal end of the war.

By that time, Stanford was seeing his popularity diminish. Elgar's music remained popular with the public (and would be so for decades), but his works were taken less seriously with each passing year by the establishment and the press. H.C. Colles, who had inherited the *Times* from Fuller Maitland, noted the importance of the generational shift and potential new directions for music, brought about more abruptly by four years of war: "As the poets of today have come from the trenches, may we not expect that the British musical future is being born in the fields of France?"[176] The post-war years would see the pastoral/folk song school of composition come into its own as a successor to the earlier Kensington movement, and though many would have wished it, it was not Vaughan Williams who took over the leadership role in an academic capacity. Hugh Allen, an organist, director of music at the University of Reading, and then director of the Leeds Festival, was chosen to head the Royal College. Holst was relieved, having noted in 1919: "Directorship of the RCM is an excellent example of the sort of big job that kills an artist. Parry sacrificed himself to save an awkward situation [...] but I dread RVW being offered something of that sort. I suppose he would decline. But he would accept if the question of self-sacrifice and duty came in as it did with Parry."[177] While Allen shared Parry's love of Brahms, he was also devoted to the new sounds of the pastoral movement, and was a long-time good friend of Vaughan Williams, ensuring that the new style would be given official sanction in academia. In his efforts to expand the College, he brought in both Vaughan Williams and Holst as part-time professors of composition,[178] so that their new ideas would take hold. Indeed, "the Allen-Vaughan Williams axis was the backbone of the Renaissance in the inter-war period. In its genteel anti-establishment instincts, it was, ironically, the *new* establishment."[179]

Due in part to Allen's efforts, music as a serious academic subject gained ground in the 1920s, something that Parry and Stanford had struggled to achieve during their tenures.[180] This new development extended outside of

1. English Music from the Later 19th Century 35

London and the traditional enclosure of Oxbridge to take hold in Wales and other regions.[181] Allen also brought in the gifted conductor Adrian Boult, a great champion of the new English music.[182] Boult was later to assume the directorship of music at the BBC, establishing the BBC Symphony Orchestra in an effort to bring up standards of playing and establish a world-class orchestra. He was highly successful, and this also gave an important new outlet for widely disseminating the works of Vaughan Williams, Holst, and others to the masses via radio, something that the purveyors of this latter-day renaissance actively encouraged.[183]

Before this, however, Vaughan Williams had produced his remarkable *Pastoral Symphony* in 1922 which, contrary to its name, did not strive to evoke images of the English countryside, but rather the war-torn fields of France. Many have since declared that the work is his War Requiem. It was a success under Boult's skillful conducting and his support for it helped significantly to set the tone for how the ongoing renaissance would develop in this new direction. Increasingly Vaughan Williams assumed the mantle of England's national composer, as we will see in chapter 3.

Throughout the 1920s, English art music inspired by folk songs and pastoral imagery was a dominant force. While Vaughan Williams and Holst in particular both experimented with many different techniques and sounds, some younger composers were still drawn into the fold of music that drew from folk and early musical traditions, as we will see. Moeran and Finzi both began to make a name for themselves, and while Philip Heseltine was far less associated with the movement (it was primarily though his friendship with Moeran), he was passionately devoted to reviving Tudor music. Colles, in his position as editor for the *Times*, did his best to spread the gospel of this new phase of the renaissance, and his assistant, Frank Howes, was the editor of the *Journal of the English Folk Dance and Song Society* from 1927 to 1945.[184]

Challenges were emerging from a variety of other sources, however. Stravinsky's music was enjoying great success in London, while Ravel continued to be popular. Satie's strange and whimsical pieces charmed many, and that most dangerous new music of all, jazz, was taking the country by storm:

> It was a new and promiscuous mixture of the tendencies so excoriated by the Renaissance in the pre-war years—neurotic Russians, the decadent French and the frivolous, degenerate—and above all, Black—music of the Americans. [...] The moral highground which Grove and Parry had gained, and which Vaughan Williams now so benignly occupied, seemed in danger of being inundated by a rising tide of alien culture.[185]

Vaughan Williams, however, had no real dislike for jazz, though he naïvely saw it as a uniquely American phenomenon that others would not be able to play or compose properly.[186] However, by the 1930s he had come to view Stravinsky as "that Russian monkey-brain."[187]

The inevitability of this change and the adoption of daring new techniques and sounds by many younger composers meant that the older adherents would also have to keep up with the times, if they wished to remain relevant. Holst had already shown himself capable of exploring many new styles and forms (as we will see in chapter 4), and even Uncle Ralph showed that he was adept in creating new works that could be positively shocking, such as his violent and dissonant *Symphony No. 4*, premiered in 1935 and dedicated to Bax, and seen by some as a warning of the storm clouds of war that many feared were gathering once again over Germany, though Vaughan Williams denied this.[188]

By the early 1930s, critics of the pastoral school were ever more vocal, such as composer and conductor Frank Bridge (1879–1941, who was passed over for a conductorship at the BBC and largely ignored by the new Kensington elite), and his young composition student, Benjamin Britten (1913–76), both of whom saw folk song influences and pastoralism as archaic and hide-bound to the new academia.[189] Britten, of course, went on to become a major force in 20th-century English music; his operas are of particular importance. He would also produce his own settings of folk songs, but in a different way than those of Vaughan Williams and others of the Edwardian age. He was highly critical of Vaughan Williams in general, decrying what he saw as the older composer's "technical incompetence."[190]

Some critics have questioned just how effective the pastoral English composers were in distancing themselves from Germanic and other influences, when many continued to use the very musical forms that had been perfected by the Germans. Hughes and Stradling argue that the very practice of seeking inspiration in folk song and dance was itself Germanic, and the structures of the composed music still relied on those traditional symphonic and orchestral styles so prevalent in German music,[191] such that "a truly autonomous English style was not possible."[192]

Percy Grainger was acutely aware of this contradiction. He had long held anti–Germanic views, and as late as 1953,[193] he wrote a letter to his friend, Danish composer and cellist Herman Sandby, decrying the persistence of Germanic musical forms, and the composers who still use them:

> Debussy, Ravel, Balfour Gardiner, Gabriel Fauré, Resphigi & myself divorced ourselves from the filthy Sonata-Symphony form. Why did you, Cyril [Scott], John Alden Carpenter join Sibelius, Carl Nielsen, Sir Hubert Parry, César Franck, in *crawling on yr knees* once more to the Germans, *accepting a German form* once more, after geniuses like Grieg, Debussy etc had repudiated? What magic is it that these Germans have that all people want to crawl on their knees before them—them, the murderers of our young men, not once, *but repeatedly*, 1860, 1870, 1914, 1938? I shall never understand it.[194]

He goes on to denounce the Germans for declaring themselves to be superior to others, when in fact, they are inferior to other "Germanics," i.e., the Nordic and English peoples.[195]

Regardless of the ultimate source of the preferred musical forms (Germanic or otherwise), the innovations that the post–1900 group of English composers introduced would be important for a far longer time than many had imagined, even as they were dismissed and criticized by the next generation after them.

For example, such music had an influence on later film scoring. Vaughan Williams wrote music for several films,[196] but another influence goes back as early as 1912–13, and his *London Symphony*. In the *Lento* (the slow second movement) for example, one can identify melodic ideas and harmonic features that would find their way into the music of Hollywood blockbusters from the 1970s onward; many have remarked on the "cinematic" feel of the music. Butterworth wrote of the movement: "The slow movement is an idyll of grey skies and secluded byways—an aspect of London quite as familiar as any other; the feeling of the music is remote and mystical, and its very characteristic beauty is not of a kind which it is possible to describe in words."[197] Holst, of course, wrote *The Planets*, and its sections would influence the writing of many science fiction movie scores,[198] especially with his innovative use of brass. The lineage of these kinds of musical motifs is found in the works of contemporary film composers such as John Williams, whose "Empire" theme from *Star Wars* owes a debt to Holst's *Mars*, and Howard Shore, whose acclaimed *Lord of the Rings* scores readily evoke the sounds of early 20th-century English pastoralism in their music for the Shire and the Hobbits.[199]

Ultimately, we can ask the question, absurd though it might seem at first: was there an English Musical Renaissance? There is no doubt that the later 19th century witnessed the beginning of a number of remarkable changes in English music. If we take the no-names and forgotten English composers from roughly 1780 to 1880, and then compare them to those whose work appeared over the next hundred years, the contrast is astonishing. We see not only the composers of this chapter (Parry, Stanford, Elgar, Sullivan, and others), but the composers who we will examine in detail in chapters 3 through 9, plus a host of others who chose different styles: Frederick Delius, Arnold Bax, John Ireland, Constant Lambert, Benjamin Britten, Michael Tippet, and many others. This extremely impressive list surely demonstrates that an important revival occurred, driven by a host of complex factors, which changed the nature and content of English art music permanently and for the better. Folk song was simply one of many ways in which this revival expressed itself.

Keith Warsop notes:

> If we look at English music up to 1914 there is an extremely wide range of compositional endeavour being greeted. [...] Those such as Vaughan Williams and Holst who looked to folk song, the Tudor composers and Purcell for their inspiration for a genuine English music were just one wing of the rising generation. Others found that the development of the German/Austrian tradition at the hands of Strauss and Mahler proved equally inspiring, while the Russian school, both nationalist and theosophist, Debussy and other French masters and the attraction of Celtic and Oriental culture (cf. Bantock, Bax and Scott) made an important contribution.

Further, he observes: "From our vantage point, with our knowledge of these and other composers, we can say emphatically that, if there was an English musical renaissance from the last quarter of the 19th century, then it advanced on broader fronts than that of the pastoral tradition."[200]

Necessarily confining this book's scope to that pastoral and folk tradition, we will now turn to the folk revival, coming as it did during a time of uncertainty and disillusionment, and seeking comfort in some form of return to an idyllic past.

2

The Revival of Folk and Early Traditions

The folk revival that became such a forceful movement from the later 19th century onward had its origins in many different sources, which came together to produce an English phenomenon that was both similar and different to those in other nations.[1] On the surface, the English revival seems to have been a yearning for a simpler time, and a longing for rural traditions that had been devastated by the Industrial Revolution. It evoked images of pastoral England, timeless folk activities, and of rustic contentment. The notion of a "merrie olde England" was emphasized, and was linked with colorful historical imagery, such as the Tudor Age, Shakespeare's works, and legends of King Arthur and Robin Hood, as well as in the literature of the time.[2] Not only folk music, but folk dance, traditional crafts, and early music were enjoying newfound popularity, and while there were obvious differences between them, they often overlapped and contributed to the whole. Of course, these disparate strands had a number of sources; there were many agendas and opinions about what these varied revivals meant and what their purposes were.

Among the issues that contributed to these movements were the upheavals of industry and the social ills that it brought, a vague fear of an Empire that had overextended itself and was in danger of retracting, the prolonged Boer War (which did not end until May 1902) bringing embarrassment to the nation, the growing power and voice of the working classes and the labor movements with their Marxist and socialist sympathies, and the emergence of rival industrial and colonial nations (such as Germany and Italy). All of these factors played a part in the unease felt by many in the middle and upper classes. Undoubtedly, some feared a loss of national identity and nationhood itself.

One solution was to look back to England's own traditions as a source of inspiration and strength, and as critics have suggested, if the appropriate source could not be found, it could be invented. Religious movements, typified by groups such as the New Crusade, wanted an end to industrialism and large towns, with their many dehumanizing aspects; as an alternative, such groups advocated a return to pastoral life and traditional crafts.[3] Socialism as well as Christianity sometimes blended in the reformers' minds, as in Thaxted in Essex, where the vicar, Conrad Noel, merged these two ideologies with a revolutionary fervor that was not always appreciated or wanted (he was later an associate of Holst's).[4] Other spiritualties cropped up, such as forms of pantheism and neo-paganism, which devoted themselves in part to a return to a rural way of living.[5] On a more mundane level, the National Trust was founded in 1895 to preserve natural areas from exploitation and degradation.[6]

Some feared that these revolutionary egalitarian ideas would undermine society, even if they supported embracing rural ideals. Kenneth Grahame, author of the beloved children's book, *The Wind in the Willows* (published in 1908), wrote the work from a "need to combat his everlasting fear (shared by many of his class and period) that the structure of society might be destroyed through social revolution."[7] His biographer, Peter Green, further notes that the book "embodies in miniature the whole essence of pre–1914 England—the smooth lawns, the river picnics, the long, sun-drenched days of idleness, the holidays in Italy, the self-assurance and stable values. The currents of change and revolution do little more than ruffle the surface of this summer stream.[...]"[8] Despite his elitism, Grahame was disappointed at the loss of country traditions. He noted in 1908, for example, that traditional Christmas mummers in the Thames Valley had largely been replaced by cheap music hall entertainments and low-brow songs.[9]

Whatever the class conflicts that might have worried those in power, the idea of an English identity rooted in a happy, rural populace fulfilled the longings of many of those seeking meaning. As Vic Gammon notes: "Most significant in this is the invention of the 'Folk' as a source of otherness, the repository of a lost traditional culture with the perceived potential through revival, to reinvigorate cultural and social life."[10]

The arts, particularly music and poetry, were especially fertile fields for new forms of expression that drew on these ideas. The belief developed that folk song was made by rural people for rural people; it had an oral, non-literate, and communal origin that was not "tainted" by commercial and other interests, unlike the varieties of popular music then in vogue.[11] This primitive quality meant that it was more in touch with the authentic soul of the nation. Folk song was more "pure" and did not quickly change over time. It could thus serve as a source of genuine inspiration and renewal for England, once it had been rescued from extinction and re-delivered to the general population in an appro-

2. The Revival of Folk and Early Traditions

priate manner.[12] A Sykes summarizes: "The Folksong Revival was part of a cultural process in which Englishness became identified with the past cultural achievements of the nation."[13]

Howes was of the opinion that the revived dual interests in folk music and early music "were roughly contemporary in origin, circa 1840; they converged at the beginning of the twentieth century to make the break with German and Italian supremacy decisive."[14] Howes, of course, witnessed the events of the time, and was biased in favor of many of its ideals and goals. He believed that the English composers of the time were able to forge a new national identity free from continental influences, a notion, as we have seen, that has been disputed.

The term "folk song," from the German *Volkslied*, and the related concept of "folklore," had been well-established in 19th-century Germany,[15] but did not appear in Victorian England before 1870.[16] Two ideas were of particular importance. As Gammon notes, "The *doctrine of survivals* sought to see the primitive within the civilised, the ancient within modern customary practices. The related *theory of origins* involved writers in a pursuit that was often very speculative and rarely definitive."[17] Folk music, in this view, was a communal activity, and collectors such as Cecil Sharp would come to have very pointed opinions about what did and did not constitute a "folk song."

The collecting of folk songs was not a new idea in Britain; interest in ballads and traditional tunes extended back at least to the 18th century. In Scotland and Ireland in particular, there were collectors seeking to gather native songs for preservation.[18] By 1805, a publisher in Newcastle produced a collection of Northumbrian bagpipe tunes, and there were other independent efforts to preserve the folk music of the north.[19] William Chappell (1809–88), an antiquarian and writer on music, published a series of editions of folk songs and broadside tunes, beginning in 1838.[20] He was also devoted to the recovery of early English music, but did not trust oral traditions, seeing them as unreliable.

In 1843, John Broadwood (1798–1865) published a small collection of Surrey and Sussex songs that were sung at festivals, including both words and music, titled *Old English Songs*.[21] He was keen to state that his transcriptions were exactly as he had heard them, and even if some of them seemed to contain musical errors, he was being faithful to their sound. Though a small effort, this was a remarkable step forward. He showed an interest in preserving songs and having them notated as they were sung by the villagers.[22] His niece, Lucy Broadwood (1858–1929), would later take up his work. In 1889, she republished his book with additions. In 1893, she collaborated with Fuller Maitland on *English County Songs*, "a landmark in the folk-song revival,"[23] containing some 92 songs from the entirety of England and beyond. Indeed, Broadwood would be a crucial figure in the movement over the next few decades, with arguably more knowledge than anyone else on the topic of folk songs during the late Victorian period. She would later be involved in the founding of the Folk Song Society, and would edit its journal until 1927, standing as president at the end of her life in 1929. A talented singer and pianist (though she never became a professional), she was also keenly interested in early music (from medieval songs to the Elizabethans, to Purcell, Bach, and Handel). She was a strong supporter of women's suffrage and had an ongoing fascination with esoteric philosophies, such as Gnosticism and Theosophy, both then in vogue.[24] She was close with Fuller Maitland and Vaughan Williams, among dozens of others, but never counted Sharp as more than an acquaintance, owing to his difficult personality and differences of opinion about various aspects of folk songs.[25] Among these differences, she had no interest in disseminating folk songs to the wider public via the concert hall. Vaughan Williams admitted that this was probably more in line with the original singers' wishes.[26]

The Folk Song Society was formally established in London on June 16, 1898; Parry and Stanford were both vice-presidents.[27] Parry delivered a lengthy inaugural speech, extolling the virtues of folk song and its importance in the place of English music. He stressed that creeping urbanization and its vulgar popular music was endangering country traditions: "And this product it is which will drive out folk-music if we do not save it.[...]"[28] Indeed the heritage of English folk songs untainted as they were by modernity, could provide, "the ultimate solution to the problem of characteristic national art."[29] Parry specifically linked folk song with English national identity and nationalism, noting that they, "are characteristic of the race, of the quiet reticence of our country folk.[...] All things that make the folk-music of the race also betoken the qualities of the race, and, as a faithful reflection of ourselves, we needs must cherish it.[...]"[30]

Parry had previously written about these connections in his *The Evolution of the Art of Music* back in 1893.[31] As the title of the work suggests, he adopted a Darwinist approach to the progression of music, an idea then very much in fashion in some circles. Music was seen by some to be representative of a culture's "progress," with the complex orchestrations of Western music naturally displaying the pinnacle of cultural achievement. Folk music, both in the larger world and at home in England, provided a priceless record of the survival of more "primitive" and unpolluted songs that could be tapped for inspiration and national pride.[32] Cecil Sharp would adhere strongly to this idea.[33]

Parry thus stressed the importance of English folk songs being bound to English identity, going back to the Middle Ages:

2. The Revival of Folk and Early Traditions 43

> The more genuinely English the folk-music, the more it breathes the genuine love of country, of freedom, of action and heartiness. From the wonderful early tune 'Sumer is icumen in' to the few uncontaminated examples of the present day the same qualities of style are apparent—a style which gay nations would call too plain and matter-of-fact, but infused with much more character, and showing more genuine taste, freshness, and variety, than almost any folk-tunes but those of the very highest standard.[34]

Despite their support for English folk music, however, neither Parry nor Stanford collected songs as their students would, or used folk melodies as a basis for their own compositions.[35]

The society itself got off to a slow start, and would not gain momentum for several years, until pushed to do so by Cecil Sharp. Indeed, Vaughan Williams admitted that in its early years, it was comprised of individuals who "discussed our traditional melodies over a cup of tea in a dilettante spirit."[36] This was despite the efforts of such musicians as Kate Lee, who has a very credible claim to being the chief architect of the new society, but who, like many women in the movement, tended to be sidelined over the years.[37] Internal divisions over the purpose of the organization may have prevented it from moving forward at the beginning, as Bearman notes: "The early Society does not appear to have had any clear policy as to what its functions and role should be [...] and one of the most interesting features of the early Society is the number and identity of those folk-music enthusiasts who did not join,"[38] including Vaughan Williams and Cecil Sharp.

On the continent, Béla Bartók became aware of the importance of folk music in Hungary from 1904 (having ignored it previously, even though he was from a rural village). He met fellow composer Zoltán Kodály, who showed him some of his methods for gathering and collecting the rich tradition of their native folk songs, and from 1905 they journeyed across Hungary and Romania to small villages and hidden towns, recording pieces on phonograph cylinders,[39] a practice that would not be adopted in England until it was introduced by Percy Grainger in 1906, and even then it was met with suspicion and dislike by many in England.[40] Other continental composers who made use of folk idioms included Janáček, Smetana, Dvořák, Tchaikovsky, Albéniz, de Falla, and Grieg.[41]

In England, the Arts and Crafts movement included an interest in reviving early music, and soon this became important to several of the folk song collectors. Arnold Dolmetsch was a friend of William Morris. He launched the first revival of early music with his work (concerts and lectures) at the Century Guild in London from 1891.[42] This was another strand that was taken up as a connection to English tradition.

Music and dance played a central role in the revival (or creation) of an old English mythology, which soon enjoyed tremendous popularity, aided and abetted by the enthusiasm of the collectors, and works such as Cecil Sharp's *English Folk-Songs: Some Conclusions*.[43] He published this book in 1907 in response to a conflict with the Board of Education and what constituted genuine folk songs to be taught to children.[44] In Sharp's view (and the movement's in general), this meant songs gathered from country folk, passed on by presumed oral tradition. In this book, Sharp advocated (as Stanford had done) the teaching of folk songs in elementary schools, to promote Englishness and a sense of national pride. He wrote:

> The discovery of English folk song, therefore, places in the hands of the patriot, as well as of the educationalist, an instrument of great value. The introduction of folk-songs into our schools will not only affect the musical life of England; it will also tend to arouse that love of country and pride of race, the absence of which we now deplore.[45]

He was also firmly of the belief that time was running out to collect and preserve these songs. Those that took up the task were, "a well-educated well-heeled set of middle-class people with a shared, sometimes amateur but more often professional, interest in music," who were "discontented with the social and artistic world in which they found themselves."[46] Their work was astonishingly successful, and by 1912, Vaughan Williams would claim that they had collected some 3,000 songs and variations.[47]

Rural life had been changing since the Victorian era, when the Industrial Revolution drew thousands away from villages and into towns and cities, and the squalor that frequently accompanied them. The reach of the "Satanic Mills" spread ever farther, and urbanization was a constant threat to the countryside.[48] Nevertheless, there were great swaths of land that seemed untouched. Ursula Vaughan Williams noted that as late as 1927, many country villages had almost no communication with the outside world, often were reached by dirt roads and paths, and the farms had no modern machines.[49] Along these roads and paths, the collectors of the late Victorian and Edwardian ages traveled, among them Lucy Broadwood, Frank Kidson, Kate Lee, Ralph Vaughan Williams, George Butterworth, Percy Grainger, and Cecil Sharp.[50]

Sharp (1859–1924) dominates as a towering figure in the folk revival at the turn of the 20th century (often through his own efforts), and he is a controversial one. Though it was by no means a one-man enterprise, his influence on the development of the movement was decisive, far-reaching, and at times ruthless. He had a clear vision of how he felt folk song and folk dance should be presented to the masses, and he made a number of enemies in doing so.[51]

Born in Camberwell, Surrey, he was the son of a merchant, James Sharp. Both James and his wife Jane were music lovers and instilled that love in their son. He was educated at Cambridge, but moved to Australia in 1882. He settled

2. The Revival of Folk and Early Traditions 45

in Adelaide where he first took up a position in banking, but then studied law, becoming an associate to Sir Samuel James Way, the Chief Justice of the Supreme Court of South Australia. However, he continued to be devoted to music, and by 1889, he resigned to undertake a musical career in full. He was able to do so having already secured various musical positions, such as assistant organist in St. Peter's Cathedral, and the leader of various choirs. In that same year, he secured the job of conductor of the Adelaide Philharmonic. He also composed and lectured at the Adelaide school of music, where he was co-director with Immanuel G. Reimann, a prominent Adelaide musician. This partnership lasted until 1891, after which Sharp decided to return to England, over the objections of many of his students, friends, and colleagues. He arrived in England in 1892, and secured a position as music teacher at Ludgrove School, a boarding and preparatory school that was founded in the same year. In 1896 he was named Principal of the Hampstead Conservatoire of Music, a part-time position that also included a residence.

As was the practice of the time, music instruction was largely based around the study of German forms and techniques. Sharp, like others, felt that there should be instruction for students in other forms, mainly in the traditions of the British Isles, and he began to investigate how this might happen. This search led him to the discovery of English folk song, which became his main focus from August 1903, when visiting his long-time friend, Charles Marson (1859–1914). Marson, whom Sharp had first met in Australia, was a Christian Socialist clergyman. While visiting Marson's home in Hambridge, South Somerset, Sharp heard John England (Marson's gardener) sing a folk song, *The Seeds of Love*.[52] Sharp was captivated, though he had long been familiar with folk songs; indeed, he probably visited Marson with the intent of collecting and recording such pieces, in contrast to the often-believed story that this incident was his great awakening.[53] As Schofield notes, "well before he did any collecting himself, he was aware that folk songs existed, he was clear what sort of songs had already been collected and he knew of some of the leading collectors of the day."[54] His decision to begin collecting may also have been in response to various criticisms of his *A Book of British Song* from 1902, in which he included some texts that many felt were unsuitable. He may have concluded that he needed to prove the value of these tunes and their words.[55]

After hearing John England's song, he was introduced to Louie Hooper and Lucy White (sisters), and also to a dairyman named Tom Sprackler. The three of them knew a good number of tunes, giving him some 40 over the next week and a half. With a further week of meetings and notating, he collected an additional 45 songs, in the Hambridge area, after which he lectured on his findings in London in November.[56] Suspecting that this was just the tip of the proverbial iceberg,⁵⁷ he returned over the holidays of 1903–04 to begin collecting in earnest.⁵⁸ He held firmly to the belief that this was a dying tradition, quite literally, as only elderly singers remembered many of the songs, and so time was of the essence in collecting as many as possible.⁵⁹ Over the next few years, he would travel widely in Somerset, collecting hundreds of songs (most with music, some only with texts). Between 1904 and 1906, he and Marson published the first three volumes of *Folk Songs from Somerset*, containing 79 of the tunes, made into arrangements with piano accompaniment.⁶⁰ While Sharp focused on the music, Marson noted the words and edited them for performing editions.⁶¹

Cecil Sharp, from the Vaughan Williams Memorial Library (by permission of the English Folk Dance and Song Society, London).

Sharp saw to it that this work was circulated in schools, in order to teach children new songs that were not of Germanic origin. His focus had always been on those songs gathered from oral tradition, in contrast to Stanford's wishes.⁶² Sharp came in for some criticism later, with charges that he and Marson had altered the words of some songs. He freely stated in 1908 that he only altered phrases which might cause offense, and that he did not expect singers to adopt the dialect of a given song's provenance, regarding it as not an essential part of that song.⁶³ This position would leave him open to some criticism; he was making the songs acceptable for a middle-class audience at the expense of losing some of their true character.

Such alterations were understandable to a certain extent, however, as some texts were more earthy in content (Sharp did note the original lyrics in his notebooks).⁶⁴ Given the social mores of Victorian and Edwardian prudery, and that some of these tunes were intended for school children, it is obvious why he would adopt such a practice. As Bearman observes, "It cannot seriously be argued that the publication of uncensored material of a sexual or scatological

2. The Revival of Folk and Early Traditions 47

nature was possible in early twentieth-century Britain—not, at least, if it was aimed at the respectable music-buying public."[65] One Douglas Goulding, who accompanied Sharp and Marson on a few of their collecting trips, noted that some of the tunes they discovered "contained verses of innocent bucolic bawdiness which Marson found delightful, but with some reluctance, had to edit."[66]

As early as 1892, Lucy Broadwood had written to the editor of *Folk-lore*, "Contributors need not be surprised to find a good set of words wedded to a vulgar modern tune, or rubbishy words joined to a fine old tune, for such is often the case, but does not detract from the value of the song."[67] Karpeles later questioned the extent of this censorship, noting, "The actual situation has been much exaggerated. An examination of Cecil Sharp's manuscript collection shows that 90 per cent of the English songs could be sung exactly as noted without bringing a blush to the cheek of the most decorous of Victorian maiden aunts."[68] Further, she notes that a later edition of songs from 1920 included some texts that had been omitted in his 1904–09 *Folk Songs from Somerset* volumes.[69]

Setting such songs to piano accompaniment (a near-universal practice among collectors and composers) was itself controversial. Since the originals were so often sung unaccompanied, it caused some to question the accuracy of delivering them to the public in this manner, effectively turning them into parlor songs. Some of the rural folk singers did not like the idea, and Vaughan Williams himself noted this, but it was generally agreed that since the parlor piano was such a fixture of middle and upper-class households, it made much more sense to produce editions of folk songs in a familiar manner that would allow them to be received favorably by their target audience.[70] Moeran would later complain that the new addition of pianos in pubs was, "an awful bogey [...] in writing down songs," as it interfered with traditional singing (making it hard for him to hear the melodies) and forced singers to adapt their songs to the tuning and scales of the instrument, thus changing them.[71]

Marson proved to be a great help in the collecting effort, as being a clergyman allowed him to introduce Sharp to strangers, many of whom were elderly and might have otherwise been suspicious of a younger man (who was also of a higher social status) wanting to interview them and have them sing for him. However, Sharp could be quite bold in simply striding up to a home, knocking on the door, and asking if anyone at home knew songs, and if they would sing them for him. While most seemed willing to share their music with him, it may be that he simply failed to record incidences of resistance, thus making it seem that the populace was more cooperative than they truly were. If any resisted, he would offer to sing something himself, which often brought them around to offering one of their own songs in response.[72] Older residents, Sharp would discover, often had knowledge of a good number of songs that had been passed on to them. He was eager to seek out anyone who might know an unusual or otherwise unknown tune. He once noted that he had persuaded a young "gypsy,"[73] Betsy Holland, to share a tune with him: "A little persuasion and she sat down on a stone, gave her baby the breast and then began a murder song that was just fascinating. Talk of folk singing! It was the finest and most characteristic bit of singing I had ever heard."[74]

Sharp's preferred method of collecting the songs was simply to notate them on paper, and write down the words. He was aware that Percy Grainger was introducing the phonograph into his work, to capture the songs exactly as they were sung, but Sharp preferred his method and told Grainger so in their correspondence, stating that he did not feel that such an accurate method was necessary or even desirable.[75] Further, as he often traveled the countryside by bicycle, it would have been impossible to transport such a large and cumbersome machine. He also felt that trying to find the original example of a given song was a hopeless endeavor; far more important to him was viewing how such songs were transmitted orally, for it was in this method that the tune truly lived.[76] In this, he also differed from Vaughan Williams, who often sought to normalize a song to a hypothetical original melody,[77] believing that "a folk-song would appear to be a series of individual variations on a common theme. A folk-song is like a tree, whose stem dates back from immemorial times, but which continually puts out new shoots."[78]

Howes notes that for Sharp, a folk song was "actually fashioned by its oral transmission; by passage through many minds whatever of individuality it once had is transformed into a communal product."[79] It was this quality which made it a truly national type of music, for it belonged to a whole community. Sharp genuinely believed in the power of this music to induce what Gammon calls a "national regeneration"; there was an almost mystical element to his belief in how these songs would lift up the populace and inspire them to do good.[80]

Not long after his efforts in song collecting began, he also became active in folk dancing, particularly Morris dancing, which would also attract the attention and devotion of the composer George Butterworth.[81] Sharp had been aware of this dance form since late 1899, when he had seen a troupe of Morris dancers, accompanied by concertina player William Kimber, in Headington Quarry (near Oxford). By 1905, he was collaborating with Mary Neal (1860–1944), a social worker, socialist, and collector of folk dances.[82] Neal had established the Espérance Club in 1895, as a cooperative to help young dressmakers. After meeting Sharp at the Hampstead Conservatoire, she had the desire to bring Morris dancing into the club to teach to the girls.[83] Using Sharp's dance notations, the project was a success, and Neal would later publish a book of the dances that the group used.[84] Sharp was highly enthusiastic about this aspect of folk revival, naïvely noting in 1906 that there was, "Nothing more characteristic of Merrie England than the Morris. It figured at all the chief village festivals & ales. Every village had its Morris dancers. Is it not worth reviving?"[85]

However, Neal and Sharp would soon have a falling out over issues of leadership in the movement, and she would eventually retire to other activities. The basis of their conflict seems to have been both ideological and personal.[86] Sharp wanted to present what he believed to be accurate representations of the dances he collected; of course some would later argue that these interpretations were no more authentic than the folk songs that he collected, especially in light of his disagreement with Grainger. Neal, by contrast was more open to "imaginative re-creation."[87] Sharp held that he had a duty to preserve dances authentically: "[...] if our folk dances are to be revived among the lettered classes it is of supreme importance that they should be taught by accredited instructors, and that only those dances should be disseminated which are the survivals of a genuine and unbroken tradition."[88] His ideal view of a Fabian society, with artistic values benevolently imposed, had no place for Neal's practice of involving enthusiastic amateurs.[89] Further, Neal was an advocate of women's suffrage, while Sharp was opposed.[90] Gammon concludes, "I am not particularly impressed with the idea that Sharp's vision constituted a sort of leftist alternative English patriotism; his romantic nationalism was, at heart, deeply conservative."[91]

Sharp shifted his focus from songs to dances for several years; he devoted himself first to Morris dancing and then to the dances of Playford's 17th-century *Dancing Master* collection.[92] From 1907, he began publishing *The Morris Book*, a series of volumes which contained his dance notations.[93] From 1911 to 1913, he brought out a work in three volumes, *The Sword Dances of Northern England*,[94] detailing the rare Northumbrian Rapper sword dance and the Yorkshire Long Sword dance, both of which were in danger of disappearing, but which underwent a revival afterward. His efforts led to a performance before the king and queen at the Chelsea Hospital grounds in 1909, which greatly pleased the royal couple.[95]

By 1911, the break with Neal was complete, and he founded the English Folk Dance Society. Neal's previous attempts to establish dance societies had failed, largely because Sharp would not support her, so she created her own Espérance Guild of Morris Dancers in 1910.[96] Sharp's response was condescending, expressing hope that they would allow themselves to be instructed by those with genuine knowledge and technique.[97] Neal shot back, writing: "I recognise no expert in Morris dancing but the traditional dancer himself, and

I recognise no expert teacher of Morris dancing but those who have been directly taught by the traditional dancer. In this sense, therefore, the teachers sent out by the Espérance Club are expert teachers."[98] Sharp considered this to be insufficient and retorted that her dance instructors "have made many grave errors."[99] Privately, his words were more severe, an example being his letter to her in July 1909. Among his other accusations, he wrote: "I blame you and I blame you very bitterly for refusing to allow them [her dance instructors] to be properly directed and controlled. Already the opinion is getting about that the Morris dance is a graceless, undignified and uncouth dance quite unfitted for educational uses.... I am not going to stand idly by any longer and allow you to make or mar the fortunes of the movement."[100] He was also successful in having her removed from directing the Stratford-upon-Avon dance summer school.[101]

Thus in 1911, Sharp established his organization in London, with the intent of preserving dances in what he believed to be their original forms, teaching them to members, certifying instructors, holding meetings and conducting research, offering instruction in schools, and establishing more branches throughout the country, under the Society's control and overview (this last showing Sharp's commitment to controlling the movement). Vaughan Williams was among those appointed to the committee.[102] The *Morning Post* noted:

> He [Sharp] had always felt the deepest responsibility in going to the folk and taking their art from them, noting it, and then disseminating it. He thought there was a very great danger that the art would suffer in the process of transferring it from the folk to another class, many of whom had an entirely different point of view. It was for those reasons that they wanted to gather people together into a society which viewed folk-dancing from a purely artistic standpoint.[103]

Ultimately, popular support for Neal faded, and galvanized behind Sharp, so that by the end of the war, she had given up her work and was concentrating on other social efforts.[104] Gammon observes that Sharp succeeded in "putting the movement firmly under middle-class (male) control and making sure folk dance 'expressed' middle-class aspirations and values."[105] Many would later see Sharp's sidelining and suppression of his rival as shameful and motivated by his own interests and ego, rather than what was good for the movement. Indeed, Sharp could be very difficult and stubborn. Neal would receive recognition for efforts late in life, however, when in 1937, she was made a Commander of the Order of the British Empire for her efforts in the folk revival[106]; Sharp received no such honors.

While this conflict raged, Sharp was engaged in various other projects. He worked with theatrical productions, such as a staging of *A Midsummer Night's Dream* in early 1914, helping to train dancers to perform in the play;

Vaughan Williams wrote approvingly of his efforts in the *Journal of the English Folk Dance Society* in May 1914.[107]

In addition to Vaughan Williams, Sharp's work also attracted the attention of various other composers of the time, chief among them Butterworth, Grainger, and Holst. The first three became actively involved in roaming the countryside in various regions, searching out folk songs from local singers much in the same manner as Sharp (though as we have seen, Grainger soon opted to make recordings, rather than just notations).[108] We will look at their efforts in the next several chapters.

With the advent of war, Sharp found that money and time were diverted away from artistic pursuits, and he had some difficulty in continuing to lecture and offer classes. He spent time in America in 1915, where he was acting as dance advisor for a production of *A Midsummer Night's Dream*. While there, his attention was drawn to a rich and unrecorded body of songs in the Appalachian region.[109] He discovered the work of Olive Dame Campbell, from Asheville, North Carolina; she had collected more than 200 songs. Sharp would later write to George Parmly Day, head of Yale University Press: "Chance brought me to America in the early days of the war [...] and while here Mrs John C Campbell of Asheville, NC, told me that the inhabitants of the Southern Appalachians were still singing the traditional songs and ballads which their English and Scottish ancestors had brought out with them at the time of their emigration."[110]

In her work, he found variants on songs he had collected, and many that had taken on a new life of their own. He wrote in a letter to Richard Aldrich, music critic for the *New York Times*: "the collection contained many interesting and illuminating variants of ballads which have been recently noted in England by members of the Folk Song Society including myself; and also variants of many ballads known to us in the older compilations [...] but which so far as we know are not now being sung in England or Scotland."[111]

He resolved to spend time in America, securing some funding from one Helen Storrow of Boston.[112] Accompanied by fellow collector, dance teacher, and social worker Maud Karpeles (1885–1976),[113] he spent considerable time during the years from 1916 to 1918 in Appalachia. He engaged in extensive field work in various states, including North Carolina (his first base of operations), Virginia, Kentucky, and Tennessee. There he searched for folk songs, which he believed had origins in England, Scotland, and Ireland, but had been brought over by settlers. He had great success in meeting the locals and learning and notating their songs, most of which he considered to be British in origin. Indeed, to Sharp, the people seemed to be in a time-warp, exhibiting 18th and 19th-ventury manners and using words and expressions that had fallen into disuse back home. He also believed that, as a result, their songs were uncorrupted by outside influences.[114]

In September of 1916, he learned of the deaths of Butterworth and other members of his Morris side, which saddened him profoundly.[115] With this grim knowledge, he sailed for England in December 1916, but soon returned to America, where he would spend much of his time until the end of 1918. The England he came back to in December of that year was much changed and devastated by the war. He often yearned to return to America, and also wanted to journey to Newfoundland to engage in similar colleting, but these ambitions never materialized.[116] The last few years of his life, he continued to devote himself to the work of promoting folk songs and dance, but increasingly, poor health limited his activities. After undertaking an exhausting touring schedule in north and south England in April and May 1924, he died in Hampstead on June 23.[117] His only regret was not living longer to finish the rest of his projects. In the immediate years after he died, the Folk Dance Society flourished and became an important part of English cultural life.[118]

After his death, Karpeles was his chief "evangelist" and champion for his theories and methods, continuing his work and compiling information for a biography. She had been devoted to him since 1909, when she and her sister Helen had enrolled in classes at the Stratford-upon-Avon Festival, under Sharp's direction. They soon formed part of the core team that worked with him. In 1913, Maud effectively became Sharp's amanuensis; by 1915, she had moved into his home.[119] They worked together closely until his death, and her efforts afterward produced three editions of his biography, in 1933, 1955, and 1967. She also took the trips to Newfoundland that he was unable to make, searching for folk songs in 1929 and 1930; in the 1950s, she would return to the Appalachians. She was honored with an OBE in 1961 for her work,[120] and stood by his methods until her death in 1976, by which time, Sharp and his colleagues were coming under considerable scrutiny and criticism for their approach.

Indeed, by the 1960s, historians and social critics were rethinking some of the established opinions about Sharp, and what he had accomplished, going further than critical views had done before. Colin Irwin sums up the differences:

> The popular image is of a charming eccentric cycling around Somerset knocking on people's doors persuading old ladies to sing him their lovely old songs so he could save them from extinction, and preserve them through his books and lectures to provide a formidable harvest for future generations to enjoy and plunder. The conflicting modernist view is of a controlling manipulator who presented a false idyll of rural England by excluding anything that didn't fit his agenda, moulding himself as an untouchable icon of the folk-song movement in the process.[121]

2. The Revival of Folk and Early Traditions 53

As Jan Marsh has noted, it perhaps seemed to these middle-class enthusiasts as if these rural poor were supposed to "remain content in their shabby, ignorant picturesqueness for the sake of wealthier and better-educated onlookers."[122]

The folk revival, particularly as exemplified by Sharp, has come in for considerable criticisms from many fronts, then as now. Sharp could be quite belligerent, and he made enemies as well as friends during his life.[123] Musicologist Sir Richard Terry (1865–1938),[124] for example, said that Sharp was akin to a "High Priest of a cult," and was "neither a folk-lorist nor an anthropologist, but he had to keep up the pose of being both. Once having formulated a theory it became a dogma with his following, and he was more or less forced into the position of having to make his folk-song 'facts' fit his folk-lore theories."[125] Arnold Bax bluntly stated that "Sharp often talked a great deal of nonsense."[126]

A.L. Lloyd, a Marxist historian and folk song enthusiast, believed that Sharp was simply creating the past as he wanted it to be, not as it really was. He was critical of Sharp's view of folk singers being almost a kind of "noble savage" living a charmed rural life. Further, he rejected the notion that collectors could essentially impose a pastoral ideal of how folk song should sound, based on middle and upper-class standards, and present it to everyone as the last word on the subject; he asserted that the working class rejected this idea, as well.[127] He also questioned the notion that these songs were uniquely English, noting that they had similarities to other, continental sources.[128] However, he still praised Sharp's commitment and his achievements.

In the 1970s and 1980s, the fiercest criticisms of Sharp came from Dave Harker, a self-described Trotskyite communist who felt that the actions of the collectors were merely exploitation of the working and lower classes by a privileged minority.[129] There was no unbroken oral tradition dating back into the shrouded past, as Sharp claimed, but rather he merely invented that idea. The songs themselves were largely drawn from printed broadsides.[130] True, they had been sung to Sharp and his colleagues, but they were of known origin. Sharp and others had merely taken these pieces and rebranded them as anonymous and collective folk songs from some romanticized past, being very selective about which ones they represented. This invented idea was then "imposed upon town and country alike for the people's own good, not in its original form, but, suitably integrated into the Conservatoire curriculum, [and] made the basis of nationalistic sentiments and bourgeois values."[131]

Harker's work was seen by some as revolutionary and by others as grossly overstated.[132] C.J. Bearman was not impressed by his analysis, and offered that scholars had been too quick to embrace his revisionist theories. Bearman argued that Harker's extreme political background had unduly influenced his views, noting with sarcasm, "To accept without question the opinion of a

Trotskyite about Sharp and his work is rather like taking one's view of the *Communist Manifesto* from a member of the British National Party."[133] He further charged that Harker had made his assumptions based on his ideological viewpoint, and had thus made the facts fit his thesis, rather than the other way around.[134] He notes that Harker has misread the statistics about where Sharp collected (villages vs. small towns or large ones), and so one of his chief criticisms, that Sharp favored certain rural sources over others to create a false impression of folk song origins, is effectively invalidated.[135] Further, as with Vaughan Williams (see below), Sharp's selectivity in what songs he chose to publish was due to who the books were intended for, i.e., a popular audience, rather than a scholarly one.[136] The charge that most songs came from printed broadsides also does not hold up to inspection, as the majority of those singers that Sharp asked about the origins of their songs said they had learned them from oral sources,[137] a conclusion also reached by Yates (see below). Bearman has issued a strong defense of Sharp, stating that his work should not be judged, "on the basis of a farrago of false statements, misconceptions, misunderstandings, suppression of the evidence, statistics that have no base, and numbers that do not add up, with its faults compounded by political prejudice and personal dislike. [...] As a tool of critical enquiry, it [Harker's work] is worse than useless."[138]

Bearman was supported in this criticism by Mike Yates, editor of the *Folk Music Journal*, who while having published Harker's original article, later came to believe that his methods were flawed, pointing out that regarding the theory of broadsides as the source for much of the music: "[...] Sharp was lax in asking singers where they learned their songs, but we do know that out of the 311 singers that he met during the period 1904–1909, sixty singers provided provenance for 77 of their songs. Only one of these songs was learned directly from a broadside, while 73 songs came directly from an oral source."[139] While this only accounts for about 20% of the singers he met, given the numbers, it is reasonable to assume that much of the other repertoire was learned in this manner as well, and not from printed material. Even if broadside ballads do account for some percentage of the tunes passed on, there is undoubtedly a good amount of material from other (and quite possibly, older) sources.[140]

Regarding Vaughan Williams, Onderdonk notes that, "On the one hand, he romanticized and idealized folksong and distorted its musical and cultural realities. On the other, he neither sentimentalized his singers nor falsified their repertories and, most importantly, he faithfully recorded the facts of folksong performance."[141] Vaughan Williams and others have been criticized for overemphasizing in their published editions those folk songs whose melodies were based on modes, the older musical scales used up through the Renaissance, rather than the more recent scales used in mainstream Western music since the 17th century.[142] A smaller percentage of these tunes were actually modal, but more of them were published. This, say some critics, was done to give folk songs a false appearance of antiquity, which helped to reinforce the collectors' argument that they were tapping into an ancient repertoire, and that these tunes were the opposite of the popular and urban songs of the time.[143]

That Vaughan Williams was fascinated by modal music is true, he admitted so, as we will see in chapter 3. However, he never denied the presence of later musical scales in folk songs, and never asserted that such songs were primarily modal, or that modes indicated great age.[144] He favored modal tunes in his presentations to represent the melodic character of these songs, which he felt were at their best when sung unaccompanied.[145] Further, the preference for publishing songs in these lesser-known modalities was made more from a desire to print unique variants of a given song, and not repeat what others had already done. Earlier publications had been far more biased in favor of tonal melodies.[146] Vaughan Williams certainly favored those songs which had versions in unusual scales, meters, or were performed for him in an exceptional manner; he readily admitted this and was not trying to deceive anyone. These features differentiated such songs from their urban counterparts, he felt, and provided a basis for the national compositional style that he wanted to establish. Folk songs came *from* the people, whereas urban popular songs were written *for* them. Therefore, his intent in favoring modal songs in publication was not to provide an encyclopedic collection of all folk songs, but rather to bring new and unfamiliar sounds to the public.

Some of Harker's fellow critics defended comparable positions, however. In 1993, Georgina Boyes published *The Imagined Village*, an assessment of the folk revival that expressed similar doubts about long-held views.[147] While well-researched, the book is nevertheless harsh in its criticisms of the movement, and again takes as a given that the entire enterprise was manufactured purely for the benefit of middle and upper-class society. Her contempt for the folk revivalists is barely concealed, and like Harker, she deems their actions to be little more than cultural appropriation, where the folk song collectors and others simply took what they wanted with virtually no regard for the people that they were drawing material from, and certainly little respect. Further, she argues that they ignored the subtle meanings and nuances of the songs (both in melody and text), taking only the elements they wanted for their new, invented tradition.[148] For the collectors, she maintains, it was about obtaining by whatever means certain pieces to save (or rather, invent) a tradition, since those people who had produced these tunes were seen as not being able to responsibly act as owners of and custodians for their own art form.[149]

There is some truth to the disregard for singers. Earlier Victorian collectors such as Kidson, notoriously did not name his singers, seeing them, as Freeman notes, as simply, "tradition-bearers without identities who could hope at best to play a minuscule role in the evolutionary development of folksong, the development of a national style of composition, and the coherent unification of English national identity."[150] Indeed, Kidson noted how he "improved" one such song to reflect how he thought it should sound in its original form: "Like all melodies by him [the anonymous signer] it is jerky and cut up. It wants all the creases ironing out and the demi-semi quavers clearing away."[151] Grainger, of course, approached collecting in the opposite manner, and was probably appalled by such attitudes.

For all of its detail, however, Boyes' book is problematic, featuring overly-broad generalizations and a conspiratorial tone, as if all collectors were simply part of a plot. She twice condemns Grainger for an incident where he obtained songs from an elderly singer without her consent, accusing him of "ruthless expropriation,"[152] but she does not discuss his remarkable work in capturing songs accurately by phonograph recording (to allow the singers to speak for themselves, akin to modern ethnomusicological practices), his sensitivity to those reluctant to sing for him, and his subsequent battles with some in the establishment to try to present his findings from this more authentic collection method. Further, Grainger demonstrated respect for his singers throughout his time as a collector,[153] which she also fails to mention. Boyes takes one youthful episode (perhaps intended mischievously, Grainger freely admitted later that he had never really grown up)[154] and effectively uses it to tarnish his entire body of work, dedicated to preserving songs accurately not only from England, but also from Denmark, New Zealand, and Polynesia. It should be noted that the old woman's daughter was happy to help Grainger in his little deception. Onderdonk notes that this kind of oversimplification attributes "a 'questionable' collecting practice to ideological factors when context and intention would indicate a less political explanation."[155] When Grainger brought one of the singers to London to record the authentic voice, he noted, "I paid for Mr Taylor to travel from Brigg (Lincs.) to London & back, & he stayed with us [...] while in London. I always took the Taylor records very seriously, for as far as I know they were the only gramophone records of a genuine English folksinger made available to the public."[156] These are not the words of a ruthless cultural appropriator.

Further, suggestions that Sharp (and others) pursued their collecting in part for money, (or were at least aware of how much wealthier they were than their singers)[157] are not completely true, at least during the early years of his work. Sharp himself wrote to Olive Dame Campbell in 1915, when presented

2. The Revival of Folk and Early Traditions   57

with the possibility of returning to America to engage in collecting field-work in Appalachia: "Like you, my enthusiasm is wholly for the subject itself. I am not out to make money, although, like you, I cannot afford to neglect that side of the question altogether. I have a wife and a family of four children dependent upon me and I am a poor man."[158] Vaughan Williams wrote in 1911 that Sharp "has given up time which might have been spent in remunerative work and the expense of travelling about the country and finding material is considerable— of course his publications bring in a little—but this is an entirely inadequate return for his outlay."[159] Karpeles stressed in 1917: "[...] he [Sharp] cannot do the collecting work and have the worry of earning a living at the same time. And, of course, there is no question but that he must go on with the collecting. That is the most important work for him to do, even though it meant that in doing it he would shorten his life by a few years."[160]

Indeed, Grainger offered a substantial portion of his considerable royalties from his immensely popular setting of the Morris tune *Country Gardens* to Sharp on more than one occasion, as a thank-you for introducing him to the piece, but Sharp declined. Grainger himself was known for giving away large amounts of his earned money to friends, family, deserving younger musicians, and charities.[161] This is not mentioned in *The Imagined Village*. To be fair to Boyes, she is correct that it was Sharp who earned a good amount of money from royalties and copyrights toward the end of his life, not his singers,[162] but he did try to compensate them in those earlier years when he was poorer. His daughter Joan remarked that he had "little business sense."[163]

Singers who had met Sharp and the others often spoke of them fondly. Louie Hooper noted in 1931 (when she was 72 years old):

> I Louie Hooper and my sister Lucy White, both of this place knew him quite well and spent many a happy hour singing to him at the vicarage Hambridge.[...] He gave me a nice concertina, I would play it. [...] He gave me a book of songs after he had mine and he said exchange was no robbery. And he wrote it in the book.... I liked him very much, he was a very kind gentleman.... He also gave the old men tobacco that used to sing to him. I often think of the days. It was a happy time.[164]

The question, of course, is whether Sharp was genuine or manipulative, or both.[165]

Conversely, Boyes provides insights that are valuable and revealing. Her overview of the power struggles in the movement during the first decade of the 20th century is illuminating and valuable. She observes that Sharp could be a difficult and determined man, who set himself up as the voice of the movement and would allow little to no dissent. As we have seen, his feud with Mary Neal is of great interest, for her intentions for folk dance were very much at odds with his, and yet in the end, his vision won out. More recently, Boyes has written a short article praising Vaughan Williams' methods in song collecting as differing from many of the established practices of the time.[166]

Regardless of their merits, it is wise to view these harshly critical works with some caution. As Gammon observes in his review:

> At its best the book [*Imagined Village*] breaks new ground; at its worst it repeats clichés and makes unsubstantiated assertions. [...] It is quite selective and narrow in focus when looking at the intellectual origins of the folk revival. [...] The aspirations of people in the past can easily seem ridiculous and naive from our vantage point, yet what are any of us without aspirations? The historian must cultivate empathy as well as critical engagement if she is to guard against contributing to the enormous condescension of posterity.[167]

Onderdonk believes that such studies "have advanced a dangerously one-sided reading that oversimplifies the motivations and achievements of the revivalists, and that ultimately exposes a weakness in their otherwise valuable materialist analysis."[168]

Vaughan Williams himself was willing to admit that through their actions, collectors and composers had rendered folk songs no longer "traditional." He had long held that music arose from enhanced speech, and that the words of these songs could not be separated from their music.[169] However, they were now being written down, analyzed, set to harmonies, arranged as instrumentals, and stereotyped, even if they were still at their best when sung unaccompanied. Such songs would no longer exist in an oral state where they could change, and were no longer the exclusive property of the rural classes. Rather they were now a part of the written tradition to which they were supposed to be in some ways opposed. However, he felt, they had taken their rightful place alongside the finest of art music, and if these traditions were dying out in their native environment, they would still live on.[170] The collectors displayed a genuine love of their subject and most often of the people they came into contact with, and many idealized country life and its traditions in the genuine hope for a more egalitarian society,[171] even if such thoughts might now seem idealistic at best.

Indeed, many advocates for the folk song revival were, as we have seen, socialists, particularly between the wars. The politician J. Bruce Glasier, for example, praised the work of Sharp and other collectors, enthusiastically (and naïvely) writing: "Not only was 'Merrie England' once a reality, but its reality is full of promise and instruction to us concerning the merrier England this is to be."[172] Georgia Pearce commented, "I think Mr Sharp is preaching Socialism as eloquently as our best orators."[173] For them, "'The folk' predated the classes; folk culture had the potential to be the culture of a one-nation Britain."[174] Even H.G. Sear, conductor of the Birmingham Labour Party Orchestra, and not generally involved in the folk revival, viewed folk songs and rhythms as excellent for children to learn; they would help to lead them to an appreciation of great music.[175] Ultimately, as Onderdonk observes, "the vogue for things rural was centrally sponsored by a professional middle class largely unconnected to land and industry and whose interests firmly resided in the extension of democratic reforms into every aspect of British social and economic life."[176] Contemporary criticisms of the revival from left-leaning scholars need to take into account such support from their predecessors.[177]

Graham Freeman has argued for something of a middle way in this conflict between the Marxist and revisionist camps in examining Percy Grainger, whom he notes has been used by both sides "as a stick with which to beat each other."[178] Grainger's modernist ideas would inevitably clash with the more conservative views of the folk song establishment, but he, "did not threaten the FSS, as Harker alleges, because his work threatened to undermine some nefarious ideological project dedicated to the suppression or mediation of working-class culture."[179] Their differing approaches simply meant that a split was inevitable.[180]

The folk revival waned in the 1930s, as another, greater war threatened. The threat of Nazi Germany undoubtedly made the longing for simpler times seem irrelevant, or at least unimportant in the face of imminent danger. Interest in folk tunes might have withered and died out but for the efforts of a new post-war generation, who saw potential not only in traditional music, but new ways of interpreting old songs. This "second folk revival" had clear political leanings to the left, often being allied with socialist and unionist causes. Unlike the earlier movement, the newer revivalists were very interested in the music of the 19th century, particularly urban songs, sea shanties, and working-class songs.[181]

The turmoil of the 1960s and the explosion of creativity would be a perfect match for this renewed interest in folk song, as folk music found expression in a number of new genres, such as psychedelic, electric folk, acid folk, progressive folk, medieval and Renaissance fusions (from the revived early music movement), crossovers with English progressive rock, jazz, and other styles.[182] More recently, mixed genres such as Celtic rock and folk metal, and even punk folk have established wide fan bases. The folk music revival continues, in ways that its Victorian and Edwardian originators could never have imagined.

3

Ralph Vaughan Williams (1872–1958)

Ralph Vaughan Williams, or "RVW" as he is often known, was the grand man of the English folk song and pastoral compositional school, affectionately known as "Uncle Ralph" by his friends and contemporaries. He did not single-handedly inspire interest in folk songs for his fellow composers, but his influence on English music was enormous, and any study of these composers and their work must begin with him. It would be a mistake, of course, to label him (and sometimes dismiss, as critics have done) merely as a pastoral composer, concerned only with musical visions of green fields, country life, and grazing animals. This "cow pat" composer was remarkably versatile, and while folk songs always remained dear to him, he was more than willing to try new ideas that often shocked those who heard them, his *Symphonies No. 4* and *No. 6* being among the most obvious examples.[1]

He was deeply devoted to the idea of creating a national music, one that could be identified as uniquely English. The combination of folk song, Tudor music, and a conscious breaking away from Germanic influences were all characteristics of his style, though Bach would remain his favorite composer throughout his life. He did not use existing folk songs in new compositions as often as many have assumed he did, but the idiom ingrained itself in him, and a folk song style of patterns and motifs wove its way into his work at various points throughout his life.[2]

Vaughan Williams was born on October 12, 1872, in the village of Down Ampney, in Gloucestershire. His father, the Reverend Arthur Vaughan Williams, was the vicar at All Saints Church. His mother Margaret Wedgwood was the great-granddaughter of the famed potter Josiah Wedgwood; she was also a niece of Charles Darwin.[3] With such a distinguished history, the family was very well off financially, ranking only below the landed gentry in wealth and

3. Ralph Vaughan Williams (1872–1958)

social status. As a result, Vaughan Williams would much later remark that he had been born "with a very small silver spoon in my mouth."[4] He was not surrounded by vast wealth, but his family had enough money that he never had to take a job simply to survive, unlike many of his friends, including Holst. However, he would earn no significant money from his work until after the age of 40. He was free to concentrate on music, and this undoubtedly made a tremendous difference to the time that he could devote to his art, as well as the lack of pressure to compose or teach for a living.[5] Nevertheless, he worked very hard in all of his musical undertakings, and was always willing to do as much as his colleagues who were less fortunate. He was quite generous with his money, as well, making loans or gifts to fellow musicians in need.[6]

His father died when he was only two years old, but his mother was able to raise him in the Wedgwood family home in Leith Hill, in Surrey near Dorking, south west of London.[7] As with many wealthy Victorian families, the Wedgwoods valued music, and little Ralph undertook the study of piano with his aunt at a young age. His first composition was a short effort titled *The Robin's Nest*,[8] perhaps giving some foreshadowing of the pastoral themes that would be with him for the rest of his life. From the age of seven, he began to study violin and quickly took to it. He entered the Rottingdean preparatory school in 1883, with more musical skill than most of his classmates. Here, his teacher introduced him to the music of J.S. Bach, igniting a life-long devotion to his music.[9] He once got into some trouble for playing his violin after bedtime, causing the other boys to dance, until they were interrupted by the unhappy school masters, though he does not seem to have been severely punished for this.[10]

His instruction continued at Charterhouse from January 1887, where he was able to practice on a proper church organ, as well as play in the school orchestra, both violin and viola (the latter becoming a much-loved instrument to him).[11] By this time, he was already so enamored of music that he could think of nothing else that he wished to do, and he especially desired to develop his compositional skills. Bearing in mind, as we have seen, that music was not a particularly well-received profession for the upper classes of the time, it was remarkable that he was so determined.

Significantly, it was during his years at Charterhouse (1887–90) that he lost any religious beliefs that he might have had. At first, he held to a fairly strong atheism, modifying this over the years to a "cheerful agnosticism,"[12] but he never returned to the church or belief; music was his religion. It is all the more remarkable given this that he was to be so associated with English church music throughout his life, indeed, taking on the task of compiling a new Anglican hymnal (see below). Over his long life, he would write numerous pieces with religious texts, including his *Mass in G minor*. Heffer observes: "He was all too susceptible [...] to the aesthetic beauty of Anglican ritual, of the Prayer Book, the King James Bible, and church music. His recognition of its quality was part of his instinctive sympathy with the culture of England.[...]"[13] A few years later at Cambridge, he ran afoul of the authorities for not attending Chapel (mandatory at the time).[14]

Like many of his friends, he was attracted to the music of Wagner, which aroused in him a quasi-mystical reaction, as he was later to write in his *Musical Autobiography*.[15] He observed, on hearing *Die Walküre* for the first time:

> [...] I experienced no surprise, but rather the strange certainty that that I had heard it all before. There was a feeling of recognition [...] which comes to us all in the face of great artistic experiences. I had the same experience when I heard an English folk-song, when I saw Michelangelo's *Day and Night*, when I suddenly came upon Stonehenge or had my first sight of New York City—the intuition that I had been there already.[16]

Upon leaving Charterhouse, he enrolled in the new Royal College of Music, a pivotal moment in his life. He initially intended to take up the viola as a professional orchestra player, but his family viewed this as somewhat unseemly for a young man of his rank (one of the few occasions where they objected to his course of study), and suggested that he focus on the organ instead.[17] More significantly, he was given the opportunity to study composition with Hubert Parry, who as we have seen, was one of the principal musical figures of the time. Though Parry was enthusiastic for the music of Beethoven, it was a love that Vaughan Williams did not share.[18] Nevertheless, he recognized a certain "Englishness" in Parry's own compositions, and came to see himself as learning from a tradition of English composers that dated back to the Tudor Age, however broken that lineage might have been,[19] noting that "he [Parry] has passed on the torch to us, and it is our duty to keep it alight."[20] The idea of a renaissance in English music was certainly in his mind.

Yet, by the time Vaughan Williams left the College in October 1892 to take up a place at Trinity College, Cambridge, he was firmly enamored of Wagner, like many young composers, and in contradiction to some of the older generation. At Cambridge, he studied both history and music,[21] and became interested in Fabian socialism, though he would never express overly political ideas (Sharp also identified with the Fabian movement).[22] He took his BMus Degree in 1894, and a history degree in 1895.[23] Deciding to return to the Royal College, he abandoned the idea of pursuing an organist's career, owing to a lack of technical skill, and focused instead on composition. He took up study with Charles Villiers Stanford, as Parry had assumed the position of head of the College.[24]

In 1895, Vaughan Williams met the young Gustav Holst, also studying at the College, an event that was to affect his life profoundly; for the next 40 years, the two would be best friends and would influence one another deeply. Most importantly, they would engage in "field days," where they would meet and thoroughly analyze each other's compositions, offering comments, criticisms, and suggestions.[25] They were honest, and if each felt that something was not working with the other's piece, they would say so. For many years, Vaughan Williams felt that he struggled with effective orchestration, the complex process of assigning orchestral instruments to melodic lines, and adding the appropriate "colors" to a composition. For Holst, this skill came more naturally, and well into their mature periods, he was known to have offered Vaughan Williams advice on improving the overall sound of a given piece.[26] Vaughan Williams noted what he believed to be his friend's superiority in technique: "I think he showed all he wrote to me and I nearly all I wrote to him.[...] I say 'nearly all' advisedly, because sometimes I could not face the absolute integrity of his vision, and I hid some of my worst crimes from him."[27] Indeed, "Holst scored his music in a way that ensured every instrument told, whereas Vaughan Williams's orchestral writing sometimes led to a thickness of sound that ended up obscuring some of what he had written."[28] This was a problem that Vaughan Williams felt he never completely overcame.[29] He was self-conscious about his own lack of training, noting that he, Holst, and others would gather, "at a little teashop in Kensington and discuss every subject under the sun.[...] I learnt more from these conversations than from any amount of formal teaching, but I felt at a certain disadvantage with these companions; they were all so competent and I felt such an amateur.[...]"[30] However, he underestimated his own abilities. More recent analysis of his works, including those from the early period, shows that he had considerable orchestrating skill.[31]

From 1895 onward, Vaughan Williams became increasingly interested in the style of the Tudor period, and the musical scales, or modes that characterized it. This contrasted with Holst, who was now also firmly under the spell of Wagner.[32] Vaughan Williams remained committed to Wagner's music as well, but was beginning to be aware of other influences. Both he and Holst were very interested in the music of Henry Purcell, whose opera *Dido and Aeneas* received its first revival performance in 1895, nearly 300 years after it had last been staged.

This interest in modal structures presented some problems in that Vaughan Williams was now studying composition with Stanford, the conservative who would have nothing to do with such innovations, whether from Wagner or from ancient modes. Stanford was always highly critical of his students' work, but rarely offered much in the way of helpful, constructive input. Vaughan Williams felt that he and Stanford were not a good match, and that he was not able to learn what the elder musician had to teach him. Stanford, for his part, considered Vaughan Williams' work to be ill-conceived. Vaughan Williams later noted:

> The details of my work annoyed Stanford so much [...] and the lesson usually started with a conversation along these lines: "Damnably ugly, my boy. Why do you write such things?" "Because I like them." "But you can't like them, they're not music." "I shouldn't write them if I didn't like them." So the argument went on and on and there was no time for constructive criticism. [...] He actually made me write a waltz. I was much bitten by the modes at that time, and I produced a modal waltz! I really must have been unteachable and fearfully obstinate.[33]

He would, regrettably, later withdraw and suppress much of what he had written in the 1890s, as his more mature style came into being in the 20th century.

In 1895, he secured a post as organist at St. Barnabas' Church in South Lambeth in London, somewhat ironic given both his lack of belief, and that he had abandoned the goal of becoming an organist as a profession. He took this post mainly to continue his education, since he did not need it to earn a living. He learned practical skills here, including how to deal with a choir that was not particularly talented, and a vicar who was "quite mad."[34]

At the end of that same year he made a journey to the continent, specifically to Berlin, to hear Wagner's *Ring Cycle* complete and unabridged.[35] On October 9, 1897, he married Adeline Fisher, whom he had met in Cambridge some years earlier.[36] She was a pianist and cellist, and first cousin to the writer Virginia Woolf. He always had a charmingly naïve romantic streak, according to Ursula (his second wife from 1953), quite in contrast to some of the more randy attitudes of his young friends[37]; he was very susceptible to the charms of women throughout his life. Adeline in many ways embodied his romantic ideal.[38] The European trip was also their honeymoon, and they would spend six months in Berlin, where he was able to take lessons in composition with the composer Max Bruch (1838–1920), who was very encouraging of his efforts, something that Vaughan Williams appreciated and would always take with him.[39] He would later offer similar such support to his own students, in sharp contrast to the Victorian sternness he had received from Stanford, noting, "I would rather be guilty of encouraging a fool than of discouraging a genius."[40] He believed in the importance of music education, and that all English children should learn traditional songs and dances.[41]

Returning to London (where the young couple settled in near Westminster), he was informed that as organist of St. Barnabas, he would now be required to take communion, an action which conflicted with his non-religious outlook. Not needing the money, he resigned in 1899,[42] devoting himself to composition, music criticism, and study for a higher degree at Cambridge.

While he continued to produce new music, he had not yet composed anything that would attract much public notice. In that year, he also submitted his *Cambridge Mass* to the university, the requirement to obtain his Doctor of Music. This was a title that he would cherish for his whole life, and he would not exchange it for any other; he refused a knighthood for that reason.[43] The mass itself was not performed during his lifetime, and was only finally premiered in March 2011.[44]

Acquiring this higher degree gave him increased credibility, and he was able to write and lecture more frequently.[45] However, he still felt that he was deficient, particularly in orchestration; this self-conscious attitude was interfering with his ability to compose; he was "waiting for the right spark to come along and ignite his creativity."[46] Vaughan Williams had first heard the *Enigma Variations* in 1899 and was entranced by what he considered a genuine "English" masterpiece.[47] He wrote to Elgar asking if he could study orchestration with him, however Elgar's wife replied that he was too busy, but suggested lessons with Granville Bantock instead. Vaughan Williams did not follow this advice (which he later regretted, given Bantock's immense knowledge), but rather studied Elgar's scores.[48] As we have seen, with the performance of the *Enigma Variations* and the *Dream of Gerontius*, Elgar was now enjoying the first fruits of popular and critical acclaim.

While dreaming of scoring magnificent orchestral work, Vaughan Williams found his first favorable critical reception in a song, *Linden Lea*. A setting of a poem by writer and poet William Barnes (1801–86) for voice and piano (other versions, including one for choir were made later), it was an original composition, rather than using a folk song or other source, and yet it has an immediately recognizable "folky" feel; one gets the sense of hearing an old tune. Kennedy notes that, "In 'Linden Lea' [...] Vaughan Williams developed a type of song midway between folk song and art song, for 'Linden Lea' owes as much to Schumann's 'Widmung' as to any folk tune. [...] Vaughan Williams's reputation as a song-writer was quickly established."[49] The poem's pastoral imagery and longing for the countryside would, as we have seen, become a trademark of much of the folk song revival and its composers.[50]

Linden Lea was immediately popular from its premier in 1902, and was his first published work.[51] Soon he would be known as a composer of songs and song-settings. Despite the beauty of the tune, he would later come to dislike his arrangement, an attitude typical of his view of his early work. He noted in 1925 that he had made money, or rather "ill-gotten gains of such sins of my youth as 'Linden Lea' which becomes every year more horribly popular."[52]

Vaughan Williams was already aware of folk song and that there were moves to resurrect it,[53] though he was not yet convinced that it should form the basis of a national school of composition,[54] feeling that simply borrowing existing tunes "would lead only to insincerity of expression."[55] He had first encountered folk songs as a child, through Christmas carols, and later in Broadwood's and Fuller Maitland's *English County Songs* in 1893.[56] From 1902, he was lecturing on folk songs, but not yet collecting.[57] He delivered a series of six lectures in Bournemouth that were very well received, and in hindsight, reveal the direction that he would soon take.[58] However, he would not begin to focus his efforts on that pursuit until December 1903[59] (see below).

Like Holst, he was yearning for a national music, an English music. He noted how different the circumstances were in Germany, where there was widespread support for composers and orchestras, while in England, despite the gains over the previous decade, it was not feasible to earn a living as a composer, and society still looked down on such pursuits.[60] The birth of a true native music would help to remedy this situation. He wrote to *The Vocalist* in 1902: "What we want in England is real music, even if it be only a music-hall song. Provided it possess real feeling and real life, it will be worth all the off-scourings of the classics in the world."[61]

He believed that the future of music could belong to Russia and England, and "that to get the spirit of his national tunes into his work must be good for a composer if it comes natural to him, in which case it doesn't matter if what he writes occasionally corresponds with some real 'folk tune.'[...]"[62]

His mostly legendary, "road-to-Damascus moment" occurred in December 1903. He was giving a lecture on folk song in Brentwood, in Essex. Afterward, he was invited to attend a tea at the nearby village of Ingrave, given by the vicar. Vaughan Williams was told that there were elderly members of the community who might know old songs. Sure enough, he met Charles Potiphar, a countryman who made him a tantalizing offer, agreeing to sing some old songs for Vaughan Williams if he would return the next day. Vaughan Williams eagerly did so, and on December 4, he listened to and collected his first folk song, *Bushes and Briars*.[63] Frank Dineen notes:

> Potiphar was 74 years old when they met, full of the wisdom of a long life and the lives of those who had gone before. He was the inheritor of a great store of songs and stories passed down from mouth to ear over many generations. Vaughan Williams was 31, struggling to find the musical path that would allow him to fully express the formless creative urges that surged in the depths of his soul. When Potiphar sang *Bushes and Briars* to the composer at Ingrave on 4th December, 1903, the soul of Vaughan Williams was charged with the energy of England's musical past. All vacillation as to his future path ceased. The needle of his creative compass found its magnetic north.[64]

He collected a total of 26 songs and was "converted" to the idea of the value of these old tunes, noting that previously, "I knew and loved the few

3. Ralph Vaughan Williams (1872–1958)

English folk songs which were then available in printed collections, but I only believed in them vaguely [...] my faith was not yet active."[65] It is amusing and perhaps telling that the atheist/agnostic Vaughan Williams should speak of his relationship to these pieces as a "faith" waiting to be confirmed. Only a few months after Cecil Sharp had begun his work in Somerset, Vaughan Williams wanted to hear more, and soon began in earnest to use Sharp's method, traveling the countryside and collecting songs.[66]

Vaughan Williams noted just how remarkable hearing these tunes was for all involved in their collection and preservation: "[...] we were dazzled, we wanted to preach a new gospel, we wanted to rhapsodize on these tunes just as Liszt and Grieg had done on theirs [...] we simply were fascinated by the tunes and wanted other people to be fascinated too.[...]"[67] For him, the significance of these tunes was not in that they would allow a return to a bygone era, but that they had something relevant to offer to listeners in his own time.[68] He would later write that a folk song is "an individual flowering on a common stem,"[69] in essence a small part of a much larger tradition.

The effects of this dazzling went far beyond merely anthropological fascination. Immersing himself in this world gave him exactly the direction he needed in creating his own music. By making use of folk song motifs, scales, and ideas, he altered his own output substantially, and influenced a generation of composers. The folk style imbued his work, such that he ultimately did not need to quote such melodies directly in his own pieces, but could create new ones in the same spirit.[70] In time, the pastoral, folk song style became associated with a national sound for England. In 1932, he noted that he and his friends, "found here in its simplest form the musical idiom which we unconsciously were cultivating in ourselves [...] far from fettering us, it freed us from foreign influences which weighed on us, which we could not get rid of, but which we felt were not pointing in the direction in which we really wanted to go."[71]

After the events of December 1903, he would go on to collect some 810 folk songs from a variety of locations, especially East Anglia, Sussex, and Herefordshire.[72] He became devoted to spending time traversing the countryside, going to villages and towns, seeking out anyone, especially the elderly, who might know of old tunes. He carried notebooks with him, in the hopes of notating previously unknown folk treasures. He soon suspected that the entire country held a vast collection of songs, awaiting discovery, as he noted in a letter to the *Morning Post*:

> Now I believe that Ingrave is not an exceptional village.[...] I imagine if every village, not only in Essex, but all over England, were investigated, an equally rich store of traditional song will be found [...] it is the elder people to whom we must go. [...] But

whatever is done in the way of preserving traditional music must be done quickly [...] if they [folk songs] are not soon noted down and preserved they will be lost forever.[73]

Indeed, just before his meeting with Potiphar, he was worried that these songs were in danger of being lost, and had written to the *Morning Post*, imploring local councils to take action, just as they had done in preserving historic buildings. He noted how Sharp had observed that in France, collecting folk tunes was in part overseen by the government, and that this should also be happening in England. Such correspondence would help in the formation of a national archive of folk songs (under Lucy Broadwood's direction) as one of the Folk Song Society's duties.[74]

His major compositional achievements during these song-collecting efforts were his *In the Fen Country* from 1904, and three *Norfolk Rhapsodies*, written between 1905 and 1906, which, as the title implies, were based on folk tunes he had collected in Norfolk.[75] Though *In the Fen Country* was completed in April 1904, it would not be premiered until 1909, after he had made revisions to it. It is a tone poem intended to evoke the open, often bleak landscape of East Anglia. For the *Rhapsodies*, he had originally thought to compose a "Norfolk Symphony," but later settled on the idea of separate works.[76] The first premiered in 1906, and he later revised it in 1914 (he was endlessly revising and tinkering with his works, never fully satisfied with them).[77] The second premiered the following year, but he withdrew it sometime in 1912. The third was eventually discarded, and sadly, the score no longer exists. While the first has been known in the concert repertoire since it was first performed, the second was forgotten and only reconstructed for a recording in 2002.[78]

At the same time that he was in the midst of this first great activity of collecting and the music that it was inspiring, he was introduced to Percy Dearmer, the chairman of a committee of clergymen that wanted to create a supplement to the standard hymn-book. Many felt that the one then in use was out-of-date. Dearmer, realizing the amount of work needed to compile a new collection, approached Cecil Sharp, who recommended Vaughan Williams for the task. Vaughan Williams resisted (non-believer that he was), at first saying that he knew very little about hymns, but he eventually agreed to take the job, on condition that it would not take him more than a few months to complete.[79] It ultimately took more than two years, but in the final product, *The English Hymnal*, the quality of the work was remarkable, containing works by Tudor (and later) composers such as Thomas Tallis and Orlando Gibbons, as well as folk song settings, Gregorian chant, and newly-invented melodies of his own.[80] These last were published as anonymous works, though he would finally take credit for them in the revised 1933 edition.[81] He used some of the simpler folk songs he had recently gathered and set religious texts with no music to them.[82] He banished the worst of the Victorian sentimental pieces to an appendix that he amusingly called "the Chamber of Horrors."[83] His work on hymns and folk songs is interrelated and helped to shape his developing style.[84] Holst also assisted with the editing and contributed his own arrangements, including his famous setting of *In the Bleak Mid-winter*.[85]

The result was a remarkable improvement for the quality of church music, and while he remained apart from its beliefs, he had cultivated another of those strands of English culture and music that could potentially represent a genuine rebirth of a truly English music. The use of traditional and old music went against the grain, so to speak, but gave worshippers a means of connecting to the idea of old England in a new way. He named the folk settings by their regional origins to help reinforce their "Englishness, a central goal of the project."[86] As a result, this became for him a cultural undertaking that was as important as anything to do with religion; many of these pieces were a living link to England's past.[87] Further, by showing the value of these working-class tunes to the greater population, efforts could be made to improve their lot, one of the goals of Fabian socialism and of other reformers.[88] The *Hymnal* contained Welsh hymns and those of other nations,[89] but the emphasis was certainly on the English.

Another of his inspirations was Walt Whitman, whose poetry was a favorite of many of the composers and literary-minded of the time. His words would find their way into Vaughan Williams' *Sea Symphony*, which was written over the long period of 1903 to 1909,[90] owing to his duties in compiling the hymnal and his devotion to folk song-collecting and research. It was premiered at the Leeds Festival in October 1910, on his 38th birthday.[91] Writing pieces with a sea theme was popular at the time,[92] and it received several repeat performances over the next few years.[93] He would also use Whitman's poetry in *Toward the Unknown Region*, written for choir and orchestra, which premiered in 1907.[94]

His interests in folk and early music coincided once again with a 1905 production of Ben Jonson's masque, *Pan's Anniversary*, the first staging since 1625. Vaughan Williams and Holst, assisted by Sharp, put together the incidental music, which included 17th-century dance pieces and Morris dances.[95] The music was arranged for modern instruments, as the idea of recreating old instruments was still in its infancy. Unlike Dolmetsch's advocacy, this was a practice that Vaughan Williams never thought was necessary; he often strongly resisted the very idea.[96]

In 1906, the fruits of his folk song collecting saw the light of day. In May, *The Journal of the Folk-Song Society* published a collection of 59 songs that he had gathered from traversing seven counties. He paid great tribute to their quality in the preface to the songs, saying that the effort provided, "the ever-present chance of picking up some rare old ballad or an exquisitely beautiful melody, worthy, within its smaller compass, of a place beside the finest compositions of the greatest composers.[...]"[97]

In these early years of folk song revival and enthusiasm for a native English tradition, he was also invited to be a part of a new annual event in Dorking, south of London, intended to encourage amateur music-making and offer competitions for choirs and others, all open to the public.[98] This creation, the Leith Hill Musical Festival, was destined to be one of his most cherished events, and he was a regular figure at it for more than 50 years, as a conductor, teacher, and composer of new works.[99]

By the end of 1906, as Kennedy notes, Vaughan Williams was beginning to make a name for himself, though he had yet to write the works that would make a lasting impact: "Folk song and [Walt] Whitman [...] had matured the composer's musical manner so that the Brahmsian influence [...] was never to recur. He had as yet written no major large-scale work, but he had written at least a dozen tunes which passed at once into the treasury of English song."[100] Graham Muncy observes, however, that this lack of works leaving their mark was in part due to his not more vigorously pursuing publication of his early pieces.[101] He and Adeline moved to Cheyne Walk, where he had a top-floor study overlooking the Thames opposite Battersea Park. From here, he would write the most important works of his early mature stage.[102]

While developing his personal style, he still felt that he needed more education in orchestration, saying that he was "lumpy and stodgy."[103] At the end of 1907, he went to Paris to study with Maurice Ravel (1875–1937), the French Impressionist composer, who was a brilliant pianist and would be praised for his gifts in orchestration.[104] At the time, however, he was not so famed in England, and perhaps this choice seemed odd, but it proved to be a very wise one. Ravel was three years younger than Vaughan Williams, but showed a remarkable gift for tone color and radical new sounds that were in contrast to the sometime-heaviness of the Germanic musical tradition. Vaughan Williams was able to incorporate a lighter feel into his work from then on, and also was given the confidence that composing from the piano (often looked down upon by establishment teachers and composers) was not only acceptable, but preferable in exploring new harmonic possibilities.[105] Vaughan Williams absorbed much that his teacher had to offer, and would have happily studied with him for years (he stayed in Paris for only three months). Ravel paid his student a compliment in noting that Vaughan Williams was the only one of his pupils who did not attempt to write Ravel's music,[106] and later told him that he was "a pupil of who I am proud."[107] He would visit London and Vaughan Williams in April 1909, and had a thoroughly good time, being quite taken with the city.[108] The two remained friends, and corresponded during their respective services during World War I.[109]

Upon his return, he was awash in new musical ideas. With the combination of influences from Tudor music and English folk songs, and now a new "French" means of approaching his orchestrations and colors, he was at last able to begin works which would fully break away from the Teutonic school. One of his major pieces from this time was *On Wenlock Edge*, written in 1909 as a setting of six poems by Housman for tenor, piano, and string quartet. Vaughan Williams was, as we have seen, one of many composers who would be drawn to Housman's pastoral yet melancholy verses. Michael Hurd calls this work "a turning point in the history of British music,"[110] for its blend of all of the elements that he had so far cultivated, and the drama and emotion with which he was able to imbue the songs. Housman, however, did not like the setting.[111] Other critics over the next few years would be less enthusiastic about his embrace of folk idioms, seeing the movement as backward-looking.[112]

In September 1910, Vaughan Williams premiered another of his landmark pieces, the *Fantasia on a Theme of Thomas Tallis*. It was performed at Gloucester Cathedral for the Three Choirs Festival (which had commissioned it),[113] and the composer conducted. It was a critical and popular success, and with his *Sea Symphony* being premiered a month later in Leeds,[114] Vaughan Williams was poised to be a key figure in a new generation of English composers, though Elgar still dominated public awareness.[115] The *Tallis Fantasia* is one of his best-known and most-loved works. It is a large-scale composition written for string orchestra and string quartet, based on a piece by Tudor composer Thomas Tallis (*ca*.1505–1585),[116] the psalm tune *Why fumeth in fight?*[117] that he contributed to the *Psalter* of 1567 (at the request of the Archbishop of Canterbury).[118] An otherwise minor and largely unknown tune, Vaughan Williams gave it immortality with a masterful setting that blended Tudor idioms with his new-found Impressionistic colorings. It made a strong case to represent the new English sound, and it had a profound impact on many of his contemporaries; Ivor Gurney and Herbert Howells, for example, were said to have wandered the streets for hours after hearing the first performance, so disturbed and thrilled were they over this astonishing new music.[119]

Another of those contemporaries was the composer George Butterworth, nearly 13 years younger, but also eager to explore music outside of the Germanic sphere. The two first met in Oxford during Butterworth's time of study there (1904–05), and became good friends. Butterworth was quickly won over by folk songs, and became an enthusiastic collector, with the encouragement of Vaughan Williams and Cecil Sharp.[120] The two composers remained in contact, and regarded each other's work very highly; there is little doubt that had Butterworth not been killed in the war in 1916, he would have remained a life-long friend of Vaughan Williams, as Holst would be.

Butterworth would be important in the realization of one of Vaughan Williams' next works, the *London Symphony*. It seems to have come about quite casually in 1911 during a visit, as Vaughan Williams recalled:

> He [Butterworth] had been sitting with us one evening [...] at the end of the evening, as he was getting up to go, he said in his characteristically abrupt way: "You know, you ought to write a symphony." I answered [...] that I never had written a symphony, and never intended to [the *Sea Symphony*, of course, was focused on its choral element]. I suppose that Butterworth's words stung me and, anyhow, I looked out some sketches I had made for what, I believe, was going to have been a symphonic poem (!) about London, and decided to throw it into symphonic form. I showed the sketches to George [...] and it was then that I realized that he possessed [...] a wonderful power of criticism of other men's work and insight into their ideas and motives.[121]

Michael Kennedy has suggested that he may have already been thinking in symphonic terms as early as 1910, but Vaughan Williams did write to Sharp in July 1911, noting: "I am in the middle of a great work, & unless I get stuck in it, I don't want to leave it."[122]

Vaughan Williams would later note in 1957 that the symphony was influenced by H.G. Wells' novel *Tono Bungay*, with its themes of downfall brought about by devious business practices and endless financial speculation and misdeeds: "The third movement begins, the last great movement in the London symphony, in which the trim scheme of the old order is altogether dwarfed and swallowed up. [...] England and the Kingdom, Britain and the Empire, the old prides and the old devotions [...] pass—The river passes—London passes, England passes...."[123]

The work has a sense of the effects of time, of the passing of empire, a concern that occupied the minds of many, and which certainly was one inspiration for the folk revival itself. He labored on it for the next few years, and it was finally premiered in London on March 27, 1914. The piece, with its first performance only five months before the outbreak of the war, perhaps foreshadows those international tensions and loss of innocence that the Great War would bring.

Reactions to the work were very favorable, both from his friends and the critics. Holst wrote to him afterward: "You have really done it this time. Not only have you reached the heights, you have taken your audience with you. Also you have proved the musical superiority of England to France."[124] Butterworth gave a very good review after the first performance, while acknowledging some of the criticism that Vaughan Williams was receiving. In defense of

3. Ralph Vaughan Williams (1872–1958)

Vaughan Williams' technique, which was already coming under fire from some in the establishment, Butterworth wrote:

> It would be hard to name any other first-rate composer who has 'found himself' with such apparent difficulty as Vaughan Williams, and this fact is sometimes cited against him as a proof of amateurish clumsiness; the beauty and originality of his ideas is widely recognised, but the not infrequent failure to express them clearly is usually ascribed to some inherent incapacity for perfecting a technique. It would probably be more logical to blame the actual newness of the ideas themselves, and the necessity thus created for the laborious working out of a new method [...] the absence of a characteristically native idiom may largely account for this.[...]"

However, with the arrival of the *London Symphony*, he continues, "the composer's ideas and their actual expression are really commensurate."[125]

Butterworth played a crucial role in saving the piece from being lost. He feared that, with the advent of war, the score might never be returned, being either in Leipzig at a German publisher, or with the conductor Fritz Busch. To prevent such a tragic loss, he committed himself to creating a copy of the full score (with the help of various friends), using the orchestral parts that had, luckily, remained in London. He was right to do so, as the score was never returned. His efforts saved the work for posterity, and after it was published in 1920, Vaughan Williams dedicated the piece to his memory.[126]

He was not happy with the overall scope and length, however, and would spend several years revising it (into the 1930s), and cutting out sections, to make it the more concise work that is known today, ultimately removing some 20 minutes of music. As late as 1951, he considered it "past mending—though indeed with all its faults I love it still—indeed it is my favorite of my family of 6."[127] However, there was much in the original version that has merit, and fortunately for the music-loving world, a recording of the original 1913 score is available.[128]

As he was writing this lengthy work in honor of the city he loved, he remained devoted to the folk songs he had discovered in those golden years of the Edwardian age, offering lectures such as his *English Folk Songs*,[129] wherein he tied the folk tunes to an emerging national style:

> I do not wish to advocate a narrow parochialism in music. A composer's style must be ultimately personal, but an individual is a member of a nation [...] there are already signs that some of our younger composers are finding inspiration in their native folk-songs. If this impulse leads them to develop a school of genuinely felt and sincerely expressed music, we shall owe a great debt of gratitude to those who have pointed out the way.[...] We have made the mistake in England of trying to take over, "ready-made," a foreign culture, a culture which is the result of generations of patient development, and of attempting to fit on to it our own incompatible conditions.[130]

Only by fostering interest in England's musical heritage to the younger generation, and the generation after that, he asserted, would a national style truly develop over time. In 1913, he also brought out his *Five English Folk Songs*, challenging but highly satisfying choral settings that are still greatly popular with choirs and audiences.

As the storm clouds of war were gathering, Vaughan Williams began work on what would become another of his most loved pieces, *The Lark Ascending*, based on a poem of the same name from 1881 by George Meredith. It is replete with pastoral imagery, including a violin representing the flight of the lark in a series of solos that are inspired by folk song motifs and Impressionistic ideas. There is a charm and innocence to the work that would seem rather outdated and even naïve by the time that it was premiered in its full form after the war, in 1921, despite its generally favorable reception. It is perhaps the composer's last look back to that imagined golden age during the Edwardian years, when folk songs were collected and the yearning for a rural English identity was at its height. Nevertheless, it has remained extremely popular with the public,[131] and retains its pastoral charm a century after it was written.

World War I would have a profound effect on him. He would lose friends such as Butterworth and his brother-in-law Charles Fisher. He came face-to-face with the carnage and horror of battlefield slaughter in his position in the Royal Army Medical Corps. Though he was almost 42 years old at the outbreak of the war he felt compelled to contribute to the effort, as did Butterworth.[132] Joining in December 1914, he may have lied about his age, stating that he was two years younger in order to gain admission[133]; however, it may have been that with the war not going as planned, recruiters were willing to overlook age limits.[134] He had no previous military training, so he was trained in medical assistance instead. Though he was twice the age of many of the other recruits, he was popular with his comrades, and was able to find musical work playing the organ and leading choirs.[135] Parry, for one, objected to him joining up, writing: "You have already served your country in very notable and exceptional ways and are likely to do so again: and such folks should be shielded from risk rather than exposed to it."[136]

He remained in England throughout 1915 and into 1916, being deployed in June just before the fateful Battle of the Somme (which would see Butterworth killed in August). That autumn, he was redeployed to Salonica in Greece (where Holst would also find himself at the war's end),[137] though his work was not just medical but also drudgery, including such exciting activities as filling in puddles to prevent the spread of mosquitoes, and washing red bricks.[138] This quickly bored and frustrated him, but he was able to return to England in 1917 for officer training. He was to remain at home until March 1918, when he was

3. Ralph Vaughan Williams (1872–1958)

sent to France again as a subaltern in the Royal Artillery. Eventually, he would take over the job of producing music for the troops to keep up morale, much as Holst was doing at the same time for the YMCA in Salonica and then Constantinople.[139]

He was fortunate to emerge from the conflict without injury, unlike so many of his friends and colleagues, but it had taken a toll on him, more than he was often willing to admit.[140] Butterworth's death in particular was a "profound sorrow" for him,[141] and only three of the seven men he had enlisted with had survived. As Samuel Hynes observes, "The war is not an event in history but a gap, an annihilation of prewar reality, and that neither art nor life can simply resume the old continuities when the war ends."[142]

He did not talk much about his experiences, but his music undoubtedly reflected what he had seen. One of the more dramatic examples of this is his third symphony, titled the *Pastoral*, which he would later explain was "really war-time music—a great deal of it incubated when I used to go up night after night with the ambulance wagon at Ecoivres [...] and there was a wonderful Corot-like landscape in the sunset—it's not really Lambkins frisking at all as most people take for granted."[143] As we have seen, this work was effectively his war requiem, containing many elements that evoked the bleakness of a battlefield.[144] Its slow pace throughout was certainly unconventional, and he doubted that many would like it, but it was received favorably, if misunderstood by some. Lucy Broadwood described it as "gorgeously beautiful."[145] Hearing it now, it seems to evoke many images of what had been lost, especially the realization that the pre-war world was gone forever.[146]

As the war ended, with several young composers dead or wounded, others such as Parry also dead, and Elgar entering a period of critical disdain, followed by very little creativity (owing to the death of his wife),[147] it seemed that the English music world looked to Vaughan Williams and Holst as the new leaders, a position in which they were not always happy to be. Vaughan Williams, as we have seen, was passed over to head the Royal College, to Holst's great relief.[148] It would have been very difficult for him, given the amount of time it would take away from his composition. Also, he was hardly a stuffy member of the establishment when it came to music that he liked. He once told Holst that, after hearing Holst's *Hymn of Jesus* at the beginning of 1920 (which was dedicated to Vaughan Williams), that he "wanted to get up and embrace everyone and then get drunk."[149]

He declared that Holst's work was his greatest influence, and while the two wrote in very different styles at times, many musicologists have seen evidence of this in his symphonies, including the *Pastoral*, the *Fourth*, the *Sixth*, and the *Sinfonia Antartica*.[150] He noted in his *Musical Autobiography* that his masque *Job* was almost entirely due to Holst and his comments and critiques. They spent many field days on it, and at the first rehearsals, Holst suggested changes that improved the sound.[151] Holst, for his part, considered *Job* to be Vaughan William's masterpiece.[152] Their approaches were increasingly different, perhaps because Holst had not had to witness the same horrors that Vaughan Williams had. Holst had always been more interested in unusual approaches to his music, and had a long love affair with all things oriental.[153] With pieces like *The Lark Ascending*, Vaughan Williams seemed to be looking back to an England that was now gone, whereas Holst, never quite as much under the spell of the pastoral and the folkloric as his best friend, moved forward with works such as *The Planets*.

Adrian Boult, the acclaimed conductor who would do much to champion Vaughan Williams' music during and after his life, remarked that after the war, musical tastes in England had changed, and that the Edwardian grandiosity of Elgar was no longer in fashion: "We now want our music shorter and more terse; we seem to need a sharper difference in style between the dramatic and the symphonic; and our composers usually write for smaller orchestras and on a smaller scale."[154] Indeed, he shortened Holst's *Planets* to a half hour, fearing that the audience could not take in more than that, and asked Vaughan Williams to shorten his *London Symphony*.[155]

Meanwhile, Hugh Allen had assumed the head position at the Royal Academy, and as a result, Vaughan Williams found himself in a position to help direct the flow of the English musical style (probably to a lesser extent, Holst was in the same position), though he sometimes felt inadequate for the task.[156] As we have seen, the pastoral school became dominant at the College[157] (and with it, a tendency to downplay the importance of Elgar), but it was not without its critics, especially in the aftermath of the war. Radical new continental influences could only be kept at bay for so long. Vaughan Williams probably did not set out to suppress anyone's creativity in these areas. Rather, it was more of a by-product of the consolidation of the new ideology at the College and elsewhere. He noted when defending his position in 1941: "All these young composers do is pick up a few shibboleths of the new language without understanding it, whereas if they were first thoroughly grounded in their native culture they would be able to assimilate anything that was worth while [*sic*] in these supposed new ideas into their own organism."[158] He offered advice to young composers: "[...] learn your own language first, find out your own traditions, discover what you want to do; then go to Paris, Berlin, or anywhere, rub musical shoulders with others.[...]"[159] In 1932, he further noted: "I know in my own mind that if it had not been for the folk-song movement of twenty-five years ago this young and vital school [of new composers] [...] would not have come into being."¹⁶⁰ The man who had already contributed greatly to English musical life, who generously sought to spread music far and wide, and who was a war veteran, was imbued with a kind of moral authority that he perhaps did not see in himself, but had to adopt, in any case.

Reaching back to the Tudor period for partial inspiration once again, he brought out his choral *Mass in G Minor* in 1922 (dedicated to Holst), of which he said: "There is no reason why an atheist could not write a good mass."¹⁶¹ The war had obviously not instilled any newfound religious beliefs in him. Indeed, this work is more suited to performance in a church than a concert hall, and has none of the grandiosity of the masses of 19th-century composers. It displayed once again his confidence in English tradition to help produce contemporary works.

His devotion to early music also showed in his taking over the directorship of the London-based Bach Choir in 1921 from Hugh Allen, which had been founded in 1876 to give England's first performance of the *Mass in B Minor* by J.S. Bach.¹⁶² The choir sang more than just Bach's music, of course, and Vaughan Williams took the opportunity to expand its repertoire to include not only more Tudor pieces, but also those of Holst and others.¹⁶³ Still, Bach's work was one of his prime loves. He would conduct the *St. Matthew Passion* regularly from 1923, with the Bach Choir and others.¹⁶⁴ As we have seen, despite this love, he had no interest in reviving historical performance practices, a topic that was beginning to be discussed in academic circles. The overall effect of the music was what was important, and for him, the smaller sound of Renaissance and Baroque ensembles had no real place in large concert halls, being antiquarian.¹⁶⁵

In May and June 1922, he and Adeline made a trip to the United States, where he conducted the first American performance of the *Pastoral Symphony*, given by the Litchfield County Choral Union in Norfolk, Connecticut. Invited by a wealthy patron, Carl Stoeckel,

Ralph Vaughan Williams in 1923 (courtesy of the Lewis Foreman collection).

Vaughan Williams was delighted at the opportunity. In addition to the concert, he was able to see Niagara Falls, and New York City, as well as parts of rural New England. He would develop a lasting love affair with New York, rivaling that of London,[166] and declaring it late in his life to be "the most beautiful city in the world."[167]

His newest works still reflected his belief in the traditional songs that he had devoted so much of his life to preserving. He provided music for a ballet, *Old King Cole*, at the request of the Cambridge branch of the English Folk Dance Society, premiering in June 1923.[168] He also produced another of his more famous works that summer, the *Folk Song Suite*, originally scored for the Royal Military School band, and the following year arranged for orchestra (and retitled the *English Folk Song Suite*) by one of his students, composer Gordon Jacob (1895–1984).

However, he was aware of the limitations that such works could have. There was a growing feeling among some in the critical sphere that he was becoming lost in the past. His opera *Hugh the Drover* (on which he had labored on and off for more than a decade)[169] was met with a favorable but rather cool reception, partially because its whimsical and pastoral themes (it contained both existing folk melodies and music modeled on them) seemed out of place in a Europe so badly scarred by war, and also because opera was viewed more as something continental, a genre at which the Italians and Germans excelled. It was Britten who was destined to ignite British opera as a vehicle for genius with his work *Peter Grimes* in 1945.[170] Vaughan Williams' lack of success in writing an opera that would be popular and critically-acclaimed was one of the major musical disappointments of his life.[171]

He would produce a number of works in the 1920s that showed this struggle to branch out further from his place of comfort, with varying degrees of success. Works such as the oratorio *Sancta Civitas* (1926)[172] seemed bold and forward-looking, while his opera, *Sir John in Love* (1929), based on texts from *The Merry Wives of Windsor*,[173] though using folk songs sparingly, seemed to once again be a backward retreat into the familiar.[174] Even his young friend and admirer Gerald Finzi declared it to be "the worst music V.W. has ever written."[175] Vaughan Williams defended his choice of topic simply be saying that Shakespeare was "fair game."[176] Holst seemed to fare better in this regard, producing a string of works that were very different than what was expected of him.[177] That Holst ignored all negativity that such experiments drew is one reason why he was more successful in trying out new ideas than his best friend. In 1926, Vaughan Williams produced a short work, *Six Studies in English Folksong*, for piano and cello (or other instruments), beautiful settings that if familiar, were perhaps more what people expected of him.[178]

3. Ralph Vaughan Williams (1872–1958)

Vaughan Williams' personal life was beginning to become increasingly stressful.[179] Adeline had suffered from frail health for some time; she had always had issues with head colds and the flu, as well as emotional trauma from the deaths of her brothers, Jack of complications from injuries sustained in the Boer war in 1902,[180] and Charles in the Battle of Jutland in 1916.[181] In early 1909, a high temperature coupled with improper self-care may have contributed to her first bout of arthritis,[182] which would become crippling in later years. By 1910, she was already having difficulty cycling or walking for long distances,[183] though she also had periods of nearly full recovery. Much later, in 1927, she broke her thigh in an accident, and the damage was so severe that she had to wear a body cast from her chest to her feet, rendering her effectively an invalid.[184] As a result, they decided to leave London and the home they had inhabited for some 25 years, and move south to the Dorking area, which Vaughan Williams had loved from his childhood. In 1929, they took a home outside of that town, and named it The White Gates.[185] From here, Vaughan Williams would create some of his most notable later works, with music that ironically reflected less pastoral influence, even as he had just relocated to the countryside. For all of his love of rural England, he was at heart a Londoner.[186]

With the Great Depression hitting the world's economy by 1930, he was able to weather it better than some, owing to family money. Due to any number of factors, his works now began to take on a darker tone. The first great example of this was *Job, a Masque for Dancing*, which, as the title implies, is based on the Book of Job from the Old Testament. The idea was initially proposed to Sergei Diaghilev, the Russian ballet impresario, but he rejected it as being "too English."[187] Vaughan Williams was never fond of the term "ballet,"[188] and so the new title was proposed, though the work has nothing to do with the form of the 17th-century masque. Its style was bold and inventive, at times violent and shocking. It astonished audiences when it was premiered in full in 1931, first in a private performance in July,[189] and then publicly in September, both in London. *Job* was one of several pieces that showed that he was reaching much further than he had before. The extremely difficult *Piano Concerto* is another good example, and most famously, his violent and unsettling *Symphony No. 4* (see below).

He spent the autumn of 1932 lecturing at Bryn Mawr in Pennsylvania, where the theme was "National Music." The lectures would be collected and published in 1934.[190] These would lay out his manifesto for a national musical identity for all countries, a justification for the work in which he and his colleagues had being engaging. He noted, with humor: "Those lectures are only what I have been spouting for the last 20 years—now they've appeared in print I shall never be able to spout them again."[191] He summed up his view by observing: "The art of music above all other arts is the expression of the soul of a nation [...] any community of people who are spiritually bound together by language, environment, history, and common ideals, and above all, a continuity with the past."[192] His nationalism was purely cultural, as opposed to the destructive political and military ideologies favored by the Nazis and the Soviets. During his time there, he was once again smitten with New York,[193] ten years having passed since his previous visit. Adeline had not been able to accompany him on this trip, as she was too frail and ill. In a show of support for his continued dedication to folk music and traditions as a cultural nationalist, he had been elected president of the English Folk Dance and Song Society in the same year.[194]

Vaughan Williams himself suffered an injury in June 1933, breaking his leg in two places after slipping and falling on a dark night's country walk home,[195] which caused him much inconvenience for some months. Of greater concern to him, however, was the deteriorating state of Holst's health. By the end of 1933, Holst was confined to a nursing home, suffering pain from a serious ulcer. An operation to repair it took too much of a toll on his frail system, and he died in May 1934.[196] Though Vaughan Williams had always feared the worst, he was devastated. The loss of his closest friend and musical confidante would never leave him. He wrote to Holst's widow and daughter, describing his sense of feeling lost and alone: "My only thought is now which ever way I turn what are we to do without him—every thing seems to have turned back to him— what would Gustav think or advise or do."[197] As early as 1906, he had written to Holst, declaring that if he did anything musically that was worth doing, it was because of Holst's advice and help.[198] He wrote no memorial music, but Holst's influence would be apparent in his *Symphony No. 6*, and he still had a photo of his best friend displayed when he died in 1958.[199] 1934 had already seen two other great losses for music, with both Elgar and Delius passing earlier in the year.

His most unsettling and controversial work yet was his *Symphony No. 4*. This piece was shocking and provocative when it premiered in April 1935, but much of the critical reaction was favorable.[200] Still, he noted that Holst had heard a piano reduction, and "was puzzled by most of it & disliked the rest."[201] Its intensity and dissonance led some to believe that it was a commentary on the worrying situation in Europe. His *Pastoral Symphony* had been a melancholy reflection on the effects of a terrible war, but the *Fourth* now seemed to predict a new conflict. Vaughan Williams always sternly denied this, noting, "I wrote it not as a definite picture of anything external—e.g. the state of Europe—but simply because it occurred to me like this."[202] When once asked what it was about, he replied, "F minor."[203] The work was uncharacteristic of what the music world had come to expect of him, even in light of his recent output, but in reality, it was the logical next step after ten years of experimenting.[204] Gone were all traces of folk song and a romanticized English past. Vaughan Williams himself was unsure of how he felt about the piece, but knew that it was necessary at the time, famously quipping: "I don't know whether I like it, but it's what I meant."[205] Anthony Barone has suggested that the work in some ways reflects his commitment to conservation, and a realization of what has been lost in England since the First World War: "Within this context, the Fourth Symphony is an aggressive response to the tarnished authenticity of the British pastoral landscape that was so often celebrated and memorialized in Vaughan Williams's earlier compositions."[206]

Holst never heard the completed work, and had not been there to advise him, save in the earlier stages of composition, when he had suggested that Vaughan Williams remove the "nice tunes" from the finale,[207] advice that Vaughan Williams heeded. There would be no resorting to his more familiar tropes, or giving listeners a sense of hope or relief. From these years onward, his music would always be surprising, frequently confounding critics who though that they had defined him.[208]

In May 1935, shortly after the premier of the new symphony, he received an invitation from King George V to join the Order of Merit.[209] Having previously refused a knighthood (owing in part to the obligations that came with it), he was reluctant. However, realizing that this was a great honor, the Order having only 24 members, and that it carried no such obligations,[210] he accepted. It seemed that he was now at the pinnacle of his career.[211]

The situation in Europe was becoming more worrying, however, as artists and intellectuals from Germany were fleeing to safer shores in Britain and America. By 1937, he was faced with an artistic quandary, when he was offered the Shakespeare Prize, a new award given by an anonymous merchant in Hamburg. He was honored, but could not decide his course of action, noting: "I feel bound to explain that I am strongly opposed to the present system of government in Germany, especially in regard to its treatment of artists and scholars. I belong to more than one English society whose object is to combat all that the present German *régime* stands for. Therefore am I the kind of person to whom a German University would wish to offer a prize?"[212] He did eventually accept the honor, in August, as he felt that it came with no political agenda, and he made the journey to Hamburg in June 1938 to accept it, yet he was disappointed to learn that he could not take the prize money out of the country, owing to new restrictions; he would not receive it until after the war.[213] By 1939, the Nazis had blacklisted his music.

At this time, he also became acquainted with the author and poet Ursula

Wood (1911–2007), whom he would later marry in 1953, and who would be crucial in promoting his works after his death. They began their friendship in collaboration on a proposed ballet in 1937, and it was quickly obvious to both that they wanted more. They would attend films and events together, as Adeline was too infirm, and Ursula's husband, Michael, was a military officer stationed on the Isle of Wight.[214] From the first meeting the two were smitten with each other, and soon after, they began an affair. The subject of much speculation for decades, Ursula finally confirmed it shortly before her death in October 2007.[215] Vaughan Williams remained devoted to Adeline, and specifically told Ursula that he would not leave her, but he undoubtedly felt the strain and frustration of being trapped in a domestic situation that social conventions dictated he could not leave. Their marriage had long been cool, despite his initial romantic yearnings for her. They never had children, and with her arthritis in such a serious state, physical affection was not possible. So, the presence of a young, intelligent, and beautiful writer who adored him was irresistible.[216]

She became a family friend and his "assistant." Adeline did not seem to resist, giving tacit approval to her role in Vaughan Williams' life, probably fully aware of their liaisons. Ursula became pregnant at one point (though whether by her husband or by Vaughan Williams is not certain), and obtained an illegal termination.[217] Ursula's husband died, not in the war, but of a surprise heart attack in 1942. She moved in with them at White Gates in that same year, living there during World War II, and being one of Adeline's care-givers.[218]

By 1938, Vaughan Williams was feeling worked out creatively, having produced so many new pieces of quality and variety in recent years. For a time, he thought that he might not write again, but soon new ideas were beginning to arise in his mind,[219] including sketches for a new symphony (his fifth) and his *Five Variants of "Dives and Lazarus,"* scored for strings and harp, and based on a folk song (with origins in the 16th century) that he known from his youth.[220] He noted that the variants were some of his recollections of versions he had heard and encountered. In sharp contrast to his more recent experimental output, this lovely piece looked back to his pastoral days, though perhaps handled with a greater maturity; it has remained one of his most popular works. Its sweet and nostalgic tone seemed to express some of the very things about England and its heritage that were threatened by Nazi aggression.[221] The work was commissioned by the British Council for the 1939 World's Fair (held in New York City), and the New York Philharmonic premiered it in Carnegie Hall on June 10, 1939, with Adrian Boult conducting. It received its British premiere under Boult's direction on November 1, in Bristol, as a new war was already raging; the BBC Orchestra had moved there from London due to bombing concerns.[222]

3. Ralph Vaughan Williams (1872–1958) 83

The war had a wide-reaching impact on Britain, and country-dwellers such as Vaughan Williams had to contribute their part. He was more than willing to do what he could, being far too old for active service, and under no illusions that conscientious objection was justified for this conflict. He agreed to take in London evacuees and help with continental refugees,[223] as well as donating some of his land for allotments, to grow food.[224] Indeed, he gained a newfound passion for gardening and chicken-farming. He was trained in firefighting and also took part in night watches for air raids.[225] He helped with the digging of an air-raid shelter at their home, as well as a nearby ditch, as an ominous last line of defense in case of an invasion. He felt that more than ever, the idea of national music was important, to draw people together. He pointed out that for some years, Germany had been engaged in producing "home music," employing composers to create music for amateurs; seeing no reason not to borrow a good idea from the enemy, he advocated for this practice in Britain.[226] He joined the committee of the Council for the Encouragement of the Arts (later renamed the Arts Council), and in 1943, assumed the presidency of the Committee for the Promotion of New Music.[227] The National Gallery in London held daily concerts to boost morale, something of which he approved.

He also lobbied (unsuccessfully) to keep fellow composer Michael Tippett, who was a conscientious objector, from jail for refusing to work in any way for the war effort. Vaughan Williams disagreed with this stance, but felt that composers were already serving in their own manner,[228] just as Parry had stressed to him back in 1914. He also stood up for Alan Bush, whose political views meant that his music was banned by the BBC.[229] Looking back to the years before that first conflict, it must have seemed a world away; his friend George Trevelyan noted that it had been an "age of gold," as opposed to the "age of iron" that they now had to witness.[230]

For the first time, he was employed in the writing of film music, specifically for a movie titled *49th Parallel*, an anti–Nazi propaganda film released in 1941. It starred such actors as Laurence Olivier and Leslie Howard, and was at least partially aimed at convincing the United States to enter the war. He found that he enjoyed this process immensely, and he would work on several other film scores in his remaining years.[231]

Perhaps his greatest work during the war period was his celebrated *Symphony No. 5*, which was in total contrast to the previous one. It is mostly a calm and serene piece, reminiscent at times of the sounds of the *Pastoral Symphony*. Indeed, some saw it as his returning "to his earlier manner."[232] He took some musical ideas from an opera, *The Pilgrim's Progress*, (on which he would work in small ways for decades), and while there are no specific folk songs, it has some of that idiom.[233] The symphony was premiered on June 24, 1943, in

Ralph Vaughan Williams and Ursula Wood at Epsom Parish Church, mid–1940s (courtesy of the Lewis Foreman collection).

London. In the midst of a dark war, it probably gave many a hope for a brighter future, as allied successes were already mounting.[234] However, while some saw it as a prediction of peace, they were mistaken (as with the belief that the previous symphony predicted war), since Vaughan Williams had first conceived the idea in 1938.[235] The work was famously dedicated "without permission" to

Sibelius, who later expressed his delight with it, replying: "Please accept my most cordial thanks for your great kindness which I consider a great honour to me."[236] Some felt that this majestic work was a musical farewell; having reached the age of 70 the previous year, he would now go into retirement, a notion that Kennedy describes as "laughable" with hindsight.[237] Indeed, the remaining 15 years of his life would be some of his busiest, with four more symphonies, ten film scores, and an astonishing amount of travel well into his 80s. The *Symphony No. 5* was perhaps a breath between the violent and intense fourth and sixth. Ursula later claimed that all of the symphonies from *No. 5* onward were "hers."[238]

His second cousin, Ralph Wedgwood, had noted on Vaughan Williams' 70th birthday that he still had much to contribute, offering as an analogy that the last works of Rembrandt and Titian were among their best.[239] Vaughan Williams continued his busy musical war work with a commission in September 1944, *A Thanksgiving for Victory*; with the success of D–Day and the push against German forces, it was now clear that victory was at hand, though, of course, it would not be until May of the following year that it was final.[240]

In October 1947, he celebrated both his 75th birthday and his 50th wedding anniversary, though Adeline was frail and crippled with arthritis. She would go through periods of feeling better and partially recover, but then have another set-back with some injury or illness,[241] but at least her mind never failed her. However, the strain on him must have been immense, and as she deteriorated, he certainly was grateful for the company of Ursula.

The years immediately after the war saw him very busy with committees and societies,[242] and there was a flurry of performances of his works, as the nation's musical life gradually returned to normal. He came to believe that a form of federalism would be necessary to prevent the kinds of wars that he had witnessed. He advocated for a European union long before it was a fact.[243] He brought out a new and even more challenging work, his *Symphony No. 6*, which was premiered on April 21, 1948. The work was a landmark achievement, more so than his fourth, announcing to the world that he had no intention of going into a quiet retirement or retreating to gentle pastoralism. Like the fourth, it was violent, intense, and shocking, containing elements of Holst's experimentation; his friend would no doubt have been pleased with it. Also like its two predecessors, it was conceived as a piece without program (theme). For some, however, its ending seemed to represent the violent aftermath of a nuclear conflict, though again, Vaughan Williams would deny any such connection, and become quite irritated at those who called it his "war symphony."[244] He wrote: "It never seems to occur to people that a man might just want to write a piece of music."[245] Without a doubt, however, it resonated strongly with a public that had just been through such an ordeal, receiving at least a hundred performances in the next few years, and though it contains no trace of pastoralism, it certainly was the kind of national music that Britain craved and even needed.

In 1949, he returned once again to folk song repertoire, with his *Folk Songs of the Four Seasons*, a choral work for women's voices, written for the National Federation of Women's Institutes. It received a grand performance on June 15, 1950, when three thousand members of the Federation sang it at the Royal Albert Hall[246]; there were more performers than audience members.[247]

Vaughan Williams was beginning to suffer from some deafness, always a major concern for musicians and composers; the story of Beethoven's tragedy is well known to every music student. This was a source of frustration, and though he would use hearing aids and an ear trumpet in later life, he never went completely deaf.[248]

Adeline was now bedridden and failing in health. She would have very bad days, and then seem to recover slightly, but both of them knew that she had a limited amount of time. He left for London to supervise a student choir rehearsal on May 10, 1951, and she died that day.[249] He grieved for the loss, writing shortly afterward to a friend (whose husband had also recently died), "We are both alone now—I go on with my work as usual which is what she wants I feel sure."[250] Yet he was certainly not alone, though of course, he and Ursula had to keep their affair private. Shortly after Adeline's death, however, the two were able to spend more time together openly.[251] By finally laying his infirm wife to rest, he gained a new lease on life, no longer being tied to the country house, or limited in how far or for how long he could travel.[252] He had missed London greatly, and now could spend more time there.[253] Ursula's youthful presence gave him much-needed energy, and he would produce more large-scale works over the next seven years than anyone would have thought possible. His sense of experimentation and whimsy can be seen in pieces such as the *Romance for Harmonica and Orchestra* (1952)[254] and the *Tuba Concerto* (1954).

He and Ursula traveled to France, where they visited Paris and Normandy; he had been to Mont Saint-Michel 70 years previously, and had surprisingly, never flown, but found the sensation rather thrilling. It was the first of many trips they would take, including to Italy, America, Greece, Ireland, Austria, Majorca and many more; he was making up for lost time. At the beginning of 1953, they had decided to marry, their age difference being of no consequence. This gave him the added opportunity to return to London permanently, and Ursula noted with amusement that he questioned the 21-year length for the lease on the house, feeling that it was "rather short." She noted that they both felt immortal at the time,[255] and that over the next few years, he was delighted to reconnect with so many friends and colleagues.[256]

Not done with music by any means, he continued to produce at a remarkable rate, the next major work being his *Sinfonia Antartica*, based on thematic material he had written for the film *Scott of the Antarctic*.[257] Boult was not convinced that it completely qualified as a symphony,[258] and the reaction, while favorable, was nothing like what had been stirred up by his sixth.[259] The piece premiered in January 1953, and on February 7, he and Ursula had a small and private wedding that they successfully managed to keep quiet and mostly free of press inquiries.[260]

Returning from a trip to Italy, he completed a work for the coronation of Queen Elizabeth II. He was one of ten composers asked to write music for the event, an attempt at replicating a collection of madrigals in honor of Queen Elizabeth I, the *Triumphs of Oriana*.[261] More travel followed, to Rome in the spring of 1954, and then to New York, where he delivered lectures at Cornell University. Not content with just seeing the east coast of America, he had arranged an entire tour, including Toronto, Buffalo, Detroit, Ann Arbor, Chicago, St. Louis, and then, remarkably, a train journey across the country to Los Angeles, where they also spent time having a holiday in Santa Barbara, and visiting the Grand Canyon, before returning to Buffalo, New York.[262]

Nineteen fifty-five saw another symphony. Again some questioned whether it truly qualified as such, owing to the form of the first movement not corresponding to what it "should" be, but he was adamant that it was simply a matter of interpretation, and so there the matter rested.[263] In these last years, he was still seen by many as the head of the musical establishment, even if younger composers resented his place, while critical reception grew more hostile. Kennedy observes, "one can pinpoint 1954 as the *annus horribilis* in which Vaughan Williams's reputation took its first serious knocks."[264]

His musical standing had been in a difficult place for a few years, as Muncy notes. *The Pilgrim's Progress*, an opera which had been his life's work in some ways (he began composing it as far back as 1906) premiered in 1951 and was poorly received, perhaps even a critical flop. In 1954, his large-scale Christmas cantata, *Hodie*, also met with hostile critical reviews, thus cementing the downturn of his reputation.[265]

However, he was still lauded and engaged in important work. He received the Albert Medal of the Royal Society of Arts (a first for a musician)[266] in 1955, and inaugurated the RVW Trust in November 1956. The Trust was endowed with the money from his performing rights royalties, and it set out to promote performances of new music by deserving composers.[267] A few months earlier, while on a holiday with Ursula in Majorca (their traveling continued at a seemingly relentless pace), he was saddened to hear of the death of Gerald Finzi, for whom he had great respect and affection.[268]

By 1958, he was still working as much as ever, and the premiere of his *Symphony No. 9* occurred on April 2. As so often the case, it was a challenging work, especially for those who still wanted to put him into various boxes. It surprisingly contained some elements of folk song, and he had originally conceived a programmatic theme, involving a vision of Stonehenge and the Salisbury Plain, but he later removed the suggestions of specific themes. Others heard the darker elements of it as the composer's acceptance of his impending mortality,[269] though this may be influenced by the hindsight of his death later that year. Critical reaction was not favorable, and the composer was entering into that period of neglect, yet before his death. It was as if the vultures were circling, awaiting the end. He shrugged it off, in part, saying, "I don't think they can quite forgive me for still being able to do it at my age."[270] Harold Fromm rather bluntly offers the thesis that "[…] it is not implausible to infer that the combination of [Vaughan Williams'] nativism and anti-modernism might have been responsible for his being written off by America's avant-garde academics and taste-setters who bullied our musical sensibilities for almost a century despite the antipathies of the musical public to serialism."[271] Ultimately, Mellers suggests that together, his nine symphonies offer "a vision of Albion—of the making of an Englishman (himself), and of the making of twentieth-century Britain."[272]

More travel followed, first to Naples[273] and then what was to be a final visit to various English locations.[274] He continued working through the summer, planning another opera,[275] his persistence in the face of some failure in the area being most admirable! On the night of August 25, 1958, he went to bed with the intention of attending a recording of his *Symphony No. 9*, conducted by Adrian Boult the next day. Ursula ends her biography with these poignant words: "we did not guess that before dawn, death, not sleep, would claim him."[276] She noted in a letter to friends that he had been restless that evening and had trouble breathing, so a doctor had given him a sedative, but he slipped away.[277] Ultimately, it may have been for the best, she maintained, as he was losing both his hearing and sight, and had been diagnosed with prostate cancer the year before.[278]

The loss to English music was immense and for many, unbelievable. Uncle Ralph, despite growing critical hostility, labored on year after year, and it seemed that the 21-year lease on their home might well need to be renewed. A funeral service and remembrance occurred at Westminster Abbey on September 19, and his ashes were interred in the North Choir Aisle.

Vaughan Williams was fortunate to have such a strong advocate for his music as Ursula. His works, as we have seen, were already somewhat neglected and even insulted in the critical sphere, but beginning in 1964, she brought out her landmark biography, published along with Kennedy's in-depth study of his music in the same year.[279] This was the beginning of a revival for a man who was out of fashion for far less time than many composers after their deaths.[280]

His music is too varied to be categorized in any one convenient designation. Known for his work in folk song, he also used shocking dissonance and was interested in new developments over the decades of his long life. If some of his music is nostalgic, he never personally shied away from the modern world, and indeed, unlike many of his friends, he preferred London city life to that of the country. Right into the year of his death, he argued, "Our own folk song and dance has proved, beyond doubt, that we are not 'the land without music.'"[281] Maud Karpeles would note in her obituary: "In his own compositions he did not, as has sometimes been supposed, set out to imitate folk music, but its idiom became for him the point of departure whence he set forth in his search for the forms which would give substance to his heaven-sent vision."[282]

Though he was quite willing to experiment with newer musical styles and conventions, he always wrote the music that he wanted to write, noting that, ultimately, "there are no canons of art except that contained in the well-worn tag, 'to thine own self be true.'"[283]

4

Gustav Holst (1874–1934)

Holst, lifelong close friend of Vaughan Williams and as devoted in his own way to folk songs and the countryside, is best-known for a work that has little to do with folk traditions or pastoralism, *The Planets*. He was equally interested in Indian culture and religion, going so far as to learn some Sanskrit in order to be able to translate ancient texts from the Rig Veda and set them to music. Throughout his life, he experimented with new ideas and influences, never wanting to repeat himself, and he disregarded critical assessments of his work. He embraced his family's adopted home with a passion and like so many of the others in this book, was devoted to the revival and preservation of English traditions. His daughter Imogen (a prolific composer in her own right) was a great advocate for the man and his music, and her biographies and other writings about him give us a very personal, if subjective, look into his life.[1]

Holst was born in Cheltenham on September 21, 1874, christened Gustavus Theodore von Holst, named after his grandfather and great-uncle respectively. Though the family originally came from Scandinavia, his great-grandfather, Matthias, was a well-respected pianist, harp instructor, and composer who was attached to the Russian Imperial Court in St. Petersburg. For what seem to be political reasons, he was obliged to flee from Russia, and he settled in London. His son Gustavus Valentine followed his father's profession in teaching harp and piano, but settled in Cheltenham in Gloucestershire in the early 1830s. Holst's parents were Adolph (son of Gustavus), an organist at a local church and a fine piano player, and Clara Lediard, who had been one of Adolph's students (and had married him against her father's wishes). So, young Holst was born into a musical family, though his father was somewhat distant and stern, preferring to spend his spare time away practicing. Clara was rather frail, suffering from a nervous disposition. She gave birth to a second son, Emil, but died of heart disease and edema (swelling under the skin) in February 1882, when Holst was only seven years old.[2]

His father was resolved to leave the unhappy home behind and resettled the family in another house in Cheltenham. In 1885, Adolph married another of his students, Mary Stone, who was a devotee of Theosophy, a spiritualist movement promoted by the Russian mystic, writer, and occultist Helena Blavatsky.[3] Her enthusiasm for topics such as reincarnation and spiritualism may have stirred young Holst's interest, as well,[4] reemerging later when he became fascinated with Indian and Eastern Spirituality.[5] She was rather neglectful of him and Emil, however, and later of her own children by Adolph, Matthias and Evelyn, preferring to focus her time on her philosophical studies and metaphysical speculation.[6]

Holst was a delicate child, perhaps inheriting some of his mother's ill health; this was exacerbated by Mary's neglect. He suffered from bouts of asthma and poor eyesight, and both problems were ignored for some time.[7] A condition in his right arm and hand, neuritis, would bother him for the rest of his life, preventing him from pursuing a career as a pianist, though he studied piano, organ, violin, and trombone.

His education at the Cheltenham Grammar School was not a particularly happy one, though he did do quite well on his exams.[8] In spite of these unsettled years and his physical ailments, he took an active interest in music, learning organ and attempting composition, though as with so many composers, he came to despise his youthful output, labeling even his attempts as a student at the Royal College as "Early Horrors."[9] Indeed, as a boy he once conceived of setting an ancient Roman story to music for choir and orchestra, and labored on it for some time. Once, when the rest of the family was out, he went to the piano and played through what he had written so far. He was appalled by what he heard and how different it sounded than he thought it would; he abandoned the piece and never worked on it again.[10]

Nevertheless, he continued to try his hand at composing (placing well in some local competitions for new works),[11] and he progressed as a keyboardist. His father encouraged him, including him in some local orchestras. After Holst failed to earn a place at Trinity College of Music in London (a fact that would irritate the college in later years when it was brought up), Adolph sent him to Oxford to study counterpoint with George Frederick Sims, the organist of Merton College. His composing abilities continued to improve.[12]

He returned from Oxford after a few months, and soon secured an appointment as organist to a small church in the village of Wyck Rissington in the Cotswolds, a remarkable achievement for one so young. He also began to conduct, which he boldly attempted with no knowledge, and seems to have done well enough, learning as he went along.[13] His various activities required much time being outdoors, walking between towns and villages. He grew fond of the hilly landscape in the Cotswolds, and despite his frail nature, he became an enthusiastic walker. He never lost his love for this land, and rural themes inspired his music in later years, as they would with so many of his colleagues.

In July 1892, he had the opportunity to travel to London to hear a performance of *Die Götterdämmerung*, Wagner's climactic opera in the *Ring Cycle*. He was dazzled by its epic nature and the power of its musical ideas[14]; he had never heard anything like it. He became fully devoted to Wagner's music after befriending Fritz Hart, a fellow student at the Royal College,[15] and for a long time afterward, Wagner's music would be a guiding force in his own work, until it began to be a detriment, as we will see below. He continued to show promise with his own compositions, winning praise from the local press, such as the *Echo*, who reported about his comic opera *Landsdown Castle* that he showed signs of genius. The *Gloucester Chronicle* called him "remarkable" and possessed of great talent.[16]

Emboldened by these remarks, he submitted the piece to the Royal College of Music, in the hopes of winning a scholarship. However, they were not so enthusiastic about the work, and offered him nothing. Adolph was now determined that his son would receive a proper musical education and borrowed £100 from a relative to send his son to the College for at least few years (Holst eventually did win a small scholarship that allowed him to stay there until 1898). He traveled to London and passed the entrance exam, entering in May 1893.[17] He took up residence in Hammersmith (an area that would always be important to him), and befriended a number of fellow students, including John Ireland (later Moeran's teacher), and Samuel Coleridge-Taylor, the gifted young composer of Sierra Leone Creole ancestry.[18]

Unfortunately, his neuritis was affecting him badly, and he came to realize that he would not be able to study piano seriously. Discouraged, he was offered the alternative of concentrating on the trombone.[19] Holst took to this with great enthusiasm and skill, and it eventually enabled him to earn a living as a professional player after leaving the college. It offered other benefits, such as allowing him to make extra money while still a student by playing in seaside bands and chamber groups, giving him an insider's view on how individual instruments worked in the context of the larger orchestra. This would help him in his own scoring and orchestration.[20] Further, it seems to have alleviated, if not cured, his asthma, as he built up his breath strength.[21] His breathing improved to the point that he was able to ride his bicycle from London back to Cheltenham, a distance of some 97 miles,[22] trombone on back, no doubt causing quite a stir among the locals.

It was during his time at the Royal College that he met and befriended his fellow student, Ralph Vaughan Williams, who returned in 1895 after three years away, as we have seen, studying history at Cambridge. They were fast friends from their initial meeting, and quickly took a great interest in each other's works, offering criticism, suggestions, and acclaim where it was warranted; they met on planned "field days" to review each other's progress. This would continue throughout their lives. Both often felt that they learned more from each other and their fellow students than they did from sitting in long lectures. Their youthful enthusiasm prompted them to meet and talk about topics far beyond music, which in turn fed back into their musical interests and compositional ideas.

Among the ideas that attracted Holst was socialism, particularly as espoused by William Morris, whose egalitarian ideas about education and work he found deeply appealing. He became a member of the Socialist Society, and went to lectures at Morris' home at Kelmscott House in Hammersmith.[23] He met and listened to Bernard Shaw and Morris himself, among others.[24] Holst had already set poems by Morris and the political atmosphere in the society seemed an ideal match for his interests. Indeed, he was invited to direct the Hammersmith Socialist Choir in 1897, and he brought in a variety of unusual musical works for them to learn and sing, including Elizabethan madrigals (showing his own growing interest in early music), as well as Baroque pieces, Mozart, Wagner, and even some of his own works; it was an ideal environment to try out his choral compositions. Significantly, one of the young singers was a soprano named Isobel Harrison, and he found himself hopelessly smitten with her; she was less enamored of him initially, but he befriended her and in time they loved one another and became engaged.[25] She did insist that he shave off the beard he had grown to look older when applying for musical jobs.[26]

Holst declined an extension on his Royal College scholarship in 1898, and set out on his own, determined to make his way as a composer and musician, and earn enough so that he and Isobel could be married. He would find this more difficult than he had initially thought. Making a living solely through composition was a virtual impossibility at the time, particularly for those just beginning their careers. Composers generally did not receive royalties or fees for performances of their works, and commercial recordings were still decades away. What money they did make came through the sales of their works to publishers, who were not always eager to take a risk on a new, untested musical voice. Holst was able to earn money through his trombone playing in seaside resorts, with both the Scottish Orchestra and the Carl Rosa Opera Company, but it was not a large amount, and he had to travel a good deal.[27]

Nevertheless, he and Isobel were married on June 22, 1901, and moved into two rooms above a shop in Shepherds Bush close to Hammersmith.[28] They were prepared to endure a frugal lifestyle, but on August 21, 1901, his father died (probably due to excessive drinking) and left him some money.²⁹ However, the estate was not settled until early 1903, and in the meantime, he continued working and touring as a professional trombonist.

While hardly enough to keep them for long, it eased the pain when he finally received it, and allowed them to go on holiday to Germany in March 1903, visiting his second cousin, Matthias, in Berlin. While there, he had the opportunity to immerse himself in the city's considerable musical culture, which both pleased and troubled him.³⁰ He felt overworked and unhappy with having to do so much orchestral playing, taking him away from composing and improving his technique and overall output. He also felt that something else was lacking, and that he and Vaughan Williams were not working hard enough or training enough. He wrote to Vaughan Williams from Berlin about this, and his words seem prophetic with hindsight: "I have been trying to think where we (you and I) are and what we ought to do. [...] To begin with, I think we crawl along too slowly. [...] So something must happen and we must make it happen."³¹ In a second letter, he observes:

> I feel it would be so splendid to "go into training" as it were, in order to make one's music as beautiful as possible. And I am sure that after a few months' steady grind we should have made the beginning of our own "atmosphere," and so we should not feel the need of going abroad so much. For it is all that makes up an "atmosphere" that we lack in England. [...] Here, people actually seem anxious to hear new music; still more wonderful, they even seem anxious to find out all about a new composer! That in itself would work a revolution in England.³²

The best solution was to write more, he believed, once telling Vaughan Williams, "We ought to be writing now what will enable us to write well later on."³³

This remarkable set of thoughts shows him yearning for a dramatic change, not only in their own lives, but in English musical life, and foreshadows their soon-to-be-fascination with folk melodies and early music. His notions of what were possible in English music had also been stirred by exposure to Elgar's works. He later noted in his popular lecture "England & Her Music" (which he delivered numerous times over the years in various forms) that while 1880 was typically accorded the approximate beginning of the English Musical Renaissance, for him personally it was some two decades later when he first heard Elgar's *Enigma Variations*, saying, "I felt that here was music the like of which had not appeared in this country since Purcell's death."³⁴ In the same lecture, he observed a problem throughout English history: "A fitting epitaph to nearly every great English composer: 'Fifty years after his death English music was as if he had never existed.'"³⁵ This perception was something that he and Vaughan Williams were determined to change.

At the end of 1903, as we have seen, Vaughan Williams began his great

4. Gustav Holst (1874-1934)   95

interest in English folk song, and Holst would soon follow.[36] Holst had already been showing signs of pastoral leanings in his *Cotswolds Symphony* of 1900,[37] with its slow movement written in memory of William Morris, and his *Walt Whitman Overture* from 1899 (though both were more indebted musically to continental influences). Imogen notes, however, that such works possess a longing that is unable to express adequately. Holst did not yet have enough of a distinct voice to produce what he wanted.[38] Reviews were mostly favorable of the *Walt Whitman* premiere, but the *Times* noted that the piece was lacking some originality, and its overall purpose was unclear.[39] Further, Holst could not interest most publishers in his music, prompting his frustration when he saw the opposite situation for young composers in Berlin.[40]

Back in London (after a stop for two weeks in Paris on the way home), he continued to struggle with this conflict. While he was searching for an English solution to the problem, he had also become fascinated with another topic entirely, that of Indian culture and Hindu beliefs. India, of course, was the jewel of the British Empire's colonies, and so hardly a strange or unfamiliar subject to many; Cheltenham was home to many retirees who had worked for the Civil Service in India.[41] Shortly after leaving college, he had read a book, *Silent Gods and Sun-Steeped Lands*, by R.W. Fraser, that introduced him to the dazzling world of Hindu gods and goddesses and their wonderful stories.[42] He was determined to learn more, and soon discovered the poetry of the *Rig Veda*, an ancient collection of hymns, stories, and prayers in Sanskrit.[43] He learned enough Sanskrit from his teacher, one Dr. Mabel Bode, of the School of Oriental Languages at the London Institution, to make simple translations of the texts.[44]

As Imogen notes, he was never able to travel to India, and probably did not study Indian music,[45] but this work fired his imagination, inspiring such pieces as his symphonic poem *Indra*, (written in Berlin in 1903), his opera *Sita*, based on the *Ramayana* (on which he labored between 1899 and 1906, after first reading Fraser's work), the *Vedic Hymns* (for voice and piano), the *Choral Hymns from the Rig Veda*, *The Cloud Messenger* (for orchestra and chorus), and his chamber opera *Savitri* (composed in 1908, but not premiered until 1916).[46] Short notes that some of his invented melodies do bear a resemblance to those in Indian ragas.[47] These pieces allowed him another means to move away from the Teutonic conventions that were still in place in England, though *Sita* contains its fair share of "Wagnerian bawling,"[48] as Holst himself readily admitted. In these early years, however, he once again found that there seemed to be little interest in such new ideas.

He would also experiment later with Middle Eastern motifs[49] that he heard on a trip to Algeria in 1908. He had been ordered by his doctor to rest in a warm climate, which would help his painful hand. Vaughan Williams, then in

Paris studying with Ravel, offered up £50 for him to take a month-long holiday in the North African climate, cautioning him not to be burdened down with thoughts of what he should be working on, and instead just to enjoy the time away.[50] So Holst boarded a ship with his bike and went off in search of rest and new experiences.[51] He encountered music that was unfamiliar and strange, far removed from the sanitized orientalist music that had occasionally been heard in Victorian and Edwardian concert halls or international exhibitions previously. With a bit of difficulty (owing to the unfamiliar way the music was played), he wrote down some of what he found, making him, if unintentionally, a folk song collector in the Maghreb. Bartók would visit the same region five years later, and also be inspired by the music he heard.[52] Later, Holst incorporated some of these melodies into his compositions. The main result was his *Beni Mora* suite (originally conceived as a ballet, but reworked), which perplexed and annoyed some listeners at its London premier in 1912. In one of his more daring feats, Holst wrote the final movement, *In the Street of Ouled Naïls* (named for the street in the Algerian town of Biskra), based on a simple four-note melody he had heard played there for some two-and-a-half hours.[53] The music repeats the melody 163 times, and features a number of ingenious ways of harmonizing the tune. He envisioned the movement as depicting a procession into an oasis, where the simple, repetitive tune was mingled with other sounds and songs as it made its way through the settlement.[54] Despite mild bewilderment, some were very impressed with the work, including the young composer Percy Grainger, who had also been collecting English folk songs for years.[55]

Drawing of Gustav Holst (courtesy of the Lewis Foreman collection).

Later, in 1915, Japanese dancer Michio Ito asked him to write a set of dances based on traditional Japanese tunes that he whistled while Holst listened and took notes, the result being his *Japanese Suite*.[56] Holst felt that these varied interests and influences in his music were beneficial, and that the wider the range of subject matter that composers used, the more they could (paradoxically) display their own nationalism.[57]

With finances still a great difficulty, he was thrown a lifeline in the form of a job offer to teach at James Allen's Girls' School in Dulwich (a post previously held by Vaughan Williams) in south London in 1904, and shortly after, he received another offer, the appointment to musical director at St. Paul's Girls' School in Hammersmith.[58] With these new posts, he gained not only some credibility, but also financial improvement. In 1907, he would also take on the musical directorship at Morley College, which had been founded to offer education to people from working-class backgrounds[59]; it would be a place of importance to him for many years. Later, Holst and Isobel were able to move into a Regency home on the Thames, in Barnes, in south-west London, which gave him a quiet room in which to work and compose.[60]

In the years of his first teaching appointments, he had found one answer to his longings for a revolution of sorts in England. It was Vaughan Williams' own discovery of English folk song, and its potential for transforming the content of English art music. Holst had not previously considered the value of English folk music, tending to regard existing tunes as primarily Scottish or Irish in origin.[61] As Imogen notes, he had "been brought up on the popular fallacy that 'folk songs are either bad or Irish.'"[62] However, when he learned that there was a vast amount of native music in England, and heard its quality, he knew that he wanted to be a part of the efforts to revive and disseminate these tunes.[63] He did not have the time or means to go on song-collecting trips like Vaughan Williams or Sharp, but he followed their work and findings with great interest.[64] For Holst, this was another of the ways that he could break free of continental influence, though it would always reside alongside his other musical interests, rather than dominating them; he was perhaps less of a romantic about England's past than some of his friends. However, the compact simplicity of the melodies appealed to him, given that they did not always fit the rigid requirements of art music's restrictions and sensibilities.[65]

His first attempts at making folk song arrangements have been described by Imogen as "painful,"[66] but he learned from his mistakes and progressed, being convinced of their value. Perhaps inspired by Vaughan Williams' first *Norfolk Rhapsody*, he tried using songs in an orchestral work titled *Two Selections of Folksong*, later divided into *Songs of the West* and the *Somerset Rhapsody*.[67] Again, Imogen notes that *Songs of the West* "was a distressing failure,"[68] because he did not yet know how to incorporate such melodies skillfully and in a convincing way; they were just a string of songs without logical connections. However, a performance of the work at the Pump Room in Bath in February 1906 met with an enthusiastic reception and a good review in the *Bath Chronicle*.[69]

He became friends with Cecil Sharp, who asked him to make arrangements for voice and piano of a collection of songs from Hampshire, and in these he was more successful, following Sharp's template of musical form and occasional watered-down texts so as not to offend Edwardian sensibilities.[70] Sharp also encouraged him to write an orchestral work based on various Somerset tunes, and he used some of his earlier material to produce his *Somerset Rhapsody* (1906–07) that incorporated four songs: *Sheep Shearing Song*,[71] *High Germany*, *The True Lover's Farewell*, and *The Cuckoo*.[72] Holst noted that the structure for the piece "grew out of a suggestion of a pastoral countryside becoming filled with human activities but surviving them all."[73] This latter piece was more successful musically, and was widely performed, while *Songs of the West* fell into obscurity and was not published.[74] By 1910, the *Somerset Rhapsody* was receiving very good reviews. Holst called a performance of the piece on April 6, "my first real success."[75] Reviewers said that it was the best piece in the concert, a masterpiece of setting, and the best English work in some time.[76] The *Daily Telegraph* noted: "There is real charm in his utterance of what presumably are Somerset folk-tunes—very lovely and characteristic they are—and the cleverness and wit in his union of the two themes [...] is exquisite in its fancy, delicacy and point. [He is] at the outset of a career that may lead to heights unapproachable by his comrades."[77]

The effect of studying and incorporating folk song idioms and ideas into his music had improved his work in many ways. Imogen Holst notes, "As a result of arranging so many folk songs, his own music became simpler and more direct. [...] In his harmonies he managed to get rid of nearly all those chromatic sequences that had cluttered up so much of his music during the years when he had imitated Wagner. Now, at last, he was free to find his own way of expressing himself."[78] Short observes that studying these folk melodies meant that "his love affair with Romantic megalomania was over; he had simplified his musical style as a result of his contact with English folk-song."[79] Similarly, Zachary Woolfe notes: "It was when a third interest [after Wagner and Indian culture]—English folk song—entered the mix that Holst's work became more interesting. His style grew both clearer and stranger, the vocal lines simultaneously incantatory and direct."[80] His *Suite No. 2 in F* from 1911 took the practice of folk song adaptation further, making use of two songs, *Dargason* and *Greensleeves*, in the *Finale*, which were combined masterfully to harmonize with each other.[81] He absorbed the folk idioms so well that his original melodies could fool listeners into thinking they were traditional ones, though late in life, he no longer had interest in making settings of folk songs, feeling he had done enough.[82]

He found the marriage of words and music in many of these songs sometimes troubling, and though there was indeed an "English language identity" in them, he often felt that the lyrics were not worthy of the melodies.[83] This was a common enough perception, as we have seen, with the result that words were sometimes altered to fit in with what polite society considered proper, and were not sung in the accents of the regions from which they originated.

His interest in textual relationships to melody was furthered when Vaughan Williams introduced him to medieval music, specifically plainsong (popularly known as "Gregorian chant"), though he may already have had some exposure to it at the Royal College, while studying organ with William Hoyte.[84] Vaughan Williams, as we have seen, drew on such melodies when assembling his *English Hymnal*, and Holst was once again smitten with a style that was serene and pure, deceptively simple but rich and fascinating. His interest in plainsong and the hymns constructed around it (a practice that dated back to the Middle Ages) inspired some of his own works, such as his setting of *Psalm 86*, and remained a life-long interest.[85] In addition to medieval repertoire, he was very fond of Elizabethan madrigals and lute songs, and took part in the revival of Ben Jonson's masque *Pan's Anniversary*, for the Shakespeare birthday celebrations in Stratford-upon-Avon in 1905, providing settings of various 16th-century pieces at Vaughan Williams' request.[86] He later noted that with the publication of Thomas Morley's madrigals in 1913, he was never quite the same, which was a good thing.[87]

He considered the Elizabethan practice of wide-spread amateur music-making to be crucial to living in a cultured and civilized manner.[88] He was always eager to teach and encourage everyone to take up instruments or singing, stating that "'Amateur' should not be a term of reproach."[89] He was also devoted to the music of Henry Purcell (1659–96), and was able to stage a performance of his masque *The Fairy Queen* on June 10, 1911, its first since the end of the 17th century.[90] It was met with great enthusiasm by both the audience and all of the performers involved. Vaughan Williams introduced the program, and its success encouraged other groups to take up Purcell's music.[91] Like Vaughan Williams, he was equally fond of Bach.[92]

The following month, he conducted his *Phantastes Suite* at the Queen's Hall; in the audience were King George V and Queen Mary. Holst later withdrew it, feeling that it had too much color and was mostly for effect, but the king reportedly smiled and seemed to enjoy it. Holst had been exposed to the daring new music of Stravinsky (*The Firebird*), and soon would hear the controversial *Five Pieces for Orchestra* by Schoenberg, whose new atonal music, lacking a definable tonal center, would shock and outrage the first audiences and critics who heard it. Holst drew from both of these sources when crafting his most celebrated work, *The Planets*.[93] His early title was *Seven Pieces for Large Orchestra*, recalling Schoenberg's.[94] Vaughan Williams had no interest in atonal music, writing as late as 1956, "it seems to me the most astonishing bit of mechanical pedantry which has ever been dignified by the name of art [...] apparently one must not use any succession of notes which sounds agreeable to the cultivated ear."[95]

Like Vaughan Williams, Holst loved the outdoors and walking, and the two took a number of holidays over the years, though he was also very fond of going on long, solitary excursions, which increased in his later years, when he often enjoyed taking a train or car part of the distance to a concert or other engagement, and then walking the remaining distance through the open country.[96] Just after Christmas 1913, he was walking in Essex, and came to the village of Thaxted, situated almost equidistantly between the triangle formed by Cambridge, Chelmsford, and Colchester; it had many scenic and historic buildings from the 14th to the 16th century, and small village charm. Despite the winter landscape (or perhaps because of it), he was taken with the place, and desired to move to the area, bringing his wife and young daughter, Imogen, to live in a 300-year-old cottage about two miles south of the village. The quiet atmosphere and setting were perfect for his needs as a composer. There was no automobile traffic, and the only sounds were those of the country: the wind, the animals, and the bees.[97] It was in this rented bit of rural charm that he began work on *The Planets*.[98]

The idyllic setting was not without some difficulties, however. When the war came, his name, "von Holst" aroused suspicion among some locals, who wondered why he was living so far out, what he was doing on those long walks, and what he was saying when he was seen speaking to locals. Irrational fears took over (Was he a spy? German spy paranoia was rampant at the time), and some neighbors complained to the police, who could find nothing wrong or suspect in his activities. This kind of distrust of all things German was to be expected, but he made efforts to endear himself to the locals, working with the church choir to improve their singing, and to introduce them to early music, particularly that of the Elizabethan composers, since the choir was already familiar with plainsong.[99]

He was able to convince the village to let him bring his musicians from the London schools where he taught to put on an amateur festival of instrumentalists and singers at Whitsun (Pentecost), which was immediately popular and fondly remembered, becoming an annual gathering (though it would move to different locations in the next few years).[100] The first festival on June 10–12 in 1916 was grey and rainy, but the participants made the best of it indoors, reviving folk songs, folk dances, Elizabethan music, and general good cheer.[101] These kinds of community gatherings celebrating all things English and traditional were very much at the heart of the movement. Vaughan Williams wrote to him from France, saying, "I sometimes feel that the future of musical England rests with you [...]" due to Holst's dedication to bringing such arts to the people.[102]

The advent of the war did not cause trouble for Holst alone. Almost immediately, harsh measures were enacted, such as the banning of all German music from concert programs, and German musicians were effectively fired from British orchestras, an unfair action that was eagerly seized on by British musicians who felt that only they had the right to play in such groups. It did not matter if a given German musician was the best qualified for the job. Other ridiculous assertions of nationalism crept in, such as a "compromise" to ban only German music written after 1870 (when Germany was unified). This presented equally silly problems, such as which pieces by Brahms had been written before this date, and which after, for example. If a piece was begun in 1869, but not completed until 1870, was it acceptable? What about Handel? He was German, but lived most of his life in England? Was his music "English" enough?[103]

Holst was, mercifully, able to steer clear of most of this. Indeed, with the war ongoing, he felt called to be in service, though like Vaughan Williams, he was too old for combat duty, and his medical conditions (neuritis and poor vision) made him unsuitable for conscription in any case. He did experience the effects first-hand, however, since Morley College was near Waterloo station, a prime target for German Zeppelin bombers. The basement of the college was designated as an air raid shelter. From 1916 onwards, and on several occasions, those warned of a possible attack from above would descend into the basement to find Holst conducting Renaissance choir music practice, which often turned into impromptu concerts that were greatly appreciated.[104]

However, eventually his sense of duty called him to perform a more active service, and in 1918, the YMCA sent him to the Eastern Mediterranean to be a musical organizer for their educational efforts among the troops being demobilized, a morale booster for the war-weary.[105] Most of them were to be sent home over the ensuing months, but the process took time. Imogen notes that it was then that he dropped the use of "von" from his name,[106] likely owing to the negative feelings that it might arouse among the soldiers. Indeed, he was refused a position in Holland because of it, so on September 18, 1918, he legally changed his name, removing a designation to which his family had little claim, anyway.[107] The irony was probably not lost on him that when he was a student, his German name was seen by some as an advantage to his being taken more seriously.[108] This did not prevent occasional cruel remarks about his heritage from bigoted members of the press. In 1928, music critic Dyneley Hussey wrote: "His share of foreign blood may well account for something strange and alien in his works. [...] There is something cold-blooded and repellent even in his best music."[109] Vaughan Williams defended Holst in asserting that race was only one small factor in what made one a national composer, and that Holst was as entitled as any to be considered an Englishman.[110]

Stationed in Salonica (Thessaloniki), he found that it was certainly no Eastern holiday as some had thought. From 1919, he was in Constantinople (Istanbul), just as the centuries-old Ottoman Empire was crumbling away, overseeing musical activities for both singers and instrumentalists, organizing concerts and competitions.[111] He missed the fourth annual Whitsun Festival, but tried to inject some Englishness into the culture of his temporary home, teaching Elizabethan pieces and folk songs among other music.[112] In both locations the troops were enthusiastic for his efforts, grateful that someone had thought of them.[113] It was not always a good experience, however; the night before his departure for Constantinople, his kitbag was stolen, which held letters, his diaries, and music sketches. They were never recovered[114] (he always kept a notebook for jotting down ideas, and one wonders what fragments were lost on this occasions).

Prior to leaving for this work, he had been treated on September 29, 1918, to a private performance of his new piece, *The Planets*, by a wealthy patron and musical admirer, Henry Balfour Gardiner, a composer in his own right.[115] Gardiner was generous with his wealth, for example, buying the French home that Delius resided in, so that the composer might stay there permanently. Holst had first conceived of the idea of his planetary suite while in Spain and Majorca with Gardiner in 1913.[116] Also present on this holiday was the writer Clifford Bax, brother of the composer Arnold (who joined them, as well). Clifford had a great interest in astrology, and Holst soon took up the study of it, becoming a skilled reader and caster of horoscopes.[117] *The Planets* was destined to become his most famous and celebrated work, and in some ways it would haunt him and overshadow his later compositions.[118] It has influenced generations of film composers, particularly in the science fiction genre.[119]

After that first performance, reaction was ecstatic, and Holst received a standing ovation. Adrian Boult had conducted, and done so superbly, making an excellent name for himself.[120] By October 1920, the work was a major success, having finally had a performance of the complete suite in London, though Holst was never one to bask in adoration. Indeed, it made him uncomfortable, and his overall indifference to both praise and harsh critiques allowed him to continue to compose what he wanted without the risk of having it molded by public or critical opinion. At the performance of his *Ode to Death* in Leeds on October 6, 1922, he "was astonished to find that he was now regarded as a celebrity, and after the concert had to be escorted to the police station until mobs of admirers and autograph-hunters had dispersed."[121] He was not fond of social gatherings and hated publicity, interviews, and photographs; he did not even like having to take bows at the end of concerts. Further, he would not accept honorary degrees or vice-presidencies of organizations, fearing that even the superficial duties of such things would take away precious time from composition, time that he always set aside from his teaching and conducting duties.[122] The negative aspect of such a stance was that it contributed to his declining popularity as the 1920s progressed.[123]

Despite the benefits that more money brought to him, he was not one to hoard material possessions, showing perhaps that his interest in Eastern philosophies had become more of a personal conviction. Long country walks, and time well spent with good friends were far more meaningful.

Gustav Holst, by Herbert Lambert (reproduced with the permission of the Wilson Cheltenham Art Gallery & Museum / The Holst Birthplace Museum, Cheltenham).

Though he was an avid reader, his library was small; he often borrowed books or gave away the ones he had when he no longer needed them.[124] He did have one possession that he valued highly, Beethoven's tuning fork, which had been given to him as a gift by an admirer. He left it in his will to Vaughan Williams, who in turn had promised to leave it to his young friend, the composer Gerald Finzi, but Finzi died before Vaughan Williams did.[125] In 1993 Ursula Vaughan Williams donated it to the British Library, with "the hope that all musicians will feel that in belonging to this treasure house it belongs to them all." It now resides there, next to the manuscript for Beethoven's *Ninth Symphony*, an appropriate resting place.

Success and popularity took their toll on Holst, who found himself increasingly in demand. Whether due to fatigue or carelessness, he fell off of a platform while conducting a rehearsal for a commemorative concert for music of the Elizabethan composers William Byrd and Thomas Weelkes (two of his favorites)[126] at Reading University College on February 20, 1923. He hit the back of his head and suffered a concussion. He took some rest, but only superficially, and soon he suffered a nervous breakdown and had to cease all activities for several weeks.[127] He was given clearance to go on a journey to America at the end of April, where he spent a few months as a guest lecturer and conductor at the University of Michigan in Ann Arbor.[128] He liked the institution and the town greatly; the feeling was mutual. The university offered him the post of Professor of Music, but he respectfully declined, being too attached to England, and not wanting to disrupt his family with such a momentous move.[129]

He and Isobel returned from America in June. However, in the autumn, he began to suffer from headaches, probably a residual effect of the concussion. The pain and the fatigue that accompanied them interfered with his heavy work load, for from 1919, he had taken on teaching duties at not only Reading, but also the Royal College of Music, which required considerable more attention than his girls' school teaching, which he also continued.[130] This extra teaching meant that work on his serious compositions often had to wait until the summer holiday.[131] However, he brought a great amount of enthusiasm to his responsibilities, and was especially devoted to the rediscovered music of the Elizabethans, both part-songs and lute songs. His assertion, for example, that John Dowland was the equal of Schubert in songwriting was met with some astonishment, yet today few would doubt that this is true.[132] Like so many in the folk song movement, Tudor music also held great appeal for him. As we will see in chapter 7, the rather infamous composer Philip Heseltine (using the name Peter Warlock, and who interestingly detested Holst's music) was a key figure in the revival and publication of accurate modern editions of long-forgotten Tudor music, transcribed from manuscripts in the British Museum.

Holst was committed to teaching his whole life, and greatly enjoyed seeing adult amateurs flourish. For children, he wanted music to be enjoyed, not a tedious course of academic study. He also felt that it deserved as much attention as other school subjects (even in those days, there were those who felt that music education was frivolous and of no value for their children). He was a kind teacher who did not demean his students and orchestras, but nevertheless expected excellence from them. He felt that the teacher and the student should be comrades, who worked closely together, as had been done in the medieval and Renaissance periods, to foster that excellence.[133] Vaughan Williams wrote in 1937 that Holst maintained that "art is not for all but only for a chosen few—but the only way to find those few is to bring art to everyone."[134]

Conducting caused a terrible strain on his already-damaged arm, which he said often felt "like a jelly overcharged with electricity."[135] He found the first recording sessions of *The Planets* to be particularly exhausting; after one session he was so tired, he could not walk upstairs to go to bed.[136] His recent popularity meant that publishers were now interested in his work, and wanted his older music.[137] This required considerable time and effort to revise and correct his scores, made more stressful by publishing deadlines preventing him from giving them the attention they deserved. As 1923 progressed, he felt increasingly ill, suffering from insomnia and headaches as he continued to overwork himself. He made the decision to retreat to the country for absolute rest, only going into London to teach one day a week.[138] A chance to ease his burden came with the gift of £1,500, which allowed him to give up several of his work duties.[139] In many ways, this was a relief for him, as he finally had a chance to escape from under the mountain of stress and responsibility that his career had piled on him. Other large sums came his way over the next few years; for his 50th birthday in 1924, a selection of friends and colleagues contributed to another monetary donation of £350, and the following year Yale University awarded him the Henry Elias Howland Memorial Prize, and a check for $1,350.[140] Gardiner also generously gave him £8 a week.[141]

Having retreated to Thaxted (he and his family now lived in a house in the village, larger but still quiet and peaceful), he initially suffered from head pains and high sensitivity to noise, and eventually his doctor ordered him to spend the rest of the year not working at all and living alone in the country.[142] Giving up teaching was difficult for him, but he found that simply being in the Thaxted area, taking in the air, and going for walks in an unhurried and non-stressed manner did wonders for his wellbeing and outlook, and he desired to begin writing music again. He was finally able to concentrate solely on composition, which made him happier than he had been for some time; he was living a true composer's life at last.[143] His time away throughout 1924 led to new works such as the *Choral Symphony* (based on Keats' works) and a short comic opera, *At the Boar's Head*, using Shakespeare texts from both parts of *Henry IV* and two of his sonnets. For this work, he adapted music from the dance collection of Playford from the mid–17th century, as well as tunes from Sharp's collections, and a few of his own.[144]

Both pieces were poorly received by the public when they premiered in 1925, however.[145] Some felt that his new opera was almost a cheat because it contained so much music that was early and not his own. One reviewer said that he had made too many assumptions about the audience's familiarity with the texts, and another complained that essentially nothing happened story-wise for the hour running time of the work.[146] Finzi felt that the music worked, but not the staging.[147] Likewise, Holst's *Choral Symphony* met with critical disdain from Cecil Gray: "Holst presents the melancholy spectacle of a continuous and unrelieved decline [...] the *Choral Symphony* is probably Holst's worst [work]."[148] He further stated that it contained some of the dullest and most pretentious music yet written.[149] Even Vaughan Williams only gave it a lukewarm reception.[150]

For some, Holst was simply guilty of not re-writing *The Planets* with each new piece. He neither cared nor responded to such criticisms, but it did mean that his popularity had noticeably declined since the early 1920s,[151] something that would alarm most artists, but that undoubtedly pleased him, as it meant fewer public engagements and annoying press interviews. He had no desire to perpetuate this popularity. Rather, he almost wanted to create new works that would not be well-received at first, and this damaged his reputation over time.[152] He once remarked to Clifford Bax: "Some day I expect you will agree with me that it's a great thing to be a failure. If nobody likes your work, you have to go on just for the sake of the work. And you're in no danger of letting the public make you repeat yourself. [...] [If an artist is] a failure he stands a good chance of concentrating upon the best work of which he's capable."[153]

He was well enough to go back to teaching in a limited way in early 1925, but the reduced workload and attention were also a relief. The noise and fast pace of London were now considerably more irritating to him.[154] However, during the course of 1925, he gradually added more to his schedule, until it was back to the level it had been before,[155] an obvious mistake in judgment, but he would not be deterred. His health improved, he traveled far and wide across the country, walked, and immersed himself in his work. He once joked to a friend, "I am at present flourishing in health owing to a strict regime of early to bed and late to rise."[156] His head no longer hurt, his sensitivity to crowds and noise had decreased, and he took on the additional position of lecturing at Liverpool University once a week.[157] He also moved into a large Elizabethan farm house named "Brook End," a few miles south of Thaxted, with the financial assistance of Gardiner.[158]

As he recovered, he turned his attention to other works. Despite his many ventures into other musical styles, he still returned to using folk melodies and motifs in some works, such as the choral ballets *The Golden Goose* (based on a Grimm's fairy tale), which incorporated country dance tunes,[159] and *The Morning of the Year*, which was dedicated to the English Folk Dance Society, and used various old songs, often in new ways.[160] The latter work portrayed themes of spring, and rituals of mating. Perhaps he intended it to be a kind of *Rite of Spring* (which he had seen many years before), though it certainly did not have the shocking power of Stravinksy's work; Short compares it to the style of Copland, but also calls parts of it "too bland and folksy."[161]

Regardless of criticisms from the establishment, Cheltenham honored Holst with a festival of his music, held on March 22, 1927. The outpouring of goodwill, praise, and congratulations from friends, family, and fans completely overwhelmed him, and he remembered it always. It was very well attended, and enough money was left over afterward to commission a painting of Holst, which now hangs in his birthplace museum in the city.[162]

Also in 1927, he composed the tone poem *Egdon Heath*, based on the fictitious location of a bleak heath in Thomas Hardy's novels of Wessex.[163] Hardy set his novel *The Return of the Native* there, and the location also appears in his *The Mayor of Casterbridge*. Holst had set some of Hardy's poetry to music as a younger man, with the poet's consent and best wishes; the two later became friends in the 1920s, traveling the countryside together on various occasions.[164] Interestingly, Hardy first heard *The Planets* from a copy of the recording owned by T.E. Lawrence.[165]

Egdon Heath was commissioned in the spring by Walter Damrosch, conductor of the New York Symphony Orchestra, and Holst finished it by July, very quick work for an extended piece (it runs at more than twelve minutes). The orchestra had wanted a full symphony, but Holst gave them, "something as far removed from a conventional symphony as possible,"[166] again not wanting to repeat himself by writing another *Planets*. Despite its rural setting, it contains little of the folk song aesthetic, instead presenting the bleakness of the landscape, with haunting melodies and dissonances, and a sense of austerity and mystery. Holst prefaced the score with a quote from *Return of the Native* that encapsulates what he was trying to communicate: "A place perfectly accordant with man's nature—neither ghastly, hateful, nor ugly; neither common-place, unmeaning, nor tame; but, like man, slighted and enduring; and withal singularly colossal and mysterious in its swarthy monotony!"[167]

Vaughan Williams was initially unsure about the piece, but he grew to admire it, and believed that Holst was correct in ignoring his suggestions for improvement.[168] Audiences and critics were less sure. Many complained about its quiet moments, and some felt that it was too repetitive.[169] Isobel was equally ambivalent about the piece, saying to the conductor Hugh Allen: "[...] how I wish you could stop Gustav writing music like this, and get him back to his old style."[170] Holst, typically, ignored his detractors (and presumably, his wife), firmly convinced that it was his best work to date[171]; he frequently said this about any new major composition of his, but he settled on *Egdon Heath* as being his finest work, and held to this belief until his death.[172]

This would be a pattern over the last years of his life: his closest friend Vaughan Williams would frequently be unclear of what he was trying to express musically, though he did once again come to Holst's defense against what he saw as the unfair reception of the *Choral Fantasia* in 1931. Written for the Three Choirs Festival,[173] and originally conceived as an organ concerto, his reworked effort was not well-received by the audience or the reviewers. Its unusual harmonies, melodies, and dissonances were difficult for some to understand or appreciate, and the press response was almost universally negative. Angered by this, Vaughan Williams wrote a rather forceful and blunt letter to Holst, praising the work's beauty, and adding: "I just want to tell the press [...] that they are misbegotten abortions."[174]

Holst once again dismissed criticisms and planned for a holiday in Vienna and Prague over the Christmas season and New Year of 1927–28. Throwing himself into the musical life of both cities, he also visited Leipzig in Germany (home to Bach) before returning in January.[175]

One of his more unique projects as the New Year dawned was *The Coming of Christ*, a modern liturgical drama that was performed in Canterbury Cathedral at Pentecost (Whitsun) 1928, at the request of George Bell, Dean of Canterbury. Getting the project launched had proven difficult, however, as there was opposition to it on religious grounds from some quarters. Indeed, as the date of the performance drew near, those with strongly-held religious beliefs (we might well call them fundamentalists) wrote letters of protest, predicting harsh consequences from God. The work was effectively the first liturgical drama to be staged in an English cathedral since the Reformation, and was a Catholic practice, so one can see why some devout Anglicans were opposed to the idea, especially given that Canterbury is the supreme cathedral in the Anglican Church. Happily, no such divine judgments were forthcoming, and the performances were hugely successful, drawing in excess of 6,000 people. It was a welcome change from some of the criticisms his work had attracted of late.[176]

By the spring of 1928, however, his creativity had dried up, and he was unable to meet commissions and produce new work. Acknowledging that it was unfair to those who were expecting new works from him, he eventually resolved to take a long holiday to Italy to clear his head, departing in December for Rome. He took in large parts of the country, journeying as far south as Sicily, and as far north as Verona, before passing though Switzerland and France on his way back in late March 1929.[177] He was barely home before setting off again to America (having been invited while he was in Italy), to meet hectic commitments in New Haven, Connecticut, and New York.[178] He finally returned to England in early May.[179] He was done traveling, having written to his wife that he wanted "to live a humdrum monotonous existence with lots of routine work [...] and occasional conducting jobs and three-day walks—I want this for the next three or four years!"[180]

Despite his declining popularity in England, he was awarded the gold medal of the Royal Philharmonic Society in April 1930 (one month after Vaughan Williams had received the same award).[181] Much of 1931 would prove to be disappointing to him, as he had another period of writer's block, and began to worry if he would ever compose again.[182]

However, in another show of admiration and support, Harvard University invited him to be a guest, offering the post of Horatio Lamb Lecturer in Composition to him in 1932 from February to May. He accepted, as well as the opportunity to conduct his own works in a concert with the Boston Symphony Orchestra.[183] He also spent time in New York, and found that he was still something of a celebrity there; he had to go to press interviews, sit for photographs, and be involved in social gatherings, all things he continued to hate.[184] He had written to Duncan McKenzie at Oxford University Press, requesting that he act as an agent for the trip, and McKenzie agreed. Holst further asked: "I rather hope that you won't get me too many engagements! I am not as strong as I was and public engagements are best for me if they come singly. Normally I lead a very quiet life.[...]"[185] He later wrote to Vaughan Williams noting that if not for McKenzie, he would have had to hand out forms, on which was printed: "Dear Sir or Madame, I'll see you damned before I'll conduct, lecture, dine, be interviewed, be photographed.[...]"[186]

He further noted: "New York fascinates and sometimes terrifies me. One can compare Cambridge Massachussetts [sic] with Cambridge England but New York is like nothing else I know."[187] He observed the excessive use of telephones, which were almost like an addiction to many (what would he have made of the modern world's obsession with cell phones?), and declared that the city was, "an amazing place to visit but give me Emma [Hammersmith] for living in."[188] Harvard, by contrast was less hectic, and he enjoyed both teaching and composing there. Unfortunately, his poor health became a problem again. He returned from Washington D.C (where he had been lecturing) to Boston, feeling faint and ill. On March 27, he was sent to a doctor and diagnosed with hemorrhagic gastritis, caused by a duodenal ulcer. This required cancelling all of his commitments and necessitated several weeks of recovery time.[189] During this period, he admitted to reaching an absolute low, but felt that this was a good thing, for it gave him clarity. He noted to Vaughan Williams: "[...] as soon as I reached the bottom I had one clear, intense and calm feeling—that of overwhelming Gratitude. And the four chief reasons for gratitude were Music, the Cotswolds, RVW, and having known the impersonality of orchestral playing."[190] His condition improved gradually, and at the end of April, he had the opportunity to hear a concert of his works performed as a tribute, which pleased him greatly; he described it as the happiest night that he had in the United States.[191] He also felt well enough to return to Ann Arbor to conduct, re-connecting with friends made on his previous visit in 1923.[192] He remained at Harvard until the end of May and then took a ship from New York back to London.[193]

He was told to take things easier and continue to recover, though he did engage in a good amount of work in the autumn of 1932, attending concerts and trying to write new music; he was less successful in this, as his physical conditions made it difficult for him to sit for long periods and compose.[194] However, he suffered some form of relapse at the end of the year (becoming ill on Boxing Day after a long walk at Thaxted), and he would spend much of 1933 convalescing, visiting clinics, staying at nursing homes, and living on a restricted diet. His condition was quite painful at times, and made doing anything else very difficult, though he did manage to write some new works, such as his *Brook Green Suite*, which he composed while in the hospital[195] (not being physically active seems to have at least stimulated his mind). Possibly named for the place where he had been married, it is a chamber orchestra piece. He wrote it for the students of the junior orchestra at St. Paul's Girls School, easy enough for them to perform, but not simply children's music; he wanted them to be challenged. The work is tonal, light, and pastoral at times, with suggestions of folk song motifs; many of these were likely melodies of his own invention,[196] but at least one was drawn from a tune he jotted down while in Sicily in 1929, watching a marionette show.[197]

By the end of 1933, his fragile health deteriorated more, and he was too ill to attend a performance of his short opera, *The Wandering Scholar*,[198] in January 1934. He did hear an informal performance of *Brook Green* in March.[199] This was to be the last concert of his own music that he attended; his actual last concert was in Oxford, a program of Cotswold folk music.[200]

His ulcer had not healed properly and he was now faced with leading a restricted life if he continued in the way things had been. By the end of April, he decided to have another operation. He was told that he could have surgery, but would likely continue as an invalid. Alternately, he could elect to undergo a more complex procedure to remove the ulcer completely, which would potentially see him return to full health in time. There were risks, but he went ahead with the decision. He could not bear to remain in his restricted life, when he so loved walking, travel, teaching, and meeting with friends.[201] Indeed, he found it amusing that at this very time, he received an offer to go to Honolulu to conduct for four months.[202]

His operation was scheduled for the end of May. It was successful, but the doctors informed his friends and family that they would need to keep a close watch on him for the next three days; beyond that, his recovery would be slow. However, the procedure had taken a heavy toll on his system, and he died on May 25. Michael Short has recently suggested that his condition was more serious than was acknowledged at the time, and that he may have been suffering from some form of cancer.[203]

Isobel had not left his side, though he did not recognize her. She would later say that his passing was peaceful, painless, and a mercy, because by not trying to correct the problem, he would have had to live as an invalid, which would have been terrible for him.[204] He was cremated and his ashes were interred in Chichester Cathedral on June 24, below the memorial to Thomas Weelkes, the madrigalist he had so admired.[205] His death was a shock to those close to him. They had known that it was a risky procedure, but none of them believed that he would not survive it. Vaughan Williams was, of course, devastated, having lost his closest friend, but he saw to it that the Gustav Holst Memorial Fund was established, and later, the Holst Room at Morley College.[206] Tributes to him began to flow in, where he had been ignored in life. His work was seen as pioneering where previously, it had simply been disappointing or not up to standard.

In the years after his death, he suffered from the inevitable neglect that often seems to occur as a composer's work is forgotten. Boult did his part to keep Holst's memory alive, performing *The Planets* and other works when he could, as did some others, though the bulk of the task fell to Imogen, who would champion her father's work for the rest of her life. By the later 1930s, his music was already largely ignored (a state of affairs that he himself had predicted), which prompted her to write the first edition of his biography in 1938, but it would take many years to convince the establishment and the public that his work was worthwhile.[207] The advocates of experimental and avant-garde music had no time for him or Vaughan Williams, whom they saw "as antediluvian representatives of the native 'cow-pat' school of composition,"[208] though as we have seen, Britten was an admirer, and worked with Imogen to help edit and preserve his works. By the 1960s, interest was again growing in his music, thanks in great part to his daughter's efforts. She died in 1984.

Holst produced a remarkably varied body of work, drawing from numerous influences and ideas. His devotion to amateurs and musical education for all was admirable, and he showed little worry about critical opinion, or composing what audiences wanted to hear. His sentiments following that first festival in Thaxted perhaps sum up his world view as well as anything that he composed. Completely satisfied with the way things had developed, he wrote a very happy letter to his colleague, the composer and music educator W.G. Whittaker, concluding with: "Music, being identical with heaven, isn't a thing of momentary thrills, or even hourly ones. It's a condition of eternity."[209]

5

George Butterworth (1885–1916)

Of the composers and musical individuals surveyed in this work, George Butterworth suffered the cruelest fate. A young composer of great promise, a skilled folk dancer, and an avid collector of folk songs, his life was tragically cut short at the age of 31. He was killed by a sniper's bullet to the head on August 5, 1916, during the Battle of the Somme, the largest and bloodiest battle of World War I. Like other composers who died young and in their prime, we can only speculate about what he might have achieved had he survived the war and returned to resume his music and dance activities. He left only a small selection of pieces behind and destroyed many of his earlier works.[1]

Butterworth did not have a long career and his output is small compared to his friends and contemporaries. He had made the decision to take up the music profession seriously only later in his short life, and his most productive period was brief, between 1910 and 1914. Making matters worse for musicologists, he destroyed the majority of what he had written prior to this time, just before embarking on his fateful trip to the trenches of France. We do not know how many pieces this included, and can only guess at what was lost. Further, he also composed nothing at all after enlisting in the army, giving his full attention to the war effort.[2] Despite this, he was an important, if minor, figure in the early 20th-century movement for a new English music. As Barlow notes, "His few works are, almost without exception, of a supremely musical character, revealing a truly indigenous style, liberated by and large from continental influences."[3]

Though only small amounts of his music survive, his work in the field of folk song collection and the preservation of folk dances was significant. While not as extensive as the findings of Sharp, Vaughan Williams, or Grainger, he nevertheless made important contributions to the ever-growing catalog of preserved folk songs at the time, his books comprising several hundred items of both music and dance.

George Sainton Kaye Butterworth was born on July 12, 1885, in Paddington, London, the only child of Sir Alexander Kaye Butterworth and Julia Marguerite Wigan. His father, a lawyer of good standing (who received his knighthood in 1914), was destined to outlive him by 30 years, dying in 1946 at the advanced age of 92.[4] His mother had musical talent, being a professional singer prior to her marriage; she had received vocal training from Charlotte Helen Sainton-Dolby, the wife of a French violinist, Prosper Sainton (and whose family name was given to George).[5] The family left London in 1891 and relocated to York, where Alexander took the job of lawyer for North Eastern Railway (and would eventually become the general manager), a lucrative and prestigious position.[6] However, George would not spend much time in the city as he grew older, being away at Aysgarth Preparatory School in North Yorkshire from 1896 to 1899.

At this young age, he already displayed impressive musical and compositional skills, including ability on the piano and organ. His mother arranged for lessons with a noted German teacher, Christian Gollieph Padel.[7] He also had a talent for making hymn settings, and when he was at school, he sent home some examples, presumably to show his progress.[8] He possessed great skill in physical activities, particularly sports such as cricket,[9] and he seemed naturally to have assumed leadership positions, a trait that would feature again in his military service.[10] His abilities earned him a place at Eton in 1899,[11] when he won a King's scholarship,[12] a prestigious honor. Once there, he continued to do well in music and various games, but as Barlow notes, "his academic record was not exceptional."[13] He clearly preferred sports and music, which later would be perfectly combined in his love of folk dancing. By 1902, his tutor, Robert Booker wrote to Alexander "[...] it is very unpleasing to have to teach a boy who finds everything useless, or a bore, or unintelligible[...]"[14] though Booker was overall quite supportive of Butterworth's efforts. Though his artistic interests were interfering with his academic studies, he returned for his final year and improved substantially.[15]

It was at Eton in 1903 that he conducted his first orchestral composition, *Barcarolle*, which he later destroyed.[16] After a few years of experimenting, he made his first serious attempts at composition, and he completed various early works at this time, including a violin sonata and a string quartet, which presumably were also lost in his pre-war purge.[17] One of his instructors, Thomas Dunhill, noted after Butterworth's death that "He was one of the best pupils I ever had."[18] Interestingly, Butterworth is only recorded as having participated in five concerts during this time, with the repertoire heavily slanted toward the continental (and the Teutonic), including works by Chopin, Schumann, Schubert, Wagner, and Mozart,[19] showing once again how much this repertoire dominated the English music scene and educational institutions in the Victorian period and shortly after.

Butterworth toyed with the idea of taking a year off after Eton to go to a music academy in Germany (he hoped to win a scholarship), but Booker did not believe this to be a good idea, and so Butterworth remained and concentrated on his studies.[20]

In the autumn of 1904, he was admitted to Trinity College at Oxford to read Greats (Classics), but he proved not to be the budding Classical scholar that his family might have hoped for (his father wanted young George to follow him into the legal profession, and this course was a good point of study to begin that career path).[21] Indeed, his interest in academics was often secondary to his devotion to music.[22] He was thrilled to attend Elgar's lecture on February 7, 1905, for example. This was followed by a performance at the Musical Club, which was also attended by both Elgar and Parry, and other concerts soon after.[23] Such a musical atmosphere was no doubt what he craved, but he also threw himself into sports and games again, and his studies suffered somewhat.[24] He earned only a Class III degree in *Literae Humaniores* in 1908. His tutor was aware that he was intelligent and gifted, and that his average marks were not a true reflection of his actual abilities.[25]

He was so engrossed in musical activities that he became President of the Oxford University Musical Club,[26] where he soon became known for a firm hand and even an autocratic approach, but he never seems to have made enemies, and in fact, his popularity only grew.[27] Stephen Banfield notes that he "grew up a gruff, blunt Yorkshireman,"[28] which may account for some of this directness. It was obvious by this time that he had his heart set on a career in music, however that might play out.[29] His father did not approve, but he could not dissuade his son from the decision, and so eventually consented.[30] Sir Alexander would later lament after this son's death that he had opposed him in this, thus hindering him from pursuing his goal earlier.[31] Rippin suggests that this opposition may have been beneficial, for if Butterworth had been given more formal and rigid training in music, rather than being able to pursue it independently, "he might never have achieved anything worthwhile."[32] He composed, studied conducting, took private piano lessons, and sang in choirs when he could.[33] He was also an avid collector and reader of scores, possessing the Beethoven symphonies, and the complete works of Bach, the latter a very expensive 21st birthday gift from his parents.[34]

It was during his time at Oxford that his musical focus was to change significantly, through his meeting and befriending several influential musicians and composers, most importantly, both Ralph Vaughan Williams and Cecil Sharp. In 1906, Vaughan Williams found Butterworth to be already enthusiastic about folk songs, the younger man having heard Parry talk on the subject, as well as learning about them from his friend Francis Jekyll (see below).[35] Vaughan Williams told Butterworth about his ongoing efforts to collect these songs, which further aroused his interest.[36] From that time on, Butterworth's focus became directed toward collecting and preserving folk songs, and incorporating those ideas and motifs into his own music; he also joined the Folk Song Society in that same year, and the Oxford Folk Music Society[37] soon after. He and Vaughan Williams became close friends and admirers of one another's work.[38] Hugh Allen would note that, "The high value that each set upon the other's opinion, and the independence of view which each maintained and cherished, did more than anything else to bring out the latent power of [Butterworth], and set him on the road to great achievement in composition."[39] Allen and Butterworth also became good friends, and even after his time in Oxford, Butterworth would visit Allen at his home, where he also socialized with and befriended Adrian Boult,[40] among others. Vaughan Williams noted that in those early years, Butterworth's creativity was hindered by "the 'Oxford manner' in music—the fear of self-expression which seems to be fostered by academic traditions,"[41] but that in time, he overcame this limitation.

Indeed, Barlow and Murphy note a curious and amusing anecdote that says much about the emerging reaction among English composers against Teutonic musical dominance, whether via the use of folk music or in other ways. Barlow writes that, "In about 1906, Hugh Allen remarked to Reginald Lennard on seeing the two young men [Butterworth and his friend R.O. Morris] approaching Blackwell's bookshop: 'there goes more red revolution than in the whole of Russia,' by which he meant that hostile reaction to the British musical establishment, then quite prevalent."[42]

Hostile to the establishment or not, Butterworth knew when he left Oxford in 1908 that he would have to find a means of gainful employment in music, beyond just composition. He did not have the luxury of Vaughan Williams' "small silver spoon," and he did not regard himself as a sufficiently talented pianist to pursue it as a career.[43] The problem was that composition was by far his preferred form of musical expression (as is so often the case with composers through the ages). Indeed, when he had a new musical idea, he was known to have become engrossed in it, devoting all of his time to working on it. When the piece was finished, however, a kind of mild depression would set in, and he would be disillusioned with life for a time, or perhaps rather with the prospect of having to return to the real world until a new theme or idea presented itself.[44]

His efforts to secure musical employment led him first to take up music criticism. He was employed at the *Times*, as an assistant music critic to J.A. Fuller Maitland.[45] During the period of 1908–09, he lived in London, though somewhat surprisingly, his life is not well documented at this time, and he seems to have done little in the way of performing or composing. While he executed his duties as a critic with skill, knowledge, and perception, he quickly grew dissatisfied with the work and desired to move on.[46]

Musical criticism not being to his liking, he tried his hand at teaching, taking a post at Radley College, a boys' boarding school near the village of Radley, just south of Oxford.[47] He only remained in this position for one academic year, from 1909–10, but during his time there, he was well-liked and did much to improve the status of its music education, including introducing proper piano instruction and creating a choral society in 1910.[48] As usual, he also excelled at sports. However, he quickly grew bored and felt constrained by the stiffness of the school's protocols and traditions. Such a small-town environment, with its lack of any opportunities beyond the school itself would not have suited someone of his talent and ambition. Nevertheless, he did find time for some composition, probably including his *Suite for String Quartet*.[49]

He decided to leave the school in 1910, and begin studying music again, feeling that his technique was not yet up to the standards that he wanted. It happened that his parents relocated from York to Chelsea in London that year, which coincided with his desire to return to London and resume study. He would live at their London home until 1914.[50]

He entered the Royal College of Music in October 1910 to improve his piano and organ skills, as well as undertake more advanced study of music theory and composition. However, in a now familiar pattern, he found the program not to be to his liking, and he left about a year later, in 1911.[51] The quality of the music he was studying did not please him. Perhaps it was too Germanic in focus while he longed to explore the possibilities of Englishness in his work. Perhaps, as at Radley, he felt too confined with the structure. Murphy suggests that it was also due to composition not being easy for him, and feeling inadequate in his technique[52]; he did take private lessons from composer Charles Wood in an effort to improve. Further, Parry praised his work, feeling that he had great promise.[53]

Whether or not he was depressed about this string of disappointments, he seems to have had a good sense of humor, and was willing to keep trying.[54] Banfield notes that while perhaps his dissatisfaction and aimlessness have been over-emphasized, his father's wishes for his career and his mother's death must have had a great impact on him[55] Julia died of Hodgkin's disease on January 29, 1911. She had been devoted to and supportive of him for his whole life, and had served as something of a buffer between him and Alexander.[56] Losing her undoubtedly affected him deeply.

Despite the assertion that "he was almost certainly gay,"[57] his sexual orientation is not clear. He certainly did not form a close friendship with any woman other than his mother and Dorothea Mavor (his father's new fiancée, see below), unless they were as part of a couple, such as Ralph and Adeline Vaughan Williams, and Cecil and Constance Sharp. He had no known romantic or sexual relations with women, and seems to have preferred the company of other men. Maud Karpeles was completely enamored of him, but he showed no mutual interest in her.[58] If he was homosexual, he seems never to have acted on those feelings, and probably remained celibate for his whole life.[59]

Interestingly, two months after his mother's death, Butterworth composed a setting of Oscar Wilde's poem *Requiescat* (written in 1881, probably for his sister who had died some years before).[60] This is an unusual choice of words and poet, but given his grief, and Wilde's well-known sexual orientation, perhaps he was trying to express many feelings.[61] In his time in the public school environment, he certainly would have been surrounded with the idea that sports and classical studies encouraged moral virtue and "manliness."[62] This, along with a denigration of more "feminine" feelings, may have led him in part to adopt his outward stance of a "gruff Yorkshireman."[63] In any case, the tragedy of early 1911 would be a preface to a substantial wave of composition over the next few years. Murphy notes that "a dam had burst and Butterworth was impelled to make sense of his life as a composer."[64]

Upon leaving the Royal College, he devoted himself intensely to the folk song and dance movement, and found there greater contentment and artistic fulfillment than he had yet known. Indeed, he had for some years been very content when collecting folk songs, and like Sharp, Vaughan Williams, and Grainger, he roamed the countryside on many occasions, searching out old tunes, writing out their lyrics, and notating the melodies. He would continue this practice, which he had begun in 1906, until the spring of 1913. His most active times were during the summer months, with 1907 to 1910 being particularly fruitful years. He traveled to nearly a dozen English counties, including Sussex, where he gathered the most songs.[65] He accompanied Vaughan Williams on some excursions, including three trips to East Anglia in 1910 and 1911, but these yielded only a small number of tunes.[66] However, some of these were subsequently published in the *Journal of the Folk-Song Society* (in 1910 and 1913), along with songs that Butterworth had collected on his own.[67] A trip to Norfolk in December 1911 led to an amusing incident recalled by Ursula Vaughan Williams, and worth recounting in detail:

> One night, in a pub where they [Vaughan Williams and Butterworth] had found several singers, one of them suggested it would be much quicker if he rowed them across the water than that they should bicycle round the Broad [a network of rivers in Norfolk and Suffolk] by road. [...] They piled their bicycles into the boat and started. Their ferryman rowed with uncertain strokes, raising his oar now and then to point at distant lights. [...] Before long they realized they were always the same lights and that he was taking them round and round in circles. The night air after the frowsty bar parlour and the beer had been fatal, and he was thoroughly drunk. Eventually they persuaded him to let them row. Luck guided them to a jetry among the reeds. By this time their singer was sound asleep and did not wake even when they extricated their bicycles from under him. So they tied the boat up and left him there while they bicycled down an unknown track and found their way back to Southwold. The singer survived and was found in the same pub the next evening. But this time they did not accept his offer of a short cut by water.[68]

This story presents a vivid picture of rural life at the time, as well as showing the class divide between those who still sang the old songs, and those who were setting out to preserve them, though Butterworth never made any mention of such things. He seemed genuinely enthusiastic about the work, though his allegiance was to Sharp in the resulting differing agendas that caused friction between various collectors.[69] Lucy Broadwood noted on her first meeting with Butterworth that he had collected hundreds of folk songs, though this was likely an exaggeration.[70]

Another of Butterworth's collaborators in folk song collecting was Francis Jekyll (pronounced "Jeekyll"), known by his friends as "Timmy."[71] Like Butterworth, he was an Eton and Oxford man, who worked for both the British Museum and the Ministry of Information at different stages of his life. Though largely forgotten today, he was important at the time, contributing at least 34 found songs, some of which are of very high quality; Butterworth considered him a helpful partner, and the feeling was mutual. After Butterworth's death, Jekyll noted: "Some of my happiest days were those which we spent together, tramping the Sussex Downs and collecting songs."[72]

George Butterworth in Leeds, 1913 (courtesy of Anthea Ionides).

5. George Butterworth (1885–1916)   119

Butterworth was, perhaps curiously, less interested in preserving texts with complete fidelity, and was known to have altered them, even changed words, to make the poems fit musical meters more accurately. He had no qualms about submitting such altered pieces for publication, suppressing, for example, verses that were considered too bawdy or scurrilous for late Edwardian sensibilities; as we have seen, this was actually a requirement for publication.[73] However, he was always meticulous in notating the melodies accurately, writing them out simply in his books and then adding the structures of musical notation (key signatures, time signatures, etc.), as was required by the standards of the time.[74] This followed Sharp's model, rather than Grainger's.

He was equally interested in the preservation and popularizing of English folk dance. He had the opportunity to see the Espérance Club perform in April 1907 at the Queen's Hall in London, and was delighted by the dances and songs.[75] In 1911, he attended the Folk Dance Summer School at Stratford-upon-Avon, which is where he probably began working with Sharp.[76] In December of that year, at about the same time that he and Vaughan Williams were being ferried about aimlessly in the dark by an inebriated folk singer, Sharp formed the English Folk Dance Society in London, and Butterworth was immediately brought into the fold as a committee member.[77] From 1912, he began to collaborate with Sharp on the collecting of folk dances.[78] He was particularly adept at folk and Morris dancing, and he performed in Sharp's Morris men's side, which held its first public performance in February 1912. This activity continued almost weekly until the outbreak of the war, and the dancers frequently accompanied Sharp to offer demonstrations during his lectures. This included two foreign trips, to Brussels in 1913 and Paris in early 1914.[79] Sharp was rather relentless in trying to get publicity for the team, and this alienated some (such as Lucy Broadwood), as he was known to do.[80]

The group was filmed in August of 1912, but this does not survive. In June of the same year, some of Butterworth's other dancing was also captured on film, featuring him in a solo Morris dance, along with Cecil Sharp and the Karpeles sisters in a group dance. The device used to film them was the Kinora, a kind of early home movie camera. Several of the spools containing the dancing sequences were not discovered until the 1980s at Cecil Sharp House in London (the home of the English Folk Dance and Song Society), and are probably the only film records of Sharp dancing. They provide an invaluable record that shows Butterworth's skill in executing various difficult dances.[81] Readily available through an internet search, these short films make for fascinating viewing. They are charming vignettes that put a human face to this young, athletic man, who displays a great love and skill for the dances. As instructional films, they are as useful now as they would have been then.[82]

Butterworth's efforts at collecting dances yielded very good results. Beginning in Oxfordshire and the Midlands, he was able to find and preserve a number of Morris dances and their tunes, which were in danger of dying out. He recorded some of these in his *Diary of Morris-dance hunting* (noted between April 13 and 24, 1912).[83] Unfortunately, the men who knew them were frequently quite elderly, and having not danced some of them in decades (sometimes as long as 50 years), many could barely remember the steps or the melodies. As such, they produced uneven demonstrations. At times, the dances were well presented, though not often enough. Butterworth himself said that some of them were "quite clear, others unintelligible, and the joins are bad."[84] Despite these frustrations, he persevered and with patience, was able to collect an impressive selection of dances, steps, and tunes over the course of a few years, which earned him the gratitude of many of the older dancers.[85] Butterworth and Sharp also journeyed to the North East of the country to record sword dances in the working-class communities of the industrial regions. Sharp later published these as a three-volume set.[86]

Butterworth was very proud of his abilities as a folk dancer, and in those years seems to have found the niche that he had been seeking. Here at last was a place where he could shine doing something that he loved. Indeed, he claimed to be the only one who could dance a certain difficult Morris move, the double caper.[87] He once told Reginald Lennard, who had referred to him as a musician, "I'm not a musician, I'm a professional dancer."[88] This remarkable statement shows a very changed man from the one who had entered the Royal College to perfect his keyboard and compositional technique only a few years earlier.

Despite this new-found identity in the folk dance world, he did remain committed to folk song collection, as well as music and composition, producing the works for which he is best known between 1910 and 1914. He also had a gift for recognizing the musical strengths and weaknesses of others, such as when he encouraged Vaughan Williams to compose a symphony, as we will see below.

In all, Butterworth achieved much in a short time. The manuscripts of his folk collections (edited by Michael Dawney in 1976)[89] contain 460 distinct items in total: 306 folk songs, 134 dances (with music and step notations), and 29 arrangements of folk songs for piano (with some overlap). He also copied many tunes and dance steps from Playford's 17th-century *Dancing Master* (which he had viewed at the British Museum) into modern notation.[90] Only a small number of his assembled folk songs were published in his lifetime, but the dances were published in full, in collaboration with Cecil Sharp.[91] While the number of songs he collected was small compared to those of Vaughan

Williams (810 songs) and Sharp (over 3,300), he accomplished much in those few years and made a lasting impact on the movement.[92]

A small collection of his work, *Folk Songs from Sussex*, was published during his lifetime, containing eleven songs that he had gathered and arranged between 1906 and 1909; four of these were collected by Jekyll. Butterworth used an earlier variant version of one of the songs, *Roving in the Dew* (that Jekyll had also discovered), in the first of his *Two English Idylls* (see below). Three other songs would find their way into various works by Vaughan Williams.[93] He also brought out his song-cycle, *Love Blows as the Wind Blows*, based on poems by the Victorian poet William Ernest Henley (1849–1903). These songs were a mixture of original material and folk song-influenced motifs,[94] but they would not be published until 1921, and were not performed in his lifetime.[95] In 1914, he rearranged them for voice and orchestra, which was to be the last work he would complete.[96] He was working on a new piece, the *Fantasia for Orchestra*, but it remained unfinished; it contains elements of both folk song and Impressionism, and has now been completed and recorded.[97]

Butterworth also submitted a number of songs for publication to the *Journal of the Folk Song Society*, but some were rejected because they did not match what the Society considered to be folk songs, and some had texts which were deemed inappropriate.[98] Again, we see a tendency to want to make such findings conform to specific ideas about what the nation's folk heritage entailed, dismissing those parts that were outside of those ideas. This, of course, did a great disservice to the authentic traditions by trying to force them into predetermined boxes, rather than letting them speak for themselves, warts and all.

In general, Butterworth and Sharp were in agreement on the methods of folk song collecting. Sharp, as we have seen, has been criticized for some of his approaches; these criticisms were leveled against him in his own time. Percy Grainger, as we will see, was more forward-looking in his methods of recording the songs, and disagreed with Sharp's views, which he felt were inadequate. He preferred to use the new technology of the phonograph to make audio recordings (which he viewed as more objective and authentic), a practice largely rejected by Sharp, Vaughan Williams, and Butterworth.[99] Butterworth held to Sharp's more conservative approach, and perhaps naively to the ideals of a romanticized rural England. Indeed, the songs that he collected are almost exclusively from rural communities and villages, and he virtually ignored any similar traditions that might be found in larger towns and cities; urban folk songs held no interest for him.[100] Butterworth was simply more comfortable in the country rather than in the city, and whether that life was idealized or not, the slower pace and the pleasures and pastimes of rural folk spoke deeply to him. Reginald Lennard noted that he had once suggested to Butterworth that an ideal occupation for him would be that of a country inn keeper, which would give him the more relaxed pace of life away from the city, allowing for composition and immersion in the folk traditions that he so loved.[101] Whether Butterworth ever seriously entertained this idea is not known. In any case, the idealistic view of a lost England would soon be challenged and destroyed by the horrors of the Great War, wherein Butterworth and so many of his young colleagues would perish.

George Butterworth in Stratford-upon-Avon, 1914 (courtesy of Anthea Ionides).

When the declaration of war came in August of 1914, Butterworth was again at Stratford, participating in one of Sharp's folk dance summer schools.[102] He did not immediately rush to join, and he declined an offer from his father for a safe commission, feeling that it was unfair to those who did not have such an option; he briefly considered taking a civil job.[103] Further, his immediate attention was on his father's fiancée, Dorothea Mavor, who was still in Germany (in a spa town near Frankfurt), and needed to get home. Fortunately, she was able to make her way to Belgium and then on to England by the end of the first week of August.[104] On returning to London at the end of August, he, along with several friends, enlisted in the Duke of Cornwall's Light Infantry, joining as a private. Immediately they were dispatched to Bodmin in Cornwall, and then to Aldershot (south-west of London) for basic training.[105]

It may be somewhat difficult for modern readers to understand the enthusiasm with which the young generation signed up for active service, though of course, we have the hindsight of the effects of so many 20th-century conflicts. At the time, it was genuinely believed by most that this would be a minor affair, over by Christmas 1914, and with minimal casualties.[106] H.G. Wells, for one, wrote a series of articles in which he confidently stated that this would be the "War that will End War,"[107] a tragically laughable proposition when seen through the lens of later 20th-century history. Further, English schools, colleges, and universities had long played up the role of manliness, as we have seen, but also explicitly tied such roles to a love of country and empire. Public schools often instructed boys who came from military families, so a career as an officer was almost a foregone conclusion for some. This attitude was not limited to the elite, however, as Murphy notes: "Strict discipline, patriotic belligerence, the British imperial ideal and, often, overt xenophobia were promoted equally in the state elementary schools."[108] Colleges such as Eton furthered these attitudes, effectively dividing the country's young men into officers and troops, a handy division for recruitment as the war began.[109] The emphasis was on physical fitness, "manliness," and cultivating leadership skills.[110] Universities, such as Oxford, continued such attitudes by training the leaders of tomorrow. Butterworth and his friends would have been inundated with these messages during their long years of study. Outside of schools, the Boy Scouts also emphasized outdoor skills and patriotism. Murphy notes: "around a third of boys born after 1900 belonged to the Boy Scouts and it is probable that the movement had a role in preparing the British people for the forthcoming war."[111]

He seems to have once again been afflicted by restlessness, even though he had found much contentment in the folk song and dance movements. After a period of great creative output, he was slowing down, and the enthusiasm for his recent work was dwindling. R.O. Morris noted after his death: "[...] there came a time when he felt that, so far as he was concerned at least, all that could be done had been done [in terms of collecting folk songs] and life began to assume an aspect of increasing perplexity for him [...] there were struggles and heart-searching. War seemed to provide the release."[112]

He and certain friends were eventually granted commissions, and he became a second lieutenant, though he remained in England for nearly a year.[113] While he was happy about this, the lack of any action left him agitated and restless; again, he was growing bored and desired to move on. The paperwork was tedious and the lack of supplies was irritating.[114] In this case, he was eager to go into active service. He kept a detailed diary during his military years, but did very little musically, leaving that life behind for the new one.[115] He made no mention of music in the diary, though he did collect some songs from the Durham miners under his command, and came to respect them and regard them as friends, despite the difference in their social stations.[116] The war had the effect of equalizing the men who fought in it. Class distinctions were of no importance during the life-or-death situations in the trenches, and this egalitarianism helped break down class divides in the years after the conflict.[117] Butterworth also maintained an interest in the political situation in England, and its effects on the war.[118]

The call to arms came at last in August 1915, when his unit was moved to France.[119] He saw little of combat for quite some time, though occasionally a few young men, including from among his friends, were killed. After a brief respite back in England in January 1916, he returned to France and his battalion was moved to the Somme Valley, where it saw real combat in July.[120]

Butterworth was unexpectedly promoted to being in charge of his company, after the previous commanding officer was wounded. He rose to the challenge, and led the group with great skill, being recommended for, and receiving, the Military Cross, "for commanding his company with great ability and coolness"[121] at Pozières between July 17 and 19, without regard for his personal safety. In this place, facing chaos and death, he had found a purpose, as meaningful as any he had searched for back in England. At the end of the month, he was wounded by shrapnel in the back, but it was not serious enough for him to be sent away from the front line.[122] Ironically, had the wound been worse and required further treatment, it would have saved his life.

At the beginning of August, the brigade was moved again to the front, to begin an attack on a trench called Munster Alley (which was ultimately successful). It was here that Butterworth met his tragic fate in the pre-dawn hours of August 5. Brigadier-General Henry Page Croft wrote to Butterworth's father, describing his heroism in those last moments:

> I went up to the farthest point reached with Lieut. Kaye-Butterworth. The trench was very low and broken and he kept urging me to keep low down. I had only reached the Battalion Headquarters on my return when I heard poor Butterworth, a brilliant musician in times of peace and an equally brilliant soldier in times of stress, was shot dead by a bullet through the head. So he, who had been so thoughtful for my safety, had suffered the same fate he had warned me against only a minute before.[123]

The battle situation and the proximity to the enemy line made it so that it was not possible to recover his body to bring back for burial.[124] He and another victim were therefore buried near Munster Alley, but no trace of the grave remains today. The nearby Thiepval Memorial does contain his name among the fallen,[125] and the trench where he fell was named Butterworth's Trench in his honor. Ultimately, of those dancers who were a part of Sharp's troupe, half (including Butterworth) were killed in the Battle of the Somme, which gives a sense of the appalling loss of life and how it affected everyone.[126] His father and stepmother were informed on August 9, with a final confirmation on August 18.[127] Few in the army knew of his musical career, and were surprised when they learned of it.[128]

Butterworth was mourned by those who knew him, especially by Vaughan Williams, who had lost a close friend. He wrote to Holst in 1916 from France (where he was then serving): "I sometimes dread coming back to normal life with so many gaps—especially of course George Butterworth.[...]"[129] He also wrote to Sir Alexander to express his condolences and praise his son's talent.[130]

5. George Butterworth (1885–1916) 125

Vaughan Williams felt that the younger composer had shown a unique ability to express himself honestly through his music. Butterworth left his remaining manuscripts to Vaughan Williams, who was keen to have them published as a memorial, and he wrote to Sir Alexander expressing this desire shortly after the terrible incident. He wanted to examine them first, however, and this would almost certainly necessitate waiting until the war was finished.

Cecil Sharp, when hearing the news while in Appalachia, noted in his diary entry for September 2, 1916: "In the evening the mail came from England and brought me the terrible news about poor George Butterworth's death. Go to bed feeling very very sad."[131] He noted on September 6 that Maud was not well, writing: "Probably only indigestion but she has suffered a good deal."[132] She was no doubt devastated by the loss. Further bad news came the following day: "There the English mail reached us and I read the awful news of poor [Reginald] Tiddy's death. Now that he Butterworth, Lucas & Wilkinson have gone I seem to have lost all my pillars except one—V[aughan] Williams and any day something may befall him. I feel too sad to get to work to do anything."[133] Thankfully, his fears for Vaughan Williams were unfounded.

Sir Alexander saw to it that a tribute to his son, the *George Butterworth, 1885–1916, Memorial Volume*, was privately published in 1918. It contained letters, recollections, tributes from friends (including Vaughan Williams), and other pieces of information, and was distributed to his friends and colleagues.[134] Lucy Broadwood summed up Butterworth's contributions well when she wrote in response to receiving her copy: "[...] the pre-war compositions of our younger composers, like your son and Ralph Vaughan Williams, seem like something prophetic of this present tragedy of the world."[135]

Others spoke highly of Butterworth in the years after his death. Finzi noted in 1922 that his music was, "the most intimate & sweet (in the fine sense) that I know: It sums up our countryside as very little else has ever done."[136] Ernest Moeran, in a defense of Benjamin Britten's living in the United States during World War II (for which Britten was criticized), wrote in 1941, in a letter to the *Musical Times*: "The death of Butterworth in 1915 [*sic*] was a tragedy, the nature of which no country with any pretensions to the preservation of culture and a respect for art can afford a recurrence."[137] Moeran, who survived the war with a head injury, was bitter about the massive loss of young life and the waste of so much potential.[138] Hugh Allen was equally disgusted: "What a loss as a musician—and specially as a friend. His dear wayward manner, that friendly scowl, that tenderly gruff voice—all gone to pay a rotten debt to a bloody-minded lot of miscreants."[139] Clearly, the king-and-country patriotism extolled so loudly before the war had left a very bad taste in the mouths of many when confronted by the horrid realities of the trenches. They were no longer shy about dissenting.

In considering his lost potential, we will examine some of Butterworth's surviving output. Barlow has divided it into four categories: early compositions, settings of Housman poems, the folk song collections and arrangements, and the "late" works to 1914.[140] Realistically, this covers a total of only about five years. The amount of surviving music is depressingly small, since, as we have seen, Butterworth's intense self-criticism led him to suppress and destroy much of his work.

Butterworth's relationship to the poems of Housman is of interest, and of all of the composers who adapted these words to their compositions, his settings are frequently considered to be among the best. He produced two song cycles of Housman poems, *Six Songs from "A Shropshire Lad"* (published in 1911) and *Bredon Hill and Other Songs* (published 1912). Both song cycles were composed between about 1909 and 1911, though some settings may have dated from his time in Oxford. He donated the autograph manuscripts of the works to Eton College in 1912, and had considered making them into one collection, but eventually settled on releasing them in two separate cycles.[141]

The *Shropshire Lad* songs secured Butterworth's reputation, though not every review was complimentary when they first premiered in June 1911.[142] Perhaps surprisingly, he did not incorporate existing folk songs into these settings, but rather supplied original melodies, though some of these certainly do follow folk motifs and melodic ideas. His setting of "On the Idle Hill of Summer" from the *Bredon Hill* cycle, is the most complex of his songs, and as Barlow notes, has more in common Wagner, Debussy, and the later Romantic style than it does with the idioms of English folk song.[143] The text of this piece is particularly poignant and ironic. It describes a young man who lazily dreams on a country hill while hearing soldiers march off to battle. While aware of the terrible fate that awaits them, he decides to join them. Butterworth could not have asked for a better description of his own destiny:

> On the idle hill of summer,
> Sleepy with the flow of streams,
> Far I hear the steady drummer
> Drumming like a noise in dreams.
>
> Far and near and low and louder
> On the roads of earth go by,
> Dear to friends and food for powder,
> Soldiers marching, all to die.
>
> East and west on fields forgotten
> Bleach the bones of comrades slain,
> Lovely lads and dead and rotten;
> None that go return again.

5. George Butterworth (1885–1916)

> Far the calling bugles hollo,
> High the screaming fife replies,
> Gay the files of scarlet follow:
> Woman bore me, I will rise.[144]

Butterworth left behind four orchestral works: *Two English Idylls*, the rhapsody: *A Shropshire Lad* (which is distinct from his song settings), and *The Banks of Green Willow*. All of these pieces but *A Shropshire Lad* incorporated into their musical structures folk songs that he had collected on his trips into the countryside. The songs were not exact replicas of the tunes he had discovered, but rather were, "an idealised version suitable for orchestral development."[145]

The *Two English Idylls* belong to the earlier phase of surviving Butterworth compositions.[146] The first *Idyll* contains three folk songs, all from Sussex: *Dabbling in the dew* (a popular piece surviving in many versions), *Just as the tide was flowing* (collected by Butterworth in 1907), and *Henry Martin* (also collected by Butterworth in 1907). The second *Idyll* makes use of material from one folk song, *Phoebe and her dark-eyed sailor* (which Butterworth collected in April 1907, also in Sussex). The pieces were premiered in Oxford at the Town Hall on February 8, 1912, and were very well-received, though Butterworth expressed annoyance that the harpist on that occasion had played her part exactly the opposite of what he had requested her to do.[147] His perfectionism never ceased, along with his tendency to lapse into being that blunt Yorkshireman.

His rhapsody, *A Shropshire Lad*, is considered by many to be his greatest work, and while begun sometime in 1909–10, it was not completed until 1911, and would not be performed until 1913.[148] Though certainly inspired by his settings in the song cycle, he wrote that this rhapsody was, "in the nature of an orchestral epilogue to [the] two sets of Shropshire Lad songs." He intended it "to express the home-thoughts of the exiled 'Shropshire Lad.'"[149] Drawing thematic material from his song, *The Loveliest of Trees* (from his *Six Songs* cycle), he did not use any existing folk tunes as a basis for the composition, but his original composed melodic structures are very reminiscent of the folk style. The work premiered in Leeds on October 2, 1913; Vaughan Williams, and possibly Elgar, were in the audience.[150] The response was overwhelmingly positive and Butterworth was regarded by those in attendance as a major new voice in English music, the work being described as "remarkable" and "full of wonderful beauty and poetry."[151] Despite the acclaim, he was still filled with self-doubt, and had not wanted any biographical information about himself to be included in the concert program.[152] In the post-war years, the piece enjoyed much popularity, and would be lovingly viewed, not as a sign of great things to come, but as a melancholy reminder of what might have been.[153]

The Banks of Green Willow, dating from 1913, incorporated three musical themes, two folk songs and an original composition.[154] The folk songs were a tune of the same name (which Butterworth collected in 1907, and later recorded on cylinder in 1909, in Basingstoke, Hampshire)[155] and *Green Bushes* (which Percy Grainger had discovered in 1906).[156] Butterworth described the piece as a "musical illustration to the folk-ballad of the same name."[157] This is somewhat remarkable, given that the ballad itself is very dark, telling the story of a young woman who becomes pregnant by a sea captain, steals money from her parents, and runs away to join him on his ship; there she delivers the child. However, the presence of a wrong-doer on board does not bode well for the ship's safety, according to ancient tradition. She resigns herself to being thrown overboard with her infant as a sacrifice, so that they may drown at sea, and thus help the ship avoid disaster.[158]

Butterworth made melodic alterations to his versions of the tune to fit the piece, and may also have worked with other variants, combining them into a new theme.[159] The work premiered in February 27, 1914, conducted by Adrian Boult. Butterworth directed a performance in Oxford the next day, and it premiered in London on March 20. This is thought to be the last time that Butterworth heard his own music performed live.[160]

As we have seen, he also played an important role in the development of Vaughan Williams' *A London Symphony*, suggesting the idea to his older friend in a casual manner, almost as an afterthought, as Vaughan Williams would later observe.[161] Butterworth was very interested in how the work developed, and he gave feedback to Vaughan Williams, which the latter greatly prized, whether it was in praise or constructively critical. Butterworth wrote the program notes for the first performance. It was premiered on March 27, 1914, and on hearing it in its full realization, he wrote an article about it for the Royal College of Music magazine shortly after,[162] offering a summary of the work's movements as well as a defense of Vaughan Williams' compositional style and ability, which was coming under scrutiny and criticism at this time for being deficient. He noted, that the concert was "perhaps as good a 'first performance' as it would be possible to obtain."[163] His enthusiasm for the work led to his efforts to save it from being lost in pre-war Germany,[164] and it is also possible that some of his honest criticisms of the length of the symphony's *Finale* may have led Vaughan Williams to make the edits and cuts down to the final edition that is now best known.[165] However, after hearing it, he also wrote to Vaughan Williams telling him that those parts of the final movement that had concerned him initially no longer did, which seems to contradict his magazine review.[166]

Vaughan Williams always valued his younger friend's opinions. His wife Adeline noted in her own correspondence to Sir Alexander (probably in 1916) after Butterworth's death that Vaughan Williams relied on his friend's input for his compositions, and he was especially pleased when Butterworth approved. He was never able to fully accept that his friend was gone and all of the music he might have composed was now lost.[167]

Their friendship extended into a mutual interest in the revival of early music. In the summer of 1912, a choral group known as the Palestrina Society (which included Butterworth) formed to focus on repertoire from the 16th century. The group asked Vaughan Williams to be their conductor, and proceeded to explore the then-unknown works of various Renaissance masters, along with folk song arrangements made by Vaughan Williams himself. Ursula Vaughan Williams records that her husband was delighted to take part in this venture, seizing the opportunity to learn more about 16th-century music. The group also performed some of his newer works.[168]

In summary, Butterworth made a small but lasting impact in a brief time. He is a minor composer in the history of the era, but an important one. We do not know what might have been had he returned from the war. Would he have resumed composition, perhaps trying his hand at larger-scale works, and joining the ranks of Vaughan Williams and Holst as one England's most revered national composers? Or would he have turned toward more continental influences, even Impressionism, as he had hinted at in his song cycles and his unfinished orchestral fantasia?[169] Perhaps, like Sibelius, he might have fallen "silent," abandoning composition and distancing himself from his work completely, as the process of writing was often difficult for him. His extensive purge of his juvenilia and some later works shows a composer burdened by self-criticism and doubting his abilities. He desired to be remembered only for specific works, should he not return, and he may have had a sense of impending doom in going off to the war.[170]

Had he survived, he might have at least delved deeper into the folk song and dance world that he loved so much, but in this too, he was already showing signs of feeling unfulfilled. If he was wrestling with issues of identity, purpose, and especially sexuality, there may well have been no remedy in a restrictive society that was only slowly beginning to loosen some of its tight Victorian bonds. The answers to these questions were taken from us by a bullet on that early August morning, and we must be content with the little that we have from this sensitive, restless man who showed signs of genius, and whose influence and importance were only truly appreciated in the decades after his untimely death.

Vaughan Williams wrote that ultimately, he was a true English composer, and that English traditions were in his blood: "Indeed, he could no more help composing in his own national idiom than he could help speak his own mother tongue."[171]

6

Ernest J. Moeran (1894–1950)

Ernest Moeran and Philip Heseltine (Peter Warlock) may be one of English music history's unlikelier duos, but their friendship in the 1920s was of great importance to both, and they influenced one another, for better or worse. Of the two, Moeran was far more involved with the collection of folk songs and incorporating their idioms into his work, though Heseltine's devotion to Tudor music and interest in Celtic tunes, among other repertoires, certainly earns him a place in this book as a figure of importance. We will examine the life and works of Moeran in this chapter, and Heseltine in the next.[1] Both chapters will consider their time spent living together in the village of Eynsford, south of London.

The standard biography has long been that of Geoffrey Self. Recently, however, Ian Maxwell has uncovered significant evidence to show that many of the assumptions about Moeran's life are incorrect, based on anecdotes and errors of memory and interpretation; Maxwell terms these mistakes "the Moeran myth."[2] Among the long-held assumptions about his life are: that Moeran came from a non-musical family and never considered music as a career in early life; that he was badly wounded by shrapnel to the head during World War I, having a metal plate inserted into his skull, which later caused him to have mood swings and exhibit erratic behavior; that he lived meagerly on a disability pension as a result; that he made little impact in the music world during the 1920s; and that his music was mostly derivative.[3] Maxwell challenges these notions, and several more. His findings require a reappraisal of Moeran's biography. It appears that some of these misconceptions (significantly, the war wound story) came from two early overviews of Moeran written by Philip Heseltine in 1924, and a longer essay in 1926,[4] written when the two were sharing a home. This information must have originated with Moeran himself, which makes untangling fact from fiction a more difficult task. This chapter will therefore survey both Moeran's life as it most often has been represented, and include references to Maxwell's work to counter those assumptions.

6. Ernest J. Moeran (1894–1950)

Ernest John Moeran (known to friends and family as "Jack") was born on December 31, 1894, in Heston, Middlesex. He was the son of an Irish father, Joseph (a clergyman from Dublin, whose family left Ireland when he was an infant), and a mother, Ada Esther, from Norfolk (who would outlive him). This mixed parentage and these two locations were to have a significant impact on his life and his work; both came from privileged backgrounds that provided an ideal setting for his advancement.[5] His mother's family was very wealthy, and she was able to secure for him a regular monthly income from about 1920. This freed him, like Vaughan Williams, from the burden of having to work for a living, and allowed him to devote his full time and attention to composing.[6] Despite this luxury, he went through several periods beginning in the mid-1920s during which he composed little or nothing. Indeed, composition often seemed to be a burden for him, as he required very specific conditions in which to work, and he was frequently unhappy with the results.

Though Moeran had an older brother who would also find his calling in the church, Moeran was not religious, and while he would later write some sacred music, he was always critical of it and of the beliefs it celebrated. It is often reported that his father was appointed to pastoral duties in the village of Bacton-on-Sea in Norfolk, a remote setting near the coast and north east of Norwich, however, records show that it was actually in Salhouse, twenty miles south and much closer to Norwich.[7] Thus, the notion that the young Moeran grew to love the Bacton area, its people, and the marshy fens from a young age can be questioned.[8]

Moeran was probably educated at home until about the age of ten, and may have begun music lessons as early as five or six years of age.[9] For decades, most scholars have assumed that Moeran grew up in a non-musical environment. Indeed, he seems to have told this story, for when Heseltine wrote about him in the mid-1920s, he included this bit of information, and must surely have heard it directly from the source. Strangely, this is almost certainly untrue, as Moeran's mother's family displayed considerable musical interest and talent.[10] Ada both played piano and sang, and the teenage Moeran already showed some notable skills with composition, something that would have been highly unlikely if he were an autodidact. Maxwell offers the hypothesis that Moeran may have deliberately obscured his background and musical training from Heseltine, so as to better fit in with his friend and appear to be more like him.[11] He may even have felt some guilt about coming from a privileged background with the kinds of musical advantages that Heseltine did not have.[12]

After the family moved to Salhouse in 1905, he was sent up the coast to Cromer to attend boarding school at Suffield Park Preparatory, remaining there until 1908 (his parents moved away to Surrey in 1907, but he stayed in the area for an additional year), continuing his education and developing his musical skills.[13] By the age of thirteen, he moved on to Uppingham School (between Peterborough and Leicester), where he further studied violin and piano, going so far as to form a string quartet. He was also experimenting with composition (and may have been for some time), including a lengthy piano sonata and three string quartets. Like Butterworth, he would later destroy these pieces, as he was filled with self-criticism and distaste for his youthful work,[14] and seems to have wanted to discourage any idea that he learned music from an early age.[15] Some believe that it may have been during this time that he first developed his interest in folk music and began collecting songs, though this is not certain.[16]

By 1912, he was ready for higher music education, and entered the Royal College of Music in September[17]; he also joined the Oxford & Cambridge Musical Club in October. This was an important gentlemen's club whose members included Vaughan Williams, Butterworth (who had been an active member, as we have seen), and Adrian Boult, among many others, as well as honorary members such as Parry and Elgar. It was to be an important affiliation for him in years to come, and its devotion to chamber music certainly had an influence on his own work.[18] At the College, Moeran focused on composition and began study, like so many before him, with Stanford.[19]

In the period that he was there, he discovered the music of Elgar and Delius, both of which would impact him greatly. However, as we have seen with Butterworth, this was soon to be a bad time for young men wanting to make long-term plans for their lives. His attention would be diverted by the crisis in Europe.

Indeed, the outbreak of the war interrupted his studies, and he enlisted at the end of September 1914, joining the Royal Norfolk Regiment as a dispatch motorcycle rider (Moeran and Heseltine would both have a life-long love affair with motor bikes and racing cars). This was an important development, as Robert Weedon notes:

> Motorbikes were a new innovation in modern warfare, but the motorcycle dispatch rider's life was a dangerous and uncertain one. With telephone communications still unreliable and likely to be severed every time a shell exploded on a communication trench, the army still relied heavily on antiquated methods as pigeons to deliver memos, orders and other messages to the front lines. The comparative speed and precision allowed by a dispatch rider meant that they were in high demand.[20]

This was a dangerous occupation, leaving the riders open to gunfire and bombs as they rode between destinations, however Moeran's was a Territorial Force regiment that was not immediately deployed to France.[21]

By June of 1915, he had been promoted to the rank of second lieutenant,[22] and then to lieutenant by the latter half of 1916.[23] During this time, he was able

6. Ernest J. Moeran (1894–1950)

to continue some of his regular musical activities, including concert-going, folk song studies, and composing,[24] including his set of *Four Songs from "A Shropshire Lad"* in 1916, his earliest known set of surviving songs. Like so many other composers, he was drawn to Housman's simple, somber, and enigmatic verses, though his exact reasons for doing so at this time are uncertain.[25] Another work possibly dating from this time is his *String Quartet in E-Flat*, part of which may have originally been intended for a musical competition.[26]

He was finally deployed to France and was at the front by 1917, but would only spend some five months there.[27] On May 3 of that year at the Second Battle of Bullecourt, he suffered a head injury; one version of the story is that a shell exploded near him, but it seems more likely that a bullet hit his motorcycle and fragmented. Fortunately for him and music-lovers alike, he survived. Self has asserted that shrapnel lodged in his head that could not be removed, adding that treatment at the time for such an injury was severe and not guaranteed, involving attaching a metal plate to his damaged skull. Having this intrusion would be damaging, not only physically, but certainly psychologically. This has become one of the standard stories about Moeran; it is used to explain some of his more erratic behaviors later in life, and many believe that it contributed to his premature death by a cerebral hemorrhage in 1950.[28] The argument put forth by Self and others is that the effects of his head injuries were exacerbated by heavy drinking, making him incoherent and belligerent at times; his coordination suffered as he aged. Further, it seemed that even a small amount of alcohol could quickly leave him appearing to be intoxicated.[29] Self has quoted private medical correspondence which was of the opinion that patients with head injuries such as Moeran was presumed to have should not have been drinking at all, because the effects of intoxication could be amplified and made worse. Mood swings, headaches, irrationality, and even a tendency to violence were all real risks. Indeed, some of Moeran's behavior would later be embarrassing to his friends and wife, and his irresponsibility would alienate those around him as he declined in later years.[30] In a 1947 Irish radio interview about his music, his answers are sometimes hesitant, and he seems to struggle with his speech, taking pauses as if searching for words that he cannot find immediately.[31]

More recently, however, Ian Maxwell has convincingly argued that this injury was not as severe as has been previously thought,[32] countering a widely-held assumption that has been used over many decades to explain multiple aspects of Moeran's life, from his personal affairs to his compositions. That he was injured is certain, but the severity has been misrepresented. Heseltine was the first to portray the injury as a severe war wound in 1924, but then it was stated to be merely a wound in his 1926 biography. The earlier description may have been Heseltine's attempt to portray Moeran in a positive light, as a kind of war hero.[33]

Moeran himself would claim, "[...] I ought to be a teetotaller (sic) on account of five lumps of shrapnel in my head.[...]"[34] His brother made the similar claim that shrapnel was too close to his brain to be removed, information he presumably received from Moeran.[35] This would seem to confirm that shrapnel was lodged in his skull, and that alcohol had a negative effect on him because of it. However, the records indicate that while the initial diagnosis was determined to be a shrapnel wound, this was altered a few days later to a gunshot wound, which an x-ray revealed had left a small metal fragment near the vertebra.[36] Significantly, it was not judged to be serious, or requiring an operation, so he was discharged and sent home on leave a mere three weeks after the event; there was no mention of any damage to his skull.[37] A few months later in August, Moeran was in London performing a very technically demanding piano piece for the Musical Club, further evidence that he was not suffering from any serious side effects.[38] Two days after this performance, a further medical exam declared him healed except for some minor pain, and he was declared to be fit to return to Home Service, as opposed to being redeployed in France.[39] By the end of the year, the pain had worsened, however, and a new x-ray did reveal some "fine pieces of metal" that had been missed in the previous scan, indicating that they must have been quite small.[40] A reassessment of the injury indicated that it initially had been more serious than thought, but was not now.[41] The larger piece was later removed in March or May of 1918; the records are rather confusing as to the date of the operation, though it may have been postponed from the earlier date.[42]

During this time, he was stationed at Boyle, County Roscommon, a garrison in Northern Ireland. This was his first experience with a country that he heard about from his father, and that he would grow to love deeply. As he had only a small number of duties, he probably spent some time traveling in the area and seems to have collected some Irish folk songs, as well as worked on new compositions. His time there probably influenced the writing of his orchestral work, *In the Mountain Country*, which he had originally titled *Cushinsheeaun*, the name of a village in County Mayo.[43] His unit returned to England in the autumn, and though the war soon ended, he applied to enter the air force. However, he was discharged in January 1919, and given a clean bill of health.[44] There is no mention of a metal plate in his head, or of shrapnel fragments that were too embedded to remove. Though these stories must have originated with Moeran himself, there is no evidence for them. Maxwell suggests that the metal plate story may have been invented by Moeran as a means of covering up his alcoholism, and that his story about living on a disability pension as a result

6. Ernest J. Moeran (1894–1950)

of his war injury may have been a means of hiding his family income. Further, there is no medical evidence that he suffered from post-traumatic stress disorder, and his time at the front was minimal, compared with many others.[45] PTSD as a condition was unknown at the time, but undoubtedly afflicted a portion of those who lived through the horrors of the trenches. Britain did recognize shell shock from 1915, a condition believed to be caused by exposure to the explosions of artillery shells, and tens of thousands of veterans were treated for it in the years after the war ended.[46]

Certainly, the war would have affected him, and he must have felt a sense of loss and waste in the aftermath of the conflict, particularly in the snuffing out of so many promising young lives, such as George Butterworth's.[47] Self maintains that these feelings were reflected in many of his pieces after the war, what he calls "a certain introspective, bleak quality—may be traced back to the trauma of those years in the 1914–18 War."[48] However, since Moeran's time on the front was quite limited, Self may be reading something into his music that is not there.

Moeran was no doubt eager to return to a full musical life. One story related that he briefly worked as a music teacher at his old school Uppingham, but this, like so many other aspects of his biography, seems to be based on faulty evidence. A photo purporting to show him in the school orchestra at the time more likely dates from 1911, and so cannot be used as evidence for his activities. Further, the school has no record of him being employed, nor did its obituary for him mention any post-war time activities there.[49]

He seems to have spent some additional time in Ireland from May 1919, taking in the country and gaining inspiration for his work.[50] However, he was eager to resume his studies at the Royal College, entering again in 1920. At this time, he studied composition with John Ireland (who, despite his name was English, from near Manchester), though it seems that these lessons took place at Ireland's home, and the two became good friends.[51] Ireland was to have a great influence on Moeran's compositional style, particularly the latter's piano works. He has been called an "English Impressionist," drawing from the works of Debussy and Ravel (Moeran would soon be attracted to Ravel's music, as well), rather than from the folk songs that inspired Vaughan Williams, Holst, and Butterworth. Some of his pieces do have an "English" feel to them, however, and he was fond of the landscapes of both Sussex and the Channel Islands.[52]

Moeran seems to have been happy during this time. While immersing himself in London's musical life, he also indulged his passion for driving fast vehicles, winning a Gold Medal from the Motor Cycling Club in a speed trial from 1922.[53] He and author Robert Gibbings enjoyed a motorcycle tour in the Pyrenees in 1920,[54] and he began a friendship with the Irish composer and conductor Hamilton Harty, who would remain a supporter throughout his life.[55] It was during these years that he also met and befriended Philip Heseltine (Peter Warlock), which had both good and bad results. We will examine their friendship below.

Moeran was very active in the London music scene, and would participate often in the Music Club events over the next decade. Indeed, the connections he made from knowing many important and influential members assured that he would soon make a name for himself as a young composer.[56] He staged a concert of his own music in early 1923, which attracted a decent audience and was generally well received.[57] He produced a number of works in these years, including his *Rhapsody No. 1*, which drew from similar ideas as previous rhapsodies by Vaughan Williams and Butterworth (see below). The music has a very strong folk song feel to it, though the melodies seem to be entirely of his own creation. This would be a feature of his music over his entire career, as Maxwell notes, with more than half of his original output containing thematic material that had folk song qualities.[58]

He had collected some folk songs before the war[59] (probably by the time he was enrolled in the Royal College),[60] but by 1921, he became seriously engaged in gathering tunes from Norfolk, traveling the countryside by bicycle. There, he learned of a certain singer, Bob Miller. Moeran was eager to meet then man, noting: "I soon fixed an appointment to spend the evening in his company at a local inn, and he gave me a splendid batch of songs, some of which were hitherto unpublished. Moreover, by his enthusiasm and personality, he opened the way to a series of convivial evenings at which I found that the art of folk-singing, given a little encouragement, had by no means died out."[61] He published eighteen songs (one as a variant version) in *The Folk Song Journal* in 1922. In all, he collected about 70 songs.[62]

Philip Heseltine's profile of Moeran for the *Musical Bulletin* in 1924 detailed the composer's interest in gathering the folk tunes of his native region. It is worth quoting at length here, for it sums up Moeran's dedication to the practice, which differed somewhat from his predecessors, being devoted to collecting the authentic songs, not sanitizing them to make them acceptable to polite society:

> It was about this time [1920] that Moeran discovered that the tradition of folk-singing was still vigorously alive in the district of Norfolk. [...] His familiarity with the neighbourhood gave him facilities which are often denied to the stranger, and his collection of songs, which now number considerably over a hundred, is undoubtedly one of the finest that has yet been made in any part of the kingdom. [...] He collects these songs from no antiquarian, historical, or psychological reasons, but because he loves them and the people who sing them. [...] For him, as for them, the song itself is the thing—a thing lives, a part of the communal life of the country; and, indeed, it is a much more heartening

musical experience to sit in a good country pub and hear fine tunes trolled by the company over their pots of beer than to attend many a concert in the West End of London. It is no good appearing suddenly at a cottage-door, notebook in hand [...] holding up your hands in pious horror at any verses of a song which may conflict with the alleged tastes of a suburban drawing-room; nor should you spoil the ground for other collectors (as someone has tried to do in Norfolk, its seems) [Vaughan Williams?] by forgetting that old throats grow dry after an hour's singing. The scholarly folk-lorist has his own reward, but he does not get in touch with the heart of the people.[63]

Heseltine further remarked on this commitment to the authentic integrity of the songs when he mentioned one of Moeran's Norfolk settings, *Down by the Riverside*, which was in 5/4 time, that is, a cycle of five beats, rather than the more typical duple or triple rhythms,[64] noting that "any suspicion of it being a possible distortion of triple or quadruple time is dispelled by the decisive thump with which mugs come down on the table or boots come down on the floor to mark the rhythm."[65] He also noted Moeran's use of folk song-like tunes in his compositions, describing it as "naturally apparent," as well as some traces of Gaelic folk song, which in general he felt were being over-used by composers of the time, and thus were less welcome in Moeran's music.[66] He joined Moeran for a "folk song hunt" on at least one occasion, in September 1923; he mentioned that they took a phonograph to obtain sound samples.[67] Moeran's commitment to folk song collecting was cemented when he was elected as a committee member of the Folksong Society in December 1923.[68]

For his part, Moeran held that the singers and their land were closely linked. He discovered that the best place to obtain examples of authentic tunes was the village pub, at least in Norfolk. At these gatherings, elder singers were respected and had precedence, and the locals recognized the ownership of certain songs by certain singers.[69] His offers to meet people at their homes were usually refused, and the singer would then make a counteroffer to meet at the inn for a demonstration.[70] Conversely, he later discovered that in Ireland, the preference was the opposite, with private meetings between him and various singers being the norm.[71]

Moeran's own recollections on how he came to know that folk music could serve as a useful starting point for composers, and then to use it in his work, are somewhat conflicting. He stated in different instances that he came to his realization during an unexpected concert in London. In 1946, he wrote that he had gone to St. Paul's Cathedral on a winter's evening to hear a performance of a Bach Passion, but it was sold out, so he found another performance, and "grudgingly" handed over a shilling to hear a Balfour Gardiner concert of contemporary English composers. Not expecting to be impressed, he wrote that:

Among other works I heard was a rhapsody of Vaughan Williams, based on songs recently collected in Norfolk by this composer. It was my first experience of a serious orchestral composition actually based on English folksong, and it caused a profound effect on my outlook as a young student of musical composition. This, and many other works which I encountered at these concerts, though not all based on actual folk-music, seemed to me to express the very spirit of the English countryside as I then knew it. My home at this time was in Norfolk, where my father was a vicar of a country parish, so I determined to lose no time in rescuing from oblivion any further folksongs that remained undiscovered.[72]

This experience, he said, awoke in him a way of combining an interest in folk songs with a method of incorporating them into new music in creative ways.

The problem with this account, as Maxwell notes, is that it conflicts with an earlier version of the story related by Heseltine, wherein he claimed that it was Delius' *Piano Concerto* in the spring of 1913 that had such a profound effect on Moeran, after failing to get in to hear Brahms' *Requiem*.[73] These are clearly two different accounts, and may well represent Moeran having difficulty recalling certain events by the 1940s. Indeed, Maxwell's search of contemporary newspapers revealed that there was indeed a performance of Bach's *St. Matthew Passion* in March 1913, and later that evening a performance including Delius' *Piano Concerto* in one of Gardiner's concerts. This is obviously a combination of aspects of the two stories above and shows that Moeran was not remembering things properly. A concert including two of Vaughan Williams' *Norfolk Rhapsodies* had actually taken place nearly a year earlier, in April 1912; Moeran may have been able to attend this concert, but it is not certain. Delius' concerto, however, was certainly not one of his more original pieces and contained nothing uniquely "English" in sound; it was not even particularly representative of his later works. It seems that Moeran combined these separate incidents into one account later in life, whether deliberately or not.[74]

In 1921, Moeran composed his *String Quartet No. 1*, which while indebted to Ravel, also made use of melodies in a folk style. He also completed his first orchestral work, *In the Mountain Country*. Dedicated to Harty, *Mountain Country* owes some of its structure to folk song elements, and again, while Moeran did not seem to use any existing songs, he composed musical themes in the style to give the work its folk-like feel. He undoubtedly drew inspiration from Vaughan Williams in this piece. Self has suggested that the title of the work may have been inspired by Vaughan Williams' *In the Fen Country*, and perhaps Delius' *Song of the High Hills*.[75] Here was the work of a student that, while looking back over the previous decade for inspiration, showed great promise.

By 1922, Moeran had advanced significantly in his compositional skill, enough to produce his *Rhapsody No. 1*, dedicated to John Ireland. Self has noted that the principle influences seem to be Delius, and perhaps surprisingly, Butterworth's *Shropshire Lad* rhapsody.[76] The work's beginning is similar to Butterworth's earlier piece, and the clarinet melodies at this opening have a structure much like those in the Norfolk songs that Moeran collected.[77] Indeed, the piece is "a set of variations around a lyrical modal melody clearly evocative of English folk music, which are the basis on which we are taken forward for a further ten minutes. As noted, musicologists have not found any identifiable folk tunes in the piece—though the melodies Moeran creates were realistic enough to fool a *Musical Times* reviewer in 1925."[78] Heseltine would joke in 1924 in his *Musical Bulletin* profile that the main melody of the piece was a perfect tune for setting his naughty limericks.[79]

Moeran conducted his *Rhapsody No. 2*, composed for the Norfolk and Norwich Centenary Festival in 1924, for an audience that included the queen; both he and Vaughan Williams were presented to her afterward.[80] The work continued his practice of integrating folk song motifs, drawing melodic inspirations from the traditions of both Norwich and later, Ireland. This was important to his expression, representing for the composer a kind of idealized world, a romanticized vision in music of the lands that gave him so much solace. This technique would never leave him, unlike some composers who moved on to other methods of composition as their lives and careers progressed.[81]

Moeran said that he had the old songs "in his ear" and considered them collectively to be a "fund" from which he could draw to create his own melodic ideas, rather than just repeating the tunes verbatim.[82] In 1930, Hubert Foss offered an assessment of Moeran's works that noted his ability to use folk influences, writing that "what [Moeran] learnt from English folk-music was absorbed and digested before ever he wrote his first outstanding work,"[83] and that he did not use actual folk songs but rather created melodies based on folk idioms and modes; these were essential to his style. This talent for constructing faux-folk song motifs was also true for various piano pieces from the time, such as his *Theme and Variations* from 1920. The longest of his piano works, with six variations and a *finale*, it contains elements of both English and Irish folk song. Self writes that "Moeran's theme could pass muster as one of the Norfolk tunes he was shortly to collect and arrange.[...]"[84]

He also tried his hand in 1920, as had so many others, at setting some of Housman's poems for voice and piano, which seems to have been almost an obligation for composers in those first two decades of the 20th century. He set four poems from *A Shropshire Lad*, under the title of *Ludlow Town*.[85] The final poem, "The lads in their hundreds to Ludlow come in for the fair," is especially poignant, describing a scene of young men happily attending a fair (Moeran loved market fairs), who soon will march off to war and die. The third stanza is particularly striking:

> I wish one could know them, I wish there were tokens to tell
> The fortunate fellows that now you can never discern;

> And then one could talk with them friendly and wish them farewell
> And watch them depart on the way that they will not return.[86]

Such language must have moved Moeran, who despite not having witnessed the horrors of war to the extent of his friends and colleagues, was well aware of the losses inflicted on a whole generation of England's youth.

As the 1920s progressed, he showed great promise, having made numerous excellent connections and proven that he was a composer of considerable talent and skill. However, there were already signs that he might not ultimately be as prolific and reliable as he himself would like. He produced a number of other smaller pieces, but his friendship with Heseltine, which resulted in them sharing a home together in the village of Eynsford in Kent, between 1925 and 1928, severely hampered his creative abilities, and encouraged him into alcoholism. We will examine their time there more in chapter 7, but it is worth discussing the effects these years had on his health and creativity. Maxwell refers to it as "nothing short of catastrophic."[87] After February 1925, for example, he no longer appeared at the Musical Club, and his compositional output began to dwindle, though he and Heseltine arranged for London concerts of his works (among others) in May and June.[88]

He intended to tackle the considerable work of producing his first symphony by 1925–26, but this was delayed significantly for a number of reasons, and would not reach fruition until 1937. Commissioned by Harty,[89] Moeran had made substantial progress on it and was nearing completion, when he decided to withdraw it, citing his dissatisfaction with its structure. He resolved to re-compose large sections of it, though some parts of the original work made it into the final version over a decade later. This was a remarkable turn of events; Moeran was effectively turning down the opportunity for a huge career boost with a famed conductor's support.[90] Moeran's proposed symphony was probably nowhere near ready by its due date, not just because of his overly-critical assessments, but also because he was in no shape to finish it.[91]

The reality was that the distractions of his life at the cottage were interfering with his ability to compose. He needed absolute quiet and isolation to work properly, and life in Eynsford was anything but those two conditions. Maxwell suggests that the primary reason he did not simply leave this environment for one more suitable for his needs was that he was already falling into alcoholism[92]; Heseltine's dominant personality did not help matters. Moeran later commented that he "lost faith" in his abilities by 1926, and the longer he put things off, the harder it was to get going again.[93] His withdrawal from musical life, and failure to produce any major works, meant that the establishment gradually forgot about him and moved on. His lack of participation in Musical Club activities may have been due to his now living too far away, but it may also have been due to some antagonism toward the organization by Heseltine, who was not eligible for membership and was thus an outsider. Given his acidic tongue about so many aspects of the musical scene at the time, he can hardly have had good things to say about it, and this may have influenced Moeran's decision to limit his involvement.[94] Moeran would eventually be dismissed from the club in 1930.[95]

From 1927, Moeran's relationship with Heseltine may have changed somewhat, and perhaps he came to realize that the living situation was not in his best interest. He seems to have spent more time at his parents' home in Ipswich, which continued into 1928.[96] The effects of Eynsford were significant, however; he had not been an alcoholic before then and afterward, he was diagnosed as such; it is logical to theorize that his attempts to match Heseltine's excessive drinking had gone terribly wrong and left him with a condition from which he would never recover.[97]

After the Eynsford situation ended, he lived in Ipswich and then London, and began to be more productive again, despite a motoring accident in 1929 and another accident the following year on a ship from Corsica to France in 1930, which left him needing a long time to recuperate. Originally diagnosed as water on the knee, and then as localized tuberculosis, he was bed-ridden until November.[98] This actually helped his creativity. Due to the physical limitations, he was able to spend much of his time composing, largely in his head, since he could not sit at a piano.

Indeed, the 1930s would see some of his more celebrated works.[99] In 1931, he brought out the orchestral piece, *Lonely Waters*, in both an instrumental and a vocal version (an earlier version of this may have existed in 1924, as Heseltine had referred to it then). Dedicated to Vaughan Williams, this is one of the few pieces directly based on a Norfolk song from "certain inns in the Broads district," as he indicated in the score. He preferred the vocal version, but indicated that the singer need not be classically-trained. Indeed, all that was required was a good, clear voice.[100] This again shows his affinity for the authentic sound of the voice, rather than hearing it through the filter of art music.

Heseltine's untimely death in December 1930[101] certainly affected and haunted him. However, it may ultimately have been helpful for his recovery. Immediately after it happened, he wrote to Edith Jones, Heseltine's mother, saying, "I have very few really close friends, & Philip was one of the closest. [...] His loss will mean a terrible gap to me when I get back again to normal life & find he is no longer there."[102]

Moeran was certainly quite bitter at how his friend had been neglected in his last year, which he believed may have contributed to Heseltine's demise, as he wrote in February 1931: "The musical profession as a whole is to be blamed for allowing a man of his genius to exist very nearly in penury."[103] In 1931, he produced *Whythorne's Shadow*, a short orchestral piece, often grouped with *Lonely Waters*, based on a part-song by the Tudor composer Thomas Whythorne (1528–1595). It was a re-done work, the first version having been lost during Moeran's drinking binge in Brussels in 1929; he, Heseltine, and others had gone to France to meet Delius, but somehow Moeran got lost along the way, ended up passed out on a street, probably did not meet with Delius on that occasion.[104] The piece as it later existed may be a memorial to Heseltine. Certainly its Tudor basis could be seen as a tribute to his friend, who was so devoted to 16th-century English music.[105] However, he did not like to speak about Heseltine in the months and years after his death, and tried to avoid the subject.[106] His *String Trio* may also be in honor of Heseltine (though it was begun before his death),[107] while the *Sonata for Two Violins* from 1930 contains his usual use of folk song themes, but is considered a major breakthrough in his mature compositional style, being free of Delius' influence to a greater degree.[108] Folk music remained important enough to him that he was elected again to the committee of the Folk-Song Society in 1931,[109] and collected new tunes near his home in Ipswich, which resulted in his *Six Suffolk Folksongs* in that same year, arranged for voice and piano.[110]

For some time, it has been believed that Moeran's whereabouts are difficult to determine between 1930 and 1935.[111] Whether in mourning for Heseltine, or needing to take long periods for himself in isolation (as well as convalesce after his accidents), he is said to have spent time in the Cotswolds, in an attempt to reappraise his work and style.[112] However, there is no real evidence for this assumption, as Maxwell shows, and the story (another aspect of the "Moeran myth") may have arisen over some confusion about his parents' address.[113]

Importantly, it was during this time that he was drawn to Ireland as a source of inspiration, finding the landscape of County Kerry in southwest Ireland much to his liking. It provided him with the peace and quiet that he needed to create. He had once explained: "I find that 'inspiration' arrives as a result of concentrated thought in complete solitude amid natural surroundings which seem to be conducive to the germination of musical ideas, such as long rambles over the countryside."[114] He once claimed that his ideal job would have been to monitor a railway crossing in some remote location, where only two trains would pass through per week.[115]

Marsh has noted, "Unless he was actually living in the place and amongst the people from which the music originated, Jack Moeran could not find the inspiration to compose. His was a dual ancestry, and even though he was later to produce his greatest work in the mountain country of Southern Ireland, there are still constant reminders of the East Anglian county with its wide horizons, tall church towers and windswept dunes."[116] He drew much inspiration being in solitary areas, though in his music, he rarely attempts to create impressions of landscape features, unlike many of his contemporaries. He evoked the natural through his use of folk song-like motifs that are as suggestive of the people as they are of the landscape[117]; his music is often more about mood than concrete descriptions, more about his experience of a given place.[118] As Huss observes,

> [...] Welsh and Irish landscapes may after all have influenced Moeran in identifiably different ways, not through their external differences, but through Moeran's expectation and experience of different associations and responses. This explains why Moeran needed specific surroundings in order to compose: if nature is not merely an external reality, but equally a perceived, internal and personal reality, it becomes more than an external influence, it becomes the internal stimulus, the 'spark' itself. Accordingly, "nature" in Moeran's music is not really an image of nature, but a facet of Moeran's personality.[119]

Shifting away from the landscape of Norfolk to that of Ireland inevitably led to a shift in the folk song influences in his works, from English to Irish. Composer Arnold Bax would note in his obituary of Moeran that "During his first thirty years he was an Englishman and a diligent collector of East Anglian folk tunes, whilst for the remainder of his days he was almost exclusively Irish. [...] It was [...] about twenty years ago [Bax wrote in 1950] that his consciousness of his Celtic heredity was aroused."[120] His works after 1930 show a greater use of larger forms, and darker moods. Moeran found much in common between Norfolk and Kerry, despite their geographical differences. He even observed some similarities in their folk songs, noting that the fishermen of Great Yarmouth fished near Ireland, and would go ashore in bad weather, where they would seek out local pubs and homes, passing time in bad weather sharing stories and songs.[121] He loved Ireland and the feeling seems to have been mutual, as he was popular with the locals; he had found a new refuge to escape to from time to time.

Ernest Moeran (courtesy of the Lewis Foreman collection).

He noted in 1939 as he was writing his *Violin Concerto* that he was immersed in the sounds of Irish music in Kenmare, County Kerry: "I am going out to farm kitchens and out-of doors Ceilidhs [...] & soaking myself in traditional fiddling and its queer but natural embellishments and ornamentations. [...] In the 2nd movement I am planning to work some of this idiom into concerto form. I may tell you that some of these people have a terrific technique."[122]

He also tried his hand at writing religious music, a potentially lucrative market. Some of it has retained its popularity,[123] but he generally disliked what he composed, calling it "this tripe for the church."[124] His lack of belief no doubt contributed to his hostility to the genre, and as he confessed to Heseltine back in 1930, the "bilge for the church" that he wrote was only for the money.[125]

In January 1935, another sign of his alcohol problems showed when he was sentenced to confinement in a nursing home under a doctor's care for attempting to drive drunk. According to the *Times*:

> Ernest John Moeran [...] was bound over for two years at Cambridge yesterday and ordered to enter a nursing home, after he had been found *Guilty* of being drunk in charge of a motor-car at Cambridge on Saturday night. Detective-constable Cummings said that he saw Moeran staggering about Market Hill. He afterwards entered a motor-car, sat down in the driving seat, and fell forward over the wheel. He said: "It is my car, and I am going to drive home."

The article notes that this was not the first time he had experienced a run-in with the law: "[...] in August, 1929, Moeran was fined £10 at Watford for being drunk in charge of a motor-car, and in October, 1934, at Aylesbury, for a similar offence he was disqualified for driving for five years and ordered to enter a home for nine months. At Aylesbury he absconded from bail."[126]

These incidents show a rather shocking belligerence on Moeran's part, significantly dating from 1929. Clearly, his time at Eynsford had led to a dependency on alcohol, and he was exhibiting careless behavior because of it. Moeran insisted that in the 1935 incident, he had been looking for a taxi and accidentally stumbled into a private car that was not his,[127] however this sounds like the excuse of an alcoholic attempting to downplay and justify his actions after the fact. He noted that it was all very upsetting and resulted in a breakdown, right when he was in the midst of a good creative period, working at last on his abandoned symphony.[128]

By 1937, his efforts to bring out this work finally paid off, and he completed his *Symphony in G Minor*, which premiered in January 1938. Its creation spanned over a decade in time; the slow movement, the *Lento*, is very likely from the earlier stage. Indeed, Moeran claimed that some of his thematic material had been inspired by the tunes and landscape of Norfolk, including a song called *The Shooting of His Dear*. However, Self's assertion that he decided (for once) to use a specific tune about a shooting accident as the basis for the slow movement back in 1924, (only a few years after his own experiences of the war), and that the symphony thus served as a kind of war requiem for Butterworth and others, remains unproven.[129] The newer movements of the piece were probably begun from 1933, and the work was completed by January 1937,[130] during which time he was frequently in Ireland.[131]

By the 1930s and into the early war years, his ability to compose freely and frequently was diminished from what it had been in the 1920s. Indeed, as Maxwell observes, nearly half of all of his output dates from the years 1920–26, while the remainder was written over the following two decades.[132] This lack of productiveness came as a result of his years in Eynsford, and one wonders what he might have achieved had he not been so derailed from the track he was on. Also in the 1930s, Moeran became more elusive; he had never been particularly socially competent. His friends would wonder where he had gone and would be worried about him, but he would always resurface eventually. His craving for solitude increased. His drinking continued and worsened, and he suffered unusual complaints, including once injuring himself while sleepwalking.[133]

By the end of World War II, Moeran's life took a dramatic change. Two new individuals came into his life, one of which inspired his last, and some of his most celebrated, works. In 1943, he was to become friends with Lionel Hill, and the two would take up regular correspondence. These letters were later published by Hill in his book *Lonely Waters: The Diary of a Friendship with E.J. Moeran*,[134] a work which, while overly glowing in its assessment of Moeran's character, nevertheless provides valuable insights into his life in his last years.

More important at this time was a new romantic relationship. Possibly as early as 1930, he had met a young cellist named Peers Coetmore (given name Kathleen).[135] By 1943, they renewed contact and Moeran began to fall in love with her. He had always been something of a romantic, and certainly he had entertained a handful of lovers in the past. Their courtship was rather quick, and may have come about due to ulterior motives by each; they were certainly not compatible in many ways.[136] Coetmore probably found the idea of having her own personal composer to write for her very appealing, especially since Moeran was something of an established name by the 1940s. She was fiercely determined to succeed as a cellist, and his promises of being able to open doors and write new music for her to premiere undoubtedly had an effect; they almost seem like bribes to get her to spend more time with him.[137] On July 26, 1945, they married, and there may have been happiness for a few years (certainly there was for Moeran). He devoted himself thereafter to composing cello music for his wife.[138] These pieces include his *Cello Concerto* and the *Sonata for Cello and Piano*, the latter of which is considered possibly his greatest work. This single-minded devotion, however, distracted him from undertaking other projects.

Clearly she inspired him, but the relationship was not easy, and grew increasingly unhappy. Her tremendous talent meant that she was much in demand, and was traveling frequently on tours, preventing Moeran from having the true kind of artistic partnership that he wanted. It did, however, give him the opportunity to continue with his much-needed times of solitude, so perhaps for a while it was the best of both worlds. However, he struggled once again with finding an appropriate place to live and write music. He wrote to her: "trying to settle down to work in London or any big city at all is a very big experiment for me, whose whole musical and creative outlook for years past has been entirely bound up with the countryside [...] it may turn out to be absolutely essential to have somewhere also to work outside London, otherwise I might cease to be able to write at all."[139] Indeed, he still required an appropriate country setting to work. Hill notes, "the countryside, in all its moods, meant more to Jack than life itself—indeed he could not compose away from the rural scene[...]"[140]

Any early marital happiness they may have enjoyed was not to last. His drinking had expanded into full-blown alcoholism, which increasingly alienated Peers. She became critical of his behavior, which he seems to have interpreted as criticism also of his musical ability, which of course, led to more difficulties in being able to produce new work, and a retreat ever further into the bottle.[141] Repeatedly he would swear to her that he was done with drinking and had been sober for some time, but he always failed and relapsed.[142] After the completion of the *Cello Sonata* in 1947, he began to unravel. He struggled to produce a second symphony, which apparently was nearing completion, but he could not bring himself to finish it.

He did return to folk song arrangement one final time, setting his *Songs from County Kerry* for voice and piano (published in 1950), but by the end of that year, he was in Cheltenham under a doctor's care for his drinking, at the insistence of Peers. However, she was called away to an extended tour of the southern hemisphere (South Africa, Australia, and New Zealand) in 1949. It may have been this trip that Moeran used as an excuse not to finish the symphony (he would resume work on it again at the end of 1949), for he declared that what he had written simply was not good enough. She attempted once again to help him, and tried to persuade him to join her in Australia. She had hopes that he would be welcomed as a teacher and conductor there. Moeran seems to have considered the option, but kept putting off making a decision. In the end, Peers simply gave up, and though not declaring it to him, she left him to pursue her own career.[143]

He still kept in touch with her, and by early 1950, he returned to Ireland, finding a solitary place to his liking that was not far from Dublin. He believed that here he could finish work on the symphony at last.[144] Nothing was to come of it, however, for he began drinking again. By June he was in Kenmare in County Kerry, where he was able to take some work as a music instructor. His mental state had deteriorated to the point that he admitted to having few lucid moments, and feared that he would be declared insane and institutionalized. On December 1, a strong storm swept through the area. He was at the Kenmare pier that evening and fell into the water. His body was recovered, and at first it was suspected that he might have been drunk, though some said he had not touched alcohol for six months.[145]

The coroner determined that he had not drowned, but was in fact dead before he fell in, citing a heart attack as a possible cause; it was eventually determined to be a cerebral hemorrhage.[146] Some have theorized that this may have been due to his old war injury, but in view of new information on this, the explanation of alcohol damage may be sufficient. Others believed that he intended to commit suicide, being in a depressed state and worried about his metal stability; why else would he have been out on a pier in a fierce and dangerous storm? The question remains open. He was buried in Kenmare with honor and acclaim, and many turned out for his funeral.

Moeran seemed destined for greatness in the 1920s, and might well have achieved it, if he had not made the fateful decision to join Heseltine in Eynsford. It seems that in those years, he developed a dependency on alcohol that he was never able to cast off, and that in later life, this made him forgetful, difficult toward others, slow to work, undependable, manipulative, and prone to injuries. These qualities have formerly been attributed to his war wound, but given that Maxwell has shown that it was not as serious as once believed, the injury probably had less of an impact on his life than his own self-inflicted woes. We can only speculate about what he might have become had he chosen a different path.

Moeran always understood that his music was not ground-breaking, not in the avant-garde, and he was content with that. In a 1947 Irish radio interview, he spoke of his love for Ireland, and how he simply was not a part of the modernist movement, summing up his musical philosophy:

> Well my music is not considered modern music by modern standards. There is a school of very modern music—some people call it "wrong note music"—but it centres around the school of Arnold Schoenberg and the central European school of music, some people call it the school of the Atonalists, and I suppose that is the last word in modern music. [...] Frankly I don't understand it very well myself, but by what really is known as modern standards, I'm afraid that my music is considered rather old fashioned, partly maybe

because I've always been interested in traditional music. From a boy onwards, I've always been fascinated by the old songs or old fiddling and that kind of thing.[147]

Further, his approach to those old songs differed from Vaughan Williams or Sharp, perhaps having more in common with Grainger:

I have not been concerned with the artificial revival of the art. In other words, with those who set about the teaching of folk-songs in schools, or the organizing of garden fetes, etc., at which folk-songs are sometimes performed in the highly sophisticated manner of those who have never heard a real traditional singer. Well-intentioned as these efforts may be, they involve something quite apart from the art of those who have it in their bones, handed down from father to son.[148]

Right into his last years, his love of folk song and the traditions of England, as well as those of his adopted County Kerry, in all of their rawness and unsophisticated beauty, never left him.

7

Philip Heseltine / Peter Warlock (1894–1930)

Philip Heseltine is one of the most unique figures in English music from the first decades of the 20th century. He was a skilled composer of songs and small musical forms, writing under the *nom de plume* of "Peter Warlock."[1] An *enfant terrible* of the classical music scene, he gloried in his scandals and sharp wit as a music critic (he admired the music of Vaughan Williams, for example, but openly despised that of Holst), frequently making enemies and raising eyebrows wherever he went. His passion for new music and especially for the works of Delius (whom he practically worshipped in his younger years), coupled with his devotion to the rediscovery and propagation of Tudor music in scholarly editions, and his close friendship with Moeran, make him an essential composer for this study, even though he sought to avoid being labeled as only an "English" composer.[2] His devilish goateed countenance, coupled with rumors of occult workings and black magic rituals, only increased his appeal to some. He was a self-styled libertine who rejected Christian teachings in a Nietzschean fashion and sought to live for the day, though his mystical inclinations increased over the years. His strong mood swings may indicate bipolar disorder (see below), and it was probably not a surprise to some when he died in December 1930, possibly by his own hand, at the young age of 36.[3]

An exact contemporary of Moeran, he was born on October 30, 1894. By his adult years, some would have undoubtedly thought it more appropriate if he had been born one day later. He was brought into this life surrounded by the luxury of the Savoy Hotel, where his wealthy parents seem to have spent some years living in lavish surroundings (the hotel had first opened in 1889). His father died only a little over two years later, in 1897, thus leaving him solely in the care of his mother, Bessie Mary Edith Coverton (or simply Edith, who often went by the nickname "Covey"). She was from affluent Welsh stock, and in his youth, Philip would develop a love for the Welsh countryside near their home, noting as an adult that it appealed to him more than wine or women, and that being in the area made him mindful of music.[4] She was a controlling and strict woman in many ways, however, and had an unhealthy obsession with her son and his activities right into his adulthood, always trying to steer him in the direction she wanted and exert her influence. Indeed, more than 300 letters written by Heseltine to her have survived, and the earlier ones reveal a relationship that was disturbingly Oedipal, as we will see below. He became increasingly aware of this unhealthy bond, but there was little he could do to completely sever it, because he often relied on her financially.[5]

His schooling began in 1899 in London, and very soon after, he showed a great interest in music; one letter to his mother noted how he was fascinated (at the age of seven) by the layout of the orchestra, the number of players, etc.[6] He also studied piano and showed some aptitude for it.

Edith remarried in 1903, to Walter Buckley Jones, a wealthy man four years younger than her. He had studied to be a lawyer, but did not pursue it to completion, preferring to live on family money in London, though he also owned a home, Cefn Bryntalch, in the Severn Valley in Wales. The family moved here in 1908, and from this point, Heseltine became deeply enamored of all things Welsh. He and his stepfather, perhaps somewhat unusually for the time, were quite fond of each other. It may have been Walter's easy-going nature that appealed to the boy.

A year after Edith's marriage, Heseltine was sent to the Stone House Boarding School in Kent. As a child, he had a rather weak constitution at times, not showing the same robustness that the young Butterworth had for physical activity and sports (though he did play them). He continued developing his musical skills, playing piano at various school concerts, and learning about songs from Shakespeare's plays, which no doubt stimulated his later interest in the music of 16th-century England.

It was also from this point that regular letter-writing between mother and son began, revealing the nature of Edith's overbearing behavior and her possessiveness toward him. She was determined to instill a stern Christian sensibility in him, instructing him to read only the Bible in bed, and sending him other religious literature, which he gratefully received. She also sent overly-affectionate postcards, which, not being in envelopes, could easily be intercepted and read by the other boys, much to Heseltine's embarrassment and horror. After suffering from their teasing and taunts, he eventually requested that she no longer send these to him.[7] He would often write to her with absurd and unsettlingly loving prose, as Smith notes, "It is also slightly disturbing that at the age of nearly 12 he could be writing to his mother words such as these:

'I am still you [sic] own VERY *extra* loving lambkin *Phil*. I hope you don't show this letter or any of my letters to anyone.... Of course I know you wouldn't but I like to make certain that our little loving talks are quite private.'"[8]

For her part, Edith seemed to revel in this devotion and began to employ emotional blackmail to ensure that it continued, infantilizing her son and keeping him dependent on her emotionally (and later, financially). A number of letters from Heseltine, for example, were profusely apologetic. He was sorry for not writing often enough, for writing letters that were too short, or for giving the impression that he did not care to receive her correspondence. As his time at school progressed, he would often have to apologize to try to contain her emotional outbursts. His attempts at appeasement would never last, of course, and he often had to assure her more than once in a given letter of how much he loved her, while putting himself down for being cruel and selfish, and then begging her forgiveness.[9] This kind of abuse would take its toll, being a factor in his later decisions and behavior.

On his 16th birthday, she sent him, of all things, a bouquet of violets. One could hardly imagine a stranger gift for a teenage boy, even at that time! His response, which probably should have been incredulity, was instead an effusive letter, claiming, "thank you a thousand times. [...] I think I was more touched by the lovely violets you sent than by almost anything you have ever sent me.[...]"[10] One senses that this ridiculous response cannot possibly have been sincere, but would have effectively staved off her emotional blackmail for a short while.

In 1908, he was accepted into Eton, but his time was not happy there. He may have been bullied, and he may have struggled against the restrictions of such an ancient and rigid institution. He noted that his moods became dark, his studies suffered, and he came to view the Eton education, and the Oxford one that was the logical continuation of it, as a waste of time with no real value other than status. He would later describe Eton as "a scholastic sausage machine," where he was surrounded by "mental juniors," and that being in such an environment essentially killed his development academically, by the age of 15.[11] However, he was able to join the Eton College Musical Society, which further stimulated his passion for all kinds of music. He was especially fond of his piano teacher, Colin Taylor, to whom he gave much credit for encouraging his musical interests.[12] Taylor would later note that he saw something quite different about the boy.[13] Like Delius, he would become a kind of father figure and would continue to correspond with Heseltine for the rest of his life.

Regarding Delius, Heseltine learned of his music in 1908, through various fellow enthusiasts at Eton. What first started as genuine interest in a new style, was to morph into something bordering on obsession with the man and his music, even a kind of infatuation. He once wrote to his mother, "Delius comes the nearest to my own imperfect ideal of music.[...]"[14] Delius was to have a profound effect on Heseltine's life and work, though by 1929, after years of familiarity with the older composer's music, Heseltine declared, "Delius, I think wears very badly. His utter lack of any sense of construction, coupled with the consistent thickness of texture and unrelieved sweetness of harmony [...] gets on one's nerves.[...]"[15]

However, in those early days, the two developed a great friendship and corresponded regularly. Delius became another father-figure to Heseltine in his younger years, helping him with personal and musical advice during difficult times and maternal conflicts.[16] Collins maintains that "Delius and his strongly held beliefs were readily taken on board by the impressionable and fatherless Philip to the point where the opinion and invective of both become practically indistinguishable."[17]

Needless to say, his mother was not at all pleased with this relationship, though long before it had taken hold, she was curious to meet the man, and wrote to her son about her possibly being introduced to him in London in May 1911. Heseltine's reply was, of course, ecstatic:

> I cannot possibly describe how passionate a love I have for Delius and his music [...] it would be one of the very greatest pleasures and highest honors of my life to meet him. I would a thousand times rather know him than King George himself! [...] if you knew Delius, I should feel that I did also through you [...] I am so excited about this I hardly know what to do![18]

On June 16, 1911, Thomas Beecham conducted a London concert devoted entirely to Delius' music, with the composer attending. Colin Taylor was able to obtain permission for Heseltine to attend, where he would meet his mother. He wrote to her: "I am so excited I hardly know what I am doing."[19] His wish was fulfilled, and he met his idol at the intermission. He was moved to write to Delius immediately afterward, telling him how much he had enjoyed the performance, and how the music had moved him like nothing else he had ever heard. Tellingly, he noted that to hear good music was far more useful than listening to sermons, something which Delius, as a non-believer himself, probably delighted in hearing. To Heseltine's utter joy, Delius was very impressed with him and his enthusiasm, and wrote back, desiring to begin regular correspondence.[20]

This encouragement, combined with his general unhappiness with the Eton academic environment, planted the seed in Heseltine's mind that he would like to pursue a career in music, but of course, his mother had other ideas. She fully intended for him to study at a university and go into either Civil Service or study to be a stock broker (both occupations were a tradition in the family);

7. Philip Heseltine / Peter Warlock (1894–1930) 153

Delius thought this idea was ludicrous.[21] However, in lieu of staying at Eton, Heseltine proposed to his mother that he go abroad to Germany for a year, study the language, and use that as a way of preparing for his career, while being able to also study music while he was there. Perhaps this was a stalling tactic, while he devised a way to make a musical career possible. After some hesitance and consideration, she surprisingly consented, and Heseltine left for Köln in October 1911. Edith accompanied him, of course, to ensure that he was properly situated.

Along the way, they stopped in France, and Heseltine was able to meet with Delius again (who resided in Grez-sur-Loing, south of Paris), which angered Edith, who declared Heseltine to be very rude and neglectful of their French hosts. More likely, she disapproved of the friendship and was merely looking for a way to start an argument. Heseltine seems to have realized this, and later put the whole thing down to his mother's "ridiculous ideas."[22]

Once settled in Germany, he did find the abundance of musical concerts available much to his liking, though almost from the start, some things did not go well. His piano teacher was determined that he practice scale and finger exercises to the exclusion of everything else to make up for his technical deficiencies, and he quickly grew bored and frustrated. Further, his studies of the language did not yield good results, and he found he had great difficulty in carrying on even simple conversations. He wrote at length to Delius, describing his predicament. Delius responded that he thought such exercises were a waste of time, and that the young man should seek out and study theory instead. Heseltine grudgingly admitted to himself that he might have to go to Oxford, read Classics and ultimately work in Civil Service after all, but he was determined to soak up as much music as he could during his time in Germany. He also tried his hand at composing, though he was frequently not happy with the results, feeling he was more of a craftsman than an artist, unable to think of new and inspired ideas.[23]

Delius was clearly enjoying the father-like position to which young Heseltine had raised him, and their letters expanded to include other subjects, such as Delius' atheism, something that had already been stirred in Heseltine, possibly due to his mother's heavy-handed religiosity. Delius encouraged his young friend to be true to himself. The older man was a great admirer of Nietzsche, and recommended in March 1912 that Heseltine read both *The Antichrist* and *Beyond Good and Evil*. Indeed, Delius later told his biographer and amanuensis, the composer Eric Fenby:

> The sooner you get rid of all this Christian humbug the better. The whole traditional conception of life is false. Throw those great Christian blinkers away, and look around you and stand on your own feet and be a man. [...] Sex plays a tremendous part in life. It

is terrible to think that we have come into this world by some despicable physical act. Don't believe all the tommy-rot priests tell you; learn and prove everything by your own experience.[...] I am inclined to think, along with Brandes, that the whole thing [Christianity] is a myth, like William Tell. One thing is certain—that English music will never be any good till they get rid of Jesus. Humanity is incredible. It will believe anything, anything to escape reality.[24]

Heseltine had returned to England in March 1912, to study for the entrance exam for Oxford, under the tutelage of one Reverend Clarence Rolt, who also took a particular interest in his other pursuits. He learned of the young man's ever-growing infatuation with Delius, and wrote to Edith in June, expressing his concern about his undue influence, stating that "the intimacy of a Nietzschian cannot be a good thing for a boy of his age."[25]

However, by that time, Heseltine was already writing to Delius to tell him that he had completely abandoned his Christian beliefs. Rolt and Edith conspired to prevent Heseltine from meeting with Delius at the Birmingham Festival in October 1912, but were unsuccessful, and Delius encouraged him to favor music over the study of Classics; he was clearly reveling in helping the boy to rebel. As the time for Heseltine's entry into Oxford approached, he again wrote to Delius, a long letter that lamented his situation, stating his resolve to enter into a music-related career, such as criticism, at the very least. Delius supported his decision, urging him not to spend his life doing something he hated.

This was the final encouragement he needed, and he wrote back telling Delius of his determination, and his optimism that a new life truly awaited him, one that might have escaped him if he had simply done what was expected by church, society, and family. "I curse the name of Jesus," he declared to Delius in 1913, "with a loathing too bitter for expression: his blasted doctrines are at the bottom of all this kind of thing. But for you, and a very few others.[...] I should have slept through life until the last and final sleep." He noted his keen interest in sex, and hated his mother's prudishness, by which she had tried to shelter him for so long. Finally, he made a declaration of tremendous importance, one which would define the rest of his life: "I am determined to *live* my life, to drain its cup to the very dregs, to live each day, each hour [...] I am absolutely *ravenous* for Life: what I do matters not so very much, so long as I live."[26] Heseltine the young libertine had arrived, and again, his mother strongly disapproved. Their relationship became more acrimonious, and Heseltine frequently dismissed her irrationality and religious foolishness.

Despite this growing rift, he did enter Oxford in October 1913, to study Classics, but was almost immediately unhappy, which only increased. He still longed to begin a music career of some kind, despite Edith's vehement objections. Delius cautioned him that music criticism would be just as unsatisfying, and felt that the young man needed a normal job while learning more about composition. Heseltine was open to such study, and pondered seeking out Vaughan Williams[27] and Holst. It is better that the latter never materialized, for he hated Holst's work, considering him an utterly derivative composer. He remarked on Holst in 1921: "I shall continue to regard this little man as a charlatan who is only saved from detection by the fact that music, unlike words, is not actionable at law."[28]

As for Vaughan Williams, Heseltine admired some of his works, such as the *Pastoral Symphony*, which late in his life he regarded (along with Elgar's *Introduction and Allegro*) as "the best English orchestral music of this century."[29] However, while he was interested in the folk song revival to a point, he also held that such songs could be set "without the usual idiotic harmonic restrictions that faddists like Cecil Sharp, V. Williams and Co. like to impose upon themselves."[30] Vaughan Williams, he wrote, was sometimes guilty of "mistiness and vacuity" in his music,[31] but was also "a man of sincere purpose and indubitable genius who will, I feel sure, one day achieve a real master-work."[32]

His interest in folk song would be partially due to his 1920s friendship with Moeran (whom initially he had sought out to tell him that he enjoyed one of his pieces), with whom he "hunted" songs. Moeran had suggested that he try arranging folk tunes when he was at a loss for other ideas,[33] one successful example being Heseltine's arrangement of *Yarmouth Fair*, a song noted down by Moeran in Norfolk. In general, Heseltine was not obsessed with the idea of the folk revival in the way that some of his contemporaries were. He drew from many sources, and certainly enjoyed modal and early music greatly. Collins suggests that evidence of folk song idioms in some of his songs "exist because they have features in common with Warlock's established style rather than being elements he deliberately chose to emulate."[34] However, he was also intrigued by Celtic music and once noted that he wanted to do for it what Grieg had done for Norwegian songs in his *19 Norwegian Folk Tunes*, arranged for piano.[35] Indeed, Kington refers to him as an authority, with experience of hearing them sung in taverns and writing them down,[36] and notes that composer Alec Rowley "described [Heseltine's] characteristics as being distinctly English and suggestive of folk-tunes.[...]"[37] Heseltine often made use of strong melodies that were almost folk-like in nature, but were surrounded by dense harmonies, influenced by Delius and others.[38]

Returning to 1914, the outbreak of the war in August allowed him to convince his mother that Oxford was not the best place to be, given the expense. He hated the city, calling it "a foul pool of stagnation."[39] He was able to obtain an exemption from service due to his "delicate" state of mind and body, but this was not a guarantee of safety, as we will see. In a letter to Delius in October

1914, he noted: "But for my 'nervous stricture,' which of course renders me 'physically unfit for service [...] the general public pressure would probably have driven me to enlist myself: hideous though a soldier's life would be for me.[...]"[40] His examining doctor observed that he had difficulty urinating when overstimulated, and that such retention could lead to further problems. This rather odd condition, as Smith notes, could well indicate that Heseltine was faking illness to get out of service.[41] In any case, concocting this move allowed him to delay his Oxford commitments, which was the real reason to go to London, of course.[42] He briefly attempted to study Philosophy at London University, but this also went nowhere quickly.[43]

After taking up residence there, he decided to try his hand at music criticism, despite Delius' warning. Securing work with the *Daily Mail*, he withdrew from his Oxford studies. Delius warned Heseltine that a critic's life was not for him,[44] and of course, he quickly grew dissatisfied with this work, since his overly critical reviews were often not published; his words could be very acidic and harsh, indeed. He began showing signs of depression again, sinking into despair. He may have suffered from some form of bipolar disorder, as his moods could change from euphoric (mania) to utterly black, and his behavior from forward-looking and thoughtful to irresponsible and childish; we will examine these moods more below. This was not helped by the horror stories filtering back from France, and his feelings of hopelessness about civilization. He withdrew from the *Mail*, and began musicological work at the British Museum on Elizabethan music manuscripts, eventually taking his place in music history as a pioneer in the study of Tudor music, and one of the leading authorities on the subject at the time.[45] He would often do this over the years when his moods prevented him from composing. From 1918 onward, English music of the 16th and 17th centuries had a noticeable effect on his compositional style.[46]

By late 1915, another important figure entered his life, D.H. Lawrence, the controversial author whose works were frequently banned and condemned. For a time, Heseltine was under his spell, and even desired to go with him to America, to found a new community of forward-looking artists who had broken away from society's constraints. He tried to convince Delius to join them, and spent time with Lawrence in Cornwall, determined to publish his writings if no one else would. Eventually, as was the pattern in Heseltine's life, the two had a falling out, possibly over what he saw as Lawrence's attempts to interfere in his personal life, or perhaps some unflattering comments made by Lawrence in a letter.[47]

Regardless of the cause, Heseltine returned to London, and began yet another chapter of his remarkably changeable life; soon, he was championing the works of the Dutch composer Bernard van Dieren, whose unconventional music Heseltine considered to be truly new and the product of genius. Unfortunately, the majority of the London musical scene thought the exact opposite, and this difference of opinion would make Heseltine very bitter, only confirming his anti-establishment views. His attempt to mount a concert of van Dieren's works was a disaster, and the music was panned by critics, whose negative reviews seem humorous now; they described his music as "dull," "nonsense," and not worthy of hearing a second time.[48] Regardless, van Dieren's friendship and influence would be so strong that he would replace Delius in Heseltine's estimation as his idol,[49] and Heseltine would eventually name him as his heir, which caused some controversy after his death, as we will see below.

During this period in London (1916–17), he was able to obtain a further war exemption, though it would not spare him completely from the risk. He also met the Scottish composer Cecil Gray, who became a life-long friend and eventually, his first biographer. The two would at one time share a flat and live the life of carefree bohemian artists. In late 1916, he also used the pseudonym "Peter Warlock" for the first time, in the periodical *Music Student*.[50] Heseltine did not get on well with the editor, but wanted to publish the article, so a fake name was the best solution; it would be the first of many such incidences.[51] Heseltine enjoyed making up humorous names, from A. Whyte Westcott ("a white waistcoat") to Rab Noolas ("saloon bar" spelled backwards). He also collected together a list of composers and musicians with last names that might induce hysterical giggles in school boys, including: Johannes Bacfart (a 16th-century Transylvanian lutenist), Johann Joseph Fux (an Austrian Baroque composer), Ludvig Schytte (a 19th-century Danish composer), and Andreas Crappius (a late Renaissance German hymn composer).[52] This puerile activity may well induce smiles in the modern reader, but it gives some insight into Heseltine's mind, as his behavior was often thought of as immature by those who knew him. Heseltine also had a talent for dirty limericks, and wrote a huge number throughout his life. Usually, they were "Rabelaisian lampoons at the expense of various critics and composers of his times."[53]

Related to this behavior, something should be said of his many failed relationships with women. Undoubtedly due to his mother's negative influence, he had a mixed set of feelings. He could become very infatuated, even declaring himself head-over-heels in love with someone, only to drop her a few months later when the next pretty face that appealed to him came along. His first passionate crush at Oxford was one Viva Smith, a woman ten years his senior, who may have taken his virginity from him.[54] Though their affair was brief, they would continue to correspond between 1913 and 1918. Far more problematic was his on-again, off-again relationship with the young model Minnie Lucy Channing, commonly known by her nickname "Puma," due to her temperament.

This intense affair resulted in her becoming pregnant, a situation that neither of them wanted. The child was born in July 1916, but Heseltine had no interest in being a father to him. The baby's identity is something of a mystery: many modern researchers assume the child was Nigel Heseltine, the Welsh writer. Nigel himself, however, denied this, claiming that he was the product of his father having a different affair, and then being adopted by Edith.[55] Ian Parrot claims that the child, named Peter, died in infancy.[56] Smith counters that Peter was actually renamed Nigel at a later date for uncertain reasons, and is indeed the writer.[57]

Perhaps strangely, given their lack of interest in parenting and in each other, Heseltine and Puma eventually married, in December 1916; both were 22 years of age at the time. Once again, Heseltine was already bored of her and the marriage by spring 1917, a boredom which soon turned to hostility. As Smith notes, "His troubled relations with both Puma and his mother would seem to indicate an immaturity in his dealings with women, particularly those with whom he sensed any kind of emotional tie or responsibility."[58] His mother's overbearing and toxic presence in his life as a boy, however, would certainly go a long way to explaining some of this pent-up hostility, and surely some of the blame must be placed on her.[59]

As the war dragged on into 1917, a disaster occurred, when German U-boats sank crucial British supply ships, decimating national food supplies. As a result, all previous war exemptions were subjected to review. Though Heseltine's exemption seemed solid, he did not want to risk the possibility of being conscripted if he passed a new medical exam. Thus, he made the decision to flee to Dublin, Ireland, and astonishingly, to take Puma with him. He hoped that this would be a new beginning for them both, but what he found there was a strange new world of occult practices that some of his friends believed had a terrible effect on him.

Interest in occult and esoteric practices had grown sharply in the latter part of the 19th century. Spiritualism, séances, ritual magic, ancient religious teachings, spirit-tapping, automatic writing, and related disciplines were topics of great interest to certain segments of society, even if the more traditionally religious were horrified and skeptics were not convinced (indeed, many self-proclaimed mediums were exposed as frauds). Figures such as the Russian occultist Helena Blavatsky offered her doctrine, known as Theosophy, as an ancient wisdom tradition for a new time. Later, the notorious Aleister Crowley would bring forth his own system, Thelema, with its famous command: "Do what thou wilt shall be the whole of the Law. Love is the law, love under will." Crowley has erroneously been labeled as a Satanist, partially because he adopted the provocative moniker, "The Great Beast," and also because of his many scandals, but his work was defined in *The Book of the Law*, which he claimed he received from an entity named Aiwass, incorporating ideas from many sources, including ancient Egyptian beliefs and ritual magic.[60]

Heseltine entered into this confusing and mysterious world with eager enthusiasm. D.H. Lawrence had been reading and recommending Blavatsky's writings, and Heseltine would later become interested in Crowley's work, possibly being introduced to it by Meredith Star, an occultist associate of Lawrence's. Cecil Gray's daughter, Pauline, would later claim that he and Heseltine were directly involved with Crowley and his group for a time, but the evidence for this is unclear.[61] If so, they never spoke of it, recalling the magical command: "know, will, dare, be silent."[62] She also claimed that they had practiced black magic, with the intent to inflict harm on their enemies. However, Denis ApIvor maintains that the "Crowley aspect of Philip's influences was never more than a pose and a rather bad joke."[63]

During his year in Ireland, he delved deeply into occult practices, including mediumship and automatic writing, as well as ritual magic. Intriguingly, one account of a séance that he and Puma attended relates that the assistant declared that Heseltine was "dogged by evil influences. Send him away."[64] Gray believed that Heseltine's practices were causing him considerable damage, psychological and otherwise, noting that his attempts to work magical rituals were "disastrous and catastrophic,"[65] though he does not detail why or what this meant. Heseltine seems to have feared for his sanity at times, but continued with his occult studies. Smith notes that one positive effect of these workings was an awakening of a deeper sense of reality, a kind of non-religious spirituality, giving him the ability to compose better and with more confidence, perhaps removing the block that he had always struggled with in his youth.[66] Heseltine would claim in 1918 that he had received lengthy messages of profound importance from an unknown source, some of them about music.[67] It was also around this time that he first grew the

Philip Heseltine (courtesy of the Lewis Foreman collection).

beard that would be a famous part of his appearance, claiming that it offered him a kind of confidence and was one of his "little magical energy-saving devices."[68] Given his many indulgences in the world of magic and spiritualism, his pen name seemed more appropriate than ever.

Not surprisingly, his relationship with Puma deteriorated again, and only a few months after their arrival in Dublin, she seemed to have returned to Wales to live with Heseltine's mother. He wrote some vicious invective about her and continued on with his new interests.[69] He had some productive time musically, deepening his interest in early music, and writing some very fine songs, as well as studying various Celtic languages. Given that he had struggled with German, it seems surprising that he was able to gain some fluency in Irish, but he was quite determined. He also wrote his five *Folk-song Preludes* for piano in early summer, based on Celtic tunes; this set was one of his rare forays into purely instrumental music.[70]

By June 1918, he once again devoted himself to van Dieren's music, and once again, he was unsuccessful. He had a famously heated feud with the publisher Winthrop Rogers over the quality of van Dieren's work, with Rogers and his colleagues[71] dismissing much of it as "shockingly bad."[72] One declared that his music was "the work of a sick man."[73] Heseltine was, of course, enraged, firing off a long letter to Colin Taylor in reply, touching on almost everything about modern society that infuriated him, and noting that "the worst enemy of Music is the musical profession."[74]

As the war wound down, he was able to return to England in August 1918, without fear of conscription or prosecution. Like so many others, he was appalled at the loss of life and the tragic waste of a whole young generation, and his disillusionment with any notions of patriotism and materialism would stay with him for the rest of his life. Over the next few years, he would be involved in producing a periodical of importance and quality, *The Sackbut*, and he would use his pen name frequently, along with others. He had actually tricked Rogers into publishing some of his songs by writing to him as Peter Warlock. Rogers was deeply impressed by the pieces, and though he later discovered that "Warlock" was Heseltine, he kept them in print, owing to their high quality; this seemed to cool the feud between the two. Heseltine's naturally caustic nature, however, allowed for new conflicts to flare up.[75] He seemed to revel in these arguments, and in agitating the musical establishment.

He oversaw nine issues of *The Sackbut* between May 1920 and March 1921, perhaps remarkably, with Rogers' financial backing. It contained opinion, both controversial and conventional. It gave a fair hearing to early music scholarship and also promoted concerts. However, Heseltine began to feel the strain of working on it as early as August 1920, when he went to France to spend time with Delius in preparation for writing a book about his long-time hero. He returned to find that Rogers was withdrawing his financial backing, probably due to the controversial nature of some of the articles, and the negative response they had received. Heseltine was naturally livid, but determined to make the magazine a success regardless.

By March of 1921, however, he left England again, to go on a trip to North Africa, including Algiers, Biskra, the Sahara, Tunis, and then Naples with his friend, the musicologist Gerald Cooper. It may or may not be significant that Aleister Crowley had made the exact same trip some years earlier with Victor Neuberg, a poet and also a friend of Heseltine's. If there was any significance to following in their footsteps, he never explained it.[76] After a period of drunkenness in France, he returned to discover that *The Sackbut* had essentially been taken away from him, and he had no legal control at all. Finding himself with no money and no prospects, he was forced to return to Wales and live at Cefn Bryntalch in the autumn of 1921.[77]

While it was a confined existence, he was to find much solace in the Welsh countryside, and discovered that the environment very amenable to composing. Indeed, he wrote some of his more memorable pieces there between 1921 and 1923, including his enigmatic song cycle, *The Curlew*, four songs set to poetry by Yeats, and considered one of his greatest works. However, he was always mindful of his technical deficiencies and lack of proper academic training in composition.

He became increasingly occupied with transcribing and editing Elizabethan music, eventually producing versions of some 300 songs and part-songs. He was convinced that it was a marvelous repertoire, to which modern editors were not doing justice and were treating as somewhat inferior.[78] Heseltine always saw early music as having its own value, and was determined to present it in modern editions without the prejudices of his day. His work foreshadowed the attitudes of the larger early music revival some decades later. He wrote to the *Sackbut* in 1926, for example: "All good music, whatever its date, is ageless—as alive and significant today as it was when it was written."[79]

During this time, he was a prolific writer and found success in having works published by Oxford University Press, including carols which so impressed Vaughan Williams in 1922 that he wrote to Heseltine asking for some new pieces in a similar style to conclude an upcoming Bach concert in December. Heseltine obliged with his *Three Carols*, which premiered on December 19. He dedicated the work to Vaughan Williams, and they were well-received.

During the early 1920s, Heseltine, perhaps still indulging in his explorations of new sensory experiences, periodically took various kinds of drugs, including the smoking of cannabis, and possibly ingesting cocaine. However, he seems to have had a bad experience in early 1923, which caused him to abandon the practice.[80] Puma was also less and less of a factor in his life, though she had also lived at the family home, and from about the same time as he decided to forego drugs, she disappeared from his life. She would later remarry in 1929, and then die of a barbiturate overdose in Glasgow in 1943.[81]

Though he lived in Wales, he still traveled frequently. It was in September of 1923 that he went on his "folk song hunt" with Moeran, which was followed by a visit to Delius in France, and there he became more acquainted with the music of Percy Grainger (whose music impressed him), writing him in November to tell him of his admiration for the Australian man's work, and to thank him for an exchange of sheet music.[82] With his life quite busy, and enjoying success as an editor and song-writer, he felt that it was time to be back near London (and presumably, away from his mother once again). He chose the village of Eynsford in Kent as a place conducive to work, and invited Moeran to share a home with him, where they would live until 1928. A charming country village set amid rolling hills and woodland on the river Darent, it was a convenient train-ride south of London. It was also surrounded by country pubs, making it that much more appealing. Indeed, their laddish, rather debauched existence during their time in Eynsford would become almost legendary, a scandal to the local inhabitants.[83]

The two shared a cottage leased from Hubert Foss with a housekeeper,[84] a Maori man named Hal Collins (whose grandmother had allegedly been a cannibal and regretted no longer being able to indulge in the pleasures of the flesh, a lurid story that was almost certainly invented nonsense[85]), and Heseltine's mistress/girlfriend Barbara Peache, who stayed with him for the rest of his life.[86] The two had an open relationship, however. These four frequently welcomed other guests of an astonishing variety over the next few years, keeping with Heseltine's wish that it be a kind of artistic commune where creative people could come and stay for as long as they wished. Gray records that there were "poets and painters, airmen and actors, musicians and maniacs of every description [...] everyone who was in any way unusual or abnormal was sure of receiving a ready welcome at Eynsford."[87] The pastimes of such guests were fairly straightforward and included drinking, carrying on, endless parties, more drinking, and making fools of themselves. If any time was left, there was more drinking. Moeran, however, later countered that Gray only visited them on weekends, and so did not see the amount of work that Heseltine actually did at other times, one of several inaccuracies in Gray's account,[88] along with his belief that Heseltine had a split personality (see below).

Various guests describe the college fraternity-level of championship drinking and behavior that went on in the house and beyond, however.[89] Australian writer Jack Lindsay noted how Heseltine could lead these celebrations to a "staggering blind-drunk conclusion."[90] Painter Nina Hamnett, at the time involved with Moeran, noted that "Heseltine was a man who really should have lived in about 1400."[91] She also noted that on Sunday mornings, when the Baptist church next door was in its service, the raucous crowd at the cottage would put forth their own music to be disruptive, including sea songs that could be quite earthy.[92] In addition to this unruly behavior, Heseltine indulged in his love of streaking, sometimes doing so by riding his motorcycle naked through the village.[93]

Somehow, their neighbors tolerated their shenanigans for those three years, though it was not a constant party. Remarkably, Heseltine composed some of his greatest musical works at Eynsford, including his acclaimed *Capriol Suite*, as well as writing books and editing a substantial amount of early music. He thrived in the hedonistic atmosphere that was so limiting for Moeran. He also found that his work was beginning to be taken more seriously by the much-hated establishment, and his pieces were being performed in concerts, while Oxford University Press wanted to publish his songs. It seemed he had finally found something of a niche, and his genuine hard work (punctuated as it was by drinking and carryings-on) was paying off.[94]

Moeran did not fare nearly so well, however, and the lively atmosphere of the cottage, though set in a small village in the countryside, seemed antithetical to what he needed: solitude and peace. Indeed, his output essentially dried up during those years, and he was unable to produce any compositions of value. His drinking became more pronounced, however, and as we have seen, Heseltine's lifestyle may well have led him to become an alcoholic; being with such an enabling crowd only made matters worse.[95] Moeran himself noted, in a letter to Peers Coetmore: "I lost faith in myself round about 1926 and composed nothing for several years. I even nearly became a garage proprietor.[...] I had an awfully lazy period in Eynsford. If you knock off for a long time, it is frightfully hard to get going."[96] Moeran and Heseltine did occasionally collaborate, such as on the drinking song *Maltworms* from 1926, conceived, appropriately enough, at the nearby Five Bells pub.[97] Eventually, Moeran left in 1928, and was able to regain some of his compositional bearings.[98]

Though Heseltine had found a degree of acceptance at last, he did not cease from writing his acidic opinions. He soon found himself in conflict with Percy Scholes, the author of the monumental *Oxford Companion to Music*,[99] and who was about as imbedded in the establishment as one could be. Heseltine picked a fight, when he saw that Scholes had criticized the music of Liszt while admitting to being not overly familiar with it. This incensed Heseltine, who wrote, in astonishingly harsh language: "[...] things like that stinking bag of putrescent tripe, Percy A. Scholes, who is permitted to gull the readers of 'The Observer' week by week are accustomed to dismiss [Liszt's] entire life's work [...] as unworthy of serious consideration, while columns are devoted to the latest mess puked up by Gustav Holst and his miserable like."[100] Heseltine's dislike of Holst was known, but these were perhaps his harshest words yet.[101]

This war was to escalate further, when Scholes criticized three concerts organized by Moeran, which included Moeran's work,[102] as well as that of other up-and-coming composers. Heseltine lashed out in Moeran's defense and made things personal in writing to Scholes, using language that was simply never considered for a public forum in the 1920s:

> Instead of appreciating the initiative of a young and by no means wealthy musician who gives a series of concerts of new and unfamiliar music, you can only complain that they are given on a Saturday afternoon when you would like to be playing tennis instead of earning your ill-gotten living. Permit me to suggest that, abandoning the pretence that you are in any way qualified to pass judgement on music, you would be much better employed in playing tennis than reporting concerts at any time, and that you would be still better employed in buggering yourself with a pair of exceptionally well-greased bellows.[103]

Scholes was so furious that he threatened legal action against Heseltine, who responded that he was welcome to try.[104] Scholes seems to have backed down, oddly remarking that he "did not want to send a genius to gaol," indicating an unexpected level of respect for Heseltine's abilities, regardless of his abusive behavior.[105]

Heseltine seemed to have enough clout in the music world now to take such chances. He was receiving praise for his works in the press (English[106] and French[107]), and he seems to have found his stride as a composer. For example, he wrote his famed *Capriol Suite* in October 1926 (quite quickly, according to Moeran),[108] a setting of several dances from *Orchésographie*, a collection published in 1588 by Thoinot Arbeau (an anagram of his real name, Jehan Tabournot).[109] This work introduced a generation of listeners to the sounds of French Renaissance dance music, arranged artfully in three different editions: one each for piano duet, strings, and orchestra, with several "Warlockisms" added in. It remains one of his most popular pieces.[110]

In January 1927, his *Serenade* (dedicated to Delius on his 60th birthday)[111] was recorded by no less than the National Geographic Society (remarkably, this piece was chosen as its first orchestral recording), and that year also proved to be a fruitful one for song-writing. He had a lot of energy and was more prolific, both in composition and editing. In December 1927, he and poet Bruce Blunt co-wrote another of his classics, the carol *Bethlehem Down*. This was done to raise some drinking money over the holidays, and *The Daily Telegraph* obliged, paying them to print it on Christmas Eve. While they got drunk and celebrated, they did not realize at the time that this gem of a piece would become something of a holiday classic, loved and performed annually by choirs ever after.[112]

Unfortunately, things began to go wrong, as they always did. In 1928, his income was again on the decline, and though he had another creative year, the money was not coming in. By October, he realized that he had no choice but to return to his mother's home in Wales, far from the ideal choice. He grew more depressed and saw his life as a failure, despite his recent successes and critical acclaim. He, Moeran, and some other friends visited Delius in April 1929, though as we have seen, Moeran's alcohol binge and getting lost rather overshadowed the trip. The year brought Heseltine some limited work, including an invitation to conduct the *Capriol Suite* at the August 29 Proms concert in London, which apparently was laughably bad; he had to wear a borrowed suit that did not fit him, and there was little, if any, relation between his conducting and what the orchestra played. Gerald Finzi noted that he "made a pitiful exhibition of himself. He was rather drunk and completely unable to give a beat of any sort," however, Finzi liked the piece.[113] In his defense, Heseltine was opposed to the idea of composers being expected to conduct their own works noting in an interview, "Conducting is a highly technical job. Nobody expects me to sing my own songs in public. Why this curious rage for getting composers to conduct their own compositions?"[114]

The unsteady economic times culminated in the American Stock Market crash in October 1929, which caused devastation in the world economy, and Britain was not spared. What few sources of income he had soon began to dry up. His very wealthy and elderly uncle, Evelyn, died in April 1930. His estate was valued at nearly £640,000, an enormous sum at the time, which was left to the Heseltine family, though Philip Heseltine was not named in the will, and received nothing. This naturally made him very bitter, and he resolved after that to abandon his family name for good, and only be Peter Warlock in the future.[115]

By 1930, he was back in London, but his mood was generally poor, lightened only by occasional flashes of creative inspiration, particularly in July. He had no work, virtually no income, and his outlook became increasingly bleak with the passing of time. He mentioned feeling suicidal at times, but still assumed that he would emerge from his periods of blackness.[116] In November, he went on a motor trip with his friend Basil trier, who would later recall that Heseltine was on some kind of last fling, since he was also sorting through his papers and preparing to burn some of them.[117]

On December 16, Barbara Peache left in the afternoon, informing him she would be gone overnight. He met up with his friends John Goss and the van Dierens. They drank at a pub and then went back to his flat for a time. His upstairs neighbor, Mary Venn, later reported that at about 6:40 a.m. the next morning, she heard the sound of doors shutting and Heseltine speaking to someone. At about 8:20, she smelled gas, and phoned the gas company. Peache returned around 10:45, and found that she could not get in, so they called the police. They found a frightened kitten in the yard; Heseltine had a life-long love of cats, and always kept them around.[118] The animal had food, but seemed distressed. They entered the flat and found Heseltine lying on a settee, fully clothed except for his shoes, facing the wall. Gas was leaking from a pipe and the plug for it was nowhere to be seen. He was pronounced dead from coal gas poisoning at a nearby hospital, and had been so for three to four hours before he was found.[119] The most obvious explanation was suicide. It seemed likely that Venn had heard Heseltine putting out his cat with some food and speaking to it, and then closing the doors before turning on the gas. His depressed moods and occasional references to suicide certainly seemed to support this. Peache noted that he had talked of killing himself more than once, as recently as December 14, but that she did not take him seriously.[120]

However, the official explanation for his death (released December 22) stated that there was insufficient evidence to determine whether it was suicide, or due to an accident. He had made van Dieren his heir, but intriguingly, he wrote a new will just before his death (never made official), leaving everything to Winifred Baker, a nurse for whom he had great affection. This odd development led some to wonder if there was a rift between him and van Dieren. Nigel Heseltine would later claim that van Dieren had murdered him, angered as he was about Heseltine changing his will.[121] Van Dieren had certainly sponged off of Heseltine's generosity for years, taking money from him even when Heseltine did not have enough for himself; both were financially irresponsible and depended on others for support. Nigel's theory was that van Dieren, who had knowledge of chemistry, had essentially drugged Heseltine that night and then removed the gas cap to poison him. Yet van Dieren claimed he had no knowledge of such a will until he was called to testify, and this is probably true. He also stated that when he and his wife left Heseltine, he seemed fine, and not even drunk.[122] Indeed the medical exam would find no evidence of alcoholism.[123] Van Dieren believed that it was an accident, caused when Heseltine kicked off his shoes to go to sleep. Adrian Allinson, an artist and friend of Heseltine's from his post–Oxford days, believed that Heseltine's experiments in black magic had killed him, and that van Dieren had been encouraging this, but again there is no evidence.[124] Generally, Nigel's conspiracy theory is not widely supported today.

The sad fact is that suicide was an even more uncomfortable topic at that time than now, and the stigma that it would bring to a prominent family may well have been enough for it to have been glossed over as only a "possibility" in the news. Heseltine's dark moods, combined with the many things that had gone wrong for him—lack of money except from his mother, no more market for his music, being cut out of a large will, having made many enemies in the establishment—may have been enough to push him over the edge in a moment of desperation. Sadly, those moments are irreversible and we will never know what his final thoughts were. Fenby believed that he took his own life out of a feeling of despair at being creatively stuck and of seeing himself as inferior to his fellow composers.[125] John Mitchell has offered the intriguing possibility that his action may have been a "cry for help," and that he expected to be found before the gas killed him.[126]

Gray's assessment that he had a split personality, Philip Heseltine and Peter Warlock, is now widely dismissed.[127] Bruce Blunt condemned the idea as early as 1944, saying that such a thing implied some sort of Jekyll-and-Hyde personality (good Philip, evil Peter) that was patently false. Anyone with character, he said, was multi-faceted, but he was one whole person.[128] Composer Elizabeth Poston, a good friend of Heseltine's, likewise asserted that the idea was Gray's invention, when in fact, "Warlock was one of the most complete people I've ever known."[129] Gray's biography of his late friend was about himself, she maintained, not Heseltine. She further denies that he was the massive drinker that some depict him being, pointing out that no one could have done the amount of work he did as an editor, critic, and composer while drunk or hung over (reiterated by the findings of his autopsy),[130] and she felt that his compositional style was remarkably consistent over the years.[131] Percy Grainger also discounted Gray in general, writing: "I never read anything written by Cecil Gray that I approved of.[...]"[132]

Recently, Judy Marchman has argued convincingly that Helestine suffered from a form of bipolar disorder, with depressive and manic episodes.[133] His mood swings, his irrational behavior, his rifts with otherwise good friends, are all symptoms of such a condition. His falling out with Lawrence is one example, his almost hysterical reaction to criticisms of van Dieren another.[134] As early as 1915, he wrote to Viva Smith, "I myself am in the lowest depths of depressions and utter lifelessness and hopelessness to which I have ever sunk. [...] My mind is an utter fog, so that I cannot think or describe or write anything whatever."[135] He had a chance and the money to see a doctor about his condition, "but hav'nt the energy or initiative to rise up and make an appointment."[136] In August, he wrote to Delius,

> My head feels as though it were filled with a smoky vapour or a poisonous gas which kills all the finer impressions before they can penetrate to me and stifles every thought, every idea before it is born [...] it is a feeling that had been enveloping me little by little for many months past, and although there are times when I think myself rid of it but it always returns after a while more virulent than ever.[137]

Such words seem to show a serious episode of depression, one that would be repeated throughout his life. It would inhibit him from composing or doing much of anything, and then he would bounce back and have fits of astonishing creativity and productivity. Even when he was able to compose while depressed, his work was still of very good quality.[138] He frequently thrived during his years at Eynsford (while Moeran withered), for example, and "When the black mood passed he would write a song a day for a week."[139] Such mental conditions are associated with higher rates of substance abuse and suicide, as well as with greater creativity, all of which correlates with the story of his life.[140]

As is so often the case, Heseltine/Warlock was more appreciated in death than in life. Tributes to the man came from some quarters during the years following his death. The composer Constant Lambert, for example, would say that his impressive output and skill allow him "to be classed with Dowland, Mussorgsky, and Debussy as one of the greatest song-writers that music has known."[141] However, his music is not as popular today as one might expect, given its quality. Marchman maintains "that it is because of this behavior [i.e., his abrasiveness and various scandals] that Warlock was virtually shunned when he lived, and as a trickle-down effect, the reason why he is not popular today."[142] Certainly, his public feuds, harsh criticisms and insults of his peers, and tendency to pick fights earned him many enemies,[143] but surprisingly, he maintained a group of admirers.

His more than 100 songs and other pieces, his extensive and pioneering work in the field of early music scholarship, his acidic criticism, his many books and projects, and his larger-than-life personality all point to a charismatic and important individual who was mourned by many after his death, including some who did not appreciate him well enough in life. As with so many artists who leave the world at a young age, those remaining are left to wonder what he might have achieved had he lived longer.

8

Gerald Finzi (1901–1956)

Gerald Finzi presents something of a contrast to the composers of the previous three chapters. He was too young to serve (or die) in World War I like Butterworth, he did not succumb to alcoholism like Moeran, and he did not indulge in the live-fast-and-die-young lifestyle of Heseltine.[1] In some respects his life was quite sedate, ordinary, and perhaps boring by comparison. However, it was not spared tragedy, for he had lost much of his family by the time he was 18, and later in life would face his own trials in coping with a drawn-out fatal illness.

Finzi was born in London on July 14, 1901, the last of five children to a Jewish family with prominent Italian and German roots (from both the Sephardic and Ashkenazi traditions). His Mediterranean appearance and Jewish heritage mark him as an unusual man to be so closely associated with English music and Englishness in general, though he is remembered today in the same company as Vaughan Williams, Holst, and Butterworth, which is exactly what he would have wanted. He composed in a limited number of fields; he did not write symphonies, operas, or piano music. Instead, he preferred songs, shorter orchestral works, and choral pieces. Banfield observes that his music is "not so much nationalist as parochial."[2]

A non-believer (he was at best an agnostic), he stepped away from his background to embrace a different life of conservation, farming, vegetarianism, and pacifism.[3] Unlike his hero, Vaughan Williams, who reveled in city life (however much he enjoyed his folk song-collecting trips), Finzi frequently found urban environments overwhelming and sought the quiet and slower pace of the countryside, where he lived for several years, partaking of its traditions. One of his great passions was preserving and cultivating different apple varieties, and he successfully grew and saved more than 350 of them.

The Finzis had been settled for a long time in England, and he was born into comfortable, if not wealthy surroundings. His father, Jack, had studied at

University College in London. He had a great interest in natural science, but found his calling as a broker in the shipping business, negotiating the transport of cargo and the sales of ships.⁴ He also was a good singer, and no longer practiced his religion.⁵ Finzi's mother, Lizzie, came from a Germanic background, her mother having been a schoolteacher.⁶ He was the fifth of five children, though he was not cared for by the family nanny, who felt that four children had been enough, and doted instead on his older brother, Edgar. Finzi was never especially close to any of his siblings. However, his mother was devoted to him, too much so at times, recalling Heseltine's situation, though not as dramatic. She noted that even at a very young age, he adored music.⁷ Lizzie was a skilled amateur pianist and composer, and encouraged young Finzi in his musical interests.

Family happiness was not to last, however. In 1906, Jack (whose brothers were already dead) was diagnosed with a cancer in the mouth. An operation forced the removal of his right eye, and part of his jaw. This did not save him, however, and his condition worsened until he died on July 1, 1909. Deprived of any father figures at that time, the void in Finzi's life was filled by his mother. Jack had left Lizzie a good sum of money, however, so the family remained comfortable.⁸

However, tragedy hit again in July 1912 when his older brother Douglas died of pneumonia; the following year, Finzi was taken ill (probably with measles), and had to remain in the sanatorium of his boarding school, Kingswood Preparatory. He hated the school, however, and once recovered, he schemed of ways to get out of the place, including faking fainting spells. This was enough to worry his mother, having just lost Douglas, so she removed him from the school, taking him and Edgar to Switzerland for a year, where she believed the mountain air would do them good.⁹ The cruelness of fate was not done with the Finzi family, however, and word came that the eldest son, Felix had died in 1913 while working for a tea company in Assam, India, possibly a suicide from taking too much sleeping medication while suffering from depression and homesickness.¹⁰

The family eventually returned to England in 1914, with events becoming increasingly unsettled on the continent. Edgar was old enough to enlist by late 1915, and spent the next few years in the army, though a dark fate awaited him as well. Perhaps due to Zeppelin attacks on London from April 1915, Lizzie decided that she was done with the south. She relocated to Yorkshire, first to the town of Pateley Bridge, and from October 1915, the spa town of Harrogate.¹¹ The area had the advantage of being a well-known health center with good country air, and a place of culture that was far from the ravages of war.

Young Finzi would find the move very fortuitous. When his mother inquired about a music teacher, she was directed to one Ernest Farrar,[12] a young composer and organist whose works were being performed in the area, and who had many connections, among them Vaughan Williams. He took Finzi on as a student after hearing him play, though he advised him that composition was no way to earn a living; Finzi ignored him, but immediately became a devoted pupil.[13] Farrar was 30 years old, and provided a kind of stability and guidance for young Finzi, somewhere between being an older brother and a father to him, taking him to concerts and rehearsals, and occasionally long walks on the Yorkshire Moors.[14] As the clouds of war gathered, however, he felt that it was his duty to enlist. This was very upsetting to Finzi, who not only did not want to lose his friend, but also did not want to have to begin study with another teacher. Farrar had taken him to London in 1917 for a meeting with Stanford, who judged him not good enough to pursue music. Finzi would not be deterred however, and so arrangements were made for him to continue study with Edward Bairstow, organist of York Minster.[15]

Farrar was back and forth for a time, and continued to look at his young student's work, not being deployed until the last days of the war. He arrived in France in September 1918, and was sent on to the front on the 16. He was killed by machine gun fire two days later, during the Battle of Éphey,[16] another tragic loss for English music. Finzi must have been devastated, but there was more bad news in store for the family. They learned in October that Edgar had been killed on September 5, probably in the Aegean. Finzi mourned the loss of his teacher more than his brother, remaining devoted to his memory for the rest of his life. He was particularly distressed about Olive, Farrar's wife, being widowed at a young age.[17] These terrible experiences stirred feelings of pacifism in him, and like Moeran, he came to regard the war as a great artifact of human stupidity and folly. His music would always retain something of an elegiac quality, perhaps in memory of that lost generation. He was acutely aware of the transience of life, reinforced as he faced his own fate in the 1950s.

Meanwhile, Bairstow was strict but supportive of the boy, especially in the wake of tragedy, and the two initially got along better than both probably had expected. Finzi eventually called him the "beloved tyrant"[18] and they became genuine friends. Bairstow took him to Leeds to hear concerts and rehearsals, and also saw to it that some of his early compositions were performed, both at York Minster and at the Leeds Town Hall.[19] Bairstow was impressed by Finzi's approach to composition, and remarked about his student, "if only we could combine that boy's ideas with my technique!"[20]

By 1919, Finzi had developed an unlikely friendship with Vera Somerfield, an Australian artist friend of his older sister, Katie. Though she was ten years his senior and had no romantic interest in him, they enjoyed banter and teasing.

She loved traveling to the continent, which perplexed young Finzi, who felt far more at home in the English countryside. He explained these pastoral longings in a letter from April 1920, when referring to a small village that he had visited on holiday: "Great Somerford is a tiny little English village. Pigs, fields, thatched cottages, lanes, an inn, a parson, squire & about 200 inhabitants—no cinemas, theatres or barrel organs. Perfect quiet—heavenly!"[21]

Indeed, once the war ended, Finzi desired to travel more in England, and one of his first sojourns was to the revived festival of music in Glastonbury. The town and the Somerset countryside cast a spell on him, not only for the musical content of the programs (he heard works by Ireland, Elgar, and Vaughan Williams, as well as Elizabethan music and that of 17th-century composer Matthew Locke), but also for the landscape and its legendary qualities. Regarding the festival and its aims, he wrote to Vera: "How wonderful it wd be if every village were a Glastonbury."[22] He was developing a deep attraction to the English nationalist ideology, described by Banfield as: "Conservationist, parochial, historicist, liberal or socialist, anti-commercial, and broadly anti-modernist,"[23] all qualities that he would express at times throughout his life. Musically, he appreciated folk song and folk dance,[24] the work of Cecil Sharp, and above all the music of Holst and Vaughan Williams, though he was sometimes expected to justify his calling. A *Times* critic pondered in 1928 why someone with his Italian name could do "English" music so well, for example. In 1938, Finzi wrote to Busch:

> [...] shall we send Vaughan Williams back to Wales [...] or Elgar to Denmark, or Grieg to Scotland. Holst's grandfather was a political refugee. Sibelius has hardly any Finnish blood in him. Wd you not say that all these [...] at some point in their ancestry, showed that they were "adept at the adoption of extra-racial characteristics where this adaptability is needed?" The charge might be levelled at nearly anyone.[...][25]

A year after the holiday in which he wrote so enthusiastically about Great Somerford, Finzi and his mother visited Down Ampney in Gloucestershire. He recounts how important it was to see the home where Vaughan Williams had been born: "So we rang the vicarage bell & delighted the vicar by telling him that the house was the birthplace of a celebrity. (He hadn't even heard of RVW!) ... I was shown over the house from top to bottom so that there cd be no chance of missing the room where our hero was born! Many will make the pilgrimage but we are the first!"[26]

Finzi wrote to Vaughan Williams in November 1923, asking for permission to use a folk song that the older composer had collected in Herefordshire.[27] Vaughan Williams gave his consent, took a liking to Finzi, and when they met at the Glastonbury festival, he handed Finzi a note to give to Rutland Boughton, the festival's director, as an introduction. It read: "to introduce Mr Finzi. He is one of us."[28] What a thrill this must have been for the young man who so wanted to be a part of the world of his heroes! Indeed, as Banfield notes, "in attaching himself to the pastoral school of Vaughan Williams in the early 1920s, Finzi felt sure he was getting straight to the iconoclastic heart of British contemporary music."[29] In time, Vaughan Williams became a kind of father figure to Finzi; he would address his letters to "Dear Uncle Ralph."[30] For the Vaughan Williams, Finzi helped to replace the loss of Butterworth, and to a certain extent, the loss of Holst after 1934.[31]

Finzi held Holst in equally high estimation, if not more, telling Vera about *The Planets*: "For several days now I have been dancing incessantly on account of the success of Holst's great work. He is a wonderful man."[32] This is a striking contrast to Heseltine's dismissive and insulting view. As with Vaughan Williams, Finzi was to forge a friendship with Holst, and to seek his input and advice on many occasions.[33] Holst's background in coming from a family of immigrants must have given Finzi many thoughts on his own place as an English composer.[34] His compositions from this young age not surprisingly show the influence of his heroes, and though he was not a collector of folk songs in the manner of Sharp, Vaughan Williams, Butterworth, or Grainger, those modalities and melodic motifs certainly found their way into his works throughout the 1920s.[35] Indeed, he had been born a bit too late to be a part of the folk song-collecting heyday of the Edwardian years, and such bold treks into villages probably would not have suited his reserved temperament in any case. In 1926, he did note down a lavender seller's song while in London.[36]

By 1921, he had begun his first setting of poetry by Thomas Hardy (1840–1928), *By Footpath and Stile*, for baritone voice and string quartet. Adapting Hardy's poems was a periodic practice that would occupy him for years; Mellers considers his fascination with Hardy's work a "near-obsession."[37] Indeed, Finzi composed more than 50 pieces using Hardy's poems as lyrics, and had sketches for almost as many more at his death.[38] Hardy, who saw the Victorian age firsthand, was critical of the Industrial Revolution and the loss of rural life, and many of his works deal with the cruelty of fate, elegies for both the Boer War and World War I, and loss in life and love. These themes obviously spoke to Finzi. Banfield has suggested that his devotion to these poems throughout his life may have been due to his "resolve to create a musical memorial, presumably, to personal loss, as much as anything.[...]"[39] Written in the aftermath of the devastation of World War I and his own family's losses, this makes perfect sense.[40] Hardy's belief that war was wasteful and futile, his focus on the inevitable passage of time, and his love of the natural world, were all things that Finzi shared and that would stay with him for his whole life.[41]

Equally important was Finzi's discovery of the works of Ivor Gurney in

1920, who was both composer and poet, and whose own life was to be beset with tragedy and mental illness, something that saddened Finzi profoundly, as he noted in 1923.[42] Like Vaughan Williams and Elgar, Gurney was a product of Gloucestershire, a land that Finzi already greatly liked. He was deeply moved by Gurney's song *Sleep* from his *5 Elizabethan Songs* when he heard it in York in 1920, which began a life-long admiration for the man and a determination to have his work gain wider appreciation.[43] Gurney eventually died on December 26, 1937, only two days before his far more celebrated contemporary, Maurice Ravel. Finzi found it rather shameful that the newspapers gave him more attention in death than in life.[44]

By August 1921, Finzi seems to have made up his mind to leave Harrogate and city life, settling in the country that so inspired him. In May and June of 1922, he and his mother packed up and moved south. Lizzie may have been as willing to move as he was, perhaps tiring of the colder, greyer north, and she eventually settled in Suffolk for many years.

As we have seen, Gloucestershire and the Cotswolds had been for some time a stronghold of the Arts and Crafts Movement, which played an important role in the folk song-collecting activities of the early 1900s, as well as the revival of other folk traditions. The country that nurtured Vaughan Williams and Elgar, among others, also was home to untold numbers of musicians, poets, and craftspeople, many striving to keep the movement alive by creating their own personal rural utopias. The region had "picturesque, apparently organic medieval townscapes and almost feudal communities in which local materials and traditional methods were still used in building and design."[45] It is unclear that such features were the primary reasons that Finzi was drawn there, but they seem a likely lure. Further, the chance to live in and be inspired by the land that was made famous by his teachers and idols would have been irresistible.[46]

They found and settled into a somewhat dilapidated house, King's Mill in Painswick, south of Gloucester, which they moved into by July. Large and made of stone, it was situated on the outskirts of town, with a stream and views of the hills. It was the perfect spot, though it needed work. Finzi announced that he was up to the task, and set about refurbishing it. However, he soon found that he had neither the time nor the skill to complete all the work himself, if he wanted to get on with composing.[47]

From here, he was close enough to major urban centers (including London) to be able to attend concerts and other events, and begin to mingle with those other composers, directors, and conductors that comprised the world of which he was now a part. He slowly cultivated an important association with composer Herbert Howells, nine years Finzi's senior, and a member of the "in crowd." Howells is now most known for his output of Anglican Church music (influenced by both Vaughan Williams and Tudor music), though he was not especially religious. Finzi and Howells were not particularly good friends, but they spent significant time together in the mid–1920s. They did not generally influence one another's work, but rather drew from common sources.[48] He also befriended the architect Detmar Blow, a direct descendant of English composer John Blow (1649–1708), and another major figure in the Arts and Crafts Movement. Blow and his wife Winifred became almost a second family to Finzi in the years 1922–26.[49]

During his time at King's Mill, Finzi was also attracted to the early "green" ideology that was held by Arts and Crafts practitioners. Rejecting industrialization, there was also a socialist and egalitarian undercurrent to the movement, with a desire for conservation, not only of the natural world, but also of lost crafts and traditional practices. This, of course, was one impetus for the collecting and recording of folk songs and other old traditions before they were lost. Finzi gradually came to see himself as doing the same with other repertoires of English music, less so from the Tudor period than from the 18th century, though he certainly drew from 16th- and 17th-century composers in his own work.[50] His time in the country eventually allowed him to develop other passions as well. Vaughan Williams would note of Finzi in his obituary from 1956 that "he was almost as keen on reviving forgotten varieties of apples as the works of forgotten composers."[51] Bliss "added stray cats to the list of things Finzi rescued from oblivion."[52]

During these years, he devoted himself to song composition (including more Hardy poems),[53] choral music (for Bairstow), and some other pieces, including his *Severn Rhapsody* from 1923. This was his first attempt at a larger orchestral work, and it was very influenced by Vaughan Williams and Butterworth in style and folk music-infused content.[54] He had quite a talent for inventing folk-like melodies (much like Moeran) when composing what he called his "pastoral whatnots,"[55] and always acknowledged the importance of traditional songs, though he did not incorporate specific songs into his works. In 1935, for example, he wrote to Frank Howes (later President of the Royal Musical Association between 1947 and 1958): "Folksong has been to me like food, grammar or counterpoint, it helped to build me up."[56] Vaughan Williams noted: "I do not think that Finzi was a close student of folk song, his mind had turned more readily to other aspects of English music, but he could not help being influenced by it, like every other English composer who did not deliberately shut his ears to it."[57]

He completed his elegiac *Requiem da Camera* in 1924, dedicated to Farrar, but doubtless also mindful of other war victims such as Butterworth and perhaps Gurney (who had been injured). This was followed by his *Concerto for Small Orchestra and Solo Violin*, written between 1925 and 1927, but this work failed, and he later broke it up, offering the slow movement, with its pastoral, Baroque, and folk qualities, as a separate piece, the *Introit*.

However, it is often quite difficult to date many of his pieces with certainty. He was known to tinker with his music, altering it and re-arranging it years after a given piece was composed. This is as true of his short works as of the longer ones. Thus, placing his pieces in chronological order is beset with uncertainties.[58]

We do know that this was a time for immersing himself in folk cultures, and he tried his hand at dancing, though unlike Butterworth, he had very little skill for it.[59] He drew his inspiration from his rural surroundings, probably feeling that this was the only way that he could compose. At the same time, however, tensions with his controlling mother were mounting, and he was increasingly unhappy and angry with her, which did not escape the notice of his friends.[60] Clearly, he could not go on living with her, and was finding that the self-sufficiency ideal of their country life was preventing him from working in the way that he wanted.

So he resolved to relocate to London and to further his studies in composition with R.O. Morris, regarded as one of the best teachers of counterpoint in Britain (and who was Vaughan Williams' brother-in-law). He settled into a small London home in early 1926, and though Morris was absent for much of his time there, they worked together by mail.[61] He made new friends, including the composer William Busch and Moeran, who admired his work. However, Finzi frequently kept to himself, even amid the goings-on of a big city. While London afforded new opportunities, he never lost his love of the country, and often left the city to go to country festivals and on long walks.

He did form a close friendship with composer and musicologist Howard Ferguson, after a minor disaster at a Richard Strauss concert (which Strauss was conducting). The thunder machine for one of the pieces fell over (gently) into the orchestra pit. The two of them found this so amusing that they roared with laughter together after the concert, and became good friends.[62] Later, this was marred by the fact that Ferguson was gay, and Finzi, understanding this only from the mid–1940s, could never fully accept it.[63] Interestingly, Finzi never revealed to Ferguson that he had a Jewish background[64] (the developments in Germany throughout the 1930s distressed him greatly, as we will see below). The two would pour over each other's compositions (as Vaughan Williams and Holst had done), offering comments, criticism, and admiration. He was able to successfully do this with Vaughan Williams, Holst, and Howells, as well, essentially inviting himself over to their homes to share his work and solicit their opinions. They were always happy to help, probably admiring his determination to better himself.[65]

8. Gerald Finzi (1901–1956)

In early 1928, Finzi developed an illness that was at first suspected to be tuberculosis, after a period of poor health from working too hard. He was ordered into a sanatorium in Sussex for six months (which he dubbed the "Caliphate"),[66] a common procedure before the use of antibiotics. This was a potentially life-threatening situation, and his friends were shocked and worried, but ultimately the doctors reduced his diagnosis to pleurisy, and he was released in July, pronounced healthy but with the advisement to rest.[67] Spending the summer in Hundon in Suffolk, he returned to London by September, and immersed himself again in the bustle of daily city life. In 1929, he resumed his country wandering and continued his efforts on a large-scale piece, a piano concerto, which he had worked on in the sanatorium, but never completed.[68] He wrote the first two movements, but struggled with the third and abandoned it. He later refigured the first movement as the *Grand Fantasia*, and the second movement was released after his death as the *Eclogue*, a serene and beautiful work that is one of his most popular.[69] Finzi found writing slower movements easier than those of a faster tempo, which could account for a number of abandoned pieces, as we saw with his *Violin Concerto*.[70]

By 1930, he had secured a one-day-per-week teaching position at the Royal Academy of Music, which, while prestigious and providing at least some additional income, failed to interest him in any real way. Referring to it as the "Royal Crematorium,"[71] he noted that he offered, "the theory of music, harmony, the first species and such things about which I know nothing and care less. What a lot of tarradiddle & bunkum it all is."[72]

He was weary of London, and this work was not nearly enough to change his mind about it. He again took to traveling the country. On a long spring trip to the south west, he met the young economist Graham Hutton, who would also become a good friend. Though he often preferred to walk alone over great distances, Hutton, like other friends, would sometimes accompany him. In August, he took a holiday with Vera and her husband to the continent, the

Gerald Finzi, by Angus McBean (courtesy of Josephine Finzi).

last trip there that he would make. He preferred the landscapes of England to any foreign travel,[73] once declaring to Ferguson: "I feel so un-at-home out of England."[74] They visited Belgium and Germany. While in Belgium, he visited some war memorials and battlefields, no doubt a kind of personal pilgrimage, given his closeness to Farrar. While in Germany, he became acutely aware of the increasing presence of the Nazis and the threat they posed to the Jewish population.

Whenever he was back in London, he was increasingly agitated, prompting Adeline Vaughan Williams to invite him out to their Dorking home as a means of escape.[75] It was just far enough south of the city to be both rural and feasible. He readily agreed, but also desired a more permanent place to which he could escape, settling finally on renting a cottage at Lye Green in Sussex. It was on an estate where one Mrs. Black and her two daughters, Joy and Mags, also lived. While there with Hutton exploring Ashdown Forest,[76] he had an encounter that would change his life. He had lit a fire in the cottage, but was having problems with it smoking excessively. He let Mrs. Black know (who was acting as landlord), and she sent Joy over to investigate. The rest was history: "Gerald opened the door to her, and fell in love."[77] Joy was not so immediately smitten. Six years younger and a few inches taller than him (he was only 5'6"); she also came from a musical and artistic background.

Though he was completely infatuated with her, he was also conflicted about how he would engage in a relationship should such a thing come to pass, given his devotion to composition, his love of long solitary walking holidays, and his somewhat meager financial situation (as with Vaughan Williams and Moeran, family money provided some income). Nevertheless, he began to see her, and they attended concerts and other events together. Worry over how he should proceed took its toll on him, and this combined with other stresses (he had suffered periodically from insomnia) led him to the verge of a nervous breakdown, by his own account.[78] In answer to this, surprisingly, he set off on a cruise to Cairo over the Christmas holiday in 1932; Joy may have organized it for him, booking him passage on a cargo ship for the very low price of £5. This trip seems to have been as much about him making up his mind to ask Joy to marry him as it was a holiday and a chance to relax, though he enjoyed Egypt greatly, seeing things beyond the usual tourist destinations, "and drinking coffee with Sheiks!"[79]

If he was still not sure of what to do about Joy on his return, her mother's death just before his trip and the unwanted advances of another woman probably pushed him over the edge[80]; they married on September 16, 1933, in Dorking, so that Vaughan Williams and Adeline could attend.[81] Finzi's mother and older sister were noticeably absent.[82] It was all a rather unromantic affair, with

8. Gerald Finzi (1901–1956)   179

Joy quipping to the registrar that she would put away her marriage license with her dog license.[83] As they took photos outside the courthouse, Finzi stood on the steps so as not to look shorter than her.[84] Hutton would later joke that with her statuesque appearance in contrast to his short stature, Finzi was showing his love for England by marrying Britannia.[85]

Joy's influence on Finzi for the rest of his life was huge, and sometimes amusing. One account sums up at least her initial plans for him. Before they were married, he took her to visit Holst, who was now ill and dying. She later recounted: "Holst asked me to sit on his bed and tell me what I was going to make G do when I married him. I said that I thought it would be an advantage if he could be persuaded to sit down to eat his meals rather than walk around with a plate in his hand!"[86] Gerald in turn encouraged her to develop her artistic talents, and her devotion to him (as well as her share of the legacy from her mother) allowed him to continue in the life of a composer, a life that he so much wanted.[87] Overall, his sense of humor seemed to improve and he relaxed more.

Nevertheless, between the years of 1930 and 1936, he composed significantly less than he had previously, but what he did write was of high quality, and some have offered that Joy's presence helped to bring out of him a more mature style.[88] Initially, they lived in Hampstead in London, but there was always a desire to escape back to the country. When Joy and her sister sold their mother's home in Sussex, the couple began to search in earnest for a new country home. They settled on a house called Beech Knoll at Aldbourne, in Wiltshire, meant to be a temporary dwelling while they looked around for a permanent place to live. Their first son was born in July 1934 and their second in August 1936. At the second birth, Finzi, seeing that mother and child were well, is recorded as saying to her: "Good. Now no more babies. Let's get back to work."[89]

By 1935, they had moved into their country home. This was still close enough to London to attend concerts and mingle when necessary (which both of them disliked in varying degrees), but far enough out in the country to be satisfying. Its open spaces and chalk downs were perfect for Finzi's wandering tendencies. Joy noted that he was somewhat claustrophobic, which he said was due to being locked in a cupboard as a child,[90] a horrible punishment that would certainly explain his indifference to his mother and siblings throughout his life. The open spaces of Wiltshire must have been heavenly. Finzi abandoned his socialist determination to take on all of the work himself, and the couple hired various locals as help. He also seems to have backed off of his commitment to vegetarianism, adding fish and occasionally poultry to his diet.[91]

Almost immediately, however, they were looking for a more permanent

Joy and Gerald Finzi, with their sons Christopher (on ladder) and Nigel, at their home in Aldbourne, 1937 (courtesy of Josephine Finzi and the Finzi Trust).

dwelling, and located a site in 1937, the sixteen-acre Church Farm, Ashmansworth[92] (south of Newbury and west of their temporary home), with old buildings that needed demolishing or substantial renovation. Work began in early 1938, which kept Finzi very busy, and frequently exasperated in how much of his time the whole project was taking, preventing composition. The needed renovations were mostly completed over that year, and they were able to move in by early March 1939.[93]

During these years, Finzi began to seriously explore his interest in apples, and in preserving endangered varieties. He heard a radio broadcast titled "The Disappearing Apple," and wrote to the speaker, Morton Shand, thus beginning a life-long quest to find and preserve unusual types that might be hidden in orchards and unidentified. McVeagh notes: "Gerald joined in with the enthusiasm of a Vaughan Williams collecting folksongs. Good apple country and good folksong country were often the same, and some of the best was in Gloucestershire around May Hill. It was all as English as could be.[...]"[94]

While their new home became their sanctuary, the rural haven that they had always wanted, this happiness was clouded by the growing threat of another war. Finzi had for some time followed the worrying developments in Germany, which had further disrupted his attempts at regular composition. His casting off of his heritage did not prevent his outrage at what he was hearing about the treatment of Jews in central Europe, from segregation to persecution. Though he held that Judaism was a belief and not a racial heritage, he knew there many who felt otherwise. He had kept newspaper cuttings and articles since 1928 on a number of different subjects relevant to German Jews in particular, and now, ten years later, things were rapidly developing into a crisis.[95] He could not have imagined what would happen over the war years. He suffered from insomnia and bouts of worry with each new report of Nazi aggression.

Joy recorded in her journal that when Germany entered Austria on March 12, 1938, he said: "It's like watching a man done to death, only this is a civilization and the last stand of central European culture."[96] After Neville Chamberlain's trip to Munich in September, and the subsequent Munich Agreement that ceded the Sudetenland to Germany in hopeless appeasement, Joy wrote: "I can feel nothing but the suffering of humanity and the fear for the future of civilization."[97] For Finzi, the Nazis potentially heralded a new Dark Age, one that might last for centuries. During the war, he was under no illusions as to what would happen to him should they succeed in invading and occupying England, and he had requested that Joy never to mention his Jewish background to anyone they did not know.[98] He also constructed a hiding space under the stairs of his library, where he might retreat should the house ever be searched.[99] Joy also recorded that he told her one evening: "Whatever comes, we must never forget how happy we have been together."[100]

Accordingly, he set aside his devotion to pacifism and to being a conscientious objector. He noted that he would have no conflict within himself in resisting this evil in whatever way he was called to do. He resigned himself to being conscripted, but felt that artists should be able to serve in ways that benefitted the general culture, for that was what the war sought to defend. Artists were the true bearers of civilization, and that exalted position set them apart from the concerns of politics and petty day-to-day doings. For him, music ranked above all else and should not be tied to any ideology, whether it be communism, fascism, Christianity, paganism, "or any bloody rope."[101] Indeed, he agreed with a *Daily Telegraph* Letter from March 4, 1940, signed by a number of artists, including Vaughan Williams, which stated: "Our art is a measure of our civilization, and our artists its guardians."[102] Later that year, the government issued a White Paper (with Vaughan Williams' support) exempting "outstanding contributors to Art, Science, learning or Letters."[103]

After Britain declared war on Germany on September 3, 1939, the Finzis' idyllic home (and all the homes in the area) became a haven for evacuees from London, and refugees from the continent.[104] When the Battle of Britain began in earnest in the summer of 1940, the German bombings came (reaching as far as their peaceful region, with a nearby village being strafed),[105] the evacuations became permanent for the foreseeable future, and Finzi was active in the Home Guard, keeping watch three evenings a week.[106] His son Christopher relayed a remarkable story of once seeing a German airplane shot down overhead. Christopher and his brother Nigel biked over to the crash site, where they found the pilot, who had ejected. They brought him back to their home, where Joy gave him food while they all waited for police to come and take him![107]

Perhaps surprisingly, this tense time seemed to fire Finzi's creativity and determination, knocking him out of the depression, sleeplessness, and dry artistic periods that he had suffered so much over the previous years. Banfield suggests that this was due in part to his feeling a real sense of belonging for the first time, and of defending the land he loved along with everyone else, his fellow English.[108] He resumed composing and produced several pieces during 1940.

At the end of 1940, he founded his amateur string group, the Newbury String Players,

> at a concert given in Enborne Church, when live music had been shut down. There was an urgency felt by those who played and those who listened, for the need of music in time of deprivation. Supported by a yearly grant from the Arts Council and a small allocation of petrol they became a mobile body, taking music wherever it was wanted throughout the south of England in churches, halls and schools.[109]

Joy played with the group, and while it was composed mostly of locals, students, and non-professionals (mostly women), he molded them over time into a fine ensemble, capable of tackling difficult repertoire. They earned the admiration of Vaughan Williams, though not of Britten, who dismissed them as poor amateurs and Finzi as the kind of conductor who turned his back on "elitist" professionals.[110] The group would perform more than 50 concerts during the war years.

Finzi also took on the role of a music historian and scholar, focusing on lesser-known works from the 18th century, particularly from England. He made his own performing editions for the orchestra. As the Finzi Trust notes:

> His search for new music for this mainly amateur band, staunchly supported by professionals, led him to discover and edit many of the composers of the 18th century includ-

ing his volume on Boyce for the *Musica Brittanica*. His well-shaped programmes always contained that which was new, in any century including contemporary, with what was familiar—and a continuous support for English music.[111]

As the war situation worsened in 1941, it became clear that men of his age (40) were also eligible to be called up, regardless of their artistic standing; his role as an amateur orchestra leader and lesser composer would not prevent it. This grim fact brought more anxiety and the unspoken realization that he might never be able to write all of the music that he had planned, or would plan in the future, which also brought back his writer's block.[112] Somewhat surprisingly, he was offered a job with the BBC, which would have had him, "involved with a little music & much muck, office work, concert agency & all the BBC schimozzle!"[113] Even more surprisingly, he turned down the offer, opting instead to take a position in July 1941 at the Ministry of War Transport, specifically with the Foreign Shipping Relations Division. This required him to return to London, and work six days a week, with a focus on shipping to the neutral South American countries, specifically to watch enemy ship activity in neutral ports. If he noticed any significance in the fact that his job bore some resemblance to that of his father, he did not comment on it.[114]

Though he had chosen this occupation for his service, he grew to resent it, and the waste of his time. He may have wanted to compose, but it was almost impossible, as his working hours frequently extended well into the evening. He was normally able to return to Ashmansworth on three weekends out of any given month, and though his time there was short, he was committed to the Newbury String Players, who rehearsed and performed at weekends. While other musical activities were of necessity limited, he did hear a number of concerts and complete some quality compositions, such as his *Shakespeare Songs*, which he produced for Vaughan Williams' 70th birthday in October 1942. Yet, he seems to have suffered from some kind of clinical depression as the war continued, for he was always tired, never motivated, and had no new music come to him.[115] Much of what he brought out now had already existed pre-war in some form, needing only revision.[116]

Life went on, the war continued, and gradually, the Allies were gaining ground. After the D–Day invasion in June 1944, the sense grew that it was only a matter of time before Hitler's final defeat. By the beginning of 1945, Finzi was agitated and wanted to be dismissed from his service, even contacting Vaughan Williams to try to pull some strings to get him an early discharge, but his lack of affiliation with an institution prevented this.[117] He finally left the job and London for good on June 1, 1945, and returned to Ashmansworth, where he would live his remaining eleven years in relative peace, finally pursuing the life he had wanted.

In the immediate post-war years, he was able to indulge in all of his interests, from composition to book collecting (his library was enormous at his death)[118] to apple cultivation to the Newbury orchestra (which began to attract professionals).[119] He was determined to rescue good things from being lost,[120] whether rare apples,[121] rare old music,[122] or Gurney's works.[123] He declined an offer to return to the Royal Academy, but undertook other musical work to support his family (and his sons' expenses at boarding school). His music was a mixture of commissions and personal projects, and his compositions began to grow in size and scope. He wrote far more music, and on a larger scale, after the war than before it.

Newbury was increasingly becoming a more professional-sounding ensemble, and as a result, was taking up more of this time. However, finding a replacement or co-director proved difficult.[124] The Finzis enjoyed their house being empty for the first time since they had moved in, though the side-effects of the war were not over. Peace had been achieved, but there was still rationing and hard times; Hitler's defeat had been the common unifying goal for the nation, but now old problems were resurfacing. Nevertheless, Ashmansworth became a haven for all of the things they loved: music, nature, conservation, cats, a welcoming place for artists, and an idyllic country setting.[125]

In the music world, things were changing rapidly. Banfield observes: "Just as Holst and Vaughan Williams had been appointed—indeed anointed—Britain's senior composers at a stroke when the end of the First World War rendered the positions psychologically vacant, Britten was similarly appointed [...] at the end of the Second.[...]"[126] Not everyone was happy about this; Finzi and his associates came to view it as nothing more than the pronouncement of the establishment. He admitted that he was "allergic" to Britten's music, calling it "derelict & dead." While conceding that Britten displayed technical brilliance, his music was like soap bubbles that burst and disperse, and "as a rule what he brings off isn't worth a rat's dropping."[127] In this instance, the mild-mannered Finzi seemed to be channeling Heseltine in his acidity! Further, he had declared in 1942 that he would much rather listen to light movements by Fauré, Johann Strauss, or Elgar, "than all the ponderous integrity of Bruckner or the constipated integrity of Schoenberg!"[128] Unlike many of his friends, he also hated Wagner and Richard Strauss, though Berg's work intrigued him.[129]

He was praised for works such as his cantata *Dies Natalis*, composed before the war; it increased in popularity during and after it. This work evoked some of the older sound, which opposed the newer ideas cultivated by Britten and his colleagues and advocates. In some circles, Finzi was seen as outdated, essentially an imitator of Vaughan Williams' style.[130] The derogatory "cow pat" moniker was applied to Finzi, as well. This scorn extended to the types of music festivals that took place in England, with old festivals such as the Three Choirs (held annually in August in the West counties since at least 1719)[131] being seen as provincial bastions of dusty traditions, while newer gatherings in Edinburgh, Aldeburgh, and Dartington were the "trendy" festivals where important new music was happening.[132]

Nevertheless, he did receive official acknowledgements and praise. His ode, *For St Cecilia*, was commissioned by the St Cecilia Festival Committee, and performed in the Royal Albert Hall in November 1947, where it was well received. This success gave him an elevated standing with certain institutions, and a measure of respectability for some time afterward.

Regardless of such social acceptance, he remained very self-critical, as were so many of the composers of his time, and he was also known to lose interest in his pieces once they were finally completed to his satisfaction. However, he might delay work on a composition for years, starting something else and returning to the other at a later time, a problem that he readily admitted to having.[133] As we have seen, this has made compiling a chronology of his music problematic.[134] He was able to complete his *Clarinet Concerto* in 1949 despite this poor habit, his largest work to date.[135]

His *Intimations of Immortality* was a musical ode completed in 1950, but which had been formulating in his mind since 1934, again demonstrating just how long he could take to craft a piece. It was a setting of William Wordsworth's *Ode: Intimations of Immortality from Recollections of Early Childhood* (published in 1807). It is a massive composition (up to 45 minutes in length) that once again showed how Finzi had developed, and that he was capable of handling large-scale works.[136] Indeed, Banfield has noted that this was likely the definitive setting of a Wordsworth poem, a curious magnum opus for a man whom history has regarded as a second-tier composer.[137] However, at the time, some saw the work as derivative, and Finzi as not only outdated but now irrelevant.[138] A critic in *Music Review* from 1952, for example, stated: "I cannot help feeling that to write in 1950 a work so obsolescent is a singular quixotism for a composer still on the right side of fifty."[139] At least there was humor to be had; a misprint on the vocal score had the piece titled *Intimations of Immorality*, which caused much laughter.[140]

In early 1951, Finzi and Joy were in a minor car accident; it was not his first, for as a young man in 1925, he had also crashed his car (with his mother on board, who was apparently reading to him while he drove) when he swerved to avoid hitting a duck.[141] Though Joy chipped a tooth, he was unhurt, but his physical troubles were just beginning.

As early as 1946, he had noticed a small lump on the back of his neck, but took it to be a boil, acne, or some such, and gave it no further thought. That lack of attention would have fatal consequences, though in those early days, it may not have mattered. In 1951, his neck glands began to swell, and he visited a doctor who was a family friend. A biopsy of a neck gland and some bone marrow indicated non–Hodgkins lymphoma. The prognosis was not good; such cancers suppress the immune system making the patient far more susceptible to otherwise less serious infections. He was given at most ten years to live.[142] The news came as a terrible blow, though in one sense it was a relief, as they had suspected that something might be wrong for some time. He and Joy resolved to tell very few people, and to get on with things and enjoy the time that they had left together as fully as possible.[143] As we have seen, Finzi had always been haunted by the transience of life, and how fate could deliver cruel blows. He had seen his father waste away and now it would be him.

As a testament to his resolve, he vowed to continue his life and work as a scholar and lecturer, and to compose as much as possible in the time left to him. Under the death sentence, he would produce his *Cello Concerto* (possibly his greatest and most ambitious work, which he had considered writing since well before 1940), the *Grand Fantasia and Toccata* (reworking portions of an older version of the *Fantasia* from as far back as 1928), his beloved Christmas work, *In terra pax* (written as a personal project for Newbury, not for hire), and an Arts Council commission to write one of ten new vocal pieces for the coronation of Queen Elizabeth in June 1953.[144] His musicological works intensified in those years, as did his commitment to preserving the works of lesser-known 18th-century English composers, a project that gave him immense satisfaction. He contributed the edition of Boyce's Overtures to the *Musica Britannica* series,[145] always guided by the directive that he wanted to preserve things that should not be lost. This extended to his devotion to the output of both Gurney and Parry.[146] These activities often eclipsed his composition work, making it all the more remarkable that he produced what he did in those years. He made friends with a young Stanley Sadie (musicologist and editor of the monumental *New Grove Dictionary of Music and Musicians*)[147] and Julian Bream (later a world-famous guitarist and lutenist), who came to his house to discuss music and perform respectively.[148] Finzi's son Christopher was becoming a capable cellist and from 1952, was a student at the Royal Academy of Music. Christopher also accompanied his father on his lecture trips, and would later succeed him as the conductor of Newbury,[149] though it was their younger son, Nigel, who would devote his life to music.[150]

Finzi continued his friendship with Vaughan Williams (who knew about his condition), but privately felt that after the composer's 80th birthday in 1952, it was perhaps time for him to retire.[151] He may have felt some envy for his older friend's long life, one that he would not have.[152] Vaughan Williams, for his part, had never recovered from the loss of his best friend Holst in 1934, and while he regarded Finzi as a good friend, he was not a replacement, and there was always something of the teacher/student relationship between them[153]; Banfield likens it to Finzi being his musical "godson."[154]

He had reconnected with his cousin, Neville, a doctor who was able to advise him on the best course to take for treating the disease. Initially, he responded to radiation treatments well, and there was a glimmer of hope that his might be one of the rare cases of a longer-term survival. However, in September 1952, he experienced sudden and rapid lymph node swellings, and in early 1953, his X-ray treatments intensified. By October of 1953, however, his blood count results led to the diagnosis that it would be necessary to perform an operation to remove his spleen,[155] though it was possible to delay this for all of 1954.

Finzi and Joy continued to face the world with a remarkable outward show of positive attitude and energy, though his illness was taking a toll on them both. He suffered side effects including indigestion, insomnia, and a persistent cough, though he did not experience hair loss. Naturally, he was discouraged, and Joy noted his declaring in 1952: "That I of all people should have to die so soon, when I have the seeds of growth in me."[156] There was sadness and pessimism in him, and perhaps a confirmation that Hardy had been right all along.

In early 1955, he had his spleen removed, an operation that was successful and gave him some relief (he spent the days of recovery in bed composing), though he was told that this would make him more susceptible to infection. Nevertheless, he pushed ahead with his busy schedule of composing, editing 18th-century music, giving lectures, growing apples, and a multitude of other activities that would have been demanding for a healthy man, much more so for one who was losing a battle with cancer. Indeed, he was in good spirits and able to carry on with most of his work, despite regular check-ups and the constant reminder of his condition. Joy would refer to 1955 as "the year of grace."[157] He carried on, despite a rough start to 1956, even optimistically accepting commissions for work in 1957 and 1958.[158]

In late summer, the Finzis and the Vaughan Williamses attended the Three Choirs Festival with various other friends, having a grand time.[159] Finzi conducted the full version of his *In terra pax*, and in the aftermath, he and Vaughan Williams called on a local sexton, a decision that they could not have known was a terrible mistake. At least one of the sexton's children had chicken pox. A few weeks later, Finzi and Joy were having a break in East Anglia, and he began to complain of chest pains. Soon a rash developed which was identified as shingles. Poor Finzi had been infected by the child a few weeks earlier. At the time, it seemed to be a minor inconvenience that might keep him immobilized for a few weeks; however, it quickly grew more serious, developing into full-blown chicken pox.[160]

He was taken to Radcliffe Infirmary in Oxford, where his condition worsened. He now had encephalitis (inflammation of the brain). Joy visited him on September 27, and recorded in her journal: "[...] as I sat & talked with him I became quite contented, even happy, in feeling all was well with possibly the awareness of the end of his suffering. I stayed with him until the evening and shortly after I left he had another convulsion & died. The shadow has fallen."[161] She received word of his death by phone when she arrived back at their house later that evening. His *Cello Concerto* had been broadcast just one night before he died.

Tributes and sympathies were quick to come in, including from the Vaughan Williamses, who had gone to Majorca, but offered to be there for Joy, if she needed them.[162] There was no service; Finzi was cremated on October 2, and Joy kept his ashes with her until 1973, when her own sister died. Then she took both sets and scattered them on May Hill, on the border between Gloucestershire and Herefordshire, returning him forever to the land that he loved.[163] Joy lived at Ashmansworth until 1974, and then also resided at homes near Newbury, dying in 1991 at the age of 84. In 1969, the Finzi Trust was established to promote not only his music, but also that of his contemporaries, giving grants for recordings, research, and other activities.[164]

In the end, Finzi is remembered as something of a minor English composer, eclipsed by Britten and others who were more cutting-edge, dynamic, and modern. Arthur Bliss spoke fondly of him, saying, "Steeped in the literary and musical traditions of England, he expressed love for their traditions alone."[165] He displayed no influences from continental composers, and "found valueless much of what was being written in the musical world around him,"[166] though he was "extremely interested in all new developments affecting music" and "well versed in the minutiae of twentieth-century music."[167]

His music was always seen—rather unfairly—as harkening back to the older style of his friend and early model Vaughan Williams, who was still relevant enough to be composing complex symphonies in his 80s, but who would forever be associated with folk songs, and to some, the "cow pat" reputation. In Finzi's defense, John Russell noted in 1954: "His style is so different from those of his much-noised contemporaries that he is regarded as a placid backwater off the main stream; as one who (it would seem) almost perversely writes music which is a joy to perform and a pleasure to listen to."[168] Even his *Cello Concerto* was dismissed by some reviewers as little more than a tribute to Elgar, and so out-of-date as a result as to be irrelevant,[169] recalling similar sentiments about his *Intimations of Immortality*. For Finzi, these "pip-squeaks"[170] served only to alienate listeners, and he gave them no regard. He was fully aware of his artistic and technical limitations, but he stayed with what he knew, and did it superbly. His son Nigel would say that Finzi "should be considered as a 'Small/Big composer' i.e., small in terms of quantity but big in terms of content."[171]

Ultimately, whatever difficulties he faced, from losing much of his family as a child, to enduring a long, slow decline in his 50s, he did so with dignity and humor. Aware of the inexorable passage of time, he delved deeply into those things which mattered to him, and lived a full life, knowing that his limited time here made those things that much more precious and enjoyable. Joy's words sum him up very well: "Like all who have known the shadows he had an immense capacity for enjoyment. A great appreciation of many things— and infinite delight & humor. The sense of precariousness made delight an ecstasy."[172]

9

Percy Grainger (1882–1961)

Percy Grainger's importance in collecting and preserving English folk songs is without doubt, yet he lived a life very different from the other composers surveyed here. A brilliant and showy pianist from a young age, he was born in Australia, spent several years as a young man in Europe, and then moved to America, where he would live for the rest of his life, though he continued to travel frequently.

He brought a responsible sense of modern ethnomusicology to the preservation of English folk song, mirroring the model of Bartók and Kodály in Eastern Europe and using early recording equipment to capture the actual tunes of his singers, rather than merely notating down what he heard, which as we have seen, was the standard practice favored by Sharp and others. Indeed, he was not interested in Sharp's goal of creating an idealistic English heritage, but felt that the songs should speak for themselves. He would bring the same scientific sensibilities of song collection to the non–European lands that he visited, including New Zealand and other South Pacific cultures. He was also noted for his work in collecting and preserving Scandinavian folk songs in a similar manner in the 1920s, and was very fond of jazz and new music, when some of his contemporaries distrusted or even disliked these genres.

In keeping with the theme of the book, this chapter will focus primarily on his life up through his time in England (1901–14), and the results that he obtained, both as a collector and a composer. He was quite an eccentric man, both in public and in private, and we will examine some of his more quirky and humorous traits, as well as his more disturbing passions.[1]

Grainger was born on July 8, 1882, in Melbourne, Australia, which at the time was undergoing an economic boom, attracting new residents from all over the world. His father, John Harry Grainger, was a respected architect from a Durham family, and his mother, Rose Annie Aldridge, came from Adelaide. She would have a tremendous influence on his life, far too much. John was very fond of culture and music, and was skilled at painting. He was a good singer, and also oversaw the formation of Adelaide's first string quartet. This organization later became a music club headed for a time by Cecil Sharp while he was in Australia.[2]

By most accounts he was kind and cultured, but Rose had never been too taken with the idea of marriage to him, only deciding to do so under the pressures of the time.[3] Her mother Sarah was wary of John's dark hair and dark eyes, which indicated that he was not of the "pure" northern stock that she found more desirable (the whole family possessed strongly bigoted views). Rose was also concerned about this, and passed this racial prejudice onto her son, who would hold to it in one form or another for his whole life.[4] She also later admitted that she had never loved John.[5] Further he was, at least nominally, a believing Christian, while Rose and her family were atheists (another belief that her son adopted). Nevertheless, he provided for her, and their home was well kept and decorated.

However, John had a fatal flaw in being an alcoholic. He was not abusive or cruel, but his drunken episodes led to terrible arguments with Rose, and on more than one occasion, she chased him from the house with a horsewhip. Alternately, he might storm from the house completely sober, perhaps seeking comfort in the arms of a prostitute and drink, only to turn up a few days later, begging Rose's forgiveness.[6] Little Percy Grainger witnessed their arguments, which must have been very stressful and hurtful for him. However, Victorian sensibilities dictated that John and Rose had to stay together to maintain an air of respectability in the community, a common tragic occurrence for dysfunctional families of the time. A family friend who was a doctor once offered to take her and her son away with him to San Francisco, but she refused, perhaps not yet ready to abandon John despite his faults.[7]

She dominated her son and from his earliest years, and attempted to mold him into her vision of what he should be. Though John genuinely loved young Grainger and tried to show him affection (John never seems to have administered corporal punishment to his son),[8] Rose equally endeavored to prevent them from being close, jealously guarding her emotional bond and trying to drive them apart. Bird rightly refers to it as a "neurotic guardianship."[9] John was able to influence Grainger enough to instill in him a love of walking, sports, and art.[10] Indeed, John expected that his son would become an artist, given his great talent.[11] He also noted with admiration that Rose was a very talented pianist, deeply devoted to Grainger, and had taught him music very well.[12]

Rose's neurosis dated to shortly after Grainger was born, when she was given the terrible medical diagnosis of syphilis. She believed that she only could have contracted it from her husband (though he would never admit to it), which meant that he had been unfaithful to her by visiting brothels or indulging in similar unsavory encounters. This has been challenged by some researchers, however, who have suggested that Rose may have contracted the disease from an earlier encounter, and that John's own symptoms were not consistent with the disease.[13]

John had boasted that as a young man, he could have fourteen prostitutes in a single night with no problems performing, though this was certainly youthful nonsense.[14] Rose had known her husband was a philanderer, having received a letter shortly after they were married from a young woman in England claiming that he had fathered her child, a story that he admitted to at the time that she was in labor with Percy.[15]

As a result, she was terrified of passing the disease on to her son, and this no doubt contributed to her desire to keep John away from him, as well. She employed a nurse, Annie, to take on virtually all of her motherly duties. Young Grainger was very fond of Annie, who acted as something of a shield between him and his family's dysfunction. She also showered him with affection, something that Rose could and would not give. Annie was dismissed when he was five, which saddened him greatly, and from then on, Rose dominated him completely.

She took over his education, which was quite extensive for a boy of five years. His routine included English, other languages, history, and art, as well as two hours' practice every day at the piano, a regimen that lasted until he was ten. She was stern and strict about discipline, and while she accorded him some freedoms to be a small boy if he did what she wanted (such as wandering outside and playing with toy ships), if he did not practice or if he neglected his studies, she would whip him as punishment. Grainger was deeply affected by this, and after puberty, he associated such beatings with sexual stimulation. His love of masochism would last his whole life, and we will examine this unusual character trait more below. She kept him away from other children, and made him focus on music, drawing, and learning. Fortunately, Grainger loved art, and showed as much talent for it as he did for music, so these restrictions did not feel so harsh to him. He loved to draw and practiced whenever he could.

With her strong spirit and fierce sense of independence, she eventually could no longer tolerate John and their sham marriage. He had been suffering from bouts of delirium from 1888 (either from syphilis, or perhaps delirium tremens),[16] and had tried various cures and hospital visits, but they were not effective. John was advised by his doctor, Robert Hamilton Russell, to observe absolute rest, but he chose instead to leave the country, ostensibly to seek treatment in London, but also simply to have a holiday. This conveniently allowed him to leave behind Rose and, with some sadness, his young son. He set out in September 1890. Russell predicted that he would be dead by the time that the ship called in at Sri Lanka,[17] but John not only recovered, he went on to live for many more years, returning to Australia in December 1890 for a short visit, and eventually establishing himself in Perth. He kept in contact with Rose and the boy over the years, sending money occasionally, and even expressing some hope of reconciliation, but the three of them would not live together again. Young Grainger wrote to him somewhat regularly and kept him advised of his progress, but in many ways mother and son were now alone, which is exactly what she wanted. Their bond grew uncomfortably close, rather like that of Philip Heseltine and his mother. It was the two of them against the world.

Grainger's brief school experience was not happy, and lasted only three months in 1894. He was not equipped to deal with other children his age, having had no chance to socialize with them in the past. The other boys teased him mercilessly and fought amongst themselves to the point where he did not want to return, and Rose was only too happy to reclaim him into her umbrella of protection and neurotic influence. Mabel Todhunter, his governess from 1888–94, noted that "Percy, when quite small, did not get on with other children very well. They did not enter into his land of make-believe.[...]"[18] She also noted that she personally did not see Rose cane him often, and helped Rose hide John's drunkenness from the world.[19]

There were other older men in his life that had a more positive influence than his father. One was Robert Hamilton Russell, who was also a gifted amateur pianist, playing for Grainger and importantly, taking him to see concerts. It was Russell, as we have seen, who had advised John to observe total rest, but now that he was gone, Russell took an interest in the boy's development, as much as was possible with such a possessive mother. From the age of ten, Grainger studied piano and harmony with a German pianist, Louis Pabst, perhaps the finest such instructor in Melbourne. He introduced Grainger to a lifelong love of the music of Bach, so much so that Grainger would later claim that anything that was good about his interpretations of Bach he learned from Pabst.[20] The German was so fond of the boy that he and his wife thought of trying to adopt him and take him back to Europe. This would have been over the dead body of Rose, who was determined that Grainger would excel at music on her terms. She refused their offer, strangely stating that if her son were to focus so intently on piano at the expense of composition until he was 16 (Pabst's plan), it would be too late for him to become a composer, and he would relegated to being a "mere" pianist. Grainger was not happy with this, but, as always, acquiesced to her wishes.[21]

He did, however, achieve the status of a child prodigy, giving his first public performance at Melbourne's Masonic Hall in 1894, one day after his twelfth birthday. The audience and critics were astonished by his virtuosity. The city paper, the *Age* praised his ability and said that any teacher with such a pupil should be proud, predicting great things for him.[22]

In addition to his musical gifts, he was extremely intelligent and learned, reading voraciously. In time, he became a skilled painter and learned eleven languages. He was very fond of the Icelandic sagas, which he read in the original tongue; his mother's ideas about northern European purity and blue-eyed perfection no doubt helped to foster this interest. He would later claim that the *Saga of Grettir the Strong* was his greatest influence, inspiring him to, "turn back [with his music] the tide of the Hastings battle, by celebrating all seemingly Old English (Anglo-Saxon) & Norse characteristics, by ignoring, as far as possible, all seemingly Norman traits & influences & those derived from the civilization of the Roman Empire."[23] He also found great inspiration in the works of Whitman and Kipling.[24]

He would come to believe that the melodic sensibilities of Northern Europe far surpassed those of the continent, and while continental composers were able to craft ingenious and complex harmonies, they were not as skilled as their northern counterparts in writing unadorned, unaccompanied, but strong melodies.[25] This was one factor that drew him to English and then Danish folk songs.

In the months after his first public performance, Rose decided that he would be best served by studying in Europe (the Pabsts having already returned there), and so in May 1895 (after another performance in the Melbourne Town Hall, to equal acclaim), they sailed for Genoa and from there journeyed by train to Germany, settling in Frankfurt. Grainger claimed that he wanted to go to Germany rather than Italy or France, because of the linguistic and cultural affinities with the Germanic, Nordic, and Icelandic stories and cultures that he so loved, particularly the sagas. He looked forward to living among such a superior people. The chance to obtain first-rate instruction while living in this place must have been irresistible to him.

Once there he would study piano at Dr. Hochs' Conservatory, an important music school, among the highest-rated in Europe at the time.[26] However, there was soon dissatisfaction with his piano teacher, James Kwast (whom Grainger felt taught him nothing of real value) and friction with his composition teacher, Ivan Knorr (who criticized some of Grainger's innovations, and wanted his students to follow his own tastes).[27] This led to him to abandon Knorr and take up study with Karl Klimsch (whom he met through Rose's work as an English teacher). Klimsch, while not being a professional composer, was a valuable teacher and friend.[28] Grainger would regard him later as his only worthwhile instructor in composition. Though German, Klimsch was devoted to England and Scotland (taking regular summer holidays to the latter destination), and introduced Grainger to English and Scottish folk songs, years before he would take up his collecting work in England. Klimsch planted an important seed in his young student,[29] and Grainger would make several settings of various folk tunes between 1899 and 1904, before beginning to record and collect them in England.[30]

At the conservatory, he made a number of friends including Balfour Gardiner (later a patron of Holst, as we have seen), Cyril Scott, and Roger Quilter, among others.[31] These young men did not like the established way of things in the musical life of Britain and Scandinavia, and wanted changes, like many others at the time. Quilter in particular became a good friend, as did Cyril Scott, who perhaps became a kind of older brother to Grainger. On a more personal level, Kwast's daughter Mimi (also one of Rose's English language students) was groomed by her father and Grainger's mother to be his first sweetheart, though she loved another, and Grainger eventually assisted her in defying her parents' wishes and going to him in Berlin.[32] This brief contact, however, awaked in him sexual desires that he associated with his whipping punishments, which we will discuss below. Indeed, Grainger himself credited his time in Germany with three important developments: his unusual sexual desires, his philosophy of racial purity, and the development of his own musical style.[33]

Rose and Grainger were able to take a holiday during the summer of 1900, visiting many locations in Europe, one of which was Glasgow and its nearby countryside. This landscape had a profound effect on Grainger, as did the traditional culture of the Scots and the sounds of the bagpipe. He would later claim that this experience was probably the most important influence on him artistically.[34] Having already heard both Scottish and English folk songs, a strong bond with Britain was forming.

Upon returning from their lengthy holiday, Rose slipped on ice and fell, which also triggered a breakdown; she had also experienced one a few years earlier. Being now both mentally and physically incapacitated, the task fell to Grainger to support them, which he did by giving recitals and concerts. He also resolved to hold back his music, not seeking to publish his works out of fear that because they were already so unusual, he would gain a bad reputation from them and be denied access to the concert stage, noting, "[...] I vowed not to publish or (conspicuously) perform the main body of my compositions until I was forty years old; for I feared that the radical nature of much of my music would stir up animosities against me that would undermine my earning power as a pianist."³⁵ He also worried that he might hate them in his later years and regret having made them public.³⁶

Grainger continued to develop and impress as a pianist while Rose recovered, but he was increasingly dissatisfied with living in Germany. He felt that German musicians frequently did not deserve their reputation for excellence, and that the English students were the superior musicians and composers.³⁷ It became obvious that he could do very well financially in London. Further, many of his best college friends were English, and were returning home. He wanted to be where he felt the next great wave of musical activity would be. A further incentive came from Lilian Devlin, a noted Australian soprano who invited Grainger to perform in one of her concerts with fellow Australian vocalist Ada Crossley, at the time a very popular contralto.³⁸ So in 1901, he and Rose decided that they would move to London, where he would be best appreciated for his talents.

They arrived there during the summer season, and sure enough, he was an immediate sensation, a wunderkid who dazzled with his technique and quirky mannerisms.³⁹ Crossley proved to be one of his entries into the complex world of social climbing that marked the London music scene. Dame Nellie Melba, a long-time friend of Rose, was friends with many important members of the establishment, as well with aristocratic circles and their patronage, and was only too happy to assist their efforts.⁴⁰ Grainger's success was all but assured, and he was soon in demand for parties, private concerts, and many other lucrative engagements.⁴¹ These did not impress him, however, and he later wrote to Eric Fenby (Delius' amanuensis) that while many romanticized the pre-war period as a last age of elegance, innocence, and grace, he detested the behavior of these classes: "Before the war utter heartlessness seemed to me to prevail, & utterly driveling & goalless attitudes were hand fed. [...] I don't think you would have liked the years before the war if you had been a grown man in them."⁴² This view may also have contributed to his later lack of interest in Sharp's apparent romanticizing of England and its past.

High society took notice of the young virtuoso; artists now desired to paint his portrait, including the esteemed painter Jacques-Émile Blanche (a prominent artist in London at the time), and Grainger's fellow countryman, the splendidly-named Rupert Bunny; both were also talented amateur musicians. Blanche introduced Grainger to the music of Debussy, which he admired.⁴³

Grainger's fortunes continued to rise when he was brought to the attention of Queen Alexandra, wife of Edward VII. In 1903, her secretary wrote a letter to Grainger and his touring partner, cellist Herman Sandby (from Denmark), requesting that they perform at Buckingham Palace. This was a remarkable achievement for a young man barely over twenty years old. The performance was a success, and thereafter the queen often attended his public London concerts.⁴⁴

His mother was not always happy with all of this new attention, however, as it took him away from her. Indeed, in February 1902, he journeyed to Bath to perform with the Bath Pump Room Orchestra. Rose was unable to attend, and the time away was the longest that they had ever been separated. Grainger had a grand time in Bath, enjoying the company of his hosts. His return to London, however, was anything but pleasant. Rose had a near neurotic breakdown, flying into a rage and hysterics when he told her about how wonderful the trip had been. In her increasingly troubled mind, he was simply not allowed to enjoy himself without her permission and supervision. This would only get worse as the years passed, his fame increased, and her condition deteriorated.⁴⁵ Grainger attributed the underlying cause of this rage to her desire that he only take delight in "superior things," not the common-place pleasures that he had been describing to her; she saw it as a sign of betrayal and disloyalty.⁴⁶ As a result, she tried ever harder to rein in his contact with friends and social callers, not always with success, but he seems to once again have given in to her wishes. His friends' visits became increasingly infrequent, and they often wondered why he simply did not stand up to her. Why, indeed...

At this time, he came to the attention of a Mrs. Frank (Lilith) Lowrey, a wealthy socialite and arts patron, who introduced him to the queen, and who entertained King Edward on occasion (with the resulting suspicions as to the nature of their relationship). Vaughan Williams lived on the same street as she did, and she likely introduced him to Grainger.⁴⁷ Significantly, she expected sexual favors from Grainger in return for her help. He gave in, and had his first sexual experience with her. He told Rose about it, and surprisingly, she approved at first, feeling that it would be very helpful to his musical

Percy Grainger as a young man (courtesy of the Lewis Foreman collection).

career. She soon fell back into her possessiveness and jealousy, however, and put a stop to the affair, though it went on for some two years.[48]

Among others taken by the young man's gifts was the Italian composer Ferruccio Busoni, who was so impressed that he offered to teach Grainger for free if he would come to Berlin, which he did. They focused especially on Bach, and Grainger would play his transcriptions of certain works for the rest of his career. Busoni was both fond of Grainger and somewhat jealous of his talents. Further, Grainger would not give Busoni the student-to-teacher adoration that he craved. They annoyed each other, and it was not the basis for a solid friendship, even though they admired one another's talents.[49]

From this young age, he was also adopting a new approaches to music, and making experiments with his compositions that were ahead of the time, writing pieces in unusual time meters, for example, or as with his 1901 piece, *Train Music*, emulating the sound and movement of a train in music; this had been inspired by hearing the irregular rhythms of the trains he took on a holiday in southern France and Italy. While on that European tour, he heard reed instruments in Italy, and the mizmar from Egypt (a loud, oboe-like instrument, probably at the Paris Exhibition), which stimulated his interest in using the oboe, the bassoon, and the French horn extensively in his own work.[50] He would later note in a radio broadcast from June 1933:

> I firmly believe that music will someday become a "universal language." But it will not become so as long as our musical vision is limited to the output of four European countries between 1700 and 1900. The first step in the right direction is to view the music of all peoples and periods without prejudice of any kind, and to strive to put the world's known and available best music into circulation. Only then shall we be justified in calling music a "universal language."[51]

Though he had some disdain for the standard classical repertoire, he was to remain devoted to Bach's music his whole life.[52]

In 1903, he had the opportunity to tour in the southern hemisphere, including South Africa, Australia, and New Zealand (where he briefly met with his father); he was eager to revisit his come country. There are amusing accounts of his physical prowess on the tour, such as walking long distances in running shorts between cities where his group was scheduled to play. He would often set out after a concert, and rejoin his companions the following day, having walked and run while they had taken a train. This was a practice that he would continue well past his sixtieth birthday,[53] and was as common in Europe or America as anywhere else.[54] In South Africa, he once was late while walking from one location to another, and his friends were worried about him, only to see him arrive jogging alongside a band of Zulu warriors.[55] He was nothing if not a spectacular showman.

As his fame grew, he attracted the interest of conductors and other composers, such as Charles Villiers Stanford, who employed his talents in various concert programs, including performances of his own works. In the summer of 1905, he toured Denmark with his friend Herman Sandby, and Sandby's fiancé Alfhild de Luce. Grainger developed strong romantic feelings for her. Though this would never materialize, the two would remain friends for the rest of their lives.[56]

Also in 1905, he met Delius for the first time, and the two were rather astonished at the similarities of their tastes in music, as well as compositional styles.[57] Both had been unaware of these likenesses, not being familiar with each other's music previously. As with Heseltine, Delius took to the young Grainger, and championed his music on several occasions, such as during the creation of the Musical League in England, when his condition for accepting the vice-presidency (Elgar was president) was that Grainger's music be featured.[58] He wrote in 1910, "I consider Percy Grainger the most gifted of all your young composers I have met, and he is an Australian! He does quite remarkable things, and is most refreshing."[59]

Just prior to his Scandinavian adventure, he became interested in the practice of folk song-collecting in England. It was to become a true pleasure of his for the next several years, lasting in earnest until 1909, during the main years of collecting for Vaughan Williams, Butterworth, Sharp, and others. It was also a period when his compositional output was very high, and his recognition as a pianist (though not as a song collector) grew rapidly. Grainger was already weary of his concertizing, partially because of an irrational stage fright (he did not understand why he was so popular and well-received), and more strangely, because he was beginning to dislike the piano greatly, for both performance and composition.[60] Folk songs, therefore, offered him something new, a genuine interest in a practice that he felt was important. While he had known about folk music for a long time (he made his first arrangement in 1898),[61] it was his introduction to Lucy Broadwood in 1904 that kindled his interest in pursuing the work of collecting these English songs. After attending her lecture on the subject in March 1905, he approached her about undertaking the work of collection, and was happily received.[62]

He joined Broadwood and Frank Kidson in attending the North Lincolnshire Musical Competition Festival on April 10 and 11, 1905, which was held in the market town of Brigg, in North Lincolnshire. Grainger had helped to create one of the events, a folksong competition wherein the prize would be won by the best tune, which did not have to be sung by the best singer. The competition noted: "It is specially requested that the establishment of this class be brought to the notice of old people in the country who are most likely to remember this kind of song, and that they be urged to come in with the best old song they know."[63] Joseph Taylor, a 72-year-old bailiff from the village of Saxby-All-Saints, about six miles north of Brigg, was the winner. He sang a tune called *Creeping Jane*, and included a number of unusual effects, ornaments, and rhythms that impressed Kidson (the chosen judge). Taylor was perhaps the best of Grainger's source singers.[64] Grainger convinced the Gramophone Company to record Taylor's singing and release it, but the recordings had little popular appeal.[65] Second place went to a Mr. W. Hilton of Keelby (east of Brigg), 85 years old and nearly deaf, but able to produce a fine version of the tune *Come all You Merry Plowboys*; one of his other songs went on for so long that he eventually had to be escorted off the stage, being unable to properly hear the requests for him to stop.[66]

Grainger did not stay in the area for long, but he was so impressed with what he had experienced that he resolved to become a more serious collector, and to make arrangements of some of what he had notated up to that point. He was particularly interested in the songs of the Lincolnshire area, which seemed to have done a splendid job of preserving some of its folk culture. He returned there in August, and his charm won over the locals, who shared many of their songs with him. This was quite a compliment, as many older singers saw their songs as possessions, not lightly given away.[67] He was not shy about approaching strangers and asking if they knew any songs, but occasionally, he found some resistance. As we have seen, he met one stubborn elderly woman who refused to have her voice recorded, or even to sing for him at all. Grainger took some initiative and befriended the woman's daughter, who let him hide under a bed while she persuaded her mother to sing a song for her. She did so, and Grainger was able to notate the song down while in hiding.[68] One can imagine the kind of legal issues and copyright questions this would raise today. In general, however, he had a closer and friendlier relationship with singers than many of his contemporaries.

Unlike some of the other collectors, Grainger was deeply interested in each song's individual characteristics. He was not interested in sentimental or romanticized versions of tunes, like some of his colleagues. His transcriptions included details of phrasing and pronunciation, variations from verse to verse in word count or melody, etc. Further, he was not satisfied with merely notating the melodies he was hearing, and so purchased an Edison wax cylinder recorder. Grainger deserves credit for being the first collector to introduce the use of recording equipment to England when gathering these old tunes, thus adopting the methods of a modern ethnomusicologist in attempting to accurately document his subject.[69] This practice had already been ongoing in Eastern Europe, as well as America. Indeed, Bartók considered its use vital to his work of folk song-collecting in Hungary from 1905, and it may be that Grainger was inspired by his model when he began his own recording work in England in the summer of 1906; some also suggest that Grainger may have in fact inspired Bartók.[70]

There had been some initial interest in the use of recording equipment. At Broadwood's lecture, the chairman W.W. Cummings, stated: "I could almost wish for the first time in my life for a gramophone.[...] I should like them [songs] to be noted down with all their errors, and not have them changed according to the good taste, or the bad taste, or the whim or humour of those who take them down." Fuller Maitland concurred: "I think the chairman's suggestion of a gramophone is most excellent. If the Folk-Song Society were rich enough, we would buy one at once." He then added, in a condescending tone: "But we should have to put it in a back parlour for I fear the country folk would be so flabbergasted by the performance of the gramophone, to begin with, that they would be afraid to sing."[71] Grainger later found that, far from being superstitious primitives, many of his singers knew about such devices and were genuinely interested in them.[72]

Grainger was clearly taken with the idea. He wrote to Cecil Sharp in 1906: "Personally, I am very keen that the tunes I collect [...] should be publicly presented in as merely scientific a form as possible, for the time being.[...]"[73] However, Sharp had little interest in the use of new-fangled technologies or the application of ethnomusicology, being quite content to notate songs by hand. He was, of course, trying in part to transmit a sense of "merrie olde England" that was at odds with Grainger's unglamorous, warts-and-all recordings, which also threatened to expose any possible fabrications of other collectors. This is plainly stated in Sharp's letter to Grainger in May 1908, noting that, "in transmitting a song, our aim should be to record its artistic effect, not necessarily the exact means by which that effect was produced."[74] Sharp maintained that recording equipment made many singers nervous, and less able to sing freely.[75] Further, he felt that musical variations between verses were often just the singers getting "into their stride" and should not necessarily be noted down.[76] Grainger believed the opposite, noting that he was "surprised to find how very readily the old singers took to singing into the machine."[77]

As a result, he grew to dislike Sharp's approach, and his settings of songs, while still acknowledging his importance as a collector.[78] In a letter to Rose regarding some Morris dancing that he witnessed in Gloucestershire, he noted: "Yesterday evening we saw the school children do morris dances learned from Esperance Club teachers who owe all to Sharp. He has really done good work in this matter. I think the morris dances are charming. The two best [...] are just as jolly as Sharp's harmonic treatment of the tunes is revolting."[79]

He did most of his collecting by recording on only a few occasions: the summer of 1906, then April of 1908, and May of 1908, with a few other excursions scattered in.[80] That May, he also published various pieces in the *Journal of the Folk-Song Society*.[81] He included 27 songs (17 from Lincolnshire), with texts and variant melodies, and he discussed the use of recording equipment as a valuable tool for gathering these selections, observing that simply trying to cram these tunes into conventional notation often did not work, and failed to capture their natural flow and musicality. He also paid tribute to his singers, observing that they were frequently ill-treated by society and deserved better for the artistic richness that they carried.[82] By 1907, Grainger had befriended the celebrated author H.G. Wells, who was very interested in Grainger's methods, and how he noted not only songs, but also the personality traits and conduct of his signers. Wells remarked: "You are trying to do a more difficult thing than record folk-songs; you are trying to record life."[83]

Grainger always stressed that these songs should be recorded as they actually were, not as the collectors or society wanted them to be; he was far more interested in capturing the actual style of the songs, than preparing them for republication for lay singers or schools.[84] This was a completely different approach to that of Vaughan Williams, who was trying to uncover original versions of these songs, or Sharp, who wanted to choose the best versions for publication, and so could occasionally disregard some of an individual singer's variations and quirks.[85]

In contrast, Grainger observed how often the melodies, rhythm, and dynamics could vary from verse to verse, but that there was a unified sense of wholeness to the songs he heard, not merely multiple repetitions of the same tune over and over. Further, the songs often featured musical scales that were not commonly in use in art music, and the singers displayed an impressive number of vocal ornaments and tricks to emphasize various points in a story.[86] In observing how folk songs were being presented to new audiences, he noted: "[…] folk music finds its way to the hearts of the general public and of the less erudite musicians only after it has been 'simplified' (generally in the process of notation by well-meaning collectors ignorant of those more ornate subtleties of our notation alone fitted for the task) out of all resemblance to the original self."[87] Additionally, Grainger, as the atheist and Australian, did not have the culture of English church music hanging over his head, or the tendency to force the songs into the accepted church musical scales and modes as some other collectors did.[88] Indeed, he stressed that after listening to more than 400 field recordings, he observed that the songs were often characterized by their rhythmic irregularities and changes of mode and scale.[89] Indeed, he noted that the melodies were not sung in distinct modes, but were often, "one single loosely-knit modal folk-song scale,"[90] combining elements of all the modes.[91]

Freeman has observed that Grainger's interest in new musical forms allowed him to approach these folk songs in a unique way.[92] He recorded these tunes because he believed that the performance was more important than the song itself, and he wanted to capture those moments. The singers intended the variations that they made from verse to verse, and changing any aspect of their songs by notating them down and normalizing them "was tantamount to the desecration of art."[93] This was completely at odds the approach that the Folk Song Society advocated, which saw the songs themselves as national treasures existing independently of their singers.[94]

As might be expected, these positions did not rest well with some in the folk establishment. Sharp's response, as noted above, was generally negative. Further, he dismissed the importance of recording every nuance and change from verse to verse, as well as Grainger's scientific approach.[95] The editing committee (of which Grainger was a member) was also cool in their response to his article, noting the value of phonographs in collecting, but expressing that it was not yet clear that this was a technology that was superior to the human ear, and adding that it might need more time to develop. This was true; these early phonograph recordings hardly had the quality of CDs, LPs, or even 78s, and frequently were marred by much mechanical noise.

Anne Gilchrist, an expert on English and Scottish folk songs, did not view the phonograph method favorably at all, nor, as we have seen, did Cecil Sharp.[96] The committee's response thus seems to have been a stalling technique, allowing them to put off indefinitely a practice that they were not interested in utilizing. Further, Fuller Maitland was not convinced about the unusual time patterns that Grainger had noted, saying instead that they were merely stresses on certain accents, and that the songs absolutely conformed to standard musical times.[97] Certainly, one could argue that the overseers of all things folkloric were trying to dictate what these songs were supposed to be, rather than letting them be as Grainger found them.[98]

Vaughan Williams was also skeptical of the practice, though as we have seen, he tried using recording equipment in 1909, but ultimately, he only gathered some 20 songs with it. His aversion to this approach probably had more to do with his dislike of technology than with the methods involved, but he is said to have referred to Grainger's methods as "mad" and like Sharp, saw no point in notating down each difference from verse to verse, considering it to be "a waste of time."[99] Butterworth may have accompanied Vaughan Williams during these attempts in 1910.[100]

Despite Grainger's important work in the area, he was never able to devote time to transcribing many of his recordings. He undertook some effort several decades later, when the interest in the subject had diminished to the point of being seen as old-fashioned. He only committed about half of the recorded songs to manuscript form. By 1909, it was obvious that his ideas were not welcome, and so he drifted away from the English movement,[101] eventually taking his methods elsewhere, to New Zealand and Denmark. Ultimately, he collected over 300 English songs, recording 216 of them, a handful of songs from the Maori and other Polynesian cultures, and more than 170 Danish folk songs in the 1920s, again using the phonograph (see below).[102] His departure from English folk song-collecting was not, however, because he was driven away by the establishment, as some have suggested, or because of his own difficult personality, as others have offered. Rather, he had many interests and projects in mind, and needed time to explore them, time that would not allow for continued wandering of the English countryside in search of old songs.[103]

However, he never lost his devotion to folk music, and in 1926, he famously commented: "in the folk-song there is to be found the complete history of a people, recorded by the race itself, through the heartoutbursts of its healthiest output. It is a history compiled with deeper feeling and more understanding than can be found among the dates and data of the greatest historian.[...]"[104] Further, he observed in 1952:

> The greatest crime against folk-song is to "middle-class" it—to sing it with a "white collar" voice production & other townified suggestions. Whether it be true or not that the ballads originated in the knightly & aristocratic world, one thing is certain: they have come down to us solely as an adjunct of rural life & are drenched through & through with rural feelings & traditions.[105]

He noted in the 1940s, however, that monophonic folk song was not as close to him as polyphony.[106] Further, he said that he had never incorporated a folk song into one of his original compositions, but only made arrangements.[107] Britten was an admirer of his method, and would note in 1933 that he had heard radio broadcasts of "[...] two brilliant folk-song arrangements of Percy Grainger—17 come Sunday, & Father & Son [Daughter], knocking all the V. Williams and R. O. Morris arrangements into a cocked-hat."[108]

Returning to Grainger the young man, by 1906, his talent had caught the attention of the elderly Edvard Grieg, when he visited London in May. Grieg later observed in March 1907: "What is nationality? I have written Norwegian Peasant Dances that none of my countrymen can play, and here comes this Australian who plays them as they ought to be played! Here is a genius that we Scandinavians cannot do other than love."[109]

In the summer of that year, Grainger visited Grieg at his home in Norway, where the two spent time pouring over music and making plans to tour together the following year, as well as discussing forming a Norwegian Folk Song Society.[110] Grieg was greatly impressed with Grainger's folk song arrangements, and felt that English folk song would indeed provide English composers with a means of creating a national style.[111] He became a kind of a father-figure to Grainger, something that the young man still needed. Unfortunately, Grieg died on September 4, 1907; he had been ill for some time, and took a turn for the worse as summer ended. His widow, Nina, gave Grainger his gold pocket watch as a memorial keepsake, and Grainger would be devoted to performing Grieg's *Concerto in A minor* on a regular basis for the rest of his career.

He returned to Oceana in 1908–09 for a tour of Australia and New Zealand (over Rose's objections, of course), and while there, he met the folk song collector A.J. Knocks. Bringing the same enthusiasm he had to English tunes, he proceeded to help Knocks in the collection of traditional music from the Maori and other peoples of Polynesia, using recording equipment. He later noted that the part-songs of Raratonga in the Cook Islands made him feel, "a boundless enthusiasm (never before or since aroused by any other music).[...]"[112] He also transcribed three Australian aboriginal pieces while in Melbourne,[113] but curiously, showed no further interest in the native music of his country.[114] He was greatly pleased by Polynesian sounds, with their pronounced rhythms and harmonies,[115] and they would influence some of his later compositions. He was not content to stay in the region of his birth, however, and returned to England later that same year. Once in England again, he focused more on settings of folk songs, rather than continuing with the process of collecting, likely due to the resistance he had previously encountered. Ironically, most of his settings were not of the pieces that he had collected.[116]

Throughout this time he was still better known as a brilliant and flamboyant concert pianist than a composer, which was somewhat frustrating, as he was beginning to long for retirement from the stage so that he could devote himself to composition. However, this would not happen, for he would be in great demand as a performer after he moved to the Unites States. Piano recitals were simply a means to an end for him. He was a composer first, and a performer only a distant second. As a composer, he was able to work anywhere. Unlike Holst or Moeran, who needed absolute silence and peace to produce their works, Grainger was as happy writing music on a train or listening to the radio.[117]

With World War I beginning, Grainger and his mother decided to relocate to America, a safer option. Rose also reasoned that her son's career would be interrupted by staying in Europe, and Grainger "feared that the possibility of being killed would thwart his cherished ambition of becoming the first Australian composer of worth."[118] Grainger later noted in 1932: "Not willingly (not if I could help it) would I sacrifice my genius (the bloom of the Australian desert) to a lot of suburban bad blood."[119] They quickly left England and moved to New York, where Grainger was hugely successful as a pianist, playing some 100 concerts in his first year, far surpassing the amount of work he had taken in the Old World.[120] When America joined the war in 1917, Grainger enlisted in the army, despite being a conscientious objector, which had earned him much scorn from his English peers. He joined the Coast Artillery Corps, being promoted to the rank of Bandsman Second Class, where he played the oboe and saxophone, the latter being an instrument that he greatly enjoyed.[121] The unit was never involved in any combat, allowing him to remain a pacifist and focus on music.[122] He created a decent number of settings of pieces for wind band, and wrote a variety of other works during his service. Deciding that his adopted country would be his permanent home, he also became an American citizen in 1918.

He helped raise money for the war effort by playing at War Bond concerts. One of his encore pieces was to play variations on a Morris Dance tune called *Country Gardens*, which he had discovered via Cecil Sharp. It is a happy, springy tune, very light and perhaps somewhat insipid to the modern listener,[123] but at the time it was just the right piece to brighten up the dark days of war. It was very popular, so he had decided to make a piano version of it as a birthday gift for his mother in 1918.[124] It was published by Schirmer and was an instant success. It broke all of their previous sales records going back 75 years, and would do so for the next 20. By 1924, it was selling 27,000 copies annually. This brought him an enormous amount of money, but it was a double-edged sword, for he became so associated with the tune that he could not escape from it, being constantly asked to play it, and seeing it eclipse his other works.[125] If he did not perform it as an encore in his concerts, the audience would demand it and frequently would not leave until he gave in and played it. The piece became a proverbial albatross around his neck, rather like Holst's *Planets* and Ravel's *Bolero*, and he eventually hated it.

However, in characteristic form, he magnanimously offered a good share of the royalties he received from the song to Cecil Sharp, who had discovered and collected the tune, and introduced him to it. Sharp graciously refused on more than one occasion. He also offered money in 1920 to publish Sharp's Appalachian songs, writing to him:

> If you would humor [sic] me in my hope to be able to help in furthering the early publication of these English-American folksongs collected by you I assure you I would consider it a great privelege [sic], so deeply do I admire what you have done for all lovers of folksong, and so deeply are my affections engaged to both this country of North America and to the folkmusic of British origins wherever found. You can readily see that this combination of British folksongs alive in America and rescued by you appeals warmly to my heart, and I hope, therefore, that you will not consider my request impertinent and that you will not refuse to consider it.[126]

However, only after his death did Maud Karpeles accept the money to help publish *English Folk Songs from the Southern Appalachians*, which contained 274 songs in a remarkable 968 variants.[127] Despite their differences, this was a nice example of cooperation for a greater good.[128]

He was discharged from the Army in early 1919, and almost immediately went back to touring. However, he did not continue with the practice of collecting folk songs, either American or English (as Sharp had done). He collected a few negro spirituals, and made a setting of one American folk song, *Spoon River*, which was intended to be the first of several, but the project never materialized.[129] He opted instead to continue his work as a pianist and to focus on larger-scale compositions.[130] He continued to be frustrated that many saw him as a pianist who also composed, rather than as a composer who played piano.[131]

He and Rose bought a house in White Plains, just north of New York City, in May 1921. They settled in there as a more-or-less permanent base from which he could compose and set off on tours.

Rose, of course, was quite happy with his success and wealth, but continued to exert her unhealthy influence over him. There has been some speculation over the years (then and more recently) about the two being involved in an incestuous relationship, but it was actually the opposite. As we have seen, due to her disease, she avoided any physical contact with him at all in his early years, out of a paranoid fear of infecting him. Further, Grainger seemed to have no interest in her sexually, at least not explicitly, though their letters to one another are filled with adoring words that normally only lovers would say to one another; he probably also feared contracting the disease from her. Of course, syphilis cannot be transmitted by such casual contact. However, this rigid abstinence from touch meant that Grainger had no healthy form of physical

Percy and Rose Grainger in New York City, *ca.* 1919, by Count Jean De Strelecki (reproduced with permission of the Grainger Museum, Melbourne, Australia).

relationship with her in his early childhood: no hugs, being held or comforted, etc., though his nurse took on that role until he was five years old. This certainly left a negative impression on him, and perhaps influenced one of his more peculiar fetishes, for the main contact that he had from her was a horse whip if he failed to practice or study.

This appalling punishment continued until he was 15 or 16, well into his early sexual development, and it left a bizarre attachment to her. Indeed, he never hated her for punishing him, and in some ways, bonded with her over it, considering it a kind of gift, noting: "I was much lashed as a young (and as an older) boy; and I am of a grateful nature. I adore what I have experienced.[...]"[132] As the only form of physical contact with her at all, Grainger eventually translated this activity into one of love and then sexual excitement.[133] By his mid-teens, perhaps inspired by his brief interactions with Mimi (which were nonsexual), he indulged in "auto-erotic experiments in sado-masochism."[134] He saw himself as being cruel, and his music was a channel to protest the greater evils and cruelties of the world, claiming: "I am personally an example in music of everything I hate and decry."[135] This cruelty extended to the whole world, in his view, but humanity was hiding from it, using the trappings of religion to claim sanctity: "All of mankind is steeped in idolatry, taboo-madness, self-unawareness. And it will be so long as religion exists—that most fell of all human curses. Religious moralizing makes man afraid to see himself as he is (in all his cruel-lustfulness, his unfairness, his meanness)."[136]

Throughout his adult years he was devoted to sadism and masochism; he loved being whipped, which he maintained helped to relieve aggression and negative tensions. Late in life he noted: "I believe that flagelantism (like boxing, football & some other sports) is a means of turning the harsh, hostile & destructive elements in man into *harmless channels*. Much of civilisation consists of turning hostility into playfulness."[137] When he went on tour, he always took his whips with him. Though he denied it, he may have had latent homosexual feeling as well, though there is no evidence one way or another that he acted on such feelings. His longer blond hair (worn at his mother's insistence; she also treated it with hydrogen peroxide to keep it "Nordic" looking), blue eyes, and "soft" features may have been appealing to some of his young colleagues, who certainly were homosexual,[138] but we do not know if any of them approached him.

From his teenage years into old age, he was always attracted to young and teenage girls more than any other, feeling that they were still "unspoiled" sexually and by the ravages of time.[139] He also exaggerated this interest to his mother, whenever she tried to push him into marrying someone that she had chosen for him; Rose always backed off, unsettled by his deviance.[140] His strong sense of sexuality would be a driving force in his creative work. Pain coexisted with pleasure, struggle and sorrow with success and happiness. If his life did not have enough pain, he would bring more upon himself, hence his masochism. Lust was superior to love, he said, because it brought freedom.[141]

He was deeply devoted to the "northern peoples" of Europe, and was imbued with a racism that his mother's family had long carried. He harbored anti-Jewish sentiments in a German climate where such feelings were openly acceptable, though he would also later have Jewish friends and admire the works of Jewish composers such as Ernest Bloch, George Gershwin,[142] and Ravel.

In addition to learning several other languages, he was making an effort to "purify" English by dropping the use of words derived from Romance languages, particularly Latin and Greek, and replacing them with Germanic constructs, restoring English to how he believed it should have sounded, if not for the Battle of Hastings and Norman cultural impositions from 1066 onward. He called this new tongue "Blue-eyed English," and even composed a dictionary of the terms he invented. These include some remarkable and delightful creations, such as "tonery" (music), "past-lore" (history), "tone work" (musical composition), "birth-giver" (parent), "cruel-hood-worship" (sadism), and "fightwinsome" (successful). Needless to say this amazingly eccentric preoccupation failed to become popular, but it shows another of the many facets of his ingenious mind, or perhaps we should say, the "over-soul of a tone-wright."[143]

Despite his initial embrace of Germany, he found himself on the receiving end of German scorn. He was Australian, and thus by association English, and he saw that some students, as well as those older than him, were disdainful toward him. This realization caused further disillusionment, and may have made the decision to move to London that much easier. In the future, he would exclude Germany from his loves, focusing instead on the superiority of the British, the Dutch, and the Scandinavians, who were the only groups he felt were capable of performing his music properly.[144] In 1937, with a new war potentially looming, he noted that he could stand to see England lose to the Scandinavians, but not to the "swinish" Germans.[145] As late as 1958, he wrote with vitriol against all Europeans, save these northern cultures and nations.[146]

Whatever dark urges drove him, it is important to note that in his dealings with others, he was a man of great integrity and charity (such as offering Sharp the greater portion of his *Country Gardens* royalties). He was remarkably kind to those he loved. He did not drink or smoke, and was strongly in favor of equality for women. He was very generous with his money, assisting those in need, especially up-and-coming composers and musicians whose work he thought deserved greater attention.[147] He gave money to his extended family in Australia, who took advantage of his gifts on more than one occasion.[148] Despite his devotion to the idea that races should not mix,[149] he had African-American students in the United States, and saw to it that one such student and her family were provided for during a period of racial tension in 1919, when they feared to leave their home.[150] He worked very hard to preserve accurately the folk music he collected, always treating singers with the utmost dignity and respect. Bird suggests that some of these behaviors were a part of his masochism; he knew that his kindnesses would not always be repaid, and this was hurtful, therefore desirable.[151] By embracing his darker side fully, he was able to channel his disturbing feelings into his art.

The greatest shock to his life came in 1922. By then, Rose was in an advanced state of mental deterioration due to her illness, and though Grainger had more than enough wealth to care for her, he could not control her actions. She had manipulated him for so long (including feigning death or threatening suicide)[152] that he was not prepared for what happened. After confronting an accusation of incest with her son by an admirer of Grainger's in April, Rose lost control. She sent a letter to him (he was then on tour on the West Coast) on April 29, telling him that she could not think properly and asking if he knew of any such rumors about "improper love." She concocted a reason to travel down to New York, saying that she needed to make phone calls from the office of Antonia Sawyer (Grainger's manager) in the Aeolian Building. Once there, she feigned illness, asking for a drink. When the office was empty, she jumped out of the window. The office was on the 18th floor, and she fell to the rooftop of another building, 14 stories lower. She was still alive when she was discovered, but died before she could be moved.[153] Grainger received the news after a Los Angeles concert, and was devastated, having lost the woman who he would declare soon after had been like God to him as a child.[154]

He dealt with his grief by taking an extended trip to Denmark (his first trip back to Europe in eight years), where he engaged in collecting folk songs with Evald Tang Kristensen, the venerable collector who was then nearly 80 years old. Kristensen had long been interested in the accurate preservation of Danish folk songs, and probably influenced Grainger's methods when the latter discovered his work in 1906. Traveling through Jutland with Grainger's recording equipment, they gathered 80 melodies in August 1922.[155] He made another trip in 1925, collecting more than 90 additional tunes. A third trip in 1927 was less successful. Grainger found a kindred spirit in Kristensen, who had likewise been ostracized by the establishment for his use of the phonograph, and the honest notating of the songs that he found. In Denmark, as in England, there was a desire to present such pieces as they "should" be. Grainger felt that these Danish melodies might well represent a survival of medieval songs, and deserved to be recorded in an honest way.[156] When the two of them presented their findings in Copenhagen, proving that Kristensen's notations from 1860 were accurate, the other collectors simply declared that the singers had sung the tunes incorrectly, or did not remember them properly; it was hopeless.[157]

After these trips, he did no more collecting, but he retained a keen interest in folk traditions around the world, especially those in Oceana, transcribing Javanese and Balinese pieces, as well as African and Chinese songs.[158] He took an active interest in the cultures from which these songs came, extending to collecting folk art and learning skills such as Polynesian beadwork. As Tall notes: "He was one of the first true ethnologists to look beyond the surface sheen to the very soul of the people by taking part in their lives. One of the stated aims of his museum in Melbourne is as a centre for ethnic study in the Pacific."[159]

Perhaps in another response to his mother's death, he chose to become a vegetarian in 1924. However, this being a "Graingerism," it could not be without its own unique eccentricities. He swore off meat, but he disliked vegetables, which would seem to present a fairly significant problem. His solution was a rather unhealthy diet of nuts, rice, fruit, bread, cheese, cake, and ice cream.[160] Yet he thrived on it; throughout his life he maintained his physical stamina, and was able to keep his weight at a constant number for decades.[161]

He continued to let stories of his odd behaviors circulate, seeing them as good publicity. Everything from tales of his walks and runs between concert venues, to sleeping under the piano at said venues before a show, to the story that he once put on several layers of clothing and immersed himself in a bath tub in order to wash them all; these made him more endearing in the public eye.[162] As late as 1950, Robert Lewis Taylor noted, "Whenever possible, he hikes to his concert appearances, wearing run-down khaki clothing and carrying a rucksack. He is occasionally arrested for vagrancy, and he is often bitten by dogs, which seem to pick on him."[163] Further, he noted Grainger still wore the same concert suit he had bought in 1909,[164] if nothing else, a testament to his efforts to maintain his weight.

Though he still disliked having to focus so much on being a concert pianist, he was making enormous amounts of money for doing so, and from royalties. At one point in 1925, he was earning as much as $5,000 per week,[165] a staggering amount that in today's money would be equal to that of a top-selling pop star. He always lived frugally, however, buying cheap clothes, taking inexpensive trains (in second class), and donating left-over travel money to charity.[166]

In 1927, he met and fell in love with a Swedish artist, Ella Viola Ström, while returning from New Zealand to North America. She was already involved with someone, but she received news of his death when the ship reached Vancouver. Without his mother's influence and disapproval, he was finally able to step out from her shadow and make his own decisions on matters of the heart. He stayed with Ella at her home in Pevensey Bay (on the south coast of Sussex) in the summer of 1927, and proposed to her in October of the same year; she accepted.[167] His love for her was genuine, but his love for the whip had not diminished. It seems that Ella was an obliging, if not entirely enthusiastic, spouse in regards to her participation in his masochistic fantasy life, though she did leave him briefly on more than one occasion because of his tastes.[168] Their wedding on August 9, 1928, was a monumental public display, taking place during a concert in which he performed at the Hollywood Bowl (and which included the première of a piece he had written for her), in front of an audience of more than 22,000 people and a full orchestra and choir. A story later arose that Ella was completely overwhelmed, having assumed that the Hollywood Bowl was a small venue, however this is not true, as Brian Allison notes: "The wedding was announced the day before in the *Los Angeles Evening Express* in a cartoon and an article, and the premiere of *To a Nordic Princess* was also mentioned in the article."[169]

When the Depression hit, Grainger was grateful to have been offered a teaching position at New York University, which gave him a welcome income at a time when public performances were an uncertain and unreliable way of making a living.[170] Since he spent so much of his vast wealth on others, he could not rely on his savings to live on. He was able to travel in 1931 to England, where he attended a music festival organized by Arnold Dolmetsch that featured early music, in which he was very interested. The two formed a friendship that would last until Dolmetsch's death in 1940.[171] Grainger worked on an edition of Dolmetsch's 16th and 17th-century consort music in the years after he died.[172]

In 1932, the Benedictine monk Don Anselm Hughes toured the United States, lecturing on Gregorian chant. Grainger was very interested in his medieval music knowledge, and the two began a great friendship, despite the difference in their ideologies. They planned an edition of medieval pieces for choirs and chamber ensembles, titled *English Gothic Music*, and subsequently published by Schirmer.[173]

On the other end of the spectrum, he was impressed by atonal experiments (though he did not compose in that idiom himself), and was very fond of jazz, though many of his colleagues disliked it. He once invited Duke Ellington and his whole band for a performance at one of his university lectures, proclaiming him to be one of the three greatest composers of all time, along with Bach and Delius![174]

In 1932, while in Scandinavia, he and Ella put together their ideas for a Grainger museum, or "past-hoard-house," to use his preferred Anglo-Saxon term. He decided that it had to be built in Melbourne, despite the obvious expense of transporting so many items to the other side of the world. Grainger felt nostalgic for his home country and probably intended to return there eventually, though this was always thwarted by his professional commitments in America[175]; as early as about 1920, a trip to Barstow in California reminded him of the Australian outback and he was determined to paint the desert landscape.[176] The Melbourne museum would contain a miscellany of all things: letters, paintings, books, music, and instruments, both relating to him and otherwise.[177] He also wanted to donate some of his flagellation equipment and clothing, though this was obviously less well-received.

In 1937, he put out a work that many consider his masterpiece, a setting of six English folk songs for the American Bandmasters Association in a suite he called *Lincolnshire Posy*. He had collected the tunes in Lincolnshire as far back as 1905–06; using five of these, and one borrowed from Lucy Broadwood, he dedicated the work to those folk singers from whom he had received these treasures. While public taste for such things (especially in America) had changed dramatically by the 1930s, this work has remained a staple of band repertoire ever since, being especially popular in schools.[178]

The years of World War II prevented him from touring abroad extensively, and he focused instead on concerts in America, especially those for the war effort, including at hospitals and performances for the military. This kept him extremely busy, and he noted afterward that he probably spent only a few nights a month in a real bed; the other nights were spent sleeping on trains and in stations while traveling to his next destination. When Hughes was stranded in America in 1939 due to the dangers of wartime passenger ships going to and from England, Grainger offered him a place to stay in his own home.[179]

Despite his ongoing touring, he was able to devote some attention to his old folk song collections. In the summer of 1940, he assisted in the transfer of his recorded folk song cylinders to the more permanent format of acetate recordings, and these were then deposited at the Library of Congress. The collection included English, Danish, Maori, and Polynesian folk songs.[180]

However, Grainger feared that the Germans might try to invade the East Coast of the United States, and so he signed a lease for an apartment in Springfield, Missouri, where he and Ella moved in November 1940. The location proved to be useful as a central location for his tours, and more importantly, gave him a greater sense of security, especially after the Japanese bombing of Pearl Harbor in December 1941, bringing a threat to the West Coast. Indeed, he believed that both coasts were in danger of enemy invasion and that the safest place to be was in the middle of the country.[181] He and Ella managed through the war years, during which time he continued to try to have his own works published (often with little success), and took on new causes, such as championing the work of George Gershwin and working to preserve barbershop music and harmony.[182] He always wanted to go into semi-retirement as a concert pianist, and focus on these kinds of projects, as well as his own musical experimentation.

By 1946, he began to collaborate with the military band at West Point Academy, whose skill greatly impressed him, and they were eager to perform his works, though he continued to doubt his own self-worth as a composer, feeling that many of his pieces were poor and not worth anyone's time. It was for this reason that he also rejected offers of honorary doctorates, and the possibility of taking the chair of the music department in Adelaide in 1947.[183] His shift in focus on the types of venues in which he played meant that he now earned very little from his concerts, in sharp contrast to the ridiculously large amounts he had earned during the 1920s. He preferred to play his own original music in exchange for little or no money, rather than play others' music for high fees.[184] He was further despaired to see some of his published music going out of print, because it did not sell well enough.[185]

By the age of 65, he began to notice the first signs of declining health. He had always relied on his tremendous stamina and physical prowess, but now was feeling the aches and pains of growing older, and his stomach bothered him,[186] a possible early sign of the more serious illness that would develop later. By 1949, he visited a doctor near his New York home, complaining of abdominal pains. Several small growths were identified, and the doctor recommended that they be removed. Grainger ignored his advice, opting instead for a non-surgical approach with a quack doctor in New York City, a mistake that came back to haunt him.[187]

In the 1950s, he experimented intensively with his long-cherished concept of Free Music, music produced by machines that was too complex for humans to make, thus freeing music "from the tyranny of the performer."[188] He devised several such machines that were not nearly as high-tech as one might expect for such a project. Indeed, Ella once described how they would go out in the evening dressed very well, so as not to arouse suspicion while they looked through garbage cans and trash heaps for pieces of metal and wood to use in his devices.[189] Grainger was also interested in the early experiments in electronic music, but not for its own sake; rather, he believed that a machine should be specifically constructed for the piece that the composer intended. His interest in new music and electric instruments led him to discover the new genre of rock and roll, which he rather surprisingly enjoyed.[190]

9. Percy Grainger (1882–1961)   215

He continued with a fairly rigorous concert schedule, despite his ever-present protests about wanting to bring it to an end, and this took a great toll on his health during the 1950s, but his focus continued to be on small venues such as high school gymnasiums and social clubs, a drastic contrast for a man who had played at the major concert halls of Europe and before royalty and presidents. He was happy with this, however, since he had never enjoyed the limelight. He remarked in 1954: "I dislike all fame, including my own. It was one of the many delightfulnesses of my wife, when I met her on the 'Aorangi' in 1926, that she didn't know who I was."[191]

By 1953, he was diagnosed with prostate cancer, and an operation was not fully successful in stopping its spread, so he spent further time in the Mayo Clinic from 1954. He had recovered sufficiently to make another trip to Australia by 1955, and in September, he and Ella sailed for what would be a nine-month stay. Instead of nostalgia and good experiences, however, he found that his home country was changing rapidly in the post-war years, and morphing into something that he no longer recognized or liked. He had troubles with his museum, and found that it was being badly kept, while at the same time, it was not always receiving items sent to it due to strict Australian customs regulations.[192] Perhaps as some act of defiance, he left a package with a bank in Melbourne, with instructions that it not be opened until ten years after his death. It contained an essay on his sexual attitudes, with accompanying photographs.[193]

He was disillusioned with his apparent rejection by the musical establishment, noting in 1954 how, despite his many innovations, he received no credit:

> In my musical life [...] I have always met with considerable hostility or opposition. [...] No major composition of mine has ever been performed in any capitol of the world [...] unless I financed the performance myself. In spite of the fact that I have provably invented most of the formulas of modern music used by Schoenberg, Cyril Scott, Stravinsky, Gershwin [...] I have yet to ever see my name mentioned in connection with any of these innovations.[194]

He never escaped from Rose's grip. On July 3, 1957, he noted: "Beloved mother would have been 95 today. I have felt the tragic influence of her death more in this year 1957 than in any other year."[195] Even as an elderly man, her abuse and the Stockholm Syndrome–like effects it had induced in him still resonated. He would always believe that whatever genius and talent he might possess, it was a result of her upbringing.[196] Rose had written in 1916 that he was a "glorious work of art [...] I feel his genius is sacred to me and the world."[197]

His last years were spent with additional trips to Europe, including England and Scandinavia, and he still made long train journeys to perform his music across America; he never wanted to fly, owing to a belief that aircraft were limited and thus probably unsafe. He continued working into 1960, despite declining health. His last performance was in April 1960 at Dartmouth College, and perhaps fittingly, he also gave a talk titled "The Influence of Folksong on Art Music."[198]

After this, he deteriorated over the next several months as cancer began to win the war against him, finally entering a hospital in White Plains from which he would not emerge. On February 20, 1961, he died of abdominal cancer in the presence of Ella, his last words to her being, "you're the only one I like."[199] He was 78 years old. In spite of his atheism, and his request that no grand ceremony be held in his honor, there was a memorial in White Plains, and then his body was flown to Australia, where an Anglican service laid him to rest in Adelaide, presumably at the request of some family members.[200]

Grainger's strange and often tragic life leaves more questions than answers. He believed that true happiness would be found in technology, amorality, and the discarding of religion.[201] He often denigrated his music despite wanting to be accepted as a serious composer, he suffered from severe stage fright, but performed constantly. He found pleasure and love through pain, he submitted to his mentally unbalanced mother's will during their whole life together, and he never escaped his reputation as a gifted pianist, despite wanting to do so. Yet his work with English folk music was unprecedented for its time, bringing to the practice of collecting a serious ethnomusicologist's approach that was little accepted by his peers, in both England and Denmark. He was a real champion for a true concept of "world music" and never looked down on his singers. Though much of his original music is unknown today, his folk song settings are still highly regarded, and his eccentricities only add to his reputation.

Conclusion

From the later Victorian age until the Second World War, England underwent a tremendous change in the quality and quantity of its classical music output. Was this a renaissance, a true rebirth after a long stagnation since Purcell's time, or was it a more complex combination of factors (some not always benign) that allowed for a resurgence of musical activity in a controlled environment? Scholars on both sides and no sides continue to debate. Undoubtedly, there was an attempt at not just reviving or recreating, but of inventing a new tradition for Britain by rescuing traditional music from oblivion and repackaging it to the masses. Many composers embraced this practice, but many others rejected it, even showing hostility to the idea.

The composers surveyed in this book shared among them some unusual things in common. Several had difficult or controlling mothers (Heseltine, Finzi, and especially Grainger, while Butterworth's father was not especially accepting of his choices); a number of them adored cats (Vaughan Williams,[1] Finzi, and Heseltine); several of them adopted socialist politics in various degrees at certain times in their lives (Sharp, Vaughan Williams, Holst, and Finzi); all of them held agnosticism or atheism as their general outlook, despite writing religious works. Vaughan Williams and Finzi only flew for the first time late in their lives, while Grainger never wanted to fly, distrusting it as a method of transportation. Yet he embraced new music and technologies enthusiastically.

Gloucestershire was an important region for several composers, whether they were born there, lived there, or used a love of its countryside to spur their musical creativity.[2] A center for the English Arts and Crafts Movement, the county also served as an ideal inspiration for the rural imagery of the pastoral style and folk song revival. To this day, the Cotswolds have a legendary trapped-in-time quality, its famous villages being postcard-perfect snapshots of a lost rural golden age. They appear somehow magically preserved in the modern world and ready to welcome eager tourists seeking to escape for a brief time into nostalgia. These stone dwellings and their surrounding rolling hills seem to cry out for a soundtrack to complete the romance, and the music of these composers is a perfect fit in the imaginations of many music-lovers.

We might ask how much of this is merely manufactured tradition; do these symphonic folksongs and rhapsodies on early music really communicate anything authentically "English," or is this merely wishful thinking? Can someone who has never seen a photograph of the hills of Gloucestershire or the flat landscape of Norfolk listen to relevant pieces inspired by those locations and truly feel that they have understood the essence of the place? George Bernard Shaw one famously quipped, "Grieg's music does not remind me of Norway, perhaps because I have never been there."[3]

Hughes and Stradling see this as proof of a "premeditated structure of receptivity,"[4] that is, one must already be prepared with some knowledge of a place before being presented with the argument that a given piece of music represents said place. It is much easier to accept that Vaughan Williams' *Norfolk Rhapsodies* accurately evoke that region if one is told that they do so and already believes this before hearing them.

This is not a phenomenon limited to Europe. Modern listeners have heard many musical works, passages, and scales which are intended to represent certain regions of the world; China and the Middle East are obvious examples. Most who hear these melodies will not have traveled to those countries, but will have been exposed to the motifs (some would say clichés) via film, television, or indeed, works of music written to evoke the spirit of place. Whether such works accurately portray the music or the culture of these areas might never be questioned, if there is a collective agreement among those who passively listen and accept such compositions, which is common. This can certainly be to the detriment of understanding a place or a culture, if a convenient musical place-holder stands in to represent that culture as a whole. The Middle Eastern musical scale, *maqam hijaz*, for example, is used extensively and for some, frustratingly, as a representation of all Middle Eastern music and imagery, whether in film soundtracks, orchestral music, or popular songs. However, there are at least 20 other *maqamat* (scales) commonly played by Middle Eastern musicians, many of which would sound strange to Western ears, but which are no less representative of the region and its history, and meaningful to its people. Similarly, the pentatonic (five-note) scale had become, to Western ears, representative of all Chinese music, owing to its popularity in traditional repertoire.

It is perhaps best then, to say that so much of this music, which was at least in part a product of the desire to create a national English style, represents what these regions, visions, eras, folk songs, and experiences meant to the composers in question. That many others were equally attracted to their ideas and shared in the belief that these new works were uniquely English demonstrates a wide-spread need for a revived cultural nationalism in the days of a fading empire. The movement was the right one at the right time, even though it was not embraced by all. That yearning was both strengthened and damaged by the horrors of World War I, which swept away the Edwardian summer with a winter of suffering and death unlike any that had been witnessed before. In the wake of this epochal destruction of a generation, the pastoral in the arts became darker, a sad yearning for things lost forever, and a meditation on the passage of time and the inevitability of death.

As the clouds of war gathered again in the 1930s, the innocence of revived folk songs and Edwardian country days out seemed increasingly irrelevant to many. However, even in those times, many saw Vaughan Williams' music in particular as a bastion of traditional English values, and his work for patriotic films and other war-related material reinforced this. In recent decades, his music has become ever more popular, and for countless listeners, it still evokes quintessentially English sounds and emotions; this no doubt would have delighted him.

Many of the composers in this book have had their works grow in popularity in recent decades, especially in Britain. This may well indicate not only a greater recognition of their collective musical genius, but may also reveal something about contemporary views on society, history, and cultural identity. Perhaps some listeners are simply reveling in nostalgia, as their predecessors did at the beginning of the century; they may yearn for an imagined better age of greater simplicity and rural values, one that is resistant to change. Others, however, may see a continuity of tradition, that old can become new again and have relevance in any era. The huge rise in popularity of early music in Europe, the United States, and around the world since the 1950s is proof that the past need not seem so distant, and that music is a most effective means of bringing it into the present day.

Likewise, the innovations of contemporary English folk music, beginning with the second folk revival, show how traditions can be molded into new forms over time. Traditional folk songs have been combined with rock, jazz, and other genres, and have been arranged in ways wholly unlike their original forms. Folk music has been reimagined for a new age, and though it is not the same as the tunes that collectors found when they wandered the English countryside a century ago, it has been recreated as something relevant for our time. This blending of something old with something new continues the practices begun by those composers, who first sat enthralled as an older generation of traditional singers shared the wealth of their communities. That wealth was enthusiastically taken up by an Edwardian society on the verge of the modern world, with all of its horrors and drastic changes, as a way to hold onto something that seemed uniquely English. The hope for that connection still survives today.

Appendix A
A.E. Housman (1859–1936)

Many English composers of the early 20th century saw the poetry of A.E. Housman as almost ideal for setting to music. A scholar of Greek and Latin at Cambridge, he was also a gifted poet in the English language. His words evoked a mythic, idealized, rural England, and stood out to composers seeking that form of inspiration. As John Quinlan has noted: "The brevity of the lines, their essential Englishness, their pastoral atmosphere, their rhythm, and their simple spontaneity of feeling were contributing factors,"[1] for such composers.[2] Wilfrid Mellers observes that he "created pseudo-folk ballads set in a mythical Shropshire countryside, making a highly artificial deployment of simple ballad forms to deal with universal themes of death, mutability and a world lost."[3]

A reclusive man, he was tormented by conflicts in his personal life, arising from an unrequited homosexual attraction, and the societal oppression that forced him to keep such feelings secret. His sadness expresses itself in various poems, however, even if readers at the time were unaware of the hidden meanings. He is most famous for his collection, *A Shropshire Lad*, which, as we have seen, was mined for content by a large number of composers.

As a poet, he was initially very obliging of new offers of musical settings, noting to his publisher in 1907: "I always give my consent to all composers, in the hope of becoming immortal somehow."[4] This seemingly amiable relationship would sour somewhat in later years, when he discovered that Vaughan Williams had omitted two verses from his setting of the poem "Is My Team Plowing?" Vaughan Williams felt, with some condescension, that they were poorly written, and that Housman should be grateful that he had excised them.[5] Housman, however, was not happy, retorting that he wondered how Vaughan Williams would feel if he cut out two bars of his music. He also disliked some of the recordings that he heard of the settings,[6] admitting that he knew little about music and saying that it "meant nothing to him."[7] He would not allow his poems to be reprinted in concert programs,[8] and did not want composers giving their own new titles to his works.[9] Further, he objected to both artists and composers adding their interpretations to his words, saying, "The trouble with book-illustrators, as with composers who set poems to music, is not merely that they are completely wrapped up in their own art and their precious selves, and regard the author merely as a peg to hang things on, but that they seem to have less than ordinary human allowance of sense and feeling."[10]

Regardless of these antagonistic attitudes, composers of the era were eager to set his poems. By the early 1940s, more than 50 of his works had been used in more than 100 song-settings.[11] Their appeal is obvious, and the short structure makes them ideal for adaptation for voice and piano (among other possibilities). His poems were in many ways idealized visions, six of them having been composed before he had even seen the Shropshire countryside. Richard Graves notes that his depiction of the region, "is largely an imaginary land: and the real place-names were often used for romantic colouring rather than because Housman had a particular feeling for a real place."[12] There is also a deep awareness of the passing of time, the fleeting nature of youth, of death, and the extinguishing of young lives in tragic circumstances, particularly in war. In the aftermath of World War I, these verses attained a new poignancy.

Appendix B
Online Resources—
Societies and Other Organizations

There are numerous societies devoted to the music, composers, dances, and other traditions of this period, as well as publishers, record labels, and libraries. The following is a list of websites for some of the most relevant to this book. All contain a great amount of extra information, and are good places for additional resources, such as lists of composers' works, updated discographies, photographs, and musical samples and recommendations. Many offer memberships, and have journals and other resources. As of this writing (October 2015), there is no society devoted to George Butterworth, a situation that needs to be rectified.

Chapter 1

The Delius Society: http://www.delius.org.uk
The Elgar Society: http://www.elgar.org
The Stanford Society: http://www.thestanfordsociety.org

Chapter 2

Country Dance and Song Society (USA): http://www.cdss.org
Cecil Sharp House: http://www.cecilsharphouse.org
English Folk Dance and Song Society: http://www.efdss.org
Mary Neal: An Undertold Story: http://www.maryneal.org
Vaughan Williams Memorial Library: http://www.vwml.org

Chapter 3

Ralph Vaughan Williams Society: http://www.rvwsociety.com
RVW Trust: http://www.rvwtrust.org.uk
Vaughan Williams Charitable Trust: http://www.vwct.org.uk

Chapter 4

The Gustav Holst Web Site: http://www.gustavholst.info
Holst Archive at the Britten-Pears Foundation: http://www.brittenpears.org/page.php?pageid=527
Holst Birthplace Museum: http://www.holstmuseum.org.uk

Chapter 6

The Worldwide Moeran Database: http://www.moeran.net

Chapter 7

Peter Warlock Society: http://www.peterwarlock.org; see also: http://www.englishmusicfestival.org.uk/composer-organisations/peter-warlock.html

Chapter 8

Gerald Finzi Official Site: http://www.geraldfinzi.com
Gerald Finzi Trust: http://www.geraldfinzi.org
Finzi Friends: http://www.finzifriends.org.uk

Chapter 9

Grainger Museum, University of Melbourne: http://www.grainger.unimelb.edu.au
International Percy Grainger Society: http://www.percygrainger.org
Percy Grainger Society (UK): http://www.percygrainger.org.uk

Miscellaneous

Arts & Crafts Museum at Cheltenham Art Gallery and Museum: http://www.artsandcraftsmuseum.org.uk; see also: http://www.artsandcraftsmuseum.org.uk/Arts_and_Crafts_Movement/The_Arts_and_Crafts_Movement.aspx
British Music Society: http://www.britishmusicsociety.com
The Housman Society: http://www.housman-society.co.uk
The Thomas Hardy Association: http://thethomashardyassociation.org
War Composers: The Music of World War I: http://www.warcomposers.co.uk
William Morris Archive: http://www.morrissociety.org

Festivals, Labels and Publishers

Albion Music: http://www.albionmusic.com
Albion Records: http://www.albionrecords.org
Aldeburgh Music Festival: http://www.aldeburgh.co.uk

Online Resources—Societies and Other Organizations

EM Publishing: http://www.englishmusicfestival.org.uk/empublishing.html
EM Records: http://www.em-records.com
English Music Festival: http://www.englishmusicfestival.org.uk
Leith Hill Musical Festival: http://www.lhmf.org.uk
Three Choirs Festival: http://www.3choirs.org

Chapter Notes

Introduction

1. For further thoughts on "English" vs. "British," see Frank Howes, *The English Musical Renaissance* (London: Secker & Warburg, 1966), 21–23. Howes (1891–1974) was music critic with the *Times* from 1943 to 1960, and witnessed many of the musical changes, as well as being acquainted with the composers of the time. He also edited the *Journal of the English Folk Dance and Song Society* from 1927 to 1945, and was less interested in the experiments of English composers after World War II. As such, he is probably not as objective as one would wish in his assessment of the English Renaissance, but his observations are still valuable.
2. Calum MacDonald, "This Week's Composer, the English Spirit," *The Listener* 104 (September 1980): 347–48.
3. See Eric Saylor, "'It's Not Lambkins Frisking at All': English Pastoral Music and the Great War," *Musical Quarterly* 91:1–2 (2008): 39–40. Pastoral literature and art contain difficulties of definition as well, see Terry Gifford, *Pastoral: The New Critical Idiom* (London: Routledge, 1999), 1–8; Peter Marinelli, *Pastoral: The Critical Idiom*, John D. Jump, general ed. (London: Methuen & Co., 1971), 8–9; and Saylor, "Not Lambkins Frisking," 41–44. For a detailed background to the concept of the pastoral in music in general, and specifically in English culture, see Paul Andrew Hopwood, "Frank Bridge and the English Pastoral Tradition." Ph.D. thesis, University of Western Australia, 2007, 15–111. For a study comparing similar ideals in Vaughan Williams and J.R.R. Tolkien, see Gregory Martin, "'Thro Albions Pleasant Land': The 20th-Century English Musical Renaissance, J.R.R. Tolkien, and Reassessing Englishness," a piano lecture recital for Indiana University, 2007, available in PDF download from the Gerald Finzi Trust website: http://www.geraldfinzi.org/downloads/02-finzitrust/scholarship_reports/2007_GregoryMartin.pdf, accessed January 28, 2015. Like Vaughan Williams, Tolkien was deeply affected by the war, and lost many of his friends. It was inevitable that this would be reflected in *The Lord of the Rings*.
4. Saylor, "Not Lambkins Frisking," 40.
5. *Ibid.*, 40–41, and 43–44.
6. *Ibid.*, 44. See also Martin, "Thro Albions Pleasant Land," 1–2.
7. Martin, in "Thro Albions Pleasant Land," notes the fixation with darkness and winter in many of the works (including those for Christmas), as well as Tolkien's inspiration from Saxon and Viking sources, whose cultures and literature frequently allude to winter settings. Death and the passage of time are ancient preoccupations in England, see 7–8.
8. Daniel M. Grimley, "Landscape and Distance: Vaughan Williams, Modernism and the Symphonic Pastoral," *British Music and Modernism, 1895–1960*, Matthew Riley, ed. (Farnham, UK: Ashgate, 2010), 160.
9. Saylor, "Not Lambkins Frisking," 54.
10. For the more detailed list, see Lewis Foreman, "National Musical Character: Intrinsic or Acquired?" *Music and Nationalism in 20th-Century Great Britain and Finland*, Tomi Mäkelä, ed. (Hamburg: von Bockel Verlag, 1997), 75.
11. *Ibid.*, 80.
12. Giles Auty, "An Art of Our Own," *The Spectator* (May 30, 1987): 33.
13. Em Marshall, *Music in the Landscape* (London: Robert Hale, 2011). This is a richly illustrated volume that surveys composers from the late Victorian era and into the 20th century, as well as key Scottish composers.
14. See also Foreman, "National Musical Character," 78–81.
15. For a good study, see John Lucas, *Ivor Gurney* (Tavistock, UK: Northcote House, 2001). For his struggles with mental illness, see Pamela Blevins, "Ivor Gurney 'There is Dreadful Hell within Me...,'" *Journal of the British Music Society* 19 (1997): 11–27.
16. *A Downland Suite* from 1932 is a fine example, inspired by his love of the Sussex Downs.
17. See his brief biography at the *John Ireland Trust* website: http://www.johnirelandtrust.org/biography.htm, accessed November 23, 2014. For a collection of recent studies, see *The John Ireland Companion*, Lewis Foreman, ed. (Woodbridge: Boydell, 2011).
18. For a study of Howells, see Paul Spicer, *Herbert Howells* (Bridgend, UK: Seren, 1998).

19. Such as his string quartet, *In Gloucestershire*, the first version of which was lost in 1916, when he left it on a train. He re-created the piece to an extent in the 1920s, though it was certainly not a slavish imitation of Vaughan Williams or the folk song style by then. For a short biography, see Paul Andrews, "Howells, Herbert," *Grove Music Online*, Oxford Music Online. Oxford University Press: http://www.oxfordmusiconline.com/subscriber/article/grove/music/13436, accessed November 11, 2014. See also John France, "Herbert Howells: String Quartet in Gloucestershire," *British Classical Music: The Land of Lost Content*: http://land-ofllostcontent.blogspot.com/2009/08/herbert-howells-string-quartet-in.html, accessed November 11, 2014.

20. These include: Frances Allitsen (1848–1912), Dora Bright (1863–1951), Rosalind Ellicott (1857–1924), Liza Lehmann (1862–1918), Adela Maddison (1866–1929), and Maude Valerie White (1855–1937), all of whom also have entries in *Grove's Dictionary*. See Sophie Fuller, "Women Composers during the British Musical Renaissance, 1880–1918," 2 Vols., Ph.D. thesis, University of London, King's College, 1998, available online at the King's College, London website: https://kclpure.kcl.ac.uk/portal/files/2927686/263601.pdf, accessed January 22, 2014. See also Fuller, *The Pandora Guide to Women Composers: Britain and the United States, 1629–Present* (London and San Francisco: Pandora, 1994).

21. Paula Gillett, *Musical Women in England, 1870–1914: "Encroaching on All Man's Privileges"* (New York: St. Martin's Press, 2000).

22. We will discuss both more in chapter 2.

23. See chapter 4.

24. See chapter 3.

25. See chapter 1. Britten did help Holst's daughter, Imogen, in her efforts to promote her father's music, especially when she worked as his assistant from 1952 to 1964.

26. In Butterworth's case, this is a surprising oversight that needs to be remedied, despite his short life and small output.

Chapter 1

1. In this chapter when the term "English Musical Renaissance" appears, the word "renaissance" is capitalized, as it also is when it appears so in quotes from others. The word "renaissance" on its own, used as a general term (and not referring to the 15th and 16th centuries), is not capitalized.

2. For a summary, see Meirion Hughes and Robert Stradling, *The English Musical Renaissance, 1840–1940: Constructing a National Music*, 2nd edition (Manchester and New York: Manchester University Press, 1993, 2001), 45.

3. Joseph Bennet, *Daily Telegraph*, September 4, 1882. For further information, see Hughes and Stradling, *Renaissance*, 42–43. Jeremy Dibble, in "Parry, Stanford and Vaughan Williams: The Creation of a Tradition," asserts that the symphonies of Parry and Stanford, "have already demonstrated that Britain enjoyed a symphonic tradition well before the turn of the century, and that Elgar and Vaughan Williams were not the prime-movers but participants within it." *Ralph Vaughan Williams in Perspective*, Lewis Foreman, ed. (London: Albion Music for the Vaughan Williams Society, 1998), 41. See also 47.

4. J.A. Fuller Maitland, *English Music in the XIXth Century* (London: Grant Richards, New York: E.P. Dutton, 1902), available online at Archive: https://archive.org/details/englishmusicinxi00full, accessed November 5, 2014.

5. Frank Howes, *The English Musical Renaissance* (London: Secker & Warburg, 1966).

6. Peter J. Pirie, *The English Musical Renaissance* (New York: St. Martin's Press, 1979). This work focuses on the period after 1900, all the way through the late 1970s. It has come in for some criticism for many of its assumptions about the "progress of history" in composition, among other weaknesses. See for example, the excellent analysis of the book by Steve Schwartz at: http://www.classical.net/music/books/reviews/0312254350a.php, accessed November 2, 2014.

7. Michael Trend, *The Music Makers: the English Musical Renaissance from Elgar to Britten* (London: Weidenfeld and Nicolson, 1985).

8. See Hughes and Stradling, *Renaissance*, xv–xvi. We will also examine this argument as a component of the folk revival in England in the next chapter. Hughes and Stradling offer the example of composer Rutland Boughton, who in 1909, wrote an essay attacking the musical establishment for supporting some composers while ignoring others, as an example that many at the time were aware of unfair treatment, see *The English Musical Renaissance*, 228–29. Boughton was also an early critic of folk song settings, seeing them merely as appropriation of working-class songs for upper-class entertainment, see 197.

9. Hughes and Stradling, *Renaissance*. The authors note in their postlude to the second edition (at 290–97) that many British reviewers did not take kindly to their ideas, including a reviewer for the *Times* who suggested that the book should be "pulped" as a service to the nation! See 292. See also Hughes, *The English Musical Renaissance and the Press, 1850–1914: Watchmen of Music* (Aldershot: Ashgate, 2002), which discusses the role of the Victorian and Edwardian Press in creating the idea of a musical renaissance in England.

10. See, for example, Julian Onderdonk's review, which questions a number of the book's premises, in the Music Library Association's *Notes*, Second Series 52:1: 63–66. We will return to Onderdonk's assessment later in the chapter. See also the review by Mike Smith in *Tempo*, New Series 187 (1993): 27–28. He bluntly states, "It is impossible to take the bulk of this book seriously," at 28. See also Alain Frogley, "'Getting its History Wrong': English Nationalism and the Reception of Ralph Vaughan Williams," *Music and Nationalism in 20th-Century Great Britain and Finland*, 147n5, where he states: "much of [their study] is profoundly flawed, merely skating the surface of many of the more important issues, peppering its argument with half-truths, and inexplicably failing to take account of some of the most pertinent recent research on British nationalism."

11. Siobhan McAndrew and Martin Everett, "Music as Collective Invention: A Social Network Analysis of

Composers," *Cultural Sociology* 9:1 (2015): 56 –80, see especially 60–64 and 75–77.

12. According to one account, he died after being locked outside by his angry wife on a cold November night and thereafter developing a chill and fever. There are other theories, however.

13. See Frogley, "'Getting its History Wrong,'" 150–51, and *n*14.

14. George Grove, who created *Grove's Dictionary of Music and Musicians*, would write as late as 1890: "There is something expressly English in Handel's characteristics. His size, his large appetite, his great writing, his domineering temper, his humour, his power of business, all are our own. [...] In fact he preeminently belongs to England [...]" in "Handel," *Chambers' Encyclopaedia: A Dictionary of Universal Knowledge*, David Patrick, ed., vol. 5 (London: William & Robert Chambers, 1890), 542.

15. However, Arne, composed *Rule Britannia!*, the immensely popular patriotic song that became a kind of second national anthem, and worked on a version of *God Save the King*, the actual anthem. Boyce was "rediscovered" in the 1920s and 30s, and his importance is now recognized. See Ian Bartlett, "Lambert, Finzi and the Anatomy of the Boyce Revival," *Musical Times* 144:1884 (2003): 54–59. For more on Finzi and his efforts at rescuing obscure 18th-century English composers, see chapter 8.

16. "Das Land ohne Musik," after an essay of that title by the German Oscar A.H. Schmitz, written in 1914. For a detailed background see Music Web: http://www.musicweb-international.com/dasland.htm, accessed March 18, 2015.

17. Hughes and Stradling, *Renaissance*, 3.

18. On the idea of importing music to Britain, see Howes, *Renaissance*, 19.

19. Vaughan Williams "Should Music be National?" *National Music and Other Essays* (Oxford: Oxford University Press, 1934, multiple reprints through 1987), 4–5.

20. See Hughes and Stradling, *Renaissance*, 4.

21. *Ibid.*, 5.

22. The 1872 edition, H.R. Haweis, *Music and Morals* (London: Longmans, Green and Co., 1872), is available at *Archive*: https://archive.org/details/musicandmorals00hawegoog, accessed November 3, 2014, and is the version we will use in this chapter.

23. Hughes and Stradling, *Renaissance*, 6.

24. For a brief summary, see the review in *The Century Magazine* (September 1872): 645–46, available online at: www.unz.org/Pub/Century-1872sep-00645a02?View=PDF, accessed November 3, 2014.

25. Haweis, *Music and Morals*, 122.

26. *Ibid.*, 553.

27. *Ibid.*, 553–54.

28. Hughes and Stradling, *Renaissance*, 7.

29. Given Beethoven's troubled life, alcoholism, and other failings, this romanticized view of his life and conduct seems humorously misinformed: "There is no stain upon his life. His integrity was spotless; his purity unblemished ; his generosity boundless; his affections deep and lasting ; his piety simple and sincere," Haweis, *Music and Morals*, 89–90.

30. *Ibid.*, 90–91.

31. For the Victorian love affair with Mendelssohn, see Hughes and Stradling, *Renaissance*, 8–17.

32. Such as the scandals of Percy Shelley, the womanizing of Schubert and Liszt, or the drug-fueled hedonism of Berlioz.

33. See Hughes and Stradling, *Renaissance*, 11–12 and 14–16.

34. For more on Three Choirs see its website: https://3choirs.org, accessed October 1, 2014. See Hughes and Stradling, *English Renaissance*, 35, for a discussion of the importance of music festivals in England.

35. See Howes, *Renaissance*, 20.

36. For more on Sullivan's deserved place as an "architect" of the renaissance, see *ibid.*, 20–21. See also Hughes and Stradling, *Renaissance*, 18. Fuller Maitland had no interest in Sullivan's work, see Hughes, *Renaissance and the Press*, 33–34.

37. For recent works on the Exhibition, see Jeffrey A. Auerbach, *The Great Exhibition of 1851: A Nation on Display* (Newhaven, CT: Yale University Press, 1999), and Michael Leapman, *The World for a Shilling: How the Great Exhibition of 1851 Shaped a Nation* (London: Headline, 2001).

38. For a good account, see Colin Eatock, "The Crystal Palace Concerts: Canon Formation and the English Musical Renaissance," *19th-Century Music* 34:1 (2010): 87–105.

39. *Ibid.*, 96.

40. For a detailed study, see David Wright, "The South Kensington Music Schools and the Development of the British Conservatoire in the Late Nineteenth Century," *Journal of the Royal Musical Association* 130:2 (2005): 236–82.

41. See Hughes and Stradling, *Renaissance*, 19–23 for a detailed study of how the new institution came into being.

42. *Ibid.*, 20–21.

43. Howes, *Renaissance*, 29–30.

44. For more on this and its relation to musical instruction, see Richard Sykes, "The Evolution of Englishness in the English Folksong Revival," *Folk Music Journal* 6:4 (1993): 462–63.

45. A modern edition is available (London: Penguin Books, 1990).

46. Published by Macmillan, and available online at Archive: https://archive.org/details/studiesinhistor01pategoog, accessed November 3, 2014.

47. Hughes and Stradling, *Renaissance*, 22 and 43.

48. Hughes and Stradling suggest that this may have been an important influence on Cole's push for his Training School, see *ibid.*, 22–23.

49. Cyril Ehrlich, *The Music Profession in Britain since the Eighteenth Century* (Oxford: Clarendon Press, 1985), 238. For more on general nationalism in the English identity, see *Englishness: Politics and Culture* (1880–1920), Robert Colls and Philip Dodd, eds. (Dover, NH: Croon Helm, 1986).

50. See Sykes, "The Evolution of Englishness," 464.

51. Hughes and Stradling, 23.

52. See *ibid.*, 26–31 for more on Grove's fundraising activities.

53. He designed lighthouses, among other structures.

54. See Howes, *Renaissance*, 48–49, for more

information. For a more detailed biography of Grove, see, appropriately enough, Grove Online: C.L. Graves and Percy M. Young, "Grove, Sir George," *Grove Music Online*. Oxford Music Online. Oxford University Press: http://www.oxfordmusiconline.com/subscriber/article/grove/music/11847, accessed November 5, 2014.

55. Available in print version in most academic libraries, and online by subscription: www.oxfordmusiconline.com.

56. Hughes and Stradling, *Renaissance*, 24. See 23–26 for more on Grove and the *Dictionary*.

57. *Ibid.*, 26.

58. A bold statement to say the least, given the discouraging lack of surviving music in manuscripts from England before the later 14th century, in contrast to those from France, Spain, Italy, and Germany.

59. RCMA PAM 22, B 20, 1, "Music in England," *The Proposed Royal College of Music* (1882): 11–12.

60. The English, via the Anglo-Saxons have Germanic ancestry, of course, still reflected in the English language. The merger with French culture from 1066, however, fundamentally altered English identity, and art music in medieval England was most often imported from Normandy and France, for the entertainment of French-speaking rulers. It took centuries for Middle English to regain a literary standing (not fully realized until the works of Chaucer, Gower, and Langland in the 14th century), and surviving songs with music in medieval English are rare.

61. Hughes and Stradling, *Renaissance*, 28–29.

62. Grove, *The Royal College of Music* (London: Clowes, 1883), 17–18.

63. *Ibid.*, 41–42.

64. See Howes, *Renaissance*, 72. English nationalism did not mean that Germanic styles had to be discarded.

65. Hughes and Stradling, *Renaissance*, 31.

66. See Howes, *Renaissance*, 30–31, for some additional thoughts on their teaching roles.

67. See Dorothea Ponsonby, "Hubert Parry," *The Musical Times* 97:1359 (1956): 263. For a biography of Parry, see Jeremy Dibble, *C. Hubert H. Parry: His Life and Music* (Oxford: Oxford University Press, 1992). For a reassessment of his compositional method, see Michael Allis, *Parry's Creative Process* (Aldershot, Hants and Burlington, VT: Ashgate, 2002). See also Hughes and Stradling, *Renaissance*, 54, for more on Parry's declining health as his professional duties took precedence in the 1890s.

68. For recent biographies of Stanford, see Jeremy Dibble, *Charles Villiers Stanford: Man and Musician* (Oxford: Oxford University Press, 2002) and Paul Rodmell, *Charles Villiers Stanford* (Aldershot: Scolar Press, 2002).

69. See also Howes, *Renaissance*, 151.

70. Howes, *Renaissance*, 26.

71. See Derek Schofield, "Sowing the Seeds: Cecil Sharp and Charles Marson in Somerset in 1903," *Folk Music Journal* 8:4 (2004): 485. Sharp, as a Fabian socialist, initially opposed this idea, see 489, though later he too would endorse it for different reasons, writing: "Then, again, one of the first objects of education should be to arouse a spirit of patriotism in the children, to inspire them with a love of their country, with a just pride in the nation to which they belong." See Cecil Sharp, *Folk Singing in Schools* (London: English Folk Dance Society, n.d. [1913]), 13.

72. Charles Villiers Stanford, *Studies and Memories* (London: Constable, 1908), 53.

73. *Ibid.*, 55.

74. *Ibid.*, 55–57. He offered a detailed plan for the correct order of introducing songs that seems stuffy and Victorian by today's standards, but he intended it to provide the best possible introduction.

75. Lewis Foreman, "The Folk-song Society, RVW, and the Early Response of British Composers to Folksong," *Journal of the RVW Society* 14 (1999): 2, where he notes that Percy Grainger was an early critic of this approach.

76. Jeremy Dibble, "Parry, Sir Hubert," *Grove Music Online*, Oxford Music Online. Oxford University Press: http://www.oxfordmusiconline.com/subscriber/article/grove/music/20949, accessed November 8, 2014.

77. Hughes and Stradling, *Renaissance*, 37, and 56–57.

78. C.L. Graves, *Hubert Parry: His Life and Works*, 2 vols. (London: Macmillan, 1926), II, 213.

79. Bantock (1868–1946) wrote music that was frequently characterized by Orientalist influences, and often focused on Middle Eastern and Asian subjects.

80. Hughes and Stradling, *Renaissance*, 57. See also 58–59 for further conflicts and controversies over this divisive composer.

81. See Hughes and Stradling, *Renaissance*, 33–34.

82. *Ibid.*, 38–39.

83. *Ibid.*, 40–41; for an example of his own efforts in the *Strand Magazine*, see Hughes, *Renaissance and the Press*, 97–98, specifically 97n57.

84. See Hughes and Stradling, *Renaissance*, 41. For more on Fuller Maitland, see Hughes, *Renaissance and the Press*, 29–38, for his support for Vaughan Williams, see 33–34. See also Jeremy Dibble, "Fuller Maitland, J.A.," *Grove Music Online*, Oxford Music Online. Oxford University Press: http://www.oxfordmusiconline.com/subscriber/article/grove/music/10378, accessed November 5, 2014.

85. Fuller Maitland, *A Door-Keeper of Music* (London: John Murray, 1929).

86. Howes, Renaissance, 85–87. See 91-96 for various accounts of other Victorian and later efforts in reviving Tudor music. Howes' work is important but dated, and contains several naïve and amusing pronouncements, such as this one about the viola da gamba, the principle bowed instrument of Tudor and Stuart England, at 105: "It is therefore unlikely that the viol will be revived beyond the stage of antiquarian curiosity. If, then, [17th-century composer] Jenkins is to have a resurrection it must be brought about through the violin family." The viol is now immensely popular in the early music field, both with professionals and amateurs, and all of Jenkins' (and many others') consort works have been recorded and performed with viols many times over.

87. See, *ibid.*, 99, for example.

88. First published in 1899, this edition is still useful and is available in a modern, two-volume version

(Toronto: Dover, 1979). See also Fuller-Maitland, "The Notation of the Fitzwilliam Virginal Book," *Proceedings of the Musical Association* 21 (1894–5): 103–12. A full list of his publications can be found in the Grove article, see *n*54 above. See also Howes, *Renaissance*, 98 and 100.

89. See chapters 3 and 7 for Vaughan Williams and Philip Heseltine, respectively. Heseltine's work is still regarded as a valuable contribution to the editing of modern editions of long-lost Tudor composers' music.

90. See Hughes and Stradling, *Renaissance*, 43–44, for further analysis.

91. *Ibid.*, 44–45.

92. For a biography, see Margaret Campbell, *Dolmetsch: The Man and His Work* (London: Hamilton, 1975). See also the very useful summary by Brian Blood, "The Dolmetsch Story," which contains several fascinating photographs, at Dolmetsch Online: http://www.dolmetsch.com/Dolworks.htm, accessed November 5, 2014. See also Howes, *Renaissance*, 101–06, and Joel Cohen, *Reprise: The Extraordinary Revival of Early Music* (Boston and Toronto: Little, Brown, & Co., 1985), 18–22.

93. Cohen, *Reprise*, 20.

94. Quoted by Percy Grainger in "Arnold Dolmetsch: Musical Confucius," The Musical Quarterly 19 (1933): 198, reprinted in Malcolm Gillies and Bruce Clunies Ross, eds., *Grainger on Music* (Oxford: Oxford University Press, 1999), 232–45. If this is a genuine quote, it may refer to a disliking on Dolmetsch's part of Impressionism or Atonalism, or some other experiment of the early 20th century.

95. Quoted in Howes, *Renaissance*, 103.

96. Cohen, *Reprise*, 19 and the note at the bottom of the page, for example, of estrangement for some years between Arnold and his daughter Hélène. See also Howes, *Renaissance*, 102.

97. Cohen, *Reprise*, 22.

98. An issue that still divides many in the early music field today; costumes, particularly as worn by those performing medieval and Renaissance music, are often seen as gimmicky, and something that cheapens the quality of music that deserves to be taken as seriously as music from later periods.

99. Campbell, *Dolmetsch*, 41.

100. Cohen, *Reprise*, 86.

101. *Ibid.*, 21–22.

102. For more on their relationship, see Kathleen E. Nelson, "Percy Grainger and the 'Musical Confucius,'" *Musicology Australia* 33:1 (2011): 15–27.

103. See Cohen, *Reprise*, 22–23, and chapter 9.

104. See chapter 3.

105. Stanford, *Studies and Memories*, 75.

106. *Ibid.*, 76.

107. See also Hughes and Stradling, *Renaissance*, 45.

108. *Ibid.*, 46.

109. See *ibid.*, 47–49.

110. See Percy M. Young, *George Grove (1820–1900)* (London: Macmillan, 1980), 211 and 238. In 2015, the Guildhall came under fire for the sexual misconduct of one of its instructors.

111. Stephen Banfield, *Gerald Finzi: An English Composer* (London: Faber and Faber, 1997), 23.

112. *Ibid.*, 24.

113. From the website of the *Arts & Crafts Museum at Cheltenham Art Gallery and Museum*, an excellent introduction with a substantial bibliography page: http://www.artsandcraftsmuseum.org.uk, see especially: http://www.artsandcraftsmuseum.org.uk/Arts_and_Crafts_Movement/The_Arts_and_Crafts_Movement.aspx, accessed September 28, 2014. For the bibliography, see http://www.artsandcraftsmuseum.org.uk/Resources/Booklist.aspx.

114. Wilfrid Mellers, *Vaughan Williams and the Vision of Albion* (London: Barre & Jenkins, 1989), 27. For a good introduction to Morris, see the William Morris archive online at: http://www.morrissociety.org, accessed February 3, 2015. For a study of his socialist beliefs, see Irene Sargent, "William Morris: his socialist career," *The Craftsman* 1:1 (1901): 15–24, available online at the Digital Library for the Decorative Arts and Material Culture: http://digital.library.wisc.edu/1711.dl/DLDecArts.hdv01n01, accessed May 4, 2015.

115. For additional thoughts, see Robert Cecil, *Life in Edwardian England* (London: Batsford, and New York: Putnam, 1969), 124–25, and 127–28.

116. Hughes and Stradling, *Renaissance*, 53. See also 119, where they note that in 1911, composer Cecil Forsyth argued in his *Music and Nationalism* that England was little more than a "colony" of Germany, especially in opera.

117. Fuller Maitland, *English Music*, 293.

118. Michael Barlow, *Whom the Gods Love: The Life and Music of George Butterworth* (London: Toccata Press: 1997), 32*n*31. See Broadwood and Fuller Maitland, *English County Songs* (London: J.B. Cramer, 1893).

119. See Mellers, *Vision of Albion*, 31, as well as Vaughan Williams, "The Evolution of the Folk-Song," *National Music*, 45, and Vaughan Williams, "British Music," *Vaughan Williams on Music*, David Manning, ed. (Oxford: Oxford University Press, 2008), 50, reprinted from *The Music Student* (1914), see 43 for full details.

120. Vaughan Williams discussed this in his Bournemouth lectures on folk songs in 1902, see Michael Holyoake, "Towards a folk song awakening: Vaughan Williams in Bournemouth, 1902," *Journal of the RVW Society* 46 (2009): 14.

121. C.W. Orr, "Elgar and the Public," *Musical Times* 72:1055 (1931): 17–18.

122. Space precludes a detailed biography of Elgar in this work; good studies are numerous. See J. P. E. Harper-Scott, *Elgar: an Extraordinary Life* (London: Associated Board of the Royal Schools of Music, 2007), for a short introduction; see also Michael Kennedy, *Portrait of Elgar* (Oxford: Oxford University Press, 1968, 3rd edition, 1987); Jerrold N. Moore, *Elgar: Child of Dreams* (London: Faber and Faber, 2004); and Byron Adams, ed, *Edward Elgar and His World* (Princeton, NJ and Oxford: Princeton University Press, 2007). For musical analysis, see Diana McVeagh, *Elgar the Music Maker* (Woodbridge: Boydell, 2013). For Elgar in relation to the Kensington renaissance, see Hughes and Stradling, *Renaissance*, 59–74.

123. Anthony Murphy, *Banks of Green Willow: The Life and Times of George Butterworth* (Great Malvern, UK: Cappella Archive, 2012), 64n39. For more information, see J. P. E. Harper-Scott, "Elgar and the Salon," *The Victorian Web*: http://www.victorianweb.org/mt/elgar/jpehs.html, accessed November 29, 2014.

124. Arthur Jacobs, *Sir Arthur Sullivan: A Victorian Musician* (Oxford: Oxford University Press, 1984), 385.

125. Percy M. Young, *Letters to Nimrod: Edward Elgar to August Jaeger, 1897–1908* (London: Dobson, 1965), 9 and 31. See also Hughes and Stradling, *Renaissance*, 62–63.

126. See Jeremy Dibble, "Elgar and His British Contemporaries," *The Cambridge Companion to Elgar*, Daniel M. Grimley and Julian Rushton, eds. (Cambridge: Cambridge University Press, 2005), 19–20.

127. Jerrold N. Moore, *Edward Elgar, a Creative Life* (Oxford: Oxford University Press, 1984), 369. The conductor Hans Richter considered Elgar's *Symphony No. 1* to be the greatest symphony of modern times, by the greatest composer, see William H. Reed, *Elgar* (London: Dent, 1946), 97.

128. Hughes and Stradling, *Renaissance*, 63–64.

129. See Sykes, "The Evolution of Englishness," 470–71, for more thoughts on this.

130. The painfully clichéd "soundtrack" of academia and graduations in the English-speaking world.

131. Vaughan Williams, "Talk on Parry and Stanford, 1957," in *Heirs and Rebels: Letters Written to Each Other, and Occasional Writings on Music, by Ralph Vaughan Williams and Gustav Holst*, Ursula Vaughan Williams and Imogen Holst, eds. (London: Oxford University Press, 1959, rep. Cooper Square, New York, 1974), 96.

132. Michael Kennedy, *Portrait of Elgar*, 152–54.

133. Hughes and Stradling, *Renaissance*, 67.

134. See Hughes and Stradling, *Renaissance*, 67–72, for a good summary, and see also the excellent analysis by Jerrold N. Moore, "Sir Edward Elgar as a University Professor," *University of Rochester Library Bulletin*, 15:3 (1960), available online at: https://www.lib.rochester.edu/index.cfm?PAGE=3356, accessed November 6, 2014.

135. This is a widely-quoted statement, and frequently referenced. See Trend, *The Music Makers*, 31. See also Daniel M. Grimley, "'The Spirit-Stirring Drum': Elgar and Populism," *Edward Elgar and His World*, Byron Adams, ed. (Princeton, NJ and Oxford: Princeton University Press, 2007): 122n45: "Elgar seems to have been aesthetically opposed to this kind of activity [basing compositions on folk tunes], and once remarked 'I write the folk songs of this country,'" an attitude that Grimley notes might have come from his desire for popular appeal, as opposed to academic acceptance.

136. Barlow, *Gods*, 74–75.

137. Michael Kennedy, *Portrait of Elgar*, 23. Only some of the works of Purcell escaped this harsh judgement.

138. Moore, "University Professor." See also see Hughes and Stradling, *Renaissance*, 137–38.

139. John Bird, *Percy Grainger* (Oxford: Oxford University Press, 1999), 149–50. Fuller Maitland had no admiration for Elgar or Delius, see Hughes, *Renaissance and the Press*, 35–36. Vaughan Williams did speak approvingly of Elgar in *National Music*, 41–42, arguing that his music was as "English" as that of the pastoral school, in its own way.

140. Philip Heseltine, "Some Notes on Delius and His Music," *The Musical Times* 56:865 (March 1915): 137–38.

141. Letter from Delius to Philip Heseltine, March 24, 1920, in *Delius: A Life in Letters, Vol. II: 1909–34*, Lionel Carley, ed. (Aldershot: Scolar Press, 1988), 230. See also Smith, *Warlock*, 170.

142. Letter from Vaughan Williams to Lord Kennet, May 20, 1941, *Letters of Ralph Vaughan Williams: 1895–1958*, Hugh Cobbe, ed. (Oxford: Oxford University Press, 2008), 317–21, at 319, also quoted in Ursula Vaughan Williams, *R.W.V.*, 242. See also his letter to Fritz Hart, March 25, 1948, where he argues that some of Holst's struggles would have made Delius a better composer, adding more strength to his music, at 427. See also his letter to Michael Kennedy, January 13, 1955, at 552. Additionally, see Vaughan Williams, "The Evolution of the Folk-Song," *National Music*, 41, where he notes that Delius was not "English" just because Percy Grainger offered him a folk song, *Brigg Fair*, on which to base a composition. See also Hughes and Stradling, *Renaissance*, 199.

143. Bird, *Grainger*, 149. Howe in *Renaissance*, speaks unflatteringly of Delius' *Brigg Fair*, opining that he "distorted its character in the process of variation writing," 196.

144. See chapter 9, and Bird, *Grainger*, 63 and 126.

145. A survey of musical Impressionism is beyond the scope of this book. For further details, see Christopher Palmer, *Impressionism in Music* (London: Hutchinson; New York: Charles Scribner's Sons, 1973), and Jann Pasler, "Impressionism." *Grove Music Online*, Oxford Music Online. Oxford University Press: http://www.oxfordmusiconline.com/subscriber/article/grove/music/50026, accessed November 7, 2014. For individual composers' biographies, see the entries at *Grove Online*; there are far too many studies and biographies to include in this note, and these will list additional material: François Lesure and Roy Howat, "Debussy, Claude," *Grove Music Online*, Oxford Music Online. Oxford University Press, http://www.oxfordmusiconline.com/subscriber/article/grove/music/07353, accessed November 7, 2014; Barbara L. Kelly. "Ravel, Maurice," *Grove Music Online*, Oxford Music Online. Oxford University Press: http://www.oxfordmusiconline.com/subscriber/article/grove/music/52145, accessed November 7, 2014; Lewis Foreman, "Bax, Sir Arnold," *Grove Music Online*, Oxford Music Online. Oxford University Press: http://www.oxfordmusiconline.com/subscriber/article/grove/music/02380, accessed November 7, 2014; Hugh Ottaway, "Ireland, John," *Grove Music Online*, Oxford Music Online. Oxford University Press: http://www.oxfordmusiconline.com/subscriber/article/grove/music/13905, accessed November 7, 2014.

146. Ralph. S. Grover, *The Music of Edmund Rubbra* (Aldershot: Scolar Press, 1993), 14. Rubbra, a student of Holst's, was very influenced by the madrigals of Elizabethan and Jacobean England.

147. Michael White, "So Mighty, So Unmusical: How Britannia Found Its Voice," *New York Times*, February 11, 2007, online at: http://www.nytimes.com/2007/02/11/arts/music/11whit.html?pagewanted=all, accessed April 17, 2015.
148. See, for example, their friendly correspondence of great mutual admiration in the early 1950s, Cobbe, *Letters*, 506 and 545. Perhaps old age softened the differences and gave them more perspective.
149. Stephen Banfield, *Finzi*, 105.
150. Lambert, *Music Ho! a Study of Music in Decline* (London: Faber and Faber, 1934, reprinted 1966), 146. He had cordial relations with Vaughan Williams, however, orchestrating a version of the latter's *Job— A Masque for Dancing* in 1931.
151. See Vaughan Williams, "Folk Song," Manning, *Vaughan Williams on Music*, 230, reprinted from his *Encyclopedia Britannica* entry; see also 229, and Vaughan Williams, *National Music*, 24. See also 23 for his four characteristics of a folk song.
152. See, for example, Vaughan Williams' letter to the Editor of the *Radio Times*, January 6, 1933, where he considers Bax to be better than any of the other composers featured in the same concert program, including himself, Cobbe, *Letters*, 208–09. Vaughan Williams also dedicated his *Symphony No. 4* to Bax, though he did feel "doubtful" about some of Bax's later works, see Cobbe, *Letters*, 588.
153. *Ibid.*, 107.
154. Arnold Bax, "A Native British Art," *Musical Standard* 86:902 (1914): 342, also quoted in Bax, *Farewell, My Youth and Other Writings*, Lewis Foreman, ed. (Aldershot: Scolar Press, 1992), 103. See also Aidan J. Thomson, "Bax and the 'Celtic North,'" *Journal of the Society for Musicology in Ireland* 8 (2012–13): 51–87.
155. Simon Brackenborough, private email correspondence with the author.
156. Grainger "Music Heard in England," originally published in the *Australian Musical News and Digest* 39/12 (1949): 32–34, republished in Malcolm Gillies and Bruce Clunies Ross, eds., *Grainger on Music* (Oxford: Oxford University Press, 1999), 352.
157. See Meirion Harries, *A Pilgrim Soul—The Life and Work of Elizabeth Lutyens* (London: Michael Joseph, 1989), seemingly drawn from one of her lectures for the Dartington Summer School. Eric Sayler counters: "Her comment belies her jealousy at the success that pastoral music enjoyed at the expense of her own style [...]" Saylor, "Not Lambkins Frisking," 54.
158. Vaughan Williams, "The Folk Song Movement," *National Music and Other Essays* (Oxford: Oxford University Press, 1934, multiple editions through 1987), 235. See also Vaughan Williams, "Let Us Remember ... Early Days," Manning, *Vaughan Williams on Music*, 253, reprinted from *English Dance and Song*, details at 251.
159. Vaughan Williams, "Some Conclusions," *National Music*, 62.
160. See Vaughan Williams, *Musical Autobiography*, in Hubert Foss, *Ralph Vaughan Williams: A Study* (London and Sydney: Harrap, 1950), 33–34.
161. See Banfield, *Finzi*, 334, for further discussion.
162. For a thorough study of popular music hall entertainment, from the late 19th century, see James Ross Moore, "An Intimate Understanding: the Rise of British Musical Revue 1890–1920," Ph.D. thesis, University of Warwick, 2000. See Anthony Murphy, *Banks of Green Willow*, for a brief discussion of how music hall songs became in effect a new kind of folk music by the turn of the 20th century, including the widely popular 1913 song, "It's a Long Way to Tipperary," which became a theme-song for World War I. In the 1930s, Vaughan Williams would still refer to the "vulgarity of the music-hall," see "The Evolution of the Folk-Song," *National Music*, 38.
163. Hughes and Stradling, *Renaissance*, 84; see also chapter 3.
164. See chapter 9.
165. See chapter 4.
166. See chapter 7.
167. However, Moeran's injury was probably not as severe as once believed, see chapter 6. For Gurney see the Introduction, n15.
168. "Heseltine" derives from the Anglo-Saxon *Hoeseldenu*, meaning "Hazel valley." It has many variants. See *House of Names*: https://www.houseofnames.com/heseltine-family-crest, accessed May 3, 2015.
169. See chapter 4.
170. Hughes and Stradling, *Renaissance*, 85–87.
171. See *ibid.*, 87–88, for a discussion of the works that these two produced and the nature of their content.
172. Hughes and Stradling, in *English Renaissance*, argue that Irish independence ultimately strengthened the English Pastoral School after World War I, 91.
173. Recalled by L.H. Heward, see Walford Davies, et al, "Charles Villiers Stanford, by Some of His Pupils," *Music & Letters* 5:3 (1924): 203.
174. Jeremy Dibble, "Parry, Sir (Charles) Hubert Hastings, baronet (1848–1918)," *Oxford Dictionary of National Biography*, Oxford University Press: http://www.oxforddnb.com/index/101035393/Hubert-Parry, accessed November 8, 2014.
175. *Ibid.*
176. J.N. Moore, *Edward Elgar—A Creative Life* (Oxford: Oxford University Press, 1984, rep. Clarendon Press, 1999), 710.
177. Michael Short, *Gustav Holst: the Man and His Music* (Oxford: Oxford University Press, 1990), 173.
178. See Hughes and Stradling, *Renaissance*, 92–93.
179. *Ibid.*, 93.
180. *Ibid.*, 94.
181. *Ibid.*, 94–96.
182. Michael Kennedy, *Adrian Boult* (London: Macmillan, 1987, rep. 1989), 91.
183. Though interestingly, the symphony's premier concert on October 22, 1930, consisted mainly of continental music: Wagner, Brahms, Ravel, and Saint-Saëns, see "Wireless Notes and Programmes," *The Manchester Guardian* (22 October 1930): 12. For a history of the orchestra, see Nicholas Kenyon, *The BBC Symphony Orchestra—The First Fifty Years, 1930–1980* (London: BBC, 1981). For a good survey of how the BBC interacted with the composers and conductors of the 1930s, including many controversies over the efficacy of radio and what should be broadcast, see Hughes and Stradling, *English Renaissance*, 101–09.

184. We have already referenced Howes' important work on the renaissance, see *n*5 above. He gives an assessment, in *Renaissance*, of some of the major works influenced by folk song, as well as those more outside the movement but which show modal influences from the same time, at 83–84.

185. Hughes and Stradling, *Renaissance*, 100.

186. Vaughan Williams, "Some Conclusions [to National Music]," *National Music*, 70–71. His 6th Symphony, for example, contained some elements of jazz influence.

187. Letter from Vaughan Williams to Elizabeth Maconchy, February, 1935, Cobbe, *Letters*, 235.

188. See chapter 3 for reactions to this groundbreaking work.

189. Hughes and Stradling, *Renaissance*, 105.

190. Letter from Britten to Grace Williams, Jan 16, 1935, in Malcolm Boyd, "Benjamin Britten and Grace Williams: Chronicle of a Friendship," *Welsh Music* (Winter 1980–81): 26. See also Michael Kennedy, "The Dark Side of Benjamin Britten," *The Spectator*, February 23, 2013, online at: http://www.spectator.co.uk/arts/arts-feature/8847791/the-great-hater, accessed April 24, 2015. For more on Britten's specific criticism of Vaughan Williams and the pastoral school, see Graham Freeman, "'Into a cocked-hat': The Folk Song Arrangements of Percy Grainger, Cecil Sharp, and Benjamin Britten," *Grainger Studies: An Interdisciplinary Journal* 2 (2012): 42–44. Ironically, Vaughan Williams was later to speak approvingly of Britten's own folk song arrangements, see 48.

191. Hughes and Stradling, *Renaissance*, 156–63.

192. Ibid., 159.

193. See chapter 9 for more on Grainger's disillusionment with Germany and all things German.

194. Letter from Percy Grainger to Herman Sandby, September 19, 1953, quoted in Bird, *Grainger*, 285–86.

195. Ibid., 286. Grainger always felt that music should not be constrained by these rigid, "classical" forms, see 69–70.

196. See chapter 3, *n*231.

197. Butterworth, "Vaughan Williams *London Symphony*," *RCM Magazine* 10:2 (1914): 44–46, quoted in Barlow, *Gods*, 169–71.

198. Holst's own attempts at writing film music were not successful, however, see chapter 4.

199. See also Banfield, *Finzi*, 458, for thoughts on Finzi's relation to later film composers.

200. Keith Warsop, "Brian and the alternative English musical renaissance," Havergal Brian Society Website: http://www.havergalbrian.org/alternative.htm, accessed November 10, 2014.

Chapter 2

1. See, for example, Arthur Knevett, "Cultural and Political Origins of the Folk-Song Society and the Irish Dimension," *Folk Music Journal* 10:5 (2015): 592–608, which considers the English revival in relation to Irish nationalism and Celtic nationhood. I am grateful to Katie Heathman for drawing my attention to this article.

2. For a detailed and illustrated study of late Victorian and Edwardian uses of medieval stories, see Velma Bourgeois Richmond, *Chivalric Stories as Children's Literature: Edwardian Retellings in Words and Pictures* (Jefferson, NC: McFarland, 2014). See Murphy, *Green Willow*, 107n31, for examples of contemporary literature of the time extolling the idyllic themes of rural England. See also the overview by Richard Sykes, "The Evolution of Englishness in the English Folksong Revival," *Folk Music Journal* 6:4 (1993): 446–90. See also Robert Colls and Katie Heathman, "Music of Englishness: National Identity and the First Folk Revival," *Oxford Handbook of Musical Identities*, David Hargreaves, Raymond MacDonald, and Dorothy Miell, eds. (Oxford: Oxford University Press, 2016), no page range as of this writing. I am grateful to Ms. Heathman for allowing me to read this insightful article in advance of its publication.

3. Cecil, *Edwardian England*, 128.

4. See chapter 4, *n*100. H.G. Wells also supported this movement, see Cecil, *Edwardian England*, 128. The socialists were particularly interested in the folk song revival, primarily in the inter-war period, see Duncan Hall, *'A Pleasant Change from Politics': Music and the British labour movement between the wars* (Cheltenham, UK: New Clarion Press, 2001), 11, and 140–45. Conservatives and fascists would also stake their claim to the practice, see 141. On fascism, see also Georgina Boyes, *The Imagined Village: Culture, Ideology and the English Folk Revival* (Manchester: Manchester University Press, 1993, revised and reprinted Leeds: No Masters Co-operative, 2010); this latter edition is the one referenced in this chapter, 157–58.

5. Though it would not be until the mid-20th century that neo-pagan religions would begin to grow. Gerald Gardner introduced his religion of Wicca (influenced by earlier British societies such as the Golden Dawn), following the repeal of anti-witchcraft laws, and Ross Nichols redefined Druidry as a spiritual movement (until then an arts and culture movement) by introducing Celtic myths and beliefs, and structuring his own group, the Order of Bards, Ovates, and Druids, into the three divisions noted by Classical commentators. On Gardner, see Philip Heselton, *Witchfather: A Life of Gerald Gardner*, 2 vols. (Loughborough, Leicestershire: Thoth, 2012). On Nichols, see the OBOD website: http://www.druidry.org/about-us/ross-nichols-founder, accessed January 4, 2015.

6. For the National Trust online, see: http://www.nationaltrust.org.uk, accessed January 4, 2015.

7. Peter Green, *Kenneth Grahame: A Biography* (Cleveland: John Murray, 1959), 247. See also 243 and 262 for further discussion of his defense of the old social order.

8. Ibid., 290.

9. Cecil, *Edwardian England*, 126–27.

10. Vic Gammon, review of Georgina Boyes, *The Imagined Village*, in *Albion: A Quarterly Journal Concerned with British Studies* 26: 2 (1994): 391.

11. The oral aspects of these songs were often stressed as one of their most important features, see Sykes, "The Evolution of Englishness," 457–58. On

their similarity to some popular songs, see 459–60. On the purity of rural life as opposed to the "un-Englishness" of the urban one, see 473. Vaughan Williams held to this view, and likened folk song to language in "British Music," reprinted in *Vaughan Williams on Music*, 45, originally published in *The Music Student* 7:1–4 (1914): 5–7, 25–27, 47–48, and 63–64.

12. For additional thoughts on this, see Sykes, "The Evolution of Englishness," 446 and 448–50. On the belief in the unchanging nature of folk song, see 473–74. Parry and Vaughan Williams would hold to this notion.

13. Ibid., 472.

14. Howes, *Renaissance*, 68.

15. See Vic Gammon, "Cecil Sharp and English Folk Music," *Still Growing: English Traditional Songs and Singers from the Cecil Sharp Collection*, Steve Roud, Eddie Upton and Malcolm Taylor, eds. (London: English Folk Dance & Song Society, 2003), 12–13, also available online at: http://www.academia.edu/5310311/Cecil_Sharp_and_English_Folk_Music, accessed January 28, 2015. For the idea of "Volksmusik," as envisioned by Carl Engel and its influence in England, see Hughes and Stradling, *Renaissance*, 77–78.

16. Vic Gammon, "Folk Song Collecting in Sussex and Surrey, 1843–1914," *History Workshop* 10 (1980): 72.

17. Ibid., 12.

18. Howes notes this in *ibid.*, 75–76.

19. Ibid., 78. He observes that since some of the songs collected in the north are found in Scotland and a few more southerly songs are also known, "English folk-song is much less regional than the early collectors thought," a view certainly not held by all.

20. Howes, *Renaissance*, 81 and 88–89.

21. For a survey of collecting in two fertile regions for songs from this time to the start of World War I, see Gammon, "Folk Song Collecting in Sussex and Surrey," 61–89. For list of key song collectors other than Vaughan Williams, see 62–63. He notes at 67 that this area would yield, "something over 850 songs or parts of songs collected from something like 160 to 170 singers in Sussex and Surrey before the First World War." For a comprehensive listing, see "The Full English," which "contains over 44,000 records and over 58,000 digitised images from the archives of 19 of the most important and influential collectors in the UK." http://www.vwml.org/browse/browse-collections-full-english, accessed January 7, 2015.

22. Howes, *Renaissance*, 77.

23. Ibid., 78. See Broadwood and Fuller Maitland, *English County Songs* (London: J.B.Cramer & Co., 1893). For a detailed summary, see E. D. Gregory, "Before the Folk-Song Society: Lucy Broadwood and English Folk Song, 1884–97," *Folk Music Journal* 9:3 (2008): 384–392. Two earlier books had appeared shortly before, Frank Kidson's *Traditional Tunes* (Oxford: Taphouse & Son, 1891), and W.A. Barrett's *English Folk Songs* (London and New York: Novello, 1891), online at Archive: https://archive.org/details/imslp-folk-songs-barrett-william-alexander, accessed March 22, 2015.

24. See also chapter 7, for Philip Heseltine's interest in and involvement with esoteric movements.

25. For an excellent survey of Broadwood's early years, see E. David Gregory, "Before the Folk-Song Society," 372–414. For a full-length biography, see Dorothy de Val, *In Search of Song: The Life and Times of Lucy Broadwood* (Farnham, UK: Ashgate, 2011). See also de Val, "The Transformed Village: Lucy Broadwood and Folksong," *Music and British Culture, 1785–1914: Essays in Honour of Cyril Ehrlich*, Christina Bashford and Leanne Langley, eds. (Oxford: Oxford University Press, 2000), 341–66; and Vaughan Williams, "Lucy Broadwood, 1858–1929," *Journal of the English Folk Dance and Song Society* 5:3 (1948): 136–8, reprinted in Manning, ed., *Vaughan Williams on Music* (Oxford: Oxford University Press, 2008), 257–60. In this article, he claims that Broadwood, "misunderstood what she thought to be his patronizing attitude of the townsman towards the countryman [...]" at 259. For information on Broadwood in Britain's National Archives, see: http://discovery.nationalarchives.gov.uk/details/rd/e44bc842-b5cc-4218-8917-9dc0d560d2e4, accessed January 4, 2015.

26. Vaughan Williams, "Lucy Broadwood, 259–60.

27. Murphy, *Green Willow*, 49. See also Gammon, "Folk Song Collecting in Sussex and Surrey," 74.

28. Hubert Parry, "Inaugural Address," *Journal of the Folk-Song Society* 1 (1899): 1–3. (Nendein, Liechtenstein: Kraus Reprint, 1975, originally pub. 1898), 1. See also Murphy, *Green Willow*, 49–50, and Boyes, *Imagined Village*, 25–27, being mindful of her acidic tone.

29. Ibid.

30. Ibid.

31. See Hubert Parry, *The Evolution of the Art of Music*, 4th ed. (London, Kegan Paul, 1905), available online at Archive: https://archive.org/details/4thevolutionofar00parruoft, accessed January 3, 2015.

32. See Martin Clayton, "Musical Renaissance and its Margins in England and India, 1874–1914," *Music and Orientalism in the British Empire, 1780s to 1940s: Portrayal of the East* (Aldershot, UK: Ashgate, 2007), 75–76.

33. See Vic Gammon, "Cecil Sharp and English Folk Music," 14–15.

34. Parry, *Evolution*, 76.

35. See Howes, *Renaissance*, 73.

36. Vaughan Williams, "Cecil Sharp—An Appreciation," in Cecil Sharp, *English Folk-Song: Some Conclusions*, 4th ed. (London: Methuen, 1954), v–vi, reprinted in Manning, *Vaughan Williams on Music*, 270.

37. For a study of Lee and her efforts in creating the society, see C. J. Bearman, "Kate Lee and the Foundation of the Folk-Song Society," *Folk Song Journal* 7:5 (1999): 627–43. She found herself at odds with one A.P. Graves, who wanted to claim the idea of the society for himself, but it does seem that Lee did more of the work, see 633–35. Lucy Broadwood was not on good terms with her, see 638–39.

38. Ibid., 637.

39. For a short summary of their work, see the Kodály Institute page, "Ethnomusicology" at: http://kodaly.hu/zoltan_kodaly/ethnomusicology, accessed May 6, 2015.

40. See chapter 9. Some have argued that Grainger may have inspired Bartók to take up the practice.

41. See also Sykes, "The Evolution of Englishness," 468.
42. Banfield, *Finzi*, 69.
43. Banfield, *Finzi*, 72. See *n*36 above for publication details.
44. See Sykes, "The Evolution of Englishness," 481–82, for some of the problems with this.
45. Sharp, *English Folk-Song*, 136. See also the letter of Vaughan Williams to the Folk Song Society, November 1906, regarding some confusion over the methods proposed by the Board of Education to include folk songs in the school curriculum, Cobbe, *Letters*, 57–58. With the help of Vaughan Williams, Sharp was eventually appointed as a Government Inspector of Schools in 1919, see Julian Onderdonk, "The composer and society: family, politics, and nation," *Cambridge Companion to Vaughan Williams*, Alain Frogley and Aidan J. Thomson, eds. (Cambridge: Cambridge University Press, 2013), 14.
46. Gammon, "Folk Song Collecting in Sussex and Surrey," 63 and 83.
47. Vaughan Williams, "English Folk Songs," Manning, *Vaughan Williams on Music*, 187.
48. On the issue of urban and industrial folk songs, see Sykes, "The Evolution of Englishness," 451–52. These tended to be ignored, as they did not fit in with the collectors' goals.
49. Ursula Vaughan Williams, *R.W.V.*, 168. For a fascinating look at rural England in 1901, see the memoirs of Roland Meredith, who devoted much time to walking the countryside and visiting towns and villages, in *Edwardian England*, The Way Things Were, Andrew Pagett, ed. (London: Brockhampton Press, 1999).
50. These were among the most well-known, but by no means were they the only ones. For two studies on less famous, but still important collectors, see Michael Pickering, "Janet Blunt—Folk Song Collector and Lady of the Manor," *Folk Music Journal* 3:2 (1976): 114–49; and Ivor Clissold, "Alfred Williams, Song Collector," *Folk Music Journal* 1:5 (1969): 293–300.
51. A glowing biography of Sharp is Maud Karpeles, *Cecil Sharp: His Life and Work* (Chicago: University of Chicago Press, 1967). Karpeles, as Sharp's longtime associate, naturally presents him in a positive light. The first Sharp biography was A. H. Fox Strangways, with Maud Karpeles, *Cecil Sharp* (London: Oxford University Press, 1933, rep. 1980 by Da Capo Press). A shorter, but useful summary is Vic Gammon, "Cecil Sharp and English Folk Music," 2–23.
52. For the tune, see Howes, *Renaissance*, 80.
53. See Schofield, "Sowing the Seeds," 491–92. See also Gammon, "Cecil Sharp and English Folk Music," 6. Both agree that the idea that this encounter with John England was purely serendipity was not true, and was manufactured later.
54. *Ibid.*, 488. See also 503.
55. *Ibid.*, 489–490.
56. For an account of Sharp's collecting over the next few days, see *ibid.*, 494–97. For his lecture, see 498–500.
57. Marson would confess that he was unaware of how many songs were still known just in his village, writing that he was in "Stygian ignorance of the wealth of Art which that village contained," Cecil Sharp and Charles Marson, *Folk Songs from Somerset* (London: Simpkin, Marshall, Taunton: Barnicott and Pearce, 1904): xiii–xiv.
58. Karpeles, *Cecil Sharp*, 33.
59. Gammon summarizes in "Cecil Sharp and English Folk Music," 6.
60. Cecil Sharp and Charles Marson, *Folk Songs from Somerset* (1904–09). Sharp would add two additional volumes in 1909 and 1911.
61. Schofield, "Sowing the Seeds," 501–02.
62. See chapter 1 and Schofield, "Sowing the Seeds," 487. Sharp may have been the first to teach children songs of oral tradition in the 1890s.
63. Sharp, *Folk-Songs of England*, vol. 1 (London: Novello, 1908), preface not numbered, second page.
64. Butterworth was guilty of the same types of alteration, see chapter 5.
65. C.J. Bearman, "Cecil Sharp in Somerset: Some Reflections on the Work of David Harker," *Folklore* 113:1 (2002): 24–25.
66. Douglas Golding, "Odd Man Out," Newall MSS, AL Marson/MPS 15, Vaughan Williams Memorial Library, noted in Schofield, "Sowing the Seeds," 502.
67. Letter from Broadwood to the editor, "Folk-Songs and Music," *Folk-lore* 3:4 (1892): 553.
68. Maud Karpeles, "Cecil Sharp: Collector and Restorer of English Folk Music," *Journal of the English Folk Dance and Song Society* 8:4 (1959): 181.
69. *Ibid.* Sharp came in for criticism of some of the texts he included in his *Book of British Song* from 1902, specifically that they were unsuitable for children. Some of this was due to the Church of England's influence, see Schofield, "Sowing the Seeds," 489–90.
70. See Mellers, *Vision of Albion*, 30. For Vaughan Williams' use of the piano in his folk song settings, see Elizabeth Poston, "R. V. W.'s Piano Accompaniments," *Folk Music Journal* 2:3 (1972): 169–71. See also Imogen Holst, "Cecil Sharp and the Music and Music-making of the Twentieth Century," *Journal of the English Folk Dance and Song Society* 8:4 (1959): 189–90; and Vaughan Williams, "Traditional Arts in the Twentieth Century," *English Dance and Song* 2:6 (1938): 98–99, reprinted in Manning, *Vaughan Williams on Music*, 243–44. He had some disdain for the drawing-room music of the time, and said so in his sixth Bournemouth talk in 1902, see Michael Holyoake, "Towards a folk song awakening: Vaughan Williams in Bournemouth, 1902," 15.
71. See Roy Palmer, "Neglected Pioneer: E.J. Moeran (1894–1950)," *Folk Music Journal* 8:3 (2003): 349.
72. Sharp, "Hampstead Lecture Notes," November 26, 1903, 17–18, quoted in Schofield, "Sowing the Seeds," 497. See also Karpeles, *Cecil Sharp*, 46–47.
73. "Gypsy" in this case may refer to the Romanichal, an offshoot of the continental Roma who arrived in England beginning in the 16th century. Many have lighter skin and hair than their continental counterparts. Sharp may have also been speaking of a more generic traveling community.
74. Karpeles, *Cecil Sharp*, 41-42, quoting a note

that he made on July 21, 1907. See also Francis M. Etherington, "Cecil Sharp: Some Personal Reminiscences," *Journal of the English Folk Dance and Song Society* 8:4 (1959): 195. For more details on Sharp's interactions with "gypsies" and travelers, see Yvette Staelens, "English Folk Music on the Margin—Cecil Sharp's Gypsies," online at: http://eprints.bournemouth.ac.uk/18360/1/Tomar_pix_sergio.pdf, accessed April 29, 2015.

75. On this issue, see chapter 9.

76. See the discussion in Howes, *Renaissance*, 74–75.

77. See Julian Onderdonk, "Vaughan Williams's folksong transcriptions: a case of idealization?" *Vaughan Williams Studies*, 124–27. However, see also 133–36, for a discussion of how Vaughan Williams would attempt, at different times, to transcribe the song as it was, or to find an idealized version, depending on circumstances and the quality of the sung performance.

78. Vaughan Williams, "English Folk Songs," a lecture first printed in *The Music Student* 4 (1912): 6–11 et al, reprinted with additions in Percy Young, *Vaughan Williams* (London: Dennis Dobson, 1953), 200–17, and reprinted in full in Manning, *Vaughan Williams on Music*, 185–200, at 195.

79. *Ibid.*, 75.

80. See Gammon, "Cecil Sharp and English Folk Music," 15–16. See also Sykes, "The Evolution of Englishness," 477.

81. See chapter 5. For detailed surveys of how Sharp became involved in the folk dance revival, see Roy Judge, "Cecil Sharp and Morris 1906–1909," *Folk Music Journal* 8:2 (2002): 195–228; Paul Burgess, "The Mystery of the Whistling Sewermen: How Cecil Sharp Discovered Gloucestershire Morris Dancing," *Folk Music Journal* 8:2 (2002): 178–194; and Vic Gammon, "'Many Useful Lessons': Cecil Sharp, Education and the Folk Dance Revival, 1899–1924," *Cultural and Social History* 5:1 (2008): 76.

82. Burgess, "Mystery of the Whistling Sewermen," 179.

83. For a detailed account of her efforts, see Roy Judge, "Mary Neal and the Espérance Morris," *Folk Music Journal* 5:5 (1989): 545–91. This article is an excellent comprehensive study of Neal and her group. For their meeting, see 549–52. See also Boyes, *Imagined Village*, 72–79. For Neal's autobiography, see Mary Neal, *As a Tale that is Told*. Summary: http://www.vwml.org/browse/as-a-tale-that-is-told-mary-neals-autobiography; Facsimile: http://media.efdss.org/docs/MaryNealAutobio.pdf, accessed November 14, 2014.

84. Mary Neal, *The Espérance Morris Book: A Manual of Morris Dances, Folk-songs, and Singing Games* (London: J. Curwen, 1910). The group still exists in modern times, now known as New Esperance, and still limited to women members only. See the organization's website for more information: http://www.newesp.org.uk, accessed November 12, 2014. See also Burgess, "Mystery of the Whistling Sewermen," 179–80.

85. Sharp, notes for a lecture given at the Espérance Club, November 15, 1906, quoted in Burgess, "Mystery of the Whistling Sewermen," 185.

86. See Murphy, *Green Willow*, 100. For an overview, see Derek Schofield, "'Revival of the Folk Dance: An Artistic Movement': The Background to the Founding of The English Folk Dance Society in 1911," *Folk Music Journal* 5:2 (1986): 215–219. Neal dated the rift to November 1907, when an article on Morris dance appeared in *Punch*, see Roy Judge, "Mary Neal and the Espérance Morris," 553–54. By 1909, they were becoming quite angry with each other, see 556–57. See also Judge, "Cecil Sharp and Morris," 212–13, and 224, and Boyes, *Imagined Village*, 81–85.

87. *Ibid.*, 54 and see also 63n24.

88. Letter from Cecil Sharp to the *Morning Post*, April 1, 1910, quoted in Murphy, *Green Willow*, 100.

89. Murphy, *Green Willow*, 100. On Sharp's essential political views, many of which were socialistic, see Gammon, "Folk Song Collecting in Sussex and Surrey," 82. See also Sykes, "The Evolution of Englishness," 483, and Boyes, *Imagined Village*, 82.

90. See Judge, "Mary Neal and the Espérance Morris," 558.

91. Vic Gammon, "'Many Useful Lessons,'" 76. See also Karpeles, *Cecil Sharp*, 19.

92. For an online edition, see: http://www.izaak.unh.edu/nhltmd/indexes/dancingmaster, accessed February 28, 2015.

93. See Sharp and Herbert C. MacIlwaine, *The Morris Book: a History of Morris Dancing, With a Description of Eleven Dances as Performed by the Morris-Men of England* (London: Novello, 1907, rep. 2010). On the publication of the second volume leading to further conflict, see Judge, "Mary Neal and the Espérance Morris," 559.

94. All three were originally published by Novello, and are available online at Archive:
Volume 1: https://archive.org/details/sworddancesofnor01shar.
Volume 2: https://archive.org/details/sworddancesofnor112shar.
Volume 3: https://archive.org/details/sworddancesofnor113shar, accessed November 13, 2014.

95. *Ibid.*, 73.

96. See Schofield, "Revival of the Folk Dance," 216. Judge's survey, "Mary Neal and the Espérance Morris," 545–91, is an excellent overall introduction.

97. Cecil Sharp, "A Guild of Morris Dancers," *Morning Post*, April 1, 1910, quoted in Schofield, "Revival of the Folk Dance," 216.

98. Mary Neal, "The Revival of English Folk Dances: Miss Mary Neal's Views," *Morning Post*, May 5, 1910, quoted in Schofield, "Revival of the Folk Dance," 217. See also Judge, "Mary Neal and the Espérance Morris," 563–64, for more background on the conflict.

99. Cecil Sharp, "English Folk-Dances," *Morning Post*, May 10, 1910, quoted in Schofield, "Revival of the Folk Dance," 217.

100. Letter from Sharp to Mary Neal, July 26, 1909, quoted in Judge, "Mary Neal and the Espérance Morris," 559.

101. See Gammon, "Cecil Sharp and English Folk Music," 7.

102. See Ursula Vaughan Williams, *R.W.V.*, 150–51, for more details.

103. *The Morning Post*, December 7, 1911, quoted in Schofield, "Revival of the Folk Dance," 215.

104. For a summary, see Judge, "Mary Neal and the Espérance Morris," 573–75. Neal would later claim that she had misunderstood the masculine aspects of Morris dancing, which may have been one of the reasons for her defeat, see 575. Interestingly, Sharp saw no problem with women taking part in Morris dances, but felt that teams should be kept to separate genders, and in his typically condescending fashion, he stated that women's dances would only approximate those of men, see Sharp, *Folk Dancing in Schools* (London: English Folk Dance Society, n.d. [1912–13]), 11.

105. Gammon, "'Many Useful Lessons,'" 94.

106. Judge, "Mary Neal and the Espérance Morris," 576.

107. Murphy, *Green Willow*, 147–48. See also Sykes, "The Evolution of Englishness," 481.

108. For a small but good selection of their findings, see Ralph Vaughan Williams, Cecil J. Sharp, G. S. K. Butterworth, Frank Kidson, A. G. Gilchrist and Lucy E. Broadwood, "Songs Collected from Sussex," *Journal of the Folk-Song Society* 4:17 (1913): 279–324.

109. For a detailed account, see the lengthy overview by Michael Yates, "Cecil Sharp in America: Collecting in the Appalachians," *Musical Traditions* (1999), available online: http://www.mustrad.org.uk/articles/sharp.htm, accessed November 13, 2014. See also Evelyn K. Wells, "Cecil Sharp in America," *Journal of the English Folk Dance and Song Society* 8:4 (1959): 182–85.

110. Letter from Sharp to George Parmly Day, August 15, 1917, quoted in Yates, "Cecil Sharp in America."

111. Letter from Sharp to Richard Aldrich, June 26, 1915, quoted in *ibid.*

112. Storrow was a prominent philanthropist and an active Girl Scout leader.

113. Karpeles was extremely important as his assistant, and after his death, she worked to ensure that his Appalachian collections were published, as well as writing a biography. She also published extensively her own work in the field. For more on Karpeles, see David Atkinson, "Resources in the Vaughan Williams Memorial Library: The Maud Karpeles Manuscript Collection," *Folk Music Journal* 8:1 (2001): 90–101. The nature of her relationship with Sharp (platonic or romantic) is unclear, see 93. For online resources, including her papers and the video of her dancing with Sharp and Butterworth, see the Vaughan Williams Memorial Library: http://www.vwml.org/vwml-projects/vwml-the-full-english/vwml-full-english-collectors/vwml-maud-karpeles, accessed November 13, 2014. She and her sister Helen, were both active in the folk dance movement, were committed Fabian socialists, and strong supporters of Sharp's efforts, see Murphy, *Green Willow*, 102–03.

114. Sharp's journal entry for August 13, 1916, quoted in *ibid*. Sharp's Appalachian diaries can be found online at the Vaughan Williams Memorial Library: http://www.vwml.org/browse/browse-collections-sharp-diaries, accessed November 13, 2014.

115. See chapter 5, *n*133, for Sharp's journal entry for September 7, 1916, quoted in *ibid*. The names of the fallen that he mentions are Reginald Tiddy, George Butterworth, George Lucas, and George Jerrard Wilkinson. Reginald Tiddy (1879–1916), a Classics don at Oxford, was deeply interested in Morris dancing, and had used family wealth to finance a dance hall with a wooden sprung floor for the Oxford Folk Music Society, see Murphy, *Green Willow*, 73–74.

116. Michael Yates, "Cecil Sharp in America."

117. For a discussion of his last years after World War I, see Karpeles, *Cecil Sharp*, 172–93.

118. See Boyes, *Imagined Village*, 95–97.

119. Atkinson, "Maud Karpeles Manuscript Collection," 90.

120. *Ibid.*, 91–92.

121. Colin Irwin, "Folk's man of mystery: is Cecil Sharp a folk hero or villain?" *The Guardian*, March, 24, 2011: http://www.theguardian.com/music/2011/mar/24/cecil-sharp-project-folk-hero-villain, accessed November 11, 2014.

122. Jan Marsh, *Back to the Land: The Pastoral Impulse in England, from 1880 to 1914* (London: Quartet Books, 1982), 29.

123. For some criticisms from Sharp's contemporaries, see Gammon, "Cecil Sharp and English Folk Music," 17–19. See also Kidson's critical remarks, noted in Boyes, *Imagined Village*, 59n55, and 66–69.

124. Terry himself collected folk songs and also was active in the revival of Tudor church music.

125. Letter from Sir Richard Terry to A. H. Fox Strangways, November 2, 1932, Box 3, Cecil Sharp Correspondence, VWML, quoted in Gammon, "Cecil Sharp and English Folk Music," 25.

126. Arnold Bax, *Farewell, My Youth* (London: Longmans, Green, & Co., 1943), 16.

127. A.L. Lloyd, *Folk Song and the Collectors*, BBC Radio 3, September 26, 1983, quoted in Michael Barlow, *Whom the Gods Love*, 95.

128. A.L. Lloyd, *Folk Song in England* (London: Lawrence & Wishart, 1967), 46–47, and 83–88. See also Sykes, "The Evolution of Englishness," 453.

129. See Dave Harker, "Cecil Sharp in Somerset—Some Conclusions," *Folk Music Journal* 2:3 (1972): 220–40, and more significantly, his book, *Fakesong: The Manufacture of British Folk Song, 1700 to the Present Day* (Milton Keynes UK and Philadelphia, U.S.: Open University Press, 1985). For his communist views, see the latter work, 256–57. For similar views, see Christopher Shaw and Malcolm Chase, "The Dimensions of Nostalgia," *The Imagined Past: History and Nostalgia*, Christopher Shaw and Malcolm Chase, eds. (Manchester: Manchester University Press, 1989), 1–17; and Eric Hobsbawm and Terence Ranger, eds., *The Invention of Tradition* (Cambridge: Cambridge University Press, 1983). For more general studies on leftist criticism of the folk revival, see Michael Pickering, "Recent Folk Music Scholarship in England: A Critique," *Folk Music Journal* 6:1 (1990): 37–64; and Pickering and James Porter, "Muddying the Crystal Spring: From Idealism and Realism to Marxism in the Study of English and American Folk Song," *Comparative Musicology and Anthropology of Music*, Bruno Nettl and Philip V. Bohlman, eds. (Chicago: Chicago University Press, 1991), 113–30.

130. See Harker, "Introduction," *Rhymes of Northern Bards*, John Bell, ed. (Newcastle-upon-Tyne: Frank Graham, 1971), li. See also Bearman, "Cecil Sharp in Somerset," 25–30. Broadsides dated back to the 16th century, and were widely popular in England into the 19th, being printed sheets of paper containing news propaganda, and especially songs and ballads. Their heyday was the 17th and 18th centuries, and thousands of songs were transmitted in this way. For a general survey with musical examples, see Claude M. Simpson, *The British Broadside Ballad and its Music* (New Brunswick, NJ: Rutgers University Press, 1966).

131. Harker, "Cecil Sharp in Somerset," 240. See also Onderdonk, "The composer and society," 11–13.

132. For Gammon's opinion, which is critical but less so, see Gammon, "Cecil Sharp and English Folk Music," 20.

133. C.J. Bearman, "Cecil Sharp in Somerset," 31. See also his "Who Were the Folk? The Demography of Cecil Sharp's Somerset Folk Singers," *Historical Journal* 43:3 (2000): 751–75, and his Ph.D. thesis, "The English Folk Music Movement 1898–1914," University of Hull, 2001.

134. The central thesis of "Cecil Sharp in Somerset." See also Gammon's summary, Gammon, "Cecil Sharp and English Folk Music," 21.

135. Bearman, "Cecil Sharp in Somerset," 14–16.

136. *Ibid.*, 18–19 and 22.

137. Bearman offers considerable detail on this in *ibid.*, 25–30.

138. *Ibid.*, 31.

139. Michael Yates, "Jumping to Conclusions," *Enthusiasms* 36 (2003), available online: http://www.mustrad.org.uk/enth36.htm, accessed November 13, 2014.

140. See also Vaughan Williams, "The Evolution of the Folk-Song," *National Music*, 33, and 31, which discusses the adaptation of existing tunes to new words.

141. Onderdonk, "Vaughan Williams's folksong transcriptions," 121, see also 123. See also Onderdonk, "The composer and society," 15.

142. Onderdonk has written an excellent rebuttal to the notion that Vaughan Williams manipulated the results of his findings, in "Vaughan Williams and the Modes," *Folk Music Journal* 7:5 (1999): 609–626, which contains some of the same text from "Vaughan Williams's folksong transcriptions." See also Sykes, "The Evolution of Englishness," 478–81.

143. Onderdonk, "Vaughan Williams and the Modes," 611, referencing as an example Vic Gammon's work, "Folk Song Collecting in Sussex and Surrey." For an analysis of this charge, see 612–615. However, see also Graham Freeman, "'It Wants All the Creases Ironing Out': Percy Grainger, the Folk Song Society, and the Ideology of the Archive," *Music and Letters* 92:3 (2011): 420–21 for some counter-arguments to Onderdonk.

144. See *ibid.*, 615–16, for several good examples. See also his "Preface" to a collection of folk songs in *Journal of the Folk-Song Society* 2:8 (1906): 141–42, where he notes that the older modes seem to be more characteristic of rural areas, while later scales are more common in towns, but admits, "this suggestion is merely empirical and founded on very partial evidence." He also stated that the appearance of modes in folk songs was "frequent," see Vaughan Williams, "Folk-Song," *Encyclopedia Britannica* IX, 14th ed. (London: Encyclopedia Britannica, 1929), 447, but by this he does not seem to mean that they were the most commonly-used musical scales.

145. *Ibid.*, 616. On his preference for unaccompanied performances, see n170 below.

146. See Onderdonk, "Vaughan Williams and the Modes," 616–18 for several examples, and 619–20 for a study of the ratio of tonal songs to modal ones. There was a gradual shift from the former to the latter in published collections after 1904, most likely due to the desire to avoid duplication.

147. Georgian Boyes, *The Imagined Village*. See 58n14, for a listing of works critical of the folk song collectors.

148. See, for example, *ibid.*, 49–50.

149. *Ibid.*, 14.

150. Graham Freeman, "'It Wants All the Creases Ironing Out,'" 432.

151. See Roy Palmer, "Kidson's Collecting," *Folk Music Journal* 5 (1986): 168. He also altered texts that he found offensive, see Freeman, "'It Wants All the Creases Ironing Out,'" 413–14.

152. *Ibid.*, 48–49, and 54.

153. See chapter 9. For an example of his praise for a singer named George Gouldthorpe, see David Wilson-Johnson, "Grainger's Songs," *Percy Grainger Companion* (London: Thames Publishing, 1981), 122, though some might also see his comments as a bit condescending. In "The Impress of Personality in Traditional Singing," *Journal of the Folk-Song Society* 3:12 (1908): 163–66, he profiled three of his favorite singers and offered all singers sincere thanks for their contributions to the art of folk song, and their charming personalities, at 164.

154. See, for example his discussion about his own cruelty and sadism, where he remarks, "[...] I have simply remained like a boy instead of growing up to be that tiresome thing 'a proper young man,'" drawn from "Bird'sEye View of the Together-Life of Rose Grainger and Percy Grainger (1947)," Grainger Museum, Melbourne, reprinted in full in *Self-Portrait of Percy Grainger*, Malcolm Gillies, David Pear, and Mark Caroll, eds. (Oxford: Oxford University Press, 2006), 56.

155. Onderdonk, "Vaughan Williams and the Modes," 610.

156. Grainger, "The London Gramophone Co. (Now 'His Master's Voice') & the Joseph Taylor Folksong Records (1932)," in "Sketches for my Book 'The Life of My Mother & Her Son,'" September 22, 1932, W35–89, Grainger Museum, reprinted in *Self-Portrait of Percy Grainger*, 129. See also 130, where he writes of Taylor's genius and an uncaring public that ignored him. For some further thoughts on Grainger's relation to the folk song "establishment" and his place in the feud between Marxists and revisionists, see Freeman, "'It Wants All the Creases Ironing Out,'" 410–36.

157. See Boyes, Imagined Village 53–55, though she concedes at 54: "there is no suggestion that collectors made a fortune from their activities [...]"

158. Letter from Sharp to Olive Dame Campbell,

September 27, 1915, quoted in Yates, "Cecil Sharp in America."

159. Letter from Vaughan Williams to Gilbert Murray (Professor of Greek at Oxford), April 25, 1911, Cobbe, *Letters*, 78.

160. Letter from Maud Karpeles to Mrs. Storrow, November 4, 1917, Box 7, Folder B, Item 32, Cecil Sharp Correspondence, VWML, quoted in Gammon, "Cecil Sharp and English Folk Music," 15. See also Karpeles, *Cecil Sharp*, 33, where she notes that during his first seven years of collecting, he paid for all of his own expenses while working full-time, collecting songs only at weekends and holidays.

161. For details, see chapter 9.

162. See Boyes, *Imagined Village*, 50. See also Hall, '*A Pleasant Change from Politics*,' 142, though he seems to regard Sharp as having a very good business sense.

163. Joan Sharp, "Memories of Cecil Sharp," *Journal of the English Folk Dance and Song Society* 8:4 (1959): 192.

164. Letter from Louie Hooper, October 12, 1931, solicited from Strangways and Karpeles as a general invite to anyone who had known Sharp during his collecting days, in order to gather more information. Reprinted in Karpeles, *Cecil Sharp*, 38.

165. See Gammon, "Cecil Sharp and English Folk Music," 10.

166. Georgina Boyes, "'An individual flowering': Ralph Vaughan Williams' work in Folklore," *Journal of the RVW Society* 46 (2009): 7–8.

167. Vic Gammon, review of *The Imagine Village*, 390–392. See also Gammon, "Cecil Sharp and English Folk Music," 20–21.

168. Onderdonk, "Vaughan Williams and the Modes," 610.

169. On this see Martin, "Thro Albions Pleasant Land," 10 and 14.

170. Vaughan Williams, "The Evolution of the Folk-Song," *National Music*, 38. He believed that the act of singing folk songs began to die out from about 1860, see Vaughan Williams, "English Folk Songs," *Vaughan Williams on Music*, 197. See also his "Introduction to *Classic English Folk Songs*," Manning, *Vaughan Williams on Music*, 291, where he states: "The ideal way to sing an English folk song, of course, is unaccompanied," though he allows that for some, a simple piano or guitar part is also suitable. Reprinted from *Classic English Folk Songs*, Vaughan Williams and A.L. Lloyd, eds. (London: English Folk Dance and Song Society, 2003), ix–xii. See also Maud Karpeles' obituary, "Ralph Vaughan Williams, O.M. October 12, 1872—August 26, 1958," *Journal of the English Folk Dance and Song Society* 8:3 (1958): 122. Gammon notes in "Folk Song Collecting in Sussex and Surrey," at 84, that there were traditions of part-song and harmony singing in some communities, as well, and that these tended to be ignored by collectors.

171. See Onderdonk, "The composer and society," 8–19 for further thoughts. Many of these middle class reformers saw the upper class as irresponsible, with no sense of a duty to society. See 24n26 for details about Vaughan Williams' support of and aid to marginalized groups, including women, Jews, and "gypsies," (travelers).

172. Glasier, in *The Labour Leader*, August 21 (1908): 529. The week previously, he had praised Sharp in "To Free the Towns and Revive the Villages. The Restoration of the Joy of Life," *The Labour Leader*, August 14 (1908): 513. Both quoted in Gammon, "Folk Song Collecting," 81.

173. Pearce, in *The Clarion*, May 24 (1907): 3. Quoted in Gammon, "Folk Song Collecting," 81.

174. Hall, '*A Pleasant Change from Politics*,' 143.

175. Ibid., 144.

176. On this, see Onderdonk, "Vaughan Williams and the Modes," 623.

177. See also Onderdonk, "The composer and society," 11–12. On the rejection of Vaughan Williams' socialist beliefs as inadequate by some revisionists, see 16.

178. Freeman, "'It Wants All the Creases Ironing Out,'" 435.

179. Ibid. See also 420 for his discussion of Grainger's role as something of a hero to Marxist historians.

180. Ibid., 424–45, and 434–35.

181. For some discussion, see Michael Brocken, *The British Folk Revival 1944–2002* (Aldershot: Ashgate, 2003), 25–42, and Britta Sweers, *Electric Folk: The Changing Face of English Traditional Music* (Oxford: Oxford University Press, 2005), 31–8. The second folk revival is obviously out of the range of this book's topics for discussion, but makes for fascinating reading.

182. See Sweers, *Electric Folk*.

Chapter 3

1. For an analysis of all nine of his symphonies, see Lionel Pike, *Vaughan Williams and the Symphony* (Woodbridge: Boydell, Toccata Press, 2003). For more thoughts on responses to his music and the tendency to categorize him as hopelessly "English," see Alain Frogley, "'Getting its History Wrong': English Nationalism and the Reception of Ralph Vaughan Williams," *Music and Nationalism in 20th-Century Great Britain and Finland*, 145–61, especially 148 for the qualities of Vaughan Williams' music that often lead to his association with Englishness. The same article, updated with with some differences, appears as "Constructing Englishness in Music: National Character and the Reception of Ralph Vaughan Williams," *Vaughan Williams Studies*, Alain Frogley, ed. (Cambridge: Cambridge University Press, 2008), 1–22. For a detailed study of nationalism in a selection of his early art songs, see Renée Chérie Clark, "Aspects of National Identity in the Art Songs of Ralph Vaughan Williams before the Great War," Ph.D. thesis, University of Illinois at Urbana-Champaign, 2014.

2. For a thorough discussion and analysis, see Elsie Payne, "Vaughan Williams and Folk-song: the relation between folk-song and other elements in his comprehensive style," *Journal of the RVW Society* 13 (1998): 3–10, and *Journal of the RVW Society* 14 (1999): 17–21, reprinted from the *Music Review* 15:2 (1954): 103–26. She notes that his earlier compositions diverged into two types: direct quotations of folk songs and those which make indirect use of the folk style, at 3. Indeed, 39 of his compositions (apart from

English Hymnal settings) quote directly from folk songs, see 4. For his use of Tudor and medieval themes, see *RVW Society* 14, at 17. Much of the music he wrote that contained direct borrowings of folk songs was written before World War I. For an invaluable list and overview of the various folk songs that he used in his works, see Adam Harvey, "English Folk Songs and Other traditional Tunes in the Works of Ralph Vaughan Williams: A Checklist," *Journal of the RVW Society* 54 (2012): 3-9.

3. Ursula Vaughan Williams' biography is the starting point for studies of Vaughan Williams, *R.V.W. A Biography of Ralph Vaughan Williams* (Oxford: Clarendon Press, 1964, rep. 1995). She devotes the first chapter to discussing the distinguished heritage of the families, 1-7. Young Ralph knew his granduncle Charles Darwin, who visited on several occasions, see 12-13 and 17-18. Ursula, his wife in his last years, had unprecedented access to his papers, letters, and other material.

4. Vaughan Williams to Lord Kennet, May 20, 1941, in response to Kennet's son, Wayland Young, expressing the wish to take up composition full time. Vaughan Williams advised against it, saying that it would not provide a proper income, and it was only the "small silver spoon" from his family's status that allowed him to do so. See *Letters of Ralph Vaughan Williams: 1895-1958*, Hugh Cobbe, ed., 317-21, at 318, also quoted in full in Ursula Vaughan Williams, *R.V.W.* 240-43, at 241. The family money came from investment in railways, see Onderdonk, "The composer and society," *Cambridge Companion to Vaughan Williams* (Cambridge: Cambridge University Press, 2013, 13.

5. Literature on Vaughan Williams is vast, far more than for most of the other composers studied in this book. The standard biography is Ursula Vaughan Williams, *R.V.W.* Written at the same time for the same publisher is Michael Kennedy, *The Works of Ralph Vaughan Williams* (Oxford: Clarendon Press, 1964, rep. 2002). Studies written during the composer's lifetime include Hubert Foss, *Ralph Vaughan Williams: A Study* (London and Sydney: Harrap, 1950); Percy Young, *Vaughan Williams*; Frank Howes, *The Music of Ralph Vaughan Williams* (London and New York: Oxford University Press, 1954); and Simona Pakenham, *Ralph Vaughan Williams: A Discovery of His Music* (London: Macmillan, 1957). See also James Day, *Vaughan Williams*, Master Musicians (earlier editions in 1961 and 1974; rep. Oxford: Oxford University Press, 1998). For a study of his works in the early years after his death, see A.E.F. Dickinson, *Vaughan Williams* (London: Faber and Faber, 1963). More recently see the short biography by Simon Heffer, *Vaughan Williams* (Boston: Northeastern University Press, 2000). Useful collections of studies are *The Cambridge Companion to Vaughan Williams*; and *Ralph Vaughan Williams in Perspective*, Lewis Foreman, ed. Mellers, in *Vaughan Williams and the Vision of Albion*, offers analysis of key works and theories about duality in the man and his music. Vaughan Williams wrote extensively about music. See, for example, his lectures delivered at Bryn Mawr in 1932, published as *National Music and Other Essays* (Oxford: Oxford University Press 1934, rep. 1963, 2nd edition.

1987, rep. as *National Music and Other Essays*, Oxford: Clarendon Press, 1996). More recently, see *Vaughan Williams on Music*, David Manning, ed. (Oxford: Oxford University Press, 2008), an invaluable collection of reprinted articles and essays, written between 1897 and 1958. A short biography, beautifully illustrated with photographs, is *There was a Time... Ralph Vaughan Williams: A Pictorial Journey from the Collection of Ursula Vaughan Williams*, Stephen Connock, Ursula Vaughan Williams, and Robin Wells, eds. (London: Albion Music for the Vaughan Williams Society, 2003). An important early collection of correspondence between Vaughan Williams and Holst is *Heirs and Rebels: Letters Written to Each Other, and Occasional Writings on Music*, by Ralph Vaughan Williams and Gustav Holst, Ursula Vaughan Williams and Imogen Holst, eds. For a more recent and far more thorough collection of letters, see *Letters of Ralph Vaughan Williams: 1895-1958*, Hugh Cobbe, ed.; this is an invaluable collection that offers many insights into his life. For online information, The Ralph Vaughan Williams Society is an excellent resource for all things related to Vaughan Williams, publishing a journal, and with affiliated book and musical recording companies: http://www.rvwsociety.com, accessed November 14, 2014. The society has a useful pictorial biography of Vaughan Williams by Stephen Connock at: http://www.rvwsociety.com/bio_expanded.html, accessed November 15, 2014.

6. See, for example, Ursula Vaughan Williams, *R.W.V.*, 84; he would pay term fees for deserving students. He also paid for Holst to have a holiday in Algeria in 1908, see chapter 4.

7. Vaughan Williams would inherit this property in 1944, and donate it to the National Trust, see Ursula Vaughan Williams, *R.W.V.*, 258-59, for details.

8. Kennedy, *Works*, 11.

9. See Ursula Vaughan Williams, *R.W.V.*, 22-25, for an account of his schooling. See also Heffer, *Vaughan Williams*, 6.

10. From a letter by Emma Darwin (Charles' widow), 1884, quoted in Ursula Vaughan Williams, *R.W.V.*, 23.

11. Vaughan Williams had already begun violin lessons before entering school, see Ursula Vaughan Williams, *R.W.V.*, 19. For his time at Charterhouse, see 25-30.

12. Ursula Vaughan Williams, *R.W.V.*, 29. For more on his lack of belief, see Byron Adams, "Scripture, Church, and Culture: biblical texts in the work of Ralph Vaughan Williams," *Vaughan Williams Studies*, 99-117. See also Julian Onderdonk, "Folksong arrangements, hymn tunes and church music," *Cambridge Companion to Vaughan Williams*, 153-54.

13. Heffer, *Vaughan Williams*, 7.

14. Amusingly recalled in Ursula Vaughan Williams, *R.W.V.*, 37: "I did not see you in Chapel this morning, Mr. Vaughan Williams." | "No, Sir." | "Perhaps, however, you were in the organ loft?" | "Yes, Sir, I was." | "Well, you can pray as well in the organ loft as in any other part of the Chapel." | "Yes, Sir—but I didn't."

15. Vaughan Williams, *Musical Autobiography*, in Foss, *Ralph Vaughan Williams*, 18-38, and in *National Music*, 176-94.

16. Vaughan Williams, *Musical Autobiography*, 22.
17. Ursula Vaughan Williams, *R.V.V.*, 30.
18. Though in later years he would borrow musical ideas from Beethoven for both *Job* and his *Symphony No. 4*, having no qualms about using them, see Heffer, *Vaughan Williams*, 73.
19. See Heffer, *Vaughan Williams*, 9–10. Ursula quotes him at length in writing about his studies under Parry, *R.V.W.*, 31–33. For Parry's comments on the lineage, see 32. See also Vaughan Williams' "Talk on Parry and Stanford, 1957," I. Holst and U. Vaughan Williams, *Heirs and Rebels*, 94–102.
20. Vaughan Williams, *Musical Autobiography*, 24.
21. Both Cambridge and Oxford Universities at the time were becoming recognized as centers for musical study outside of London, see Murphy, *Green Willow*, 31.
22. Margaret Cole, *The Story of Fabian Socialism* (Stanford: Stanford University Press, 1961), 134. The Fabian Society was founded in 1884 as a movement for social reform, advocating gradual changes for more social justice, rather than revolution. For a good history, see Cole's book. Vaughan Williams had been around socialist ideas all of his life; his nurse, Sarah Wager, had not only cared for the children, but imparted some of her political philosophies to them as well, apparently with the approval of the family. See Ursula Vaughan Williams, *R.W.V.*, 11.
23. Ursula Vaughan Williams, *R.W.V.*, 41.
24. *Ibid.*, 44.
25. *Ibid.*, 43. See also chapter 4.
26. This continued into the early 1930s, see Heffer, *Vaughan Williams*, 74. Ravel, with whom Vaughan Williams would study in 1908, was a master of orchestration, and his period of study with the younger Frenchman helped to improve his technique.
27. Vaughan Williams, *Musical Autobiography*, 37.
28. Heffer, *Vaughan Williams*, 20–21.
29. *Ibid.*, 20.
30. Vaughan Williams, *Musical Autobiography*, 28.
31. Graham Muncy notes, for example, "[...] we can hear the music of a technically sure and secure composer whose orchestral technique is second to none—even in the late 1890s!" private email correspondence with the author. Roy Douglas, who worked with Vaughan Williams in the 1950s, was eager to dispel the rumor that he had orchestrated the man's works in those years, see Douglas, *Working with R.V.W.* Oxford: Oxford University Press, 1972. For a brief summary, see "Roy Douglass ... an Absurd Rumor," *Journal of the RVW Society* 63 (2015): 40, an excerpt from the book.
32. See chapter 4 for more on Holst's adoration of Wagner. For Vaughan Williams and modes, see Anthony Payne, "Encompassing His Century's Dilemmas; the modality of Vaughan Williams," *Vaughan Williams in Perspective*, 154–75. Vaughan Williams also had, from childhood, a passionate interest in Norman and gothic architecture, and this crossed over well with his interest in early music, see Ursula Vaughan Williams, *R.W.V.*, 21.
33. Vaughan Williams, *Musical Autobiography*, 27–28. See also Vaughan Williams, "Talk on Parry and Stanford," I. Holst and U. Vaughan Williams, *Heirs and Rebels*, 100–101. John Ireland had similar experiences with Stanford, though Stanford at least once used Vaughan Williams' music as an example of what Ireland could not do, see Kennedy, *Works*, 78.
34. Letter from Vaughan Williams to Holst, July 1897, Cobbe, *Letters*, 15–16. See also his *Musical Autobiography*, 29.
35. By the 1950s, he felt that hearing the *Ring Cycle* once every ten years was sufficient, and for some of Wagner's other operas, once was enough! See Ursula Vaughan Williams, *R.W.V.*, 362.
36. Ursula Vaughan Williams, *R.W.V.*, 46.
37. See *ibid.*, 38–39.
38. *Ibid.*, 49.
39. *Ibid.*, 52. See also Vaughan Williams, *Musical Autobiography*, 30. See also 21 for an earlier example of such encouragement from James Noon, the mathematics professor at Charterhouse.
40. Vaughan Williams, *Musical Autobiography*, 30.
41. Ursula Vaughan Williams, *R.W.V.*, 151.
42. *Ibid.*, 58.
43. Kennedy, *Works*, 44. See also Heffer, *Vaughan Williams*, 20. He would later receive an honorary doctorate from Oxford, in 1919, see Ursula Vaughan Williams, *R.W.V.*, 135, as well as from several other universities, including from the University of Bristol in 1951, which was conferred by Winston Churchill, see 313–14.
44. See "'Forgotten' Vaughan Williams score's first concert," BBC News: http://www.bbc.co.uk/news/uk-england-cambridgeshire-12641429, accessed November 15, 2014. The *Cambridge Mass* has also not been recorded until recently, receiving a release by Albion Records in October 2014: See also Stainer & Bell: http://www.stainer.co.uk/d99.html, accessed November 15, 2014.
45. For an impressive list of his publications in *The Vocalist* in 1902, see Ursula Vaughan Williams, *R.W.V.*, 61.
46. See Heffer, *Vaughan Williams*, 19.
47. Kennedy, *Works*, 45.
48. Vaughan Williams, *Musical Autobiography*, 31.
49. *Ibid.*, 77.
50. For the words and some commentary, see: http://about.lyndenlea.info/poem.php?pg=music, accessed November 15, 2014.
51. See Kennedy, *Works*, 407.
52. Vaughan Williams to publisher J.B. McEwen, March 1925, quoted in Kennedy, *Works*, 77n1. For the full letter, see Cobbe, *Letters*, 149, and Ursula Vaughan Williams, *R.W.V.*, 157–58.
53. For example, the Vaughan Williams family maintained close ties to the Broadwoods, who lived near Leith Hill, see Ursula Vaughan Williams, *R.W.V.*, 63. Lucy Broadwood, as we have seen, had been active in collecting folk songs in the 1890s. See also Julian Onderdonk, "The composer and society: family, politics, and nation," *Cambridge Companion to Vaughan Williams*, 11.
54. See Michael Kennedy, "Ralph Vaughan Williams-The Centenary of his Birth," *Folk Music Journal* 2:3 (1972): 167. See also Elsie Payne, "Vaughan Williams and Folk-song," *Journal of the RVW Society* 13, 3. As late as 1912, he wrote that composers should take inspiration from many sources, football chants,

street cries, factory songs, etc., see "Who Wants the English Composer?" *Royal College of Music Magazine* 9:1 (1912): 11–15, reprinted in Manning, *Vaughan Williams on Music*, 39–42, at 41. It is significant that he was writing his *London Symphony* at the time.

55. David Manning, "The public figure: Vaughan Williams as writer and activist," *Cambridge Companion to Vaughan Williams*, 240.

56. Vaughan Williams, *Musical Autobiography*, 32.

57. See Tony Kendall, "Through bushes and Briars... Vaughan Williams's earliest folk-song collecting," Foreman, *Vaughan Williams in Perspective*, 50–53, for details on these activities.

58. A thorough analysis and summary of these talks is given in Michael Holyoake, "Towards a folk song awakening: Vaughan Williams in Bournemouth, 1902," *Journal of the RVW Society* 46 (October 2009): 9–15.

59. Holyoake suggest that Lucy Broadwood, who was present at one of the Bournemouth lectures, must surely have convinced him to undertake the work of song collecting, see *ibid.*, 12.

60. See Ursula Vaughan Williams, *R.W.V.*, 63.

61. Vaughan Williams, "Good Taste," *The Vocalist* 1:2 (1902): 38, reprinted in Manning, *Vaughan Williams on Music*, 24.

62. Letter from Vaughan Williams to Ralph Wedgwood, February, 1898, Cobbe, *Letters*, 23–24.

63. For a brief account, see Ursula Vaughan Williams, *R.W.V.*, 66. See also Kendall, "Through Bushes and Through Briars," Foreman, *Vaughan Williams in Perspective*, 57–58, for how Ursula's account conflicts slightly with Vaughan Williams' own; Kendall believes that Ursula's version is more accurate. For the score of the song, and some additional history, see *Folksongs Collected by Ralph Vaughan Williams*, Roy Palmer, ed. (London: JM Dent, 1983), 27–28. For more details about the family and background that led up to this meeting, see Frank Dineen, *Ralph's People: The Ingrave Secret* (London: Albion Music, 2001), a short but useful history. Elsie Payne notes that this song and "Captain's Apprentice" (both from Essex) were the most frequently used when he was borrowing folk song ideas, see Payne, "Vaughan Williams and folk-song," *Journal of the RVW Society* 13 (1998): 4. See describes them as "outstandingly vital to his musical thought."

64. Dineen, *Ralph's People*, foreword available online at: http://www.albionmusic.com/content/our-publications/ralphs-people-ingrave-secret, accessed April 3, 2015.

65. See Palmer, *Folksongs*, 27.

66. See Ursula Vaughan Williams, *R.W.V.*, 66–67 for some details of songs he collected at this time. Initially, the two did not seem to be aware of each other's efforts, see Murphy, *Green Willow*, 50.

67. Vaughan Williams, *National Music*, 46.

68. See, for example, Vaughan Williams, "The Folk-Song," *National Music*, 22.

69. Vaughan Williams, "The Evolution of the Folk-Song," *National Music*, 33.

70. For some more thoughts on this, see Lewis Foreman, "Restless Explorations; articulating many visions," Foreman, *Vaughan Williams in Perspective*, 19. See also Payne, "Vaughan Williams and Folk-song," *RVW Society* 13, 3.

71. Vaughan Williams, *National Music*, 41.

72. See Palmer, *Folk Songs*, iii–vi, for a larger listing of the counties in which Vaughan Williams collected. For some examples of the fruits of his collecting expeditions, see Ursula Vaughan Williams, *R.W.V.*, 72–73 and 83–84. For the assistance given to him by Ella Mary Leather (a somewhat forgotten figure in folk song collection), see Richard Birt, "Wise and Fair and Good as She," *Journal of the RVW Society* 13 (1998): 2 and 24. On his manuscript of collected songs, compiled between 1903 and 1913, see Onderdonk, "Vaughan Williams's folksong transcriptions," 122n7.

73. Vaughan Williams to Stewart Gowe, October 4, 1904, quoted in Ursula Vaughan Williams, *R.W.V.*, 69–70.

74. Letter from Vaughan Williams to the *Morning Post*, December 2, 1903, quoted in full in Kendall, "Through Bushes and Through Briars," Foreman, *Vaughan Williams in Perspective*, 62.

75. For an account of his collecting adventures in King's Lynn in 1905, see Edgar Samuel, "Vaughan Williams and Kings' Lynn," *Journal of the RVW Society* 14 (1999): 22–23, and James Carter, "Fisherman of King's Lynn," *Journal of the RVW Society* 14 (1999): 23–24.

76. For more analysis of the *Norfolk Rhapsodies*, see Anthony Newton, "Vaughan Williams and the Idea of Folk Song in the Norfolk Rhapsodies," *Journal of the RVW Society* 46 (2009): 3–6. See also Kennedy, *Works*, 82–84.

77. Ursula noted that in 1953, for example, he made a slight change to a second violin passage in the *London Symphony*, saying, "I've changed my ideas in forty years," Ursula Vaughan Williams, *R.W.V.*, 337.

78. The piece, edited and reconstructed by Stephen Hogger, is available on Vaughan Williams, *Pastoral Symphony*, London Symphony Orchestra, Richard Hickox, conductor, Chandos 10001, CD, 2002. See the liner notes for more on the rhapsodies and the specific folk songs that Vaughan Williams used in them. Ursula Vaughan Williams authorized this reconstruction and recording, as she would for various other pieces, for the interest of musicologists and listeners alike, feeling that enough time had passed that some of his suppressed music deserved a new hearing.

79. For Vaughan Williams' own recollection, see *The First Fifty Years: a Brief Account of the English Hymnal from 1906 to 1956* (London: Oxford University Press, 1956), a portion of which is reprinted in "Some Reminiscences of the English Hymnal," Manning, *Vaughan Williams on Music*, 115–18. He noted that, "the final clinch was given when I understood that if I did not do the job it would be offered to a well-known church musician with whose musical ideas I was much out of sympathy," at 115, where he also mentioned that he thought it would only take two months to complete. See also Ursula Vaughan Williams, *R.W.V.*, 70–72. For a study of the 100 years between 1906 and 2006, see Simon Wright, "'Pale Green of the English Hymnal!'—A Centenary Retrospective," *Brio: Journal of IAML* 43:1 (2006): 2–20. See also Ursula Vaughan Williams, *R.W.V.*, 157, where she notes that he was called upon again in 1924 to produce another hymn book, *Songs of Praise*. In 1928, he also edited the

Oxford Book of Carols. He had a great fondness for English carols and wanted to promote their use as much as folk songs, see, for example, Ursula Vaughan Williams, *R.W.V.*, 105–06 and 272. On the carol revival see Howes, *Renaissance*, 81–83.

80. For a remarkable historical recording of Vaughan Williams speaking about the process of creating the hymnal, see: https://www.youtube.com/watch?v=TtoHusbBuqQ, accessed November 15, 2014.

81. Mellers, *Vision of Albion*, 258.

82. On the presence of folk song, see Julian Onderdonk, "Folk-Songs in the English Hymnal," *Strengthen for Service: 100 Years of the English Hymnal 1906–2006*, Alan Luff, ed. (Norwich: Canterbury Press, 2005), 191–216. He notes at 201, for example, that Vaughan Williams simplified 19 of his settings to make them easy for everyone to sing; see also 203–04. See also Onderdonk, "Hymn Tunes from Folk Songs: Vaughan Williams and English Hymnody," *Vaughan Williams Essays*, Byron Adams and Robin Wells, eds. (Aldershot, UK: Ashgate, 2003), 109 and 112; and Onderdonk, "Folksong arrangements," where he notes at 136 that Vaughan Williams observed that as far back as 1601, the German composer Hans Leo Hassler may well have used a folk song in one of his chorales. For a comprehensive background on the formation of the *Hymnal* and its relations to the needs for "Englishness" at the time, see Katie Heathman, "'Lift up a living nation': Church and nation in *The English Hymnal*," MA dissertation, University of Leicester, 2012. I am grateful to Ms. Heathman for allowing me to read her work. Vaughan Williams' use of these newly-collected folk songs was an attempt to popularize them, see 23, and Onderdonk, "Folk-Songs in the English Hymnal," 192, 195, and 197.

83. Vaughan Williams, "Some Reminiscences of the English Hymnal," Manning, *Vaughan Williams on Music*, 116.

84. On this, see Onderdonk, "Hymn Tunes from Folk Songs," 103.

85. Michael Short, *Gustav Holst: The Man and His Music* (London: Oxford University Press, 1990), 54–55. See also Heathman, "Lift up a living nation," 22.

86. Heathman, "Lift up a living nation," 33–35.

87. Kennedy, *Works*, 42. See also Heffer, *Vaughan Williams*, 28–29 for more thoughts on this. Heathman notes that the Hymnal drew on both religious beliefs and the Arts and Crafts movement, "Lift up a living nation," at 9 and 19.

88. *Ibid.*, 38–39, and 54–58, for a broader discussion of Christian socialism and socialism in general. See also Onderdonk, "English Hymnal," 210–11.

89. See Onderdonk, "English Hymnal," 206–09, for a listing of the works.

90. The work was initially called *The Ocean*. He enjoyed spending time at the beach, and on one occasion in 1904, while visiting Robin Hood's Bay in Yorkshire, he nearly drowned, see Ursula Vaughan Williams, *R.W.V.*, 68–69.

91. Butterworth, Hugh Allen, Stanford, and Lucy Broadwood were all in attendance, giving their support, see Murphy, *Green Willow*, 78. Stanford, despite his many criticisms of his student's work, was the one who persuaded the Festival to perform the piece, see Vaughan Williams, "Talk on Parry and Stanford," I. Holst and U. Vaughan Williams, *Heirs and Rebels*, 101–02.

92. For example, see Stanford's *Songs of the Sea* (1904) and *Songs of the Fleet* (1910), Elgar's *Sea Pictures* (1899), Debussy's *La mer* (1905), and Frank Bridge's *The Sea* (1911).

93. See Heffer, *Vaughan Williams*, 38–39, for some appraisal and reactions. However, Vaughan Williams believed that the *Sea Symphony* had a "very doubtful reception," and that it was Hugh Allen's generosity in organizing repeat performances that helped, despite his own reservations about the work, see *Musical Autobiography*, 26.

94. See Ursula Vaughan Williams, *R.W.V.*, 78–79.

95. Ursula Vaughan Williams, *R.W.V.*, 74–75.

96. Several examples of this resistance to period instruments and practices, which could be vehement at times, can be found in Cobbe, *Letters*. See 99, 142, 391, 448, 612, and 628. He was sure Bach would have preferred the piano to the harpsichord if he had had access to one (see 628), though modern musicologists would likely dispute this.

97. Vaughan Williams, "Preface" to his folk song collection, *The Journal of the Folk-Song Society* 2:8 (1906): 141.

98. For its aims and goals, see Ursula Vaughan Williams, *R.W.V.*, 73–74.

99. Graham Muncy, private email correspondence with the author.

100. Kennedy, *Works*, 85.

101. Muncy, in private email correspondence with the author, observes: "By 1906, VW had in fact composed several large-scale and substantial works, many of which had been performed with continued performances into the second decade of the century. He even supplied a works list of them to a critic who was writing a short biography and included many early titles by which he had become known. However, he apparently did little to further these pieces by way of publication and by about 1919, they had gradually dropped from view."

102. Ursula Vaughan Williams, *R.W.V.*, 77.

103. Vaughan Williams, *Musical Autobiography*, 34.

104. Ravel's orchestration of Mussorgsky's piano work *Pictures at an Exhibition* in 1922 is one famous example of his skill. For Vaughan Williams' correspondence and impressions, see Cobbe, *Letters*, 61–63. He was particularly grateful to French music critic Michel Calvocoressi for introducing them. For a good study of his time with Ravel and its influence, see Byron Adams, "Vaughan Williams's musical apprenticeship," *Cambridge Companion to Vaughan Williams*, 38–53.

105. "Sans le piano on ne peut pas inventer des nouvelles harmonies," Ravel noted, quoted in Ursula Vaughan Williams, *R.W.V.*, 80. She details their interactions and correspondence at 79–82, including an early meeting where Ravel asked him to write a "little minuet" in the style of Mozart, and Vaughan Williams flatly refused! See 79. See also Heffer, *Vaughan Williams*, 32–33 for more on their time together.

106. Vaughan Williams noted that Ravel told him, "[…] that I was the only pupil who 'n'écrit pas de ma musique,'" quoted in Ursula Vaughan Williams, *R.W.V.*, 82. See also Heffer, *Vaughan Williams*, 35.

107. Ravel to Vaughan Williams, March 3, 1908, quoted in Ursula Vaughan Williams, *R.W.V.*, 81.
108. Ursula Vaughan Williams, *R.W.V.*, 86.
109. See, for example, Ravel's letters to Vaughan Williams, quoted in Ursula Vaughan Williams, *R.W.V.*, 118, 120, and 133.
110. Vaughan Williams, *Along the Field*, John Mark Ainsley and the Nash Ensemble, Hyperion A67168, CD, 2002, liner notes by Michael Hurd.
111. See Ursula Vaughan Williams, *R.W.V.*, 82.
112. For examples, see Aidan J. Thomson, "Becoming a national composer: critical reception to c. 1925," *Cambridge Companion to Vaughan Williams*, 62.
113. Ursula Vaughan Williams, *R.W.V.*, 88.
114. Though it would not receive its London premiere until February 4, 1913, see Ursula Vaughan Williams, *R.W.V.*, 107. On the importance of these festivals and the rise of importance of instrumental music, even at those mainly focused on choral music, see Charles Edward McGuire, "Vaughan Williams and the English Music Festival: 1910," *Vaughan Williams Essays*, 235–68. Having two of his major works premiered by two major festivals in the same year was something that would not happen again, see 261.
115. See Kennedy, *Works*, 108–09; Vaughan Williams was still not well-known provincially. See also Thomson, "Becoming a national composer," 59–60. See also 64–65 for reactions, both favorable and otherwise, to the *Tallis Fantasia*.
116. Tallis was a gifted and praised composer of the time, living from the reign of Henry VIII well into that of his daughter, Elizabeth I, and managing to navigate the religious and political turmoil of 16th-century England.
117. Connock, et al, *There was a Time*, 17.
118. See Ursula Vaughan Williams, *R.W.V.*, 88. Vaughan Williams had included another of Tallis' melodies in the *English Hymnal* project a few years earlier. McGuire suggests in "English Music Festival" that the *Fantasia* is "a composition designed in part to give an Anglican balance to Elgar's Catholic *Gerontius*," at 260.
119. See Paul Spicer, *Herbert Howells* (Bridgend: Seren, 1998), 22 and 116. For a more detailed discussion of the fantasia and its effect on its young listeners, see Rob Young, "Cloud of Knowing," June 11, 2010, *Guardian* online: http://www.theguardian.com/culture/2010/jun/12/vaughan-williams-fantasia-theme-tallis, accessed May 5, 2015. See also *The Passions of Vaughan Williams*, directed by John Bridcut (2008, BBC 4), unfortunately not commercially available at the moment.
120. See chapter 5 for more details.
121. Michael Barlow, *Whom the Gods Love*, 120, quoting from the *Butterworth Memorial Volume*, 92–93 (see chapter 5). There are other versions of this story. For a slightly different account, see also Ursula Vaughan Williams, *R.W.V.*, 95. For Vaughan Williams' shortened account see "George Butterworth," *National Music*, 245. In this same passage Vaughan Williams also noted that he had previously sketched out movements for other symphonic ideas, but that these were, "all now happily lost."
122. See Vaughan Williams, *A London Symphony: The Original 1913 Version of the Symphony No. 2*, London Symphony Orchestra, Richard Hickox, conductor, Chandos 9902, 2001, compact disc, liner notes by Stephen Connock (6–11), and Michael Kennedy (11–13), 11.
123. H.G. Wells, *Tono-Bungay*, 1908–09. Various versions are available online, including at Project Gutenberg: http://www.gutenberg.org/files/718/718-h/718-h.htm, accessed November 17, 2014. For information on the influence of this work on the symphony, see Connock, liner notes, *A London Symphony*, 7. See also Frogley, "H.G. Wells and Vaughan Williams's 'London Symphony': Politics and Culture in fin-de-siécle England," *Sundry Sorts of Music Books: Essays on the British Library Collections*, Chris A. Banks, Arthur Searle, and Malcolm Turner, eds. (London, 1993), 299–308.
124. Letter from Holst to Vaughan Williams, March 29, 1914, I. Holst and U. Vaughan Williams, *Heirs and Rebels*, 43, also quoted in Ursula Vaughan Williams, *R.W.V.*, 111.
125. Butterworth, "Vaughan Williams London Symphony," *RCM Magazine* 10:2 (1914), 44–46, reprinted in Barlow, *Gods*, 169–71, at 169–70. See also Butterworth's letter to Vaughan Williams, March 28, 1914, Cobbe, *Letters*, 94. For other reviews and reactions, see Thomson, "Becoming a national composer," 66.
126. Michael Barlow, *Gods*, 122. For correspondence on the efforts to reconstruct the work, see Cobbe, *Letters*, 102–05. The 1920 version was highly regarded, see Thomson, "Becoming a national composer," 68–69.
127. Letter from Vaughan Williams to John Barbirolli, October 6, 1951, Cobbe, *Letters*, 487. He would compose three more symphonies over the next few years.
128. See *n*122 above. This recording is a remarkable restoration of the earliest version of the work, and while it was not the one that Vaughan Williams intended for posterity, it provides great insight into how he originally conceived the piece.
129. Given January 10, 1912, see Ursula Vaughan Williams, *R.W.V.*, 100.
130. Vaughan Williams, "English Folk Songs," a lecture first printed in *The Music Student* 4 (1912): 6–11, et al, reprinted with additions in Young, *Vaughan Williams*, 200–17, and reprinted in full in Manning, *Vaughan Williams on Music*, 185–200, at 198 and 199.
131. Listener polls for classical radio in Britain have longed ranked the work as among the favorites.
132. On this, see Ursula Vaughan Williams, *R.W.V.*, 132.
133. Murphy, *Green Willow*, 164.
134. Muncy, private email correspondence with the author: "When VW joined up on 31 December, the strict criteria were perhaps beginning to be relaxed as desperation was setting in," with older recruits, like Vaughan Williams, being placed in non-combat positions.
135. Ursula recounts his war-time experiences in *R.W.V.*, 115–32. On his relationship to others, see 117–18.
136. Parry to Vaughan Williams, January 19, 1915, quoted in Ursula Vaughan Williams, *R.W.V.*, 117.

137. See chapter 4.
138. Noted by his army friend Henry Steggles in *The R.C.M. Magazine*, 55:1 (1959): 24, quoted in Ursula Vaughan Williams, *R.W.V.*, 124. See also Heffer, *Vaughan Williams*, 49. For more on his time there, see Alan K. Aldous, "Ralph Vaughan Williams in Salonika," *Journal of the RVW Society* 16 (1999): 7–8.
139. See chapter 4.
140. Heffer, *Vaughan Williams*, 50. See also Ursula Vaughan Williams, *R.W.V.*, 132.
141. Ursula Vaughan Williams, *R.W.V.*, 122.
142. Samuel Hynes, *A War Imagined: The First World War and English Culture* (London: Pimlico, 1992), 129.
143. Letter from Vaughan Williams to Ursula Wood (later Vaughan Williams), October 4, 1938, Cobbe, *Letters*, 265, also quoted in Ursula Vaughan Williams, *R.W.V.*, 121. See also Murphy, *Green Willow*, 196. Philip Heseltine, once joked that Vaughan Williams' music was, "a little too much like a cow looking over a gate," see Robert Nichols, "At Oxford," *Peter Warlock: A Memoir of Philip Heseltine*, Cecil Gray, et al. (London: Jonathan Cape, 1934), 78–79, though Heseltine admired the symphony, see chapter 7. He later called it "the highest point yet reached by an Englishman" and "the best English orchestral music of the century," see Barry Smith, *Peter Warlock: The Life of Philip Heseltine* (Oxford: Oxford University Press, 1994) 236 and 258; see also 115. For other negative reactions to the work, see Eric Saylor, "Not Lambkins Frisking," 48.
144. For a detailed analysis of the work and both its pastoral and modernist characteristics, see Daniel M. Grimley, "Landscape and Distance: Vaughan Williams, Modernism and the Symphonic Pastoral," 147–74. Heffer offers some observations in *Vaughan Williams*, 56–57. See also Kennedy, *Works*, 169–72.
145. Lucy Broadwood to Vaughan Williams, January 29, 1922, quoted in Ursula Vaughan Williams, *R.W.V.*, 140.
146. See Grimley, "Landscape and Distance," 148–51, for some of the more critical responses, generally born out of a misunderstanding of the work.
147. She died of lung cancer in April, 1920.
148. See chapter 1.
149. Vaughan Williams to Holst, 1925 (no other date), quoted in Short, *Gustav Holst*, 186. See also Ursula Vaughan Williams, *R.W.V.*, 136–37.
150. See Short, *Gustav Holst*, 336.
151. Vaughan Williams, *Musical Autobiography*, 38, quoted in I. Holst and U. Vaughan Williams, *Heirs and Rebels*, 76. See also Short, *Gustav Holst*, 284–85. See also Jon C. Mitchell, *A Comprehensive Biography of Composer Gustav Holst, with Correspondence and Diary Excerpts* (Lewiston, NY: Mellen, 2001), 399–400.
152. Imogen Holst, *Gustav Holst: A Biography* (London: Oxford University Press. 1938, revised 1969), 147.
153. See chapter 4.
154. Heffer, *Vaughan Williams*, 52.
155. Michael Kennedy, *Adrian Boult* (London: Hamish Hamilton, 1987), 68.
156. See Ursula Vaughan Williams, *R.W.V.*, 136.
157. See Frogley, "Constructing Englishness in Music," 15, for more on the importance of the Pastoral school in post-war Britain.
158. Vaughan Williams to Lord Kennet, May 20, 1941, Cobbe, *Letters*, 320, also quoted in Vaughan Williams, *R.W.V.*, 243. Showing that he was not languishing in the past, he became president of the Committee for the Promotion of New Music in 1943, which he joked was the "Society for Prevention of Cruelty to New Music," see Ursula Vaughan Williams, *R.W.V.*, 256–57.
159. Vaughan Williams, "Nationalism and Internationalism," in *National Music*, 158–59. See also "Tradition," at 59, and "Should Music Be National?" at 11.
160. Vaughan Williams, "The Evolution of the Folk-Song," in *National Music*, 47. See also his "Talk on Parry and Stanford," I. Holst and U. Vaughan Williams, *Heirs and Rebels*, 99, where he restates the same sentiments as late as 1957.
161. Ursula Vaughan Williams, *R.W.V.*, 138, and Heffer, *Vaughan Williams*, 54. For some additional background and analysis, see Mellers, *Vision of Albion*, 68–75. See also Thomson, "Becoming a national composer," 74, where he calls it one of "the 'first fruits' of the Tudor revival in England." Vaughan Williams did set more religious texts in the post-war period, see Clark, "Aspects of National Identity," 313.
162. The choir is still very active. See its website: www.thebachchoir.org.uk, accessed November 17, 2014.
163. See Ursula Vaughan Williams, *R.W.V.*, 139–40, for a background on the choir and his work with it.
164. Ursula Vaughan Williams, *R.W.V.*, 148.
165. See *n*96, and Cobbe, *Letters*, 99. This was something of a naïve view, appropriate for his time but not ours. These days, period performance groups of all sizes are ubiquitous and have produced stunning results in the effort to recreate the sound of early music from the medieval, Renaissance, and Baroque periods.
166. See Ursula Vaughan Williams, *R.W.V.*, 142–45, for his correspondence with Holst and Adeline's letter to her sister, Cordelia, detailing more of their experiences.
167. Ursula Vaughan Williams, *R.W.V.*, 348.
168. Ursula Vaughan Williams, *R.W.V.*, 149–50. Though he did not like traditional ballet, other forms of pairing music with dance appealed to him, as in *Job*. See *n*188, below.
169. See Murphy, *Green Willow*, 149 for some of its folk influences.
170. For some recent studies of this important work, see *The Making of Peter Grimes: Essays and Studies*, Paul Banks, ed. (Woodbridge: Boydell, 2000).
171. Often his operas were first worked on by student groups, which perhaps caused them to be perceived as amateur pieces, see Ursula Vaughan Williams, *R.W.V.*, 176. He was further convinced (against popular opinion) that opera should be translated, even if this meant losing the poetry of the original, see 108.
172. A work which he would later claim was his favorite of his choral pieces, see Ursula Vaughan Williams, *R.W.V.*, 162 and 391. See also Cobbe, *Letters*, 347 and 410.

173. Holst had produced a similar work, *At the Boar's Head*, which was met with equal coolness, see chapter 4.
174. See Ursula Vaughan Williams, *R.W.V.*, 174–75, for Vaughan William's own thoughts, in his *Preface to Sir John in Love*. He notes at 175, "out of a total of 120 minutes of music, the folk tunes occupy less than 15." Heffer provides some useful commentary on both works in *Vaughan Williams*, 66–69.
175. Gerald Finzi, letter to Howard Ferguson, April 10, 1928, in *Letters of Gerald Finzi and Howard Ferguson*, Ferguson and Michael Hurd, eds. (Woodbridge: Boydell, 2001), 26.
176. Vaughan Williams, *Preface*, quoted in Ursula Vaughan Williams, *R.W.V.*, 174. Shakespeare was another love of his, and he provided suggestions and repertoire for incidental music to various plays, see, for example, 103–04.
177. See chapter 4.
178. For a short analysis, see John Barr, "The Folk Songs of Ralph Vaughan Williams's *Six Studies in English Folksong*," *Journal of the RVW Society* 13 (1998): 14–15. He discusses how these settings were in some ways ideal versions of the tunes, rather than faithful adaptations, emphasized by the fact that they are instrumental.
179. Ursula also notes that from the mid-1920s, he began to put on weight, owing to a love of sweets, pies, and fatty foods, and that the slim and fit figure was gone forever, see 166. The stress of his personal life may also have contributed to this.
180. Ursula Vaughan Williams, *R.W.V.*, 62.
181. *Ibid.*, 122. After his death, she wore black for the rest of her life. She would later grieve for the loss of her sister's niece, Honorine Williamson, in a London air raid in September 1940; she had been like a daughter to the Vaughan Williams for several years, see 235–36.
182. *Ibid.*, 85.
183. *Ibid.*, 90.
184. *Ibid.*, 169.
185. Heffer, *Vaughan Williams*, 70–71. For more details, see Ursula Vaughan Williams, *R.W.V.*, 171–72, and 178. They would eventually buy the property in 1933.
186. Ursula Vaughan Williams, *R.W.V.*, 179. This has been noted by most studies of the composer's life.
187. Ursula Vaughan Williams, *R.W.V.*, 183.
188. In 1912, he had been approached by the eccentric and brilliant American dancer Isadora Duncan, to create music for a choral ballet based on a new translation of *The Bacchae* (the ancient story of Dionysius, the Greek god of wine). Vaughan Williams was charmed by her dancing and her rejection of traditional ballet style, which he disliked even then, and agreed to the collaboration. She would occasionally take him about London at night in her car, stopping to take walks and dazzle the locals. Sadly, nothing came of the work, except for one piece, *Where is the Home for Me?* Isadora, being flighty and mercurial, vanished from his life and he lost track of her. See Ursula Vaughan Williams, *R.W.V.*, 94 and 105. On his preference for the term "masque" for *Job*, see his letter to Edwin Evans of December 14, 1930, Cobbe, *Letters*, 184.

189. See Ursula Vaughan Williams, *R.W.V.*, 188. There was an additional performance in Oxford, which he did not attend. On his relationship to the dancers and staging, see 187. Holst was very involved in offering his critiques and opinions of *Job*, see Mitchell, *Comprehensive Biography of Composer Gustave Holst*, 398–90.
190. Vaughan Williams, *National Music*, cited multiple times in these chapters. For his time there, see Ursula Vaughan Williams, *R.W.V.*, 191–93, and Heffer, *Vaughan Williams*, 76–78. Manning notes that these lectures did not so much define national music, but were, "an explanation of what Vaughan Williams would wish national music to be in an ideal world," see David Manning, "The public figure," 244.
191. Vaughan Williams to Imogen Holst, 1935, quoted in Ursula Vaughan Williams, *R.W.V.*, 204, but not found in Cobbe's collection.
192. Vaughan Williams, "Some Conclusions," *National Music*, 68.
193. See, for example, his letter to Maud Karpeles, quoted in Ursula Vaughan Williams, *R.W.V.*, 193, where he describes the tragic and classical beauty of the city as viewed from atop the Empire State Building.
194. Heather de Savage, "Chronology," *Cambridge Companion to Vaughan Williams*, xix.
195. Ursula Vaughan Williams, *R.W.V.*, 195.
196. For more details on Holst's declining health, see chapter 4.
197. Letter to Isobel and Imogen Holst, May 25, 1934 (the day Holst died), Cobbe, *Letters*, 227. See also Ursula Vaughan Williams, *R.W.V.*, 200. Adeline would help in giving her own assessments of his work, see 208. See also Kennedy, *Works*, 241. As late as February 5, 1953, he wrote to composer Sydney Waddington: "I feel lost without you or Gustav to look over my things & tell me where to get off [...]" Cobbe, *Letters*, 518. Waddington had offered him a similar role in assessing his compositions, see Vaughan Williams, *Musical Autobiography*, 36.
198. Letter from Vaughan Williams to Holst, July 1906, Cobbe, *Letters*, 51.
199. Kennedy, *Works*, 241.
200. On this, see *ibid.*, 243–46. For a good study of the work, and the events leading up to it, see Anthony Barone, "Modernist Rifts in a Pastoral Landscape: Observations on the Manuscripts of Vaughan Williams's Fourth Symphony," *Musical Quarterly* 91:1–2 (2008): 60–88.
201. Letter from Vaughan Williams to Adrian Boult, August 19, 1934, Cobbe, *Letters*, 239. See also Barone, "Modernist Rifts," 74. Finzi also heard the piano run-through and those of many other of Vaughan Williams' works, see Banfield, "Vaughan Williams and Gerald Finzi," Foreman, *Vaughan Williams in Perspective*, 208.
202. Vaughan Williams to R.G. Longman, December 1937, quoted in Kennedy, *Works*, 247. See also 245, and Ursula Vaughan Williams, *R.W.V.*, 190. In contrast, his *Dona Nobis Pacem* from the same year was a call for peace based on his own wartime experiences, and the prospect of new conflict.
203. Michael Kennedy, "Fluctuations in the response

to the music of Ralph Vaughan Williams," *Cambridge Companion to Vaughan Williams*, 283.

204. For further thoughts on this, see Kennedy, *Works*, 264–65.

205. Kennedy, *Works*, 246. He notes that Vaughan Williams made this remark during rehearsals for the first performance, and that Adrian Boult confirmed its authenticity. For his detailed thoughts on the work, see his letter to R.G. Longman, December 1937, where he restates his uncertainty about whether he likes it, but it was what he "wanted to do *at the time*," Cobbe, *Letters*, 254–55, also quoted in Kennedy, *Works*, 246–47. Heffer has suggested that Vaughan Williams suffering two successive injuries, the broken leg and then a septic cut, both of which required convalescence, may have caused much frustration and anger which found its way into the work, see *Vaughan Williams*, 83. Holst's death, and the increasing strain of his marriage may have also contributed.

206. Barone, "Modernist Rifts," 64–65. See also 86n20.

207. Kennedy, *Works*, 239. See also Ursula Vaughan Williams, *R.W.V.*, 205.

208. See Vaughan Williams, *R.W.V.*, 194, for Frank Howes' assessment.

209. It was founded by King Edward VII at his coronation in 1902, to be "given to such persons, subjects of Our Crown, as may have rendered exceptionally meritorious services in Our Crown Services or towards the advancement of the Arts, Learning, Literature, and Science or such other exceptional service as We are fit to recognise." See the *British Monarchy* website: http://www.royal.gov.uk/MonarchUK/Honours/OrderofMerit/OrderofMerit.aspx, accessed November 20, 2014.

210. As he would later remark in his letter from Vaughan Williams to Rutland Boughton, July 9, 1952, Cobbe, *Letters*, 502–03. Vaughan Williams also castigates Boughton for his seeming support of the Soviet Union, saying that the Soviets are the antithesis of true socialism and communism. See also his letter to Boughton from December 20, 1950, 470–72, and 472, n1 and n2. For more background on Boughton, see Duncan Hall, '*A Pleasant Change from Politics*,' 26, 126–31, 140, and 144. See also Vaughan Williams' brief letter to Imogen Holst on accepting the award, and hoping that her father would approve, June 7, 1935, Cobbe, *Letters*, 238. See also Hughes and Stradling, *English Musical Renaissance*, 242–44.

211. See Ursula Vaughan Williams, *R.W.V.*, 207–08.

212. Letter from Vaughan Williams to Hermann Fiedler, July 1937, Cobbe, *Letters*, 249. See also his related letters at 250–51. Also quoted in Ursula Vaughan Williams, *R.W.V.*, 217.

213. Ursula Vaughan Williams, *R.W.V.*, 221–22.

214. For some details of their first meeting, see Ursula Vaughan Williams, *R.W.V.*, 218–19, which takes on the feel of an autobiography from this point in her book.

215. Two documentary films, *The Passions of Vaughan Williams*, directed by John Bridcut, and *O Thou Transcendent*, DVD, directed by Tony Palmer (2007, UK: Tony Palmer Films), reveal new details about his private life. Bridcut's summary of his film can be read online: http://www.dailymail.co.uk/femail/article-567375/Vaughan-Williams-wife-mistress-shared-bed.html, accessed November 20, 2014. See also the filmmaker's website: http://www.johnbridcut.com/filmdetail.php?film=3&pic=28#chosenpic, accessed November 20, 2014.

216. See, for example, his letter to Ursula of October 4, 1938. She had sent him a poem, which he was returning because it was "rather too personal to show around, though I like it (and your hair)." Cobbe, *Letters*, 265. See also Harold Fromm, "Against Representation: Ralph Vaughan Williams and the Erotics of Art," *Hudson Review* 63:2 (2010): 286.

217. The pregnancy is discussed in both *Passions* and *O Thou*. On thoughts of their being childless, and how Finzi might have taken on some of that role, see Banfield, "Vaughan Williams and Gerald Finzi," Foreman, *Vaughan Williams in Perspective*, 220.

218. She recounts the "numbing shock" of this event and describes how Adeline said "I don't want you to feel far from us," in Ursula Vaughan Williams, *R.W.V.*, 247. See also 248.

219. Ursula Vaughan Williams, *R.W.V.*, 222.

220. The tune has many alternate titles, depending on geographical location, see Kennedy, *Works*, 278. See also Heathman, "Lift up a living nation," 24.

221. See Heffer, *Vaughan Williams*, 98 and 112–13, and Kennedy, *Works*, 278.

222. Ursula Vaughan Williams, *R.W.V.*, 230.

223. Ursula Vaughan Williams, *R.W.V.*, 224. See also 236, for conditions with refugee artists. Various friends and relations would stay with them during the war, see Ursula Vaughan Williams, *R.W.V.*, 259.

224. Gerald Finzi and his wife would engage in similar activities from their country home, while he also worked in London, see chapter 8.

225. On his bombing and fire duties, see Ursula Vaughan Williams, *R.W.V.*, 233 and 253. On growing food, see 229 and 237–38. See his letter to Wood of July 1940 on his fire brigade training, Cobbe, *Letters*, 301, involving a real fire and creeping along on his stomach with an axe and hosepipe.

226. Vaughan Williams, "The Composer in Wartime," 1940," I. Holst and U. Vaughan Williams, *Heirs and Rebels*, 92.

227. See his foreword for the Society's brochure from March 1954, Cobbe, *Letters*, 540–41. See also Heffer, *Vaughan Williams*, 102 and 105.

228. See Ursula Vaughan Williams, *R.W.V.*, 255. Vaughan Williams did write to Tippett on December 17, 1941, rebuking him for his stance, pointing out that Finzi and others were contributing to bringing the war to an end without fighting, so why was he not? See Cobbe, *Letters*, 329–30. See also his letters to Granville Bantock from August 21 and 29, 1940, on securing release for interred German musicians, whom he saw as no threat, Cobbe, *Letters*, 302–04.

229. Letter from Vaughan Williams to the Director-General of the BBC, March 9, 1941, Cobbe, *Letters*, 314. See also Ursula Vaughan Williams, *R.W.V.*, 239.

230. Letter from George Trevelyan to Vaughan Williams, on the death of their mutual friend Maurice Amos in 1940, quoted in Ursula Vaughan Williams, *R.W.V.*, 233.

231. Films with his music: *49th Parallel* (1940); *Coastal Command* (1942); *The People's Land* (1943); *The Story of Flemish Farm* (1943); *Stricken Peninsula* (1945); *The Loves of Joanna Godden* (1946); *Scott of the Antarctic* (1948); *The Dim Little Island* (1949); *Bitter Springs* (1950); and *The England of Elizabeth* (1955). He had long been a fan of the cinema, see Ursula Vaughan Williams, *R.W.V.*, 239. For a list of his other patriotic war-time music, see Clark, "Aspects of National Identity," 303n557. For a good study of how music was used to further the war effort, see Kate Guthrie, "Propaganda Music in the Second World War: John Ireland's *Epic March*," *Journal of the Royal Musical Association* 139:1 (2014): 137–75. While focusing on Ireland's piece, it offers a detailed general discussion of the subject.

232. Ursula Vaughan Williams, *R.W.V.*, 254. Some were elated by this, others not as much. For further background on the work's themes and possible folk song connections, see Murray Dineen, "Vaughan Williams's Fifth Symphony: Ideology and Aural Tradition," *Vaughan Williams Essays*, 17–27.

233. Dineen, "Vaughan Williams's Fifth Symphony," 23–25.

234. Including Adrian Boult, who noted in a letter to Vaughan Williams from June 27, 1943, "Ann & I both feel that its serene loveliness is completely satisfying in these times & shows, as only music can, what we must work for when this madness is over." Cobbe, *Letters*, 360.

235. Kennedy, *Works*, 279.

236. Letter from Sibelius (in translation) to Vaughan Williams, June 18, 1946, Cobbe, *Letters*, 401.

237. Kennedy, *Works*, 279. For his analysis of the work, see 279–83. Some ideas for the symphony also found their way into his *Oboe Concerto*, from 1944. See also Ursula Vaughan Williams, *R.W.V.*, 273.

238. Ursula once said that all of his symphonies from the *Fifth* onward were "hers," in that, regardless of program or lack thereof, they were effectively dedicated to her. See *Passions of Vaughan Williams*.

239. See Ursula Vaughan Williams, *R.W.V.*, 251. Finzi noted some of the pieces dedicated to Vaughan Williams and broadcast on his birthday (he was in the studio) with amusingly blunt commentary, calling one work "ghastly," another "fussy and uninteresting," and another "balls." See his letter to Howard Ferguson, October 12, 1942, *Letters of Gerald Finzi*, 231–32.

240. Ursula Vaughan Williams, *R.W.V.*, 261. The work was apparently misplaced after Vaughan Williams delivered it, and was not found for six months, after which he had to quickly revise and orchestrate it, see his letter to Victor Hely-Hutchinson at the BBC, May 14, 1945, Cobbe, *Letters*, 385. For some thoughts on Vaughan Williams' image as a "national composer" in response to the war effort, see Frogley, "'Getting its History Wrong,'" 159.

241. See, for example, Ursula Vaughan Williams, *R.W.V.*, 253, 261, 266, 269, 294, and 295. Adeline was prone to such accidents and ailments.

242. See Ursula Vaughan Williams, *R.W.V.*, 264–65, and 277.

243. On his federalist views, see Ursula Vaughan Williams, *R.W.V.*, 234 and 361. He also refused to sign an artists' peace petition in 1950, noting the growing Soviet threat, see 303, and n210 above. See his letter to Iris Lemare of October 4, 1940, outlining some of his positions on a European Union, Cobbe, *Letters*, 306–07. See also Onderdonk, "The composer and society," 22.

244. Letter from Vaughan Williams to Frank Howes, August 10, 1949, Cobbe, *Letters*, 433.

245. Michael Kennedy, *Works of Ralph Vaughan Williams*, 302, see also n1. See also Ursula Vaughan Williams, *R.W.V.*, 283.

246. Vaughan Williams, *Early and Late Works*, Royal Scottish National Orchestra, Martin Yates, conductor, Epoch CDLX 7289, 2012, compact disc, liner notes by Lewis Foreman (3–8), 4. A portion of the work was later made into an instrumental orchestral suite by Roy Douglas, and published in 1956. See Vaughan Williams' letter to Douglas of April 23, 1952, regarding the type of orchestra needed, Cobbe, *Letters*, 498. See also Ursula Vaughan Williams, *R.W.V.*, 292. For a reprint of Vaughan Williams' program notes for the first performance, see Manning, *Vaughan Williams on Music*, 369–70.

247. Ursula Vaughan Williams, *R.W.V.*, 299.

248. See, for example Ursula Vaughan Williams, *R.W.V.*, 278–79.

249. See Ursula Vaughan Williams, *R.W.V.*, 309.

250. Letter from Vaughan Williams to Elizabeth Trevelyan, May 21, 1951, Cobbe, *Letters*, 484. For another such letter, see Ursula Vaughan Williams, *R.W.V.*, 310.

251. See Ursula Vaughan Williams, *R.W.V.*, 311.

252. He had felt at the time of her death that he was too old to travel, see Ursula Vaughan Williams, *R.W.V.*, 311 and 318, but this would soon change.

253. Ibid., 313.

254. See Ursula Vaughan Williams, *R.W.V.*, 324.

255. Ursula Vaughan Williams, *R.W.V.*, 331.

256. Ursula Vaughan Williams, *R.W.V.*, 370.

257. See his letter Alan Frank at OUP, December 31, 1952, regarding his re-use of the film music, Cobbe, *Letters*, 512–13. See also Ursula Vaughan Williams, *R.W.V.*, 279–80, for more on the film, as well as 286–87, and 293. For analysis, see Kennedy, *Works*, 360–62.

258. Vaughan Williams maintained that it was, see his letter to Frank Howes, April 18, 1955, Cobbe, *Letters*, 558. Finzi also held that it was not a "true" symphony, see his letter to Vaughan Williams, January 22, 1953, Cobbe, *Letters*, 514–15.

259. For favorable reactions, see Kennedy, *Works*, 322–24.

260. See Cobbe, *Letters*, 516 for a copy of the printed wedding invitation, dated February 1, 1953.

261. Collected by Thomas Morley (1557/8–1602) in 1601. Gerald Finzi was among those who also contributed to this new effort, but both he and Vaughan Williams did not consider their works a complete success, see chapter 8 and Ursula Vaughan Williams, *R.W.V.*, 328. She gives a vivid account of the coronation at 333–34.

262. Vaughan Williams seemed to have spontaneously come up with the idea of visiting both Rome and the Grand Canyon one day late in 1953, see Ursula

Vaughan Williams, *R.W.V.*, 342. For her account of Rome, see 345–46. For the American tour, see her lively account at 348–58.

263. See Kennedy, "Fluctuations in the response," 293–94. The conductor John Barbirolli came to his defense and declared that the work was, indeed a symphony. See also Heffer, *Vaughan Williams*, 137.

264. Kennedy, "Fluctuations in the response," 290. This article is a good overview of critical reception throughout his life, see 275–98. See also Heffer, *Vaughan Williams*, 132.

265. Muncy, private email correspondence with the author.

266. Ursula Vaughan Williams, R.W.V., 362.

267. For the Trust website, see: http://www.rvwtrust.org.uk, accessed February 16, 2015. See also Ursula Vaughan Williams, *R.W.V.*, 377.

268. See chapter 8, and Ursula Vaughan Williams, *R.W.V.*, 376. Vaughan Williams had hoped that Finzi would be a member of the committee, see his letter to Finzi, May 31, 1956, Cobbe, *Letters*, 584.

269. Heffer, *Vaughan Williams*, 143, see also Kennedy, Works, 343 and 269–70.

270. See Kennedy, "Fluctuations in the response," 295, and Kennedy, *Works*, 343.

271. Harold Fromm, "Against Representation," 279. On his neglect being related to nationalism and the slow decline of British power and influence, see Frogley, "Constructing Englishness in Music," 2–4 and 20–22, and "'Getting its History Wrong,'" 159–61.

272. Mellers, *Vision of Albion*, 75–76.

273. Ursula provides a splendid narrative for the trip in *R.W.V.*, 392–94.

274. Ibid., 394–95.

275. Ursula and Ralph planned to spend September working on it, see *ibid.*, 398.

276. Ursula Vaughan Williams, *R.W.V.*, 399.

277. Letter from Ursula Vaughan Williams to Vera Mackenzie and Molly Hodge, September 4, 1958, Cobbe, *Letters*, 643–44.

278. Cobbe, *Letters*, 532.

279. For Vaughan Williams' thoughts about his biography and a study of his works, see Ursula Vaughan Williams, *R.W.V.*, 379–80. He favored Ursula writing his biography, and Michael Kennedy writing about his music, which is exactly what happened. He had corresponded with Kennedy since 1945, and finally met him in 1952, and the two formed a lasting friendship, see 316–17.

280. See Kennedy, "Fluctuations in the response," 296, for more on this.

281. Vaughan Williams, "The Diamond Jubilee of the Folk Song Society," *Journal of the English Folk Dance and Song Society* 8:3 (1958): 124, published posthumously. Percy Grainger wrote a short note to congratulate the Society in the same issue, at 124.

282. Maud Karpeles, "Ralph Vaughan Williams, O.M. October 12, 1872—August 26, 1958." *Journal of the English Folk Dance and Song Society* 8:3 (1958): 122.

283. Vaughan Williams, *Musical Autobiography*, 25.

Chapter 4

1. Imogen was very involved in teaching, and was Benjamin Britten's assistant in the 1950s. She was an artistic director for the Aldeburgh Festival, and wrote extensively on several aspects of music. Her works on her father include: *Gustav Holst: A Biography*; *The Music of Gustav Holst* (London: Oxford University Press, 1951, revised 1985 to include *Holst's Music Reconsidered*); *Heirs and Rebels: Letters Written to Each Other, and Occasional Writings on Music*, by Ralph Vaughan Williams and Gustav Holst; and *Holst*, Great Composers Series (London: Faber & Faber, 1974, 2nd ed. 1981). Her biographies are hindered slightly by a lack of detailed notes and sources. For studies of Imogen, see Christopher Grogan and Rosamund Strode, *Imogen Holst: A Life in Music*, 6 parts, parts 5 and 6 with Christopher Tinker (Woodbridge: Boydell, 2010). For other essential studies on Holst, see Michael Short, *Gustav Holst: The Man and His Music*, as well as the very detailed work of Jon C. Mitchell, *A Comprehensive Biography of Composer Gustav Holst, with Correspondence and Diary Excerpts*, and the useful bibliographic guide by Mary Christison Huismann, *Gustav Holst: A Research and Information Guide* (New York and Abingdon: Routledge, 2011). For a short but useful study, see Michael Short, "Gustav Holst: An Evaluation," *Journal of the RVW Society* 11 (1998): 2–4. For online resources on Holst's life and works, see Colin Matthews, "Holst, Gustav," *Grove Music Online*, Oxford Music Online: http://www.oxfordmusiconline.com/subscriber/article/grove/music/13252, accessed October 5, 2014 (which has an extensive bibliography), and Kenric Taylor's *Gustav Holst* website: http://www.gustavholst.info, accessed October 5, 2014. On Holst's learning Sanskrit, see Imogen Holst, *Holst: A Biography*, 22–23, and Short, *Gustav Holst*, 37–38. There is also the documentary, *Holst: In the Bleak Midwinter*, DVD, directed by Tony Palmer (UK: Isolde Films, 2011). Unlike Palmer's Vaughan Williams film, *O Thou Transcendent*, this production is less of a chronological biography than a series of lengthy musical excerpts with historical anecdotes. The archival film footage of interviews with Imogen is very valuable, as are the commentaries from Michael Short and others (giving new information), but the work feels overly long, and slightly unsatisfying. Many of the performances are supplemented with odd choices of visual imagery, which some might not consider suitable for younger audiences.

2. Short, *Gustav Holst*, 8–11, and Mitchell, *Comprehensive Biography*, 2–3.

3. We will discuss Blavatsky and her movement more in chapter 7, in the discussion of Philip Heseltine's occult interests and alleged practices.

4. Imogen Holst, *Holst, Great Composers*, 15, see also Short, *Gustav Holst*, 77.

5. He never spoke of his own beliefs, beyond saying he was attracted to Hindu concepts. Perhaps like Vaughan Williams, he remained a "hopeful agnostic." His early years were spent in Cheltenham, where a large number of retirees from Civil Service jobs in India lived, so this may have stimulated his interest as well, see the DVD *Holst: In the Bleak Midwinter*. Late

in life, he noted that he had tried to read the biblical prophets, but "they have too much Hitler in them for my taste," Letter from Holst to Imogen, January 31, 1934, Holst Foundation, quoted in Mitchell, *Comprehensive Biography*, 598.

6. Short, *Gustav Holst*, 11, and Mitchell, *Comprehensive Biography*, 3–4.

7. Imogen Holst, *Holst: A Biography*, 7.

8. According to Michael Short, Holst was "hopeless" at sports and games, see the DVD, *Holst: In the Bleak Midwinter*. See also Mitchell, *Comprehensive Biography*, 4.

9. Imogen Holst, *Holst*, Great Composers, 19.

10. Short, *Gustav Holst*, 13, and Mitchell, *Comprehensive Biography*, 4.

11. For more on these early compositions, see Mitchell, *Comprehensive Biography*, 5–8.

12. *Ibid.*, 16. Despite the relatively dreary nature of the lessons, Holst greatly enjoyed them and his time in Oxford, see Imogen Holst, *Holst: A Biography*, 8.

13. Imogen Holst, *Holst*, Great Composers, 16.

14. Short, *Gustav Holst*, 17.

15. Imogen Holst, *Holst: A Biography*, 11.

16. Short, *Gustav Holst*, 17–19.

17. *Ibid.*, 19.

18. Coleridge-Taylor was a fascinating figure in English music at the turn of the 20th century. For two recent biographies, see Jeffrey Greene, *Samuel Coleridge-Taylor: a Musical Life* (London: Pickering and Chatto, 2011), and Geoffrey Self, *The Hiawatha Man: the Life & Work of Samuel Coleridge-Taylor* (Aldershot, UK: Scolar Press, 1995).

19. See Mitchell, *Comprehensive Biography*, 9.

20. For an amusing story about Holst drinking alcohol and inadvertently playing the wrong part on trombone during a performance at a party, see Imogen Holst, *Holst: A Biography*, 15–16.

21. Imogen Holst, *Holst*, Great Composers, 19.

22. Short, *Gustav Holst*, 22.

23. See Mitchell, *Comprehensive Biography*, 11–12.

24. Shaw, a leading critic, was committed to the idea that art, especially theater, must elevate and instruct, not merely entertain. It was fine for it to make money, but it must do so in a way that did not pander to the least common denominator. See Cecil, *Edwardian England*, 189 and 192–93.

25. Imogen Holst, *Holst*, Great Composers, 21–23. See also Short, *Gustav Holst*, 29–30, and Imogen Holst, *Holst: A Biography*, 16–17, where she also notes at 17 that Holst was not a committed socialist throughout his life, and admitted to being a fence-sitter on some issues: "although he admired William Morris the man, he found that the glamour of his romantic medievalism soon wore off." See also 117–18 about his ambivalence during the general strike of 1926.

26. Short, *Gustav Holst*, 31, and Imogen Holst, *Holst: A Biography*, 17.

27. See Mitchell, *Comprehensive Biography*, 15–16, 21–22, and 26–27.

28. Imogen Holst, *Holst*, Great Composers, 27.

29. Short, *Gustav Holst*, 42.

30. See *ibid.*, 46–47.

31. Holst to Vaughan Williams, 1903, quoted in Imogen Holst, *Holst: A Biography*, 179–82.

32. Holst to Vaughan Williams, 1903, I. Holst and U. Vaughan Williams, *Heirs and Rebels*, 17.

33. Recalled by Vaughan Williams in *Musical Autobiography*, 34.

34. Quoted in Short, *Gustav Holst*, 127. For the complete lecture "England and Her Music," see I. Holst and U. Vaughan Williams, *Heirs and Rebels*, 49–52.

35. "England & her Music," *Heirs and Rebels*, 49. See also Mitchell, *Comprehensive Biography*, 305.

36. On the timing of this introduction, see Imogen Holst, "Holst's Debt of Gratitude to Vaughan Williams," *Folk Music Journal* 2:3 (1972): 171–72.

37. See Mitchell, *Comprehensive Biography*, 24, for a summary.

38. Imogen Holst, *Music of Gustav Holst*, 6.

39. See Short, *Gustav Holst*, 44.

40. Imogen Holst, *Holst*, Great Composers, 29.

41. See n5.

42. According to Imogen Holst; Short proposes that it may have been a volume from Friedrich Max Müller's *The Sacred Books of the East*, see Short, *Gustav Holst*, 37.

43. The Rigveda or Ṛgveda, is one of the four canonical sacred texts, śruti, of Hinduism, collectively known as the Vedas. It is one of the oldest surviving texts in an Indo-European language.

44. Imogen Holst, *Holst: A Biography*, 22, and Short, *Gustav Holst*, 37–38.

45. Imogen Holst, *Holst*, Great Composers, 25. He may have heard Indian music at some point, however, see Martin Clayton, "Musical Renaissance and its Margins in England and India, 1874–1914," *Music and Orientalism in the British Empire*, 78 and 81, see also 77.

46. For an analysis of his Indian-inspired works from 1906 to 1912 see Imogen Holst, *Music of Gustav Holst*, 16–25. See also Mitchell, *Comprehensive Biography*, 22–24; for *The Cloud Messenger*, see 90.

47. Short, *Gustav Holst*, 41, 67, and 78. See 76–80.

48. Imogen Holst, *Music of Gustav Holst*, 16.

49. As a boy, Holst once had the chance to play an Egyptian flute with a unique melodic scale, which may have been an early stimulus to his later interests, see Short, *Gustav Holst*, 12. This instrument may have been the cane flute known as the nay, but it is notoriously difficult to play, being simply a hollow cane tube with finger holes; the sound is made by blowing at the edge down the tube, like a Japanese shakuhachi. It takes quite a bit of practice to produce a sound, much less develop a good tone, so it seems more likely that he found some kind of simple fipple flute.

50. Short, *Gustav Holst*, 73. For the letter from Vaughan Williams encouraging this holiday, see I. Holst and U. Vaughan Williams, *Heirs and Rebels*, 42.

51. See Imogen Holst, *Holst: A Biography*, 32–33, for the text of letters written to his wife while there. See also Mitchell, *Comprehensive Biography*, 80–82.

52. Imogen Holst, *Holst: A Biography*, 74–75.

53. This was possibly played on the mizmar, a loud reed instrument common throughout the Middle East. Other accounts suggest that the instrument was a flute, so it may have been a nay or a qusaba, traditional Middle Eastern flutes, the latter of which is more common in the Maghreb in North Africa, and has a limited

musical scale, like the melody of the third movement. Imogen Holst also noted that he included a bit of an Algerian tune in a theme in the *Intermezzo* from his *St. Paul's Suite*, see Alan Gibbs, "New Light on Holst and Friends: Manuscript Discoveries at St Paul's Girls' School," *Tempo* 60:237 (2006): 46. See also Mitchell, *Comprehensive Biography*, 89 and 91, and for the *St. Paul's Suite*, see 114–15.

54. Short, *Gustav Holst*, 86.

55. Grainger was a great admirer of Holst, writing to Imogen from Melbourne on February 22, 1954, to ask her for copies of sheet music of various works by him. He recalled hearing *Beni Mora* in 1912, and said he enjoyed it more than any other such work based on a Middle Eastern theme. He wanted to include Holst's works in his new museum; see the letter quoted in full in Mitchell, *Comprehensive Biography*, 352–53. Unfortunately, many pieces were not in print at the time. For a further summary of Holst's Algerian visit, see Imogen Holst, *Music of Gustav Holst*, 137–38.

56. Ito (1893–1961) was a famed dancer and choreographer who spent much time in Europe and then the United States. For more information, see the Michio Ito Foundation online: http://www.michioito.org, accessed October 12, 2014. For more on the *Japanese Suite*, see Short, *Gustav Holst*, 132.

57. Short, *Gustav Holst*, 132–33.

58. St. Paul's would remain important to him for years, as he was able to use a sound-proof room to work in. See Imogen Holst, *Holst: A Biography*, 42. On James Allen's School, see Mitchell, *Comprehensive Biography*, 43–46.

59. Imogen Holst, *Holst, Great Composers*, 29–30. He was apparently accepted there after giving a lecture that included a discussion on the horrors of the bagpipe! See the DVD *Holst: In the Bleak Midwinter*. For a detailed survey of Holst's involvement with the College, see Mitchell, *Comprehensive Biography*, 65–78. Morley College still exists, and continues to offer music education to those from non-musical backgrounds, see http://www.morleycollege.ac.uk, accessed March 5, 2015.

60. *Ibid.*, 33.

61. As a child, he had heard Irish and Scottish tunes at his family's music evenings, and he listened to a street musician play an old Northumbrian tune, see Short, *Gustav Holst*, 11–12.

62. Imogen Holst, *Holst: A Biography*, 27.

63. See Imogen Holst, *Holst, Great Composers*, 35, and Imogen Holst, *Music of Gustav Holst*, 12–15, the latter offering a survey of his earliest attempts in folk song settings.

64. See Imogen Holst, "Gustav Holst's Debt to Cecil Sharp," *Folk Music Journal* 2:5 (1974): 400–01.

65. Short, *Gustav Holst*, 64.

66. Imogen Holst, *Music of Gustav Holst*, 12.

67. Short, *Gustav Holst*, 64.

68. Imogen Holst, *Music of Gustav Holst*, 14.

69. Short, *Gustav Holst*, 65.

70. See Imogen Holst, "Gustav Holst's Debt to Cecil Sharp," 403, for a copy of one of Holst's letters to Sharp regarding folk song arrangements.

71. This song in fact appears to be from a 1715 stage play, *Country Lasses*, with music by the English composer John Barrett (*ca.* 1674—*ca.* 1735). See Imogen Holst, *Music of Gustav Holst*, 138.

72. Christopher Mowat, liner notes to Holst, *Beni Mora, et al*, Naxos 8.553696, CD, 1997. See also Imogen Holst, "Gustav Holst's Debt to Cecil Sharp," 401.

73. Quoted in Imogen Holst, *Holst, Great Composers*, 35. Holst, unlike many of his contemporaries, was often more fascinated with the bleakness of certain country settings, as evidenced in pieces like *Egdon Heath*.

74. Short, *Gustav Holst*, 65.

75. Holst to the BBC, July 30, 1928, quoted in Short, *Gustav Holst*, 88.

76. *Ibid.*

77. *Daily Telegraph*, April 7, 1910, quoted in *ibid.*, 88.

78. Imogen Holst, *Holst, Great Composers*, 36. Mitchell notes in *Comprehensive Biography*, that this is not completely true, as Holst continued to use some of these Romantic musical concepts in *Savitri* and other works, see 51.

79. Short, *Gustav Holst*, 73. For a further summary of his folk song influences and the early works that came from them, see Mitchell, *Comprehensive Biography*, 51–53, and 55–56.

80. Zachary Woolfe, "When Holst Read the Mahabharata," *New York Times*, May 11, 2012: http://www.nytimes.com/2012/05/12/arts/music/an-evening-of-holst-by-the-little-opera-theater-of-new-york.html, accessed October 6, 2014.

81. Short, *Gustav Holst*, 92–93.

82. He made an exception for a set of twelve Welsh folk songs which greatly pleased him, see Imogen Holst, *Holst: A Biography*, 146.

83. *Ibid.*, 65. See also 141, and Imogen Holst, *Holst: A Biography*, 106.

84. Short, *Gustav Holst*, 20, 151. Hoyte and Holst did not initially get along, and Holst's father lectured him on it, see Mitchell, *Comprehensive Biography*, 9.

85. Imogen Holst, *Holst, Great Composers*, 38–39. See also Short, *Gustav Holst*, 54–55.

86. Short, *Gustav Holst*, 56.

87. *Ibid.*, 115.

88. *Ibid.*, 69.

89. Holst, "Certain Possibilities of the School Orchestra," *The Music Student*, February 1916, reprinted in I. Holst and U. Vaughan Williams, *Heirs and Rebels*, 57. He treated professionals and amateurs equally.

90. Mitchell, *Comprehensive Biography*, 106–07.

91. Short, *Gustav Holst*, 93–95. See also Imogen Holst, *Holst: A Biography*, 39.

92. Holst claimed to have had a kind of mystical experience when he first heard Bach's *Mass in B Minor* in 1893, see Marshall, *Music in the Landscape*, 100.

93. Short, *Gustav Holst*, 101–02. See also 116–17, and 118–21. For a comprehensive analysis of *The Planets*, see Richard Greene, *Holst: The Planets*, Cambridge Music Handbooks, Julian Rushton, general ed. (Cambridge: Cambridge University Press, 1995). Currently, it is the most recorded English piece; there are more than 200 recordings of the work worldwide.

94. Short, *Gustav Holst*, 120.

95. Letter from Vaughan Williams to Michael

Kennedy, August 18, 1956, Cobbe, *Letters*, 590. See also Michael Kennedy, *Works*, 337 and 376. Moeran confessed that this "wrong note music" was not for him, see chapter 6.

96. Short gives a large number of examples in *Gustav Holst*, of Holst's extensive walking holidays at all times of the year and in any kind of weather, both in England and abroad. For some examples, see 177, 196 (with Vaughan Williams), 245–46, 249, 253, 279, 282, 287, 288, 290, 291, 296–76 (in France), 299, 301, 315–16, and 317. See also Imogen Holst, *Holst: A Biography*, 124–26.

97. Imogen Holst, *Holst, Great Composers*, 40. See her "Gustav Holst in Thaxted, *Journal of the RVW Society* 11 (1998): 6, for a brief but useful summary of his time there. See also Short, *Gustav Holst*, 117–18.

98. Short, *Gustav Holst*, 118.

99. Imogen Holst, *Holst, Great Composers*, 40–41.

100. This was partially due to the controversial socialist, bordering-on-communist views of Thaxted's vicar, Conrad Noel. Many felt that this was inappropriate and did not want to go to Thaxted, see Short, *Gustav Holst*, 136, 158, and 187. Noel's church flew the red flag and refused to fly the Union Jack, seeing it as a symbol of imperialism, see the DVD, *Holst: In the Bleak Midwinter*. Holst accepted his friend's more radical views, and played a role in the liberalization of the types of music acceptable in a church, including secular performances, see Short, 150. However, he referred to some of Noel's rants as "Conrad's comic Gospel of hate," in a letter to Vally Lasker, December 18, 1918, Holst Foundation, quoted in Mitchell, *Comprehensive Biography*, 156; see 139–44, 154–56, and 217 for more on the Whitsuntide Festival and Conrad Noel. See also Michael Goatcher, "Mr. Von and Dr. Vaughan," *Journal of the RVW Society* 11 (1998): 12, for more on Noel and the controversy surrounding him.

101. *Ibid.*, 41–42. See also Short, *Gustav Holst*, 138–40.

102. Letter from Vaughan Williams to Holst, June 1916, Cobbe Letters, 109. See also I. Holst and U. Vaughan Williams, *Heirs and Rebels*, 45. In another letter to Holst from late June, 1916, he expressed a belief that Holst's work in this area was authentic, unlike the efforts of Rutland Boughton, which were a "sham imitation," see Cobbe, *Letters*, 109–110.

103. Short, *Gustav Holst*, 124–25.

104. *Ibid.*, 153–54.

105. See Mitchell, *Comprehensive Biography*, 160–61 for Percy Scholes' letters to Holst regarding his acceptance.

106. Imogen Holst, *Holst, Great Composers*, 46. See also Short, *Gustav Holst*, 159–60.

107. See Imogen Holst, *Holst: A Biography*, 52.

108. See Short, *Gustav Holst*, 159–60, and 243.

109. Dyneley Hussey, "English Musicians: 8. Gustav Theodore Holst," *Landmark* 10:2 (1928): 119–22, quoted in Short, *Gustav Holst*, 214.

110. Vaughan Williams, "Gustav Holst: An Essay and a Note," *National Music*, 133.

111. For a series of letters written to Isobel and Vaughan Williams from Salonica and Istanbul, see Imogen Holst, *Holst: A Biography*, 54–77. See also Mitchell, *Comprehensive Biography*, 171–80, and 188–89.

112. Imogen Holst, *Holst, Great Composers*, 46–47. See also Short, *Gustav Holst*, 173–74, for some details on the music competition he oversaw while in Turkey.

113. Short, *Gustav Holst*, 166. See 164–75 for more details.

114. *Ibid.*, 171.

115. For details of the rehearsals and production, see Short, *Gustav Holst*, 161–62, and Imogen Holst, *Holst, Great Composers*, 50–51. For an account of how Boult first met Holst, see Short, *Gustav Holst*, 154–55. Gardiner was, for a time, also a collector of folk songs in Hampshire, see Murphy, *Green Willow*, 80.

116. Imogen Holst, *Holst, Great Composers*, 48. See also Short, *Gustav Holst*, 41–42.

117. For more details of the Iberian trip, see Short, *Gustav Holst*, 111–113, and Mitchell, *Comprehensive Biography*, 118–22; for more on his astrological interests, see Mitchell, *Comprehensive Biography*, 126–27. Holst never again used astrology as a source of inspiration, but continued to cast horoscopes for friends, see 134. See also Short, *Gustav Holst*, 43–44, where she remarks that he called the practice his "pet vice."

118. For an analysis of the music and some additional background, see Imogen Holst, *Music of Gustav Holst*, 32–41, and Short, *Gustav Holst*, 121–34.

119. *Mars* was used in a BBC radio serialization of H.G. Wells' *War of the Worlds*, for example, and one can certainly detect the influence of that same piece in certain themes in the *Star Wars* movies. Holst tried his hand at film composition as well, with disappointing results, as the film, *The Bells*, was not released and his score for it has disappeared; see Short, *Gustav Holst*, 296–98, and Imogen Holst, *Holst: A Biography*, 150. For a more detailed survey, see Mitchell, *Comprehensive Biography*, 409–18.

120. See Mitchell, *Comprehensive Biography*, 183–85 for correspondence between Holst and Boult. See 220–22 for reaction to the first full performance.

121. Short, *Gustav Holst*, 205.

122. Imogen Holst, *Holst, Great Composers*, 55. See also Mitchell, *Comprehensive Biography*, 227–35 and 297–98, Short, *Gustav Holst*, 217, and Imogen Holst, *Holst: A Biography*, 83–84.

123. Short, *Gustav Holst*, 190–91.

124. Imogen Holst, *Holst: A Biography*, 164. This was in sharp contrast to his young friend Gerald Finzi, who hoarded thousands of books for his country home, see chapter 8.

125. Finzi died in 1956, Vaughan Williams in 1958. See chapter 8 for Finzi's life and works. For the letter of June 5, 1949 offering the tuning fork to Finzi, see Cobbe, *Letters*, 451–52.

126. On Weelkes, see Holst, "My Favourite Tudor Composer," *The Midland Musician*, January 1926, reprinted in I. Holst and U. Vaughan Williams, *Heirs and Rebels*, 52–55.

127. Short, *Gustav Holst*, 207–08.

128. For a thorough listing of correspondence related to this American invitation and his injury, see Mitchell, *Comprehensive Biography*, 245–87.

129. Short, *Gustav Holst*, 210. See also Mitchell, *Comprehensive Biography*, 265–87, for detailed reprints of the letters regarding his time there and his refusal of the offer.
130. Short, *Gustav Holst*, 179. See also Imogen Holst, *Holst*, Great Composers, 59, and Mitchell, *Comprehensive Biography*, 198–203.
131. See Vaughan Williams, "Introductory Talk to Holst Memorial Concert," Manning, *Vaughan Williams on Music*, 300, reprinted from a BBC Broadcast on June 22, 1934, and Bernard Shore, *The Orchestra Speaks* (London: Longmans, Green, 1938), 139–41. Vaughan Williams believed that this limited time actually focused his concentration and produced better work.
132. Imogen Holst, *Holst*, Great Composers, 83.
133. For various accounts of Holst's approach to music education, see Short, *Gustav Holst*, 53, 57–62, 69–70, 97–98, and 179–80. See also Mitchell, *Comprehensive Biography*, 58, 62n40, and 207–210.
134. Letter from Vaughan Williams to Imogen Holst, September 19, 1937, Cobbe, *Letters*, 252–52.
135. See Imogen Holst, *Holst*, Great Composers, 60.
136. Short, *Gustav Holst*, 215. On the process of recording the work, see Mitchell, *Comprehensive Biography*, 290–93.
137. This had begun with the popularity of *The Planets*. Suddenly, his old works, which had been ignored for so long, were in demand. See Short, *Gustav Holst*, 197.
138. Imogen Holst, *Holst: A Biography*, 88–89.
139. Short, *Gustav Holst*, 217–18, and Mitchell, *Comprehensive Biography*, 302.
140. *Ibid.*, 228. Holst would later act as a go-between for wealthy patrons and young musicians, setting up anonymous donations from the former, so that they could continue their work, see Imogen Holst, *Holst: A Biography*, 140. See also Mitchell, *Comprehensive Biography*, 355–56.
141. Mitchell, *Comprehensive Biography*, 304.
142. Imogen Holst, *Holst: A Biography*, 90–92. See also his letter to Whittaker of February, 1924, reprinted in Mitchell, *Comprehensive Biography*, 303.
143. See Imogen Holst, *Holst: A Biography*, 103–04, and Mitchell, *Comprehensive Biography*, 304.
144. Short, *Gustav Holst*, 227. See also Imogen Holst, *Holst: A Biography*, 110 and 113, and Imogen Holst, "Gustav Holst's Debt to Cecil Sharp," 402.
145. See reactions and correspondence about both in Mitchell, *Comprehensive Biography*, 306–10.
146. For a full account, see Short, *Gustav Holst*, 230–32.
147. Letter from Finzi to Howard Ferguson, April 22, 1928, *Letters of Gerald Finzi*, 29.
148. Cecil Gray, 1925, quoted in Short, *Gustav Holst*, 237. Gray, a Scottish composer and music critic, was particularly harsh on Holst at this time.
149. *Ibid.*, 239. For other negative reactions, see Imogen Holst, *Holst: A Biography*, 115–16.
150. Letter from Vaughan Williams to Holst, n.d., 1925, I. Host and Ursula Vaughan Williams, *Heirs and Rebels*, 60–61.
151. *Ibid.*, 240–41.
152. See Hubert Foss, "Holst: the bringer of Paradox," *Listener* 28:714 (1942): 381.
153. Imogen Holst, *Holst: A Biography*, 81.
154. Imogen Holst, *Holst*, Great Composers, 64.
155. Short, *Gustav Holst*, 230.
156. Letter from Holst to Harold Brooke, November 22, 1926, BL Add. 57953, quoted in *ibid.*, 248.
157. Imogen Holst, *Holst: A Biography*, 117.
158. Mitchell, *Comprehensive Biography*, 315.
159. Short, *Gustav Holst*, 245.
160. *Ibid.*, 249.
161. *Ibid.*
162. *Ibid.*, 251–53. See also Imogen Holst, *Holst: A Biography*, 122–23.
163. Hardy's poetry would also be of great importance to Finzi, see chapter 8.
164. For specific visits with Hardy that inspired his choice of subject, see Short, *Gustav Holst*, 201, 246, and 256. Holst would later claim that it was not any particular meeting, but rather the years that the two knew one another, Hardy's works, and the heath itself, see 265. See also Holst's letter regarding *Egdon Heath* to his American friend, Austin Lidbury, quoted in Imogen Holst, *Holst: A Biography*, 126–27.
165. Holst to Austin Lidbury, August 11, 1927, quoted in Imogen Holst, *Holst: A Biography*, 126–27.
166. Phillip Cooke, "On Gustav Holst's 'Egdon Heath'...": http://www.phillipcooke.com/on-gustav-holsts-egdon-heath, accessed October 7, 2014.
167. Thomas Hardy, *Return of the Native* (London: Macmillan, 1911), 6. See also Short, *Gustav Holst*, 253–54, where he describes the work as ending with "a ghostly pastoral folk-tune echoing an atavistic past." For further analysis, see Imogen Holst, *Music of Gustav Holst*, 80–84.
168. Vaughan Williams, *Royal College of Music Magazine*, 1934, quoted in I. Holst and U. Vaughan Williams, *Heirs and Rebels*, 64.
169. See Short, *Gustav Holst*, 264, for some examples, and Imogen Holst, *Holst: A Biography*, 130–31. It did not do well in New York, London, or Paris, see Mitchell, *Comprehensive Biography*, 390–91.
170. Short, *Gustav Holst*, 264. See also Thomas Armstrong, "Mr. H.," *Music in Education* 38:368 (1974): 163–65.
171. Imogen Holst, *Holst*, Great Composers, 72–73.
172. Short, *Gustav Holst*, 265. For details on the commission and the initial mixed reaction to the piece, see Mitchell, *Comprehensive Biography*, 325–52.
173. See chapter 8 for more on this important festival.
174. Letter from Vaughan Williams to Holst, September 1931, I. Holst and U. Vaughan Williams, *Heirs and Rebels*, 77.
175. For details of the trip, see Short, *Gustav Holst*, 262–63, Imogen Holst, *Holst: A Biography*, 128–29, and Mitchell, *Comprehensive Biography*, 317–19.
176. See Short, *Gustav Holst*, 259–60 and 268–70.
177. See *ibid.*, 273–79 for details of the trip and the writer's block that led to it, and Imogen Holst, *Holst: A Biography*, 133–36, as well as Mitchell, *Comprehensive Biography*, 356–57, and 366.
178. For an example of his crowded schedule in New York, see Mitchell, *Comprehensive Biography*, 379–83. Such large gatherings and packed agendas must have driven him to distraction!

179. On his time there, see Mitchell, *Comprehensive Biography*, 357–85.
180. Holst to Isobel, April 12, 1929, quoted in Short, *Gustav Holst*, 280.
181. Elgar and Delius had received the award in 1925, see Mitchell, *Comprehensive Biography*, 396–97.
182. Imogen Holst, *Holst: A Biography*, 149. See also Mitchell, *Comprehensive Biography*, 419–20.
183. Short, *Gustav Holst*, 302. See Mitchell, *Comprehensive Biography*, 421–23, 426–99, for a detailed survey of his time in New York and Harvard, leading up to his illness.
184. Imogen Holst, *Holst, Great Composers*, 78. See also Imogen Holst, *Holst: A Biography*, 119.
185. Letter from Holst to Duncan McKenzie, December 4, 1931, quoted in Short, *Gustav Holst*, 303.
186. Letter from Holst to Vaughan Williams, April 15, 1932, I. Holst and U. Vaughan Williams, *Heirs and Rebels*, 80, written just after he had been released from the hospital and was recovering from gastritis.
187. Letter from Holst to Vally Lasker (a piano teacher at St. Paul's school and long-time friend), January 29, 1932, quoted in Short, *Gustav Holst*, 304. The relationship between Holst and Lasker is somewhat unclear. They grew much closer in his later life, and wrote to one another frequently. He would sometimes stay at her home, but it does not seem that they engaged in an affair, see Mitchell, *Comprehensive Biography*, 424–25. Holst and Isobel had often been separated, however, due to his wander-lust as much as any other reasons, and perhaps their marriage cooled over time, see 423.
188. Letter from Holst to Vally Lasker, January 29, 1932, Holst Foundation, quoted in Mitchell, *Comprehensive Biography*, 450.
189. *Ibid.*, 310. For Holst's account, see his letter to Vaughan Williams, April 15, 1932, I. Holst and U. Vaughan Williams, *Heirs and Rebels*, 81. See also Imogen Holst, *Holst: A Biography*, 156–57.
190. Letter from Holst to Vaughan Williams, April 15, 1932, I. Holst and U. Vaughan Williams, *Heirs and Rebels*, 81.
191. See Mitchell, *Comprehensive Biography*, 510–12.
192. For more detail, see *ibid.*, 523–41.
193. For a full account, see Short, *Gustav Holst*, 309–13.
194. Mitchell, *Comprehensive Biography*, 552–53.
195. See *ibid.*, 574–76.
196. For a short history and analysis, see the *Gustav Holst* website: http://www.gustavholst.info/compositions/listing.php?work=25, accessed October 7, 2014.
197. Short, *Gustav Holst*, 277 and 323.
198. For some background on this work, see Mitchell, *Comprehensive Biography*, 388–89.
199. See *ibid.*, 602–03.
200. Imogen Holst, *Holst: A Biography*, 167.
201. *Ibid.*, 165–66.
202. *Ibid.*, 168.
203. Short, interview in the DVD *Holst: In the Bleak Midwinter*.
204. Short, *Gustav Holst*, 327–28. See also Mitchell, *Comprehensive Biography*, 605, Isobel's reply to Vaughan Williams, June 3, 1934, Cobbe, *Letters*, 227n3 (to Letter 247).
205. Short, *Gustav Holst*, 328.
206. See Mitchell, *Comprehensive Biography*, 606–08, for details of the Holst Room, which survived the bombings of World War II and still exists today as a resource and memorial.
207. Short, *Gustav Holst*, 332.
208. *Ibid.*, 333.
209. Imogen Holst, *Holst, Great Composers*, 43. The full text of the letter is in Imogen Holst, *Holst: A Biography*, 47–48. A collection of their letters is housed at the University of Glasgow library. For more information, see http://special.lib.gla.ac.uk/exhibns/month/sep2004.html, accessed March 5, 2015. See also *Gustav Holst: Letters to W. G. Whittaker*, Michael Short, ed. (Glasgow: University of Glasgow Press, 1974).

Chapter 5

1. A very good introductory study to Butterworth, with analysis of his principal works, is Michael Barlow, *Whom the Gods Love: The Life and Music of George Butterworth*. For a more recent and comprehensive biography, see Anthony Murphy, *Banks of Green Willow: The Life and Times of George Butterworth* (Great Malvern, UK: Cappella Archive, 2012), which offers details about Butterworth's early life, and of Edwardian society in general. For a brief earlier biography, see Ian A. Copley, *George Butterworth and His Music: A Centennial Tribute* (London: Thames Publishing, 1985). Butterworth's short life has meant that there is not a great amount of remaining study to be done, but several other useful articles have appeared over the years. See Stephen Banfield, "Butterworth, George," *Grove Music Online*, Oxford Music Online. Oxford University Press: http://www.oxfordmusiconline.com/subscriber/article/grove/music/04467, accessed September 12, 2014. See also Barlow's earlier work, "George Butterworth: The Early Years," *Journal of the British Music Society* 5 (1983): 89–100 (he incorporated various portions of this article into his later book); see also his brief overview, "George Butterworth and the Folksong Revival," *English Dance and Song* 47:3 (1985): 10–11. A selection of the folk songs that Butterworth collected can be found in Michael Dawney, "George Butterworth's Folk Music Manuscripts," *Folk Music Journal* 3:2 (1976): 99–113. An earlier, brief biography can be found in John Rippin, "George Butterworth 1885–1916," *The Musical Times* 107:1482 (1966): 680–682, and 107:1483 (1966): 769 and 771. A catalog of Butterworth's works compiled by Kenneth L. Thompson can be found in the latter issue, at 771–72, and a more detailed listing (with information on composition dates, first performances, and publication) is in Barlow, *Gods*, 137–43.
2. See Rippin, "Butterworth," 107:1483 at 771. Rippin suggests that his destruction of earlier works may have been due to feeling that anything he wrote prior to his discovery and cataloging of folk songs was not worth keeping, see 771.
3. Barlow, *Gods*, 13.

4. *Ibid.*, 21.
5. Prosper Sainton (1813–1890), spent much time in England, and was associated with Mendelssohn, Liszt, and Wagner, among others. Charlotte was a gifted vocalist who had entered the Royal Academy of Music in 1831. See the *Oxford Dictionary of National Biography* for further information, accessed September 10, 2014: http://www.oxforddnb.com/index/101024520/Prosper-Sainton. For a more detailed family history, see Murphy, *Green Willow*, 5–8.
6. For more on their home in York, see Murphy, *Green Willow*, 9.
7. *Ibid.* See also 11; he was allowed to practice on the school organ.
8. Barlow, *Gods*, 22. He also notes at *n*12 that three of these survive. Sir Alexander compiled a collection of miscellany concerning his son, *Scrapbook of Letters, etc., concerning George Butterworth, 1903–1916*, Bodleian MS. Eng. Misc. c. 435, which contains these tunes. See also Murphy, *Green Willow*, 11.
9. See Murphy, *Green Willow*, 27.
10. Barlow, "Early Years," 89.
11. Eton, founded in 1440 by King Henry VI, retains a hallowed air as one of Britain's most prestigious boarding schools, the educational institute of future prime ministers (19 to date) as well as the upper echelons of the British establishment.
12. Murphy, *Green Willow*, 11 and 15. On his time at Eton, see 13–29.
13. Barlow, *Gods*, 24. He was also said to have had perfect pitch, see *Gods*, at 25.
14. Robert Booker to Alexander Butterworth, March 26, 1902, from Bod. MS Eng c.3296, *ff*. 21–24, quoted in Murphy, *Green Willow*, 20.
15. See Murphy, *Green Willow*, 21.
16. The work was well-received, see Murphy, *Green Willow*, 23, and it is unfortunate that this and other works are now lost.
17. Barlow, "Early Years," 90, and *Gods* 26. For the quartet, see also Murphy, *Green Willow*, 28. This is not the same piece, the *Suite for String Quartette*, that is housed in the Bodleian Library (Bod., Mus MS c. 297), see 35. For some analysis of this work, see 104–05, as well as 108 *n*35.
18. Barlow, *Gods*, 26, referring to a letter in the *Scrapbook*, *f*. 41. See also Murphy, *Green Willow*, 16–17.
19. Barlow, *Gods*, 25–26, citing the *Eton College Chronicles*.
20. See Murphy, *Green Willow*, 23–24.
21. For a detailed account of his Oxford years, see Murphy, *Green Willow*, 31–64. For some thoughts on Classics at Oxford, see Cecil, *Edwardian England*, 150. There was a growing feeling that the university was a "playground for the idle rich"; indeed, one-quarter of those at Magdalen College did not earn a degree, see 151; see also 152 for more on university elitism.
22. Murphy, *Green Willow*, 35.
23. *Ibid.*, 36–37.
24. *Ibid.*, 37.
25. Barlow, "Early Years," 90, and Rippin, "Butterworth," 107:1482, at 681.
26. See Murphy, *Green Willow*, 35 and 41.
27. So wrote Hugh Allen, organist of New College, in "George Butterworth and his Work," *The Times Literary Supplement* 797 (April 26, 1917): 201, in the *Scrapbook*, *ff*. 132–33, also cited in Barlow, *Gods*, 27*n*20. See also Murphy, *Green Willow*, 75–76, regarding his personality, quoted from the *Memorial Volume*, 11.
28. Banfield, "Butterworth." See also *n*62 below.
29. See Murphy, *Green Willow*, 53, 54, and 57; he found his course tedious and uninspiring, and he had no intention of becoming a lawyer.
30. See *ibid.*, 57–58 for the strained relationship with his father at this time.
31. *Ibid.*, 58.
32. Rippin, "Butterworth," 107:1482, at 681.
33. Murphy, *Green Willow*, 59–60.
34. *Ibid.*, 44.
35. Private correspondence with Anthony Murphy.
36. See Vaughan Williams, *Musical Autobiography*, 37.
37. See Murphy, *Green Willow*, 74; Sharp and Vaughan Williams were among those invited to lecture at Oxford Society events.
38. See Murphy, *Green Willow*, 51 and 55.
39. Allen, "Butterworth and his Work," *Times Literary Supplement* 797 (April 26, 1917): 201. See also Murphy, *Green Willow*, 51.
40. See Barlow, *Gods*, 28*n*23 for details of their first meeting. See also Murphy, *Green Willow*, 34, where he notes the influence that Allen would have on the young Butterworth. See also 39 and 133.
41. Vaughan Williams, "George Butterworth," *National Music*, 246.
42. Barlow, *Gods*, 31. See also Murphy, *Green Willow*, 38–39. Morris would eventually marry Emmie Fisher in February 1915, the older sister of Adeline, thus becoming Vaughan Williams' brother-in-law. Butterworth was probably the best man, see *Green Willow*, 170.
43. Murphy, *Green Willow*, 61.
44. Rippin, "Butterworth," 107:1482, at 681.
45. For more on Fuller Maitland, see chapter 1.
46. See Murphy, *Green Willow*, 67.
47. *Ibid.*, 70.
48. *Ibid.*, 71; this was due largely to his efforts.
49. Private correspondence with Anthony Murphy. Murphy has informed me that this piece has been recorded, "by the Bridge Quartet and an orchestral version by Kriss Russman has recently been recorded by the BBC National Orchestra of Wales." For a more detailed survey of Butterworth's time at Radley, see Barlow, *Gods*, 32–36.
50. Murphy, *Green Willow*, 76–77. See also 148.
51. Dawney suggests that he left the program much sooner, see "Folk Music Manuscripts," 99, and *n*1.
52. Murphy, *Green Willow*, 78.
53. *Ibid.*, 77, quoting from Parry's comments in the *Memorial Volume*, 8.
54. Barlow, *Gods*, 37–38. See also R.O. Morris' observation, Murphy, *Green Willow*, 160.
55. Banfield, "Butterworth."
56. See Murphy, *Green Willow*, 85 and 89.
57. Banfield, "Butterworth." See Murphy, *Green Willow*, 26, for an interesting discussion about Eton's institutionalized misogyny and the unspoken undercurrent of homoeroticism among some students. It

was thought that physical exercise was a good "outlet for unruly passions." Perhaps this was one reason that Butterworth excelled at sports and dance. He once spoke at length about the deficiencies of the female gender, though this was somewhat tongue-in-cheek, see 25–26. School headmasters were often required to be in Holy Orders, and many parents felt that this was helpful in preventing boys from engaging in homosexual activities, see Cecil, *Edwardian England*, 148.

58. Murphy, *Green Willow*, 161.
59. *Ibid.*, 161.
60. Murphy, *Green Willow*, 85–86.
61. For a brief analysis of the song, see Barlow, *Gods*, 41–42, and Barlow, "Early Years," 94. Murphy suggests in *Green Willow* at 86 that this "choice of texts was most probably dictated by mood and feeling rather than an attempt to help rehabilitate Wilde's reputation at this time." For Housman's feeling about Wilde's ordeal, see Murphy, *Green Willow*, 40.
62. This idea was increasingly coming under criticism, see Cecil, *Edwardian England*, 146. On sexism in the culture and the contrast of British "manliness" with the more "feminine" continent, see Sykes, "The Evolution of Englishness," 489 n93. Cecil Sharp was notoriously sexist, as were some of the other revivalists, despite the important presence of women in their movement.
63. See Murphy, *Green Willow*, 17 and 26.
64. *Ibid.*, 86.
65. Other English counties included Berkshire, Buckinghamshire, Hampshire, Herefordshire, Kent, Norfolk, Oxfordshire, Shropshire, Suffolk, and Yorkshire. For some examples of these "hunts," see Murphy, *Green Willow*, 103, 119, 131–32.
66. Barlow, "Folksong Revival," 10. See also Barlow, *Gods*, 82.
67. *Ibid.*
68. Ursula Vaughan Williams, *R.V.W.*, 98–99.
69. Murphy, *Green Willow*, 56 and 103. One of Butterworth's rivals, a Miss Dorothy Marshall referred to him as "the egregious Butterworth."
70. Barlow, *Gods*, 84. Jekyll may have introduced Butterworth to her, see Murphy, *Green Willow*, 63 n16.
71. Murphy, *Green Willow*, 38.
72. *Scrapbook, f.* 73. See also Barlow, *Gods*, 79. A brief biography of Jekyll can be found in Lewis Jones, "Francis Jekyll (1882–1965)—Forgotten Hero of the First Folk Song Revival," *English Dance and Song* (June 2000), available online at: http://folkopedia.efdss.org/images/3/3c/Francis_Jekyll.pdf, accessed September 14, 2014. See Murphy, *Green Willow*, 60–61, 65, 67–68, 70, 76, and 79 for accounts of some of their collecting outings.
73. See Murphy, *Green Willow*, 106, for one such example. See also chapter 2.
74. Dawney, "Folk Music Manuscripts," 102.
75. Quoted in Murphy, *Green Willow*, 55.
76. Murphy, *Green Willow*, 100. Vaughan Williams would attend these as well, and even participate in the dancing, though he had none of Butterworth's athletic grace, see 133 and 154n7. See also 120; Vaughan Williams was working on incidental music for Shakespeare plays and would have seen Butterworth there.

77. Dawney, "Folk Music Manuscripts," 99–100. He would return again in 1912 and thereafter, see Murphy, *Green Willow*, 120.
78. Barlow, "Folksong Revival," 10, and Murphy, *Green Willow*, 111–12. See also chapter 2.
79. For more details, see Murphy, *Green Willow*, 147,.
80. See Murphy, *Green Willow*, 129n39, for a listing of Broadwood's opinion in its original manuscript form.
81. For a complete summary of Butterworth's Morris and other dancing activities as well as more information on the Kinora spools, see Barlow, *Gods*, 75–79, and Murphy, *Green Willow*, 118–19, and 128n24. See also Vic Gammon, "'Many Useful Lessons': Cecil Sharp, Education and the Folk Dance Revival, 1899–1924," 84–85.
82. See Mike Heaney, "Two Films from the Past," *English Dance and Song* 45:3 (1983): 20–21, and Heaney, "Butterworth Dancing," *The Morris Dancer* 15 (1983): 7–12, for more on these important films.
83. This was published privately by his father in *George Butterworth, 1885–1916, Memorial Volume* (York and London, 1918). See Murphy, *Green Willow*, 112–17 for an excellent summary of his April dance "hunt." See also n85 below.
84. Russell Wortley and Michael Dawney, eds. "George Butterworth's Diary of Morris Dancing," *Folk Music Journal* 3:3 (1977): 200.
85. For further information on specific traditions and dances that Butterworth discovered and documented, see Barlow, *Gods*, 87–91.
86. Cecil Sharp, *The Sword Dances of Northern England*, Maude Karpeles, ed. (London: Novello, 1911–13, 2nd edition 1950–51). See also Murphy, *Green Willow*, 118.
87. Russell Wortley, "The Bucknell Morris," *English Dance and Song* 41:2 (1979): 11.
88. Barlow, *Gods*, 91, referencing *George Butterworth—The Man and His Music*, BBC Home Service, 14 July 1942. See also Murphy, *Green Willow*, 132.
89. See n1 above.
90. For an additional breakdown of the collection, see Dawney, "Folk Music Manuscripts," 101. See also Barlow, "Folksong Revival," 10.
91. *Ibid.*, 102. See also Barlow, *Gods*, 86n29, for a complete list of subsequent reprints of the dances.
92. Barlow, *Gods*, 91. For a complete listing of the songs and dances collected, see *Gods*, 147–63, which also includes publication details.
93. *A lawyer he went out, Seventeen come Sunday*, and *Tarry Trowsers*, used in Vaughan Williams' *Folk Songs of the Four Seasons*, *English Folk-Song Suite*, and *A Sea Symphony* respectively. For a more detailed analysis of the collection, see Barlow, *Gods*, 79–81. See also Murphy, *Green Willow*, 121–22.
94. See Murphy, *Green Willow*, 122–26 for analysis.
95. *Ibid.*, 126.
96. See Murphy, *Green Willow*, 149–50.
97. Private correspondence with Anthony Murphy: "the unfinished Orchestral Fantasia has now been 'completed' and recorded by Kriss Russman with the BBC National Orchestra of Wales." It will be released

in 2016 for Butterworth's death centenary. For an analysis of the work, see Murphy, *Green Willow*, 150–51.
98. See Murphy, *Green Willow*, 131.
99. See chapter 9 for Grainger's considerable efforts in recording folk singers. See also Murphy, *Green Willow*, 79 and 154n2.
100. It is significant that urban and industrial folk songs held little or no interest for many collectors, see Sykes, "The Evolution of Englishness in the English Folksong Revival,"451–52.
101. Barlow, *Gods*, 134, referencing *George Butterworth—The Man and His Music*.
102. These summer dancing schools were popular and attracted many names, including Vaughan Williams, see Ursula Vaughan Williams, *R.W.V.*, 95. See also Murphy, *Green Willow*, 152–53.
103. Murphy, *Green Willow*, 158.
104. *Ibid.*, 157–58.
105. Barlow, *Gods*, 125–26.
106. See, for example, Murphy, *Green Willow*, 170.
107. Murphy, *Green Willow*, 159–60.
108. Murphy, *Green Willow*, 14.
109. See *ibid.*, 159–60, for some discussion on class and placement in the military. For many lower-class individuals, military service was a preferable alternative to factory work, or low wages as a country laborer.
110. *Ibid.*, 14–15.
111. *Ibid.*, 101.
112. R.O. Morris, *Memorial Volume*, 9, quoted in Murphy, *Green Willow*, 160. See also 161.
113. See Murphy, *Green Willow*, 166, for some further thoughts on their decision to become officers, as well as 168–69. It took at least this long to train new recruits, Anthony Murphy, private correspondence.
114. Murphy, *Green Willow*, 173.
115. Parry received a commission to set the opening of William Blake's work *Milton a Poem* in early 1916, and thought initially to pass it off to Butterworth, but took up the work upon learning that the younger man had once again left for France, see Murphy, *Green Willow*, 184–85. More popularly known as "Jerusalem," it contains the famous opening lines: "And did those feet in ancient time | Walk upon England's mountains green."
116. The diary forms a significant portion of the *Memorial Volume*, at 15–80. On the Durham miners, see Barlow, *Gods*, 133, and Murphy, *Green Willow*, 186 and 190.
117. See Murphy, *Green Willow*, 1. Initially, however, the mixing of social classes was resisted, and attempts were made to create battalions of men from similar backgrounds, at the request of those in the upper classes, see Peter Doyle, *First World War Britain* (Oxford: Shire Publications, 2012), 33.
118. See for example Murphy, *Green Willow*, 2 and 188. He could be quite sarcastic and acid-tongued about politicians.
119. Barlow, *Gods*, 125–28, gives a much more detailed overview of his time in training.
120. The Battle of the Somme was the greatest tragedy of the war for Britain. The initial assault resulted in more than 20,000 British troop deaths in one morning, with an additional 40,000 wounded.

Murphy gives a good summary in *Green Willow*, 191–96. By the end of it, more than one million men on both sides had been killed or wounded, see 213. See also the multimedia site *First World War*: http://www.firstworldwar.com/battles/somme.htm, accessed December 1, 2014. Murphy has suggested to me in private correspondence that Butterworth probably minimized some of his experiences, downplaying how much action the unit was seeing.
121. Letter from Lt. Col. H, Wilkinson to Sir Alexander, recorded in the *Scrapbook*, *f.* 11, and quoted by Barlow in *Gods*, 130 and *n*17. See also Murphy, *Green Willow*, 194 and 195; he was twice recommended for his heroic actions. Sir Alexander would receive his son's ribbon on August 10, see Murphy, *Green Willow*, 207.
122. Murphy, *Green Willow*, 197. Murphy informs me in private correspondence that Butterworth purposely downplayed the injury in his letter home; further, his death is still commemorated annually at Pozières, on August 5 or close to the date.
123. *Memorial Volume*, 80, quoted by Barlow in *Gods*, 131. Murphy provides a detailed and harrowing account of Butterworth's last hours in *Green Willow*, 198–200.
124. Murphy, *Green Willow*, 203.
125. Barlow, *Gods*, 131–33.
126. For a listing of deaths from the Morris side and elsewhere, see Murphy, *Green Willow*, 208–10.
127. See Murphy, *Green Willow*, 203–05, for the content of the letters.
128. Murphy, *Green Willow*, 207–08.
129. Letter from Vaughan Williams to Holst, autumn 1916, U. Vaughan Williams and I. Holst, *Heirs and Rebels*, 45.
130. Letter from Vaughan Williams to Sir Alexander, August 16, 1916, Cobbe, *Letters*, 110–11.
131. Sharp's diaries are available online from VWML: http://www.vwml.org/browse/browse-collections-sharp-diaries.
For this entry, see http://www.vwml.org/browse/browse-collections-sharp-diaries/browse-sharpdiary1916#recordnumber=264, both accessed December 1, 2014. See also Chapter 2.
132. http://www.vwml.org/browse/browse-collections-sharp-diaries/browse-sharpdiary1916#recordnumber=268, accessed December 1, 2014.
133. http://www.vwml.org/browse/browse-collections-sharp-diaries/browse-sharpdiary1916#recordnumber=269, accessed December 1, 2014.
134. Murphy, *Green Willow*, 211–212. See also *n*83 for publication details. For Vaughan Williams' tribute and a letter to Sir Alexander of December 2, 1917, see Cobbe, *Letters*, 116–17.
135. Lucy Broadwood, *Scrapbook*, *ff*. 132–33, quoted in Murphy, *Green Willow*, 212.
136. Letter from Finzi to Vera Sommerfield, May 1922, quoted in Stephen Banfield, *Gerald Finzi: An English Composer*, 31. See also Banfield, "Butterworth." See also Murphy, *Green Willow*, 97, for Finzi's opinion of Butterworth's Housman settings.
137. October issue of 1941, reprinted in Geoffrey Self, *The Music of E.J. Moeran* (London: Toccata Press, 1986), 20–21. We will discuss Moeran in detail in

chapter 6; Butterworth's style may have influenced one of his early works, the *First Rhapsody for Orchestra*.

138. See chapter 6.
139. Cyril Bailey, *Hugh Percy Allen* (Oxford and London: Oxford University Press, 1948), 139.
140. Barlow, *Gods*, 39.
141. *Ibid.*, 56. Barlow provides a thorough overview of the songs with musical analysis at 56–71. For background and analysis see Murphy, *Green Willow*, 88–97. See also 41; Butterworth and Jekyll were both determined to set Housman's poems.
142. See *Ibid.*, 57, for a dismissive *Morning Post* review, for example. See also Banfield, "Butterworth," for some further considerations on the structure of the Housman songs.
143. Barlow, *Gods*, 71. See also Murphy, *Green Willow*, 96.
144. Housman, *A Shropshire Lad* (London: K. Paul, Trench, Treubner, 1896), published online at: http://www.bartleby.com/br/123.html, accessed September 15, 2014. See also *Collected Poems*, 51, and Appendix A.
145. Dawney, "Folk Music Manuscripts," 103.
146. See Murphy, *Green Willow*, 81 and 97 for the precise dating of both works.
147. Barlow provides musical analysis of the pieces in *Gods*, at 45–50.
148. See Barlow's overview of the work, *ibid.*, 98–108.
149. Program notes written by Butterworth for the London performance of March 20, 1914. Printed in the *Memorial Volume*, 114, and quoted in Barlow, *Gods*, 99.
150. See Murphy, *Green Willow*, 136–38, for details about the event.
151. See Barlow, *Gods*, 105–06, and Murphy, 138–40, for more detailed reviews.
152. Butterworth to Herbert Thompson, 1912, quoted in Murphy, *Green Willow*, 134. See also 140; it seems that success embarrassed him.
153. *Ibid.*, 108.
154. For some analysis, see Murphy, *Green Willow*, 140–41.
155. The British Library has this wax cylinder recording online at: http://sounds.bl.uk/World-and-traditional-music/Ethnographic-wax-cylinders/025M-C0037X1631XX-0100V0, accessed September 15, 2014.
156. Barlow, *Gods*, 109.
157. From the program notes to the premier performance on March 20, 1914. These were included in the *Memorial Volume*, at 114–15. Barlow also includes this reference in *Gods*, 109.
158. For an analysis of the song and different versions of the tune and lyrics, see the online resource *Mainly Norfolk: English Folk and Other Good Music*: http://mainlynorfolk.info/lloyd/songs/thebanksofgreenwillow.html, accessed September 15, 2014.
159. See Barlow, *Gods*, 109, for an example of the variant.
160. *Ibid.*, 111. He offers an analysis of the themes at 108–111.
161. See chapter 3, and Ursula Vaughan Williams,

R.V.W., 95, quoting from the private memoir to Butterworth. See also Murphy, *Green Willow*, 87.
162. This is reprinted in full in Barlow, *Gods*, 169–71.
163. *Ibid.*, 170. See also chapter 3.
164. See Murphy, *Green Willow*, 152.
165. The London Symphony Orchestra, under the direction of Richard Hickox, presented a world premiere recording of the original 1913 version, released by the Chandos label in 2001, with the permission of Ursula Vaughan Williams. CHAN9902.
166. For the text of that letter, see Ursula Vaughan Williams, *R.V.W.*, 111.
167. *Scrapbook, f.* 104, quoted in Barlow, *Gods*, 124.
168. Ursula Vaughan Williams, *R.V.W.*, 105, and Murphy, *Green Willow*, 121. Interestingly, Butterworth was not moved by Gregorian chant, finding a service he attended in 1906 to be "beautifully sung" but "passionless," see 45.
169. See Barlow, *Gods*, 134.
170. See Murphy, *Green Willow*, 170.
171. Vaughan Williams, "George Butterworth," *National Music*, 247.

Chapter 6

1. For a brief comparison of their works and styles, see Gerald Cockshott, "Warlock and Moeran," *Composer* 33 (1969): 1–4.
2. Published works on Moeran are relatively few, the most accessible being Geoffrey Self, *The Music of E.J. Moeran* (London: Toccata Press, 1986). See also his addenda in "E.J. Moeran: Unpublished Letters and Songs," *British Music: Journal of the British Music Society* 16 (1994): 33–43, and "E.J. Moeran: Unpublished Letters and Songs Postscript," *British Music* 17 (1995): 63. Ian Maxwell, the editor of *British Music*, has recently completed a doctoral thesis at Durham University, "The Importance of Being Ernest John: Challenging the Misconceptions about the Life and Works of E. J. Moeran." This is available online at Durham E-Theses: http://etheses.dur.ac.uk/10752, accessed January 12, 2015. Maxwell has discovered various errors in Self's work, and this reappraisal is essential to understanding Moeran's life. He also provides a good summary of earlier Moeran studies at 24–42, and additional source material from 42–47. Other books include Lionel Hill, *Lonely Waters: The Diary of a Friendship with E J Moeran* (London: Thames, 1985), a collection of correspondences between Moeran and the author in the 1940s, and Stephen Wild, *E. J. Moeran* (London: Triad Press, 1973); this was based on his MA dissertation, and included interviews with Moeran's widow, Peers Coetmore; her recollections were not always accurate. For a study of Moeran's relationship to the natural world and using it as a source of inspiration, see Fabian Gregor Huss, "The Construction of Nature in the Music of E. J. Moeran," *Tempo* 63:248 (2009): 35–44. For online information, see Anthony Payne, "Moeran, E.J.," *Grove Music Online*, Oxford Music Online, Oxford University Press: http://www.oxfordmusiconline.com/subscriber/article/grove/music/48243, accessed September 16,

2014. A useful online resource is the *Worldwide Moeran Database*: http://www.moeran.net/index2.html, accessed September 16, 2014. Though not currently being updated, it still contains good information. The biography has links to several articles, some long out-of-print: http://www.moeran.net/Biography.html, accessed September 16, 2014.

3. For a detailed list, see Maxwell, "The Importance of Being Ernest John," 20.

4. Philip Heseltine, "Newcomers: E. J. Moeran," *The Chesterian* 36 (January 1924): 124, and "E. J. Moeran," *The Music Bulletin* 6:6 (June 1924): 170–74. The longer work is Heseltine, *E. J. Moeran* (London: J & W Chester, 1926). See Maxwell, "The Importance of Being Ernest John," 24–27 for a summary of some of these early details.

5. Maxwell, "The Importance of Being Ernest John," 63–64.

6. See *ibid.*, 48–50, and 197–99 for details. This generosity lasted for some 20 years. For a detailed study of his family history, see 51–63.

7. *Ibid.*, 65, referencing *Crockford's Clerical Directory for 1905* (London: Horace Cox, 1905), 962.

8. For this view, see Self, *E.J. Moeran*, 17.

9. Maxwell, "The Importance of Being Ernest John," 66, 67, and 70.

10. See, for example, Maxwell, "The Importance of Being Ernest John," 57–59, and 73–74; some of these relatives probably visited the Moeran home when he was a child.

11. For more details, see *ibid.*, 67–69. Moeran's brother recalled that their parents wanted him to become an engineer, see 68; however, this is unlikely, see 76 and 79.

12. Heseltine's mother strongly objected to his decision to pursue a musical career (wanting him to go into the Civil Service), while Delius encouraged it, much to her dismay, see chapter 7.

13. Little information survives from this period, see Maxwell, "The Importance of Being Ernest John," 74–75. His parents' move was caused by his father's health problems and the decision to retire from the ministry, see 76.

14. Self, *E.J. Moeran*, 17–18. For more detailed summary of his time at Uppingham, see Maxwell, "The Importance of Being Ernest John," 76–79.

15. Maxwell, "The Importance of Being Ernest John," 74.

16. See Aloys Fleischmann, "The Music of E.J. Moeran," *Envoy: A Dublin Review* 4:16 (1951): 61. However, see also Maxwell, "The Importance of Being Ernest John," 94–95.

17. *Royal College of Music Students Register*, No. 10 1911–1914, RCM Records & Archives MS P35.03, 3768, referenced in Maxwell, "The Importance of Being Ernest John," 80.

18. On the Musical Club and Moeran's membership, see Maxwell, "The Importance of Being Ernest John," 81–88, and 106–07.

19. *Ibid.*, 107.

20. Robert Weedon, "E.J. Moeran's War," *War Composers: The Music of World War I*, available online at: http://www.warcomposers.co.uk/moeranbio.html, accessed September 17, 2014.

21. Maxwell, "The Importance of Being Ernest John," 114.

22. E. J. Moeran, Military Record: Commission, National Archives WO 374/48245 C457620, noted in Maxwell, "The Importance of Being Ernest John," 154 *n*253.

23. Maxwell, "The Importance of Being Ernest John," 154.

24. For examples of his activities and work at that time, see *ibid.*, 115, 117–18, and 149–51.

25. *Ibid.*, 120–21. For a more detailed analysis of these songs, see 122–33.

26. See *ibid.*, 133–54 for a detailed survey of the work. Maxwell concludes that part of it may have been intended for a competition run by Walter Wilson Cobbett (1847–1937), who sought to revive the Tudor and Stuart form of the phantasy or fancie (but as envisioned and reinvented by Cobbett himself) by commissioning composers to create new works in this style, bringing contemporary sensibilities to them, and submitting them for awards. He held five chamber music competitions in total, taking place every few years between 1905 and 1919. For a thorough study of Cobbett and his competitions, see Betsi Hodges, "W.W. Cobbett's Phantasy: A Legacy of Chamber Music in the British Musical Renaissance," DMA thesis, University of North Carolina at Greensboro, 2008. While Maxwell posits that Moeran may have submitted work for the 1917 "folk song phantasy" competition, Hodges makes no mention of Moeran entering this or any of the others.

27. Maxwell, "The Importance of Being Ernest John," 149.

28. Self, *E.J. Moeran*, 19–20.

29. *Ibid.*, 20.

30. *Ibid.*, 19–20, quoting an assessment from a private medical opinion. See also 233–34 for some accounts of his unreliability from those who knew him.

31. From a 1947 interview for Irish radio with Eamonn Andrews; the recording and transcript of which are available at the Moeran Database: http://www.moeran.net/Writing/Radio-Interview.html, accessed September 18, 2014.

32. See his detailed research in Maxwell, "The Importance of Being Ernest John," 154–65.

33. For these differing assessments in 1924 and 1926, see *ibid.*, 156–57.

34. Letter from Moeran to George Parker, February 10, 1935; quoted in Geoffrey Self, "E.J. Moeran—Unpublished Letters and Songs," *British Music* 16 (1994): 34.

35. On both of these accounts, see Maxwell, "The Importance of Being Ernest John," 157–58.

36. E. J. Moeran Military Record, Arrival Report, National Archives WO 374/48245 C457620, quoted in Maxwell, "The Importance of Being Ernest John," 161. See also 168.

37. Maxwell, "The Importance of Being Ernest John," 161.

38. Oxford & Cambridge Musical Club Archives, Oxford University Library Dep.c.967, 129, noted in *ibid.*, 161 and *n*284.

39. E. J. Moeran Military Record, Medical Board Report—Smallburgh, 9/8/17, National Archives WO 374/48245.

C457620, noted in Maxwell, "The Importance of Being Ernest John," 163 and n286.
40. E. J. Moeran Military Record, Medical Board Report—Wroxham, 1/1/18, National Archives WO 374/48245.
C457620, noted in Maxwell, "The Importance of Being Ernest John," 164 and n291.
41. Maxwell, "The Importance of Being Ernest John," 165.
42. See *ibid.*, 166–67.
43. Recalled in a letter from Moeran to Aloys Fleischmann, February 10, 1937, and sourced by Maxwell in "The Importance of Being Ernest John," 170 n302. See also 207–210 for more background on the piece.
44. E. J. Moeran Military Record, Protection Certificate, 7 January 1919, National Archives WO 374/48245.C457620, noted in Maxwell, "The Importance of Being Ernest John," 181n319.
45. For his convincing conclusions, see Maxwell, "The Importance of Being Ernest John," 181–86.
46. For a recent study of the phenomenon, see Peter Leese, *Shell Shock: Traumatic Neurosis and the British Soldiers of the First World War* (New York and Basingstoke: Palgrave Macmillan, 2002).
47. See chapter 5.
48. Self, *E.J. Moeran*, 21.
49. For the photo and analysis, see Maxwell, "The Importance of Being Ernest John," 188–89.
50. See *ibid.*, 193–95.
51. See Moeran's recollection in Evan Senior, "E.J. Moeran," *Australian Musical News and Digest* (1 May 1950): 31.
52. Ireland's *Downland Suite*, for example, certainly evokes the Sussex countryside. For a brief biography, see Hugh Ottaway, "Ireland, John," *Grove Music Online*, Oxford Music Online: http://www.oxfordmusiconline.com/subscriber/article/grove/music/13905, accessed September 17, 2014. For a collection of essays, see *The John Ireland Companion*, Lewis Foreman, ed. (Woodbridge: Boydell, 2011). For his fondness for the countryside, see Em Marshall, *Music in the Landscape*, 138–51.
53. Self, *E.J. Moeran*, 23.
54. See Martin J. Andrews, *The Life and Work of Robert Gibbings* (Bicester, UK: Primrose Hill Press, 2003), 53, and Robert Gibbings, *Coming Down the Wye* (London: Dent, 1947), 1–2. See also Maxwell, "The Importance of Being Ernest John," 206–07, for some details of how they may have met.
55. For an overview of Harty, see Michael Kennedy, "Harty, Sir Hamilton," *Grove Music Online*, Oxford Music Online. Oxford University Press: http://www.oxfordmusiconline.com/subscriber/article/grove/music/12488, accessed September 17, 2014.
56. See Maxwell, "The Importance of Being Ernest John," 200–03, 205, 211–12, and 219–20, for a survey of some of his activities during the early years of the 1920s.
57. *Ibid.*, 228–29. However, see chapter 7 for Percy Scholes' review and the furious response it elicited from Heseltine.
58. *Ibid.*, 222.
59. This is a matter of some controversy, and once again, the facts seem to be obscured by Moeran misremembering aspects of his early work. See Maxwell, "The Importance of Being Ernest John," 94–95.
60. *Ibid.*, 96–97. The first collecting probably occurred in July 1915, see 106 and 118–19.
61. Christopher Palmer, *Delius: Portrait of a Cosmopolitan* (London: Duckworth, 1976), 166.
62. Moeran, "Moeran Norfolk Collection," *Folk Song Journal* 7:26 (1922): 1–24. See Self, *E.J. Moeran*, 48n14 for a complete list of his songs, including the singer and the place and date each song was collected. See also the list in Roy Palmer, "Neglected Pioneer: E.J. Moeran (1894–1950)," *Folk Music Journal* 8:3 (2003): 357–61. This article gives a good sampling of first-person accounts from Moeran about his folk song work. For a broader view of folk song transmission in Norfolk, related to Moeran's work, among others, see Christopher Heppa, "Harry Cox and his Friends: Song Transmission in an East Norfolk Singing Community, c. 1896–1960," *Folk Music Journal* 8:5 (2005): 569–93. See also Maxwell, "The Importance of Being Ernest John," 96 and 118.
63. Heseltine, "Introductions XVIII: E J Moeran," *The Music Bulletin* 6:6 (1924): 170–174, also reprinted at the *Moeran Database*: http://www.moeran.net/Biography/Warlock1924.html, accessed September 17, 2014. On not censoring the texts, see also Palmer, "Neglected Pioneer," 352 and 355, where Moeran noted that he would like to see complete editions of authentic texts published, "in which nothing worth while [sic] is glossed over or left out for reasons of squeamishness or timidity."
64. These two rhythmic patterns had dominated Western music since the Middle Ages. For a detailed study of 5/4 rhythms in traditional English tunes, see Vic Gammon and Emily Portman, "Five-Time in English Traditional Song," *Folk Music Journal* 10: 3 (2013): 319–346.
65. Heseltine, "Introductions," 173. See also Heseltine, "E J Moeran," *Moeran Database*.
66. Heseltine, "E J Moeran," *Moeran Database*.
67. In a letter to Bernard van Dieren, the Dutch composer and music critic, who Heseltine would later make his heir in his will, which led to some controversy. Self, *E.J. Moeran*, 44.
68. "Annual General Meeting, 1923," *Journal of the Folk-Song Society* 7:27 (1923): xi.
69. See Heppa, "Harry Cox and his Friends," 578.
70. See Moeran, "Some Folk Singing Today," *Journal of the English Folk Dance and Song Society* 5:3 (1948):152, where he notes: "I have tried it time and again, only to be met with the proposal to meet the following Saturday at an inn." See also Roy Palmer, "Neglected Pioneer," 349.
71. Self, *E.J. Moeran*, 47.
72. Moeran, "Folk Songs and some Traditional Singers in East Anglia," *The Countrygoer* 7 (Autumn 1946), available online at the Moeran database. http://www.moeran.net/Writing/FolkSongs.html, accessed September 28, 2014. For other slight variations of the story, see Christopher Palmer, *Delius*, 166, and Roy Palmer, "Neglected Pioneer," 346.
73. See 89–90, drawing from Heseltine's account in "E. J. Moeran," *The Music Bulletin*, 172.

74. For a more detailed survey, see Maxwell, "The Importance of Being Ernest John," 88–93, as well as 95 and 118–19.
75. For an analysis of the work, see Self, *E.J. Moeran*, 32–34. Self is rather unfairly critical of the piece, citing what he believes is "the dullness of its principal ideas" (at 32), but nevertheless recognizing its fine orchestration (at 33).
76. *Ibid.*, 34. He provides a full analysis at 34–36.
77. *Ibid.*, 36.
78. *Moeran Database*: http://www.moeran.net/Orchestral/FirstRhapsody.html, accessed September 17, 2014. See also Maxwell, "The Importance of Being Ernest John," 222.
79. *Moeran Database*: http://www.moeran.net/Orchestral/FirstRhapsody.html.
80. *The Times*, issue 43798 (December 30, 1916): 10.
81. See Self, *E.J. Moeran*, 57–60. However, see also Maxwell, "The Importance of Being Ernest John," 20 and 30.
82. Correspondence between Michael Bowles and Self, detailed in Self, *E.J. Moeran*, 53.
83. Hubert Foss, "E. J. Moeran: A Critical Appreciation," *The Musical Times* (January 1930): 26.
84. Self, *E.J. Moeran*, 39.
85. "When smoke stood up from Ludlow" (no. 7), "Farewell to barn and stack and tree" (no. 8), "Say, lad, have you things to do?" (no. 24), and "The lads in their hundreds to Ludlow come in for the fair" (no. 23).
86. From the 1896 edition, available online at: http://www.bartleby.com/123/23.html, accessed September 17, 2014.
87. Maxwell, "The Importance of Being Ernest John," 241.
88. See *ibid.*, 248–51.
89. See Maxwell, "The Importance of Being Ernest John," 251.
90. For further discussion, see Rhoderick McNeill, "Moeran's Unfinished Symphony," *The Musical Times* 121:1654 (December, 1980): 771–73, and 775–77.
91. Maxwell, "The Importance of Being Ernest John," 254.
92. *Ibid.*, 251–53 and 253n495.
93. See chapter 7.
94. A plausible theory, see Maxwell, "The Importance of Being Ernest John," 258–59.
95. *Ibid.*, 259 and n514, and 269.
96. *Ibid.*, 260–61.
97. *Ibid.*, 261–63, and 262n523, which contains details about Moeran's 1948 diagnosis. See also 276.
98. *Ibid.*, 270. See also Heseltine's letters to Arnold Dowbiggin of June 18, 1930, and July 1, 1930, in Smith, ed., *Collected Letters of Peter Warlock*, 4 vols. (Woodbridge: Boydell, 2005), IV, 272, and IV, 274 respectively.
99. For an assessment of his output at this time, see Self, *E.J. Moeran*, 73–101, and Maxwell, "The Importance of Being Ernest John," 270–71.
100. Self, *E.J. Moeran*, 53. On the dating of the piece, see 54, and for other aspects, see 54–57.
101. See chapter 7 for details.
102. Letter from Moeran to Edith Buckley Jones, December 27, 1930, Heseltine Papers, Add.MS 964, British Library, London, quoted in Maxwell, "The Importance of Being Ernest John," 279. One can sense feelings of loss similar to those of Vaughan Williams, first with Butterworth in 1916, and then with Holst in 1934.
103. Letter from Moeran to Arnold Dowbiggin, February 18, 1931, quoted in Self, *E.J. Moeran*, 74.
104. Eric Fenby is unclear about this, noting that Moeran eventually did arrive at the destination of his companions (Delius' home) by taxi, but that Delius had gone in, having had enough company for the day. Eric Fenby, *Delius as I Knew Him* (London: Charles Birchall, 1936, reprinted Cambridge University Press, 1981, and Dover, 1994), 63.
105. See the *Moeran Database*: http://www.moeran.net/Orchestral/WhythornesShadow.html, accessed September 18, 2014. See also Self, *E.J. Moeran*, 87–90, and Barry Smith, *Peter Warlock: The Life of Philip Heseltine* (Oxford and New York: Oxford University Press, 1994), 235. Moeran himself produced Tudor-influenced pieces such as *Phyllis and Corydon*, see Hughes, *English Musical Renaissance*, 250–51.
106. Self, *E.J. Moeran*, 234.
107. See Maxwell, "The Importance of Being Ernest John," 282 and n545.
108. On these two pieces, see also Rhoderick McNeill, "A Critical Study of the Life and Works of E. J. Moeran," Ph.D. thesis, University of Melbourne, 1983, 114 quoted in Maxwell, "The Importance of Being Ernest John," 282. See also 285–86.
109. "Annual General Meeting," *Journal of the Folk-Song Society* 8:35 (1931): xii.
110. For more on his folksong settings, see Roy Palmer, "E.J. Moeran and Folksong," liner notes to Moeran, *Complete Solo Folksong Arrangements*, BMS 438CD, CD, 2010, 3–17.
111. Self, *E.J. Moeran*, 75.
112. Payne, "Moeran, E.J."
113. Maxwell, "The Importance of Being Ernest John," 280–81.
114. Leonard Duck, "Inspiration: Fact and Theory," *The Musical Times* 94:1319 (1953): 13.
115. Self, *E.J. Moeran*, 232. He was very fond of trains, see Marshall, *Music in the Landscape*, 210.
116. Barry Marsh, "E.J. Moeran in Norfolk," *Moeran Database*: http://www.moeran.net/Jackinnorfolk.html, accessed September 18, 2014.
117. For a longer discussion, see Huss, "The Construction of Nature," 37–38, and 40–41.
118. *Ibid.*, 42.
119. *Ibid.*, 44.
120. Bax, "E.J. Moeran, 1894–1950," *Music and Letters* 32:2 (1951): 126.
121. Palmer, "Neglected Pioneer," 354. See also Self, *E.J. Moeran*, 102–03.
122. Quoted in Lewis Foreman, liner notes to Moeran: *Violin Concerto, Lonely Waters, and Wythorne's Shadow*, Chandos CHAN8807, CD, 1990.
123. Self, *E.J. Moeran*, 75–76.
124. *Ibid.*, 81.
125. Letter to Heseltine dated November 5, 1930 (shortly before his death), partially reprinted in Self, *E.J. Moeran*, 236.

126. "Composer's Motoring Offence," *The Times* issue 46968 (January 22, 1934): 4, quoted in Maxwell, "The Importance of Being Ernest John," 290–91.
127. Letter from Moeran to George Parker, February 10, 1935; quoted in Self, "E.J. Moeran—Unpublished Letters and Songs," 34.
128. *Ibid.*
129. Self, *E.J. Moeran*, 130–31. See also chapter 5.
130. For Self's history of the work and an analysis see *ibid.*, 102–33. For the *Lento*'s folk music sources, see 118–22. However, See Maxwell, "The Importance of Being Ernest John," 35, 121, and 291.
131. Moeran considered it essential to be in Ireland to complete the work, see Marshall, *Music in the Landscape*, 209.
132. Maxwell, "The Importance of Being Ernest John," 333.
133. Moeran confessed this with embarrassment in an August 1940 letter to Aloys Fleischman, also quoted in Self, *E.J. Moeran*, 157.
134. See n2 above for the publication details.
135. Though given that he was recovering from his fall at the time, he would not likely have been doing much socializing, see Maxwell, "The Importance of Being Ernest John," 296. This may be another misremembered event.
136. See Maxwell, "The Importance of Being Ernest John," 296. For details of their blossoming relationship, see 299–314.
137. See examples in *ibid.*, 302–06; Coetmore may also have been looking for a father figure, see 306. Moeran's suggestion that they co-write music together would have been impossible, given his slowness, self-criticism, and refusal to obey deadlines, see 307.
138. Her influence on his work is described in detail in Self, *E.J. Moeran*, 186–220.
139. Letter from Moeran to Peers Coetmore, January 27, 1945, quoted in Rhoderick McNeill, "Moeran's unfinished Symphony," *The Musical Times* (December 1980): 771.
140. Lionel Hill, *Lonely Waters*, 37. See also Maxwell, "The Importance of Being Ernest John," 314, where he notes that this need for solitude was bordering on obsessive. Curiously, he had a talent and enthusiasm for mushrooming, and in England could identify those that were edible, see Marshall, *Music in the Landscape*, 211.
141. For several instances of his alcoholism and its embarrassing public consequences, see Self, *E.J. Moeran*, 234–36.
142. See, for example, Maxwell, "The Importance of Being Ernest John," 308.
143. Self, *E.J. Moeran*, 221–24.
144. See Huss, "The Construction of Nature," 42; Moeran was by then convinced that he could not write the work except in Ireland.
145. See Marshall, *Music in the Landscape*, 211.
146. Self, *E.J. Moeran*, 228–29.
147. 1947 interview for Irish radio with Eamonn Andrews, *Moeran Database*: http://www.moeran.net/Writing/Radio-Interview.html, accessed September 18, 2014.
148. Quoted in Roy Palmer, "Neglected Pioneer," 354–55, original citation (n69) missing from the article. See also Huss, "The Construction of Nature," 43.

Chapter 7

1. Heseltine wrote mostly vocal music, and only a handful of instrumental pieces, including his famed *Capriol Suite* and the *Serenade for String Orchestra*. For a list and study of these works, see I.A. Copley, "The Published Instrumental Music of Peter Warlock," *The Music Review* 25:3 (1964): 209–23.
2. See Peter J. Reynolds, "Peter Warlock: His Contemporaries & their Influence," *British Music Society Journal* 7 (1985): 49.
3. There are a number of studies on Heseltine. The definitive biography to date is Barry Smith, *Peter Warlock: The Life of Philip Heseltine*, which contains a good amount of original reprinted source materials, particularly letters from Heseltine to others, giving unique insights into the man and his life. Heseltine was a prolific letter-writer, and Smith has also edited his letters in a separate edition: *The Collected Letters of Peter Warlock*. See also Smith's *Frederick Delius and Peter Warlock: A Friendship Revealed* (Oxford: Oxford University Press, 2000), a collection of the correspondence between the two. The earliest work on Heseltine was Cecil Gray, *Peter Warlock: A Memoir of Philip Heseltine* (London: Jonathan Cape, 1934), which, while useful as a primary source by as friend, has been criticized for its attempts at psychoanalysis and trying to portray Heseltine as a split personality, a theory not generally accepted now. A good listing of the books about him, as well as collections of his writings, can be found at the website of the Peter Warlock Society: http://www.peterwarlock.org, accessed September 18, 2014; the bibliography is at: http://www.peterwarlock.org/PWBOOKS.HTM. An invaluable collection of essays is David Cox and John Bishop, eds., *Peter Warlock: A Centenary Celebration* (London: Thames, 1994). See also Brian Collins, *Peter Warlock: The Composer* (Aldershot, UK: Scholar Press, 1996). Barry Smith also wrote the Grove article, which is a useful, if brief, summary of his life and works: "Warlock, Peter," *Grove Music Online*, Oxford Music Online. Oxford University Press: http://www.oxfordmusiconline.com/subscriber/article/grove/music/29912, accessed September 19, 2014. For a chronological listing of his songs, see Kenneth Avery, "The Chronology of Warlock's Songs," *Music & Letters* 29:4 (1948): 398–405, and Kenneth Avery, "The Chronology of Warlock's Songs," *Music & Letters* 29:4 (1948): 398–405. For a musical edition, see Peter Warlock and Michael Pilkington, *Songs 1911–1930*, 8 vols. (London: Thames, 2004 and 2005). For a discussion of Heseltine's mental problems and how they related to his music, an invaluable study is Judy O. Marchman, "Peter Warlock (1894–1930): A Contextual Analysis of his Art Songs Related to Symptoms of Mental Illness," DMA thesis, University of Miami, 2013.
4. Smith, *Peter Warlock*, 5 and see his letter to Cecil Gray, November 19, 1921, Smith, *Collected Letters*, III, 384.
5. *Ibid.*, 6. Smith reprints lengthy excerpts from many of his letters throughout the book.
6. Letter to Edith from Florence Peck, British Library, BL Add. MS 57964, quoted in Smith, *Peter Warlock*, 7. See *Centenary Celebration*, 37, for the complete text of the letter.

7. Smith, *Peter Warlock*, 9–10.
8. Smith, *Peter Warlock*, 10. For the full letter from Heseltine to Edith, September 23, 1906, see Smith, *Collected Letters*, I, 92–94.
9. See Smith, *Peter Warlock*, 10–11 for an early example, as well as 16–17 for a disturbing example of the self-blame and assurance of his love. For representative letters, see Smith, *Collected Letters*, I, 74–75 (December 12, 1906), and 98 (May 20, 1908).
10. Letter from Heseltine to Edith, October 31, 1910, Smith, *Collected Letters*, I, 247, also quoted in Smith, *Peter Warlock*, 17.
11. Alec Rowley, "The Music of Peter Warlock," *Musical Mirror* (August 1927). I have not been able to view this source, and Smith, in *Peter Warlock*, lists two conflicting sets of pages for it: 183–84 (at 302n47) and 83 and 88 (at 330 in the bibliography). The reader will have to investigate to determine the correct citation.
12. See, for example, the letter from Heseltine to Delius, March 25, 1912: "Colin Taylor is a splendid man: I owe most of my love for music to him." Smith, *Collected Letters*, II, 11.
13. Smith, *Peter Warlock*, 13–15.
14. Letter from Heseltine to Edith, October 7, 1910, Smith, *Collected Letters*, I, 240, also quoted in Smith, *Peter Warlock*, 18.
15. Letter from Heseltine to Colin Taylor, January 19, 1929, Smith, *Collected Letters*, IV, 218. Vaughan Williams had similar opinions, see chapter 1. See also Smith, *Peter Warlock*, 257–58, for thoughts on what may have prompted this about-face in his opinion of the man he had idolized.
16. For a study of their relationship, see Barry Smith, *Frederick Delius and Peter Warlock: A Friendship Revealed*.
17. Collins, *Peter Warlock*, 3.
18. Letter from Heseltine to Edith, May 25, 1911, Smith, *Collected Letters*, I, 283–84, also quoted in Smith, *Peter Warlock*, 19–20.
19. Letter from Heseltine to Edith, June 15, 1911, Smith, *Collected Letters*, I, 291, also quoted in Smith, *Peter Warlock*, 20.
20. Smith, *Peter Warlock*, 21–22.
21. See Gray, *Peter Warlock*, 53.
22. *Ibid.*, 22–25, and 44. See also Marchman, *Contextual Analysis*, 48.
23. Smith includes lengthy excerpts of the correspondence between Delius and Heseltine, as well as much more detail in *ibid.*, 25–31.
24. Eric Fenby, *Delius*, 179–80. This caused Fenby great distress, and the two argued about it for some time, see especially 170–84. See also Fenby (in conversation with David Cox) "Warlock as I Knew Him," *Composer* 82 (1984): 19–23. He notes at 22 that both Heseltine and Grainger made him feel uncomfortable, that there was something sinister about them. For Grainger's peculiar activities, see chapter 9. It may be significant that both Heseltine and Grainger were dominated by their mothers to an unhealthy extent. See also Heseltine's letter to Colin Taylor of August 9, 1918, where he equates the concept of "Antichrist" with modern materialism, and states that darkness and light must exist in balance. Antichrist denies truth, while Christianity affirms a lie, which is just as bad. Smith, *Collected Letters*, III, 189–90. See also Peter J. Reynolds, "Contemporaries & their Influence," 48.
25. Letter from Clarence Rolt to Edith, June 7, 1912, BL Add. MS 57964, quoted in Smith, *Peter Warlock*, 33.
26. Letter from Heseltine to Delius, February 17, 1913, Smith, *Collected Letters*, II, 87–92, at 88–90, also quoted at length in Smith, *Peter Warlock*, 42–43.
27. Smith, *Peter Warlock*, 61. See 49–63 for a full summary of his Oxford year.
28. Letter from Heseltine to Fritz Hart, November 15, 1921, Smith, *Collected Letters*, III, 381, also quoted at length in Smith, *Peter Warlock*, 67. He also held that Holst had stolen his musical ideas from Vaughan Williams, the superior composer, see his letter to Delius of March 15, 1920, Smith *Collected Letters III*, 263, and 264n2.
29. Letter from Heseltine to Taylor, January 19, 1929, Smith, *Collected Letters*, IV, 218, also quoted in Smith, *Peter Warlock*, 258. He also made a piano reduction of the *Pastoral Symphony*, see Reynolds, "Contemporaries & their Influence," 57. See also Smith, *Peter Warlock*, 115.
30. Letter from Heseltine to Taylor, July 17, 1917, Smith, *Collected Letters*, III, 86. This was 12 years earlier than his praise of the *Pastoral Symphony*, quoted in Smith, *Peter Warlock*, 115. He may have been showing the influence of Delius in this opinion, for his idol had no interest in Vaughan Williams' music at all, see 170, and chapter 1.
31. Letter from Heseltine to Gray, June 15, 1918, Smith, *Collected Letters*, III, 161, see also 165n18 for the original source of his description; also quoted in Brian Collins, "Lillygay," *Centenary Celebration*, 144.
32. Letter from Heseltine to Fritz Hart, November 15, 1921, Smith, *Collected Letters*, III, 381.
33. See Moeran's account in Smith, *Peter Warlock*, 215–16, private letter of the Peter Warlock Society.
34. Collins, "Lillygay," *Centenary Celebration*, 144.
35. Beryl Kington, "Alec Rowley and Recollections of Peter Warlock," *A Centenary Celebration*, 220. For his interest in Celtic music, such as Cornish repertoire, see his letter to Cecil Gray, April 7, 1918, Smith, *Collected Letters*, III, 124–28.
36. Kington, "Recollections," 220, undoubtedly from his association with Moeran.
37. *Ibid.*, 221.
38. See Reynolds, "Contemporaries & their Influence," 52, who observes that this technique passed from Grieg to Delius to Heseltine. See also Copley, *Music of Peter Warlock*, 54, for the central importance of melody in his songs.
39. Letter from Heseltine to Delius, March 24, 1914, Smith, *Collected Letters*, II, 279.
40. Letter from Heseltine to Delius, October 18, 1914, Smith, *Collected Letters*, II, 445, also quoted in Smith, *Peter Warlock*, 64.
41. Smith, *Peter Warlock*, 65.
42. In his letter to Delius of October 18, 1914, he declares, "I have left Oxford forever!" Smith, *Collected Letters*, II, 445.
43. Marchman, *Contextual Analysis*, 56.
44. See Smith, *Peter Warlock*, 58–59.

45. *Ibid.*, 70–75. See Reynolds, "Contemporaries & their Influence," 55–56. See also Heseltine, "On Editing Elizabethan Songs," *Musical Times* 63:953 (1922): 477–80.
46. Hold, *Parry to Finzi*, 333. See also Marchman, *Contextual Analysis*, 87–89.
47. For a detailed study of their friendship and eventual falling out, see Ian A. Copley, *A Turbulent Friendship: A Study of the Relationship between D.H. Lawrence and Philip Heseltine ('Peter Warlock')* (London: Thames, 1983), and Smith, *Peter Warlock*, 76–94.
48. *Ibid.*, 102. Heseltine's admiration of and friendship with van Dieren is discussed in detail at 93–120.
49. For a discussion of their relationship, see Alastair Chisholm, "Bernard van Dieren: Friendship and Influence," *Centenary Celebration*, 160–65.
50. For theories on the adoption of the name, see Marchman, *Contextual Analysis*, 11–13. He would first compose under this name in 1918, see 101.
51. Peter Warlock, "Notes on Goossens' Chamber Music," *Music Student*, Camber Music Supplement, 22a (1916): 23–24. See Smith, *Peter Warlock*, 103.
52. For a longer list, see Smith, *Peter Warlock*, 104.
53. Patrick Mills, "It Started with a Limerick (or, How the Peter Warlock Society came into existence)," *A Centenary Celebration*, 249. The article at 248–51 is illuminating and amusing. Smith also sprinkles a generous sampling of these poetic gems throughout *Peter Warlock*. See also Smith, *Peter Warlock*, 233–34, for a remarkable account of how Heseltine once typed out a series of limericks on a roll of toilet paper and then rolled it back up!
54. For some thoughts on the psychological impact of this relationship, see Marchman, *Contextual Analysis*, 52–55.
55. Nigel Heseltine, *Capriol for Mother* (London: Thames, 1992), 123.
56. Ian Parrott, *The Crying Curlew: Peter Warlock: Family & Influences* (Llandysul, Dyfed: Gomer Press, 1994), 24–25.
57. Smith, *Peter Warlock*, 106–07.
58. *Ibid.*, 109.
59. He may have had some sadistic inclinations toward women, as well, see *ibid.*, 267–68.
60. For a biography of Blavatksy, see Daniel H. Caldwell, *The Esoteric World of Madame Blavatsky: Insights into the Life of a Modern Sphinx* (Wheaton, IL: Quest Books, 1991). See also the *Blavatsky Study Center*: http://blavatskyarchives.com, accessed September 22, 2014, which, despite its overly colorful, 1990s design style, is a useful resource. For Crowley, see the detailed biography by Richard Kaczynski, *Perdurabo: The Life of Aleister Crowley* (Berkeley, CA: North Atlantic Books, 2010, revised and expanded). See also the *Aleister Crowley Foundation* online: http://aleistercrowleyfoundation.net, accessed September 22, 2014.
61. Pauline Gray, *Cecil Gray: His Life and Notebooks* (London: Thames, 1989), 29.
62. Heseltine mentioned Crowley in his letters only a few times. See Smith, *Collected Letters*, II, 335; III, 196; and IV, 103. In the last letter, written to Norman Mudd (a disciple of Crowley's who was his PR consultant) dated October 2, 1924, Heseltine offers him advice for Crowley to acquire legal representation.
63. Denis ApIvor, "Memories of 'The Warlock Circle,'" *Centenary Celebration*, 187–96.
64. Douglas Goldring, *Odd Man Out: The Autobiography of a 'Propaganda' Novelist* (London: Chapman and Hall, 1935), 182.
65. Nigel Heseltine, *Capriol*, 167.
66. Smith, *Peter Warlock*, discussed in detail at 131–34. See also 140–41. See also Barry Smith, "Peter Warlock and the Occult," *South African Journal of Musicology* 13 (1993): 71–80.
67. Gray, *Peter Warlock*, 198. See also Smith, *Peter Warlock*, in Heseltine's letters to Gray, 151–53. Gray seems to have considered them to be demonic, see also 155. For an interesting study of how his song "The Bayly berith the bell away" may have been interpreted by Heseltine to refer to a Black Mass, see Ernest Kaye, "Witches and Warlock," *Centenary Celebration*, 166–70. David Cox doubts this, in "The Maidens Come," *Centenary Celebration*, 171–74.
68. Heseltine to Colin Taylor, July 19, 1918, Smith, *Collected Letters*, III, 573, also quoted in Smith, *Peter Warlock*, 153 and Gray, *Peter Warlock*, 170–71. Gray described his beard in August 1918 as "huge unkempt […] which, though real, looked as if it were false. He looked, in fact, like an exaggerated caricature of a Bolshevik and a German spy combined […]" Gray, *Peter Warlock*, 199.
69. Smith, *Peter Warlock*, 121–24.
70. For a study of these pieces, see Copley, "Published Instrumental Music," 212–16.
71. The composers John Ireland, Frank Bridge, Roger Quilter, and Anthony Bernard.
72. Letter from Rogers to Colin Taylor, July 19, 1918, Smith, *Collected Letters*, III, 197, also quoted in Smith, *Peter Warlock*, 146.
73. Smith, *Collected Letters*, III, 197.
74. This remarkable letter is quoted at length in Smith, *Peter Warlock*, 147–49. For his annotations in direct response to Rogers' letter, see Smith, *Collected Letters*, III, 198–99.
75. See Smith, *Peter Warlock*, 158–86, for a full account of the "Sackbut saga."
76. *Ibid.*, 179–80. Perhaps he was again "being silent" in the magical sense about his activities.
77. *Ibid.*, 184–87.
78. See *ibid.*, 195–95 for some of his songs written during this time, and 195–98 for his work on Elizabethan music.
79. See Warlock, "The Editing of Old English Songs," parts 1 and 2, *The Sackbut* 6 and 8 (1926): 183–86 and 215–20, quoted in Smith, *Peter Warlock*, 197. On the early music revival, see Joel Cohen and Herb Snitzer, *Reprise: The Extraordinary Revival of Early Music*.
80. Smith, *Peter Warlock*, 210–11.
81. *Ibid.*, 211.
82. Letter from Heseltine to Grainger, November 18, 1923, Smith, *Collected Letters*, IV, 86.
83. See Smith, *Peter Warlock*, 221–52, for a complete account. For Moeran's own reminiscences of his time there, see Gerald Cockshott, "E. J. Moeran's

Recollections of Peter Warlock," *The Musical Times* 96:1345 (1955): 128–30.

84. For Foss' description of the goings-on in his cottage after Hesseltine and Moeran moved in, see "The Warlock Gang," *The London Symphony Orchestra Observer* (November 1951): 99–100, where he notes: "[...] it was acutely, sometimes insanely, alive; each day it blossomed into a new unpredictable, semi-exotic flower. It was not exemplary, but it contained genius. The inmates and many visitors were joined in a pursuit of art. [...] They just were brilliant, eccentric, passionately alive [...]"

85. Collins was actually a gifted musician and artist. For a brief study of his life, see Frank Callaway, "Hal Collins and the Warlock Connection," *Centenary Celebration*, 242–47. See also Cockshott, "Recollections of Peter Warlock," 129; Collins could not read music but some of his piano improvisations were remembered and "salvaged" by Heseltine.

86. Gray, *Peter Warlock*, 254–55.

87. *Ibid.*, 255.

88. Cockshott, "Recollections of Peter Warlock," 128.

89. See some examples in Maxwell, "The Importance of Being Ernest John," 253*n*495.

90. See Smith, *Peter Warlock*, 223, drawing from a detailed account from Jack Lindsay, *Fanfrolico and After* (London: Bodley Head, 1962), 82–84.

91. The full account is in Nina Hamnett, *Is She a Lady?: A Problem in Autobiography* (London: Allan Wingate, 1955), 22–33, the specific instance is quoted in Smith, *Peter Warlock*, 224.

92. Smith, *Peter Warlock*, 224.

93. For other instances of Heseltine's nudism-for-shock and humor, see Smith, *Peter Warlock*, 73.

94. For more examples, see *ibid.*, 228–30.

95. The composer Herbert Howells blamed Heseltine for Moeran's drinking, see Christopher Palmer, *Herbert Howells: A Centenary Celebration* (London: Thames, 1992), 354–55. Howells disliked Heseltine, also blaming him for negative reactions to the premier of his *Piano Concerto no.2 in C* on April 27, 1925, which may or may not have a basis in truth, see Jonathan Clinch, "'Tunes all the Way'? Romantic Modernism and the Piano Concertos of Herbert Howells," *The Music of Herbert Howells*, Phillip A. Cooke, David Maw, eds. (Woodbridge: Boydell, 2013), 177–78.

96. Letter from Moeran to Peers Coetmore, possibly 1948, quoted in Self, *Moeran*, 63.

97. See Cockshott, "Recollections of Peter Warlock," 129.

98. For some comparisons of their song writing, see Stephen Banfield, "Moeran, Warlock and Song," *Journal of the British Music Society* 23 (2001): 51–55. In all, Heseltine wrote some 119 songs over about a twelve-year period, in addition to his work as an editor and letter writer.

99. Percy Scholes, *Oxford Companion to Music* (Oxford: Oxford University Press, 1970, reprinted 1985). The later editions included many changes, and a current online edition is now available at Oxford Music Online: http://www.oxfordmusiconline.com/, accessed September 23, 2014.

100. Letter from Heseltine to Robert Nichols, February 24, 1925, Smith, *Collected Letters*, IV, 118, also quoted in Smith, *Peter Warlock*, 230–31.

101. Holst, as we have seen in chapter 4, always took criticism in stride, and paid no real attention to it.

102. See chapter 6.

103. Letter from Heseltine to Percy Scholes, June 14, 1925, Smith, *Collected Letters*, IV 130–31. See also III, 104*n*9 for an explanation of the origins of this insult. Also quoted in Smith, *Peter Warlock*, 231.

104. Letter from Heseltine to Scholes, June 20, 1925, Smith, *Collected Letters*, IV, 132. Scholes remarked that Heseltine had sent him obscene postcards and made prank phone calls as well, see 132*n*1.

105. *Ibid.*, n1.

106. See Lewis Foreman, "Peter Warlock's Reception by the Press," *A Centenary Celebration*, 227–41.

107. See Paul Ladmirault, "Peter Warlock: A Great English Composer," *Chantecler* (1927), trans. David Cox and printed in *A Centenary Celebration*, 58–63.

108. See Copley, "Published Instrumental Music," 218.

109. For more on the dance collection, see http://graner.net/nicolas/arbeau/, accessed February 15, 2015.

110. Heseltine also contributed to the published edition of the original dances in 1925. See Smith, *Peter Warlock*, 241–42, for some analysis, as well as Copley, "Published Instrumental Music," 218–23.

111. For a short analysis, see Copley, "Published Instrumental Music," 216–17.

112. See *ibid.*, 249 for how the carol came about, and 279 for his rearrangement of it for solo voice in November/December 1930.

113. Letter from Finzi to Howard Ferguson, September 6, 1929, *Letters of Gerald Finzi*, 61 and n10.

114. Interview with the *Evening News*, December 17, 1929, quoted in Smith, *Peter Warlock*, 263 (who lists the interview at 323*n*35 as being December 17, 1930, but this would have been one day after his death).

115. Smith, *Peter Warlock*, 270.

116. See, for example, his letter to Winifred Baker of June 15, 1930, where he notes, "My mind is slowly awakening from its torpor and I hope to be able to get through a considerable deal of work during the next few weeks." Smith, *Collected Letters*, IV, 271. However, two weeks later, he was again consumed by depression; see his letter to Baker of June 30, Smith, *Collected Letters*, IV, 273.

117. Smith, *Peter Warlock*, 273–76.

118. For more on his love of felines, see *ibid.*, 255–56.

119. Smith offers a detailed analysis of his death and the inquest that followed in "The Mystery of Philip Heseltine's Death," *Centenary Celebration*, 64–83. For Venn's testimony, see 69.

120. *Ibid.*, 77.

121. Nigel Heseltine, *Capriol*, 71–72. See also Smith, *Peter Warlock*, 281.

122. Smith, *Peter Warlock*, 284.

123. The post mortem is reprinted in Smith, "Mystery," 82.

124. See Robert Beckhard, "Notes from an American

on a 1950s Warlock Odyssey," *Centenary Celebration*, 204.

125. Fenby, "Warlock as I knew Him," 23.

126. Private correspondence with John Mitchell (Peter Warlock Society): "[...] although [Warlock] deliberately turned on the gas tap himself, he may have subconsciously anticipated that his suicide attempt may have been foiled—he made a lot of noise when he secured the flat, and he was expecting Barbara back fairly soon after. Could he have had it in the back of his mind that his actions might have been interrupted, either by his landlady or Barbara? [Was he] making what turned out to be an unheeded 'cry for help'? We shall never know, of course!"

127. For Gray's summary, see "Peter Warlock," *Centenary Celebration* 49–52. Fenby also sympathized with this view, see Fenby, "Warlock as I Knew Him," 22. Denis Aplvor, in "Philip Heseltine (Peter Warlock): A Psychological Study," *Music Review* 46:2 (1985): 118–132, argues that Heseltine consciously adopted two different personas, when it suited him, and to help him face life's challenges.

128. Bruce Blunt, *The World Goes By*, BBC Home Service, December 16, 1944.

129. Elizabeth Poston, "Dispelling the Jackals," BBC Broadcast, 1964, reprinted in *Centenary Celebration*, 10.

130. Ibid., 12.

131. Smith, *Peter Warlock*, 154.

132. Quoted by Beckhard in "Notes from an American," *Centenary Celebration*, 202.

133. Marchman, "Contextual Analysis." For a detailed analysis, see 111–34, and the conclusion at 119–20. Other writers have concluded similarly, see Kay R. Jamison, *Touched with Fire: Manic-Depressive Illness and the Artistic Temperament* (New York: Free Press, 1993), 267–269.

134. See Marchman, "Contextual Analysis," 10–11, for example.

135. Letter from Heseltine to Viva Smith, May 7, 1915, Smith, *Collected Letters*, II, 373.

136. Ibid.

137. Letter from Heseltine to Delius, August 22, 1915, Smith, *Collected Letters*, II, 376.

138. Marchman, "Contextual Analysis,"140–41.

139. Cockshott, "Recollections of Peter Warlock," 128. In the summer of 1930, he wrote one song, *The Fox*, with the words also being written at the same time, in 18 hours, see Copley, *Music of Peter Warlock*, 143.

140. Marchman, "Contextual Analysis," 118, and see 128–29, for his suicidal inclinations.

141. Constant Lambert, "Master of English Song," *Radio Times* 59:770 (1938): 12–13.

142. Marchman, "Contextual Analysis,"131. See also 145.

143. See *ibid.*, 131–34, for several examples.

Chapter 8

1. Indeed, he had no interest in Heseltine's bohemian activities; musically, he admired the *Capriol Suite*, but found *The Curlew* "mildly decadent." See Banfield, *Finzi*, 105.

2. Stephen Banfield, "Finzi and Wordsworth," *The Clock of the Years: An Anthology of Writings on Gerald and Joy Finzi Marking Twenty-Five Years of the Finzi Friends Newsletter*, Rolf Jordan, ed. (Lichfield, UK: Chosen Press, 2007), 131.

3. There are two excellent biographies of Finzi available. The first is Stephen Banfield, *Gerald Finzi: An English Composer*; the second is Diana McVeagh, *Gerald Finzi: His Life and Music* (Woodbridge: Boydell, 2005). Also of importance is Howard Ferguson and Michael Hurd, eds., *Letters of Gerald Finzi and Howard Ferguson* (Woodbridge: Boydell, 2001), which collects the correspondence of these two close friends over the years. For a shorter introduction and a catalog of works, see John C. Dressler, *Gerald Finzi: a Bio-Bibliography* (Westport, CT: Greenwood Press, 1997). McVeagh also wrote the Grove article, "Finzi, Gerald," *Grove Music Online*, Oxford Music Online. Oxford University Press: http://www.oxfordmusiconline.com/subscriber/article/grove/music/09689, accessed September 27, 2014. For some further thoughts on Finzi abandoning his heritage (and probably not for good reasons), see Banfield, *Finzi*, 493–96, and McVeagh, *Finzi*, 255.

4. McVeagh, *Finzi*, 4. For a history of the Finzi family, see McVeagh, *Finzi*, 3–6 and Banfield, *Finzi*, 2–10.

5. Banfield, *Finzi*, 5.

6. For more on Lizzie's background, see *ibid.*, 6–9.

7. McVeagh, *Finzi*, 5–6.

8. Banfield, *Finzi*, 6, and McVeagh, *Finzi*, 6–7.

9. McVeagh, *Finzi*, 7–8, and Banfield, *Finzi*, 12.

10. McVeagh, *Finzi*, 8.

11. Banfield, *Finzi*, 13–14, and McVeagh, *Finzi*, 8–9.

12. For a biography of Farrar, see Robert Weedon, "Ernest Bristow Farrar—a biography," at the *War Composers* page: http://www.warcomposers.co.uk/farrarbio.html, accessed September 27, 2014. See also Donald Webster "Ernest Bristow Farrar, 1885–1918," *Clock of the Years*, 185–93.

13. McVeagh, *Finzi*, 9, and Banfield, *Finzi*, 14–15.

14. Banfield, *Finzi*, 17.

15. McVeagh, *Finzi*, 14, and Banfield, *Finzi*, 18.

16. http://www.warcomposers.co.uk/farrarbio.html, see also Banfield, *Finzi*, 20–21.

17. Banfield, *Finzi*, 20–21.

18. McVeagh, *Finzi*, 15.

19. See *ibid.*, 15–16, for more on their relationship, and Banfield, *Finzi*, 15. See Banfield, 19, for details about Finzi's compositions, and McVeagh, 19–20 for Bairstow's role in getting young Finzi's music performed.

20. McVeagh, *Finzi*, 20.

21. Quoted in McVeagh, *Finzi*, 18, and Banfield, *Finzi*, 22. For more in their relationship, see McVeagh, 17–18, and Banfield, 22–23.

22. Letter from Finzi to Vera, June 19, 1920, quoted in McVeagh, *Finzi*,18, and Banfield, *Finzi*, 31.

23. Banfield, *Finzi*, 23–24. See also 30–31 for some of Finzi's own thoughts on the issues.

24. Vaughan Williams noted that Finzi "was an enthusiastic country dancer," and he and his wife

would organize summer country dance events at their home, see Vaughan Williams, "Gerald Finzi: 1901–1956," Manning, *Vaughan Williams on Music*, 323, reprinted from the *Journal of the English Folk Dance and Song Society*, 8:1 (1956): 57.

25. Letter from Finzi to Busch, November 11, 1938, quoted in McVeagh, *Finzi*, 97.

26. Letter from Finzi to Vera, April 4, 1921, quoted in McVeagh, *Finzi*, 20.

27. See Hugh Cobbe, "The Correspondence of Gerald Finzi and Ralph Vaughan Williams," *Clock of the Years*, 196–97. See also Cobbe, *Letters of Ralph Vaughan Williams*, 140. For some further background on this, see Robert A. Weedon, "'Why do I go on doing these things?' The Continuity and Context of Gerald Finzi's Extended Choral Works," MA dissertation, Durham University, 2012, 42–43, and 46.

28. McVeagh, *Finzi*, 20. For an overview of their friendship, see Stephen Banfield, "Vaughan Williams and Gerald Finzi," Foreman, *Vaughan Williams in Perspective*, 202–21.

29. Stephen Banfield, "Vaughan Williams and Gerald Finzi," 202.

30. See Cobbe, "Correspondence," *Clock of the Years*, for examples. Some 200 letters between them survive, see 200.

31. *Ibid.*, 198–99.

32. Letter from Finzi to Vera, November, 1920, quoted in Banfield, *Finzi*, 32.

33. See, for example, Ursula Vaughan Williams, *R.W.V.*, 196–97.

34. See Banfield, *Finzi*, 24–27, for a discussion on Jewish identity and assimilation, and how Finzi fit into this as he desired to be thought of as "English."

35. See *ibid.*, 34, and then 35–57, for detailed analyses of many of his songs from the early 1920s.

36. *Ibid.*, 391.

37. Mellers, *Vision of Albion*, 245.

38. Banfield, *Finzi*, 53. Finzi was so attracted to Hardy that he knew he would never be able to set all of the poems that he wanted to, see 173. For a detailed study of the two, see Christopher Stunt, "Hardy and Finzi," *Clock of the Years*, 153–84. Stunt places the number of Hardy songs at 44, see 164–65, and 165n25 for his reasons.

39. *Ibid.*, 54. See also 53. For an introduction to Hardy, see *The Thomas Hardy Association*, an excellent online resource: http://thethomashardyassociation.org, accessed September 28, 2014.

40. See McVeagh, *Finzi*, 23, for some further thoughts on the individual poems that Finzi selected for inclusion.

41. *Ibid.*, 174. See also Stunt, "Hardy and Finzi," *Clock of the Years*, 161–64.

42. McVeagh, *Finzi*, 25.

43. Ivor Gurney Society online: http://www.ivorgurney.org.uk/biography.htm, accessed October 3, 2014. See also Banfield, *Finzi*, 393. Another work from the same time, Gurney's *Gloucestershire Rhapsody*, was composed in 1919–20 and influenced by Elgar and Vaughan Williams, but it would not be heard in its entirety for some 90 years. The rhapsody was premiered at the Three Choirs Festival in August, 2010. See the *Classical Iconoclast* for a description: http://classical-iconoclast.blogspot.com/2010/08/big-scoop-inor-gurney-premieres-at-3.html, accessed October 3, 2014. Though not yet available in a commercial recording, this very fine piece was released on a free CD, *An Elegy For War*, that accompanied *BBC Music Magazine* 22:9 (May 2014), performed by the BBC Scottish Symphony Orchestra, conducted by David Parry, BBCMM371, CD, 2014. Information on the recording is at the Discogs site: http://www.discogs.com/Frank-Bridge-Ivor-Gurney-An-Elegy-For-War/release/5722991, accessed February 18, 2015. The recording can be found online by searching.

44. Letter from Finzi to Howard Ferguson, January 1, 1938, *Letters of Gerald Finzi*, 169. See also Banfield, *Finzi*, 396–97.

45. Banfield, *Finzi*, 70.

46. For more thoughts on this, see *ibid.*, 60–62.

47. McVeagh, *Finzi*, 24.

48. For a thorough study of the Finzi-Howells relationship, see Banfield, *Finzi*, 62–66.

49. For more on Blow and Finzi, see Banfield, *Finzi*, 68–70.

50. See Weedon, *Gerald Finzi's Extended Choral Works*, 52, for a discussion of how the neo-classical style may have influenced Finzi's work, even as he resisted many continental musical developments.

51. Vaughan Williams, Arthur Bliss, and Graham Hutton, "Mr Gerald Finzi: a many-sided man," *The Times* (October 3, 1956): 13.

52. Banfield, *Finzi*, 69. For the original quote, see Arthur Bliss, "Gerald Finzi: An Appreciation," *Tempo*, New Series 42 (Winter 1956–57): 6. See also Banfield, *Finzi*, 67–69 for more on Finzi's relationship to the movement. Finzi was very fond of cats, see McVeagh, *Finzi*, 13, 37, 48–50, 168, and 223 for several charming examples.

53. For some early analysis of Finzi's songwriting style, see N. G. Long, "The Songs of Gerald Finzi," *Tempo*, New Series 2 (December 1946): 7–11, and C.M. Boyd, "Gerald Finzi and the Solo Song," *Tempo*, New Series 33 (Autumn 1954): 15–19. More recently, see Trevor Hold, *Parry to Finzi*, 395–421. For some analysis of the relation between words and music in his pieces, including Hardy, see Edward Cline, "The Composers' Use of Words: The Language and Music of Gerald Finzi," *The Journal of the British Music Society* 14 (1992): 8–24.

54. See Banfield, *Finzi*, 85–87 for some analysis, though it is subjective and critical. Vaughan Williams was impressed with the work, considering it "well worth doing," see Banfield, "Vaughan Williams and Gerald Finzi," 206.

55. See Banfield, "Finzi Centenary Lecture," *Clock of the Years*, 4. See also Banfield, "Vaughan Williams and Gerald Finzi," 205.

56. Letter from Finzi to Howes, October 25, 1935. See Frank Howes, "Recent Work in Folk Music," *Proceedings of the Musical Association* 64 (1938): 47. Later, during his lecture years, he would not give much time to folk songs in his talks, possibly wanting to distance himself from what was seen by the 1950s as a quaint and outdated practice.

57. Vaughan Williams, "Gerald Finzi: 1901–1956,"

Manning, *Vaughan Williams on Music*, 323, reprinted from the *Journal of the English Folk Dance and Song Society*, 8:1 (1956): 57. See also Weedon, "Gerald Finzi's Extended Choral Works," 46, where he notes that Finzi's only use of an actual folksong was what prompted his letter to Vaughan Williams in 1923, asking for permission to use his collected version. After that, Finzi was so dissatisfied with the result, that he did not use any folk song, or another composer's melody, again.

58. McVeagh, *Finzi*, 24. See also Banfield, *Finzi*, 112.

59. McVeagh, *Finzi*, 26.

60. See Banfield, *Finzi*, 25, for some instances, including one account "that he was almost sadistic towards later," and that later on he "all but disowned her."

61. See *ibid.*, 98–99, and 110. See also Banfield, "Vaughan Williams and Gerald Finzi," Foreman, *Vaughan Williams in Perspective*, 206–07.

62. See the amusing account in Ferguson, "People, events, and influences," in *The Music of Howard Ferguson: A Symposium*, Alan Ridout, ed. (London: Thames Publishing, 1989), 8–9. See also McVeagh, 47–48. The collection of their correspondence, *Letters of Gerald Finzi and Howard Ferguson*, Ferguson and Michael Hurd, eds., reveals much about musical life in England from the 1920s to the 1950s, as well as their own personalities. On the Strauss concert incident, see 3.

63. For more on this, see *Letters of Gerald Finzi*, 237. The two continued to correspond, however, only Ferguson's letter from then seems to survive.

64. Banfield, *Finzi*, 109.

65. McVeagh, *Finzi*, 50.

66. See for example his letter of June 15 to Howard Ferguson, *Letters of Gerald Finzi*, 40.

67. McVeagh, *Finzi*, 55, and Banfield, *Finzi*, 115–16.

68. From Finzi's time in the sanatorium, Ferguson would routinely address him as "Dave" in letters, a reference to Finzi's struggle with his piano concerto being like David vs. Goliath, see *Letters of Gerald Finzi*, 43.

69. For some analysis of the *Grand Fantasia* and reactions to it, see McVeagh, *Finzi*, 58–61, and 121.

70. See also Banfield, "Vaughan Williams and Gerald Finzi," Foreman, *Vaughan Williams in Perspective*, 215, for his affinities with Vaughan Williams.

71. Em Marshall, *Music in the Landscape*, 219.

72. Letter from Finzi to Ferguson, January 7, 1930, quoted in McVeagh, *Finzi*, 63.

73. For more on this, see Banfield, *Finzi*, 172.

74. Letter from Finzi to Ferguson, September 23, 1935, quoted in McVeagh, *Finzi*, 76.

75. *Ibid.*, 68.

76. Banfield, *Finzi*, 165.

77. McVeagh, *Finzi*, 68.

78. Banfield, *Finzi*, 173.

79. Letter from Finzi to Ferguson, December 24, 1932, quoted in Banfield, *Finzi*, 173. For more on this trip, see Banfield, 173–74, and McVeagh, *Finzi*, 69–70.

80. For slightly differing accounts of this, see Banfield, *Finzi*, 174, and McVeagh, *Finzi*, 70.

81. See Cobbe, "Correspondence," *Clock of the Years*, 198, for some details on the wedding's location, and Vaughan William's amusing response to concerns about his then-broken ankle and ability to navigate steps. See also Cobbe, *Letters*, 215.

82. Christopher Finzi notes that in fact, Gerald "loathed" his sister and felt that his mother "had the brains of a chicken," see "Remembering Gerald Finzi," *Clock of the Years*, 20.

83. Banfield, *Finzi*, 176, and McVeagh, *Finzi*, 72. See also Banfield, "Vaughan Williams and Gerald Finzi," Foreman, *Vaughan Williams in Perspective*, 211–212. Joy joked about looking for the bride.

84. Banfield, *Finzi*, 176.

85. McVeagh, *Finzi*, 71.

86. Joy Finzi, letter to Banfield, 1984, quoted in Banfield, *Finzi*, 175.

87. For more thoughts on their relationship and her support, see *ibid.*, 177–180, and McVeagh, *Finzi*, at 257.

88. *Ibid.*, 161–62.

89. McVeagh, *Finzi*, 82.

90. Banfield, *Finzi*, 217.

91. McVeagh, *Finzi*, 74.

92. This area is very close to Highclere Castle, where the popular television drama *Downton Abbey* is filmed. The British show chronicles events in a stately home during the 1910s and 1920s, when so many of these composers were active.

93. See Banfield, *Finzi*, 237–39 for details of the whole overwhelming but rewarding process. See also McVeagh, *Finzi*, 90.

94. McVeagh, *Finzi*, 84–85, and Banfield, *Finzi*, 420. For a short history of English apple cultivation in the century between 1850 and 1950, see Alan Davidson, "Apples: The Apple Connoisseurs," *Los Angeles Times*, September 20, 1990: http://articles.latimes.com/1990-09-20/food/fo-675_1_apple-varieties, accessed September 30, 2014.

95. McVeagh, *Finzi*, 89–90.

96. *Ibid.*, 91.

97. *Ibid.*, 93. See also Banfield, *Finzi*, 259.

98. Banfield, *Finzi*, 259.

99. McVeagh, *Finzi*, 112.

100. *Ibid.*, 99.

101. Letter from Finzi to Robin Milford, December 30, 1940, quoted in McVeagh, *Finzi*, 119. See also Banfield, *Finzi*, 284.

102. Quoted in McVeagh, *Finzi*, 110.

103. *Ibid.*

104. *Ibid.* 107.

105. Banfield, *Finzi*, 274.

106. McVeagh, *Finzi*, 115.

107. Christopher Finzi, "Remembering Gerald Finzi," *Clock of the Years*, 19. He also relates other stories, such as observing the beginning of the invasion of France, and that German POWs were sent to work on their home, which resulted in amicable conversations.

108. Banfield, *Finzi*, 274–75.

109. "Newbury String Players," *Gerald Finzi Trust* online: http://www.geraldfinzi.org/01-about/articles_04.php, accessed September 30, 2014. See also Banfield, *Finzi*, 282–86 for more details, and McVeagh, *Finzi*, 128.

110. Banfield, *Finzi*, 285. Joy joked that Finzi had poor coordination in general, and that when conducting, "you'd feel that his arms might go round the wrong way." See Michael A. Salmon, "Starshine over Distant Fields," *Clock of the Years*, 66.
111. "Newbury String Players," *Gerald Finzi Trust* online. See also Weedon, *Gerald Finzi's Extended Choral Works*, 52–53.
112. Banfield, *Finzi*, 275, and McVeagh, *Finzi*, 121.
113. Finzi to William Busch, July 18, 1941, quoted at length in Banfield, *Finzi*, 277–78. See also McVeagh, *Finzi*, 123.
114. Banfield, *Finzi*, 278–80.
115. For more details on this, see McVeagh, *Finzi*, 131–32.
116. *Ibid.*, 133.
117. See *ibid.*, 139, and Banfield, *Finzi*, 310–11. See also Ursula Vaughan Williams, *R.W.V.*, 265–66.
118. It contained more than 4,000 volumes, donated to the Reading University Library (now the Finzi Book Room), while his antiquarian books were donated to St. Andrews University, see Banfield, "Finzi Centenary Lecture," *Clock of the Years*, 9.
119. See McVeagh, *Finzi*, 184–85.
120. See *ibid.*, 174–75 for more thoughts on this.
121. See *ibid.*, 143–44 for a list of some of the varieties, and his work with them. See also Banfield, *Finzi*, 419–21.
122. See McVeagh, *Finzi*, 151, and 182–83 for his work with the music of Boyce, Arne, and others.
123. *Ibid.*, 142. See also Cobbe, "Correspondence," *Clock of the Years*, 199–200.
124. Joy discussed this in 1952, see Banfield, *Finzi*, 316.
125. See *ibid.*, 75, for more observations on this.
126. *Ibid.*, 323.
127. Letter from Finzi to Tony Scott, December 16, 1945, quoted in McVeagh, *Finzi*, 145. He would nevertheless continue to follow Britten's career and works over the years.
128. Letter from Finzi to Busch, June 16, 1942, quoted in Banfield, *Finzi*, 295.
129. Anthony Scott, "Gerald Finzi as a Tutor of Composition," *Clock of the Years*, 42. See also Weedon, *Gerald Finzi's Extended Choral Works*, 51.
130. See Banfield, "Vaughan Williams and Gerald Finzi," Foreman, *Vaughan Williams in Perspective*, 215, for some thoughts on this.
131. For more on the Three Choirs Festival, see its website: https://3choirs.org, accessed October 1, 2014.
132. Banfield, *Finzi*, 325–26.
133. Joy readily admitted that this was a problem, and that he would wait for a given problem in a piece to work itself out in his subconscious, rather than trying to force the issue, see Salmon, "Starshine Over Distant Fields," *Clock of the Years*, 65.
134. McVeagh, *Finzi*, 175–76.
135. For an analysis, see Banfield, *Finzi*, 360–68.
136. For an analysis, see *ibid.*, 369–88.
137. See *ibid.*, 386–88, for some thoughts on what drew Finzi to this work, and to Wordsworth in general.
138. McVeagh, *Finzi*, 191–92.
139. Hans Redlich, *Music Review* 13 (1952): 242–43, quoted in Banfield, *Finzi*, 373.
140. One account says that Vaughan Williams noticed this while attending a rehearsal and began "to rumble with laughter," McVeagh, *Finzi*, 186, while the other says that tenor Eric Greene noticed it during a rehearsal, and soon the whole choir was laughing, Banfield, *Finzi*, 370. Both accounts may be correct.
141. Banfield, *Finzi*, 95 and 388.
142. McVeagh, *Finzi*, 198, Banfield, *Finzi*, 422–23.
143. McVeagh, *Finzi*, 198, Banfield, *Finzi*, 423.
144. McVeagh, *Finzi*, 213, Banfield, *Finzi*, 438–43.
145. *Musica Britannica*, a multi-volume collection of printed music editions devoted to historical British repertoire: "was founded in 1951 as an authoritative national collection of British music. It is designed to stand alongside existing library editions, and to explore the vast heritage of material still largely untouched by them, thus making available a representative survey of the British contribution to music in Europe. Although its chief purpose is an accurate and scholarly presentation of the original texts, it is also intended to provide a basis for practical performance." New volumes continue to be added to the collection. See the website for more details: http://www.musicabritannica.org.uk, accessed October 2, 2014.
146. For an extended discussion of Finzi's activities in all of these areas in his last years, see Banfield, *Finzi*, 389–421.
147. Updated and available online via membership at: http://www.oxfordmusiconline.com.
148. Banfield, *Finzi*, 216.
149. *Ibid.*, 316. Christopher, or "Kiffer" as he was known, also went to prison for three months for his conscientious objection, refusing to do National Service or make an appeal on religious grounds, McVeagh, *Finzi*, 234.
150. Josephine Finzi, in private correspondence with the author, notes: "Although he [Christopher] was a trained cellist, he did not pursue this as a career, whereas Nigel was a professional violinist, and toured with major orchestras, as well as playing with the Newbury String Players from time to time."
151. McVeagh, *Finzi*, 419.
152. See Banfield, "Vaughan Williams and Gerald Finzi," Foreman, *Vaughan Williams in Perspective*, 218. He seemed to have some tension with Ursula, as well, perhaps because of her revitalizing influence on Vaughan Williams.
153. Banfield, *Finzi*, 212.
154. *Ibid.*, 493. See also Banfield, "Vaughan Williams and Gerald Finzi," Foreman, *Vaughan Williams in Perspective*, 219, where he notes that some of this relationship may have been an example of "the small man attaching himself to the great one." See also 220.
155. McVeagh, *Finzi*, 219, Banfield, *Finzi*, 424–25.
156. Joy Finzi's journal, quoted in Banfield, *Finzi*, 426.
157. McVeagh, *Finzi*, 243.
158. *Ibid.*, 249.
159. The Finzis had been regular attendants at the Festival for many years. For his relationship with this event, see Anthony Boden, "Gerald Finzi at the Three Choirs Festival," *Clock of the Years*, 233–241, especially 234 and 238.
160. McVeagh, *Finzi*, 249–50.

161. Banfield, Finzi, 482. The full text of her account of his last days is at 479–82.
162. For various letters and Vaughan Williams' tribute written for the *Times* on October 3, 1956, see Cobbe, *Letters*, 592–95.
163. *Ibid.*, 485, and McVeagh, *Finzi*, 251.
164. The organization's website is at: http://www.geraldfinzi.org, accessed October 3, 2014.
165. Arthur Bliss, "Gerald Finzi: An Appreciation," 5.
166. *Ibid.*
167. Alan Walker, "Gerald Finzi (1901–1956)," *Tempo*, New Series 52 (1959): 10.
168. John Russell, "Gerald Finzi: An English Composer," *Tempo*, New Series 33 (Autumn 1954): 15. See also 10. See Weedon, "Gerald Finzi's Extended Choral Works," 138, where he notes that Finzi's choral style continued in the 1950s to be tailored for the choir festival, an institution that was sagging in popularity by then, further adding to perceptions of his irrelevance.
169. Banfield, *Finzi*, 469.
170. In his splendid letter to Anthony Milner, August 12, 1956. See Banfield, *Finzi*, 469–72 for more on his defense against these criticisms.
171. Josephine Finzi, in private correspondence with the author.
172. Joy to Diana McVeagh shortly after Finzi's death, quoted in Banfield, *Finzi*, 179.

Chapter 9

1. The best short biography of Grainger is John Bird, *Percy Grainger* (Oxford: Oxford University Press, 1999, revised from an earlier edition), an excellent overview, slightly hindered by infrequent and incomplete footnote citation. Bird is a passionate defender of Grainger and is not shy about expressing his annoyance that Grainger's work has been neglected in the decades since his death. He notes in his preface at xvi: "We cannot, of course, be expected to take seriously anyone with the name of 'Percy,' now can we?" Further and even more caustically, at xx: "Could it be that these 'experts' [music critics and historians] know so much about music that they can no longer enjoy it? Would the world of music be a happier and healthier place if these university departments were to be burnt to the ground (having salvaged the libraries first) and their staff put out to doing something useful like sweeping streets or cleaning out toilets?" Philip Heseltine would approve! For collections of shorter studies, see *The Percy Grainger Companion*, Lewis Foreman, ed. (London: Thames, 1981); *The New Percy Grainger Companion*, Penelope Thwaites, ed. (Woodbridge, UK: Boydell, 2010); and Wilfrid Mellers, *Percy Grainger*, Oxford Studies of Composers (Oxford: Oxford University Press, 1992). For a good selection of Grainger's own writings, see *Grainger on Music*, Malcolm Gillies and Bruce Clunies Ross, eds. (Oxford: Oxford University Press, 1999). For personal recollections, see *Portrait of Percy Grainger*, Malcolm Gillies and David Pear, eds. (Rochester, NY: University of Rochester Press, 2002). For his own autobiographical musings (which often are fascinating and occasionally disturbing), see *Self-Portrait of Percy Grainger*, Malcolm Gillies et al, eds. For a fine collection of images and a short summary of his life (though with a few errors), see Robert Simon, *Percy Grainger: The Pictorial Biography* (Winston-Salem, NC: SD Publications, 1987). For a study of how Grainger's relationship with English folk song-collecting related to his own modernist approaches, see Graham Freeman, "'That Chief Undercurrent of My Mind': Percy Grainger and the Aesthetics of English Folk Song," *Folk Music Journal* 9:4 (2009): 581–617.

2. Bird, *Grainger*, 4–5.
3. Rose Grainger, in *Portrait of Percy Grainger*, 6. She stated that she was "Impelled by some fate to marry an Englishman whose physical attraction & mental outlook never appealed to me. Married Life—unhappy -experiencing both physical & mental Cruelty."
4. Bird, *Grainger*, 5.
5. Percy Grainger, *Photos of Rose Grainger and of 3 Short Accounts of Her Life* (Frankfurt: privately published, 1923), quoted in Bird, *Grainger*, 5–6. For background on this unusual publication, see 213.
6. Bird, *Grainger*, 7.
7. *Ibid.*, 7.
8. See, for example, Grainger, "My Father in Childhood," from "Grainger's Anecdotes," 423–85, Grainger Museum, Melbourne, reprinted in *Self-Portrait of Percy Grainger*, 24.
9. Bird, *Grainger*, 8.
10. *Ibid.*, *Grainger*, 16. Grainger was very fond of drawing and painting, and would remain so his whole life.
11. Brian Allison, private correspondence with the author.
12. John Grainger, in *Portrait of Percy Grainger*, 4.
13. Allison, private correspondence with the author: "Rose was brought up in a hotel and she may have been sexually active prior to meeting John. Syphilis is only usually contagious during the primary stage. The fact that Percy writes of his father having an affair with a woman in Brighton makes most people jump to the conclusion that JHG gave it to Rose. The microbiologist wife of the late architecture historian, George Tibbits (who did the first research into JHG's work), even challenges the notion that JHG had syphilis—his symptoms were consistent with the effects of periods of excessive drinking and later in life, crippling arthritis."
14. Bird, *Grainger*, 4. Allison, in private correspondence with the author, adds: "[...] John would have been about 16, which makes this claim highly implausible. Apart from anything else, where would a 16-year-old get the money to pay 14 prostitutes?"
15. See *ibid.*, 6 and 7.
16. Allison, private correspondence with the author.
17. *Ibid.*, 16–17.
18. Mabel Todhunter, in *Portrait of Percy Grainger*, 7.
19. *Ibid.*, 8–9.
20. Grainger, from notes on Pabst, Grainger Archives, White Plains, November 23, 1936, quoted in Bird, *Grainger*, 23–24.

21. Bird, *Grainger*, 24.
22. Quoted in *ibid.*, 25.
23. Grainger, "Aldridge-Grainger-Ström Saga," quoted in Bird, *Grainger*, 12. He would later be convinced that composers with blue eyes were by far the best, and embarked on a rather odd project to photograph composers' eyes. Vaughan Williams was among these subjects, see 266. Grainger referred to him as a genius, and gave praise to his *4th*, *5th*, and *6th symphonies*, see Grainger, "Music Heard in England," *Grainger on Music*, 353.
24. For Kipling's influence, see Grainger, "John H. Grainger (1956)," Museum Legend, Grainger Museum, Melbourne, reprinted in *Self-Portrait of Percy Grainger*, 17. See also Bird, *Grainger*, 63 and 67. Kipling inspired some 40 of Grainger's pieces, see Stephen Lloyd, "Grainger 'In a Nutshell,'" *Percy Grainger Companion*, 15.
25. See Grainger, "The Influence of Anglo-Saxon Folk Music," originally published as "Music Number in the Evening Post (New York)," October 30, 1920, 1–2. This was a condensed version of a lecture he had given in Portland Maine on October 4, 1910, republished in *Grainger on Music*, 113–120. See especially 113–116. He notes at 116: "But we shall be doing no injustice to the great musical geniuses of Continental Europe if we assert that their great progress in emotional expressiveness by means of an ever more and more subtle use of harmony, dynamics, and orchestral tone color was accompanied by a comprehensive atrophy of melodic and rhythmic inventivity."
26. See Bird, *Grainger*, 32, for a list of the impressive faculty and others associated with it over those years.
27. See Bird, *Grainger*, 34–36 for more details of both teachers.
28. See Lewis Foreman, "Grainger and His Contemporaries," *New Percy Grainger Companion*, 176–78, for more on his influence on Grainger.
29. Bird, *Grainger*, 38. See also David Tall, "Grainger and Folksong," *Percy Grainger Companion*, 55.
30. See Tall, "Grainger and Folksong," 55–56, for more details of the pieces he set.
31. See Lloyd, "Grainger 'In a Nutshell,'" 16, for more about these friends, known as the "Frankfurt Group."
32. For more on Mimi, see Bird, *Grainger*, 43–45.
33. *Ibid.*, 48. For more on his stylistic development, see 65.
34. *Ibid.*, 46.
35. Grainger, *Legend* to "Percy Aldridge Grainger's Published Compositions, 1st Editions," ts., November 2, 1938, 1. See Lloyd, "Grainger 'In a Nutshell,'" 19, for Delius' help in convincing him to overcome this hesitancy.
36. See *The Throne* magazine interview, *Portrait of Percy Grainger*, 49.
37. See, for example, Grainger, "English pianism and Harold Bauer (1945)," *Grainger on Music*, 341.
38. Bird, *Grainger*, 72.
39. See Lloyd, "Grainger 'In a Nutshell,'" 16–17.
40. Bird, *Grainger*, 74.
41. *Ibid.*, 72–73.

42. Letter from Grainger to Fenby, December 6, 1936, quoted in Bird, *Grainger*, 73.
43. Bird, *Grainger*, 65.
44. *Ibid.*, 76.
45. *Ibid.*, 77–78. For an account of the Bath Incident and more on Rose's jealously, see Grainger, "Bird's Eye View," *Self-Portrait of Percy Grainger*, 47–48.
46. Grainger, "Bird's Eye View," *Self-Portrait of Percy Grainger*, 47–48.
47. Bird, *Grainger*, 83. See also 112–13 for an account of evening musical gatherings involving Grainger, Vaughan Williams, Holst, Bax, and others.
48. *Ibid.*, 84–85. For Grainger's explicit account of the affair, see "Mrs L and My Early London Days," in "Ere-I-Forget," 384–19, Grainger Museum, Melbourne, reprinted in *Self-Portrait of Percy Grainger*, 93–100.
49. For a longer overview of the Grainger/Busoni relationship, see Bird, *Grainger*, 86–93.
50. Bird, *Grainger*, 69.
51. Radio broadcast, WVED, Grainger Museum transcript, June 30, 1933. See also Richard Franko Goldman, "Some Notes on Percy Grainger," *Studies in Music* 10 (1976): 11, and Roger Covell, "Percy Grainger—A Personal View," *Studies in Music* 10 (1976): 13.
52. Mellers, *Percy Grainger*, 49–51.
53. Bird, *Grainger*, 96.
54. See *ibid.*, 79, for more examples. See also 50 for some examples of similar feats when he was a student in Germany.
55. *Ibid.*, 99–100.
56. *Ibid.*, 103–06.
57. For Grainger's recollection of this and his "giving" of *Brigg Fair* to Delius, see John Amis, ed. "Interview with Percy Grainger," *Studies in Music* 10 (1976): 6, from a BBC recording on July 1, 1959.
58. Bird, *Grainger*, 150. For their first meeting, see 63. See also 125–26, 149, and 214. For a study of their friendship, see Lionel Carley, "Impulsive Friend: Grainger and Delius," *Percy Grainger Companion*, 31–50.
59. Letter from Delius to Ethyl Smith, 1910, *Portrait of Percy Grainger*, 52–53.
60. On his stage fright in later years, see Grainger, "What is Behind my Music," in "Grainger's Anecdotes," 423–88, Grainger Museum, Melbourne, reprinted in *Self-Portrait of Percy Grainger*, 168, where he notes that even in 1954, going in for an operation which might kill him made him less afraid than playing for an audience. See also Bird, *Grainger*, 113–14 and 287; on his dislike of the piano, see 115–16.
61. See Stephen Varcoe, "Singing Grainger Solo," *New Percy Grainger Companion*, 46.
62. Bird, *Grainger*, 117. See also Tall, "Grainger and Folksong," 56.
63. Quoted in Bird, *Grainger*, 117.
64. For more on Taylor and Lincolnshire, see Patrick O'Shaughnessy, "Percy Grainger: The English Folk-song Collection," *Studies in Music* 10 (1976): 19–21.
65. *Ibid.*, 21. See also chapter 2.
66. See Lady Winefride Elwes' recollection of the event (and of the following year) in *Portrait of Percy Grainger*, 46–48. See also Bird, *Grainger*, 117–18.

67. 118. Moeran encountered this sentiment in Norfolk, as well, see chapter 6.
68. Bird, *Grainger*, 119. See also chapter 2 for some modern criticism of this incident.
69. For a brief survey, see Michael Yates, "Percy Grainger and the Impact of the Phonograph," *Folk Music Journal* 4:3 (1982): 265–75. See also C.J. Bearman, "Percy Grainger, the Phonograph, and the Folk Song Society." *Music and Letters* 84 (2003): 434–55.
70. See Bird, *Grainger*, 121, and 242, for relations between the two in the 1930s. See also Lewis Foreman, "Grainger and His Contemporaries," *New Percy Grainger Companion*, 174.
71. See Tall, "Grainger and Folksong," 58–59. See also chapter 2.
72. Tall, "Grainger and Folksong," 59. See also Freeman, "That Chief Undercurrent," 610–11.
73. Letter from Grainger to Sharp, November 2, 1906, quoted in Bird, *Grainger*, 122.
74. Music from the People, BBC Radio, June 26, 1985, quoted in Barlow, *Gods*, 93n43. See also Yates "Impact of the Phonograph," 269. The full letter is at 267–70.
75. Yates, "Impact of the Phonograph," 268.
76. *Ibid.*, 270.
77. Grainger, "Collecting with the Phonograph," *Journal of the Folk-Song Society* 12 (1908): 147.
78. Grainger considered them overly simplistic, which was true, given that they were often intended for school children. Grainger's approach was considerably more complex and avant-garde. For examples of his settings contrasted with Sharp's, see Freeman, "'Into a cocked-hat,'" 36–42.
79. Letter from Grainger to Rose, August 1, 1909, quoted in Bird, *Grainger*, 124–25. See also Amis, "Interview with Percy Grainger," 6, for his recollections about how using a phonograph caused no real upset or harm at all. Even Vaughan Williams acknowledged that some of Sharp's piano accompaniments for songs, "Occasionally [...] seem to be bad." See Vaughan Williams, "Cecil Sharp's Accompaniments," *Vaughan Williams on Music*, 234.
80. Tall, "Grainger and Folksong," 59. For his collecting outside of Lincolnshire during this time, see Gwilym Davies, "Percy Grainger's Folk Music Research in Gloucestershire, Worcestershire, and Warwickshire, 1907–1909," *Folk Music Journal* 6:3 (1992): 339–58. For a small selection of songs in sheet music from his various collection regions, see R.S. Thomson, "Songs from the Grainger Collection," *Folk Music Journal* 2:5 (1974): 335–51.
81. Grainger, "Collecting with the Phonograph." *Journal of the Folk-Song Society* 12 (1908): 147–62.See also O'Shaughnessy, "The English Folk-song Collection," 21.
82. See O'Shaughnessy, "The English Folk-song Collection," 23.
83. Grainger "The Impress of Personality in Unwritten Music," *Musical Quarterly* 1 (1915): 416–35, reprinted in *Grainger on Music*, 47. He had previously written the similarly-titled "The Impress of Personality in Traditional Singing," *Journal of the Folk-Song Society* 3:12 (1908): 163–66, a brief survey of three of his best singers.

84. See his interesting short note, "Congratulations to the Folk Song Society," *Journal of the English Folk Dance and Song Society* 8:3 (1958): 124, for its 60th anniversary. By this time, he praises the "scientific" approach taken, being able to study the same song transcribed 14 years apart (by Broadwood and Vaughan Williams) and to compare the two.
85. See Onderdonk, "Hymn Tunes from Folk Songs," 118, 120, and 124.
86. On this, see O'Shaughnessy, "The English Folk-song Collection," 24. See also Bird, *Grainger*, 127–30.
87. Percy Grainger, "The Impress of Personality in Unwritten Music," originally published in *Musical Quarterly* 1 (1915): 416–35, reprinted in *Grainger on Music*, 45.
88. See Tall, "Grainger and Folksong," 56 and 58.
89. Grainger, "The Impress of Personality in Unwritten Music," 50.
90. Grainger, "Collecting with the Phonograph," 158.
91. See Freeman, "'Into a cocked-hat,'" 35–36, and Freeman, "That Chief Undercurrent," 599–600.
92. Freeman, "That Chief Undercurrent," 582.
93. *Ibid.*, 599. See also 609.
94. *Ibid.*, 595. See also 596–99.
95. See Yates, "Impact of the Phonograph," 269. See also Bird, *Grainger*, 130–31. For an account of how sensitively Grainger dealt with elderly singers, see 122.
96. See examples in Yates, "Impact of the Phonograph," 266–69. See also Freeman, "'It Wants All the Creases Ironing Out,'" 426–29, 431, and 433–34.
97. On these responses, see Tall, "Grainger and Folksong," 61 and 63.
98. See Freeman, "'It Wants All the Creases Ironing Out,'" 416–19, and Freeman, "That Chief Undercurrent," 592–94.
99. Yates, "Impact of the Phonograph," 274n9.
100. See Barlow, *Gods*, 92–94, for more information. See also chapter 5.
101. See O'Shaughnessy, "The English Folk-song Collection," 22.
102. David Tall, "Grainger and Folksong," *Percy Grainger Companion*, 55. See also Paul Jackson and Barry Peter Ould, "Towards a Universal Language: Grainger and Early Music; Granger and World Music," *New Percy Grainger Companion*, 79–81.
103. See Freeman, "'It Wants All the Creases Ironing Out,'" 424–25, and 434–35, for more discussion on Grainger's departure from English folk song-collecting.
104. Deborah Bierne, Grainger interview, *Success Magazine* (January 1926): 54–55. See also Freeman, "That Chief Undercurrent," 590–91, for his opinion that folk songs were the equal of "art" music.
105. Preface to *Bold William Taylor* (December 1952), in Grainger, *Thirteen Folksongs* (London: Thames Publishing, rep. 1982), also in *The Grainger Society Journal* 3:1 (1980): 9, quoted in Tall, "Grainger and Folksong," 69.
106. See James Michael Floyd, ed. "An Interview with Percy Grainger, 15 May 1946," *Tempo* 61: 239 (2007): 21.
107. Amis, "Interview with Percy Grainger," 5.

108. Christopher Palmer, ed., *The Britten Companion* (London: Faber and Faber, 1984), 73. For more on Britten's admiration of Grainger's new method of setting folk songs, see Freeman, "'Into a cocked-hat,'" 42 and 45–46. See also Gillies and Pear, *Portrait of Percy Grainger*, 139.

109. Quoted in the newspaper *Kjobenhavn*, March 15, 1907, see Bird, *Grainger*, 133–134, also noted in Simon, *Pictorial Biography*, 5.

110. Bird, *Grainger*, 138.

111. Letter from Grieg to Grainger, August 11, 1907, quoted in Bird, *Grainger*, 140. See also Lewis Foreman, "Grainger and His Contemporaries," *New Percy Grainger Companion*, 173–74, and Grieg in *Portrait of Percy Grainger*, 50–51.

112. Grainger, "Native Art and Stage Fright," Museum Legend, December 9, 1938, Grainger Museum, Melbourne, reprinted in *Self-Portrait of Percy Grainger*, 215. For a detailed study of these songs and musical transcriptions, see Paul Jackson, "Percy Grainger's Aleatoric Adventures: The Raratongan Part-Songs," *Grainger Studies: An Interdisciplinary Journal* 2 (2012): 1–32.

113. Tall, "Grainger and Folksong," 63.

114. Allison, private correspondence with the author, notes that Grainger transcribed, "three of the original recordings collected by anthropologist (Walter) Baldwin Spencer 1860–1929—Grainger did not appear to express much interest in indigenous Australian music, in fact the only written reference I can think of is noting that he had transcribed Spencer's recordings."

115. See his letter to Roger Quilter, January 31, 1909, quoted in Bird, *Grainger*, 147–48.

116. Tall, "Grainger and Folksong," 63.

117. See, for example, Bird, *Grainger*, 180. He only saw piano-playing as a means to an end, i.e., to support his composing, see 231–32. Like Finzi, it is often difficult to date his compositions, as he could take years in writing them, make new arrangements later, etc.

118. Lloyd, "Grainger 'In a Nutshell,'" 19.

119. Grainger, "The London Gramophone Co. (Now 'His Master's Voice') & the Joseph Taylor Folksong Records (1932)," in "Sketches for my Book 'The Life of My Mother & Her Son,'" September 22, 1932, W35-89, Grainger Museum, Melbourne, reprinted in *Self-Portrait of Percy Grainger*, 130. Seeing England as a land that willingly sacrificed genius without regret, he had no desire to be one of them.

120. Bird, *Grainger*, 179.

121. Allison, private correspondence with the author, notes that "the saxophone family was to feature in a lot of his future arrangements. There are a number of photographs taken of PG in fatigues carrying a soprano sax. We also have pictures of him playing at the Interlochen summer music camps with noted saxophonists. He was to even arrange early music for saxophone quartet."

122. Bird, *Grainger*, 185–86.

123. Grainger has long been criticized for a certain level of saccharine and kitsch in his music. For a good survey, see Peter Tregear, "'Nostalgia is not what it used to be': Exploring the kitsch in Grainger's Music," *Grainger Studies: An Interdisciplinary Journal* 1 (2011): 97–113.

124. *Ibid.*, 187. See also Mellers, *Percy Grainger*, 55–56.

125. See Bird, *Grainger*, 159.

126. Letter from Grainger to Sharp, November 2, 1920, quoted in Michael Yates, "Cecil Sharp in America." See also Yates "Impact of the Phonograph," 272,.

127. Michael Yates, "Cecil Sharp in America." For the work, see Maud Karpeles, ed., *English Folk Songs from the Southern Appalachians*, 2 vols. (New York and London: Oxford University Press, 1932).

128. Tall, "Grainger and Folksong," 64. See Yates "Impact of the Phonograph," 272, for Grainger's praise of Sharp's overall work. See also Bird, *Grainger*, 217.

129. See also Jackson and Ould, "Universal Language," 81.

130. Tall, "Grainger and Folksong," 63–64.

131. Bird, *Grainger*, 188. See also 192.

132. Grainger, "Bird's-Eye View," *Self-Portrait of Percy Grainger*, 56.

133. Grainger allowed that this may have been the case, but was not sure that it was the only reason, see "Notes on Whip-Lust," Grainger Museum, Melbourne, reprinted in *Self-Portrait of Percy Grainger*, 166–68.

134. Grainger, "Bird's-Eye View," *Self-Portrait of Percy Grainger*, 49.

135. Newspaper interview, date uncertain, in the possession of Bird, and quoted in Bird, *Grainger*, 49–50. He also once claimed that he was "full of violence," see 258.

136. Grainger, "The Things I Dislike," Grainger's Anecdotes, 423–87, August 1, 1954, Grainger Museum, Melbourne, reprinted in *Self-Portrait of Percy Grainger*, 155–56. This is a remarkable rant of invective that begins with him claiming to hate "almost everything," at 149, and includes playing piano, teaching (150–51), smokers and drinkers (152), and especially "forcefulness," which he describes in detail at 156–57.

137. Grainger, "To Whoever Opens the Package," *Self-Portrait of Percy Grainger*, 160–61.

138. Bird, *Grainger*, 50.

139. See Grainger, "Bird's Eye View," *Self-Portrait of Percy Grainger*, 57, where he discusses in detail how he felt about females of different ages, with the youngest being pure, clean, natural, sweet, and nice, all qualities that he admired and held up as ideal.

140. Bird, *Grainger*, 153–54. See also Grainger, "Bird's-Eye View," *Self-Portrait of Percy Grainger*, 57. For Grainger's brief engagement to his student Margot Harrison in 1912, see *ibid.*, 172–73.

141. See Grainger, "Bird's Eye View," *Self-Portrait of Percy Grainger*, 46. See also Bird, *Grainger*, 53–57, for excerpts of his own writings about these inner conflicts.

142. Bird, *Grainger*, 60.

143. For an extended list of his invented words, and some further insights into his many quirks, see James Conway, "A Percy Grainger Glossary": http://strangeflowers.wordpress.com/2011/02/20/a-percy-grainger-glossary, accessed October 16, 2014.

144. Grainger, "Ere-I-Forget," Grainger Museum, Melbourne, quoted in Bird, *Grainger*, 183.

145. Bird, *Grainger*, 212.

146. *Ibid.*, 183.

147. For his thoughts on this generosity, see

Grainger, "Money Spent," *Self-Portrait of Percy Grainger*, 130–31.
  148. See *ibid.*, 115, for the appalling and greedy behavior of some of his extended family in Adelaide.
  149. See, for example, Grainger, "The Truly Nordic Life," in "The Aldridge-Grainger-Ström Saga," December 3, 1933, W37-173 to 37-177, Grainger Museum, Melbourne, reprinted in in *Self-Portrait of Percy Grainger*, 138–43. He notes at 141 (19) that it was necessary "to hinder the breeding of Nordics with other races," using his own family as an example, and referring to himself as a "bastard outcome" because of racial mixing. See also 142 (24), where he proposes giving up certain regions in the United States to non-Nordic races where they might live separately and not mix with Nordics.
  150. Bird, *Grainger*, 194. Interestingly, he considered Africans to be one of the "beautiful races," see Grainger, "Pure Nordic Beauty," in "The Aldridge-Grainger-Ström Saga," November 15, 1933, W37-119 to 37-121, Grainger Museum, Melbourne, reprinted in in *Self-Portrait of Percy Grainger*, 132–33.
  151. *Ibid.*, 62.
  152. For a particularly galling example, see *ibid.*, 200.
  153. For a full summary, see *ibid.*, 201.
  154. Grainger, "Thought Mother was 'God.' Something of This Still Remains," in "Sketches for my Book 'The Life of My Mother & Her Son,'" November 16, 1923, W35-62, Grainger Museum, reprinted in *Self-Portrait of Percy Grainger*, 35–36. While he was in the Netherlands afterward, Vaughan Williams paid him a surprise visit to offer his condolences, see Ursula Vaughan Williams, *R.W.V.*, 142.
  155. See Grainger's own account, "Facts about Percy Grainger's Year in Europe," August 24, 1923, Grainger Museum, Melbourne, reprinted in *Self-Portrait of Percy Grainger*, 240–43.
  156. Tall, "Grainger and Folksong," 64. For some extra details of the 1922 trip, see Bird, *Grainger*, 208.
  157. Bird, *Grainger*, 157–58.
  158. He would claim that Chinese and Japanese music felt more like his "own natural music," see Floyd, "An Interview with Percy Grainger," 19 and n10.
  159. Tall, "Grainger and Folksong," 66.
  160. Simon, *Pictorial Biography*, 8. See also Bird, *Grainger*, 13, for a discussion of his unusual childhood diet, and 221 for his adult diet and other minutiae that he recorded in his diaries. For Rose's comments on his diet in 1921, see *Portrait of Percy Grainger*, 98. See also Sparre Olsen's account at 151: "Grainger was a vegetarian. He loved the Norwegian goat cheese and lingonberries. He did not care for tobacco, liquor, coffee, and tea."
  161. He noted in "How I Became a Meat-Shunner," *American Vegetarian* 4 (1946): 4, how he did not like the killing of animals for food, and that at that time, aged 64, he was never sick and could work 16-hour days.
  162. See *ibid.*, 221–22 for other accounts of his eccentricities.
  163. Robert Lewis Taylor, *The Running Pianist* (New York: Doubleday, 1950), 1. See also 2–4 and 7, for more on his arrests for vagrancy among other stories.
  164. *Ibid.*, 7.
  165. Simon, *Pictorial Biography*, 9, see also Bird, *Grainger*, 126.
  166. Bird, *Grainger*, 181.
  167. For more details of their meeting and courtship, see Bird, *Grainger*, 227–30.
  168. See Grainger's strange and revealing missive, "Read This If Ella Grainger or Percy Grainger Are Found Dead Covered with Whip Marks," August 21, 1932, Grainger Museum, Melbourne, reprinted in *Self-Portrait of Percy Grainger*, 123–24. He notes at 124, "[...] she panders to both my flagellistic cravings— she lets me whip her & she whips me herself." See "Sex-Life," *Self-Portrait of Percy Grainger*, 117–122, for his explicit accounts of their sexual relations. See also Bird, *Grainger*, 235.
  169. Allison, private correspondence with the author. Images of the announcement (a cartoon and an article) are in Simon, *Pictorial Biography*, 67.
  170. For some of his lecture content, as it relates to early and world music, see Jackson and Ould, "Universal Language," 73.
  171. For Grainger's friendship with Dolmetsch, see Kathleen E. Nelson, "Percy Grainger and the 'Musical Confucius,'" *Musicology Australia* 33:1 (2011): 15–27. For Grainger's own article on his friend, see Percy Grainger, "Arnold Dolmetsch: Musical Confucius," *The Musical Quarterly* 19 (1933): 186–98. Sparre Olsen wrote that "Old Dolmetsch embraced Grainger as a father would his beloved son, and it was quite evident that both had a mutual respect and admiration for one another." See *Portrait of Percy Grainger*, 153.
  172. Nelson, "Musical Confucius," 22–24. See also Jackson and Ould, "Universal Language," 74–75, and 77.
  173. For a good study of Grainger's interest in early music, see Malcolm Gillies, "Grainger, early music, democracy, and freedom," *Grainger Studies* 1 (2011): 21–33. For his medieval work with Hughes, see 27. See also Jackson and Ould, "Universal Language," 75–76. See also Hughes' recollections of Grainger in *Portrait of Percy Grainger*, 136–38. For those of Gustav Reese on Grainger's interest in the *Worcester Fragments* material, see 134–35.
  174. Bird, *Grainger*, 239–40. See also Grainger "The Influence of Anglo-Saxon Music," 117, where he notes, "I doubt if a greater tonal poet and more intrinsic musician has ever put pen to paper than Frederick Delius [...]"
  175. *Ibid.*, 243.
  176. *Ibid.*, 195.
  177. See *ibid.*, 239 and 243–44 for more details. In 1951, he also had the odd idea of shipping over wooden and papier-mâché mannequins of himself, Ella, and various others, to stand in the museum; for an amusing account, see 283. For the museum's website, see: http://www.grainger.unimelb.edu.au, accessed October 28, 2014.
  178. For an extended analysis of this work, see Thomas P. Lewis, "A Source Guide to the Music of Percy Grainger," available online at the *International Percy Grainger Society* website: http://www.percy

grainger.org/prognot6.htm, accessed October 28, 2014. See also O'Shaughnessy, "The English Folksong Collection," 23.

179. Bird, *Grainger*, 255.
180. *Ibid.*, 256.
181. *Ibid.*, 256–57.
182. *Ibid.*, 268–59.
183. *Ibid.*, 264.
184. He claimed that higher fees brought higher expectations, which made his self-consciousness and stage fright worse, see Grainger, "The Lower the Fee, the Better I Play," in Deemths ((Opinions)) Book I, section 21, October 28, 1941, Grainger Museum, Melbourne, reprinted in *Self-Portrait of Percy Grainger*, 221–22.
185. See Bird, *Grainger*, 269 for more details. It is ironic that it was Grainger's impressive music sales that had kept some of these publishers in business during the Depression.
186. *Ibid.*, 263.
187. *Ibid.*, 270. Allison, in private correspondence with the author, notes, "He sought alternative medicine on the advice of Cyril Scott."
188. Bird, *Grainger*, 274. See 271–80, and 290–91, as well as 218–19, for more on Free Music and his machines. For a good online example, see Simon Crab, "The 'Free Music Machine.' Percy Grainger & Burnett Cross, USA/Australia, 1948," at *120 Years of Electronic Music*: http://120years.net/wordpress/the-free-musicmachinepercy-grainger-burnett-crossusaaustralia 1948-2/, accessed November 1, 2014. Vaughan Williams and others thought that he was squandering his talents and would not be able to extricate himself from this new direction, see 280.
189. Lloyd, "Grainger 'In a Nutshell,'" 21.
190. Particularly the new rock and roll films, see Bird, *Grainger*, 275. Martin Bernstein, Grainger's colleague at New York University, mentions that Grainger had a good opinion of jazz and rock and roll, though he may be confusing the two. See *Portrait of Percy Grainger* 133. One wonders what Grainger might have made of the advancements in rock music in the 1960s and 70s, particularly in the genres of psychedelic and progressive rock, the latter with its use of synthesizers and complex musical structures. It is quite possible that bands such as the Beatles, the Doors, Yes, King Crimson, Genesis, and Jethro Tull would have appealed greatly to him, had he lived a decade longer to hear them.
191. Grainger, "The Things I Dislike," *Self-Portrait of Percy Grainger*, 149.
192. See Bird, *Grainger*, 287–90 for a detailed account of this disappointing trip.
193. For the text, see Grainger, "To Whoever Opens the Packages Marked 'Do Not Open until 10 years after My Death,'" May 10, 1956, Grainger Museum, Melbourne, reprinted in *Self-Portrait of Percy Grainger*, 160–62.
194. Letter from Grainger to Kaare K. Nygaard, March 5, 1954, in *The All-Round Man: Selected Letters of Percy Grainger, 1914–1961*, Malcolm Gillies and David Pear, eds. (Oxford: Clarendon Press, 1994), 263–64.
195. Bird, *Grainger*, 294. See also 284: this lingering influence may well have contributed to him self-sabotaging his efforts.
196. *Ibid.*, 145–46.
197. Recalled by Sir Peter Pears in "A Personal Introduction to Percy Grainger," *Percy Grainger Companion*, 25.
198. Bird, *Grainger*, 295.
199. *Ibid.*, 296.
200. He had made the unusual request that his skeleton be donated to the University of Melbourne for potential display in his museum, but this never happened, which is probably just as well. See Bird, *Grainger*, 295.
201. On this, see Mellers, *Percy Grainger*, 61.

Conclusion

1. For a charming account of Vaughan Williams' relations with cats, see Ursula Vaughan Williams, *R.V.W.*, 341–42.
2. See Hughes and Stradling, *English Renaissance*, 184–87.
3. Stephen Banfield, "Aesthetics and Criticism," *The Romantic Age, 1800–1914*, *The Athlone History of Music in Britain*, Nicholas Temperley, ed. (London: Athlone Press, 1981), 472.
4. Hughes and Stradling, *English Renaissance*, xx.

Appendix A

1. John Quinlan, "A.E. Housman and British Composers," *The Musical Times*, 100:1393 (1959): 137–38.
2. See Murphy, *Green Willow*, 40–41. Houseman's works are readily available online. A good print edition is *The Collected Poems of A.E. Housman*, Wordsworth Poetry Library, Michael Irwin, ed. (Ware, Herts, UK: Wordsworth Editions, 1994, rep. 2005). For a biography, see Norman Page, *A.E. Housman: A Critical Biography* (London: Macmillan, 1983).
3. Mellers, *Vision of Albion*, 33.
4. Richard P. Graves, *A.E. Housman—The Scholar Poet* (Oxford and London: Oxford University Press, 1981), 117.
5. Vernon Butcher, "A. E. Housman and the English Composer," *Music & Letters* 29:4 (1948): 333–34.
6. Percy Withers, *A Buried Life: Personal Recollections of A. E. Housman* (London: Jonathan Cape, 1940), 82–83. See also Barlow, *Gods*, 54–55.
7. Graves, *A.E. Housman*, 82.
8. Butcher, "English Composer," 329.
9. *Ibid.*, 336–37.
10. See William White, "A. E. Housman and Music," *Music & Letters* 24:4 (1943): 210. White argues that Housman's musical sensibilities were very rudimentary and never developed, hence his caustic remarks, see 219.
11. *Ibid.*, 208.
12. Graves, *A.E. Housman*, 105.

Bibliography

Adams, Byron. "By Season Seasoned: Shakespeare and Vaughan Williams," *Journal of the RVW Society* 10 (October 1997): 28–30.

———. "'Music in the air': Vaughan Williams, Shakespeare, and the Construction of an Elizabethan Tradition." In *Let Beauty Awake: Elgar, Vaughan Williams and Literature*, edited by Julian Rushton, 96–107. London: Elgar Editions, 2010.

———. "Scripture, Church, and Culture: Biblical Texts in the Work of Ralph Vaughan Williams." In *Vaughan Williams Studies*, edited by Alain Frogley, 99–117. New York: Cambridge University Press, 1996.

———. "Vaughan Williams's Musical Apprenticeship." In *The Cambridge Companion to Vaughan Williams*, edited by Alain Frogley and Aidan J. Thomson, 29–55. Cambridge: Cambridge University Press, 2013.

———, ed., *Edward Elgar and His World*. Princeton: Princeton University Press, 2007.

———, and Robin Wells, eds. *Vaughan Williams Essays*. Aldershot: Ashgate, 2003.

Aldous, Alan K. "Ralph Vaughan Williams in Salonika." *Journal of the RVW Society* 16 (October 1999): 7–8.

Allen, Hugh. "George Butterworth and His Work." *The Times Literary Supplement* 797 (April 26, 1917): 201, also in Alexander Butterworth, ed. *Scrapbook of Letters, Etc., Concerning George Butterworth, 1903–1916*, Bodleian MS. Eng. Misc. c. 435, *Ff*. 132–33.

Allis, Michael. *Parry's Creative Process*. Aldershot: Ashgate, 2002.

Allison, Brian. "John Harry Grainger: Architect and Civil Engineer." *University of Melbourne Collections* 1 (November 2007): 38–45.

Amis, John, ed. "Interview with Percy Grainger." *Studies in Music* 10 (1976): 4–8, from a BBC recording on July 1, 1959.

Andrews, Martin J. *The Life and Work of Robert Gibbings*. Bicester, UK: Primrose Hill Press, 2003.

"Annual General Meeting." *Journal of the Folk-Song Society* 7:27 (1923): xi.

"Annual General Meeting." *Journal of the Folk-Song Society* 8:35 (1931): xii.

Aplvor, Denis. "Memories of 'The Warlock Circle.'" In *Peter Warlock: A Centenary Celebration*, edited by David Cox and John Bishop, 187–96. London: Thames, 1994.

———. "Philip Heseltine (Peter Warlock): A Psychological Study." *Music Review* 46:2 (1985): 118–132.

Armstrong, Thomas. "Mr. H." *Music in Education* 38:368 (1974): 163–65.

Atkinson, David. "Resources in the Vaughan Williams Memorial Library: The Maud Karpeles Manuscript Collection." *Folk Music Journal* 8:1 (2001): 90–101.

Auerbach, Jeffrey A. *The Great Exhibition of 1851: A Nation on Display*. New Haven, CT: Yale University Press, 1999.

Auty, Giles. "An Art of Our Own." *The Spectator* (May 30, 1987): 33–34.

Avery, Kenneth. "The Chronology of Warlock's Songs." *Music & Letters* 29:4 (1948): 398–405.

Bailey, Cyril. *Hugh Percy Allen*. Oxford: Oxford University Press, 1948.

Banfield, Stephen. "Aesthetics and Criticism." In *The Romantic Age, 1800–1914*. The Athlone History of Music in Britain, edited by Nicholas Temperley, 455–73. London: Athlone Press, 1981.

———."Finzi and Wordsworth." In *The Clock of the Years: An Anthology of Writings on Gerald and Joy Finzi Marking Twenty-Five Years of the Finzi Friends Newsletter*, edited by Rolf Jordan, 130–42. Lichfield, UK: Chosen Press, 2007.

———. "Finzi Centenary Lecture." In *The Clock of the Years: An Anthology of Writings on Gerald and Joy Finzi Marking Twenty-Five Years of the Finzi Friends Newsletter*, edited by Rolf Jordan, 2–12. Lichfield, UK: Chosen Press, 2007.

———. *Gerald Finzi: An English Composer*. London: Faber & Faber, 1997.

———. "Moeran, Warlock and Song." *Journal of the British Music Society* 23 (2001): 51–55.

———. "On Interpreting Housman." *The British Music Society Newsletter* 9 (1981): 4–11.

———. "Vaughan Williams and Gerald Finzi." In *Ralph Vaughan Williams in Perspective: Studies of an English Composer*, edited by Lewis Foreman, 202–21. Somerset: Albion Music, 1998. Also in *Journal of the RVW Society* 10 (October 1997): 2–7.

Banks, Paul, ed. *the Making of Peter Grimes: Essays and Studies*. Woodbridge: Boydell, 2000.

Barker, Ernest, ed. *The Character of England*. Oxford: Clarendon Press, 1947.

Barlow, Michael. "George Butterworth and the Folksong Revival." *English Dance and Song* 47:3 (1985): 10–11.

———. "George Butterworth: The Early Years." *Journal of the British Music Society* 5 (1983): 89–100.

———. *Whom the Gods Love: The Life and Music of George Butterworth*. London: Toccata Press, 1997, published in paperback, 2009.

Barone, Anthony. "Modernist Rifts in a Pastoral Landscape: Observations on the Manuscripts of Vaughan Williams's Fourth Symphony." *Musical Quarterly* 91:1–2 (2008): 60–88.

Barr, John. "The Folk Songs of Ralph Vaughan Williams's Six Studies in English Folksong." *Journal of the RVW Society* 13 (October 1998): 14–15.

Bartlett, Ian. "Lambert, Finzi and the Anatomy of the Boyce Revival." *Musical Times* 144:1884 (2003): 54–59.

Bax, Arnold. "E.J. Moeran, 1894–1950." *Music and Letters* 22:2 (1951): 125–27.

———. *Farewell, My Youth*. London: Longmans, Green, & Co., 1943.

———. *Farewell, My Youth and Other Writings*, edited by Lewis Foreman. Aldershot: Scolar Press, 1992.

Bearman, Christopher J. "Cecil Sharp in Somerset: Some Reflections on the Work of David Harker." *Folklore* 113:1 (2002): 11–34.

———. "The English Folk Music Movement 1898–1914," Ph.D. thesis, University of Hull, 2001.

———. "Kate Lee and the Foundation of the Folk-Song Society." *Folk Song Journal* 7:5 (1999): 627–43.

———. "Percy Grainger, the Phonograph, and the Folk Song Society." *Music and Letters* 84 (2003): 434–55.

———. "Who Were the Folk? The Demography of Cecil Sharp's Somerset Folk Singers," *Historical Journal* 43:3 (2000): 751–75.

Beckhard, Robert. "Notes from an American on a 1950s Warlock Odyssey." In *Peter Warlock: A Centenary Celebration*, edited by David Cox and John Bishop, 197–206. London: Thames, 1994.

Bierne, Deborah. Interview with Percy Grainger. *Success Magazine* (January 1926): 54–55.

Bird, John, *Percy Grainger*. London: Faber & Faber, 1982.

Birt, Richard. "Wise and Fair and Good as She: An Appraisal of Ella Mary Leather—The Forgotten Gatherer of Folk Lore." *Journal of the RVW Society* 13 (October 1998): 2 and 24.

Blake, Andrew. *The Land Without Music: Music, Culture and Society in Twentieth-Century Britain*, Music and Society. Manchester: University of Manchester Press, 1997.

Blevins, Pamela. "Ivor Gurney 'There Is Dreadful Hell Within Me….'" *Journal of the British Music Society* 19 (1997): 11–27.

Bliss, Arthur. "Gerald Finzi: An Appreciation." *Tempo*, New Series 42 (Winter 1956–57): 5–6.

Boden, Anthony. "Gerald Finzi at the Three Choirs Festival." In *The Clock of the Years: A Gerald and Joy Finzi Anthology Marking Twenty-Five Years of the Finzi Friends Newsletter*, edited by Rolf Jordan, 233–241. Lichfield, UK: Chosen Press, 2007.

Boult, Sir Adrian. *Boult on Music: Words from a Lifetime's Communication.* London: Toccata Press, 1983.
Boyd, C.M. "Gerald Finzi and the Solo Song." *Tempo*, New Series 33 (Autumn 1954): 15–19.
Boyd, Malcolm. "Benjamin Britten and Grace Williams: Chronicle of a Friendship," *Welsh Music* (Winter 1980–81): 7–38.
Boyes, Georgina. *The Imagined Village: Culture, Ideology and the English Folk Revival.* Leeds: No-Masters Co-operative Press, 2010.
———. "'An individual flowering': Ralph Vaughan Williams' Work in Folklore." *Journal of the RVW Society* 46 (October 2009): 7–8.
Broadwood, Lucy. *English Traditional Songs and Carols.* London: Boosey, 1908.
———. Letter to the editor, "Folk-Songs and Music." *Folk-Lore* 3:4 (1892): 551–53.
———, and J. Fuller Maitland. *English County Songs.* London: J.B. Cramer, 1893.
Brocken, Michael. *The British Folk Revival 1944–2002.* Aldershot: Ashgate, 2003.
Burckhardt, Jakob. *The Civilization of the Period of the Renaissance in Italy* (modern edition in English). London: Penguin Books, 1990.
Burgess, Paul. "The Mystery of the Whistling Sewermen: How Cecil Sharp Discovered Gloucestershire Morris Dancing." *Folk Music Journal* 8:2 (2002): 178–194.
Burton, Humphrey, and Maureen Murray. *William Walton: The Romantic Loner.* Oxford University Press, 2002.
Busselberg, Paul. *A Justification for the Study of Folk Song Settings, or the Arrangement as a Valid Composition.* DMA dissertation, Rice University, 2007.
Butcher, Vernon. "A.E. Housman and the English Composer." *Music & Letters* 29:4 (1948): 329–39.
Butterworth, Sir Alexander Kaye, ed. *George Butterworth, 1885–1916, Memorial Volume.* York and London: privately published, 1918.
———, ed. *Scrapbook of Letters, Etc., Concerning George Butterworth, 1903–1916,* Bodleian MS. Eng. Misc. c. 435.
Butterworth, George. "Vaughan Williams *London Symphony.*" *RCM Magazine* 10:2 (1914): 44–46.
Butterworth, Neil. *Ralph Vaughan Williams: A Guide to Research,* Garland Composer Resource Manuals 21. New York: Garland Publishing, 1990.
Caldwell, Daniel H. *The Esoteric World of Madame Blavatsky: Insights into the Life of a Modern Sphinx.* Wheaton, IL: Quest Books, 1991.
Callaway, Frank. "Hal Collins and the Warlock Connection." In *Peter Warlock: A Centenary Celebration,* edited by David Cox and John Bishop, 242–47. London: Thames, 1994.
Calloway, Edwin Sand. *A Comparative Study of Three Song Cycles Based on A.E. Housman's a Shropshire Lad by Ralph Vaughan Williams, George Butterworth and Arthur Somervell.* DMA dissertation, University of Alabama, 2001.
Campbell, Margaret. *Dolmetsch: The Man and His Work.* London: Hamilton, 1975.
Carley, Lionel. "Impulsive Friend: Grainger and Delius." In *The Percy Grainger Companion,* edited by Lewis Foreman, 31–50. London: Thames Publishing, 1981.
———, ed. *Delius: A Life in Letters, Volume I: 1862–1908.* London: Scolar Press, 1983.
———, ed. *Delius: A Life in Letters, Volume II: 1909–1934.* London: Scolar Press, 1988.
Carter, James. "Fisherman of King's Lynn." *Journal of the RVW Society* 14 (February 1999): 23–24.
Cecil, Robert. *Life in Edwardian England.* London: Batsford, and New York: Putnam, 1969.
Chisholm, Alastair. "Bernard Van Dieren: Friendship and Influence." In *Peter Warlock: A Centenary Celebration,* edited by David Cox and John Bishop, 160–65. London: Thames, 1994.
Clark, Renée Chérie. "Aspects of National Identity in the Art Songs of Ralph Vaughan Williams Before the Great War." Ph.D. thesis, University of Illinois at Urbana-Champaign, 2014.
Clayton, Martin. "Musical Renaissance and Its Margins in England and India, 1874–1914." In *Music and Orientalism in the British Empire, 1780s to 1940s : Portrayal of the East,* edited by Martin Clayton and Bennett Zon, 71–93. Aldershot: Ashgate, 2007.
Clinch, Jonathan. "'Tunes all the way'? Romantic Modernism and the Piano Concertos of Herbert Howells." In *The Music of Herbert Howells,* edited by Phillip A. Cooke and David Maw, 170–84. Woodbridge: Boydell, 2013.
Cline, Edward. "The Composers' Use of Words: The Language and Music of Gerald Finzi." *The Journal of the British Music Society* 14 (1992): 8–24.

Clissold, Ivor. "Alfred Williams, Song Collector." *Folk Music Journal* 1:5 (1969): 293–300.

Cobbe, Hugh. "The Correspondence of Gerald Finzi and Ralph Vaughan Williams." In *The Clock of the Years: A Gerald and Joy Finzi Anthology Marking Twenty-Five Years of the Finzi Friends Newsletter*, edited by Rolf Jordan, 196–203. Lichfield, UK: Chosen Press, 2007.

———, ed. *Letters of Ralph Vaughan Williams*. Oxford and New York: Oxford University Press, 2008.

Cockshott, Gerald A. "E. J. Moeran's Recollections of Peter Warlock." *Musical Times* 96:1345 (1955): 128–30.

———. "Warlock and Moeran." *Composer* 33 (1969): 1, 3–4.

Cohen, Joel. *Reprise: The Extraordinary Revival of Early Music*. Boston and Toronto: Little, Brown, & Co., 1985.

Cole, Margaret. *The Story of Fabian Socialism*. Stanford, CA: Stanford University Press, 1961.

Coleman, Stanley M. "The Dual Personality of Philip Heseltine." *Journal of Mental Science* 155 (1949): 456–66.

Collins, Brian. "Lillygay." In *Peter Warlock: A Centenary Celebration*, edited by David Cox and John Bishop, 140–53. London: Thames, 1994.

———. *Peter Warlock: The Composer*. Aldershot, UK: Scholar Press, 1996.

Colls, Robert, and Katie Heathman. "Music of Englishness: National Identity and the First Folk Revival." In *Oxford Handbook of Musical Identities*, edited by David Hargreaves, Raymond MacDonald, and Dorothy Miell, no page range as of this writing. Oxford: Oxford University Press, 2016.

———, and Philip Dodd, eds. *Englishness: Politics and Culture (1880–1920)*. Dover, NH: Croon Helm, 1986.

"Composer's Motoring Offence," *The Times* issue 46968 (January 22, 1934): 4.

Connock, Stephen. "The Edge of Beyond." *Journal of the RVW Society* 16 (October 1999): 3–6.

———, Ursula Vaughan Williams, and Robin Wells, eds. *There Was a Time—Ralph Vaughan Williams: A Pictorial Journey from the Collection of Ursula Vaughan Williams*. Somerset: Albion Music, 2003.

Copley, Ian A. *George Butterworth and His Music: A Centennial Tribute*. London: Thames Publishing, 1985.

———. *The Music of Peter Warlock*. London: Dennis Dobson, 1979.

———. "The Published Instrumental Music of Peter Warlock." *The Music Review* 25 (1964): 209–23.

———. *A Turbulent Friendship: A Study of the Relationship Between D.H. Lawrence and Philip Heseltine ('Peter Warlock')*. London: Thames, 1983.

———. "Warlock and Delius: A Catalogue." *Music and Letters* 49 (1968): 213–18.

———. "The Writings of Peter Warlock (Philip Heseltine) (1894–1930): A Catalogue." *Music Review* 29 (1968): 288–99.

Covell, Roger. "Percy Grainger—A Personal View." *Studies in Music* 10 (1976): 12–13.

Cox, David. "The Maidens Come." In *Peter Warlock: A Centenary Celebration*, edited by David Cox and John Bishop, 166–70. London: Thames, 1994.

———, and John Bishop, eds. *Peter Warlock: A Centenary Celebration*. London: Thames, 1994.

Crockford's Clerical Directory for 1905. London: Horace Cox, 1905.

Cubbin, Sue. *"That Precious Legacy": Ralph Vaughan Williams and Essex Folksong*. Chelmsford: Essex Records Office, 2006.

Cudworth, "Charles" (Cyril). "The 'Shropshire Lad' and English Music." *Music* 1 (1952): 11–14.

Davies, Gwilym. "Percy Grainger's Folk Music Research in Gloucestershire, Worcestershire, and Warwickshire, 1907–1909." *Folk Music Journal* 6:3 (1992): 339–58.

Davies, Walford, et al. "Charles Villiers Stanford, by Some of His Pupils." *Music & Letters* 5:3 (1924): 193–207.

Dawney, Michael. "George Butterworth's Folk Music Manuscripts." *Folk Music Journal* 3:2 (1976): 99–113.

Day, James. *Vaughan Williams*. Master Musicians Series. Oxford: Oxford University Press, 3rd edition, 1998.

de Val, Dorothy. *In Search of Song: The Life and Times of Lucy Broadwood*. Aldershot: Ashgate, 2011.

———. "The Transformed Village: Lucy Broadwood and Folksong." In *Music and British Culture, 1785–1914: Essays in Honour of Cyril Ehrlich*, edited by Christina Bashford and Leanne Langley, 341–66. Oxford and New York: Oxford University Press, 2000.
Dibble, Jeremy, *C. Hubert H. Parry: His Life and Music.* Oxford: Oxford University Press, 1992.
———. *Charles Villiers Stanford: Man and Musician.* Oxford: Oxford University Press, 2002.
———. "Elgar and His British Contemporaries." In *The Cambridge Companion to Elgar*, edited by Daniel M. Grimley and Julian Rushton, 15–23. Cambridge: Cambridge University Press, 2005.
———. "Parry and Vaughan Williams: Ideas, Impressions and Influences." *Journal of the RVW Society* 9 (June 1997): 4–5, 14; and 10 (October 1997): 32–33.
———. "Parry, Stanford and Vaughan Williams: The Creation of a Tradition." In *Ralph Vaughan Williams in Perspective: Studies of an English Composer*, edited by Lewis Foreman, 25–47. Somerset: Albion Music, 1998.
Dickinson, A.E.F. *Vaughan Williams.* London: Faber and Faber, 1963.
Dineen, Frank. "The Priming of Miss Locksie." *Journal of the RVW Society* 13 (October 1998): 16–19.
———. *Ralph's People: The Ingrave Secret.* London: Albion Music, 2001.
Dineen, Murray. "Vaughan Williams's Fifth Symphony: Ideology and Aural Tradition." In *Vaughan Williams Essays*, edited by Byron Adams and Robin Wells, 17–27. Aldershot: Ashgate, 2003.
Douglas, Roy. *Working with R.V.W.* Oxford: Oxford University Press, 1972.
Douglass, Keith. "Herbert Howells and Ralph Vaughan Williams," *Journal of the RVW Society* (June 1997): 11 and 22.
Doyle, Peter. *First World War Britain.* Oxford: Shire Publications, 2012.
Dressler, John C. *Gerald Finzi: A Bio-Bibliography.* Westport, CT: Greenwood Press, 1997.
Dreyfus, Kay, ed. *The Farthest North of Humanness: Letters of Percy Grainger 1901–14.* Melbourne: Macmillan Australia, 1985.
Duck, Leonard. "Inspiration: Fact and Theory." *The Musical Times* 94:1319 (1953): 11–14.
Eatock, Colin. "The Crystal Palace Concerts: Canon Formation and the English Musical Renaissance." In *19th-Century Music* 34:1 (2010): 87–105.
Edgar, Alan, Frederic Dickinson, and Alan Gibbs, eds. *Holst's Music—A Guide.* London: Thames, 1995.
Ehrlich, Cyril. *The Music Profession in Britain Since the Eighteenth Century.* Oxford: Clarendon Press, 1985.
Etherington, Francis M. "Cecil Sharp: Some Personal Reminiscences." *Journal of the English Folk Dance and Song Society* 8:4 (1959): 194–96.
Fenby, Eric. *Delius as I Knew Him.* London: Charles Birchall, 1936, reprinted Cambridge University Press, 1981, and Dover, 1994.
——— (in conversation with David Cox). "Warlock as I Knew Him." *Composer* 82 (1984): 19–23.
Ferguson, Howard. "People, Events, and Influences." In *The Music of Howard Ferguson: A Symposium*, edited by Alan Ridout, 7–15. London: Thames Publishing, 1989.
———, and Michael Hurd, eds. *Letters of Gerald Finzi and Howard Ferguson.* Woodbridge: Boydell, 2001.
Finzi, Christopher. "Remembering Gerald Finzi." In *The Clock of the Years: A Gerald and Joy Finzi Anthology Marking Twenty-Five Years of the Finzi Friends Newsletter.*, edited by Rolf Jordan, 17–26. Lichfield, UK: Chosen Press, 2007.
Fleischmann, Aloys. "The Music of E.J. Moeran." *Envoy: A Dublin Review* 4:16 (1951): 60–66.
Floyd, James Michael, ed. "An Interview with Percy Grainger, 15 May 1946." *Tempo* 61: 239 (2007): 18–26.
Foreman, Lewis. "The Folk-Song Society, RVW, and the Early Response of British Composers to Folk Song," *Journal of the RVW Society* 14 (February 1999): 2–7.
———. *From Parry to Britten: British Music in Letters, 1900–1945.* London: Batsford, 1987.
———. "Grainger and His Contemporaries." In *The New Percy Grainger Companion*, edited by Penelope Thwaites, 171–80. Woodbridge: Boydell, 2010.
———. "National Musical Character: Intrinsic or Acquired?" In *Music and Nationalism in 20th-Century Great Britain and Finland*, edited by Tomi Mäkelä, 65–85. Hamburg: von Bockel Verlag, 1997.

———. "Peter Warlock's Reception by the Press." In *Peter Warlock: A Centenary Celebration*, edited by David Cox and John Bishop, 227–41. London: Thames, 1994.
———. "Restless Explorations; Articulating Many Visions." In *Vaughan Williams in Perspective*, 1–24. Colchester, UK: Albion Music, 1998.
———, ed. *The John Ireland Companion*. Woodbridge: Boydell, 2011.
———, ed. *The Percy Grainger Companion*. London: Thames Publishing, 1981.
———, ed. *Vaughan Williams in Perspective: Studies of an English Composer*. Colchester, UK: Albion Music, 1998.
Forsyth, Cecil. *Music and Nationalism: A Study of English Opera*. London: Macmillan, 1911.
Foss, Hubert. "E. J. Moeran: A Critical Appreciation." *The Musical Times* (January 1930): 26–29.
———. "Holst: The Bringer of Paradox." *Listener* 28:714 (1942): 381.
———. "Introductions: Xix Philip Heseltine." *The Music Bulletin* 6 (1924): 202–206.
———. *Ralph Vaughan Williams: A Study*. London and Sydney: Harrap, 1950.
———. "The Warlock Gang," *The London Symphony Orchestra Observer* (November 1951): 99–100.
Francmanis, John. "National Music to National Redeemer: The Consolidation of a 'Folk-Song' Construct in Edwardian England." *Popular Music* 21 (2002): 1–25.
Freeman, Graham. "'Into a cocked-hat': The Folk Song Arrangements of Percy Grainger, Cecil Sharp, and Benjamin Britten." *Grainger Studies: An Interdisciplinary Journal* 2 (2012): 33–54.
———. "'It wants all the creases ironing Out': Percy Grainger, the Folk Song Society, and the Ideology of the Archive." *Music and Letters* 92:3 (2011): 410–36.
———. "'That chief undercurrent of my mind': Percy Grainger and the Aesthetics of English Folk Song." *Folk Music Journal* 9:4 (2009): 581–617.
Frogley, Alain, "Constructing Englishness in Music: National Character and the Reception of Ralph Vaughan Williams." In *Vaughan Williams Studies*, edited by Alain Frogley, 1–22. New York: Cambridge University Press, 1996.
———. "'Getting its history wrong': English Nationalism and the Reception of Ralph Vaughan Williams." In *Music and Nationalism in 20th-Century Great Britain and Finland*, edited by Tomi Mäkelä, 145–61. Hamburg: Bockel, 1997.
———. "H.G. Wells and Vaughan Williams's 'London Symphony': Politics and Culture in Fin-De-Siécle England." In *Sundry Sorts of Music Books: Essays on the British Library Collections*, edited by Chris A. Banks, Arthur Searle, and Malcolm Turner, 299–308. London: British Library, 1993.
———. "Rewriting the Renaissance: History, Imperialism and British Music Since 1840." *Music & Letters* 84:2 (2003): 241–57.
———, ed. *Vaughan Williams Studies*. New York: Cambridge University Press, 1996.
———, and Aidan J. Thomson, eds. *The Cambridge Companion to Vaughan Williams*. Cambridge: Cambridge University Press, 2013.
Fromm, Harold. "Against Representation: Ralph Vaughan Williams and the Erotics of Art," *Hudson Review* 63:2 (2010): 277–86.
Fulcher, Jane F. *The Composer as Intellectual: Music and Ideology in France, 1914–1940*. Oxford: Oxford University Press, 2005.
Fuller, Sophie. *The Pandora Guide to Women Composers: Britain and the United States, 1629-Present*. London and San Francisco: Pandora, 1994.
Fuller Maitland, J.A. *A Door-Keeper of Music*. London: John Murray, 1929.
———. *Fitzwilliam Virginal Book*, 2 vols., corrected by Blanche Winogron. Toronto: Dover, 1979.
———. "The Notation of the Fitzwilliam Virginal Book." *Proceedings of the Musical Association* 21 (1894–5): 103–12.
Gammon, Vic. "Cecil Sharp and English Folk Music." In *Still Growing: Traditional Songs and Singers from the Cecil Sharp Collection*, edited by Steve Roud, Eddie Upton, and Malcolm Taylor, 2–23. London: English Folk Dance & Song Society, 2003. Also available online, accessed January 28, 2015: http://www.academia.edu/5310311/Cecil_Sharp_and_English_Folk_Music.
———. "Folk Song Collecting in Sussex and Surrey, 1843–1914." *History Workshop Journal* 10 (1980): 61–89.
———. "'Many useful lessons': Cecil Sharp, Education and the Folk Dance Revival, 1899–1924." *Cultural and Social History* 5:1 (2008): 75–98.

_____. Review of Georgina Boyes, *The Imagine Village*. *Albion: A Quarterly Journal Concerned with British Studies* 26:2 (1994): 391.
_____, and Emily Portman. "Five-Time in English Traditional Song." *Folk Music Journal* 10:3 (2013): 319–346.
Gelbart, Matthew. *The Invention of 'Folk Music' and 'Art Music': Emerging Categories from Ossian to Wagner*. New Perspectives in Music History and Criticism. Cambridge: Cambridge University Press, 2007.
Gibbings, Robert. *Coming Down the Wye*. London: Dent, 1947.
Gibbs, Alan. "New Light on Holst and Friends: Manuscript Discoveries at St Paul's Girls' School." *Tempo* 60:237 (2006): 44–58.
Gifford, Terry. *Pastoral: The New Critical Idiom*. London: Routledge, 1999.
Giles, Judy, and Tim Middleton, eds. *Writing Englishness: An Introductory Sourcebook on National Identity*. London: Routledge, 1995.
Gillett, Paula. *Musical Women in England, 1870–1914: "Encroaching on All Man's Privileges."* New York: Palgrave Macmillan, 2000.
Gillies, Malcolm. "Grainger, Early Music, Democracy, and Freedom." *Grainger Studies* 1 (2011): 21–33.
_____, and David Pear, eds. *The All-Round Man: Selected Letters of Percy Grainger 1914–61*. Oxford: Clarendon Press, 1994.
_____, and David Pear, eds. *Portrait of Percy Grainger*. Rochester, NY: University of Rochester Press, 2002.
_____, and Bruce Clunies Ross, eds. *Grainger on Music*. New York: Oxford University Press, 1999.
_____, et al., eds. *Self-Portrait of Percy Grainger*. Oxford: Oxford University Press, 2006.
Goatcher, Michael. "Mr. Von and Dr. Vaughan." *Journal of the RVW Society* 11 (February 1998): 12–15.
Goldman, Richard Franko. "Some Notes on Percy Grainger." *Studies in Music* 10 (1976): 10–11.
Goldring, Douglas. *Odd Man Out: The Autobiography of a 'Propaganda' Novelist*. London: Chapman and Hall, 1935.
Grace, Harvey. "Butterworth and the Folksong Revival." *The Listener* 28:704 (1942): 61.
Grainger, Percy. "Arnold Dolmetsch: Musical Confucius." *The Musical Quarterly* 19 (1933): 186–98.
_____. "Bird's Eye View of the Together-Life of Rose Grainger and Percy Grainger (1947)." In *Self-Portrait of Percy Grainger*, edited by Malcolm Gillies, et al, 42–77. Oxford: Oxford University Press, 2006.
_____. "Collecting with the Phonograph." *Journal of the Folk-Song Society* 12 (1908): 147–62.
_____. "Congratulations to the Folk Song Society." *Journal of the English Folk Dance and Song Society* 8:3 (1958): 124.
_____. "English Pianism and Harold Bauer (1945)." In *Grainger on Music*, edited by Malcolm Gillies and Bruce Clunies Ross, 338–46. Oxford: Oxford University Press, 1999.
_____. "Facts About Percy Grainger's Year in Europe." In *Self-Portrait of Percy Grainger*, edited by Malcolm Gillies, et al, 240–43. Oxford: Oxford University Press, 2006.
_____. "How I Became a Meat-Shunner." *American Vegetarian* 4 (1946): 4.
_____. "The Impress of Personality in Traditional Singing." *Journal of the Folk-Song Society* 3:12 (1908): 163–66.
_____. "The Impress of Personality in Unwritten Music." In *Grainger on Music*, edited by Malcolm Gillies and Bruce Clunies Ross, 43–64. Oxford: Oxford University Press, 1999. _____. "The Influence of Anglo-Saxon Folk Music." In *Grainger on Music*, edited by Malcolm Gillies and Bruce Clunies Ross, 113–20. Oxford: Oxford University Press, 1999.
_____. "John H. Grainger (1956)." In *Self-Portrait of Percy Grainger*, edited by Malcolm Gillies, et al, 15–19. Oxford: Oxford University Press, 2006.
_____. "The London Gramophone Co. (Now 'His Master's Voice') & the Joseph Taylor Folksong Records (1932)." In *Self-Portrait of Percy Grainger*, edited by Malcolm Gillies, et al, 128–30. Oxford: Oxford University Press, 2006.
_____. "The Lower the Fee, the Better I Play." In *Self-Portrait of Percy Grainger*, edited by Malcolm Gillies, et al, 221–22. Oxford: Oxford University Press, 2006.

———. "Mrs L and My Early London Days." In *Self-Portrait of Percy Grainger*, edited by Malcolm Gillies, et al, 93–100. Oxford: Oxford University Press, 2006.
———. "Music Heard in England." In *Grainger on Music*, edited by Malcolm Gillies and Bruce Clunies Ross, 349–55. Oxford: Oxford University Press, 1999.
———. "My Father in Childhood." In *Self-Portrait of Percy Grainger*, edited by Malcolm Gillies, et al, 24–26. Oxford: Oxford University Press, 2006.
———. "Native Art and Stage Fright." In *Self-Portrait of Percy Grainger*, edited by Malcolm Gillies, et al, 214–15. Oxford: Oxford University Press, 2006.
———. "Notes on Whip-Lust." In *Self-Portrait of Percy Grainger*, edited by Malcolm Gillies, et al, 166–68. Oxford: Oxford University Press, 2006.
———. "Percy Aldridge Grainger's Published Compositions, 1st Editions." ts., November 2, 1938.
———. *Photos of Rose Grainger and of 3 Short Accounts of Her Life by Herself*. Frankfurt: privately published, 1923.
———. "Preface to *Bold William Taylor* (December 1952)." *The Grainger Society Journal* 3:1 (1980): 7–9.
———. "Pure Nordic Beauty." In *Self-Portrait of Percy Grainger*, edited by Malcolm Gillies, et al, 132–36. Oxford: Oxford University Press, 2006.
———. "Read This If Ella Grainger or Percy Grainger Are Found Dead Covered with Whip Marks." In *Self-Portrait of Percy Grainger*, edited by Malcolm Gillies, et al, 123–24. Oxford: Oxford University Press, 2006.
———. *Thirteen Folksongs*. London: Thames Publishing, reprinted 1982.
———. "Thought Mother Was 'God.' Something of This Still Remains." In *Self-Portrait of Percy Grainger*, edited by Malcolm Gillies, et al, 35–36. Oxford: Oxford University Press, 2006.
———. "To Whoever Opens the Packages Marked 'Do Not Open Until 10 Years After My Death.'" In *Self-Portrait of Percy Grainger*, edited by Malcolm Gillies, et al, 160–62. Oxford: Oxford University Press, 2006.
———. "The Truly Nordic Life." In *Self-Portrait of Percy Grainger*, edited by Malcolm Gillies, et al, 138–43. Oxford: Oxford University Press, 2006.
———. "What Is Behind My Music." In *Self-Portrait of Percy Grainger*, edited by Malcolm Gillies, et al, 168–69. Oxford: Oxford University Press, 2006.
Graves, C.L. *Hubert Parry: His Life and Works*, 2 vols. London: Macmillan, 1926.
Graves, Richard Perceval. *A.E. Housman—The Scholar-Poet*. Oxford and London: Oxford University Press, 1981.
Gray, Cecil, et al. *Peter Warlock: A Memoir of Philip Heseltine*. London: Jonathan Cape, 1934.
Gray, Pauline. *Cecil Gray: His Life and Notebooks*. London: Thames, 1989.
Green, Peter. *Kenneth Grahame: A Biography*. Cleveland: John Murray, 1959.
Greene, Jeffrey. *Samuel Coleridge-Taylor: A Musical Life*. London: Pickering and Chatto, 2011.
Greene, Richard. *Holst: The Planets*, Cambridge Music Handbooks, Julian Rushton, general editor. Cambridge: Cambridge University Press, 1995.
Gregory, E. David. "Before the Folk-Song Society: Lucy Broadwood and English Folk Song, 1884–97." *Folk Music Journal* 9:3 (2008): 372–414.
———. *The Late Victorian Folksong Revival: The Persistence of English Melody, 1878–1903*. Plymouth, UK: Scarecrow Press, 2010.
———. *Victorian Songhunters: The Recovery and Editing of English Vernacular Ballads and Folk Lyrics, 1820–1883*. Lanham, MD: Scarecrow Press / Rowman & Littlefield, 2006.
Grimley, Daniel M. "Landscape and Distance: Vaughan Williams, Modernism and the Symphonic Pastoral." In *British Music and Modernism, 1895–1960*, edited by Matthew Riley, 147–74. Farnham, UK: Ashgate, 2010.
———. "'The spirit-stirring drum': Elgar and Populism." In *Edward Elgar and His World*, edited by Byron Adams, 97–123. Princeton: Princeton University Press, 2007.
Grogan, Christopher, and Rosamund Strode. *Imogen Holst: A Life in Music*, 6 parts, parts 5 and 6 with Christopher Tinker. Woodbridge: Boydell, 2010.
Grove, George. "Handel." *Chambers' Encyclopaedia: A Dictionary of Universal Knowledge*, edited by David Patrick, vol. 5, 541–43. London: William & Robert Chambers, 1890.

———. "Music in England." *The Proposed Royal College of Music*, RCMA PAM 22, B 20, 1 (1882): 11–12.
———. *The Royal College of Music*. London: Clowes, 1883.
Grover, Ralph. S. *The Music of Edmund Rubbra*. Aldershot: Scolar Press, 1993.
Guthrie, Kate. "Propaganda Music in the Second World War: John Ireland's *Epic March*." *Journal of the Royal Musical Association* 139:1 (2014): 137–75.
Hall, Duncan. *'A Pleasant Change from Politics': Music and the British Labour Movement Between the Wars*. Cheltenham, UK: New Clarion Press, 2001.
Hamnett, Nina. *Is She a Lady?: A Problem in Autobiography*. London: Allan Wingate, 1955.
Hardy, Thomas. *Return of the Native*. London: Macmillan, 1911.
Harker, David. "Cecil Sharp in Somerset: Some Conclusions." *Folk Music Journal* 2:3 (1972): 220–40.
———. *Fakesong: The Manufacture of British "Folksong" 1700 to the Present Day*. Milton Keynes, UK: Open University Press, 1985.
———. "Introduction." *Rhymes of Northern Bards*, edited by John Bell. Newcastle-upon-Tyne: Frank Graham, 1971.
Harper-Scott, J. P. E. *Elgar: An Extraordinary Life*. London: Associated Board of the Royal Schools of Music, 2007.
Harries, Meirion. *A Pilgrim Soul—The Life and Work of Elizabeth Lutyens*. London: Michael Joseph, 1989.
Harrington, Paul. "Holst and Vaughan Williams: Radical Pastoral." In *Music and the Politics of Culture*, edited by Christopher Norris, 106–27. London: Lawrence & Wishart, 1989.
Hattersley, Roy. *The Edwardians*. New York: St. Martin's Press, 2005.
Harvey, Adam. "English Folk Songs and Other Traditional Tunes in the Works of Ralph Vaughan Williams: A Checklist." *Journal of the RVW Society* 54 (June 2012): 3–9.
———. "Folk Song in the English Folk Song Suite." *Journal of the RVW Society* 57 (June 2013): 12–16.
———. "Folk Song Identification in the Works of Vaughan Williams: Some Confusion." *Journal of the RVW Society* 53 (February 2012): 11–15.
Heaney, Mike. "Butterworth Dancing." *The Morris Dancer* 15 (1983): 7–12.
———. "Two Films from the Past." *English Dance and Song* 45:3 (1983): 20–21.
Heathman, Katie. "'Lift up a living nation': Church and Nation in the *English Hymnal*," MA thesis, University of Leicester, 2012.
Heffer, Simon. *Vaughan Williams*. Boston, MA: Northeastern University Press, 2000.
Heppa, Christopher. "Harry Cox and His Friends: Song Transmission in an East Norfolk Singing Community, C. 1896–1960." *Folk Music Journal* 8:5 (2005): 569–93.
Heseltine, Nigel. *Capriol for Mother: A Memoir of Philip Heseltine (Peter Warlock)*. London: Thames, 1992.
Heseltine, Philip. *E. J. Moeran*. London: J & W Chester, 1926.
———. "The Editing of Old English Songs," parts 1 and 2. *The Sackbut* 6 and 8 (1926): 183–86 and 215–20.
———. "Introductions Xviii: E. J. Moeran." *The Music Bulletin* 6:6 (June 1924): 170–74.
———. "Newcomers: E. J. Moeran." *The Chesterian* 36 (January 1924): 124.
———. "Notes on Goossens' Chamber Music." *Music Student*, Chamber Music Supplement, 22a (1916): 23–24.
———. "On Editing Elizabethan Songs." *Musical Times* 63:953 (1922): 477–80.
———. "Some Notes on Delius and His Music." *The Musical Times* 56:865 (1915): 137–42.
———, and Michael Pilkington, ed. *Songs 1911–1930*, 8 vols. London: Thames, 2004 and 2005.
Heselton, Philip. *Witchfather: A Life of Gerald Gardner*, 2 vols. Loughborough, Leicestershire: Thoth, 2012.
Hill, Lionel. *Lonely Waters: The Diary of a Friendship with E J Moeran*. London: Thames, 1985.
Hinnells, Duncan. "The Making of a National Composer: Vaughan Williams, OUP and the BBC." Ph.D. thesis, Oxford University, 1999.
Hobsbawm, Eric, and Terence Ranger, eds. *The Invention of Tradition*. Cambridge: Cambridge University Press, 1983.

Hodges, Betsi. "W.W. Cobbett's Phantasy: A Legacy of Chamber Music in the British Musical Renaissance," DMA dissertation, University of North Carolina at Greensboro, 2008.

Hold, Trevor. *Parry to Finzi: Twenty English Song-Composers*. Woodbridge: The Boydell Press, 2002.

———. "Peter Warlock: The Art of the Song-Writer." *Music Review* 36 (1975): 248–299.

Holden, A. W. and J. R. Birch. *A. E Housman—A Reassessment*. London: Palgrave Macmillan, 1999.

Holst, Imogen. "Cecil Sharp and the Music and Music-Making of the Twentieth Century." *Journal of the English Folk Dance and Song Society* 8:4 (1959): 189–90.

———. *Gustav Holst, a Biography*. London and New York: Oxford University Press, 2nd edition, 1969.

———. "Gustav Holst at Thaxted." *Journal of the RVW Society* 11 (February 1998): 6.

———. "Gustav Holst's Debt to Cecil Sharp." *Folk Music Journal* 2:5 (1974): 400–03.

———. *Holst*, Great Composers Series. London: Faber & Faber, 1974, 2nd edition 1981.

———. "Holst's Debt of Gratitude to Vaughan Williams." *Folk Music Journal* 2:3 (1972): 171–72.

———. *The Music of Gustav Holst*. London: Oxford University Press, 1951, revised 1985 to include *Holst's Music Reconsidered*.

Holyoake, Michael. "Towards a Folk Song Awakening: Vaughan Williams in Bournemouth, 1902." *Journal of the RVW Society* 46 (October 2009): 9–15.

Hopwood, Paul Andrew. "Frank Bridge and the English Pastoral Tradition." Ph.D. thesis, University of Western Australia, 2007.

Howes, Frank. *The English Musical Renaissance*. London: Secker & Warburg, 1966.

———. *The Music of Ralph Vaughan Williams*. London and New York: Oxford University Press, 1954.

———. "Recent Work in Folk Music." *Proceedings of the Musical Association* 64 (1938): 39–69.

Hughes, Meirion. *The English Musical Renaissance and the Press 1850–1914: Watchmen of Music*. Aldershot: Ashgate, 2002.

Huismann, Mary Christison. *Frederick Delius: A Guide to Research*. New York and London: Routledge, 2004.

———. *Gustav Holst: A Research and Information Guide*. New York and London: Routledge, 2011.

Hull, Robert. "A Bibliography of the Settings of Poems from 'A Shropshire Lad' and 'Last Poems' by A.E. Housman." *Dominant* (1928): 26–29.

Hunt, Duncan. "A Few Reflections on Vaughan Williams, Englishness and the National Culture." *Journal of the RVW Society* 5 (February 1996): 15–16.

Hurd, Michael. *Vaughan Williams*. The Great Composers. London: Faber and Faber, 1970.

Huss, Fabian Gregor. "The Construction of Nature in the Music of E. J. Moeran." *Tempo* 63:248 (2009): 35–44.

Hussey, Dyneley. "English Musicians, 8: Gustav Theodore Holst." *Landmark* 10:2 (1928): 119–22.

Hynes, Samuel. *A War Imagined: The First World War and English Culture*. London: Pimlico, 1992.

Irwin, Michael, ed. *The Collected Poems of A.E. Housman*. Wordsworth Poetry Library. Ware, Herts, UK: Wordsworth Editions, 1994, reprinted 2005.

Jackson, Paul. "Percy Grainger's Aleatoric Adventures: The Raratongan Part-Songs." *Grainger Studies: An Interdisciplinary Journal* 2 (2012): 1–32.

———, and Barry Peter Ould. "Towards a Universal Language: Grainger and Early Music; Granger and World Music." In *The New Percy Grainger Companion*, edited by Penelope Thwaites, 73–86. Woodbridge: Boydell, 2010.

Jacobs, Arthur. *Sir Arthur Sullivan: A Victorian Musician*. Oxford: Oxford University Press, 1984.

James, Elizabeth. "James Carter, Fisherman of King's Lynn." *Journal of the RVW Society* 14 (February 1999): 23–24.

Jameson, Michael. *Ralph Vaughan Williams: An Essential Guide to His Life and Works*. London: Pavilion Publishing, 1997.

Jamison, Kay R. *Touched with Fire: Manic-Depressive Illness and the Artistic Temperament*. New York: Free Press, 1993.

Jefferson, Alan. *Sir Thomas Beecham: A Centenary Tribute*. London: Macdonald and Jane's, 1979.

Jordan, Rolf, ed. *The Clock of the Years: A Gerald and Joy Finzi Anthology Marking Twenty-Five Years of the Finzi Friends Newsletter*. Lichfield, UK: Chosen Press, 2007.

Joyce, William Brooke. "Listening Inside the Memory Palace." Ph.D. thesis, Princeton University, 2005.

Judge, Roy. "Cecil Sharp and Morris 1906–1909." *Folk Music Journal* 8:2 (2002): 195–228.
_____. "Mary Neal and the Espérance Morris." *Folk Music Journal* 5:5 (1989): 545–91.
Juneau, Roger. "Appearances and Reality: A Survey of RVW CD Covers." *Journal of the RVW Society* 14 (February 1999): 14–16.
Kaczynski, Richard. *Perdurabo: The Life of Aleister Crowley*. Berkeley, CA: North Atlantic Books, 2010, revised and expanded.
Karpeles, Maud. "Cecil Sharp: Collector and Restorer of English Folk Music." *Journal of the English Folk Dance and Song Society* 8:4 (1959): 179–81.
_____. *Cecil Sharp: His Life and Work*. Chicago: University of Chicago Press, 1967.
_____. *Cecil Sharp's Collection of English Folk Songs*. Oxford: Oxford University Press, 1974.
_____. *An Introduction to English Folk Song*. London; Oxford University Press, 1973.
_____. "Ralph Vaughan Williams, O.M. October 12, 1872—August 26, 1958." *Journal of the English Folk Dance and Song Society* 8:3 (1958): 121–122.
_____, ed. *English Folk Songs from the Southern Appalachians*, 2 vols. New York and London: Oxford University Press, 1932.
Kaye, Ernest. "Witches and Warlock." In *Peter Warlock: A Centenary Celebration*, edited by David Cox and John Bishop, 166–70. London: Thames, 1994.
Kendall, Tony. "Through Bushes and Through Briars…: Vaughan Williams's Earliest Folk-Song Collecting." In *Ralph Vaughan Williams in Perspective: Studies of an English Composer*, edited by Lewis Foreman, 48–68. Somerset: Albion Music, 1998.
Kennedy, Michael. *Adrian Boult*. London: Macmillan, 1987, reprinted 1989.
_____. *A Catalogue of the Works of Ralph Vaughan Williams*. Oxford: Oxford University Press, 1996, reprinted 1998).
_____. "Fluctuations in the Response to the Music of Ralph Vaughan Williams." In *The Cambridge Companion to Vaughan Williams*, edited by Alain Frogley and Aidan J. Thomson, 275–98. Cambridge: Cambridge University Press, 2013.
_____. *The Life of Elgar, Musical Lives*. Cambridge: Cambridge University Press, 2004.
_____. *Portrait of Elgar*. Oxford: Oxford University Press, 1968, 3rd edition 1987.
_____. "Ralph Vaughan Williams-The Centenary of His Birth." *Folk Music Journal* 2:3 (1972): 167–68.
_____. *the Works of Ralph Vaughan Williams*. Oxford: Clarendon Press, 1964, reprinted 1992.
Kenyon, Nicholas. *The BBC Symphony Orchestra—The First Fifty Years, 1930–1980*. London: BBC, 1981.
Kidson, Frank. *Traditional Tunes*. Oxford: Taphouse, 1891.
_____, and Mary Neal. *English Folk Song and Dance*. Cambridge: Cambridge University Press, 1915.
Kington, Beryl. "Alec Rowley and Recollections of Peter Warlock." In *Peter Warlock: A Centenary Celebration*, edited by David Cox and John Bishop, 213–24. London: Thames, 1994.
Knevett, Arthur. "Cultural and Political Origins of the Folk-Song Society and the Irish Dimension." *Folk Music Journal* 10:5 (2015): 592–608.
Koehne, James. "Vaughan Williams and the Value of Nostalgia." *Journal of the RVW Society* 7 (October 1996): 10–11, reprinted from *Quadrant* (Jan-Feb 1995): 31–33.
Kumar, Krishan. *The Making of English National Identity*. Cambridge: Cambridge University Press, 2003, reprinted 2006.
Ladmirault, Paul. "Peter Warlock: A Great English Composer." *Chantecler* (1927), translated by David Cox. Reprinted in *Peter Warlock: A Centenary Celebration*, edited by David Cox and John Bishop, 58–63. London: Thames, 1994.
Lambert, Constant. *Music Ho! A Study of Music in Decline*. London: Faber and Faber, 1934, reprinted 1966.
Leach, Gerald. *British Composer Profiles: A Biographical Dictionary and Chronology of Past British Composers 1800–2010*, 3rd edition, edited and revised by Ian Graham-Jones. Upminster, UK: British Music Society, 2012.
Leapman, Michael. *The World for a Shilling: How the Great Exhibition of 1851 Shaped a Nation*. London: Headline, 2001.
Leese, Peter. *Shell Shock: Traumatic Neurosis and the British Soldiers of the First World War*. New York and Basingstoke: Palgrave Macmillan, 2002.

Lewis, Thomas P. *Source Guide to the Music of Percy Grainger*. White Plains, NY: Pro-Am Music Resources, 1991.

Lindsay, Jack. *Fanfrolico and After*. London: Bodley Head, 1962.

Lisano, Deborah Bowden. "Symphony No. 5 as a Summary of Ralph Vaughan Williams's Philosophy of the English Composer." Ph.D. thesis, University of Georgia, 2004.

Lloyd, A.L. *Folk Song in England*. London: Lawrence & Wishart, 1967.

Lloyd, Stephen. "Grainger 'In a Nutshell.'" In *The Percy Grainger Companion.*, edited by Lewis Foreman, 15–21. London: Thames Publishing, 1981.

Long, N. G. "The Songs of Gerald Finzi." *Tempo*, New Series 2 (December 1946): 7–11.

Lucas, John. *Ivor Gurney*. Tavistock, UK: Northcote House, 2001.

MacDonald, Calum. "This Week's Composer, the English Spirit." *The Listener* 104 (September 1980): 347–48.

Malisse, Peter. "Waiting for the Genius: The English Musical Renaissance (1880–1925). History, Memory, Identity." Ph.D. thesis, KU Leuven, Belgium, 2014.

Manning, David. "The Public Figure: Vaughan Williams as Writer and Activist." In *The Cambridge Companion to Vaughan Williams*, edited by Alain Frogley and Aidan J. Thomson, 231–48. Cambridge: Cambridge University Press, 2013.

_____, ed. *Vaughan Williams on Music*. Oxford: Oxford University Press, 2007.

Marchman, Judy O. "Peter Warlock (1894–1930): A Contextual Analysis of His Art Songs Related to Symptoms of Mental Illness." Ph.D. thesis, University of Miami, 2013.

Marinelli, Peter. *Pastoral: The Critical Idiom*. John D. Jump, general editor. London: Methuen & Co., 1971.

Marsh, Jan. *Back to the Land: The Pastoral Impulse in England, from 1880 to 1914*. London: Quartet Books, 1982.

Marshall, Em. *Music in the Landscape: How the British Countryside Inspired Our Greatest Composers*. London: Robert Hale, 2011.

Matthews, Colin. "Holst Out of Context." *Journal of the RVW Society* 11 (February 1998): 5.

McAndrew, Siobhan, and Martin Everett. "Music as Collective Invention: A Social Network Analysis of Composers." *Cultural Sociology* 9:1 (2015): 56–80.

McGuire, Charles Edward. "Vaughan Williams and the English Music Festival: 1910." In *Vaughan Williams Essays*, edited by Byron Adams and Robin Wells, 235–68. Aldershot: Ashgate, 2003.

McNeill, Rhoderick. "A Critical Study of the Life and Works of E. J. Moeran." Ph.D. thesis, University of Melbourne, 1983.

_____. "Moeran's Unfinished Symphony." *The Musical Times* 121:1654 (1980): 771–73 and 775–77.

McVeagh, Diana. *Elgar the Music Maker*. Woodbridge: Boydell, 2013.

_____. *Gerald Finzi: His Life and Music*. Woodbridge: Boydell, 2006.

Mellers, Wilfrid. "Delius and Peter Warlock." *Scrutiny* 5 (1937): 384–97.

_____. *Percy Grainger*, Oxford Studies of Composers. Oxford: Oxford University Press, 1992.

_____. *Vaughan Williams and the Vision of Albion*. Somerset: Albion Music, 1997, 2nd edition, revised and expanded, London: Travis & Emery, 1998.

Mills, Patrick. "It Started with a Limerick (Or, How the Peter Warlock Society Came into Existence)." In *Peter Warlock: A Centenary Celebration*, edited by David Cox and John Bishop, 248–51. London: Thames, 1994.

Mitchell, Jon C. *A Comprehensive Biography of Composer Gustav Holst, with Correspondence and Diary Excerpts*. Lewiston, NY: Mellen, 2001.

Mitchell, Kevin. "'All things are written in the mind': Perspectives on Thomas Hardy and Ralph Vaughan Williams." *Journal of the RVW Society* 15 (June 1999): 18–21.

Moeran, Ernest J. "Moeran Norfolk Collection." *Folk Song Journal* 7:26 (1922): 1–24.

_____. "Some Folk Singing Today." *Journal of the English Folk Dance and Song Society* 5:3 (1948): 152–54.

Moore, James Ross. "An Intimate Understanding: The Rise of British Musical Revue, 1890–1920." Ph.D. thesis, University of Warwick, 2000.

Moore, Jerrold N. *Edward Elgar, a Creative Life*. Oxford: Oxford University Press, 1984, reprinted Clarendon Press, 1999.

———. *Elgar: Child of Dreams*. London: Faber and Faber, 2004.
Morris, Alice L. "A Stylistic Comparison of Peter Warlock's Songs." MA dissertation, Kansas State University, 1970.
Muncy, Graham, and Robin Barber. *Ralph Vaughan Williams: A Bibliography*. RVW Society, 1995.
Murphy, Anthony. *Banks of Green Willow: The Life and Times of George Butterworth*. Malvern: Cappella Archive, 2012.
Neal, Mary. *The Espérance Morris Book: A Manual of Morris Dances, Folk-Songs, and Singing Games*. London: J. Curwen, 1910.
Nelson, Kathleen E. "Percy Grainger and the 'Musical Confucius.'" *Musicology Australia* 33:1 (2011): 15–27.
Newton, Anthony. "Vaughan Williams and the Idea of Folk Song in the Norfolk Rhapsodies." *Journal of the RVW Society* 46 (October 2009): 3–6.
Noakes, Tony. "Vaughan Williams and Delius." *Journal of the RVW Society* 6 (June 1996): 20.
Nowell-Smith, Simon. *Edwardian England, 1901–1914*. London: Oxford University Press, 1964.
Onderdonk, Julian. "The Composer and Society: Family, Politics, and Nation." In *The Cambridge Companion to Vaughan Williams*, edited by Alain Frogley and Aidan J. Thomson, 9–28. Cambridge: Cambridge University Press, 2013.
———. "The English Musical Renaissance, 1860–1940: Construction and Deconstruction." *Notes—Quarterly Journal of the Music Library Association*, Second Series 52:1: 63–66.
———. "Folk Songs in the English Hymnal." In *Strengthen for Service: 100 Years of the English Hymnal, 1906–2006*, edited by Alan Luff, 191–216. Norwich: Canterbury Press, 2006.
———. "Folksong Arrangements, Hymn Tunes and Church Music." In *The Cambridge Companion to Vaughan Williams*, edited by Alain Frogley and Aidan J. Thomson, 136–56. Cambridge: Cambridge University Press, 2013.
———. "Hymn Tunes from Folk Songs: Vaughan Williams and English Hymnody." In *Vaughan Williams Essays*, edited by Byron Adams and Robin Wells, 103–28. Aldershot, UK: Ashgate, 2003.
———. "Ralph Vaughan Williams's Folk Song Collecting: English Nationalism and the Rise of Professional Society." Ph.D. thesis, New York University, 1998.
———. "Vaughan Williams and the Modes." *Folk Music Journal* 7:5 (1999): 609–626.
———. "Vaughan Williams's Folksong Transcriptions: A Case of Idealization?" In *Vaughan Williams Studies*, edited by Alain Frogley, 118–38. New York: Cambridge University Press, 1996.
Orr, C.W. "Elgar and the Public." *Musical Times* 72:1055 (1931): 17–18.
O'Shaughnessy, Patrick. "Percy Grainger: The English Folk-Song Collection." *Studies in Music* 10 (1976): 19–24.
Page, Norman. *A.E. Housman: A Critical Biography*. London: Macmillan, 1983.
Pagett, Andrew. *Edwardian England. The Way Things Were*. London: Brockhampton Press, 1999.
Pakenham, Simona. *Ralph Vaughan Williams: A Discovery of His Music*. London: Macmillan, 1957.
Palmer, Christopher. *Delius: Portrait of a Cosmopolitan*. London: Duckworth, 1976.
———. *Herbert Howells: A Centenary Celebration*. London: Thames, 1992.
———. *Impressionism in Music*. London: Hutchinson; New York: Charles Scribner's Sons, 1973.
———, ed. *The Britten Companion*. London: Faber and Faber, 1984.
Palmer, Roy. "Kidson's Collecting." *Folk Music Journal* 5 (1986): 150–75.
———. "Neglected Pioneer: E.J. Moeran (1894–1950)." *Folk Music Journal* 8:3 (2003): 345–61.
———, ed. *Folksongs Collected by Ralph Vaughan Williams*. London: JM Dent, 1983.
Parrott, Ian. *The Crying Curlew: Peter Warlock: Family & Influences*. Llandysul, Dyfed: Gomer Press, 1994.
Parry, Hubert. "Inaugural Address." *Journal of the Folk-Song Society* 1 (1899): 1–3. Reprinted Nendein, Liechtenstein: Kraus Reprint, 1975, originally published 1898.
Payne, Anthony. "Encompassing His Century's Dilemmas; the Modality of Vaughan Williams." In *Vaughan Williams in Perspective*, edited by Lewis Foreman, 154–75. Colchester, UK: Albion Music, 1998.
Payne, Elise. "Vaughan Williams and Folk-Song: The Relation Between Folk-Song and Other Elements in His Comprehensive Style." Part 1, *Journal of the RVW Society* 13 (October 1998): 3–10. Part 2, *Journal of the RVW Society* 14 (February 1999): 17–21.

Pear, David, ed. *Facing Percy Grainger*. Canberra: National Library of Australia, 2006.
Pears, Peter. "A Personal Introduction to Percy Grainger." In *The Percy Grainger Companion*, edited by Lewis Foreman, 23–30. London: Thames Publishing, 1981.
Pickering, Michael. "Janet Blunt—Folk Song Collector and Lady of the Manor." *Folk Music Journal* 3:2 (1976): 114–49.
———. "Recent Folk Music Scholarship in England: A Critique." *Folk Music Journal* 6:1 (1990): 37–64.
———, and James Porter. "Muddying the Crystal Spring: From Idealism and Realism to Marxism in the Study of English and American Folk Song." In *Comparative Musicology and Anthropology of Music*, edited by Bruno Nettl and Philip V. Bohlman, 113–30. Chicago: Chicago University Press, 1991.
Pike, Lionel. *Vaughan Williams and the Symphony*. London: Toccata Press, 2003.
Pirie, Peter J. *The English Musical Renaissance*. New York: St. Martin's Press, 1979.
———. "The 'Georgian Composers,' Music in Britain." *A Quarterly Review* 69 (1965): 23–27.
Ponsonby, Dorothea. "Letter to the Editor: Hubert Parry." *The Musical Times* 97:1359 (1956): 263.
Poston, Elizabeth. "Dispelling the Jackals." BBC Broadcast, 1964. Reprinted in *Peter Warlock: A Centenary Celebration*, edited by David Cox and John Bishop, 9–16. London: Thames, 1994.
———. "R. V. W.'S Piano Accompaniments." *Folk Music Journal* 2:3 (1972): 169–71.
Quinlan, John. "A.E. Housman and British Composers." *Musical Times* 100:1393 (1959): 137–38.
Radke, Melanie. "Folk Influences in Concert Repertoire for the Violin: A Performer's Perspective." MMus dissertation, Elder Conservatorium of Music, University of Adelaide, 2007.
Rayborn, Tim. "Peter Warlock and Music of the 16th and 17th Centuries." *Early Music America Magazine* 22:1 (Spring 2016): 42–45.
———. "Ralph Vaughan Williams and Early Music." *Ralph Vaughan Williams Society Journal* 65 (2016): 7–11.
Redlich, Hans. Review of Finzi's *Intimations of Immortality*. *Music Review* 13 (1952): 242–43.
Reed, William H. *Elgar*. London: Dent, 1946.
Revill, George. "The Lark Ascending: Vaughan Williams's Monument to a Radical Pastoral." *Landscape Research* 16:2 (1991): 25–30.
Reynolds, Peter J. "Peter Warlock: His Contemporaries and Their Influence." *British Music Society Journal* (1985): 48–58.
Richmond, Velma Bourgeois. *Chivalric Stories as Children's Literature: Edwardian Retellings in Words and Pictures*. Jefferson, NC: McFarland, 2014.
Rippin, John. "George Butterworth 1885–1916." *The Musical Times* 107:1482 (1966): 680–682, and 107:1483 (1966): 769 and 771.
Robinson, Suzanne and Kay Dreyfus, eds. *Grainger the Modernist*. Aldershot: Ashgate, 2015.
Rodmell, Paul. *Charles Villiers Stanford*. Aldershot: Scolar Press, 2002.
Ross, Ryan. "Ralph Vaughan Williams and the Pastoral Mode." Ph.D. thesis, University of Illinois, 2012.
Rowley, Alec. "The Music of Peter Warlock." *Musical Mirror* (August 1927): 83 and 88, or 183–84 (see 264n11).
Rushton, Julian, ed. *Let Beauty Awake: Elgar, Vaughan Williams and Literature*. London: Elgar Editions, 2010.
Russell, John. "Gerald Finzi: An English Composer." *Tempo*, New Series 33 (1954): 9–15.
Salmon, Michael A. "Starshine Over Distant Fields." In *The Clock of the Years: A Gerald and Joy Finzi Anthology Marking Twenty-Five Years of the Finzi Friends Newsletter*, edited by Rolf Jordan, 63–69. Lichfield, UK: Chosen Press, 2007.
Samuel, Edgar. "Vaughan Williams and King's Lynn." *Journal of the RVW Society* 14 (February 1999): 22–23.
Savage, Heather de. "Chronology." In *The Cambridge Companion to Vaughan Williams*, edited by Alain Frogley and Aidan J. Thomson, xvii–xx. Cambridge: Cambridge University Press, 2013.
Savage, Roger. *Masques, Mayings and Music-Dramas: Vaughan Williams and the Early Twentieth-Century Stage*. Woodbridge: Boydell, 2014.
Saylor, Eric. "'It's not Lambkins frisking at all': English Pastoral Music and the Great War." *The Musical Quarterly* 91:1–2 (2008): 39–59.

_____. "The Significance of Nation in the Music of Ralph Vaughan Williams." Ph.D. thesis, University of Michigan, 2003.
Schofield, Derek. "Ralph Vaughan Williams on Lucy Broadwood." *English Dance and Song* 70:2 (2008): 12–14.
_____. "'Revival of the folk dance: An artistic movement': The Background to the Founding of the English Folk Dance Society in 1911." *Folk Music Journal* 5:2 (1986): 215–219.
_____. "Sowing the Seeds: Cecil Sharp and Charles Marson in Somerset in 1903." *Folk Music Journal* 8:4 (2004): 484–512.
Scholes, Percy. *Oxford Companion to Music*. Oxford: Oxford University Press, 1970, reprinted 1985.
Scott, Anthony. "Gerald Finzi as a Tutor of Composition." In *The Clock of the Years: A Gerald and Joy Finzi Anthology Marking Twenty-Five Years of the Finzi Friends Newsletter*, edited by Rolf Jordan, 39–44. Lichfield, UK: Chosen Press, 2007.
Scott, Derek. *The Singing Bourgeois: Songs of the Victorian Drawing Room and Parlour*, 2nd ed. Aldershot: Ashgate, 2001.
Scowcroft, Philip L. *British Light Music, a Personal Gallery of 20th Century Composers*. Binsted, Hampshire: Dance Books, 2013.
Self, Geoffrey. "E.J. Moeran: Unpublished Letters and Songs." *British Music: Journal of the British Music Society* 16 (1994): 33–43.
_____. "E.J. Moeran: Unpublished Letters and Songs Postscript." *British Music: Journal of the British Music Society* 17 (1995): 63.
_____. *The Hiawatha Man: The Life & Work of Samuel Coleridge-Taylor*. Aldershot, UK: Scolar Press, 1995.
_____. *The Music of E.J. Moeran*. London: Toccata Press, 1986.
Senior, Evan. "E.J. Moeran." *Australian Musical News and Digest* (May 1, 1950): 30–31.
Sharp, Cecil. *English Folk Song: Some Conclusions*. London: Simpkin, Novello, 1907.
_____. *English Folk Songs, Collected and Arranged with Pianoforte Accompaniment by Cecil J. Sharp*. London: Novello, 1916.
_____. *Folk Dancing in Schools*. London: English Folk Dance Society, n.d. [1912–13].
_____. *Folk Songs of England*, vol. 1, London: Novello, 1908.
_____. *The Sword Dances of Northern England*, edited by Maude Karpeles. London: Novello, 1911–13, 2nd edition 1950–51.
_____, and Herbert C. MacIlwaine. *The Morris Book: A History of Morris Dancing, with a Description of Eleven Dances as Performed by the Morris-Men of England*. London: Novello, 1907, reprinted 2010.
_____, and Charles L. Marson. *Folk-Songs from Somerset*, 5 series. London: Simpkin, Marshall, Hamilton, Kent, 1904–09.
Sharp, Joan. "Memories of Cecil Sharp." *Journal of the English Folk Dance and Song Society* 8:4 (1959): 191–93.
Shaw, Christopher, and Malcolm Chase. "The Dimensions of Nostalgia," In *The Imagined Past: History and Nostalgia*, edited by Christopher Shaw and Malcolm Chase, 1–17. Manchester: Manchester University Press, 1989.
Shore, Bernard. *The Orchestra Speaks*. London: Longmans, Green, 1938.
Short, Michael. "Gustav Holst: An Evaluation." *Journal of the RVW Society* 11 (February 1998): 2–4.
_____. *Gustav Holst: The Man and His Music*. Oxford: Oxford University Press, 1990.
_____, ed. *Gustav Holst: Letters to W. G. Whittaker*. Glasgow: University of Glasgow Press, 1974.
Simon, Robert. *Percy Grainger: The Pictorial Biography*. Winston-Salem, NC: SD Publications, 1987.
Simpson, Claude M. *The British Broadside Ballad and Its Music*. New Brunswick, NJ: Rutgers University Press, 1966.
Smith, Barry. *Frederick Delius and Peter Warlock: A Friendship Revealed*. New York and Oxford: Oxford University Press, 2000.
_____. "The Mystery of Philip Heseltine's Death." In *Peter Warlock: A Centenary Celebration*, edited by David Cox and John Bishop, 64–83. London: Thames, 1994.
_____. "Peter Warlock and the Occult." *South African Journal of Musicology* 13 (1993): 71–80.
_____. *Peter Warlock: The Life of Philip Heseltine*. Oxford: Oxford University Press, 1994.

———, ed., *The Collected Letters of Peter Warlock (Philip Heseltine)*, 4 vols. Woodbridge: Boydell, 2005.

———, ed. *The Occasional Writings of Philip Heseltine (Peter Warlock)*, 4 vols. London: Thames, 1998.

Smith, Mike. Review of Hughes and Stradling, *The English Musical Renaissance, 1840–1940*. *Tempo*, New Series 187 (1993): 27–28.

Spicer, Paul. *Herbert Howells*. Bridgend, UK: Seren, 1998.

Stanford, Charles Villers. *The National Song Book*. London: Boosey, 1906.

———. *Studies and Memories*. London: Constable, 1908.

Steggles, Henry. "From Henry T. Steggles." *The R.C.M. Magazine* 55:1 (1959): 21–24.

Stradling, Robert. "England's Glory: Sensibilities of Place in English Music, 1900–1950." In *The Place of Music*, edited by George Revill, Andrew Leyshon, and David Matless, 176–96. New York: The Guilford Press, 1998.

Stradling, Robert, and Meirion Hughes. *The English Musical Renaissance, 1860–1940*. Manchester and New York: Manchester University Press, 1993, reprinted 2001.

Strangways, A. H. Fox, in collaboration with Maud Karpeles. *Cecil Sharp*. London: Oxford University Press, 1933, reprinted by Da Capo Press, 1980.

Stunt, Christopher. "Hardy and Finzi." In *The Clock of the Years: A Gerald and Joy Finzi Anthology Marking Twenty-Five Years of the Finzi Friends Newsletter*, edited by Rolf Jordan, 153–84. Lichfield, UK: Chosen Press, 2007.

Sweers, Britta. *Electric Folk: The Changing Face of English Traditional Music*. Oxford: Oxford University Press, 2005.

Sykes, Richard. "The Evolution of Englishness in the English Folksong Revival." *Folk Music Journal* 6:4 (1993): 446–90.

Tall, David. "Grainger and Folksong." In *The Percy Grainger Companion*, edited by Lewis Foreman, 55–69. London: Thames Publishing, 1981.

Taylor, Robert Lewis. *The Running Pianist*. New York: Doubleday, 1950.

Thomson, Aidan J. "Bax and the 'Celtic North.'" *Journal of the Society for Musicology in Ireland* 8 (2012–13): 51–87.

———. "Becoming a National Composer: Critical Reception to C. 1925." In *The Cambridge Companion to Vaughan Williams*, edited by Alain Frogley and Aidan J. Thomson, 56–78. Cambridge: Cambridge University Press, 2013.

Thomson, R.S. "Songs from the Grainger Collection." *Folk Music Journal* 2:5 (1974): 335–51.

Thompson, Kenneth. "A Butterworth Catalogue." *The Musical Times* 107:1484 (1966): 771–72.

Thwaites, Penelope, ed. *The New Percy Grainger Companion*. Woodbridge: Boydell, 2010.

The Times, issue 43798 (December 30, 1916): 10 (Vaughan Williams and Moeran presented to the queen).

Tolley, David. "RVW and the Nation's Heritage." *Journal of the RVW Society* 3 (July 1995): 14–15.

Town, Stephen. *An Imperishable Heritage: British Choral Music from Parry to Dyson*. Aldershot: Ashgate, 2012.

Tregear, Peter. "'Nostalgia is not what it used to be': Exploring the Kitsch in Grainger's Music." *Grainger Studies: An Interdisciplinary Journal* 1 (2011): 97–113.

Trend, Michael. *The Music Makers: The English Musical Renaissance from Elgar to Britten*. London: Weidenfeld and Nicolson, 1985.

Van Dieren, Bernard. "Philip Heseltine." Obituary, *Musical Times* 72 (1931): 117–19.

Varcoe, Stephen. "Singing Grainger Solo." In *The New Percy Grainger Companion*, edited by Penelope Thwaites, 46–57. Woodbridge: Boydell, 2010.

Vassall, David, and John Bishop, eds. *Peter Warlock: A Centenary Celebration*. (London: Thames, 1994.

Vaughan Williams, Ralph. "British Music." In *Vaughan Williams on Music*, edited by David Manning, 43–56. Oxford: Oxford University Press, 2007.

———. "Cecil Sharp—An Appreciation." In *Vaughan Williams on Music*, edited by David Manning, 269–71. Oxford: Oxford University Press, 2007.

———. "Cecil Sharp's Accompaniments." In *Vaughan Williams on Music*, edited by David Manning, 233–34. Oxford: Oxford University Press, 2007.

Bibliography

———. "The Composer in Wartime, 1940." In *Heirs and Rebels*, edited by Imogen Holst and Ursula Vaughan Williams, 90–93. Westport, CT: Greenwood Press, 1980 reprint.
———. "The Diamond Jubilee of the Folk Song Society." *Journal of the English Folk Dance and Song Society* 8:3 (1958): 123–24, published posthumously.
———. "English Folk Songs." In *Vaughan Williams on Music*, edited by David Manning, 185–200. Oxford: Oxford University Press, 2007.
———. *The First Fifty Years: A Brief Account of the English Hymnal from 1906 to 1956.* London: Oxford University Press, 1956.
———. "Folk Song." In *Vaughan Williams on Music*, edited by David Manning, 29–34. Oxford: Oxford University Press, 2007.
———. "Folk-Song." *Encyclopedia Britannica* IX, 14th edition, 447–48. London: Encyclopedia Britannica, 1929.
———. "George Butterworth." In *National Music and Other Essays*. Oxford: Oxford University Press, 1934, reprinted 1987, 245–47.
———. "Gerald Finzi: 1901–1956." In *Vaughan Williams on Music*, edited by David Manning, 323. Oxford: Oxford University Press, 2007.
———. "Good Taste." In *Vaughan Williams on Music*, edited by David Manning, 23–24. Oxford: Oxford University Press, 2007.
———. "Gustav Holst: An Essay and a Note." In *National Music and Other Essays*. Oxford: Oxford University Press, 1934, reprinted 1987, 129–53.
———. "Introduction to *Classic English Folk Songs*." In *Vaughan Williams on Music*, edited by David Manning, 289–292. Oxford: Oxford University Press, 2008.
———. "Introductory Talk to Holst Memorial Concert." In *Vaughan Williams on Music*, edited by David Manning, 299–300. Oxford: Oxford University Press, 2007.
———. "Lucy Broadwood, 1858–1929." *Journal of the English Folk Dance and Song Society* 5:3 (1948): 136–8.
———. *Musical Autobiography*. In Hubert Foss, *Ralph Vaughan Williams: A Study*. London and Sydney: Harrap, 1950, 18–38. Reprinted in *National Music and Other Essays*. Oxford: Oxford University Press, 1934, reprinted 1987, 176–94.
———. *National Music and Other Essays*. Oxford: Oxford University Press, 1934, reprinted 1987.
———. "Preface." *Journal of the Folk-Song Society* 2:8 (1906): 141–42.
———. "Some Reminiscences of the English Hymnal." In *Vaughan Williams on Music*, edited by David Manning, 115–18. Oxford: Oxford University Press, 2008.
———. "Traditional Arts in the Twentieth Century." In *Vaughan Williams on Music*, edited by David Manning, 243–45. Oxford: Oxford University Press, 2008.
———. "Who Wants the English Composer?" In *Vaughan Williams on Music*, edited by David Manning, 39–42. Oxford: Oxford University Press, 2008.
———, Arthur Bliss, and Graham Hutton. "Mr Gerald Finzi: A Many-Sided Man." *The Times* (October 3, 1956): 13.
———, et al. "Songs Collected From…" *Journal of the Folk-Song Society* 2:8 (1906): 143–217.
———, et al. "Songs Collected from Sussex." *Journal of the Folk-Song Society* 4:17 (1913): 279–324.
———, and A.L. Lloyd, eds. *Classic English Folk Songs*. London: English Folk Dance and Song Society, reprinted 2003.
Vaughan Williams, Ursula. *R.V.W., A Biography of Ralph Vaughan Williams*. London: Oxford University Press, 1964.
———, and Imogen Holst, eds., *Heirs and Rebels: Letters Written to Each Other and Occasional Writings on Music, by Ralph Vaughan Williams and Gustav Holst*. Westport, CT: Greenwood Press, 1980 reprint.
Walker, Alan. "Gerald Finzi (1901–1956)." *Tempo*, New Series 52 (1959): 6–10 and 18.
Weedon, Robert A. "'Why do I go on doing these things?' the Continuity and Context of Gerald Finzi's Extended Choral Works." MA dissertation, Durham University, 2012.
Wells, Evelyn K. "Cecil Sharp in America." *Journal of the English Folk Dance and Song Society* 8:4 (1959): 182–85.
White, William. "A.E. Housman and Music." *Music & Letters* 24:4 (1943): 208–19.
Whittall, Arnold. "Individualism and Accessibility: The Moderate Mainstream." In *The Cambridge*

History of Twentieth-Century Music, edited by Nicholas Cook and Anthony Pople, 364–94. Cambridge: Cambridge University Press, 2004.
Wild, Stephen. *E. J. Moeran*. London: Triad Press, 1973.
Wilson-Johnson, David. "Grainger's Songs." In *Percy Grainger Companion*, edited by Lewis Foreman, 123–36. London: Thames Publishing, 1981.
"Wireless Notes and Programmes." *The Manchester Guardian* (October 22, 1930): 12.
Withers, Percy. *A Buried Life: Personal Recollections of A. E. Housman*. London: Jonathan Cape, 1940.
Wortley, Russell. "The Bucknell Morris." *English Dance and Song* 41:2 (1979): 12–14.
_____, and Michael Dawney, eds. "George Butterworth's Diary of Morris Dancing." *Folk Music Journal* 3:3 (1977): 193–207.
Wright, David. "The South Kensington Music Schools and the Development of the British Conservatoire in the Late Nineteenth Century." *Journal of the Royal Musical Association* 130:2 (2005): 236–82.
Wright, Simon. "'Pale green of The English Hymnal!'—A Centenary Retrospective." *Brio: Journal of IAML* 43:1 (2006): 2–20.
Yates, Michael. "Percy Grainger and the Impact of the Phonograph." *Folk Music Journal* 4:3 (1982): 265–75.
Young, Percy M. *George Grove (1820–1900)*. London: Macmillan, 1980.
_____. *Letters to Nimrod: Edward Elgar to August Jaeger, 1897–1908*. London: Dobson, 1965.
_____. *Vaughan Williams*. London : Dennis Dobson, 1953.

Online Resources

Aleister Crowley Foundation online, accessed September 22, 2014: http://aleistercrowleyfoundation.net.
Andrews, Eamonn. Interview with E.J. Moeran. Moeran Database, accessed September 18, 2014: http://www.moeran.net/Writing/Radio-Interview.html.
Andrews, Paul, "Howells, Herbert," *Grove Music Online*, Oxford Music Online. Oxford University Press, accessed November 11, 2014: http://www.oxfordmusiconline.com/subscriber/article/grove/music/13436.
Arbeau, Thoinot. *Orchésographie* online, accessed February 15, 2015: http://graner.net/nicolas/arbeau.
The Bach Choir, accessed November 17, 2014: www.thebachchoir.org.uk.
Banfield, Stephen. "Butterworth, George," *Grove Music Online*, Oxford Music Online. Oxford University Press, accessed September 12, 2014: http://www.oxfordmusiconline.com/subscriber/article/grove/music/04467.
Banks of Green Willow. British Library wax cylinder recording, accessed September 15, 2014: http://sounds.bl.uk/World-and-traditional-music/Ethnographic-wax-cylinders/025M-C0037X1631XX-0100V0.
Barrett, William A. *English Folk Songs*. London and New York: Novello, 1891, Archive, accessed March 22, 2015: https://archive.org/details/imslp-folk-songs-barrett-william-alexander.
Blavatsky Study Center, accessed September 22, 2014: http://blavatskyarchives.com.
Blood, Brian. "The Dolmetsch Story," at *Dolmetsch Online*, accessed November 5, 2014: http://www.dolmetsch.com/Dolworks.htm.
Bridcut, John. *The Passions of Vaughan Williams*, accessed November 20, 2014: http://www.johnbridcut.com/filmdetail.php?film=3.
_____. "Vaughan Williams, His Wife and the Mistress Who Shared Their Bed," accessed November 20, 2014: http://www.dailymail.co.uk/femail/article-567375/Vaughan-Williams-wife-mistress-shared-bed.html.
British Monarchy website, accessed November20, 2014: http://www.royal.gov.uk/MonarchUK/Honours/OrderofMerit/OrderofMerit.aspx.
Butterworth, George. "George Butterworth Collection," Vaughan Williams Memorial Library, accessed September 28, 2014: http://www.vwml.org/browse/browse-collections-full-english/browse-gb.

Bibliography (Online Resources)

Conway, James. "A Percy Grainger Glossary," accessed October 16, 2014: http://strangeflowers.wordpress.com/2011/02/20/a-percy-grainger-glossary.
Cooke, Phillip. "On Gustav Holst's 'Egdon Heath'...," accessed October 7, 2014: http://www.phillipcooke.com/on-gustav-holsts-egdon-heath.
Crab, Simon. "The 'Free Music Machine.' Percy Grainger & Burnett Cross, Usa/Australia, 1948," at *120 Years of Electronic Music*, accessed November 1, 2014: http://120years.net/wordpress/the-free-music-machinepercy-grainger-burnett-crossusaaustralia1948-2/.
"Das Land Ohne Musik." *Music Web*, accessed March 18, 2015: http://www.musicweb-international.com/dasland.htm.
Davidson, Alan. "Apples: The Apple Connoisseurs," Los Angeles Times, September 20, 1990, accessed September 30, 2014: http://articles.latimes.com/1990-09-20/food/fo-675_1_apple-varieties.
Dibble, Jeremy. "Fuller Maitland, J.A.," *Grove Music Online*, Oxford Music Online. Oxford University Press, accessed November 5, 2014: http://www.oxfordmusiconline.com/subscriber/article/grove/music/10378.
_____. "Parry, Sir Hubert," *Grove Music Online*, Oxford Music Online. Oxford University Press, accessed November 8, 2014: http://www.oxfordmusiconline.com/subscriber/article/grove/music/20949.
_____. "Parry, Sir (Charles) Hubert Hastings, Baronet (1848–1918)," *Oxford Dictionary of National Biography*, Oxford University Press, accessed November 8, 2014: http://www.oxforddnb.com/index/101035393/Hubert-Parry.
Dineen, Frank. "Foreword," *Ralph's People: The Ingrave Secret*, accessed April 3, 2015: http://www.albionmusic.com/content/our-publications/ralphs-people-ingrave-secret.
"Ethnomusicology," Kodály Institute page, accessed May 6, 2015: http://kodaly.hu/zoltan_kodaly/ethnomusicology.
First World War, accessed December 1, 2014: http://www.firstworldwar.com/battles/somme.htm.
Foreman, Lewis. "Bax, Sir Arnold," *Grove Music Online*, Oxford Music Online. Oxford University Press, accessed November 7, 2014: http://www.oxfordmusiconline.com/subscriber/article/grove/music/02380.
"'Forgotten' Vaughan Williams Score's First Concert," BBC News, accessed November 15, 2014: http://www.bbc.co.uk/news/uk-england-cambridgeshire-12641429.
France, John. "Herbert Howells: String Quartet in Gloucestershire," *British Classical Music: The Land of Lost Content*, accessed November 11, 2014: http://landofllostcontent.blogspot.com/2009/08/herbert-howells-string-quartet-in.html.
"The Full English," accessed January 7, 2014: http://www.vwml.org/browse/browse-collections-full-english.
Fuller, Sophie. "Women Composers During the British Musical Renaissance, 1880–1918." Ph.D. thesis, King's College, University of London, 1998, accessed January 22, 2014: https://kclpure.kcl.ac.uk/portal/files/2927686/263601.pdf.
Fuller Maitland, J.A. *English Music in the Xixth Century* (London: Grant Richards, New York: E.P. Dutton, 1902), Archive, accessed November 5, 2014: https://archive.org/details/englishmusicinxi00full.
Gammon, Vic. "Cecil Sharp and English Folk Music." In *Still Growing: Traditional Songs and Singers from the Cecil Sharp Collection*, edited by Steve Roud, Eddie Upton and Malcolm Taylor, 2–23. London: English Folk Dance & Song Society, 2003, accessed January 28, 2015: http://www.academia.edu/5310311/Cecil_Sharp_and_English_Folk_Music.
Grainger, Percy. "Percy Grainger Folk Song Collection," Vaughan Williams Memorial Library, accessed October 17, 2014: http://www.vwml.org/browse/browse-collections-full-english/browse-pg#
Graves, C.L., and Percy M. Young. "Grove, Sir George," *Grove Music Online*. Oxford Music Online. Oxford University Press, accessed November 5, 2014: http://www.oxfordmusiconline.com/subscriber/article/grove/music/11847.
Grove Dictionary of Music and Musicians: www.oxfordmusiconline.com. *Ivor Gurney Society* online, accessed October 3, 2014: http://www.ivorgurney.org.uk/biography.htm.

Gurney, Ivor. *Gloucestershire Rhapsody*, at *Classical Iconoclast*, accessed October 3, 2014: http://classical-iconoclast.blogspot.com/2010/08/big-scoop-inor-gurney-premiees-at-3.html.
Harper-Scott, J. P. E. "Elgar and the Salon," *The Victorian Web*, accessed November 29, 2014: http://www.victorianweb.org/mt/elgar/jpehs.html.
Haweis, H.R. *Music and Morals*. London: Longmans, Green and Co., 1872, Archive, accessed November 3, 2014: https://archive.org/details/musicandmorals00hawegoog.
Heseltine family crest, at *House of Names*, accessed May 3, 2015: https://www.houseofnames.com/heseltine-family-crest.
Holst and Whittaker letters, University of Glasgow library, accessed March 5, 2015: http://special.lib.gla.ac.uk/exhibns/month/sep2004.html.
Housman, A.E. *A Shropshire Lad*. London: K. Paul, Trench, Treubner, 1896, accessed September 17, 2014: http://www.bartleby.com/123/23.html.
Irwin, Colin. "Folk's Man of Mystery: Is Cecil Sharp a Folk Hero or Villain?" *The Guardian*, March 24, 2011, accessed November 11, 2014: http://www.theguardian.com/music/2011/mar/24/cecil-sharp-project-folk-hero-villain.
John Ireland Trust website, accessed November 23, 2014: http://www.johnirelandtrust.org.
Jones, Lewis. "Francis Jekyll (1882–1965) - Forgotten Hero of the First Folk Song Revival," *English Dance and Song* (June 2000), accessed September 14, 2014: http://folkopedia.efdss.org/images/3/3c/Francis_Jekyll.pdf.
Kelly, Barbara L. "Ravel, Maurice," *Grove Music Online*, Oxford Music Online. Oxford University Press, accessed November 7, 2014: http://www.oxfordmusiconline.com/subscriber/article/grove/music/52145.
Kennedy, Michael. "The Dark Side of Benjamin Britten," *The Spectator*, February 23, 2013, accessed April 24, 2015: http://www.spectator.co.uk/arts/arts-feature/8847791/the-great-hater.
———. "Harty, Sir Hamilton," *Grove Music Online*, Oxford Music Online. Oxford University Press, accessed September 17, 2014: http://www.oxfordmusiconline.com/subscriber/article/grove/music/12488.
Kidson, Frank. *Traditional Tunes*. Oxford: Taphouse & Son, 1891, Archive, accessed March 22, 2015: https://archive.org/details/imslp-tunes-kidson-frank.
The Kinora Films, featuring Cecil Sharp, George Butterworth, and the Karpeles sisters performing various dances, from 1912, accessed April 6, 2015: https://www.youtube.com/watch?v=bQEkXMCusuI
Lewis, Thomas P. "A Source Guide to the Music of Percy Grainger," *International Percy Grainger Society* website, accessed October 28, 2014: http://www.percygrainger.org/prognot6.htm
Lesure, François, and Roy Howat, "Debussy, Claude," *Grove Music Online*, Oxford Music Online. Oxford University Press, accessed November 7, 2014: http://www.oxfordmusiconline.com/subscriber/article/grove/music/07353.
"Lucy Broadwood," in Britain's National Archives, accessed January 4, 2015: http://discovery.nationalarchives.gov.uk/details/rd/e44bc842-b5cc-4218-8917-9dc0d560d2e4.
"Lynden Lea," accessed November 15, 2014: http://about.lyndenlea.info/poem.php?pg=music.
Mainly Norfolk: English Folk and Other Good Music, accessed September 15, 2014: http://mainlynorfolk.info/lloyd/songs/thebanksofgreenwillow.html.
Marsh, Barry. "E.J. Moeran in Norfolk," Moeran Database, accessed September 18, 2014: http://www.moeran.net/Jackinnorfolk.html.
Martin, Gregory. "Thro Albions Pleasant Land": The 20th-Century English Musical Renaissance, J.R.R. Tolkien, and Reassessing Englishness," a piano lecture recital for Indiana University, 2007, available in PDF download from the Gerald Finzi Trust website, accessed January 28, 2015: http://www.geraldfinzi.org/downloads/02-finzitrust/scholarship_reports/2007_GregoryMartin.pdf.
Matthews, Colin. "Holst, Gustav," *Grove Music Online*, Oxford Music Online, accessed October 5, 2014: http://www.oxfordmusiconline.com/subscriber/article/grove/music/13252.
Maud Karpeles collection. Vaughan Williams Memorial Library, accessed November 13, 2014: http://www.vwml.org/vwml-projects/vwml-the-full-english/vwml-full-english-collectors/vwml-maud-karpeles.
Maxwell, Ian. "The Importance of Being Ernest John: Challenging the Misconceptions About the

Bibliography (Online Resources)

Life and Works of E. J. Moeran." Ph.D. thesis, University of Durham, 2014. Durham E-Theses, accessed January 12, 2015: http://etheses.dur.ac.uk/10752.

McVeagh, Diana. "Finzi, Gerald," *Grove Music Online,* Oxford Music Online. Oxford University Press, accessed September 27, 2014: http://www.oxfordmusiconline.com/subscriber/article/grove/music/09689.

Michio Ito Foundation online, accessed October 12, 2014: http://www.michioito.org.

Moeran, Ernest J. "Folk Songs and Some Traditional Singers in East Anglia." *The Countrygoer* 7 (Autumn 1946), *Moeran Database,* accessed September 28, 2014: http://www.moeran.net/Writing/FolkSongs.html.

———. "Rhapsody No. 1," *Moeran Database,* accessed September 17, 2014: http://www.moeran.net/Orchestral/FirstRhapsody.html.

———. "Whythorne's Shadow," *Moeran Database,* accessed September 18, 2014: http://www.moeran.net/Orchestral/WhythornesShadow.html.

Moore, Jerrold N. "Sir Edward Elgar as a University Professor," University of Rochester Library Bulletin, 15: 3 (1960), online and accessed November 6, 2014: https://www.lib.rochester.edu/index.cfm?PAGE=3356.

Morley College, accessed March 5, 2015: http://www.morleycollege.ac.uk.

Musica Britannica: http://www.musicabritannica.org.uk.

National Trust online: http://www.nationaltrust.org.uk.

Neal, Mary. *As a Tale That Is Told,* accessed November 14, 2014. Summary: http://www.vwml.org/browse/as-a-tale-that-is-told-mary-neals-autobiography; Facsimile: http://media.efdss.org/docs/MaryNealAutobio.pdf

New Esperance Morris Dance, accessed November 12, 2014: http://www.newesp.org.uk.

"Newbury String Players," Gerald Finzi Trust online, accessed September 30, 2014: http://www.geraldfinzi.org/01-about/articles_04.php.

Order of Merit. British Monarchy website, accessed November 20, 2014: http://www.royal.gov.uk/MonarchUK/Honours/OrderofMerit/OrderofMerit.aspx.

Ottaway, Hugh. "Ireland, John," *Grove Music Online,* Oxford Music Online. Oxford University Press, accessed November 7, 2014: http://www.oxfordmusiconline.com/subscriber/article/grove/music/13905.

Parry, Hubert. *The Evolution of the Art of Music,* 4th edition. London, Kegan Paul, 1905, Archive, accessed January 3, 2015: https://archive.org/details/4thevolutionofar00parruoft.

Pasler, Jann. "Impressionism." *Grove Music Online,* Oxford Music Online. Oxford University Press, accessed November 7, 2014: http://www.oxfordmusiconline.com/subscriber/article/grove/music/50026.

Pater, Walter. *Studies in the History of the Renaissance.* London: Macmillan, 1873. Archive, accessed November 3, 2014: https://archive.org/details/studiesinhistor01pategoog.

Payne, Anthony. "Moeran, E.J.," *Grove Music Online,* Oxford Music Online, Oxford University Press, accessed September 16, 2014: http://www.oxfordmusiconline.com/subscriber/article/grove/music/48243.

Pearson, Jonathan. "The Music of Ralph Vaughan Williams on Cd/Dvd," at the *Ralph Vaughan Williams Society* website, accessed December 3, 2014: http://www.rvwsociety.com/RVCD_database_pearson_adobe.pdf.

Playford, John. *Dancing Master,* accessed February 28, 2015: http://www.izaak.unh.edu/nhltmd/indexes/dancingmaster.

"Prosper-Sainton." *Oxford Dictionary of National Biography,* accessed September 10, 2014: http://www.oxforddnb.com/index/101024520/Prosper-Sainton.

"Ralph Vaughan Williams: An Annotated Bibliography, 1996–2014," accessed March 3, 2015: http://www.rvwsociety.com/biblio2014.pdf.

Review of *Music and Morals. The Century Magazine* (September 1872): 645–46, available online, accessed November 3, 2014: www.unz.org/Pub/Century-1872sep-00645a02?View=PDF.

"Ross Nichols," OBOD website, accessed January 4, 2015: http://www.druidry.org/about-us/ross-nichols-founder.

Sargent, Irene. "William Morris: His Socialistic Career," *The Craftsman* 1:1 (1901): 15–24, available online at the *Digital Library for the Decorative Arts and Material Culture*, accessed May 4, 2015: http://digital.library.wisc.edu/1711.dl/DLDecArts.hdv01n01.

Scholes, Percy. *Oxford Companion to Music*: http://www.oxfordmusiconline.com.

Schwartz, Steve. Review of Pirie's *English Musical Renaissance*, accessed November 2, 2014: http://www.classical.net/music/books/reviews/0312254350a.php.

Sharp, Cecil. *Appalachian Diaries*. Vaughan Williams Memorial Library, accessed November 13, 2014: http://www.vwml.org/browse/browse-collections-sharp-diaries.

———. "Cecil James Sharp Collection," Vaughan Williams Memorial Library, accessed November 12, 2014: http://www.vwml.org/browse/browse-collections-full-english/browse-cjs2#.

———. *The Sword Dances of Northern England*, 3 vols. Archive, accessed November 13, 2014: Volume I: https://archive.org/details/sworddancesofnor01shar; Volume II: https://archive.org/details/sworddancesofnor112shar; Volume III: https://archive.org/details/sworddancesofnor113shar.

Smith, Barry. "Warlock, Peter," *Grove Music Online*, Oxford Music Online. Oxford University Press, accessed September 19, 2014: http://www.oxfordmusiconline.com/subscriber/article/grove/music/29912.

Staelens, Yvette. "English Folk Music on the Margin—Cecil Sharp's Gypsies," accessed April 29, 2015: http://eprints.bournemouth.ac.uk/18360/1/Tomar_pix_sergio.pdf.

Vaughan Williams, Ralph. *A Cambridge Mass*, accessed November 15, 2014: http://www.stainer.co.uk/d99.html.

Warsop, Keith. "Brian and the Alternative English Musical Renaissance," *Havergal Brian Society Website*, accessed November 10, 2014: http://www.havergalbrian.org/alternative.htm.

Weedon, Robert. "E.J. Moeran's War," *War Composers: The Music of World War I*, accessed September 17, 2014: http://www.warcomposers.co.uk/moeranbio.html.

———. "Ernest Bristow Farrar—A Biography," *War Composers: The Music of World War I*, accessed September 27, 2014: http://www.warcomposers.co.uk/farrarbio.html.

Wells, H.G. *Tono-Bungay*, 1908–09. Various versions are available online, Project Gutenberg, accessed November 17, 2014: http://www.gutenberg.org/files/718/718-h/718-h.htm.

White, Michael. "So Mighty, So Unmusical: How Britannia Found Its Voice," *New York Times*, February 11, 2007, accessed April 17, 2015: http://www.nytimes.com/2007/02/11/arts/music/11whit.html?pagewanted=all.

Woolfe, Zachary. "When Holst Read the Mahabharata," *New York Times*, May 11, 2012, accessed October 6, 2014: http://www.nytimes.com/2012/05/12/arts/music/an-evening-of-holst-by-the-little-opera-theater-of-new-york.html.

Wrobel, Elinor, curator. "Percy Grainger: The Passionate Folklorist and Ethnomusicologist," accessed May 5, 2015: http://grainger.unimelb.edu.au/

Index

Page numbers in **_bold italics_** indicate pages with illustrations.
Books and musical compositions appear
under the listing of their individual author or composer.

Albéniz, Isaac 43
Albert, the Prince Consort 15, 22
Aldeburgh Music Festival 185, 224, 250n1
Aldrich, Richard 51
Alexandra, Queen of England 196
Allen, Hugh 34–35, 76, 77, 107, 115, 125, 244n91, 244n93
Allinson, Adrian 166
American Bandmasters Association 213
Arbeau, Thoinot 164; *Orchésographie* 164; see also Heseltine, Philip, *Capriol Suite*
Arne, Thomas 12; *Rule Britannia!* 229n15; see also Finzi, Gerald
Arts and Crafts Movement 6, 24–25, 43, 174, 175, 217, 224, 244n87; see also Morris, William
Arts Council 83, 182, 186

Bach, Johan Sebastian 12, 19, 21, 23, 42, 60, 61, 77, 99, 108, 114, 137, 138, 161, 193, 198, 212, 244n96; *Mass in B Minor* 77, 252n92; *St. Matthew Passion* 77, 137, 138
Bacon, Francis 22
Bairstow, Edward 171, 175
Baker, Winifred 166, 266n116
Bantock, Granville 20, 38, 65, 230n79
Barnes, William 65
Barrett, John 252n71
Bartók, Béla 32, 43, 96, 190, 200–01, 235n40
Bath Pump Room Orchestra 97, 197
Bax, Arnold 31, 32, 36, 37, 38, 53, 102, 143, 233n152
Bax, Clifford 102, 106
Bayreuth 27
BBC 35, 36, 83, 183, 233n183, 253n119
BBC National Orchestra of Wales 256n49, 257n97
BBC Symphony Orchestra 35, 36, 82
Beecham, Sir Thomas 32, 152
Beethoven, Ludwig von 12, 14, 17, 19, 62, 86, 103, 114, 229n29, 242n18

Bennet, Joseph 11, 21
Berg, Alban 184
Berlioz, Hector 27, 30, 229n32
Birmingham Festival 154
Birmingham Labour Party Orchestra 58
Blake, William 258n115
Blanche, Jacques-Émile 196
Blavatsky, Helena 91, 158, 159, 250n3; see also Theosophy
Bliss, Arthur 31, 175, 188
Bloch, Ernest 209
Blow, Detmar 175
Blow, John 175
Blunt, Bruce 164, 167
Bode, Dr. Mabel 95
Boer War 39, 79, 173
Booker, Robert 113, 114
Boughton, Rutland 31, 172, 228n9, 248n210, 253n102
Boult, Adrian 35, 76, 83, 87, 88, 102, 111, 115, 128, 132, 248n205, 249n234
Boy Scouts 123
Boyce, William 12, 183, 186, 229n15; see also Finzi, Gerald
Brahms, Johannes 12, 19, 20, 34, 70, 101, 138; *Requiem* 138
Bream, Julian 186
Bridge, Frank 19, 31, 36
British Museum 13, 22, 104, 118, 120, 156
British Musical Renaissance see English Musical Renaissance
Britten, Benjamin 10, 31, 36, 37, 78, 111, 125, 182, 184, 188, 204, 228n25, 250n1; *Peter Grimes* 78
Broadwood, John 41; *Old English Songs* 41
Broadwood, Lucy 9, 26, 41–42, 44, 47, 66, 68, 75, 118, 119, 125, 199, 201, 213, 235n25, 235n37, 242n53, 243n59, 244n91; *English County Songs* 26, 41, 66

299

Bruch, Max 64
Brussels Conservatoire 22
Bunny, Rupert 197
Burckhardt, Jakob 16; *The Civilization of the Period of the Renaissance in Italy* 16
Busch, Fritz 73
Busch, William 172, 176
Bush, Alan 83
Busoni, Ferruccio 198
Butterworth, Sir Alexander Kaye: 2, 3, 5, 7, 8, 10, 25, 26, 31, 33, 34, 37, 44, 48, 51, 52, 71–75, 112–129, 132, 135, 136, 138, 145, 150, 169, 173, 175, 176, 199, 203, 217; *George Butterworth, 1885–1916, Memorial Volume* 125, 257n83
Butterworth, George 2, 5, 7, 8, 10, 25, 26, 31, 33, 34, 37, 44, 48, 51, 52, 71–73, 74, 75, 112–129, **118, 122**, 132, 135, 136, 138, 145, 150, 169, 173, 175, 176, 199, 203, 217, 223, 244n91, 255n2, 256n42, 257n69, 257n76, 258n115, 258n120, 258n122, 259n168; Butterworth's Trench 124; childhood and education 113–14; death 124–25; *Diary of Morris-dance hunting* 120; Duke of Cornwall's Light Infantry 122; folk song collecting 112–13, 115, 117–19, 120–21, 123, 127, 128, 129; *Folk Songs from Sussex* 121; Military Cross, awarded 124; Morris and folk dancing 112, 113, 117, 119–20, 122, 124; Munster Alley 124; music criticism 116; sexual orientation 117, 129, 256–57n57; teaching at Radley College 116; Thiepval Memorial 124; war experiences 122–25; **Works**—*The Banks of Green Willow* 127–28; *Barcarolle* 113; *Bredon Hill and Other Songs* 126; *Fantasia for Orchestra* 121, 257–58n97; *Love Blows as the Wind Blows* 121; *Requiescat* 117; *A Shropshire Lad* 127; *Six Songs from "A Shropshire Lad"* 126; *Suite for String Quartet* 116, 256n17; *Two English Idylls* 121, 127
Byrd, William 12, 103

Campbell, Olive Dame 51, 56
cats 166, 175, 184, 217, 268n52, 276n1
Chamberlain, Neville 181
Channing, Minnie Lucy ("Puma") 157–58, 159, 160, 162
Chappell, William 41
Christianity 14, 16, 40, 45, 61, 149, 150, 153–54, 181, 191, 264n24
church music 9, 13, 16, 18, 21, 61, 62, 69, 100, 144, 174–75, 202, 238n124
Church of England (Anglican Church) 62, 108, 131, 154, 216, 236n69, 245n118, 253n100
Cobbett, Walter Wilson 260n26
Coetmore, Peers 145, 146, 163, 259n2, 263n137
Cole, Sir Henry 16, 17, 229n48
Coleridge-Taylor, Samuel 19, 92, 251n18
Colles, H.C. 34, 35
Collins, Hal 162, 266n85
Committee for the Promotion of New Music 83, 246n158
Constantinople (Istanbul) 75, 102; *see also* Holst, Gustav
Cooper, Gerald 161
Cornell University 87
Cotswolds 91–92, 95, 109, 142, 174, 217–18
Coverton, Bessie Mary Edith ("Covey") 149–51,
152–53, 154, 155, 157, 158, 160, 162, 165, 167; *see also* Heseltine, Philip
Cowen, Frederic 21
Croft, Brigadier-General Henry Page 124
Crossley, Ada 196
Crowley, Aleister 158–59, 161, 265n62; Aiwass 159; *The Book of the Law* 159; *see also* Thelema
Crystal Palace 15
Cummings, W.W. 201

Daily Telegraph 98, 165, 181, 228n3
Damrosch, Walter 107
Dartington Music Festival 185, 233n157
Darwin, Charles 60, 241n3
Darwinism 42
Day, George Parmly 51
Dearmer, Percy 68
Debussy, Claude 4, 9, 31, 36, 38, 126, 125, 168, 196
de Falla, Manuel 43
Delius, Frederick 5, 10, 29, 30, 37, 80, 102, 132, 138, 142, 149, 151–52, 153–54, 155, 156, 157, 161, 162, 164, 165, 167, 196, 199, 212, 223, 232n139, 232n142, 255n181, 260n12, 262n104, 264n30, 264n38; **Works**—*Brigg Fair* 30, 232n142, 232n143, 272n57, 274n174; *Piano Concerto* 138; *Song of the High Hills* 138
de Luce, Alfhild 199
Devlin, Lilian 196
Diaghilev, Sergei 79
Dolmetsch, Arnold 21, 22–23, 25, 43, 69, 212, 231n94, 275n171
Dowland, John 12, 104, 168
Downton Abbey 269n92
Duncan, Isadora 247n188
Dunhill, Thomas 113
Dvořák, Antonín 43

Easter Rising 33
Edinburgh Music Festival 185
Edward VII, King of England 18, 27, 49, 196, 197, 248n209
Edwardian era 5, 9, 32–33, 36, 44, 59, 73, 74, 173, 219, 220, 234n2, 236n49
Elgar, Caroline 26, 27, 75, 246n147
Elgar, Edward 1, 5, 19, 26–29, **28**, 31, 33, 34, 37, 65, 71, 75, 76, 80, 94, 114, 127, 132, 172, 174, 184, 188, 199, 223, 228n3, 232n135; 232n137, 232n139, 255n181, 268n43; Peyton Lectures 28–29; **Works**—*Caractacus* 27; *Coronation Ode* 27; *The Dream of Gerontius* 26, 65, 245n118; *Enigma Variations* 26, 27, 65, 94; *In the South* 26; *Introduction and Allegro* 155; *Pomp and Circumstance Marches* 27; *Violin Concerto* 29
Elizabeth I, Queen of England 22, 23, 87, 245n116; *The Triumphs of Oriana* 87
Elizabeth II, Queen of England 87
Ellington, Duke 212
Embleton, Henry 27
Encyclopedia Britannica 21
England, John 45, 236n53
English Folk Dance and Song Society 3, 35, 80, 119, 223, 227n1
English Folk Dance Society 49, 78, 106, 119
English language 5, 58, 98–99, 192, 195, 209, 221,

Index

230*n*60, 234–35*n*11; *see also* Granger, Percy, "Blue-eyed English"
"Englishness" in music 1, 12, 21, 41, 44, 62, 69, 76, 102, 116, 169, 234–35*n*11, 240*n*1, 244*n*82, 258*n*100
Espérance Club 48, 50, 119, 201; *see also* Neal, Mary; Sharp, Cecil
Espérance Guild of Morris Dancers 49–50; *see also* Neal, Mary; Sharp, Cecil
Eton College 113, 114, 118, 123, 126, 151, 152, 153, 256*n*11, 256*n*57
Eton College Musical Society 151

Fabian socialism 49, 62, 69, 230*n*71, 238*n*113, 242*n*22; *see also* Sharp, Cecil; socialism
Farrar, Ernest 33, 171, 175, 178
Farrar, Olive 171
Fauré, Gabriel 184
Fenby, Eric 153, 167, 196, 262*n*104, 264*n*24
Ferguson, Howard 176, 178, 267*n*3, 269*n*62, 269*n*63, 269*n*68
Finzi, Christopher ("Kiffer") *180*, 182, 186, 269*n*82, 269*n*107, 270*n*149, 270*n*150
Finzi, Douglas 170
Finzi, Edgar 170, 171
Finzi, Felix 170
Finzi, Gerald 2, 5, 7, 8–9, 31, 35, 78, 87, 103, 105, 125, 165, 169–89, *177*, *180*, 217, 224, 247*n*201, 248*n*217, 248*n*224, 248*n*228, 249*n*239, 249*n*261, 250*n*268, 253*n*124, 267–68*n*24, 268*n*38, 268*n*52, 268–69*n*57, 269*n*68, 269*n*82, 270*n*110, 271*n*168; agnosticism 169, 217; apple farming 9, 169, 175, 180–81, 184, 187; cancer diagnosis 185–86; cats, love of 175, 184, 217, 268*n*52; childhood and education 170–71; Church Farm, Ashmansworth 180–81, 183, 184, 188; death 9, 187–88; Jewish background 169, 176, 181; and Jews in Germany 178, 18; mother, difficulties with 170, 176, 178, 179, 269*n*60, 269*n*82; *Musica Britannica* 183, 186, 270*n*145; personal library 270*n*118; travel 172, 177–78; Vaughan Williams, friendship with 172–73, 176, 178, 183, 186–87, 188, 270*n*152, 270*n*154; and World War II 181–82, 183, 269*n*107;
Works—*Cello Concerto* 186, 188; *Clarinet Concerto* 185; *Concerto for Small Orchestra and Solo Violin* 175–76, 177; *Dies Natalis* 184; *Eclogue* 177; *For St Cecilia* 185; *Grand Fantasia and Toccata* 186; *In terra pax* 186, 187; *Intimations of Immortality* 185, 188; *Introit* 175–76; *Requiem da Camera* 175; *Severn Rhapsody* 175; *Shakespeare Songs* 183
Finzi, Jack 169–70
Finzi, Joy (née Black) 178–80, *180*, 181, 182, 184, 185, 186, 187–88, 189, 269*n*83, 270*n*110
Finzi, Katie 171
Finzi, Lizzie 170, 171, 172, 174, 176, 178, 179, 185, 269*n*82
Finzi, Neville 187
Finzi, Nigel 179, *180*, 182, 186, 189, 270*n*150
Finzi Trust 3, 182–83, 188, 224
Fisher, Charles 74
Fisher, Emmie 256*n*42
flute, Egyptian/Middle Eastern 251*n*49, 251*n*53
"the Folk" 50, 58
folk dance 2, 6, 8, 25, 36, 39, 43, 44, 48–50, 51, 52, 57, 64, 69, 89, 100, 105, 106, 112–13, 117, 119–20, 122, 123, 124, 129, 172, 176, 201, 206, 223, 237*n*84, 237*n*86, 238*n*104, 238*n*113, 238*n*115, 256–57*n*57, 257*n*76, 258*n*102, 267–68*n*24; see also Butterworth, George; Morris dance
folk song, oral tradition, in transmission 19, 40–41, 44, 46, 47–48, 53, 54, 55, 58, 67–68, 98–99, 136–37, 206, 234*n*11, 236*n*62, 240*n*170
Folk Song Society 42, 51, 68, 115, 142, 201, 203, 236*n*45
Foss, Hubert 139, 162, 266*n*84
Fraser, R.W. 95; *Silent Gods and Sun-Steeped Lands* 95
Fuller Maitland, J.A. 11, 15, 21, 25–26, 34, 41, 42, 66, 116, 201, 203, 229*n*36, 232*n*139; *A Door-Keeper of Music* 21; *English County Songs* 26, 41, 66; *Fitzwilliam Virginal Book* 21

Gardiner, Henry Balfour 36, 102, 105, 106, 137, 138, 195, 253*n*115
Gardner, Gerald 234*n*5
George V, King of England 81, 99, 152
Germanic musical influences in England 4, 5, 7, 11, 12, 14, 16, 18, 19, 20, 24, 25, 32, 33, 34, 36–37, 38, 41, 45, 46, 60, 66, 70, 71, 78, 83, 101, 116, 196, 230*n*64, 231*n*116
Gershwin, George 209, 214, 215
Gibbings, Robert 135
Gibbons, Orlando 68
Gilbert and Sullivan 14, 15; *see also* Sullivan, Arthur
Gilchrist, Anne 203
Glasier, J. Bruce 58, 240*n*172
Glastonbury Music Festival 172
Gloucestershire 60, 90, 172, 174, 181, 188, 201, 217, 218, 273*n*80
Goossens, Eugene Aynsley 31
Goss, John 166
Goulding, Douglas 47
Grahame, Kenneth 40; *The Wind in the Willows* 40
Grainger, John Harry 190–91, 192–93, 198, 271*n*3, 271*n*13
Grainger, Percy 2, 5, 7, 9, 10, 23, 26, 29, 30, 32, 33, 36–37, 43, 44, 48, 49, 51, 56, 57, 59, 96, 112, 117, 119, 121, 128, 148, 162, 167, 173, 190–216, *197*, *207*, 217, 224, 239*n*153, 239*n*154, 239*n*156, 252*n*55, 264*n*24, 271*n*1, 272*n*23, 272*n*25, 272*n*60, 273*n*78, 274*n*114, 274*n*117, 274*n*121, 274*n*123, 274*n*136, 274*n*139, 275*n*149, 275*n*154, 275*n*160, 275*n*161, 275*n*168, 275*n*174, 275*n*177, 276*n*184, 276*n*185, 276*n*190, 276*n*200; Annie (his nurse) 192; as artist 191, 192, 194, 213, 271*n*10; atheism 202, 216, 217; "Blue-eyed English," invented language 209; Cecil Sharp, relationship with 48, 49, 51, 57, 121, 190, 196, 201, 202–03; childhood and education 191–94; diet 211, 275*n*160; early music, interest in 23, 210–11, 212, 274*n*121, 75*n*171; eccentric behaviors 190, 198, 209, 211; family life, troubled 191–93; folk song collecting in Denmark 56, 204, 210–11, 216; folk song collecting in England 7, 9, 26, 43, 48, 49, 51, 56, 59, 96, 112, 117, 119, 121, 128, 190, 195, 199–204, 205, 206, 213, 216; folk song collecting in Oceana 56, 190, 204, 205; folk song settings 195, 199, 200, 204–05, 206, 213, 216, 273*n*78, 274*n*121; Folk Song

302　　　　　　　　　　　　　　　　　Index

Society, disagreements with 43, 59, 203–04, 206–07, 209; Free Music 214, 276*n*188; generosity 57, 206–07, 209–210, 212; Grieg, friendship with 204–05; health 198, 211, 214, 215, 215; jazz, interest in 190, 212, 276*n*190; machine music 214, 276*n*188; marriage 212, 214, 215, 216; mother (Rose), difficult relationship with 190–93, 197–98, 205, 207–08, 210, 212, 215, 216; mother's suicide 210, 211, 215; Northern Europe, devotion to 191, 194, 208, 209; phonograph, in collecting folk songs 43, 48, 56, 121, 200–04, 210; photographing composers 272*n*23; as pianist 9, 190, 193–94, 195–96, 199, 204–06, 207, 211, 212, 213, 214, 215, 216, 274*n*136; racism 209, 210, 275*n*149; rock and roll, interest in 214, 276*n*190; sadomasochism 9, 192, 195, 208, 210, 212, 213, 274*n*133, 275*n*168; sexual attitudes 192, 195, 197–98, 207, 208–09, 215, 275*n*168; stage fright 199, 216, 272*n*60, 276*n*184; United States, settling in 190, 205–06, 207, 213; wealth 206–07, 209–10, 211, 212, 276*n*185; world music, interest in 198, 275*n*158; World War I service 205–06, 274*n*121; **Works**—*Country Gardens* 57, 206, 209; *Lincolnshire Posy* 213; *Spoon River* 207; *To a Nordic Princess* 212; *Train Music* 198
Grainger, Rose 9, 190, 191–93, 194, 195, 196, 197–98, 201, 205–06, 207, **207**, 208, 210, 211, 212, 215, 216, 271*n*3, 271*n*9, 271*n*13
Grainger Museum in Melbourne, Australia 3, 211, 213, 215, 224, 252*n*55, 275*n*177, 276*n*200
Gray, Cecil 105, 157, 159, 162, 167, 254*n*148, 263*n*3, 265*n*67, 265*n*68
Gray, Pauline 159
Great Depression 79, 212, 276*n*185
Great Exhibition of 1851 15
Grieg, Edvard 30, 36, 43, 67, 155, 172, 204–05, 218, 264*n*38; *Concerto in A minor* 205; *19 Norwegian Folk Tunes* 155
Grieg, Nina 205
Grove, George 11, 17, 18, 20, 21, 24, 30, 35, 229*n*14; *Dictionary of Music and Musicians* 17, 21, 25, 186
Guildhall School of Music 24, 231*n*110
Gurney, Ivor 9, 33, 34, 71, 173–74, 175, 184, 186, 268*n*43; *5 Elizabethan Songs* 174; *Gloucestershire Rhapsody* 268*n*43; *Sleep* 174

Hamnett, Nina 163
Handel, George Frideric 12, 17, 18, 21, 26, 42, 101, 229*n*14
Hardy, Thomas 107, 173, 175, 187, 224, 254*n*164, 268*n*38, 268*n*39; *By Footpath and Stile* 173; *The Mayor of Casterbridge* 107; *The Return of the Native* 107
Hart, Fritz 92
Harty, Hamilton 136, 138, 140
Harvard University 109
Hassler, Hans Leo 244*n*82
Haweis, the Reverend H.R. 13, 14, 16; *Music and Morals* 13, 229*n*29
Henry VI, King of England 256*n*11
Henry VIII, King of England 245*n*116
Heseltine, Nigel 158, 166
Heseltine, Philip 2, 5, 7, 8, 10, 12, 21, 30, 33, 35, 104, 130, 131, 132, 133–34, 136–37, 138, 139, 140–42, 144, 147, 149–68, **159**, 169, 170, 173, 184, 193, 199, 217, 224, 231*n*89, 233*n*168, 246*n*143, 263*n*1, 263*n*3, 264*n*24, 265*n*53, 265*n*62, 265*n*67, 266*n*85, 266*n*95, 266*n*98, 266*n*104, 267*n*1; and alcohol 140–41, 162–63, 165, 166, 167; atheism 149, 153–54; bipolar disorder 149, 156, 167–68, 266*n*116; birth 149; cats, fondness for 166; Cefn Bryntalch 150, 161; childhood and education 150–52; death, controversy 166–67; Delius, admiration of 10, 30, 149, 151–54, 156, 157, 161, 164, 165; drug use 161–62; in Dublin, Ireland 158–60; Ernest Moeran, friendship with 8, 130, 133–34, 136–37, 140–42, 147, 149, 155, 162–63, 164, 165; Eynsford 130, 140, 141, 147, 162–63, 168; folk songs 136–37, 155, 160, 162; Jekyll-and-Hyde personality 167; limericks 139, 157, 265*n*53; mother, problematic relationship with 150–51, 152–53, 154, 157, 158, 162, 167; as music critic 149, 154–55, 156, 167, 168; North Africa, travel to 161; occult interests 8, 149, 158–59, 265*n*67; as Peter Warlock 149, 157, 160, 165, 167; pseudonyms 157, 160; *The Sackbut* 160–61; Tudor music, interests and work 8, 12, 21, 35, 130, 142, 149, 156, 161; World War I exemption 155–56, 157, 158, 160; **Works**—*Bethlehem Down* 164–65; *Capriol Suite* 163, 164, 165; *The Curlew* 161, 267*n*1; *Folk-song Preludes* 160; *Maltworms* (with Moeran) 163; *Serenade* 164; *Three Carols* 161; *Yarmouth Fair* 155
Highclere Castle 269*n*92
Hill, Lionel 145, 146
Hilton, W. 200; *Come All You Merry Plowboys* 200
Hitler, Adolf 183, 184, 250–51*n*5
Holland, Betsy 48
Holmes, Henry 24
Holst, Adolph 90, 91, 92, 93–94, 252*n*84
Holst, Clara Lediard 90
Holst, Emil 90, 91
Holst, Gustav 2, 5, 7, 8, 9, 12, 19, 24, 25, 26, 28, 30–31, 32, 33, 34, 35, 36, 37, 38, 40, 51, 61, 62–63, 66, 69, 72, 74, 75–76, 77, 78, 80, 81, 85, 90–111, **96**, **103**, 124, 129, 135, 149, 155, 164, 169, 172, 173, 176, 179, 184, 187, 194, 205, 206, 217, 224, 228*n*25, 232*n*142, 247*n*197, 251*n*20, 251*n*49, 252*n*55, 252*n*59, 252*n*61, 252*n*73, 252*n*92, 253*n*100, 254*n*140, 254*n*164, 255*n*187, 264*n*28; agnosticism 250*n*5; Algeria 95–96; and amateur musicians 99, 100, 104, 111; astrology, interest in 102, 253*n*117; Beethoven's tuning fork 103; childhood and education 90–92; concussion 103–04, 105; death 110–11; "England & Her Music" 94; failure, thoughts on 106; fame, unhappy with 102–03, 104–05, 106, 109; family history 90–91; family name controversy 33, 100, 101; field days with Vaughan Williams 63, 76, 93; folk songs 8, 26, 35, 38, 51, 90, 95, 96, 97, 98, 100, 102, 110; Hammersmith Socialist Choir 93; health problems 80, 91, 92, 101, 106, 109, 110, 179; Indian and Hindu culture, interest in 8, 90, 91, 95, 98, 250*n*5, 251*n*43, 251*n*45; Royal Philharmonic Society medal 108; St. Paul's Girls School 97, 104, 110, 252*n*58; socialist views 93, 217, 251*n*25, 253*n*100; teaching 34, 97, 99, 102, 103, 104, 105, 106, 109, 110; texts and music 98–99, 105; Thaxted 40, 100, 105, 106, 110, 111, 253*n*100; trombone playing 91,

Index

92, 93, 251*n*20; United States travel 104, 108, 109; walking and love of outdoors 91–92, 100, 103, 105, 106, 107, 110; Whitsun Festival 100, 102; YMCA service 33, 75, 101; **Operas**—*At the Boar's Head* 105; *Landsdown Castle* 92; *Savitri* 95, 252*n*78; *Sita* 95; *The Wandering Scholar* 110; **Works**—*The Bells* (film score) 253*n*119; *Beni Mora–In the Street of Ouled Naïls* 96, 252*n*55; *Brook Green Suite* 110; *The Coming of Christ* 108; *Choral Fantasia* 107–08; *Choral Hymns from the Rig Veda* 95; *Choral Symphony* 105–06; *The Cloud Messenger* 95; *Cotswolds Symphony* 95; *Egdon Heath* 107, 252*n*73, 254*n*164; *The Golden Goose* 106; *Hymn of Jesus* 75; *In the Bleak Mid-winter* 69; *Indra* 95; *Japanese Suite* 96; *The Morning of the Year* 106; *Ode to Death* 102; *Phantastes Suite* 99; *The Planets* 8, 31, 37, 76, 90, 99, 100, 102, 104, 106, 107, 111, 173, 206, 252*n*93, 253*n*119, 254*n*137, 253*n*119; *Psalm 86*, 99; *Seven Pieces for Large Orchestra* see *The Planets*; *Somerset Rhapsody* 97, 98; *Songs of the West* 97, 98; *Suite No. 2 in F* 98; *Two Selections of Folksong* 97; *Vedic Hymns* 95; *Walt Whitman Overture* 95
Holst, Imogen 9–10, 90, 95, 97, 98, 100, 101, 111, 228*n*25, 250*n*1, 252*n*55
Holst, Isobel (née Harrison) 93, 94, 97, 100, 104, 107, 108, 111, 225*n*187
Holst Birthplace Museum 3, 107, 224
Holst Room, Morley College 111, 255*n*206
Hooper, Louie 45, 57, 240*n*164; see also White, Lucy
Housman, A.E. 71, 126, 133, 139–40, 221–22, 224, 257*n*61, 276*n*10; *A Shropshire Lad* 126, 127, 133, 139, 221
Howard, Leslie 83
Howard-Jones, Evlyn 31
Howells, Herbert 9, 31, 71, 174–75, 176, 266*n*95; *In Gloucestershire* 228*n*19
Howes, Frank 11, 35, 41, 48, 175, 227*n*1, 230*n*86, 234*n*184
Hoyte, William 99, 252*n*84
Hughes, Don Anselm 212, 213 *English Gothic Music* (with Percy Grainger) 212
Hutton, Graham 177, 178, 179

Impressionism, in music 7, 8, 9, 25, 31, 32, 70, 71, 74, 121, 129, 135, 231*n*94, 232*n*145
Industrial Revolution 2, 14, 24–25, 33, 39, 40, 44, 59, 120, 173, 175
Ireland 4, 5, 33, 41, 51, 86, 131, 134, 135, 137, 139, 142, 143, 145, 147, 158, 159, 263*n*131, 263*n*144
Ireland, John 8, 9, 19, 28, 31, 37, 92, 135, 138, 172, 242*n*33, 261*n*52, 265*n*71
Ito, Michio 96, 252*n*56

Jaeger, August 27
Janáček, Leoš 32, 43
jazz 35, 59, 190, 212, 219, 234*n*186, 276*n*190
Jekyll, Francis 115, 118, 121
Jenkins, John 230*n*86
Jones, Walter Buckley 150
Jonson, Ben 69, 99; *Pan's Anniversary* 69, 99
Journal of the English Folk Dance and Song Society 35, 42, 51, 69, 117, 121, 136, 202, 227*n*1

Journal of the Folk-Song Society 69, 117, 121, 202, 239*n*144, 239*n*153, 261*n*68, 262*n*109, 273*n*83
Judaism see Finzi, Gerald

Karpeles, Helen 52, 119, 238*n*113
Karpeles, Maud 9, 47, 51, 52, 57, 89, 117, 119, 207, 236*n*51, 238*n*113, 240*n*164
Kennedy, Michael 89, 250*n*279
Kidson, Frank 44, 56, 199, 200
Kimber, William 48
Kinora film 119, 257*n*81
Kipling, Rudyard 194
Klimsch, Karl 194–95
Knocks, A.J. 205
Knorr, Ivan 194
Kodály, Zoltán 43, 190
Kristensen, Evald Tang 210–11
Kwast, James 194, 195
Kwast, Mimi 195

Lambert, Constant 31, 37, 168, 233*n*150
Lasker, Vally 255*n*187
Lawrence, D.H. 156, 159, 167
Lawrence, T.E. 107
Lee, Kate 43, 44, 235*n*37
Leeds Festival 27, 28, 34, 69
Leith Hill Musical Festival 70, 225
Lennard, Reginald 115, 120, 121–22
Leopold, Duke of Albany 17
Lindsay, Jack 163
Liszt, Franz 67, 163–64, 229*n*32, 256*n*5
Lloyd, A.L. 53
London Board of Schools 19
London University 156
The Lord of the Rings (films) 37
Lowrey, Lilith 197
Lutyens, Elisabeth 32, 233*n*157

Mackenzie, Alexander 20, 21, 25, 27, 29
Marson, Charles 45, 46, 47, 236*n*57; *Folk Songs from Somerset* see Sharp, Cecil
Marxism 39, 53, 59, 239*n*156
Mavor, Dorothea 117, 122, 124
medieval music 4, 17, 42, 43, 59, 68, 99, 100, 210–11, 212, 230*n*60, 231*n*98, 246*n*165, 259*n*168; see also *Sumer Is Icumen In*
Melba, Dame Nellie 196
Mendelssohn, Felix 12, 14, 16, 21, 24, 256*n*5
Meredith, George 74
Meredith, Roland 236*n*49
Miller, Bob 136
Ministry of War Transport 183
mizmar, Middle Eastern reed instrument 198, 251*n*53
Moeran, Ada Esther 131
Moeran, Ernest John 2, 5, 7, 8, 9, 10, 19, 30, 31, 33, 35, 47, 92, 125, 130–48, **143**, 149, 155, 162–63, 164, 165, 168, 169, 171, 175, 176, 178, 205, 224, 260*n*26, 261*n*59, 261*n*63, 262*n*104, 263*n*137, 263*n*140; accidents 145, 147; alcoholism 8, 133, 134, 140, 141, 144, 145, 146, 147, 163, 165, 169; atheism 131, 144; childhood and education 131–32; death 147; disability pension, controversy 130, 134–35; drunk driving 144; Eynsford 130, 140,

141, 144, 145, 147, 162–63, 168; family wealth 131, 134–35, 260n6; folk song collecting 47, 130, 134, 136–37, 139, 148; folk song motifs in composition 5, 8, 30, 31, 136, 137–38, 139, 141, 142, 143, 146, 260n26; injury in war 8, 33, 125, 130, 133, 134–35, 147; in Ireland 5, 134, 135, 137, 139, 142, 143, 145, 147, 263n131, 263n144; metal plate in head, controversy 130, 133, 134; "Moeran myth" 130, 142; motorcycle dispatch rider during World War I 132–33; natural world, influence and need for 134, 135, 138, 142, 143, 144, 146; Philip Heseltine, friendship with 8, 130, 133–34, 136–37, 140–42, 147, 149, 155, 162–63, 164, 165; social awkwardness 145, 263n135; **Works**—*Cello Concerto* 145; *Down by the Riverside* 137; *Four Songs from "A Shropshire Lad"* 133; *In the Mountain Country* 134, 138; *Lonely Waters* 141, 142; *Ludlow Town* 139; *Rhapsody No. 1* 136, 138–39; *Rhapsody No. 2* 139; *Six Suffolk Folksongs* 142; *Sonata for Cello and Piano* 145–46, 147; *Sonata for Two Violins* 142; *Songs from County Kerry* 146; *String Quartet in E flat* 133; *String Quartet No. 1*, 138; *String Trio* 142; *Symphony in G Minor* 144–45; *Theme and Variations* 139; *Violin Concerto* 144; *Whythorne's Shadow* 142
Moeran, Joseph 131, 134, 138
Morley College 97, 101, 111, 252n59
Morley, Thomas 99, 249n261
Morris, R.O. 115, 123, 176, 204, 256n42
Morris, William 24, 25, 43, 93, 95, 224, 251n25
Morris dance 8, 48–50, 52, 57, 69, 119–20, 124, 201, 206, 223, 237n84, 237n86, 238n104, 238n115; *see also* Butterworth, George; Karpeles, Maude; Neal, Mary; Sharp, Cecil
Motor Cycling Club 135
Mozart, Wolfgang Amadeus 12, 24, 93, 114, 244n105
Munich Agreement 181
music halls 14, 18, 32, 40, 66, 233n162
Musica Britannica 186, 270n145
Musical Antiquarian Society 21
The Musical League 29, 199
Mussorgsky, Modest 168, 244n104

National Training School of Music 16
National Trust 40, 241n7
nationalism, in music 17, 18, 24, 38, 42, 80, 97, 101, 169, 172, 219, 228n10, 230n64, 231n116
Nazi Germany 59, 80, 81, 82, 83, 178, 181, 182
Neal, Mary 48–50, 57, 223, 237n84, 237n86, 238n104; *see also* Espérance Club; Espérance Guild of Morris Dancers
Neuberg, Victor 161
New York University 212
Newbury String Players 182, 183, 184, 186, 270n150; *see also* Finzi, Gerald
Nichols, Ross 234n5
Nietzsche, Friedrich 149, 153, 154; *The Antichrist* 153; *Beyond Good and Evil* 153
Noel, Conrad 40, 253n100
North Lincolnshire Musical Competition Festival 199–200
Norwich Centenary Festival 139

Olivier, Laurence 83
Orr, C.W. 26
Oxford & Cambridge Musical Club 114, 132, 134, 140–41
Oxford Companion to Music 163, 266n99; *see also* Scholes, Percy
Oxford History of Music 21
Oxford University Press 109, 161, 163; Duncan McKenzie 109

Pabst, Louis 193, 194
Padel, Christian Gollieph 113
Palestrina Society 129
Parratt, Walter 18
Parry, Hubert 11, 14–15, **15**, 17, 18, 19, 20, 21, 24, 25, 26, 27, 28, 30, 33, 34, 35, 36, 37, 42, 43, 62, 74, 75, 83, 114, 115, 116, 132, 186, 228n3, 230n67, 235n12, 258n115; *The Evolution of the Art of Music* 42; *Jerusalem* 258n115; *Prometheus Unbound* 14–15, 20
pastoralism, in art and music 5–6, 7–8, 9, 10, 24, 31–32, 33, 34, 35, 36, 37, 38, 40, 53, 60, 61, 65, 67, 71, 74, 76, 78, 79, 81, 82, 85, 86, 90, 95, 98, 110, 173, 175–76, 217, 219, 221, 227n3, 232n139, 233n157, 233n172, 234n190, 264n30; winter themes 227n7
Pater, Walter 16; *Studies in the History of the Renaissance* 16
Peache, Barbara 162, 166
Pearce, Georgia 58; *see also* socialism
period instruments and ensembles 22–23, 231n98, 244n96, 246n165
phonograph, for recording folk songs 43, 48, 56, 121, 137, 200, 201, 203–204, 210, 273n79
physical fitness and sports, in schools 113, 114, 116, 117, 150, 251n8, 257–57n57
piano, use in folk music 47, 236n70, 240n170
Playford, John 49, 105, 120; *Dancing Master* 49, 120
Ponsonby, Dorothea 18
Poston, Elizabeth 167
Potiphar, Charles 66, 68
Purcell, Henry 4, 12, 15, 17, 18, 21, 26, 38, 42, 63, 94, 99, 217, 232n137; *Dido and Aeneas* 63; *The Fairy Queen* 99

Quilter, Roger 195, 265n71

Raleigh, Sir Walter 22
Ravel, Maurice 4, 5, 9, 31, 35, 36, 70–71, 96, 135, 138, 174, 206, 209, 242n26, 244n104, 244n105, 244n106
Reimann, Immanuel G. 45
Rigveda 90, 95, 251n43; *see also* Holst, Gustav
Rogers, Winthrop 160, 161
Rolt, the Reverend Clarence 154
Romanichal 236n73
Rowley, Alec 155
Royal Academy of Music 16, 20, 76, 177, 184, 186
Royal Albert Hall 86, 185
Royal Army Medical Corps 33, 74; *see also* Vaughan Williams, Ralph
Royal College of Music 16, 17, 18, 20, 22, 23, 24, 26, 34, 62–63, 75, 76, 91, 92–93, 95, 99, 104, 116, 117, 120, 128, 132, 135, 136

Index

Royal Musical Association 175
Rubbra, Edmund 31, 232n146
Ruskin, John 24
Russell, Robert Hamilton 192, 193

Sadie, Stanley 186
St. Paul's Cathedral 34, 137
Sainton, Prosper 113, 256n5
Sainton-Dolby, Charlotte Helen 113, 256n5
Salonica (Thessaloniki) 74, 75, 102, 253n111; see also Holst, Gustav
Sandby, Herman 36, 196–97, 199
Sawyer, Antonia 210
Schoenberg, Arnold 99, 147, 184, 215; *Five Pieces for Orchestra* 99
Scholes, Percy 163–64, 261n57, 266n104
Schubert, Franz 104, 114, 229n32
Schumann, Robert 65, 114
Schuster, Frank 26
Scott, Cyril 36, 38, 195, 215
Sear, H.G. 58–59
second folk revival 59, 240n181
Shakespeare, William 22, 39, 78, 99, 105, 150, 247n146; *Henry IV* 105; *A Midsummer Night's Dream* 50–51; *The Merry Wives of Windsor* 78
Shand, Morton 180
Sharp, Cecil 3, 25, 26, 32, 41, 42, 43, 44–54, **46**, 56–57, 58, 62, 67, 68, 69, 71, 72, 97, 98, 105, 112, 115, 117, 118, 119–20, 121, 122, 124, 125, 148, 155, 172, 173, 190, 191, 196, 199, 201, 202, 203, 206–07, 209, 217, 223, 230n71, 236n45, 236n51, 236n53, 236n62, 236n69, 236n73, 238n104, 238n113, 240n162, 257n62, 273n79; *A Book of British Song* 45, 236n69; *English Folk Songs from the Southern Appalachians* 207; *English Folk-Songs: Some Conclusions* 44; *Folk Songs from Somerset* 46, 47, 236n57; *The Morris Book* 49; *The Sword Dances of Northern England* 49
Sharp, Constance 117
Sharp, James 44
Sharp, Jane 44
Sharp, Joan 57
Shaw, George Bernard 20, 27, 93, 218, 251n24
Shore, Howard 37
Shropshire 221, 222
Sibelius, Jean 36, 84–85, 129, 172
Sims, George Frederick 91
Smetana, Bedřich 43
Smith, Viva 157, 167
socialism 6, 19, 25, 39, 40, 45, 48, 58–59, 62, 69, 93, 172, 175, 179, 217, 230n71, 234n4, 237n89, 238n113, 240n177, 242n22, 248n210, 251n25, 253n100; see also Fabian socialism; Pearce, Georgia
Somerfield, Vera 171–72, 173, 177
Sprackler, Tom 45
Stanford, Charles Villiers 14, 15, 17, 18–20, **19**, 21, 23, 25, 26, 27, 28, 30, 33–34, 37, 42, 43, 44, 46, 62, 63–64, 132, 171, 199, 223, 228n3, 242n33, 244n91; *Savonarola* 20; *The Veiled Prophet* 20
Star, Meredith 159
Star Wars 37, 253n119
Stock Market crash of 1929 79, 165, 212; see also Great Depression

Stoeckel, Carl 77
Storrow, Helen 51, 238n112
Stratford-upon-Avon dance summer school 50, 52, 119, 122; see also Butterworth, George; Sharp, Cecil
Strauss, Johann 184
Strauss, Richard 27, 29, 38, 176, 184
Stravinsky, Igor 35, 36, 99; *The Firebird* 99; *Rite of Spring* 106
Ström, Ella Viola 211–12, 213, 214, 215, 216; see also Grainger, Percy
Sullivan, Arthur 14, 15, 16, 27, 37; see also Gilbert and Sullivan
Sumer Is Icumen In (medieval song) 17, 43

Tallis, Thomas 12, 68, 71, 245n116, 245n118; *Why fumeth in fight?* 71
Taylor, Colin 151, 152, 160, 264n12, 264n24
Taylor, Joseph 200, *Creeping Jane* 200
Terry, Sir Richard 53, 238n124
Thaxted, Essex 40, 100, 105, 106, 110, 111, 253n100
Thelema 158; see also Crowley, Aleister
Theosophy 42, 91, 158; see also Blavatsky, Helena
Thomas, Arthur Goring 21
Three Choirs Festival 15, 71, 107, 187, 225, 270n159
Times 21, 25, 29, 34, 35, 95, 116, 144, 227n1, 228n9
Tippett, Michael 31, 83, 248n228
Todhunter, Mabel 193
Tolkien, J.R.R. 227n3, 227n7
Tudor music 4, 8, 11, 21, 23, 26, 29, 35, 38, 42, 60, 62, 63, 68, 71, 77, 93, 99, 100, 102, 103, 104, 130, 142, 149, 156, 161, 172, 175, 230n86, 231n89, 232n146, 238n124, 260n26

University College, London 170
University of Birmingham 28, 29
University of Cambridge 20, 27, 44, 62, 64, 65, 93, 221, 242n21
University of Durham 23
University of Leeds 28
University of Liverpool 106
University of Melbourne 224
University of Michigan, Ann Arbor 104
University of Oxford 20, 27, 71, 91, 114–15, 118, 123, 126, 151, 153, 154, 155, 156, 157, 166, 238n115, 242n21, 242n43, 256n21
University of Reading 34, 103

van Dieren, Bernard 156–57, 160, 166, 167, 261n67
Vaughan Williams, Adeline 64, 70, 77, 79, 80, 82, 85, 86, 117, 128–29, 178, 247n181, 248n218, 256n21, 256n42
Vaughan Williams, the Reverend Arthur 60, 61
Vaughan Williams, Ralph 1, 2, 5, 7, 8, 9, 10, 12, 13, 19, 21, 23, 25, 27, 28, 30–31, 34, 35–36, 37, 42, 51, 57, 60–89, **77**, **84**, 90, 92–93, 94, 95–96, 97, 99–100, 101, 102, 103, 104, 106, 107–08, 109, 111, 115, 117, 124–25, 127, 128–29, 131, 132, 136, 139, 141, 149, 155, 161, 169, 171, 172–73, 174, 175, 176, 178, 181–82, 183, 184, 186–87, 188, 197, 217, 219, 221, 223, 228n3, 234–35n11, 242n26, 242n31, 243n79, 244n90, 244n96, 244n104, 245n114, 246n158, 246n171, 247n188, 248n205, 257n76, 258n102, 270n140, 275n154, 276n188; agnosticism 6, 61–

306 Index

62, 67, 217, 250n5; Albert Medal of the Royal Society of Arts 87; atheism 6, 61–62, 64, 67, 77, 217, 241n14; birthplace 60–61, 172; carols 66, 161, 243–44n79; childhood and education 61–62; death 88–89; family 60–61, 62, 85, 241n3, 242n53, 242–43n54; field days with Holst 63, 76, 93, 247n197; folk song collecting 7, 26, 44, 47, 48, 50, 54–55, 58, 66–68, 69–70, 73, 94–95, 97, 112, 115, 117–18, 119, 120–21, 137, 148, 173, 199, 202, 203, 236n45, 237n77, 272n23, 273n79; folk song influence and motifs in his music 31–32, 38, 43, 60, 62, 67–68, 69, 71, 73–74, 76–77, 78, 81, 82, 83, 86, 88, 89, 97, 135, 203, 240n1, 240–41n2, 244n82, 247n174; at Ingrave 66, 67, 243n63; modal music 54–55, 63–64, 239n144, 239n146; nationalism in music 35, 60, 65–66, 67, 73–74, 79–80, 83, 86, 102, 247n190; Order of Merit 81; political views 62, 85, 217, 240n171, 242n22, 248n210, 249n243; at the Royal College 24, 62–63, 92–93; Shakespeare Prize 81; travels 64, 77–78, 79–80, 81, 86, 87, 88, 217, 249n252, 249–50n262; wealth of family 60–61, 79, 115, 241n4, 241n7; White Gates 79, 82, 83, 178; World War I service 33, 35, 74–75, 80, 101, 125, 245n134; World War II service 82–83, 248n225, 248n228; **Film Music**—*49th Parallel* 83; *Scott of the Antarctic* 87, 249n231; **Folk song settings**—*English Folk Song Suite* 78, 257n93; *Five English Folk Songs* 74; *Five Variants of "Dives and Lazarus"* 82; *Folk Songs of the Four Seasons* 86, 257n93; *Six Studies in English Folksong* 78, 247n178; **Operas**—*Hugh the Drover* 78; *The Pilgrim's Progress* 83, 87; *Sir John in Love* 78, 247n174; **Symphonies**—*London Symphony* 37, 72–73, 76, 120, 128, 243–44n54, 243n77, 245n121, 245n128; *Pastoral Symphony* 35, 77–78, 80, 83, 155, 243n78, 246n143, 264n29; *Sea Symphony* 69, 71, 72, 244n93, 257n93; *Sinfonia Antartica* 75, 87; *Symphony no. 4* 36, 75, 79, 80–81, 85, 233n152, 242n18; *Symphony no. 5* 82, 83–85, 249n234; *Symphony no. 8* 87, 250n263; *Symphony no. 9* 88; **Works**—*Cambridge Mass* 65, 242n44; *Dona Nobis Pacem* 247n202; *Fantasia on a Theme of Thomas Tallis* 71, 245n118; *Hodie* 87; *In the Fen Country* 68, 138; *Job, A Masque for Dancing* 76, 79, 233n150, 242n18, 246n168, 247n188, 247n189; *The Lark Ascending* 74, 76, 245n130; *Linden Lea* 65; *Mass in G minor* 62, 77; *Norfolk Rhapsodies* 68, 97, 137–38, 218; *Old King Cole* 78; *On Wenlock Edge* 71; *Piano Concerto* 79; *The Robin's Nest* 61; *Romance for Harmonica and Orchestra* 86; *Sancta Civitas* 78; *A Thanksgiving for Victory* 85, 249n240; *Toward the Unknown Region* 69; *Tuba Concerto* 86; *Where Is the Home for Me?* 247n188; **Writings and editions**—*English Folk Songs* 73; *The English Hymnal* 68–69, 99, 240–41n2, 243n79, 244n82, 245n118; *National Music and Other Essays* 79, 232n139, 232n142, 240n170,

241n5, 245n121, 247n190; *see also* Royal Army Medical Corps
Vaughan Williams, Ursula (née Wood) 10, 44, 64, 81–82, **84**, 85, 86, 87, 88, 103, 117, 129, 241n3, 243n78, 248n216, 248n218, 248n238, 250n275, 250n279, 270n152
Venn, Mary 166
Victorian era 5, 7, 9, 11, 12, 13, 14, 16–17, 32, 41, 42, 44, 46, 47, 64, 96, 114, 129, 173, 191, 217, 227n113, 228n9
Volkslied 41

Wagner, Richard 12, 13, 17, 20, 25, 27, 29, 30, 62, 63, 64, 92, 93, 95, 98, 114, 126, 184, 242n35, 256n5; *Ring Cycle* 20, 62, 64, 92, 242n35
Walton, William 31
Warlock, Peter *see* Heseltine, Philip
Way, Sir Samuel James 45
Wedgwood, Josiah 60
Wedgwood, Margaret 60, 61
Wedgwood, Ralph 85
Weelkes, Thomas 12, 103, 111
Wells, H.G. 72, 122, 202, 234n4, 253n119; *Tono Bungay* 72; *War of the Worlds* 253n119
West Point Academy Military Band 214
White, Lucy 45, 57; *see also* Hooper, Louie
Whitman, Walt 69, 70, 194
Whittaker, W.G. 111
Wigan, Julia Marguerite 113
Wilbye, John 12
Wilde, Oscar 117, 257n61; *Requiescat* 117
Williams, John 37
Wood, Charles 116
Wood, Ursula *see* Vaughan Williams, Ursula
Woolf, Virginia 64
Wordsworth, William 24, 185; *Ode: Intimations of Immortality from Recollections of Early Childhood* 185
World War I 5, 6, 7, 8, 9, 30, 33–34, 35, 50, 51, 52, 71, 72, 73, 74–75, 76, 77, 78, 80, 81, 100, 101–02, 112, 119, 122–26, 129, 130, 132, 133–34, 135, 140, 145, 155–56, 157, 158, 160, 169, 170, 171, 172, 173, 175, 178, 184, 205–06, 219, 222, 224, 227n3, 233n162, 247n202, 258n117, 258n120; Battle of Epehy 171; Battle of Jutland 79; Battle of the Somme 8, 74, 112, 124, 258n120; Second Battle of Bullecourt 133
World War II 36, 59, 80, 81, 82–85, 145, 181–83, 184, 209, 213–14, 217, 219, 248n223, 248n228, 269n107; Battle of Britain 82–83, 182, 183, 248n225, 248n228, 269n107; D-Day 85, 183

xenophobia, British 123

Yale University 105
Yeats, William Butler 161
YMCA 33, 75, 101

www.ingramcontent.com/pod-product-compliance
Lightning Source LLC
Chambersburg PA
CBHW051209300426
44116CB00006B/490